The Paintings of Quinten Massys

The Paintings of Quinten Massys
with Catalogue Raisonné

LARRY SILVER

PHAIDON · OXFORD

Phaidon Press Limited, Littlegate House, St. Ebbe's Street, Oxford, 0X1 1SQ

First published in Great Britain 1984

First published in the United States of America in 1984 by Rowman & Allanheld, Publishers, under the imprint Allanheld & Schram

British Library Cataloguing in Publication Data

Silver, Larry
The paintings of Quinten Massys
1. Massys, Quinten
I. Title II. Massys, Quinten
759.9493 ND673.M4/

ISBN 0-7148-2346-5

Printed in the United States of America

In loving memory of
Ruth M. Sprecher
and
Abner Schram

Contents

List of Illustrations

Plates

Preface

The purposes of the pictures made by Quinten Massys within the urban complex of Antwerp occupy center stage in this text. Thus a number of remarks about the painter's changes of technique or his use of visual models—either 15th or 16th century, Netherlandish or Italian—will appear more strictly confined to the catalogue section than is customary in such monographs. "Style," when it is discussed in the main text, will be considered as a conscious employment of visual formulas or conventions in association with the task at hand: the purpose of the image, either as an icon, an altarpiece for a specific group, a secular satire, or a portrait. The text is organized along the lines of these pictorial types and functions. Consideration of artistic tasks is intended here to bridge the frequent polarization of form from content by art historians and to restore the sense of the artist's intention, insofar as it can be inferred from his work. Unlike a modern painter, who can serve as an informant about his work to the contemporary scholar, Massys has left behind few documents or extrinsic indications of his interests, personal affiliations, or beliefs. What little has been preserved in the way of documents will be examined in the Introduction, along with some background information on the city, Antwerp, in which Massys lived and worked. In the chapters that follow, attention will be given, wherever possible, to the patrons, the people who specifically commissioned a work of art; but we must recall, even where such information is recoverable, that both patrons and painter belonged to a common culture. This book tries to establish fully what the premises were for that culture and how art-making by artists like Massys played its part in the definition and confirmation of that culture.

A book should profess its limits and liabilities at the outset. Most of the limitations here result from the choice of a single artist. Ideally, a host of other detailed monographs would be pieced together to create a composite picture of the patrons and circumstances of artworks. Still, one must begin somewhere, and Massys offers the possibility of a case study. This book began as a doctoral dissertation (Harvard University, 1974) that once aspired to be a definitive monograph. Left over from that project are the *catalogue raisonné* and chronological armature of Massys's works. Since that time, however, new interests of the more contextual sort described above have intervened, and a large, lavish monograph on the artist (by A. de Bosque) has reduced the need for a traditional approach to this single painter.

Massys, however, remains a worthy subject for study because of his active and varied participation in the culture of his day. Maker of altarpieces for both local guilds and confraternities, exporter of altarpieces to kings and merchants in both Portugal and Germany, portraitist of both scholars and prosperous burghers, and one of the first important painters of secular subjects, Massys managed to produce examples of every kind of picture known to the Netherlands of his day. He serves, therefore, as a good index of the possibilities of art-making during his lifetime, and he also made contact with many of the important individuals or groups in his urban, cosmopolitan culture in Antwerp. He had assimilated the heritage of fifteenth-century Flemish painting as well as more recent innovations of famed contemporaries from elsewhere, Dürer and Leonardo. Chapter 9 will begin with Massys as an index to art and its purposes and will attempt to demonstrate his individual significance by comparisons to other important artists of the day, such as Gossaert and Joos van Cleve. In every case, the goal is to "read" the attitudes implicit in these Flemish paintings and to define the limits and range of their audience—their context of communication.

Like all scholarly works, this book depends upon its predecessors. Newton's maxim about standing on the shoulders of giants is applicable here, for the titans of the study of Netherlandish art have already contributed much to our understanding of the Antwerp master. In particular the great achievements of Max J. Friedländer, Ludwig von Baldass, K. G. Boon, and Erwin Panofsky deserve mention. Other specialists have contributed full-scale studies to Massys: Walter Cohen, Hugh Broadley and, most recently, A. de Bosque. All have served as an indispensable foundation for this book, which primarily seeks to ask new cultural questions rather than to offer any corrections or amendments to such a fine heritage of scholarship on Massys. Two other models, particularly influential on the author's thinking about images and their purposes, should be mentioned here: Sixten Ringbom's *Icon to Narrative,* cited throughout, and the excellent recent parallel study by Michael Baxandall, *The Limewood Sculptors of Renaissance Germany.* The works of historians, too, have been critical, particularly in unraveling that wonderful complex of world order and behavior that we call "late medieval piety." Here again the notes reveal how fundamental has been the dependence on such outstanding studies as the books by Delaruelle, Moeller, Ozment, and Oakley.

Individual scholars have enhanced the pages of this text in subtle ways that do not show up in footnotes. In particular, the wonderful community of scholars (truly the proper phrase, for once) in the field of Netherlandish art have been a source of constant inspiration and have offered both general and specific criticisms. The most important of them are friends as well as colleagues: Keith Moxey, Peter Parshall, Sandra Hindman, David Freedberg, Elizabeth McGrath, Peter Schabacker, James Mundy, Kristin Belkin, John Hand, and Martha Wolff. My original teacher for this material and the man who suggested Massys as a dissertation topic (long before there was a graduate student who required one) was Herbert Kessler, whose constant encouragement and friendship mean even more than his shining example. Seymour Slive supervised the original dissertation and added much to its clarity and precision; he, too, has offered considerable encouragement through the years. Egbert Haverkamp-Begemann, J. R. Judson, Horst Gerson, and Irving Lavin were senior colleagues whose belief and support meant much at critical moments. Jan Piet Filedt Kok, Gary Schwartz, and Josua Bruyn in Holland and Carel van de Velde in Antwerp greatly assisted researches in a once strange, now familiar, land of Massys. Lorne Campbell generously shared his researches prior to publication. Other friends and scholars have richly added to this book: Susan Smith, Christiane Andersson, Natalie Davis, Gavriel Moses, Shelly Errington, Carl Pletsch, Bill Sewell, Ron Inden, Leonard Barkan, Richard Wendorf, and Joel Snyder. Harry Rand deserves a sentence all to himself, but he will have to share it with Archie Rand.

Institutions, and the individuals within them, have been more than generous over the many years that this book has been in the making. First, the museums and staffs and the private collectors who own Massys pictures have been extraordinarily helpful in offering their paintings, their files, and their hospitality to scholars such as the author. Crucially important, too, have been the library and faculty of the Warburg Institute, the world's greatest scholarly haven and research facility. For financial support, but for much more than that, the Danforth Foundation (especially Lillie Mae Rose) and the Samuel H. Kress Foundation (Mary Davis) deserve credit for a dissertation, for this book, and for an entire graduate school education. Postdoctoral research has been made possible by other generous institutions: the Institute for Advanced Study in Princeton and the National Gallery of Art, with the gracious assistance of Robert and Clarice Smith. Perhaps the most generous institution of all is the Silver Family of Waco, Texas, who never failed to supplement the above agencies with both financial and moral support at critical moments. This book is inadequate recompense to them for such lengthy and burdensome investment.

My wife, Elizabeth Silver-Schack, merits twofold thanks. It was she who delayed this book with marvelous alternative projects, and it was she alone who made its ultimate completion possible. Typically, she wants me to acknowledge our cat, who served as an organic paperweight during the writing of this manuscript.

Finally, I would like to thank especially Mr. and Mrs. Abner Schram for being much more than publishers. Their patience and humanity helped to pry the book loose at last. Finally, Janet Johnston's fair firmness bettered it and brought it into production.

"The excellence of every art must consist in the complete accomplishment of its purpose."

Inscription, facade of Victoria and Albert Museum, London

"I shall not labor in vain if I set down that which may be useful for painting. For the art of painting is employed in the service of the Church and by it the sufferings of Christ and many other profitable examples are set forth. It preserves also the likeness of men after their death . . . The attainment of true, artistic, and lovely execution in painting is hard to come unto; it needs long time and a hand most free and practiced. Whosoever, therefore, is not gifted in this manner, let him not undertake it; for it comes by inspiration from above."

Albrecht Dürer
Food for Young Painters

1

Introduction: The Artist and His Home Town

A rough Cyclop blacksmith was I before,
But when my sweetheart was also courted by a painter,
She made me understand with some reproach,
That the thundering blows on the anvil were less pleasing to her
Than the silent play of brushes,
The force of love made me a painter.
The truth of this is indicated by a little anvil,
Which I selected for a signature on my pictures.
As Cypris obtained from Vulcan the arms for her son,
O great poet, You have made a clever painter from a blacksmith.[1]

The historical reality of Quinten Massys is shrouded in legend. Almost no contemporary account survives to provide evidence of his activities or character. Consequently, myths have developed to explain the young Quinten's choice of painting as a vocation. One finds Massys praised as a self-taught master, guided only by his own genius.

The earliest of these tales concerning Massys' profession emerges from the poem cited above. According to this version, Massys began his adult life as an apprentice smith but was won over to the gentler craft of painting by his young fiancée's aversion to the rude and sweaty life of the forge. This particular poem adorned the alleged portrait of Massys that was published with other such portraits in the 1572 book of famous Netherlandish artists by Domenicus Lampsonius: *Pictorum aliquot celebrium Germaniae inferioris elogiis.*[1] Lampsonius's versified eulogies were accompanied by engraved effigies made by Hieronymus Wierix, a professional print-maker who seems to have used a famous, lost self-portrait of Massys (see Catalogue: Documented Lost Works, no. 3) as the source for this particular image.[2] Lampsonius's text furnished the basis for the "biographical" background of Carel van Mander's account of the artist in the latter's Vasari-like compendium of artists' lives, the *Schilderboek* *Pl. 20*
(1604), in which the artist's famous *St. John altarpiece* (1508–11; F. 1, cat. 11) is mentioned for the first time. Van Mander is also the first to insist that Massys studied with no other artist, an exception to the prevailing guild system of apprenticeship then practiced in the Netherlands.

The very earliest reference to Massys predates Lampsonius by five years. It is a citation in Lodovico Guicciardini's *Descrittione di tutti i Paesi Bassi altrimenti detti Germania inferiore,* where the artist is mentioned briefly among other notable Netherlandish painters and is called "Master of Louvain."[3] A local Louvain chronicler, J. Molanus, writing in 1575 in his *Historiae Lovaniensium,* also describes Massys as a Louvain native and refers to the artists's humble beginnings as a blacksmith. Molanus is also the first writer to associate Massys with the other major altarpiece for which he is known today, the
Pl. 1 *St. Anne altarpiece* from Louvain (1507–9; F. 2, cat. 10)

> Quintinus Mesius [sic; the spelling also used by Lampsonius] was also a smith, who worked with his hammer on the mass which surrounds the baptismal font in St. Peter's [Louvain]. Craftsmen still marvel at this. Then he moved to Fantum and found an excellent teacher in Rogerius so that he finally was called to Antwerp on account of his art. From his hand stems the Louvain altar of St. Anna, the Antwerp alter of Mary, which was spared by the iconoclasts on account of its artistic merit.[4]

The historical circumstances of this "Mary altar" of Antwerp correspond with the later version of van Mander concerning the *St. John altarpiece,* although whether Molanus was referring to the same triptych is uncertain.

During the 17th century in Antwerp, Massys became almost a cult figure among admirers of art, for he was regarded as the founder of the local school of painting, which was then climaxing with the career of Peter Paul Rubens.[5] In 1629, the first centennial of Massys' death was marked by a ceremony and the erection of a relief plaque and inscription on the facade of the Antwerp cathedral. The benefactor of this memorial was Cornelis van der Geest, a wealthy art collector who was especially fond of Massys and considered the centerpiece of his own extensive art collection to be Massys' late
Pl. 58 *Madonna of the Cherries* (F. 67, cat. 50; now lost).[6] Van der Geest's plaque dubs Massys "incomparabilis artis Pictor" and repeats the blacksmith legend: "in his time a smith and afterwards a famous painter."[7] Local Antwerp admiration for this painter-patriarch continued unabated at mid-century, when there appeared two different biographies and appreciations of Massys. In 1648, Franchoys Fickaert published *Metamorphosis, or the Wonderful Transformation and Life of the Revered Mr. Quinten Matsys Artistic Smith and Painter in Antwerp.* The "metamorphosis," of course, again refers to the changeover from smith to painter, which today would be considered a complete transformation of lifestyle. Fickaert's book was dedicated to Peter Stevens, close friend of van der Geest and himself the owner of several Massys paintings.[8] The second Massys book of the mid-17th century appeared in 1658. Published by Antwerp art restorer Alexander van Fornenbergh, its title is even more extravagant: *The Antwerp Proteus or the Cyclopean Apelles, that is, the Life and the Artful Deeds of the Exceptional and the Esteemed Mr. Quinten Massys, Transformed from Smith into Fine Painter.*[9] It is clear from the titles of both these books that they depend strongly on the legends concerning the artist's origins and genius. Their chief importance for modern scholars is their relatively early documentation of pictures either by Massys or considered to be by him among those 17th-century collectors of Antwerp who were also the audience for such books.

Only in the middle of the 19th century did local archivists attempt to penetrate the legends surrounding Massys and to sort out surviving documentation about the artist's life.[10] It is surprising that they discovered a kernel of truth behind the myths. Quinten Massys was indeed the son of a smith.[11] His father was Joost Massys (d.1483), his mother Catherine van Kincken. Joost Massys had been in the city of Louvain for some 20 years when Quinten was born.[12] (That birthdate is not recorded but can be reconstructed from Louvain documents.) On 4 April 1491 he was declared "free" at the request of his widowed mother. This means that Quinten was younger than the legal age of majority, 25; on 10 September 1494, however, he declared that majority before the Louvain magistrates as a 28-year-old man. Quinten, therefore, was born sometime between 4 April and 10 September 1466.[13]

The artist had three siblings: Joost, the oldest, Jan, and Catherine. Joost followed the trade of his father and became a smith. There is no evidence for putting Quinten in the family foundry, but neither is there reason to assume that he avoided practicing the family trade while a young man. Despite the 17th-century accounts of poverty in the Massys household, documented donations and possessions of Joost Massys the Elder show a respectable income. Financial need was not the reason young Quinten took up painting.[14]

Unfortunately, the city of Louvain kept no regular guild records for painters before 1494, so if Massys ever enrolled there as an apprentice during his youth, that experience is lost to posterity. Van Mander's insistence that Quinten was self-taught is mainly intended as a tribute to the artist's native ability, or genius. Van Mander gives similar accounts for both Herri met de Bles and Abraham Bloemaert elsewhere in the *Schilderboek;* but this legend of self-education in the painting might also stem from van Mander's own study of the classics: Pliny's *Natural History* mentions testimony by Douris of Samos that Lysippos was just such a "masterless master."[15] Like the later, 17th-century versions of Massys' life, this story seems to stem from a Renaissance-based conception of the artist-as-genius, borrowed from the powerful models of Michelangelo and other Italians as recounted in the biographies of Georgio Vasari's *Lives,* a book well known to van Mander.[16] A related example from Vasari about the patriarch artist of his own city, Florence, recounts that Giotto was discovered by his master, Cimabue, while drawing upon a rock when he was a shepherd in the fields. In similar fashion, Cimabue's natural talent had emerged while he played truant from grammar lessons in order to make drawings "like one who felt himself compelled to do so by nature."[17]

Under the guild regulations of the time it would have been extremely improbable and professionally undesirable for Massys not to have been apprenticed to a painter. Scholars have proposed a variety of possible teachers for the young Quinten.[18] Ultimately, all these connections remain speculative, although the most logical suggestion links Massys with the dominant local painting tradition in Louvain, that of the Bouts family.[19] Although Dieric Bouts died while Massys was a child (1475), his artistic heritage was continued in Louvain by his sons, especially by Albert Bouts, some ten years older than Quinten. Yet even this supposition stands or falls upon the remaining visual evidence of Massys' earliest works, which seem to owe their greatest debt to the even more prominent school of Bruges, then led by Hans Memling.[20] Since this kind of analysis revolves more around the issue of visual influence than around documentation of actual training, Massys' apprenticeship (if any) must remain a matter for conjecture.

One fact is certain: Quinten Massys entered the St. Luke guild of painters in Antwerp in 1491, and he was duly inscribed in the *Liggeren,* or records.[21] Because he was not previously registered in Antwerp as an apprentice, Massys had probably already attained master's status elsewhere, which provides even more reason to believe that his earlier formal training had taken place in Louvain. In Antwerp, Massys is later recorded as having taken on the following apprentices:

a. Ariaen (van Overbeke? master in 1501), inscribed 1495;
b. Willem Muelenbroec, inscribed 1501;
c. Eduart Portugalois (master 1506), inscribed 1504; and
d. Hennen Boeckmakere, inscribed 1510.[22]

Even though the artist continued to be active in Antwerp for 20 years more, he is not recorded as having taken on any new apprentices during that entire time. Part of this reason might have been because his own sons, later painters of considerable talent in their own right, eventually became his assistants in a kind of undeclared apprenticeship; support for this view is provided by the fact that both Cornelis and Jan Massys received their master's patent simultaneously, shortly after the death of their father in 1531.[23] Still another reason for Massys' absence from the city records might be his marked change over those two decades from a painter of large-scale altarpieces, who required assistants, to an artist of smaller-scale and more private works.

A related issue is the presence or absence of the artist in Antwerp. Since the Antwerp guild kept no records of annual payments nor any specifics about its members, no documentation survives concerning Massys' possible travels to other parts of the Netherlands or even farther afield, such as travel to Italy, so much a part of an artist's training later in the 16th century.[24] As in the case of an artist's training, such "foreign" influences on Massys' art, in particular, can be inferred only from visual traces in his surviving works.

The earliest dated Massys painting is the large *St. Anne altarpiece* (completed 1509). Products from the artist's first 16 years can be determined only by comparison with this mature, dated work; their relative chronology to it and to each other is therefore only approximate. Inevitably, the juvenilia of an artist are the most elusive of his works, for only with great difficulty can the derivative or immature elements of such works be separated from the artist's own imitators or unidentifiable contemporaries who worked within the same idiom. To date, Massys' identified early works are few and fairly uniform: mostly small iconic images of the Virgin, influenced strongly by Bruges images. A few portrait medals, dated within the 1490s, still survive (Appendix A) and lend further evidence to the supposition that Massys had some association with Joost's forge. A number of scholars have attempted to see the artist's hand in tapestry designs from this period as a means of explaining the paucity of paintings; here, however, the evidence is largely negative.

Aside from the official guild records, only a few documents survive to tell anything about the life of Quinten Massys. It is certain that he married twice. His first wife, Alijt van Tuylt, he had wedded by 1492; she died in 1507. A document of 15 March 1508 mentions the couple's three children: Quinten, Pauwel, and Katelijne.[25] To these last two children (then minors), Massys deeded their mother's half of the property; in 1511 his fee for the *St. John* or *Lamentation altarpiece* in Antwerp was changed to an annual payment for Quinten and Katelijne.[26] In 1508 Quinten remarried. His second wife, Catherine Heyns, bore him ten children: Jan, Cornelis, Quinten, Maria, Huebrecht, Abraham, Peternella, Katelijne, Sara, and Susanna.[27] The artistic careers of the first two children of this second union have already been mentioned.

Quinten also influenced his contemporaries through his homes, two of which were considered Antwerp landmarks during his own lifetime. The first, located in the Huidenvetterstraat, was called "The Ape" *(de simme)*.[28] In his diary (5 August 1520) Dürer mentions a visit to this house during his stay in Antwerp: "I have also been Master Quinten's house."[29] On 6 August 1521 Quinten inherited property from his second wife's family, and he decided to build a second house with a gate and a garden on that site, the Schuttershofstraat.[30] This house he called "St. Quinten" after his patron saint, whose colored iron statue was placed over the door (in later years, this statue was naturally attributed to Massys, the former smith). If van Fornenbergh's account of the interior of this house can be trusted and can be attributed to Massys rather than to some later inhabitant, it was indeed a splendidly decorated site, with a frieze of Italianate ornament such as grotesques, festoons, and spirals with playing putti on its walls *en grisaille*.[31] Massys' homes attest to his relatively high income and local prominence. Genealogical researches have shown that his first wife's family were landowners in the Kempen region.[32] In short, both of Massys' marriages enhanced his wealth and position. In this connection, the apocryphal story of how Massys' wife preferred a painter to a smith indicates (if the story has even the remotest basis in fact) the importance of the artist's mate in his professional ambition.

Some of these elements when pieced together suggest a composite profile of the artist. Both the elaborate ornamentation of his dwelling and the withdrawal from active training of apprentices in his workshop imply that Massys increasingly isolated himself from the customary behavior of his profession and turned from the image and rank of craftsman to the loftier role of wealthy burgher, or *poorter*. This conjecture receives reinforcement from another important bit of negative evidence: Massys never once served as dean *(dekan)* of the Antwerp Painters' guild of St. Luke. Friedländer was the first to hypothesize that such a notable omission meant that the artist "held aloof from guild society," yet van den Branden insists, in defense of Massys, that this deanship involved only a burdensome administrative duty that would have interfered with active painting.[33] Like the denial of apprentices, the denial of deanships is negative evidence, yet it does show us a painter who spent the last two decades of his career outside the mainstream activities of his guild colleagues.[34] During this later period, the artist who had created the two great altarpieces of St. Anne and St. John increasingly retreated from this most public realm of religious painting (see Chap. 5). No other documentary evidence helps to explain such an alteration.[35] After Massys' 1517 portrait commission by Erasmus and Antwerp's town secretary, Peter Gillis (F. 36–37, cat. 58), it is also possible to adduce the importance of Massys' increasing association with Erasmus and Antwerp's Erasmian circle of humanist scholars (see Chapter 6) as an influence of the artist's redefinition of his role and profession. His abandonment of the public piety of altarpieces for a more private and personal religious imagery may be attributed to a set of altered religious values, due in part to this humanist contact of Massys. In addition, Erasmus, as well as Antwerp's literary society, the *rederijkers,* were essential to the development of Massys' moralizing, satirical secular subjects (see Chap. 7).

One other, final bit of documentation sheds light on Massys' religiosity. When the artist died of plague ("sweating sickness") in the summer of 1530, he was reported to have spent his last days in seclusion at a Carthusian monastery on the outskirts of Antwerp, in the community of Kiel.[36] The austerity and ascetic ideals of the Carthusians were combined with their insistence on a vivid, meditative reenactment of biblical events. Evidence of Carthusian religious ideals emerges from the late, half-length religious narrative pictures by Massys. Indeed, this Carthusian piety must be considered as a powerful complement to the internalized Erasmian piety that Massys discovered among the Antwerp humanist circle (see Chap. 6).

To complete the record of Massys' social contacts, mention should be made of the painter's part in the estate of his fellow artist Joachim Patinir (d. 5 October 1524). At that time "Meester Quinten Matsijs, Karel Alaerts, and Jan Buyst, all painters" were listed as "kith and kin" and guardians of the orphaned minors, two daughters of Patinir.[37] Master Joachim Patinir was called by Dürer "the good landscape painter" *(den goeden landschapschilder)* and was one of the earliest artists to make a specialty out of painting landscapes (usually inhabited by tiny figures).[38] Patinir and Massys collaborated on a large painting, signed by Patinir (now in Madrid, Prado, F. 31, cat. 26) of the *Temptation of St. Anthony;* *Pl. 114* for that work, Massys completed the larger foreground figure group, Patinir the landscape and smaller distant figures.

More important than any specific social connections of the painter is the environment in which, and for which, he painted his pictures. Early 16th-century Antwerp was truly one of history's remarkable urban settings. According to the 16th-century travelogue of Lodovico Guicciardini, "Antwerp was the truly leading city in almost all things, but in commerce it headed all the cities of the world."[39]

The foundations of that commerce—and the resulting population, prosperity, and cultural creativity—were formed by the coincidence of several major trade communities linked together in the favorable geographical center of Antwerp. Antwerp had always been a marketplace and port, located near the North Sea on a broad stretch of the River Scheldt. During the 14th century it shared with nearby Bergen-op-Zoom the annual Fairs of Brabant, an important trade conclave, particularly for staples. During the 15th century the local Flemish cloth industry and its principal port, Bruges, began to encounter stiff competition from the English, who no longer exported their fine wool to Flanders but instead began, with royal assistance, to build their own national cloth industry. Antwerp cashed in on the new trade development and imported the English cloth that did so much to undermine the ecomony of her neighboring cities in Flanders and Brabant; in 1496 the *Magnus Intercursus* (known to disgruntled Flemings as the *Malus Intercursus),* a commercial agreement between Henry VII of England and Archduke Maximilian of the Netherlands, established Antwerp as the continental depot for the sale of English cloth.[40] Rapid expansion of trade in this cloth led to major growth in Antwerp concurrently with that in the English center, London.

A second major component of the rapid growth of Antwerp was Portuguese trade in spices. At the end of the 15th century, Portuguese seafaring merchant adventurers, again led by royal support under the renowned Prince Henry the Navigator, had found the seaway to India and the Far East.[41] This broke the Italian monopoly in the spice trade, another of the pillars of Bruges trade hegemony in the Netherlands. In 1499 Antwerp was chosen as the European depot for this important new exchange. What the Portuguese depended upon for their barter in Africa and India they could also find in Antwerp: copper, a metal more highly prized in Africa than gold. The source of this copper was the third of Antwerp's cornerstones of prosperity: South German merchants, principally from Augsburg and Nuremberg. Their use of mercury in a technique known as the amalgamation process helped to separate gold and silver from copper ore.[42] Within the mines of Bohemia and Hungary, controlled by the South Germans, such intensified extractions of both silver and copper led to a major boom in the metal trade. Meeting together in Antwerp, the South Germans and the Portuguese provided the basis of a new worldwide economy, whose fulcrum of exchange was the city on the Scheldt.[43]

Antwerp's prosperity acted as a magnet for artists from all over the Netherlands. Friedländer puts the matter succinctly: "Almost every master who distinguished himself in the broad region of the Netherlands between 1500 and 1530 turns up for at least a brief sojourn in Antwerp."[44] The names of the artists preserved in the Antwerp guild records almost always point to other cities of origin for these painters: "Painters kept arriving, bringing with them ideas from Brussels, Louvain, Mons, Amsterdam, Leyden, Maubeuge—an especially large number from Holland and Bruges."[45] In this context young Quinten arrived from his native Louvain and fell under the spell of the dominant artistic school of Bruges. At the time of his arrival, the city of Antwerp had virtually no native painting tradition and had not yet fully developed the economic boom that coincided with the arrival of the Portuguese. In fact, the city was so lacking in local artistic talent that it imported the Brussels painter Colijn de Coter in 1493 to ornament the vault of the St. Luke chapel of the Antwerp painters in the Church of Our Lady.[46] The guild records from the years immediately following Massys' own membership indicate the vacuum in Antwerp painting at this time: in 1492–93, 39 new masters were accepted into the Antwerp St. Luke guild as painters, and one-third of them carried names of other cities with them into the new port of opportunity.[47]

This economic history, even for painters, might be only the material foundation for Antwerp's prosperity and of little direct interest in the study of Massys were it not for the fact that the artist enjoyed the patronage of a number of the more important parties involved in the city's boom. In particular, he seems to have made good contacts with the Portuguese trade representatives, or *factors* (see Chapter 3). Through them, Massys was commissioned to send two large altarpieces for royally founded convents in Portugal. A later private altarpiece (lost) was painted for another Portuguese merchant, Damião de Gois, who also developed humanist interests (Chap. 3; Documented Lost Works,
Pl. 37 no. 2). A small-scale, private altarpiece (F. 3, cat. 24) by Massys was made for yet another important member of the Antwerp trading community, Lucas Rem, who represented one of the principal Augsburg metal and financial families, the Welsers, in both Antwerp and Lisbon. That these were by no means isolated instances is atttested by Dürer's experiences, recorded in his diary, during his visits to Antwerp in 1520–21. The German artist was especially close to Portuguese trade representatives, in particular the factors João Brandão, whose portrait he made alongside a likeness of his black servant, and Rodrigo Fernández d'Almada, for whom he made a portrait and the oil painting *St. Jerome,* now in Lisbon (1521).[48] Dürer, of course, also enjoyed a generous reception from the German trade representatives in Antwerp, including Bernhard Stecher, the factor of the Fuggers, the largest, wealthiest, and most powerful of the Augsburg families.[49] Likewise, Dürer mentions numerous meetings with Italians, who were, with the Spanish, later defectors from their trading havens in Bruges to the newer commerce of Antwerp.[50]

The foreign communities in Antwerp added a considerable cosmopolitan atmosphere to the city. Aside from the impressive accounts of currency brought in by these groups, they enhanced possibilities for the export of Antwerp paintings and sculpture. For example, numerous Flemish-sculpted retables are found even today in small provincial churches throughout Europe, particularly in Sweden, northern France, Germany, and Spain.[53] Information about the export of painted retables and smaller pictures is not extensive; however, the career of Joos van Cleve furnishes an instructive example from the period of Massys' activity. Between the years 1515 and 1530, van Cleve sent major altarpiece retables to such faraway places as Genoa and Danzig.[52] The opportunity to send out paintings with the other export items from Antwerp was undoubtedly the basis of the massive production of paintings grouped today under the stylistic heading of "Antwerp Mannerism."[53] The strongly decorative character and the frankly exotic presentation of costumes and setting recall the forms of sculpted works for export, and occasionally such paintings adorn the wings of sculpted retables; moreover, the repetition of stock themes, such as the Nativity and the Adoration of the Magi, suggests a formulaic production geared toward a broad audience.[54] Again, Joos van Cleve offers a point of reference for the Antwerp Mannerist movement, for his triptychs of the Adoration of the Magi dating from (ca. 1515–25) are steeped in that particular stylistic idiom (see Chapter 9).[55]

Yet the Antwerp environment was surely not just a place for the production of art for export. The presence of so many national groups must also have occasioned the arrival in Antwerp of some of the art from their own countries. In particular, the Italian influences that have been detected by scholars in the later works of both Massys and Joos van Cleve might as easily have been the result of the collections of Italians in Antwerp as of trips to Italy by the Flemish painters. In the case of Massys, familiarity with Leonardo da Vinci drawings (or copies of those drawings) is demonstrated by the grotesque heads in Quinten's *Martyrdom of St. John the Evangelist* from the *St. John altarpiece* (see Chap. 2), but the source for these heads, Leonardo's *Five Grotesque Heads* (now in Windsor Castle), was one of that artist's more frequently copied studies on paper. For the same *St. John altarpiece,* Massys also used figures from Dürer's *Martyrdom of St. John the Evangelist* (B. 61), the woodcut introduction to his 1498 *Apocalypse* cycle, a work which surely required no special visit by Massys to Germany. There is simply no firm evidence for a trip by Quinten to Italy, even though other artists later in the century made such a visit a mandatory element of their training, beginning with the 1508 expedition of Jan Gossaert.[56] Prior to that time, however, the artistic exchange had been concentrated, particularly between Bruges and Florence, by way of the representatives of the Medici bank. For example, the portraits by Hans Memling (see Chap. 8) offer a strong precedent during Massys' youth for a reciprocal visual exchange between Flanders and Italy.[57] This exchange of Memling, it should be repeated, was also an artistic contact tied to commercial movement rather than to the travels of individual artists.

Pl. 15
Pl. 16
Pl. 14

Antwerp was more than a large welter of collectors making jobs possible for struggling young artists. The city must be taken as a cultural base, where both the artist and collector shared common values. Antwerp culture provided the occasions for picture-making and enabled the collectors and artists to reach consensus on what kinds of paintings properly fulfilled their purposes. Unfortunately, the records of 16th-century Antwerp are not very informative. No major city writer had the self-consciousness of the contemporary German authors to write a chronicle of his home town; it is ironic that one of the earliest full accounts of Antwerp and other Netherlandish towns of the mid-16th century is by an outsider, Lodovico Guicciardini—his *Descrittione di tutti i Paesi Bassi (Description of the Low Countries and of the Provinces thereof)* mentioned earlier.

A good place to begin investigation of Antwerp culture is through the local citywide rituals. One of the most informative of Antwerp's local ceremonies is its annual procession, or *ommegang* (literally meaning "tour"), of Our Lady on Assumption Sunday. This procession consisted of a number of wagons and scenic *tableaux,* which could vary from year to year. Fortunately, the *ommegang* of August 1520 was described by Dürer in his diary. That passage is worth quoting in full:

> On the Sunday after Our Dear Lady's Assumption I saw the great Procession from the Church of Our Lady at Antwerp, when the whole town of every craft and rank was assembled, each dressed according to his rank. And all ranks and guilds had their signs, by which they might be known. In the intervals great costly pole-candles were borne, and their long old Frankish trumpets of silver. There were also in the German fashion many pipers and drummers. All the instruments were loudly and noisily blown and beaten. I saw the Procession pass along the street, and people being arranged in rows, each man some distance from his neighbor, but the rows close one behind another. There were the Goldsmiths, the Painters, the Masons, the Broderers, the Sculptors, the Joiners, the Carpenters,

the Sailors, the Fishermen, the Butchers, the Leatherers, the Clothmakers, the Bakers, the Tailors, the Cordwainers—indeed, workmen of all kinds, and many craftsmen and dealers who work for their livelihood. Likewise, the shopkeepers and merchants and their assistants of all kinds were there. After these came the shooters with guns, bows, and cross-bows and the horsemen and foot-soldiers also. Then followed the watch of the Lords Magistrates. Then came a fine troop all in red, nobly and splendidly clad. Before them however went all the religious Orders and the members of some foundations very devoutly, all in their different robes. A very large company of widows also took part in this procession. They support themselves with their own hands and observe a special rule. They were all dressed from head to foot in white linen garments, made expressly for the occasion, very sorrowful to see. Among them I saw some stately persons. Last of all came the Chapter of Our Lady's Church with all their clergy, scholars, and treasurers. Twenty persons bore the image of the Virgin Mary with the Lord Jesus, adorned in the costliest manner, to the honor of the Lord God. In this Procession very many delightful things were shown, most splendidly got up. Wagons were drawn along with masques upon ships and other structures. Behind them came the company of the Prophets in their order and scenes from the New Testament, such as the Annunciation, the Three Holy Kings riding on great camels and on other rare beasts, very well arranged; also how Our Lady fled to Egypt—very devout—and many other things, which for shortness I omit. At the end came a great Dragon which St. Margaret and her maidens led by a girdle; she was especially beautiful. Behind her came St. George with his squire, a very goodly knight in armor. In this host also rode boys and maidens most finely and variously dressed in the costumes of many lands, representing various Saints. From beginning to end the Procession lasted more than two hours before it was gone past our house. And so many things were there that I could never write them all in a book, so I let it well alone.[58]

Some of the other wonders of the *ommegang,* omitted by Dürer, are mentioned by Voet in his discussion of a 1684 print of that year's *ommegang* by Gaspar Bouttats (1625–1703).[59] Voet states that from the beginning of the 16th century the wagons pulled such frequent images as the legendary giant of Antwerp, Druon Antigon, an elephant, a dolphin with a cupid, a great ship, a whale with Neptune, Apollo and the Muses on Mt. Parnassus, and the Virgin of Antwerp. This kind of procession can be compared to America's present-day ritual parades with their floats of giant figures and allegorical themes manned by static personifications, usually beautiful young women; sandwiched between the floats are groups of "dignitaries" riding (as befits their station) and marching groups (usually marching bands).

In Antwerp's procession, the city magistrates, two burgomasters, and sixteen aldermen *(schepenen),* two jurists, secretaries, and treasurer-recorders *(greffiers)* marched at the head of the *ommegang.* This governing body functioned for the town in conjunction with the Duke of Brabant or, more usually, his representatives: a margrave, a sheriff *(schout)* for criminal cases, and a bailiff *(amman)* for civil cases.[60] After the end of the 15th century, the college of burgomasters and aldermen consisted of both nobles and burghers *(poorters)* who were not members of guilds. These are the first rank of the groups singled out by Dürer. In terms of Massys' career, it is worth noting that some of the closest Antwerp associates of Erasmus were members of the College of Magistrates as either *stadsgreffier* (Peter Gillis, or Petrus Aegidius) or *stadssekretaris* (Cornelius de Schrijver, or Grapheus); their extensive education was an essential background for their legal and scribal duties for the city.

The majority of the marchers in the *ommegang* were members of the various official guilds of the city, arranged according to their professions. Three of the 22 guilds held a privileged position within the General Council of the City: the boatmen *(schippers),* oldest of the guilds; the mercers *(meerseniers),* richest of the guilds; and the linen-workers *(lakenbereiders),* finishers of the imported English linen. These, of course, were the most important industries in the port city. Particular guild associations had arisen during the 14th century; in addition to maintaining monopolies and standard prices during the periods between open fairs in Antwerp, they served as a kind of welfare and pension fund for members (some even had retirement homes for their aged members), much in the manner of modern trade unions.[61] Guilds took responsibility for burial, with full attendance of members, of their constituents. In addition, most of the guilds had chapels with particular religious devotions of their own.[62] Here, too, we find that Massys was a participant, because the Antwerp coopers and joiners guild had commissioned a *Lamentation* retable from the artist and placed it in their chapel. In 1511 he completed a second *Lamentation altarpiece* with wings, devoted to their patron saint, John, for the splinter guild of the joiners, who had separated themselves from the coopers in the meantime (see Chapter 2). (Both these traditional groups are cited by Dürer.) In similar fashion other guilds maintained altarpieces dedicated to their patron saints; Peter Schabacker has demonstrated that the portraitlike image of *St. Eloy* as goldsmith and jeweller (New York, Metropolitan Museum Lehmann coll.) was commissioned by the Antwerp guild of smiths to honor their patron saint.[63] The sign of membership in any guild was that characteristic and distinctive dress which Dürer observed in the colorful file of the corporations in the 1520 *ommegang*. *Pl. 119*

Massys' own painters' guild of St. Luke had begun as an association of gold- and silversmiths, painters, glassmakers, embroiderers, and enamelers as early as 1382, and received a charter as a guild in 1442.[64] At the time of Dürer's observations and Massys' membership, the guild also included the first of Antwerp's three literary guilds or "rhetoricians" *(rederijkers)*, called *De Violieren* (Gillyflower, or pink). Such "Chambers of Rhetoric" were institutions in each town in the Netherlands; the first to be called by that title originated in Oudenaarde in 1441.[65] The origins of these literary societies are obscure, but they seem to be an outgrowth of church organizations of the late Middle Ages that put on ecclesiastical dramas and pageants, and they continued to number ordained members even when fully independent of the churches in later years. Such direction remained the principal urban function of these *rederijkers*, even when their independence and secularization gave them a distinctive character in the 16th century. Most of them, like *De Violieren* (est. 1480), were named after plants. Each also had its own motto and arms; that of *De Violieren* was *uyt jonsten versaemt* ("united by friendship"). Antwerp's other two rival rhetorician groups were called *Goudbloem* (Marigold, est. 1488) and *Olijftak* (Olive Branch, est. 1510). In addition to their organization of public festivals and plays, *rederijker* contests between rival clubs were a major periodic event (at irregular intervals of several years), a kind of verbal Olympics in which neighboring towns competed against one another with compositions on a predetermined theme.[66] These contests for prizes were called Landjewels *(Landjuwelen)*, and the first one was held in Antwerp in 1515. The largest and most splendid was also hosted by Antwerp in 1561.[67] Landjewels also had a festival atmosphere and featured colorful costumes, wagons, floats, and cavalcades, like the *ommegang* itself. Their central questions were usually religious morals, such as the topic "What is the greatest favor given by God for man's salvation?" Like professional guilds, the *rederijkers* selected a leader, called in this case a "prince," who spoke the parting verses of *rederijker* poems, set rules of composition, and offered prizes to the winners of verbal contests. Most important of the officers, a "factor" composed the presentation verses of the Chamber and led most of the performances, like a modern director in the theatre. Finally, most of the chambers had a fool or jester among their number, whose importance as an image of both folly and truth-telling was central to their satirical poems. (see Chap. 7).

The typical plays performed by *rederijkers* at Landjewels and public gatherings were of two kinds: farces *(kluchten* or *esbattementen)* and serious morality plays *(zinnespelen)*. Again, the origins of these latter performances are to be found in ecclesiastical drama of the late Middle Ages, either mystery, saint, and miracle plays or the more allegorical morality plays beginning in the 14th century.[68] In the 16th century, almost all the serious dramas were allegorical in presentation; making use of personification was a frequent element in public spectacles, like the *ommegang* (see below for the figures on the wagons of the *ommegang)*.[69] Thus, unlike the classic dramas of Greece and their progeny, these moralities featured not action and causality, but independent declarations; not an unfolding succession of moments in time, but a series of scenic tableaux loosely joined around the central moral issue.[70] The classic morality play is "Everyman," originally composed in Dutch (the full Dutch title is *The Mirror of Salvation of Everyman)* but translated into English by the end of the 15th century.[71] The simple and timeless plot is the encounter of any- and everyman with Death; together they meet Society, Friends,

Kin, and Worldly Goods, then a weakened Virtue in a sickbed. By Virtue Everyman is led to Knowledge (of God), Confession, then Wisdom, Strength, and Beauty, and eventually the five senses. The moral of the play is that without Knowledge of God, man is misled by his senses and values; but after encountering Knowledge, all his faculties lead directly to God in the form of the sacrament. Properly enlightened by Virtue, mankind turns from distractions to righteousness. He then is prepared for death. This close connection between the drama and moral instruction is part of an address to the audience of the morality play; it is the viewer rather than a protagonist who is the true hero of serious *rederijker* dramas. This superindividual, generalized characterization leads to a kind of detached viewer contemplation, rather than to an Aristotelian empathy with the characters of a drama; in this regard it is entirely appropriate to a goal of moral instruction and is allied to the process of meditation upon literary tracts of theology (see below). Like the ascetic books, these plays are discursive arguments intended to produce religious insight and transformation—indeed, "conversion" in the original, literal sense—like the alteration of the characters of the play. The satirical, secular pictures of Massys (Chap. 7) often partake of this sermonizing spirit, presenting characters drawn from daily life in compromising actions or grotesque aspect in order to bring home a Christian ethical point to the viewer.

In choosing character types from daily life, however, Massys' secular images also partake of the naturalistic characterizations of the other main *rederijker* dramas, the farces *(kluchten)*. These brief comical sketches principally involved a small number of characters, often in basic domestic situations, like husband-wife or peasant-fool confrontations. Examples include a "Taming of the Shrew" where a husband subdues his shrewish wife by cloaking her in black fur and making a pack-horse out of her *(Moorkens vel van de quade wijven,* before 1538), or the occasion where a peasant "converts" to the profession and dons the attributes of a fool in order to escape from work and the domination of his wife *(De Sotslach)*.[72] Heckling and stock types drawn from everyday society characterize these farces, just as they populate the more grotesque of Massys secular images *(Ill-Matched Pair, Grotesque Old Woman;* see Chap. 7).

Rederijkers were not specifically singled out by Dürer among the groups he saw in the 1521 Antwerp *ommegang.* But another related group mentioned in the diary is the military contingent of the city: musket-shooters, bowmen, horsemen, and infantry. As in the professions, these military men were also organized into guilds, called *schuttersgilde,* or shooting companies[73] The association of *rederijkers* with these *schuttersgilde* was especially marked on festival days, as illustrated in the *Festival of St. George's Day* (1559), a print by Peter Bruegel that depicts a rural celebration in honor of the patron saint of soldiers.[74] Among the entertainments on such occasions (which included a sword dance, archery contests, and ritual enactment of the tilt between the saint and the dragon) was an outdoor performance on a temporary stage by local *rederijkers;* the play in progress appears by costume to be a *klucht.*[75] It is hardly coincidence that the pattern of the *rederijker* Landjewel was established after the model of *schuttersgilde* conclaves of the same name; the later, independent *rederijker* festivals seem to be a direct outgrowth of an earlier collaboration with militia companies. Even the idea of contests mingled with festivity and the choice of ranked officers was borrowed from the shooting companies, leading some authors to speculate that the very origins of *rederijker* chambers lay in this secular corps, rather than in the realm of church dramas.[76] According to Guicciardini, Antwerp had six militia companies of 100 members each: two chapters of the Arbalestriers (cross-bowmen), two of Archers, one of Arquebusiers (musketeers), and one of Two-Hand Swordsmen.[77] That these companies had some importance for artists can be seen from examples spanning three entire centuries in the Netherlands. The first instance is the famous Roger van der Weyden altarpiece of the *Deposition* (Madrid, Prado), commissioned not in Antwerp but in Louvain, for the Archers' guild of that city for their chapel in the Church of Notre-Dame Outside-the-Walls.[78] Around the time of Massys, an *Archery Fair,* dated on its original (now lost) frame to the year 1493, shows many of the costumed soldiers of the shooters company in festive dalliance, accompanied by the colorful central figures of two fools; the picture is attributed to the anonymous Antwerp artist known as the Master of Frankfurt.[79] The final examples of militia companies' importance are to be found in their continuing patronage of the arts during the 17th century. In Antwerp, one of Rubens's most important early altarpiece commissions was the triptych of the *Descent from the Cross* of 1611–14, commissioned for Antwerp Cathedral by the local Arquebusiers.[80] The 17th-century militia companies no longer commissioned religious art in the Calvinist Netherlands, but their group portrait commissions were the largest undertakings of such painters as Frans Hals, Bartholomeus van der Helst, and Rembrandt.[81]

The remaining organizations in Antwerp's *ommegang* were religious orders and members of foundations. The former, or course, were members of the local monastic organizations; in the 50,000 population of Antwerp in Massys' day, some 500 were monks in holy orders, including the Carthusians of nearby Kiel; the Augustine Eremites (after 1513, a leading center for Lutheran religious views during the early 1520's); the Premonstratensians of St. Michael's Abbey (admiringly mentioned and sketched by Dürer); the Cistercians (St. Salvator Priory), Dominican, Carmelite, and Minorite cloisters; and outside the walls a Victorine cloister and Beguine court.[82] Other important participants in religious life were the chapters of local parish churches, four in number: St. Walburgis (the oldest), St. James (Jakobs), St. George (Joris) and the Church of Our Lady, later elevated to the status of cathedral (in 1559; Antwerp was in the bishopric of Cambrai during Massys's lifetime).[83] These churches took on added significance because they were the sites of Antwerp's Latin schools, supported by both the chapters and the city government. The prominence of these parish churches and their chapters in city life is made vivid by their building programs during this very period. In particular, the Church of Our Lady had begun construction of its west facade in 1454; its south transept arm was completed in 1483–93, followed by the north in 1491–1519. Under the direction of Herman II de Waghemakere and his son, Dominicus, the slender north tower of Our Lady was constructed through three storeys, with special activity taking place during the period 1501–2, and the crowning of the tower in 1521.[84] Massys proudly featured the Antwerp tower of Our Lady, which already had the status of a civic symbol, in the background of the *Offering of Joachim*, exterior wing of the *St. Anne altarpiece* (1507–9; see Chap. 2); however, at the time of the painting, that tower was incomplete and Massys' imagination added the crowning pinnacle. When completed, the tower was one of Europe's tallest structures (123 m.), adorning the largest parish church, and its elaborate clockwork was named "Charles" in honor of the city's ruler, Emperor Charles V. *Pl. 8*

But the other parish churches enjoyed a similar period of prosperity and growth.[85] Like the Church of Our Lady, they were begun at the end of the 15th century and continued throughout the 16th century, sometimes completed only during the time of Rubens. The St. James Church was begun in 1491 with the west tower and the nave shortly afterwards (1496–97), also according to plans by Herman de Waghemakere, succeeded by Dominicus, then Rombout Keldermans (who also worked on Notre Dame after 1521); it lay incomplete until 1656, and the west tower was never finished. St. Walburgis, now destroyed, was reconstructed during the 16th century, beginning in 1499, but it remained uncompleted until the 1640s. A monastic church, St. Andrew (Andries) was begun after 1515 as cloister church of the Saxon Augustinians and became a fifth parish church after the Lutheran sympathies of the Augustinians caused the order to be banned from Antwerp in 1522. The St. George (Joris) Church, now destroyed, added a choir and aisles around 1500. And various monastic churches added to their buildings during this active century, including the Dominicans (1540; plan from 1517; now St. Paul's), Minorites (1492; destroyed), and Carmelites (1499; destroyed).[86]

Antwerp, then, was a town where religion was a principal enterprise, symbolized by the translation of piety into major constructions in stone. The final set of participants in the *ommegang* parade were also religious worshippers of still another kind: lay members of religious confraternities. These brotherhoods were organized along the same lines of self-help and mutual pious devotion as the trade guilds, and they endorsed a special patron saint or cult within their own private chapels. Usually, they sponsored masses in honor of their patron saint and special celebrations on their annual festivals, as well as requiem masses and burials for fellow members. Antwerp had six major confraternities of varying ages and sizes.

The confraternity of the Holy Cross was the oldest, established in the Church of Our Lady in 1375.[87] Half of its dozen members were laymen, and all were members of the aristocracy. The Holy Cross brotherhood sponsored a Friday Holy Cross mass with 14 to 16 singers on its own altar and promoted the celebration of the Invention of the True Cross (May 3) and the Elevation of the Cross (September 14). More peculiar to Antwerp was the Brotherhood of the Holy Circumcision, which was citywide and not tied to any particular church. Its membership of 24 leading citizens was established in 1427 but was enlarged to an indefinite number, dependent upon an annual membership fee. The raison d'être of the Circumcision brotherhood was the precious relic of the foreskin of Christ, which was preserved in Antwerp. By 1389 the city already had established a Circumcision chapel with the relic on its altar. According to Guicciardini, on Trinity day the city held a procession (est. 1324), led by the confraternity, of its foreskin relic.[88] Another old guild is that of "Salve Regina" confraternity of the Virgin, established in 1456 in the Church of Our Lady. Almost immediately a rival confraternity, Praise of Our Lady, based on the "Laudes" hymns, sprang up in 1478, and the two groups contended for prominence in local events like the *ommegang*.[89] Praise of Our Lady sought to sing hymns before the image of the Virgin in the cathedral and was especially devoted to musical performance for voices, chimes, and organ. Members of Praise of Our Lady included knights of the Order of the Golden Fleece, margraves, burgomasters, *ammans*, and the like, including the richest burghers of Antwerp. Membership had increased to 200 by 1505, and the prominent tradesmen of Antwerp who were brothers also attracted some of their colleagues in the foreign "nations" of Antwerp into affiliation with Praise of Our Lady.

Third oldest of the confraternities was Holy Sacrament, founded in 1446.[90] This veneration of the eucharist was a powerful devotion of the period.[91] A measure of the seriousness of the sacrament was the large tabernacle constructed to house it; in Antwerp this tabernacle was ordered by the confraternity of the Holy Sacrament in 1493. Other massive and ornate tabernacles survive in the Netherlands, the loveliest of which is the mid-15th-century turret construction in the Church of St. Peter of Louvain by Matthew de Layen.[92] Another testimony to the almost magical aura about the sacrament is the presence in prints and paintings of so many versions of the sacrament *Miracle of St. Gregory*.[93] In Antwerp after 1497 the Holy Sacrament brotherhood shared its altar with the soapmakers trade guild, whose patron saint was St. Gregory. Popular superstition then held that each mass released a tormented soul from purgatory and converted a sinner and helped to ward off danger between Sunday communions.[94]

Second oldest of Antwerp's confraternities was St. Anthony, founded in 1423. Anthony was venerated as a healer of skin diseases and of disease in general. In this capacity, the saint stood as the patron of a monastic order of hospitals.[95] A later Antwerp guild dedicated to St. Roch (1495) seems to have been specifically tied to healing the plague, for Roch, a 14th-century plague victim, gave his life for the preservation of future Christians from the plague.[96] Massys featured Roch along with another antiplague martyr, St. Sebastian, on the wings of his private altarpiece for the South German trade representative, Lucas Rem (see Chap. 3).

These Antwerp confraternities represent only the most prominent of local devotions, centered around important local relics like the Holy Foreskin, around particular therapeutic saints, around the central sacrament of the mass, and around central images of the faith, the Virgin and the Cross. Such brotherhoods were supported by the most prosperous and prominent of Antwerp's citizens, as well as by a larger populace. They help to point out the significance of the *ommegang* event which Dürer witnessed, in which such confraternities marched alongside militia companies and trade unions to honor the Virgin.

The Virgin occupied a special position of veneration in Antwerp. The accounts of the Church of Our Lady record numerous offerings to images or devotions of the Madonna, including the *ommegang* itself. Another important cult in Antwerp, second only to the foreskin as an object of veneration, was an image of the Mdonna, fixed to a tree, nicknamed the "Virgin on the Stick" *(Onze Lieve Vrouw op 't Stoksken).*[97] During the 1470s a new pedestal, a silver replica with chain, and an iron grill ornamented this famous image. These miracle-working or venerable images were by no means unique to Antwerp; they could be found during the late Middle Ages throughout the Netherlands. According to the definitive study of Netherlandish Mary veneration by Kronenburg, some 70 such images, usually ancient, were carried in procession, shown to pilgrims, and made the objects of special cults—the kind of worship condemned pointedly by Erasmus as superstitious (see Chap. 6).[98]

The image carried through the streets of Antwerp was an older version of the same kind of Madonna, and it had been featured in the *ommegang* since 1399. The procession began after an all-night vigil in the cathedral by members of the guilds in front of the sacred image of the Virgin. Not by accident was the route of that same image in the *ommegang* a round-trip circuit from the Church of Our Lady.[99] Religious processions were a characteristic form of late medieval piety in urban areas, beginning with Candlemas (Purification of the Virgin), and liturgically sanctioned sacrament processions on Rogation days (before Ascension), Holy Week, and Sacrament Sunday.[100] Protestants objected to these public manifestations of religion as a kind of degrading public amusement.[101] Such public religiosity was particularly striking when seen in full spectacle, as Dürer witnessed the *ommegang*, with music, costumes, floats, and tableaux. And the processions were administered in cities as much by the civic magistrates as by the ecclesiastical authorities; both of these groups appear prominently in the Antwerp *ommegang*. Other periods of procession usually occurred on the festival day of a patron saint of a church or confraternity or on the anniversary day of a church's foundation, the kermess (from *kerk-mis*, or church-mass) so magnificently depicted (including background processions) by Peter Bruegel in both prints and paintings.[102] Of course, venerated holy relics, like the foreskin of Antwerp or the Holy Blood at Bruges, were favored local occasions for celebrations by means of a grand procession.

Bruges's Procession of the Holy Blood, reenacted annually even today, was the grandest procession in the greatest Flemish city of Massys' day, and it undoubtedly served as the model for Antwerp's *ommegang*.[103] Like the Antwerp relic of the foreskin, Bruges's Holy Blood allegedly came from the Holy Land, a gift of gratitude by the Patriarch of Jerusalem to Count Thierry of Alsace for his role in the crusade of 1150. It was described by 13th-century eulogists as the result of Joseph of Arimathea's ministrations during the Deposition of Christ. The procession, at the beginning of each May, coincided with the beginning of the large trade fair of Bruges and provided a ceremonial hiatus in the civic calendar with parades, contests, concerts, and mystery plays. In the magnificent procession, like Antwerp's *ommegang* of a century later, marched knights, city officials, the aristocratic members of the Confraternity of the Holy Blood, local clergy, bearers of relics and standards, and all of the guilds in Bruges in special costumes made for the occasion. Like today's parades, the city presented a prize to the group with the finest decorations. Biblical scenes were staged with full costume and all of the elaborate detail described so meticulously in contemporary accounts. The procession then was both a religious manifestation and a time for civic pride and display. It was an invocation of protection by, and of special honor for, the prized and powerful local relic. In the most literal sense, this procession made the city of Bruges into a religious center, even in the literal, cosmic sense, where the boundaries between profane and sacred are dissolved in celebration.

In the same way, it is as a procession with a definite local emphasis that the Antwerp *ommegang* came to have such prominence in Antwerp's civic life. In this context lies the importance of the unidentified wagons and allegories, which Dürer could not understand as readily as he could the prophets and saints and New Testament scenes from the life of the Virgin. These, of course, were in honor of the Madonna as the center of the ceremonies (the scenes recounted by Dürer included the Annunciation, Adoration of the Magi, and Flight into Egypt) and were an outgrowth of the church mystery plays so beloved and frequent and vivid in the late Middle Ages.[104] But the unidentified, more locally significant elements of the *ommegang* can be established through the study of manuscripts that inventory the accessories of the procession and through prints recording the appearance of the procession.[105] At Antwerp each of the guilds owned its own wagon, which it regularly presented in each succeeding *ommegang*. In addition to some religious images not mentioned by Dürer—St. John the Baptist in the Desert, Holy Trinity, Last Judgment, and Hell—the *ommegang* presented allegorical imagery of the city and its features, much in the manner of modern American parades and pageants. Generally, the city of Antwerp herself was represented by a beautiful young girl, the *pucelle* of the city. Guicciardini explains the basis of this image of innocence and beauty: "The city of Antwerp is considered a maiden *[pucelle]*; that is, the inhabitants here affirm that she will never revolt against her natural prince, that she will never be sacked, nor her women violated, or preoccupied with honor."[106]

At the head of the procession of floats in 1564 was an allegory of Antwerp's river and lifeline, the Scheldt, surrounded by his tributaries and ornamented by marine plants. To the right of the Scheldt lay Mercury, the god of merchants; to the left a personification of Abundance, surrounded by various wares. In the train of the Maid of Antwerp and the Scheldt followed a group of boys and girls representing the various provinces of the Netherlands. The city's international prominence and self-consciousness were displayed by a tableau entitled the "Theater of the World," just as the facade of the trading exchange, or Bourse, of the city held the inscription: "For the service of merchants of all nations and languages."[102] This "Theater of the World" represented the four corners of the globe—Europe, Asia, Africa, and America—together with the explanation that they were interdependent and should share their resources. This conception of the four corners of the earth remained a powerful conceit during the 16th and 17th centuries, particularly in the service of glorifying the power of princes or of governments. For example, the triumphal entry (14 June 1594) of Archduke Ernest of Austria, governor-general for King Philip II, into Antwerp included among its triumphal arches and splendid decorations a representation of the four continents, designed by the Antwerp painter Martin de Vos on the arch of the Genoese merchants.[108] (Other well-known examples of the theme include Bernini's Four Rivers fountain for the Pamphilii papacy in the Piazza Navona, Rome (1648–57), and the Tiepolo ceiling painting in the Grand Staircase, Residenz, Würzburg (1750–53).)[109] The 1571 inventory of the Antwerp *ommegang* mentions a Palace of Nations wagon where Mercury, god of commerce, is seated in triumph surrounded by 12 women, who represent the commercial nations of Europe, each adding to the welfare of the others.[110] These nations read like a "who's who" of Antwerp trade deputations: Germans, Spaniards, French, Austrians, Portuguese, Florentines, Genoese, Milanese, Basques, Lucchese, English, and Scots.

Antwerp also had a tradition, like other cities in the Netherlands, of staging a magnificent triumphal procession, or Joyous Entry *(Blijde Inkomst)*, for each new prince or his designated representative; on these solemn occasions, the city was decorated with expensive triumphal arches or theaters, which formed way-stations and an elaborate program of political praise and information.[111] Financing of these triumphal entries was borne partly by the city, partly by the very "nations" singled out for praise in the *ommegang* procession. During Massys' lifetime, the most important Joyous Entry into Antwerp was that of September 1520, when the newly crowned Holy Roman Emperor Charles V came to the city as part of his inaugural circuit of the Netherlands as Emperor (he had previously visited the city upon attaining his majority and enjoyed an entry on 12 February 1515.)[112] The program for this entry was devised by Peter Gillis, the same city secretary *(greffier)* whom Massys had previously painted in the portrait diptych with Erasmus of 1517 (see Chapter 6), and by Cornelius Grapheus. Dürer describes purchasing the printed program "Entry into Antwerp" from this occasion: "The King was received with a splendid triumph—the gates very costly adorned—and with plays, great joy, and graceful maidens, whose like I have seldom seen."[113] This Triumphal Entry, then, was the secular equivalent of the *ommegang;* its ceremonial veneration of the Emperor was a token of the allegiance of the city, renewed by oaths and vows on that solemn occasion. Whereas the city reconsecrated its devotion to the Virgin in an annual ceremony, the *ommegang* procession, it made its worldly pledges to the prince one time only, shortly after his accession to the throne.[114]

Given this basic similarity, it is hardly surprising that a closer inspection of the program of the entry of Charles V would show close resemblance to the secular forms of the *ommegang.*[115] The first station of the Emperor presented the Genius of Antwerp with the three graces, their hands joined, holding together a golden apple. This symbol of the beauty and acclaim of the city of Antwerp, borrowed from the Judgment of Paris myth, was accompanied by a caption about the importance of Faith and Love in the city: "Faith and love made all these things" *(Fides et Amor haec omnia fecerunt).* At the second stage Jupiter (Homeric Jove), seated between Themis (Justice) and Cratos (Power), commands his eagle to offer a sceptre to the Emperor, with the Greek inscription reading, "Since you receive the sceptre from God, consider how you will please Him who gives you power." Meanwhile, Justice invests the Emperor with a sword, and Power presents him with a golden diadem. Gillis's interpretation of these actions reveals "the fact that Power bestows the crown means that Crowns—i.e., cities, whose figure is defined by wall and turrets—are not to be oppressed by power but rather are to be guarded by laws, so that they may acknowledge the power of the prince and feel his humanity and mildness."[116] At the third stage the Emperor meets Eusebia (Piety). At this point the Greek inscription reads: "Above all, piety glorifies the king." And in Latin, he reads: "With Caesar Carolus (Emperor Charles) piety reigns. On the ground and underfoot will lie impious ways." The fifth stage presents Justice along with Astraea, fabled virgin Justice of the Golden Age, now returned to earth to celebrate the new Golden Age, crushing underfoot "tyranny, the most horrid monster of all, especially to be hated by princes."[117] The remaining stages continue the themes of the just ruler through allegorical personifications of his virtues, such as the station where Philoponia (Love of Work) conquers Pleasures *(Voluptates),* the conceit frequently represented allegorically in art and literature as the Choice of Hercules.[118] The final stage calls for the Emperor to embrace the allegorical figures of the four continents, which we have already met in the *ommegang* procession, but omitting America, whose importance was not yet fully established in 1520. The optimistic inscription of this final imperial conceit, penned by Grapheus, reads: "He will make the world but one flock with one shepherd." This idea of a new world monarchy, headed by Charles as the new Charlemagne, was to become a hallmark of his imperial pageantry and political apologies; even his device with the Pillars of Hercules accompanied by the motto *Plus Oultre* (even further) captures this image of universal dominion.[119] James Tracy stresses the importance in Antwerp's 1520 *Blijde Inkomst* of the contractual nature of the city's relationship to her Emperor.[120] Although such triumphal entries normally consisted of tribute by a city for its ruler followed by ratification or reaffirmation of traditional civic rights and privileges, the Gillis program warns the young Charles V against tyranny and neglect of the city's liberties under law. While Spanish and Italian pageants stressed the theme of world empire, the Flemish entries based their program on a political theory that promoted shared, rational agreement *(consensus)* rather than royal *gloria* and *majestas* as the foundation of government.[121] Gillis's mentor, Erasmus (see Chap. 6), had explicitly voiced these philosophies in his *Adages* (1515):

> Fine cities are built by the people, subverted by princes . . . good laws are borne by popular magistrates, violated by princes; the people desire peace, while princes stir up war. . . . The tyranny of princes may be constrained by honest harmony among towns and townfolk.[122]

When Charles V arrived at Louvain in 1515, he confirmed the privileges of his loyal subjects with just this kind of contractual oath.[123]

Just like the power of the ruler in a triumphal entry, Antwerp's own power was one of the principal features celebrated in the *ommegang.* The maritime dominance of the city of trade was highlighted by giving a large ship float the place of honor, following the notables of the city, in the procession. The 1564 procession featured a specific merchant ship with all of its riggings, manned by a captain and Aeolus, god of the winds.[124] Antwerp thus signified that navigation was her mainstay and the source of her riches, thanks to the grace of the four winds, who appeared behind the ship. Accompanying this allegorical conceit were gods and monsters of the sea, such as Portunus, god of ports and servant of Neptune, on a giant sea horse.[125] The sea horse symbolized the need for utilization of both land and water for the prosperity of the city. Of course, Neptune was inevitably present, seated on a giant marine monster (he is visible at the right in the 1684 etching, which shows the fish spouting water from its mouth onto a startled crowd). In another tableau, Nereus and Doris portray the union of freshwater and seawater. Whales, cupids on dolphins, nereids, and tritons fill out the *ommegang* with maritime imagery.

Another standard component of the *ommegang* in Antwerp, especially by the 17th century, was the presence of classical divinities. Diana the huntress, the Judgment of Paris, or the muses on Mt. Parnassus were standard features. From the triumphal entries, we can surmise that these paid tribute to Antwerp's prowess and culture. More specifically local was the central figure from the myth of the city's origin: the giant named Druon Antigon. According to Antwerp legend, Druon lived in a castle on the Scheldt at the site of Antwerp's current commercial center.[126] He exacted a burdensome tribute from all who passed him on the river, taking at least half of their wares or else removing their hands and tossing them into the river as a sign of his power over the region. This terrible custom is credited with being the origin of the city's name, from the Dutch phrase "hand-throwing" *(handwerpen)*. The giant's hegemony was broken only through the heroism of a warrior named Brabo, according to legend a general under Julius Caesar, who refused to pay the ransom but managed to conquer Druon and to turn the tables on his antagonist by tossing the giant's own hand into the Scheldt. The province of Antwerp, Brabant, is said to take its name from this Roman hero, and ever since that time the city of Antwerp has carried on its city coat of arms two hands cut off at the wrist above a powerful castle. This story of Druon and Brabo had the status of a founding myth in Antwerp, akin to the stories of Romulus and Remus for Rome, and it was very much alive in Massys' day. Guicciardini mentions the importance of its repetition in the *ommegang* for civic pride and identity:

> Those who still cling to this origin of the name are aided by the two most solemn processions of the year, which are made in Antwerp on the days of Circumcision and of Our Lady. They have always had the custom of carrying a great statue representing this giant, behind which march those people dressed up as if each of them had a hand cut off. Moreover, they are strengthened by Latin verses written in the ancient book of Privileges of the city (but God knows when they were put forth).[124]

The legend of Druon was made the subject of the large bronze decoration atop a fountain in the prominent square before the west portal of the Church of Our Lady—a fountain that is often still attributed (without foundation) to Quinten Massys the smith;[128] above a leafy vine ornament stands Brabo in armor with the severed hand of the giant Antigon. More important, in Dürer's day it was possible to visit the local relics of the bones of the giant (which are still preserved today in the museum of the Steen, the castle built as the strategic spot which was supposed to be Druon's own dwelling site). The Dürer diary records his visit:

> I saw at Antwerp the bones of the giant. His leg above the knee is 5 1/2 feet long and beyond measure heavy and very thick, so with his shoulder blades—a single one is broader than a strong man's back—and his other limbs. The man was 18 feet high, had ruled at Antwerp and done wondrous great feats, as is more fully written about him in an old book, which the Lords of the Town possess.[129]

Aside from attesting to Dürer's own fascination with the wondrous and bizarre, this passage shows how important a relic and tourist attraction the bones of the giant were in Antwerp, a fact confirmed by the Latin verses penned for them by Cornelius Grapheus, the coauthor of the triumphal entry program for Charles V, during Massys's own lifetime.[130] Thus the sight of the giant Druon Antigon, enthroned majestically at a height of nine meters in the *ommegang*, was a crucial element of local Antwerp culture, completed by the lesser giants behind him with their hands cut off and by the final figure of Brabo, brandishing the titan's oversized hands at the end of his sword. This myth of power civilized was reenacted in Antwerp annually and offered the further suggestion of a Roman origin for the city's peaceful prosperity, continuing into the present under a new Holy Roman Emperor, Charles V. In this respect, the founding legend gave local pride a sense of importance combined with a primeval association of its welfare with the current princely dynasty.

A final element of Antwerp secular floats were live animals, most especially the most powerful of animals, the elephant. Often this sturdy elephant was present as a beast of burden, carrying the figure of Fortune, who was thus revealed to be still more powerful than the majestic animal below her.[131] The presence of other exotic animals, such as camels, not only added to the spectacle and attraction of the procession but also pointed to the worldwide trade contacts and influence of the city of Antwerp. And imaginary or hybrid animals formed an entertaining and popular form of painted decoration in many an *ommegang*, adding to the sense of magic still felt today in our more secularized society (and still very close to the surface in such familiar surviving processions as the giant dragon parade of the Chinese New Year).

Like most other municipalities of the day, Antwerp was organized according to privileges, a body of rules and statutes which defined the group and its members and spelled out both their rights and responsibilities. These groups further defined themselves with such visible distinctions as dress, places of worship, and careers. We have seen that such distinctions carried great weight in opportunities for individuals, as evidenced by the membership rolls of Antwerp's religious confraternities. In similar fashion, the reigns of government and the crafts were mutually exclusive, just as they marched separately in the *ommegang*. The trade guilds simply had no access to the civic magistrates' positions. In fact, the definition of a "freeman" (*poorter*) was that he was a burgher who was not a member of a trade guild; usually these *poorters* were the wealthy urban bourgeoisie, usually merchants, who served as the city patriciate alongside nobles and professionals, usually lawyers, in the town government. Of course, the very name *poorter* was derived from the merchant economy of Netherlandish cities like Antwerp and was ultimately derived from the Latin *portus*, port market.[132] Burghers, then, were not craftsmen, and vice versa, an important distinction in Antwerp (as opposed to other late medieval cities in the Netherlands, where *poorters* and crafts together controlled government and effectively restricted trade in a protectionist society).[133]

Against the background of modern individualism, it is worth stressing that for all these groups, the conception of identity was corporate, like the confraternities of the day—centered in the group, not the individual.[134] In Antwerp, as in other cities of the Netherlands, the ultimate source of civic independence and privilege was considered to be the ruler: originally the counts of Flanders, then the dukes of Burgundy, and in the 16th century, the Hapsburg emperors. We have already seen in the *Blijde Inkomst* of Charles V how Antwerp prided herself on her cooperation with her rulers (an accord which was sharply ruptured during the early years of the Dutch Revolution, between 1566 and 1585).[135] This was only natural, since Maximilian of Hapsburg had launched the economic boom in the city by according Antwerp a charter, dated 30 June 1488, which ordained the transfer to Antwerp from Bruges of all the commerce of the Netherlands controlled by the prince and by inviting the foreign merchants to come to Antwerp with the same privileges and protection they had formerly enjoyed at Bruges. This move and the 1496 *Magnus Intercursus*, which brought the English to Antwerp as the first of the "nations" to take up Maximilian's offer, was part of the Emperor's punishment to Bruges and other Flemish towns which had revolted against his authority on behalf of their local autonomy.[136] In this respect, Antwerp's nascent capitalist economy was tied to the centralizing tendency of the Hapsburgs against both guild protectionism and municipal particularism of her Flemish urban neighbors. Thus, the advent of Charles V was truly the occasion within Antwerp's walls for a Joyous Entry and a heartfelt oath of allegiance by the city to her lord.

Antwerp's relationship to its ruler might have been more progressive by being amicable, but it in no way contradicts the impression given by German city-states in relation to the Holy Roman Emperor. According to the researches of Heinrich Schmidt, German city chronicles of the 15th century (Lübeck, Augsburg, Nuremberg) show much the same corporate identity and pride that we have already encountered within Antwerp's own processions.[137] These German cities also held a special place, analogous to Antwerp's, within the Empire: they were imperial cities (*Reichsstädte*), which received complete autonomy from the Emperor in return for their payment of annual dues to the state.[138]

As Pirenne puts it, "The German town was only free in the sense that it exchanged the neighboring and very active authority of its lord for the distant and very feeble authority of the emperor."[139] The same could be said for Antwerp in the early 16th century, where Charles V's regent in the Netherlands was Margaret of Austria, his daughter, at the court of Brussels or Mechelen; and more locally was a third party, the *schout,* or margrave of Rijen (during this period a man named Jan van Immerseel). As a result, both the German cities and Antwerp conceived of their own boundaries as the boundaries of law and the Empire and equated their own interests with the universal interests of the Empire.[140] The free city incorporates the free individuals (defined according to their station), the Empire incorporates the city, and the Christian hierarchy of order incorporates the earthly Empire. In this view, law was itself the outcome of Christian truth, and secular events were religiously ordained.

The Empire endured as a concept in the imperial cities even when the Emperor himself was not present, because it was part of a universal law, embodied in the formal title "city of the Holy Empire" (*des heiligen reiches stett*). And the Empire was itself identified as "Christendom." This is nowhere better illustrated than in the Dürer painting of the *Madonna of the Rosegarlands,* commissioned in 1506 by the German merchants' association in Venice, the Fondaco dei Tedeschi.[141] This painting presents a vision of universal Christian brotherhood, with Emperor Maximilian kneeling on one side, the pope on the other, of the Virgin's lap. Behind the two leaders of Christianity and the Empire are the German merchants who commissioned the picture, adoring the Madonna and Child like the Antwerp burghers in the *ommegang.*

A claim could then be made that Antwerp's prosperity is the outcome of the Emperor's favor and, ultimately, could be credited to the protection of the Virgin herself. For this reason, the annual *ommegang* became a necessary renewal of that close bond with the divine. As such it was both a civic and a religious procession, and its participants felt no contradiction, no separation of church and state. Neither did they fail to recognize that the various religious confraternities, monastic orders, magistrates, and trade guilds were likewise arranged according to a divinely ordained scheme of things. But the city's self-concept as the loyal consort of her lord, the Emperor, embodied in the Joyous Entry, is subordinated there to a stress on piety and love and the duty of both parties to God, as in the German imperial cities. The standard formula was "Got, Ehre, Recht" (God, Honor, Law), and the city's citizens considered themselves to be the embodiment of all three in microcosm.

The city's construction of so many majestic religious buildings during this period is a sign not only of Antwerp's prosperity, which permitted her to sustain such expensive and lengthy undertakings, but also of her dedication to the divine favor which allowed for that very prosperity. Similarly, the various religious confraternities paid special homage to their cults and occupied specific chapel spaces within the new churches. Each and every trade guild had its own patron saint, plus its own corporate chapel to sustain its success and prosperity. Massys' own guild of St. Luke established a cult to the Seven Sorrows of the Virgin (see Chap. 3), in part because the guild possessed a cult image of the Virgin that was allegedly painted by their patron saint, Luke, the first religious artist.[142] In short, the individual was defined by his corporate identity, and that corporation was defined, in turn, by its spiritual foundation. Worldly privilege for the city came from the Emperor through his local representatives; worldly privilege of the guilds came from the city magistrates. But the ultimate sanction for each of these governmental authorities came from the ultimate, heavenly authority. Schmidt characterizes the German imperial city of the 15th century:

> The late medieval German city appears as a unified organism, closed to the outside. In it the Empire of God and the earthly Law are unbroken. It lives by the strength of its law, which is at the same time its truth. . . . The undisturbed holiness of the saints is guaranteed in the laws and privileges of the city. To preserve them is the mission of the city. Political affairs in the world are divine service; holiness and law interweave, give the city its position and the burghers the means of their lives. This life is threatened bodily with the freedom of the city.[143]

Scholars have given mixed reviews to this kind of public, urban religion. Toussaert and Delaruelle, in the most detailed investigations of late medieval piety in cities, have sketched a vision of this piety as externalized and formal, lacking in true spiritual depth.[144] The religious theater that made moral abstractions visible as personifications is seen as a symptom of the weakness of inner conviction, what Huizinga has termed "symbolism in its decline."[145] This "visual piety" often found expression in the cult of relics of saints and pilgrimages to holy sites.[146] Pilgrimages, in fact, were such a mark of piety that confraternities of travelers to famous sites, particularly Santiago de Compostela in Spain or to Jerusalem, sprang up in cities of the Netherlands. One of Massys' most handsome early portraits (1509; F. 38; cat. 53; Winterthur, coll. Reinhart) depicts such a pilgrim, who proudly displays a cartellino telling of his visit to Jerusalem (see Chapter 8). Another artist, Jan van Scorel of Utrecht (himself a canon), painted some of the earliest group portraits in the Netherlands of the Haarlem society of pilgrims.[147] (This is the very pilgrimage practice condemned as superstitious by Erasmus in his colloquy "A Pilgrimage for Religion's Sake.") *Pl. 138*

Perhaps even more revealing is the most controversial of all the late medieval forms of piety: the indulgence.[148] Bitterly denounced by Luther and other early Protestant theologians, indulgences were virtues accumulated by Christ and the saints, a spiritual treasury that could be drawn upon by living members of the Church as insurance against additional suffering in the afterlife. This doctrine had been developed by theologians of the 13th century; an indulgence was originally dispensed as the result of a particular and unusual pious deed by the worshipper, such as a fast, a series of prayers, alms, or a pilgrimage to a holy site. During jubilee years, particularly 1475 and 1500, such indulgences became widespread for pious acts or prayers and were accompanied by charitable gifts to the church. This church collection opened up the possibility for venality which came to be so vigorously asserted by the critics. In Antwerp during the jubilee year even exiles were allowed back into the city by the magistrates, and a city ordinance expressly forbade the sale or resale of such indulgences by anyone except the canons of Our Lady; moreover, the ordinance directed innkeepers not to gouge the visitors to the city and allowed begging in each of the city's seven churches.[149] Processions and communions were held out of season in Antwerp owing to the special holy occasion of the jubilee. The city also held its own special indulgences, such as the one based upon the relic of the foreskin, held on display on that day of the church year on which the civic procession also took place. Papal indulgences were often granted for the recital of certain prayers before specific images, and they were also connected with particular sites as a kind of fund-raising support based on the holy spots.[150] Unlike Germany, however, abuses of indulgences for fund raising seem not to have been major causes of complaint or of reform movements in the Netherlands; instead, they represented a continuity from earlier medieval practices of supporting the worthy houses and shrines for the saints in a city, while providing a source of shared spiritual grace to the worshippers in the same manner as a procession or any other communal worship. Charitable purchases of indulgences can be compared on a smaller scale to the activities of the wealthier burghers or corporate guilds and confraternities in endowing masses, chapels, altar-pieces, or other works of art in honor of the saints in a city church.

A final, telling example of the degree to which daily life in Antwerp was saturated with religious concepts is the annual calendar. We have already seen the local significance of Circumcision and Assumption days as the occasion for major processions and local civic festivals. And the importance of church calendar days of the specific saints of a confraternity or trade guild automatically took on special meaning for the members of those communities. But not frequently stressed in literature on medieval life is the fact that the entire yearly calendar was determined around Church festivals, as can be discerned in the zodiacally organized ecclesiastical tables still preserved in 15th-century luxury manuscripts.[151] Ordinary festival days (one-sixth of the calendar) were marked on these calendars by blue or red numbers; they usually honored Church fathers or early saints, doctors, famous popes, and local saints. Public holidays appeared in gold: some 40 days each year, plus locally special saints (*apôtres à vigile*) and the cycle of Marian festivals. In the early 16th century in the diocese of Utrecht, there were no fewer than 59 obligatory church feast days to be celebrated during the year, in addition to any particular locally designated festivals, and these provided vacation days within the populace's heavy work schedules.[152] Significantly, the Jacobus da Voragine compendium of saints' lives and deeds, *The Golden Legend,* is itself organized along the sequence of the church calendar for convenient use during the ecclesiastical year. It is a mark of the secularization of our own society that the principal days of the American calendar include Independence Day, Memorial and Veterans days, and Labor Day, as well as holidays based upon famous explorers, presidents, and heroes designated by the nation. Only Thanksgiving has the comparable status of a state-sponsored religious holiday inserted into the nameless days of the calendar.

Against this background of lay piety in the city of Antwerp, it is hardly surprising that Massys produced mostly religious pictures, and that a great many of those were isolated cult images, or icons, devoted to Antwerp's patroness, the Virgin (see Chap. 4). Given the popularity of cults of saints, it is unusual that Massys produced few images devoted to their veneration, although the early *St.*
Pl. 113 *Christopher* (Antwerp; F. 32, cat. 7; see Chap. 6) and the private *Rem altarpiece* dedicated to the Trinity,
Pl. 37 the Virgin, St. Roch and St. Sebastian (Munich; F. 3, cat. 24; made for the German merchant Lucas Rem; see Chapter 3) both fit into this widespread religious practice. Massys' corporate religious commissions for confraternities, like the Louvain brotherhood of St. Anne or the Antwerp joiners guild (Chap. 2), as well as for wealthier private individuals, are also quite natural within this urban lay religion. Even more puzzling, however, is the artist's activity after 1514 on pictures of nonreligious subjects (Chap. 7). For an indication of the cultural setting for these secular products, and their relationship to pious imagery, the best source of information is Antwerp's contemporary literature.

After the first press had been set up in the city in the 1480s by Matthias van der Goes, Antwerp rapidly became the leading publishing center of the entire Netherlands.[153] According to the indispensable bibliographical study of the years 1500–40 by Nijhoff-Kronenberg, Antwerp's 66 printers during that period represented fully half the printers in the entire Netherlands, and her total number of titles (2254—55 percent of the total) surpassed that of all other centers combined.[154] The reasons for this printing activity were, of course, linked to the overall success of Antwerp in international trade. But the consequences of such domination meant that famous authors like Erasmus made visits to the city to confer with publishers of their works (a fact of great importance for Massys, who painted
Pl. 99 Erasmus's portrait in 1517), and it meant that Latin and education in general took on a particular significance in the city.[155] But humanistic Latin editions and texts are only part of the story of printing in 16th-century Antwerp, despite the importance afforded them by modern hindsight, and publishing remained very much a business interested in reaching a larger reading market. A broader cultural picture can be established by examining books in the vernacular, the first "best-sellers" of the era of printing.

Three figures dominated Antwerp publishing during Massys' lifetime: Michiel Hillen van Hoochstraten, Willem Vorsterman, and Jan Grapheus.[156] Hillen van Hoochstraten published not only the largest number of books (532 titles) but also the largest number of texts by Erasmus; of the 2250 titles printed at Antwerp, 787 were in Dutch, and most of them prose.[157] The majority were philosophical or religious works without literary pretensions. Some works were mystical texts in prose. Perhaps the most famous of these, by anonymous Carthusian authors, date after Massys' lifetime in the 1540s: *The Great Evangelical Pearl* and *The Temple of Our Souls.*[158] Closer in time is *The Consolation of Souls (Der Sielen Troost,* 1502), a collection of *exempla.* This literature is well characterized by van Mierlo as

> purely medieval, of simple faith . . . first and foremost practical, more affective than speculative: the presentation of the Humanity and Suffering. Beside the Observant Franciscans, the Carthusians were now prominent, who appear to take the lead in mysticism, because the Netherlands and Rhenish provinces were still a region of asceticism and mysticism.[159]

Some of these early printed works had the intention of being catechisms of either general or specific application. The *Kerstenspiegel* (Mirror of Christ) of Dierc Coelde van Münster (1470) enjoyed numerous printings during the 16th century and was followed shortly thereafter by a similar *Mirror of the Christian Faith* (1478). More detailed studies concerning the new Madonna devotion of the rosary appeared with the late 15th-century spread of that cult (see Chapter 4); additional interest in the miracle of the eucharist prompted pious treatises on the sacrament of the mass. Antwerp was also the location of some of the earliest vernacular bibles in the Netherlands, beginning with the 1513 publication of the *Bibel in't corte* by Claes de Grave.

Books detailing the Passion of Christ were especially popular during this period (see Chapter V). Continuing as a major text of the late Middle Ages was the Carthusian Ludolph of Saxony's *Life of Christ,* first printed in the vernacular with 147 woodcut illustrations in Antwerp by Gerard Leeu in 1487 and reprinted many times thereafter; it contained a particularly vivid account of the Passion, along with other events from His infancy. Specialized Calvary accounts, such as the *Indulgence of the Holy City,* a series of accounts of the twelve stations, and meditations like the Seven Wounds (Antwerp, 1516) reflect empathic, late medieval emphasis on Christ's suffering. These essentially are outgrowths of the visionary literature of the 14th century, such as the writings of St. Brigitta, and of the 15th century, like the Netherlandish Franciscan Jan Brugman.

Also popular among the earliest books were volumes devoted to the Virgin. In addition to the rosary literature already mentioned, a number of specific meditational devotions focused on the Madonna. Most notable among these was the cult of the Seven Sorrows of the Virgin (see Chap. 3), a counterpart of the sufferings of Christ which selected events from the life of the Virgin that paralleled her sufferings with His. A typical juxtaposition is given by the title of a 1517 book, published in Antwerp by van Hoochstraten: *A Devout Book of the Seven Sorrows of Mary and of the Suffering of Christ.* Other similar volumes concentrated on the *Ten Virtues of Our Lady* (Antwerp, Vorsterman, 1521) or the mantle of the Virgin.

Beyond these religious prose works lay a body of secular themes called prose novels *(prozaromans)* and usually attributed to the *rederijkers.*[160] For the most part, these prose books are derivative in nature, going back to French, Latin, or German sources. They are filled with Crusader adventures, wondrous events, magic, battlefields, duels, and lovers' perils. Occasionally, realistic descriptions and moral commentaries on marital fidelity and virginal purity intrude into the stories. Many of the most popular prose novels were romances about knights and their ladies; prominent examples include *Margarieta van Lymborch* (1516), *Peeter van Provencen (Pierre de Provence), Floris ende Blanceflour* (ca. 1517), *Frederick van Jenuen* (Genoa, ca. 1518, actually a virtuous wife dressed up as a knight), *Alexander van Metz* (ca. 1518), and the *Strijt van Roncevale* (ca. 1520, based on the *Song of Roland*). Throughout these texts, knightly heroes are held up as champions of the faith, although their private erotic morality does not always live up to their public deeds; the tone sometimes resembles Boccaccio's and Chaucer's worlds of courtly adultery. But a number of these novels also present the traditional knightly virtues of decorous love combined with marvelous deeds and colorful pageantry, all in exotic locales, intermingled with the epic tales.

Georges Duby has characterized the importance of the image of the knight as a model in feudal society of the 12th century:

> On the one side was the prince (that is, the king) and near him, the clerk and the knight; on the other the masses, admiring these models of human perfection: this was the general framework of feudal society. This too was the framework for the currents of popularization and the complex phenomena of borrowings and exchanges at all levels of what, for want of a better word, we may call culture.[161]

That these images of knights still had the power to delight and to serve as models of conduct in 16th-century Antwerp is a remarkable tribute to the durability of chivalry as a cultural model, even for bourgeois city-dwellers. Yet these heroic deeds, drawn from tales of the past, were progressively being presented with seamier touches of baseness that grew out of the increasing cultural estrangement of readers who were distanced from knightly values by both social class and elapsed centuries. Even today, chivalric romances still have the power to delight modern readers, as do their American counterparts, westerns.

In contrast to the high seriousness of the knightly tales, some of the prose novels in Dutch were satirical in intent, based closely upon everyday characters and situations. Examples of this satirical vein are the translation of *Til Eulenspiegel* (the Dutch is *Ulenspieghel,* ca. 1519); *Reynaert the Fox; Broeder*

Russche, in which a devil impersonates a monk in order to work mischief in a monastery and town; and the *Pastor of Kalenberghe,* in which a young clerk becomes pastor and then reveals most of the seven deadly sins in succession. Just as the animal world of Reynard concludes with the gloomy and derisive realization that the world is full of deceitful, foxy types, and that righteousness no longer survives in the cynical and greedy world of courts and churches, so do borrowed German texts like the *Ship of Fools* (Paris, 1500; Antwerp, 1504) and *Ulenspieghel* castigate the follies and deceits of all men. Whereas the erotic made an appearance in the knightly novels, in these satires the obscene or burlesque sets the tone for the relations between the sexes. Again, the bawdiness of Boccaccio and Chaucer serve as precedents and analogues to these late medieval literary forms, but in place of the knights of the other prose tales, monks, pastors, devils, animals, and pranksters are the protagonists of this world of mockery. These satirical prose novels are distant in neither space nor time from Rabelais's *Gargantua,* but they usually lack the sense of humor of Rabelais or Erasmus's Dame Folly, and in place of irony offer only scorn, the social mockery of Carnival.[162]

The use of stock characters in everyday situations as a means of presenting a sharply critical picture of human weakness characterizes not only the satirical prose tales, but also the secular pictures of Massys. Both seem to present their social criticisms upon a firmly established moral foundation, as vivid as the personifications of a *rederijker* allegory. Both aim at instruction of the viewer with an aim toward the introduction of the practice of true Christian piety within daily affairs. Dabaene's description of the prose books shows best the spirit they share with Massys' close-up images:

> The entire presentation is simple: seeking strongly expressed effect rather than sober appreciation and nuance; intense empathy of the narrator or authors with their tales, their language resembles verbal tales, although it seems that they consciously strive for a specific form and embellishment of the text, while they more than once evoke their own world of the fifteenth and sixteenth century.[163]

A kind of hybrid work between these prose satires and lyric verses is the "moral refrain" *Vanden.X Esels* (Of Ten Asses, ca. 1522), which details ten men "who by their desperate lives are worthy of carrying asses' ears."[164] Among the ten "asses" catalogued are a man who squanders his money in bordellos (no. 1), a procurer (no. 4), a rich miser (no. 8), and a man who prides himself on the favors he has bought from women (no. 9). The author of this moralizing satire is probably its publisher, another Antwerp printer-author named Jan van Doesborch. Van Doesborch is of some importance for Massys, for he was a colleague of the artist in the Antwerp St. Luke's guild, where he was admitted in 1508 as a master illuminator *(verlichtere).* Van Doesborch was also the publisher of another rhymed moralizing tale, *Tghevecht van Minnen* (Combat of Love, 1516), which details the foolish conduct of lovers and concludes with "a remedy and counsel against infatuation": either to stifle the attraction with sheer numbers or else to seek consolation in the image of the suffering Christ.[165]

The argument has been advanced by several scholars that the authors of the prose tales are none other than the Antwerp *rederijkers,* and the principal author Anna Bijns (1493–1575), whose well-chosen motto was "more sours than sweets."[166] Her first verse anthology of 23 "refrains" appeared in Antwerp in 1528, the oldest surviving anthology *(bundel)* of its type. Several of her poems were also published in the collection published by van Doesborch (dating sometime between summer 1528 and summer 1530) and also within the verses of *Vanden.X Esels,* another van Doesborch publication.[167] Bijns is credited with a number of love lyrics that focus principally on the plaints of departed love. This versified continuation of the medieval chivalric convention of courtly love is infused not only with the female point of view for the first time, but also with the more skeptical vision of the joys of love and marriage that informs the knightly prose tales. The other major aspect of Anna Bijns's poetry corresponds to the critical reverse of her prose work: polemical poems about moral decline and the undermining of faith. Her chief villain in these complaints is Luther, who is for Bijns the devil incarnate. Her verses, then, are a kind of affirmation of the old faith and the Church, akin to the public "revivals" in the *ommegangen.* She also wrote religious verses of a more positive kind, involving reflection on the faith, or praise of Christ and the Virgin, or new year's wishes, or meditations on death.[168] These latter verses often stand very close to the spiritual prose treatises mentioned above.

Anna Bijns shared with the *rederijkers,* of whom she was a member, a characteristic pessimism about the decline of faith and a resulting decline of moral values, and a common interest in creating verse refrains, which derived from a conventional religious or courtly love tradition. Comparisons with the refrain anthologies *(bundels)* published by van Doesborch (ca. 1530) and by Jan van Styevoort (1524) show the same topics and verse forms as in Bijns's lyrics.[169] These *rederijker* refrains are classified into three categories: "joyous refrains" *(refreinen int vroede)* concerning religious subjects and moral edification; "amorous refrains" *(refreinen int amoureuze),* courtly subjects of personal feelings; and "foolish refrains" *(refreinen int sotte),* comical and satirical verses concerning vices and daily life, including a set of completely ironic verses known as "lying verses" *(leugenrefreinen).* The joyous verses include refrains on God, Christ, the Virgin, saints, death, and Judgment ("Four Last Things"), penitence, and introspection (the closest equivalent to the numerous ascetic prose treatises of the day), and admonitory poems on trust in God, endurance of suffering, and other similar virtues.[170] Frequently these verses dwelt upon the impermanence of life and the need for withdrawal from worldly concerns, the traditional medieval ideal of the *contemptus mundi.* A typical refrain of this sort is Bijns's "Dit soude ons met recht de werelt doen verleen" ("This we should rightly grant of the world") which "grants" that the world is the great deceiver, filled with inconstancy, injustice, idleness, and foolishness:

> The greatest knaves their greatest gains enhance
> And this, our world quite rightly goes and grants.[171]

Joyous poems also single out for criticism a number of specific worldly sins, including slander, envy, infidelity, hypocrisy, greed, drunkenness, and self-delusion.[172] Some of these critiques spill over into the irony of the foolish poems.

Anna Bijns was not a frequent composer of foolish poems, preferring instead to speak out directly in denunciation of worldly vanities. But other *rederijkers* found a fine outlet in their "Eat, drink, and be merry" verses, describing the pleasurable effects of drink and women in particular; these poems recall nothing so much as the counterculture literature of parody allegedly penned by the so-called "vagrants" *(vaganten),* wandering scholars of the late Middle Ages.[173] This literary genre consists of composed Latin poems on merriment and companionship and the delights of the senses.[174] During the 15th and 16th centuries, such "guild" associations as the Robijn- or Everaerts- or Aernouts-brothers traveled as singers and poets, creating their own lusty verses and parodies in the manner of *rederijker* folly poems. In addition to the preoccupations with drinking and pleasure, the folly poems also address in general the source of their creation, folly itself. One poem speaks of the proverbial stone of folly hidden in the brain of the fool and subject to growth with the victim's increasing folly. In echo of Erasmus's famous *Praise of Folly,* this poem begins, "O Moria, well renowned."[175] Other folly poems comment on the universal folly of mankind ("All Fools and None Carry Bells"; "Everyone Has a Strange Spirit Which Torments Him"); included in the catalog of the world's fools are court jesters, lovers, warriors, stay-at-homes, clergymen, and those with no time or care for their goods *(tijelooskens).*[176] Even more bitter is the "lying poem": "How It Would Go Ill in That World" *(Hoe sout dan qualick in die weerlt gaen),* which speaks of the lost golden age when honesty prevailed and tradesmen thought more of their customers than of their profit. Everyone from knights and lords to milkmaids, including all stations (clerics, procurers, lawyers, merchants, shoemakers, millers, herring salesmen) come in for the barbs.[177]

In contrast to the vice-ridden or folly-filled world of the foolish poems, the final group of lyrics, the amorous poems, presents a more romantic picture and a quest for favors by the beloved. The pain of love is expressed in these poems by means of laments about infidelity, unresponsiveness, fickleness, even about the mere absence of the beloved. Other poems confess love, praise constancy, and pray for signs of requital. Kruyskamp defines the amorous poems:

> The conception of love, as it is expressed in our refrains, is generally idealistic and more or less stylized, which is still invariably characterized as 'courtly' in the literature of the fifteenth century: glorification of the beloved and in contrast the self-abasement of the lover, who beholds his

> unworthiness and who, despite the heartlessness of his 'princess' remains ever faithful, always ready 'to serve,' fearful of and loathing of rivals *(nijders)* and prattlers *(clappers)* who hinder or threaten the success of the lover; laments about remaining 'unconsoled' (this whole conception of love for that matter means that a larger place is occupied by languishing and lamentation than by joy and jubilation); hope is still the most optimistic state of emotion of the courtly lover.[178]

The sentiment of these poems is essentially the final gasp of courtly love, known in the late Middle Ages in Dutch as *Minne.*[179] In general it is an unconsolable, ideal, and all-too-rarely fulfilled love. These *rederijker* verses often include the names of famous lovers, like the legendary figures from the prose tales of the same moment which, like the amorous poems, depend heavily on an inherited courtly medieval tradition.[180]

Rederijkers, of course, were neither knights nor courtly heroes. On the contrary, they were emphatically middle class in their outlook, even in the prose tales and amorous poems of courtly origins. As Roose describes them,

> *Rederijker* literature mirrors a *petit bourgeois* vision of life, evident in the predilection for the material repercussions of events on daily existence, in the criticism of institutions through their representatives, the sharp attention to human weaknesses and faults, the experience of love as the fundament of domesticity or as playful caressing (further and further removed from the courtly love lyric, of which the amorous refrains appear to be a continuation), in the appetite for instruction and knowledge, in upright piety [and] a complete absence of mystical aspirations. Indeed one finds exceptions; some poets give evidence of a certain intellectual standing; they have read Erasmus and show a sympathy for and a knowledge of theological questions.[181]

What remains at the center of *rederijker* literature—in prose, in verse, and in dramas—is a fundamental preoccupation with morality. On the positive side, this morality takes the form of dramatic personifications, of exemplary prose tales of knights and their faithful consorts, of joyous poems celebrating the virtues of holy figures and righteous conduct. On a more negative side, moral failures take center stage in folly poems, in prose satires, and in colorful farces. The same basic mentality can also be seen even within solemn occasions, such as the Joyous Entry of Charles V in 1520, where the young monarch establishes his authority within the city of Antwerp by promising to live up to a virtuous conduct commensurate with his high office. It is really on the basis of these promises and expected virtues that the city pays him allegiance; this lofty level of behavior is the stated source of his power, not armed might, nor claims to divinity, nor any other strength.[182] For the *rederijkers* and for the city of Antwerp in general, clearly "right makes might."

Like the emotional impact of *rederijker* verses, Massys' paintings are saturated with a forceful and intense sentiment, particularly with the artist's adoption in his later years of portraitlike half-lengths for his holy figures (see Chap. 4), religious stories (Chap. 5), saints (Chap. 6), and secular images (Chap. 7). The viewer's response might well be revulsion in the face of secular grotesques like the London *Old Woman* or the Washington *Ill-Matched Pair* or, instead, it might be tender compassion for Christ's suffering or Mary's maternal affection. But in either case, the observer is taken out of his everyday context and brought close to a charged emotional situation, a world filled with sentiment.

The activating principle of that world is morality. Resolution of a picture might appear uncertain *(Moneychanger and his Wife; Temptation of St. Anthony),* or it might be captured at a decisive moment *(Ecce Homo; Ill-Matched Pair)* that invites viewer criticism. Massys' hope is that the viewers' involvement will motivate them to a more virtuous Christian life. To engineer the proper response of his audience, Massys shows evil through ugliness in the form of grotesque caricature. By implication, most ordinary men are sinful creatures and ugly in the sight of a righteous God, for the viewer is made to feel himself as part of the pictorial world of Christ's tormentors (especially in the *Ecce Homo* images; see Chap. 5). Man's sinfulness does not derive from the Devil, as in Bosch's universe, but is rather the product of conscious choice, of submission to the seduction of worldly pleasures. The only difference between St. Anthony and the old man of the *Ill-Matched Pair* is their respective resolutions to the perennial problem of man's temptation toward lechery.

Massys does offer viewers the chance to follow the true path. He presents Christ carrying the cross and asking out of the picture for assistance. He presents Jesus as the prisoner of Pilate, asking for pardon and mercy. He presents the Madonna and Child as enthroned figures receiving the homage of angels and kings from the East. And he shows a more beautiful world, the extraordinary world of saints and holy figures, as a contrast to the grotesque faces of everyday sinfulness. The aged, venerable meditator, St. Jerome, the reflective, young convert, Mary Magdalene, or the tender and compassionate Mary are all lovely figures, whose beautiful features reflect their inner beatitude. Such figures are lifted out of the everyday world by virtue of their supreme blessedness. They are the transcendent models mankind must strive to follow.

This model of virtue, expressed visually through beauty, is what links Massys' imagery to the literature of the *rederijkers*. For both the artist and the authors of Antwerp, secular satire and joyous praise of holiness were opposite sides of the same coin: Christian ethics. Both the virtuous love poems and the visual perversions of love (the London *Old Woman*) presuppose individual wills and moral responsibility. Mankind is subject to passions yet capable of conscience. Even government itself is seen to rest upon the foundation of civil order, which is, for both ruler and subject, righteous conduct. Ultimately the inspiration for mankind is divine love—of the Madonna for her Son, of Christ for mankind in the Passion. The goal of the pious Christian is to seek and to merit the grace that comes as the natural outgrowth of divine love. To this end, the city of Antwerp organized annual *ommegangen* and venerated the sacred relics it possessed; to this end, each guild and confraternity paid homage to its own particular cult or patron saint. What is striking about both the more subjective *rederijker* verses and the more intimate half-length images of Massys is that, in contrast to the more corporate and formulaic presentations of the previous century, these new creations of the 16th century already revealed something of a new individualistic, personalized spirit within traditional forms that would characterize a later, more "modern" epoch to come.

Massys himself was acquainted with such *rederijkers* as van Doesborch, for they were fellow members of the St. Luke guild in Antwerp. Beyond this fact, the scanty biographical details concerning Massys do not permit any conclusions: for example, whether the nascent Reformation, which was to humble Cornelius Grapheus in a public recantation at the altar of Our Lady in Antwerp (1521; see Chap. 6) and which was to draw the polemical wrath of Anna Bijns against Luther, ever made much of an impression on the artist.[183] His burial with the Carthusians and numerous late Madonna icons suggest that Massys remained a loyal and pious Catholic during his final decade (Lutheranism's first decade). Associations with a learned humanist circle in Antwerp (Chap. 6) and construction of a splendid home, both expensive and ornately decorated, point to Massys' increasing sense of self-esteem and prosperity; these trends reinforce the impression gained by his conspicuous absence from deanships and apprentice lists in the St. Luke guild after 1510. But unless some other new and startling document surfaces to reveal more about this artist, our best picture of his values and attitudes is still given by the larger culture of Antwerp, revealed in both local ceremonies and literature—and by his own art.

NOTES

1. The Latin text:

> Ante faber fueram Cyclopeus ast ubi mecum / Ex aequo pictor coepit amare procus / Seque graves tuditum tonitrus postferre silenti / Peniculo objecit cauta puella mihi: / Pictorem me facit amor tudes innuit illud / Eixguus tabulis quae nota certa meis. / Sic ubi Vulcanum nato Venus arma rogarat / Pictorem e fabro Summa Poeta facis.

Quoted from Domenicus Lampsonius (Antwerp, 1572). Critical edition by J. Puraye, *Les effigies des peintres célèbres des Pays-Bas* (Liege, 1956), pp. 40–41. The translation used here is that of C. van de Waal in his edition of C. van Mander, *Dutch and Flemish Painters* (New York, 1936), p. 62. Van Mander's Flemish translation (Haarlem, 1604) of Lampsonius's Latin text reads as follows:

> Een rouw Cyclopsche Smidt heb ick gheweest te voren / Maer doe een Schilder oock mijn Vrijster vrijde snel / En dat dat Jeysken loos verwijtich my liet hooren / Dat sy op 't aenbeeldt de donderslaghen fel / Veel verder van haer wierp, als stil Pinceeler spel / Heeft my der liefden cracht een Schilder haest doen sesen, / Sulcx wijst aen waer to

zijn een cleen aenbeeldken wel, / Zijnde op mijn Tafereel een teecken uytghelesen. / Gelijk Cypris vercreegh van Mulciber voor desen / De wapens van haer soon, O grootst Poeet; als dit, / Hebt ghy een Schilder cloeck, ghemaeckt van een rouw-Smidt.

2. A. de Bosque, *Quentin Metsys*, pp. 39–42. The picture was removed from the Antwerp St. Luke guild in 1794 during the French occupation and was never returned, nor has it been located since that time. The Wierix engraving bears the superscription "Obiit Antverpiae 1529 in Carthusia ad urbis muros conditus"—the first evidence that Quinten died within the walls of Antwerp's Carthusian monastery at Kiel. The profile portrait as engraved compares closely in features and in costume with a portrait medal of the artist, dated 1495 and believed to be by Massys' own hand (see Appendix A). For the most recent discussion of the Wiericx engraving, see H. Pauwels, "Naar aanleidung van een gravure naar Quinten Metsys." pp. 248–62.

3. Cited by H. W. von Löhneysen, *Die ältere niederländische Malerei*, p. 329, no. 352. Quotes by Guicciardini in this chapter will come, for convenience's sake and for proximity to the Italian original, from the 1625 French edition, published in Amsterdam by J. Janzonium: "Quinten natif du même lien de Louvain, grand maitre de faire de beaux image et figures, entre lequelles, on
Pl. 20 voit un tableau ou est representé nostre Seigneur Jesus Christ en Notre Dame, Anvers." [the Antwerp Lamentation; see Chapter 2] (p. 98).

4. Molanus, *Rerum Lovaniensium Libri XIV*, 1575; quoted by H. Brising, *Quinten Matsys und der Ursprung des Italianismus in der Kunst der Niederlände*, p. 22, n. 2. Molanus goes into more detail in *Memoria aliquot pictorum Lovaniensium*, vol. 9, fo. 610, where he is the earliest to mention Massys as the creator of Erasmus's 1519 bronze medal portrait, and he even cites Erasmus's letters as proof ("effigiem meam fudit aere," Libro XIX epistolarum). I am grateful to Professor David Freedberg for calling my attention to this passage.

5. J. Held, "Artis Pictoriae Amator," p. 64, n. 27; F. Baudouin, *Rubens*, Eng. ed. (New York, 1977), p. 297. This was the view that basically prevailed in the two great fundamental 19th-century local surveys of Antwerp painting: M. Rooses, *Geschiedenis der Antwerpsche Schilderschool*, p. 46ff.; F. J. van den Branden, *Geschiedenis der Antwerpsche Schilderschool*, p. 40ff.: "The first Antwerp painter whose works have come down to us, is, moreover, a genius, indeed the greatest or at least the original master whom our glorious school of art has produced."

6. Held, "Artis Pictorie Amator," and Baudouin, *Rubens*. The full citation of the tombstone and the circumstances surrounding its erection are given by van den Branden, *der Antwerpsche Schilderschool*, pp. 650–53. Three paintings attributed to
Pl. 59 Massys can be seen in the Willem van Haecht painting of van der Geest receiving Archduke Albert and Irchduchess Isabella in
Pl. 58 his *Gallery* (now Antwerp, Rubenshuis; color reproductions 1,2 in de Bosque). The principal painting on display is a now-
Pl. 146 missing *Madonna of the Cherries* (F.67; cat.50). The others are a portrait, now in Frankfurt (F.46; cat.61), the *Scholar*, and a
Pl. 183 problematic portrait, the so-called *Paracelsus* (F.78; cat.supp.E), of which the original is now lost.

7. "In synen tyt grofsmidt en daernaer famues schilder."

8. Held, "Artis Pictorie Amator," p. 69, n. 35; J. Briels "Amator Pictoriae Artis, De Antwerpse Kunst-verzamelaar Peeter
Pl. 58 Stevens (1590-1668) en zijn Constkamer," *Jaarboek Koninklijk Museum Antwerpen* (1980), pp. 137-226, esp. pp. 186-94, 216.
Pl. 118 Stevens inherited the missing Massys *Madonna of the Cherries*, and he also owned the *Moneychanger and his Wife* (F.53; cat.16), now in the Louvre. For the full Dutch title of Fickaert's biography, see the Bibliography.

9. See the Bibliography for the Dutch title.

10. DeBosque, *Quentin Metsys*, pp. 14–15, 34. Van den Branden, p. 42, following van Fornenbergh, attributes the Antwerp well-cover and the baptismal font of St. Peter's of Louvain, plus one other: the iron ornament for the tomb of the English king Edward IV. Despite his important researches into the Antwerp documents of Massys' life, van den Branden's biographical sketch still reads like a *summa* of all previous tales. The earliest extensive documentary researches were made by E. van Even, *L'ancienne école de Louvain*, p. 323ff., and "Metsys, Quentin," *Biographie nationale* (Brussels, 1866–1944) vol. 14, pp. 639–77; *Notice biographique sur le peintre Quentin Metsys;* defending an Antwerp birthplace, P. Génard, *Anvers à travers les âges*, vol. 2 (Brussels, 1888) pp. 571–72; and *Nasporingen over de geboorteplaats en de familie van Quentin Massys*.

11. See de Bosque, *Quentin Metsys*, p. 37, for discussion of the orthography of the artist's name. Quinten spelled his name three different ways. "Massys" is the way his name was entered in the records of the Antwerp painters' guild of St. Luke in 1491. Furthermore, it is also the spelling of the family name in the oder documents used to trace Quinten's ancestry (de Bosque, pp. 29–33). Finally, it is the preferred spelling by his painter son Jan, who often signs his pictures JOHANNES QUINTINI MASSIIS. (For the most recent article concerning Jan, with extensive bibliography, see V. Scatt, "Johannes Quintini Massiis Pingebat," pp. 259–80; also de Bosque, pp. 66–68). Cornelis Massys, Quinten's other painter son, monogrammed his works in two ways, however: CMe or CMa, as well as COR MET (B. L. Dunbar, "The Landscape Art of Cornelis Massys;" de Bosque, pp. 69–70). "Metsys" is the spelling used by Quinten in his large-scale works (Brussels *St. Anne altarpiece;* F.2, cat.10) and in his Latinized signatures (1513 *Old Man*, F.51, cat.54; 1529 *Christ Blessing*, cat.49) on the rare occasions when he signed his works of art. The spelling "Matsys" is the rarest form, e.g., on the 1514 signature on the *Moneychanger and his Wife* (F.53, cat.16). Because of its continuous use as a family name and because it is more frequently used in scholarly literature, "Massys" is the spelling used in this book.

12. De Bosque, pp. 29–33. At least four previous generations of Quinten's ancestors have been traced by scholars. For the fullest genealogy, see F. Prims, "De Familie van Quinten Massijs," and "Quinten Massys in de Kempen," pp. 45–63; A. de Laet, "Quinten Massys, voorgeslacht, leven, en kunst," pp. 1–36. Hendrik Massys, Quinten's grandfather (d. 1475) moved to Antwerp or had dealings there as early as 1425. The presence of his descendants among Antwerp citizens led for a time to contentions that Quinten was actually born in Antwerp rather than in Louvain; for a summary of the 19th-century scholarly controversy of each city's archivists, see M. J. Friedländer, [Early Netherlandish Painting], vol. 7, pp.13–14; and n. 10, above.

13. De Bosque, p. 424, Documents nos. 1,2. Also E. van Even, *L'ancien école* pp. 323, 336. A good summary of biographical documentation on Massys can also be found in the Appendix of Broadley, "The Mature Style of Quinten Massys," pp. 247–68.

14. On Joost, see de Bosque, p. 33; de Laet, "Quinten Massys," p. 17ff. Joost was already by 1459 the chosen administrator of the smiths' corporate Chapel of St. Eloy in Louvain, and he executed commissioned works for the Louvain city hall and the commune.

15. Von Löhneysen, pp. 318, 320; E. Kris and O. Kurz, *Legend, Myth, and Magic in the Image of the Artist* (New Haven, 1979), pp. 14–20.

16. H. E. Greve, *De bronnen van Carel van Mander* (The Hague, 1903); H. Noë, *Carel van Mander en Italie* (The Hague, 1954); H. Miedema, *Karel van Mander. Den Grondt der edel vry Schilder-const* (Utrecht, 1973); also useful are the notations, concerning one of van Mander's *vitae*, by R. Vos, "The Life of Lucas van Leyden by Karel van Mander," *Nederlands Kunsthistorisch Jaarboek* 29 (1978): 459–507.

17. Kris and Kurz, *Legend, Myth, and Magic*, pp. 22–24, 26, 30.

18. Van den Branden, p. 48f.; J. de Bosschere, *Quinten Metsys*, p. 21f.; F. Prims, "Quinten Massys en de Kempen," pp. 56–63, conjecturing that young Quinten was trained as a miniaturist with a certain Pater Storm at the priory in Grobbendonk, the region of Massys' ancestors. Both van den Branden and de Bosschere rely upon Massys' origins in Louvain to suggest now-unknown Louvain artists as hypothetical masters for the youthful Quinten: Roger van der Weyden II, and the Louvain town painter *(stadsschilder)*, Hubert Stuerbout, respectively. Naturally, most of the scholarly attention has been directed at the most well known master of Louvain, Dirk Bouts (d. 1475), and his sons and other followers in the city.

19. For Massys and the Bouts tradition, see W. Cohen, *Studieu zu Quinten Matsys*, pp. 10–40; K. G. Boon, *Quinten Massys*, p. 8; Friedländer, vol. 3 (Bouts), vol. 7, pp. 14, 20–21; Friedländer, "Quentin Massys: Reflexions on His Development," pp. 52–54; de Bosque, p. 35.

20. Friedländer, vol. 6.

21. P. Rombouts and T. van Lerius, *De Liggeren der Antwerpsche Sint Lucasgilde*, vol. 1, p. 43ff.

22. Only the third apprentice has been associated with a body of paintings; see L. Reis-Santos, "Edouard Portugalois," p. 185ff.; L. van Puyvelde, "Edouard Portugalois," pp. 288–95.

23. See note 11. Also van den Branden, p. 78, with biographies of Jan and Cornelis on pp. 135–49; Friedländer, vol. 13, p. 17ff.; E. de Callatay, "Cornelis Massys, paysagiste, collaborateur de son père et de son frère et auteur de l'album Errera," pp. 49–70.

24. N. Dacos, *Les peintres Belges à Rome au XVIe siècle*, Brussels, 1964.

25. De Bosque, pp. 37, 42, and 424, Document no. 4. For relatives of the first Mrs. Massys, see Document no. 3 (13 June 1506).

26. Ibid., pp. 42 and 424, Document no. 5.

27. Ibid., pp. 42, 47, and 425, Document no. 16, a testament that names the family survivors of the artist.

28. Van den Branden, p. 78; purchased on 28 July, 1519.

29. J.A. Goris and G. Marlier, *Albrecht Dürer Diary of His Journey to the Netherlands*, p. 58.

30. De Bosque, pp. 42–43, 424, Document 7; van den Branden, pp. 122–23.

31. Dated on the wall "Anno 1528." In addition, the rooms contained heraldic columns "in the imperial style," with the words "Plus ultra." By this description, van Fornenbergh doubtless refers to the emblem of Charles V: a pair of columns representing the Pillars of Hercules and the device "yet further" *(Plus ultra)*. See E. Rosenthal, "*Plus ultra, non plus ultra* and the Columnar Device of Emperor Charles V," *JWCI* 34 (1971): 204–28.

32. See above, note 12.

33. Friedländer, vol. 7, p. 12; van den Branden, p. 79. The remuneration of the office was apparently quite small, and the duties were primarily time-consuming policing of guild regulations. See also Guicciardini (cited from the 1625 French edition, as noted above in n. 3), p. 95: "The office of these deans *(doyens)* and of their assessors and coadjutors is to be present at the city hall when there is a General Council to treat with their fellow members, and to communicate with those of their craft *(art)*, in order to see if those who are up for admission to the trade *(au metier)* are loyal, satisfactory, and capable, to promote amity and concord among them, to take cognizance of one member and another and to harmonize them, and to guard and defend them against all potential violence."

34. His younger colleague, Joos van Cleve, admitted as master only in 1511, served as dean of Massys' painters' guild in 1519, 1520, and 1525 (Friedländer, vol. 9, pp. 17–18, and Chapter 9, herein).

35. Baldass, "Gotik und Ren. im Werke des Quinten Massys," pp. 137–82.

36. Van den Branden, p. 125; de Bosque, p. 46, Document 15. The artist had appeared before the Antwerp magistrate on 13 July 1530, but already on 16 September of that year his wife is recorded as a widow (Broadley, p. 258, n. 2). From Wierix's engraving of 1572 to van der Geest and van Fornenbergh, this death date had been given as 1529. Van Fornenbergh reports the cause of death as "sweating sickness" *(zweetkoorts)* on St. Michael's Day, 1529. Also see n. 2 for Wierix's testimony concerning the Carthusians; Fickaert, p. 16; van Fornenbergh, p. 31. F.H. Mertens and K.L. Torfs, *Geschiedenis van Antwerpen*, p. 46 (without citing their source for the information) allege that the final resting place was the Carthusian monastery at Kiel. That monastery was torn down for civil defensive reasons, along with the cloisters of the Victorines and the Begijnhof Sion, in July 1542. Subsequently, the Carthusians relocated to nearby Lier (F. Prims, *Geschiedenis van het Kiel* [Wilrijk, 1938] pp. 41–42). Also cited in the chronicle, attributed to G. Bertryn, *Cronijck der Stadt Antwerpen*, ed. G. van Havre (Antwerp, 1879), p. 253 (cited by Broadley, p. 258). Mertens and Torfs mention that Burgemeester Aert van Leere and Rutgeerd van der Weyden [sic], deacon of Massys' St. Luke's guild, were also struck down by the same plague.

37. Friedländer, vol. 7, p. 46; de Bosque, pp. 63–64, and 425, Document 20. For Patinir, see R. Koch, *Joachim Patinir*.

38. Dürer's remark about Patinir is one of the first uses of the term "landscape" to be recorded; see Goris and Marlier, *Dürer Diary*, p. 23, 50, 88–89, 93; Koch, p. 3.

39. Guicciardini, 1625 edition, p. 69. Quoted by J.J. Murray, *Antwerp in the Age of Plantin and Brueghel* (Norman, Okla., 1970), p. 43; also see S.T. Bindoff, "The Greatness of Antwerp," in *New Cambridge Modern History*. Vol. 2: *The Reformation 1520–59* (Cambridge, 1958), pp. 50–69, and other works cited in Chapter 2, n. 48.

40. H. Miskimin, *The Economy of Later Renaissance Europe 1460–1600*, p. 138; O. de Smedt, *De Engelse natie te Antwerpen in de XVIe eeuw* (1496–1582) (Antwerp, 1950).

41. Miskimin, pp. 124–31; V. Magalhães—Godinho, *L'Economie de l'empire portugais aux XVe et XVIe siècles* (Paris, 1969); J.

Denucé, *Privilèges commerciaux accordés par les rois du Portugal aux Flamands et aux Allemands (XVe et XVIe siècles)* (Lisbon, 1909); A. de Burbure de Wesembeek, *La Casa de Portugal d'Anvers* (Lisbon, 1953). The basic work remains J. A. Goris, *Etude sur les colonies marchandes méridionales à Anvers (1477–1567).*

42. Miskimin, p. 31.

43. On this concept, see I. Wallerstein, *The Modern World-System,* pp. 120–21; "Antwerp [was] in the sixteenth century an 'international' market center, which linked the Mediterranean and Baltic trades with the transcontinental trade via South Germany. Not only did Antwerp coordinate much of the international trade of the Hapsburg Empire, but it was also the linchpin by which both England and Portugal were tied into the European world-economy. In addition, at this time, Antwerp became the supreme money market in Europe."

44. Friedländer, vol. 7, p. 49. For art trade in general, cf. H. Floerke, *Studien zur niederländischen Kunst- and Kulturgeschichte: Die Formen des Kunsthandels, das Atelier, und die Sammler in den Nederlanden vom 15.-18. Jahrhundert* (Munich/Leipzig, 1905); G.F. Koch, *Die Kunstausstellung,* p. 44ff.; and the fine recent sketch by L. Campbell, "The Art Market in the Southern Netherlands in the Fifteenth Century," pp. 188–98.

45. Friedländer, vol. 7, p. 50.

46. Friedländer, vol. 4, pp. 65–66; J. Maquet-Tombu, *Colyn de Coter Peintre bruxellois* (Brussels, 1937), p. 13.

47. Rombouts and T. van Lerius, vol. 1, pp. 44–46.

48. For the Brandão portrait, see Goris and Marlier, pp. 13, 85; for the Almada, pp. 80, 84, 62. See also Chapter 3.

49. Ibid., p. 57.

50. J. Goris, *Les colonies marchandes*; J. Denucé, *Italiaansche koopmansgeschlachten te Antwerpen in de XVIe-XVIIIe eeuw* (Antwerp, 1934).

51. J. de Borchgrave d'Altena, *Les Retables brabancons conservés en Suède* and *Les Retables brabancons 1450–1550*; J. Roosval, "Retables d'origine néerlandaise dans les pays nordiques," pp. 136–58; J. de Bosschere, *La Sculpture anversoise aux XVe et XVIe siécles*; K. Meinander, *Oeuvres de l'art flamande du moyen-age en Finlande* (Helsinki, 1930); H.J. de Smedt, "De verspreiding der Brabantse retables in oostelijke richting," *De Brabantse Stad* [Louvain], 1965, p. 23ff., and "De beeldhouwkunst te Antwerpen 1470–1530," *Aspekten van de Laatgotiek in Brabant,* exh.cat. (Louvain, 1971), p. 282ff.; G. Derveaux-van Ussel, *Le Retable malinois de l'église d'Odeby (Artes Belgicae)* (Brussels, 1973), esp. p. 9.

52. A rare documented example of sculpted retables with painted wings is the 1516 *St. Reinhold altarpiece* from the Danzig
Pl. 162 Church of Our Lady (Friedländer, vol. 9, p. 19, no. 20; now in Warsaw, National Museum); the wings were painted by Joos van Cleve and his workshop. On Joos van Cleve, see Friedländer, vol. 9; J. Bialostocki, "New Observations on Joos van Cleve," *Oud Holland* 70 (1955): 121–29. For Joos's altarpieces in Italy, see Friedlănder, vol. 9, no. 9 (*Adoration triptych,* Genoa, San Donato), no. 19. (*Lamentation triptych* from Genoa, Santa Maria della Pace), and no. 28 (*Adoration of the Magi* from near Genoa, San Luca d'Erba). Also discussed recently by J. Hand, "Joos van Cleve: The Early and Mature Paintings," pp. 64ff., 127ff.

53. Still basic is Friedländer, vol. 11, with extensive bibliography.

54. See in particular, J. Roosval, "Retables d'origine néerlandaise."

55. In Massys' works only the 1526 half-length New York *Adoration of the Magi* (F.8, cat. 40) and the crowded *Ecce Homo*s of Coimbra (F.196, cat. 18) and Madrid (F.10, cat. 31), both favorite Antwerp Mannerist subjects, suggest the impact of this local Antwerp form of religious narrative (see Chapter 5). Indeed, the general absence of Antwerp Mannerist formulas from Massys' later works is another measure of his indepependent values during these years.

56. N. Dacos, *Les peintres Belges à Rome.*

57. Panofsky, *ENP,* p. 349, n. 10; J. Pope-Hennessey, *The Portrait in the Renaissance,* p. 60. Both conclude that Memling's Italian patrons persuaded the Bruges artist to adopt the Quattrocento formula of an unbroken landscape behind portraits. Instead, it seems more likely that Memling's conceptualization grew naturally out of the 15th-century Netherlandish portrait type, such as van der Weyden's *St. Ivo* (London) or the related works of Christus and Bouts (Panofsky, *ENP,* p. 316). That northern formula, becoming favored by the Italian population, exerted its own impact on artists south of the Alps. Pope-Hennessey, p. 60, n. 85, admits that Memling exerted a "reciprocal" influence and links Bouts's 1462 London *Portrait of a Man* to a ca. 1500 Perugino *Self-Portrait* in the Uffizi. Memling's landscape portraits are numerous, and they predate notable Italian examples like Perugino's *Francesco dell' Opere* or Solario's *Cristoforo Longoni.* These two pictures also have more in common with Memling's work than they do with an earlier Italian portrait like Piero della Francesca's *Duke Federigo of Urbino* (Uffizi), with its profile head and elevated viewpoint, where the sitter is separated from, rather than integrated within, the background landscape. On the Medici Bank, located in Bruges until it was dissolved in 1480, see R. de Roover, *The Rise and Decline of the Medici Bank 1397–1494,* p. 317, and *Money, Banking, and Credit in Medieval Bruges,* pp. 34, 86. The Medici representative until 1465, Angelo Tani, commissioned a *Last Judgment altarpiece* (Friedländer, vol. 6, no. 8, now in Danzig, Marienkirche) from Memling; see F. de Roover, "A Prize of War: A Painting of Fifteenth-Century Merchants," *Bulletin of the Business Historical Society* 19 (1945): 3–12; J. Bialostocki, *Les Primitifs Flamands: Les Museés de Pologne* (Brussels, 1966), pp. 55–123; K.M. McFarlane, *Hans Memling,* p. 16ff. Tani's successor with the Medici Bank, Tommasso Portinari, commissioned portraits from Memling and a massive altarpiece (now in Florence, Uffizi; see Blum, p. 77ff.). The basic study remains A. Warburg, "Flandrische Kunst und florentinische Renaissance," *Gesammelte Schriften* (Leipzig, 1932), vol. 1, pp. 185–206, 370–80.

58. Goris and Marlier, *Dürer Diary,* pp. 60–62.

59. *Antwerp's Golden Age,* exh. cat., pp. 118–19, no. 105; also, S. Williams, "Les Ommegangs d'Anvers et les cortèges du Lord-Maire de Londres," and S. Williams and J. Jacquot, "Ommegangs anversois du temps de Bruegel et de van Heemskerck," *Les Fêtes de la Renaissance II. Fêtes et ceremonies au temps de Charles Quint,* ed. J. Jacquot (Paris, 1960), pp. 349–88; M. Sabbe, "De Antwerpsche ommegang," *Uit het Plantijnsche huis* (Brussels, 1924); F. Prims, "De Antwerpsche ommeganck op de vooravond van de Beeldstormerij," *Mededelingen van de Koninklijk Vlaamsche Academie* (Antwerp / Utrecht, 1946); I. van Roeder-Baumbach, *Versieringen bij blijde inkomsten gedruckt in de Zuidelijke Nederlanden gedurende de 16e en 17e eeuw* (Antwerp, 1943); *Ommegangen en blijde inkomsten te Antwerpen,* exh. cat., Antwerp, 1957.

60. Guicciardini, 1625, French ed., pp. 93–95; J.J. Murray, *Antwerp* (n. 39), pp. 31–33; J. Vanroelen, "Het Stadsbestuur," *Antwerpen in de XVIe eeuw* (Antwerp, 1975), pp. 37–54; R. Boumans, *Het Antwerps stadsbestuur voor en tijdens de Franse overheersing*

(Antwerp, 1965). A source from around the time of Guicciardini is Josse de Weert, *Chronycke van Nederlant, besonderlyck der Stadt Antwerpen 1097–1565* in *Chroniques de Brabant et de Flandre*, ed. C. Piot (Brussels, 1879).

61. R. Lauwaert, "Ambachten en nieuwe nijverheden," *Antwerpen in de XVIe eeuw* (Antwerp, 1975), pp. 143–59; Murray, pp. 161–64.

62. Prims, *Geschiedenis*, pp. 159-64; and "Altarstudieën," *Antwerpiensia* 12 (1938): 285ff.

63. P. Schabacker, "Petrus Christus' *St. Eloy*," p. 103ff.

64. Murray, pp. 151–52; van den Branden, pp. 7–39.

65. For *rederijkers* in general, J.J. Mak, *De Rederijkers*; J. van Mierlo, *Geschiedenis van De Letterkunde van de Middleeuwen*, p. 214ff. The best survey of Antwerp literature and religion during Massys' time are L. Roose, *Anna Bijns*; A. van Elslander, "Letterkunding leven in de Bourgondische tijd. De Rederijkers," p. 3ff.; Murray, p. 103ff. The *rederijker* guild motto of *De Violieren*, together with the winged bull of St. Luke, protector of the Antwerp painters' guild, adorn the 1496 double portrait by the Master of Frankfurt (F.163; Antwerp, Koninklijk Museum). See also C.P. Serrure, *De Violieren te Antwerpen* (Antwerp, 1855), pp. 103–8; F. Donnet, *Het Jonstich Versaem der Violieren* (Antwerp, 1907); L. Roose, "De Letterkunde," *Antwerpen in de XVIe eeuw* (Antwerp, 1975), p. 322ff.

66. G.J. Steenbergen, *Het Landjuweel van de Rederijkers*.

67. Ibid., pp. 202–10; Murray, p. 106; E. van Even, *Het Landjuweel van Antwerpen in 1561* (Louvain, 1861); C. Kruyskamp, ed., *Het Antwerpse landjuweel van 1561* (Antwerp, 1962).

68. W.M.H. Hummelen, *De sinnekens in het rederijkersdrama*; E.K. Chambers, *The Medieval Stage* (Oxford, 1903); K. Young, *The Drama of the Medieval Church* (Oxford, 1933); Delaruelle, Labande, and Ourliac, *L'Eglise au Temps du Grand Schisme*, p. 610ff.

69. Mak, p. 58ff.; van Mierlo, p. 255ff.; Hummelen, *De Sinnekens*; G.R. Kernodle, *From Art to Theatre* (Chicago, 1944); for the comparison of personifications in spectacle and in art, see S. Williams and J. Jacquot; I.M. Veldman, *Maarten van Heemskerck and Dutch Humanism in the Sixteenth Century* (Amsterdam, 1977), pp. 55ff., 133ff.

70. Hummelen, *De Sinnekens*, p. 221ff.; see also a useful compedium by S. Chew, *The Pilgrimage of Life* (New Haven, 1962).

71. A recent discussion with bibliography is G. Knuvelder, *Handboek tot de geschiedenis der nederlandse Letterkunde*, vol. 1, pp. 393–98.

72. Mak, pp. 70–89; van Mierlo, pp. 259–63.

73. T. Reintges, *Ursprung und Wesen der mittelalterlichen Schützengilden* (Bonn, 1963); J.D. Tracy, *The Politics of Erasmus*, pp. 75–76

74. R.van Bastelaer, *Les Estampes de Peter Bruegel l'Ancien* (Brussels, 1908), no.207; R. Klein, *Graphic Worlds of Peter Bruegel the Elder* (New York, 1963), p. 107.

75. A morality play is depicted in more serious costume by Bruegel in the background of his allegory *Temperance*, 1560, van Bastelaer no.138. The drawing for Bruegel's print is dated 1560 and is now in Rotterdam, Museum Boymans-van Beuningen; see L.Münz, *Bruegel: The Drawings* (London, 1961), no. 148; C. de Tolnay, *Die Zeichnungen des Peter Bruegel* (Berlin, 1952), no.63; and the outstanding catalog *Pieter Bruegel d.Ä. als Zeichner* (Berlin, 1975), p. 69, no.74. The performance practices pictured in the Bruegel *Temperance* are discussed by a theater specialist, J. J. Mak, in "De wachter in het Rederijkersdrama," *Oud Holland* 64 (1949): 162ff.

76. Steenbergen, p. 33ff.; Mak, *Rederijkers*, p. 11.

77. Guicciardini, 1625 ed. p. 96.

78. Blum, pp. 49–58; the Prado *Deposition* dates before 1443, when the *Edelheer altarpiece* was donated to the Louvain church and inscribed.

79. Friedländer, vol. 7, p. 55, no.164.

80. J. Martin, *Rubens: The Antwerp Altarpieces* (New York, 1969), esp. pp. 56–70; F. Baudouin, "Rubens Altarpieces before 1620," *Rubens* (New York, 1977), p. 73ff.

81. For Hals's group portraits of the Haarlem militia companies of St. Hadrian and St. George, see Seymour Slive, *Frans Hals* (London, 1970), vol.1, pp. 39ff., 69ff., 134ff., vol.1, pp. 69ff., 134ff. 39ff., and *Frans Hals Schützengilde St. Georg* (Stuttgart, 1962). On the portraits of Captain Becker's company (1639–43) and other van der Helst militia company group portraits, see J. Rosenberg, S. Slive, and E. ter Kuile, *Dutch Art and Architecture 1600–1800* 3rd ed., (Harmondsworth, 1977), pp. 319f., plus for Hals, 50ff., 63ff.. For Rembrandt's "Night Watch" of 1642, the Company of Captain Banning Cocq, see the bibliography in Rosenberg, et al, pp. 432–33, n.15, p. 462, along with the recent fine studies by C. Tümpel, "Beobachtungen zur 'Nachtwache,' " *Beiträge zur neue Rembrandt-Forschungen*, ed. O. von Simson and J. Kelch (Berlin, 1973), pp. 162–75, and E. Haverkamp-Begemann, *Rembrandt's Nightwatch* (Princeton, 1983).

82. The Dürer drawing is in Goris and Marlier, *Dürer Diary*, p. 60, Plate 7. For the religious life in Antwerp during Massys' lifetime, see C. de Clercq, "Kerkelijk leven," *Antwerpen in de XVIe eeuw* (Antwerp, 1975), p. 56ff.; Prims, *Geschiedenis, passim*.

83. De Clerq, "kerkelijk leven."

84. L. de Barsee, "De Bouwkunst in de XVIe eeuw," *Antwerpen in de XVIe eeuw* (Antwerp, 1975), pp. 362–65, bibliography n.2.

85. Ibid., pp. 365–67.

86. Ibid.

87. Prims, *Geschiedenis*, pp. 123-24.

88. Guicciardini, 1625 ed., p. 76; E. de Moreau, *Histoire de l'eglise en Belgique*, vol.4, p. 377. The legend falsely credited the illustrious Godefroid de Bouillon with fetching this Saint-Prépuce de Notre-Seigneur from the Holy Land.

89. Prims, *Geschiedenis*, pp. 126–34.

90. Ibid., pp. 134–35.

91. Especially Toussaert, *Le Sentiment religieux en Flandre à la fin du Moyen-Age*, pp. 122–203; Post, *Kerkelijke verhoudingen in Nederland voór de Refermatie* pp. 401–9; Delaruelle, p. 748ff.; de Moreau, *Histoire*, pp. 368–72; S.Axters, *De Moderne devotie, 1380–1550*, pp. 396–401.

92. De Moreau, p. 372; Blum, p. 63, ill. 54.

93. J. de Borchgrave d'Altena, "La Messe de saint Gregoire. Etude iconographique," pp. 3–34; *Die Messe Gregors des Grossen*, exhibition catalog (Cologne, 1982).

94. D. Meertens, *De godsvrucht in de Nederlanden* (Louvain, 1932), vol.3, pp. 11, 25.

95. For the Antonite order at Colmar in relation to Grünewald and for the hospitallers in general, see A. Hayum, "The Meaning and Function of the Isenheim Altarpiece: The Hospital Context Revisited," *Art Bulletin* 59 (1977): 501–17.

96. Prims, *Geschiedenis*, pp. 147–48.

97. Ibid. 137–39; de Moreau, p. 373.

98. J.A.F. Kronenberg, *Marias heerlijkheden in Nederlanden*, esp. vol.2. According to de Moreau (pp. 373–78), some 150 cults of the Virgin survived from the Middle Ages into Massys' day. The survival, especially in Louvain and Liege, of 12th-century wooden Mosan *Sedes sapientiae* figures of Virgin and Child is discussed in A. van Buren, "The Canonical Office in Renaissance Painting, part II: More about the Rolin *Madonna*," *Art Bulletin* 60 (1978); 622–24; and in J. de Borchgrave d'Altena, *Les Madones anciennes conservés en Belgique* (Brussels, 1943).

For Erasmus's views, see especially the 1526 "A Pilgrimage for Religion's sake," *The Colloquies of Erasmus*, ed. C.R. Thompson (Chicago, 1965), p. 285ff.

99. De Moreau, p. 377; also S. Williams, "Les Ommegangs d'Anvers," and other references cited in note 59.

100. Post, *KV*, pp. 393–95; Toussaert, pp. 244–67.

101. N.Z. Davis, "The Sacred and the Body Social in Sixteenth Century Lyon," 1978 (to be included in her forthcoming book on 16th-century Lyons).

102. See Bruegel's *Festival of St. George's Day*, mentioned above, n. 74. Also the print *Kermess at Hoboken* (van Bastelaer no. 208; Klein, p. 111, no. 23). Bruegel's Vienna painting of a *Peasant Dance* is also a kermess (F. Grossman, *Bruegel The Paintings*, 3rd ed. [London, 1973], p. 201). S. Alpers, "Bruegel's Festive Peasants," *Simiolus* 4(1972): 169ff., discusses folk customs in related images by Bruegel and his contemporaries.

103. Toussaert, pp. 258–66; K. Rotsaert, *De heilig-bloedprocessie* (Bruges, 1982). Bruges also held a procession to its own image of the Madonna, an August 15th parade for Notre Dame de la Poterie, celebrating a vow made in 1304 by the wives of the city to ensure the victory of their military husbands.

104. Van Mierlo, pp. 226–40. See also n. 68, above.

105. S. Williams, "Les Ommegangs d'Anvers," pp. 349–57, n. 6, 13. The prints include a mid-17th century woodcut by Jan Jegher and a 1684 etching by Gaspar Bouttats, accompanied by explanatory texts printed by Hieronymus Verdussen (*Antwerp's Golden Age*, exh.cat., pp. 118–19, no. 1050.).

106. Guicciardini, 1625 ed., p. 86.

107. J.J. Murray, p. 67. On the relationship between this *ommegang* procession and later Rubens imagery, such as the *Vienna Parts of the Earth*, see A. Joplin, "Return to the Golden Age: Three Marine Allegories by Rubens," (Master's thesis, University of Calif., 1977); also E. McGrath, "Le Déclin d'Anvers et les decorations de Rubens pour l'entrée du Prince Ferdinand en 1635," *Les fêtes de la renaissance III*, ed. J. Jacquot (Tours, 1972), p. 173ff., esp. 181-82, and "Rubens' Pompa Introitus Ferdinandi and the Traditions of Civic Pageantry" (Ph.D. dissertation, Warburg Inst., U. of London, 1972).

108. Joplin, "Return to the Golden Age"; *Antwerp's Golden Age*, pp. 46–47, nos. 17–20. America is symbolized by a young woman, holding in one hand an arrow and in the other a tomahawk, seated on an armadillo. Africa holds an olive branch and rides a crocodile. Asia sits upon a camel, while dominant Europe bestrides a globe with a sceptre in her hand and a compass and book in her lap. See H. Reinsch, *Die Zeichnungen des Martin de Vos* (Tübingen, 1967), pp. 162–63, 178. Also useful is the catalogue by H. Honour, *European Vision of America* (Cleveland, 1975), p. 112ff.

109. On Bernini, R. Wittkower, *Gian Lorenzo Bernini*, 2nd ed. (London, 1966), pp. 30, 219–20, no.50; G. Pochat, "Über Berninis 'Concetto' zum Vierströmebrunnen auf Piazza Navona," *Kunsthistorisk Tidskrift* 25 (1966): 72ff. On Tiepolo, M. Ashton, "Allegory, Fact, and Meaning in Giambattista Tiepolo's Four Continents in Würzburg," *Art Bulletin* 58 (1978): 109ff. (with bibliography); on the general theme, C. le Corbeiller, "Miss America and Her Sisters: Personifications of the Four Parts of the World," *Metropolitan Museum of Art* Bulletin N.S. 19 (1961): 211ff.

110. Williams, "Les Ommegangs d'Anvers," pp. 352–53. On Mercury's role in public allegories, McGrath, "Le Déclin d'Anvers."

111. For the entrance of Archduke Ernst, see the designs of Martin de Vos, mentioned above, n. 109, and the accompanying program description by Joannes Bochius, secretary of the city of Antwerp, illustrated by Peter van der Borcht (*Antwerp's Golden Age*, exh. cat., pp. 178–99, nos. 152–56; also A. Doutrepont, "Martin de Vos et l'Entrée triomphale de l'Archeduc Ernest d'Autriche à Anvers en 1594," *Bulletin de l'Institut historique belge de Rome* 18 (1936): 125–98. For entries during the period of Emperor Charles V, see *Fêtes et ceremonies au temps de Charles Quint*, vol.2 of *Fêtes de la Renaissance II*, ed. J. Jacquot. The 1549 Antwerp entry, organized by Cornelius Grapheus for Philip II, is described by J. Roobaert, "De seer Wonderlijcke Schoone Triumphelijcke Incompst van de Hooghmogenden Prince Philips in de Stadt van Antwerpen Anno 1549," *BMRBA* 9 (1960); 43ff.; and by Guicciardini, 1625 ed., pp. 87–89. For Rubens's designs and the 1635 triumphal entry into Antwerp of Archduke Ferdinand, see J.R. Martin, *Decorations for the Pompa Introitus Ferdinandi* (Corpus Rubenianum Ludwig Burchard XVI) (London, 1972) (with bibliography); McGrath, works cited in note 107, and "Rubens' Arch of the Mint," *JWCI* 37 (1974): 191–217. Late 16th-century Habsburg entries are discussed by T. Kaufmann, *Variations on the Imperial Theme: Studies in Ceremonial Art and Collecting in the Age of Maximilian II and Rudolph II* (New York, 1978).

Bibliography on the general topic is also extensive: I. van Roeder-Baumbach, *Versieringen bij Blijde Inkomsten gebruikt in de zuidelijke Nederlanden, Ommegangen en Blijde Inkomsten te Antwerpen*, exh. cat; J. Landwehr, *Splendid Ceremonies. State Entries and Royal Funerals in the Low Countries 1515–1791. A Bibliography* (Leyden, 1971); S. Anglo, *Spectacle, Pageantry, and Early Tudor Policy* (Oxford, 1969); R. Strong, *Splendour at Court: Renaissance Spectacle and the Theatre of Power* (London, 1973); E. Müller-Bochat, *Der allegorische Triumphzug* (Cologne, 1957); F. Yates, *Astraea: The Imperial Theme in the Sixteenth Century* (London, 1975), and *The Valois Tapestries* (London, 1959); D.M. Bergeron, *English Civic Pageantry 1558–1642* (London, 1971).

112. Prims, "De 13 Hypothesen," pp. 159–64; J.D. Tracy, *The Politics of Erasmus*, pp. 91–92.

113. Goris and Marlier, p. 68.

114. C. Geertz, "Centers, Kings, and Charisma," pp. 150–71.
115. Prims, "De 13 Hypothesen," pp. 159–64.
116. Quoted by J.D. Tracy, p. 92, from P. Aegidius and C. Grapheus, *Hypotheses sive argumenta spectaculorum quae Caesari Carolo civitatis Antwerpiensis antistites sunt edituri* (Antwerp: Hillen, 1520).
117. Ibid. On Astraea, see F. Yates, "Queen Elizabeth I as Astraea," *Astraea* pp. 29–87. (n. 111).
118. For this theme, see the Dürer engraving (B.73, ca. 1497–98) *Hercules at the Crossroads,* as interpreted by E.Panofsky in *Albrecht Dürer,* pp. 73–76, and in *Hercules am Scheidewege* (Leipzig/Berlin, 1930), pp. 166–73. The conceit of identifying a Habsburg monarch with Hercules is discussed by G. Bruck, "Habsburger als 'Herculier,' " *JKSW* N.F. 14 (1953); 191–98; W. McDonald, "Maximilian I of Habsburg and the Veneration of Hercules: On the Revival of Myth and the German Renaissance," *Journal of Medieval and Renaissance Studies* 6 (1976): 139–54.
119. F. Yates, "Charles V and the Idea of the Empire," *Astraea,* pp. 1–28; E. Rosenthal, "*Plus ultra*" (n.31).
120. Tracy, p. 92.
121. Ibid. pp. 36–47, stressing the differences in the political theories of the Netherlander Erasmus (*consensus*) and the Frenchman Budé (*maiestas*).
122. Ibid., p. 39, n.147, for this Erasmus quotation. See also the adages "The beetle searches for the eagle" (*Scarabeus aquilam quaerit*), "To exact dues from the dead" (*A mortuo tributum exigere*), "You have obtained Sparta, adorn it" (*Spartam nactus es, hanc orna*), "War is sweet to those who do not know it" (*Dulce bellum inexpertis*) and, especially, "Kings and fools are born, not made" (*Aut fatuum aut regem nasce oportere*). Also, "The duty of a prince, who takes taxes from all, is to consult the advantage of all—to preside over trials, to stamp out crime, to respect the magistrate, to amend useless laws . . . It is in this [wisdom] that the prince must so far excel other mortals, as he excels them in dignity, in wealth, in splendour, and in power" (M.M. Phillips, *Erasmus on His Times A Shortened Version of the Adages* [Cambridge, 1967], pp. 34–72, 97–140).
123. H.H. Rowan, ed., *The Low Countries in Early Modern Times* (New York, 1972), p. 12ff.; also Remi du Puys, *La Tryumphante Entrée de Charles Prince des Espagnes en Bruges 1515* ed. S. Anglo (New York, 1976).
124. Williams, "Les Ommegangs d'Anvers," p. 354.
125. Ibid., p. 355; also Joplin, "Return to the Golden Age"; McGrath, "Le declin," p. 181.
126. Williams, p. 356. Also mentioned in Guicciardini, 1625 ed., p. 70; Prims, "Antwerpsche Ommeganck", pp. 9–10.
127. Guicciardini, 1625 edition:

> After the states of Asia fell, 1300 years before the birth of Jesus, this was the worthy castle of the Giant Antigon, whom Brabo conquered on which Brabantic land, founded with great fortifications and high towers, he bestows a name; he strikes with violent power, throwing the hand outside [clima] close to the Scheldt and the sea. Now the prominent city in the entire known world is battered by surging billows of the great ocean, once endowed by the trophies of superior emperors, confident port of the rivers carries from the shore, and earth and clear sky. Fertile riches by sea, by lands, to those nations in which many live, many are amply enriched: 'Imperial, mistress, that is the true Antwerp.'

> Postquam res Asiae ceciderunt, mille trecentes
> Annis ante Jesum de sacra Virginia natum,
> Hic fuit Antigoni castrum insigne Gigantes,
> Quem Brabo devicit de quo Brabantica tellus,
> Moenibus inceptum magnis, et turribus altis,
> Cut nomen tribuit manum violenta potestas,
> Extra clima jacens, juxta Scaldam, pelagusque,
> Fluctibus Oceani quantitur surgentibus ampli,
> Nunc villa insignis toto notissima mundo,
> Caesaris excellis olim dotata trophaeis,
> Ex pelago, ex terra, et coela confisa sereno
> Insterili terralocuples portus fluviorum,
> Per mare, per terras, quae questam gentibus affert,
> Quo multi vivunt, multi ditantur abunde:
> Imperialis, hera sic est Antwerpia vera.

128. Van den Branden, p. 42, citing "tradition."
129. Goris and Marlier, p. 68.
130. B. Deneke, "Prodigien-glaube," *Albrecht Dürer 1471–1971,* exh.cat. pp. 214–15, 22–27. Guicciardini, 1625 edition, p. 70, preserves these Grapheus verses, addressed to each of the surviving bones of the giant, as follows:

> *In coxam* Tanta haec horrifici fuerit si coxa Gigantis Caetera quanta illi membra fuisse putes?
> *In dentem* Faucibus immensis dens hic stetit, ore voraci Quivisset solidos ille vocare boves.
> *In brachium* Quam fuerit forti munitus robore saevus Ille vir, id Cubiti pars monet ista sui.
> *In scapulam* Ardua terribilis scapula haec est (crede) tyrrani: Quid reris quantum sustinuisset onus?
> *In tibiam* Gestavit vastum vasta ist haec tibia corpus, Enceladum aequavit (non dubiam) ille gradu.

131. W. Heckscher, "Bernini's Elephant and Obelisk," *Art Bulletin* 29(1947): 155-82; M. Winner, "Raffael malt einen Elephanten," *Mitteilungen des Kunsthistorischen Institutes in Florenz* 11(1964), p. 71ff
132. H. Pirenne, *Early Democracy in the Low Countries,* pp. 11–12, 108–24, 156–62; F. Rörig, *The Medieval Town* (Berkeley / Los Angeles, 1967) pp. 122–60.
133. Pirenne, pp. 171–80.
134. A point forcefully argued in D. W. Robertson, *Chaucer's London* (New York, 1968), p. 5ff.; and, although he argues strongly for increase in social mobility, see the remarks on "class" and identity in F.R.H. Du Boulay, *An Age of Ambition: English Society in the Late Middle Ages* (New York, 1970), pp. 61–79. A *locus classicus* is J. Huizinga, *Waning of the Middle Ages,* pp. 56–67,

although, like Du Boulay, he sees society through a knightly lens. The confraternities in the Flemish cities of Massys' era are, however, a clear indication of corporate spirit. For a fine introduction, with bibliography, on both religious and guild organizations, cf. Toussaert, p. 478ff., Delaruelle, Labande, and Ourliac, p. 666ff., and other references in Chapter 2, note 32.

135. Most reently, G. Parker, *The Dutch Revolt* (London, 1977); also, P. Geyl, *The Revolt of the Netherlands*, 5th ed. (London, 1966); J. Wegg, *The Decline of Antwerp under Philip of Spain* (London, 1924).

136. Pirenne, pp. 187–206.

137. H. Schmidt, *Die deutschen Städtechroniken als Spiegel des bürgerlichen Selbstverständnisses im Spätmittelalter* (Göttingen, 1958); also useful are the recent observations by M. Baxandall, *The Limewood Sculptors of Renaissance Germany*, pp. 83–88, on the collective identity conveyed by a sculpted retable.

138. The importance of the independence of imperial cities and their role in the acceptance of Protestantism and its political doctrines is discussed by B. Moeller, *Imperial Cities and the Reformation* (Philadelphia, 1972), 64–101, 106.

141. Panofsky, *Albrecht Dürer*, pp. 109–13; see also the Hans Burgkmair woodcut of the Imperial eagle *(Reichsadler)* superimposed over the crucifix with all of the heraldic arms of the princes within the Holy Roman Empire (1510), and his 1508 frontispiece to Johannes Stammler's *Dialogus de diversarum gencium sectis et mundi religionibus*, a book on world religions—an image showing "Sancta Mater Ecclesia" seated with both Pope and Emperor kneeling at her feet *(Hans Burgkmair Das graphische Werk*, exh.cat., [Stuttgart, 1973], nos. 42, 28).

142. *Geschiedenis*, and *Prims*, and "De St. Lucasgilde en de zeven Weden," *Antwerpiensia* 13 (1939).

143. Schmidt, *Die deutschen Städtechroniken*, pp. 97–98.

144. Toussaert, Delaruelle, and S. Ozment, *The Reformation in the Cities* (New Haven, 1975), pp. 15-46.

145. J. Huizinga, *Middle Ages*, pp. 200-214; E. Mâle, *L'Art religieux à la fin du Moyen-Age en France;* Delaruelle, Labande, and Ourliac, p. 610ff. (with bibliography).

146. For pilgrimages and relics, Delaruelle, Labande, and Ourliac, p. 787ff.; Toussaert, p. 267ff.; Post, *KV*, pp. 395–400, and *KG*, Vol. 2, pp. 236–51, 296–97.

147. Friedländer, vol. 12, pp. 71–72; nos. 345–49, including Scorel, himself a pilgrim. This is the very pilgrimage practice condemned by Erasmus in "A Pilgrimage for Religion's Sake," C. R. Thompson, *The Colloquies of Erasmus* (Chicago, 1965), p. 285ff.

148. Delaruelle, Labande, and Ourliac, p. 810ff.; Toussaert, p. 341ff.; Post, *KV*, pp. 473–84, and *KG*, vol. 2, pp. 19–20, 42–5; Prims, pp. 152–6. The standard reference is N. Paulus, *Geschichte des Ablasses im Ausgang des Mittelalters* (Paderborn, 1923).

149. Prims, *Geschiedenis*, p. 153.

150. Ringbom, p. 23ff. The Antwerp example cited by Prims, pp. 155–56, is the 1501–02 indulgence granted for prayers directed toward the altar of the Salve Regina confraternity and based on the power of the relics of saints contained there. This practice was not substantially different from using the magical powers of local relics to stimulate pilgrimages and alms, as in the case of the relic of the Madonna's tunic at Chartres, used to help finance the construction of Chartres cathedral in the mid-12th century: O. von Simson, *The Gothic Cathedral* (New York, 1962), pp. 160–72.

151. Calendars of the 15th-century manuscripts are discussed by Toussaert, p. 339, with specific reference to a Tournai diocese volume of the Mailly family. The Catholic ordering of time by means of saints' days is sensitively discussed by N. Davis, "The Sacred and the Body Social," for 16th-century Lyons. Voragine's *Golden Legend* was organized in its anthology of saints' lives according to the ecclesiastical calendar. Utrecht's annual church calendar is cited as an example by Post, *KV*, pp. 389–90; See R. Poole, *Medieval Reckonings of Time* (London, 1921); for art, P. Perdrizet, *La Calendrier Parisien à la fin du Moyen âge d'apres le Breviaire et les Livers d'Heures* (Paris, 1937).

152. Post, *KV;* Toussaert, pp. 326ff. 338–40: "One spoke, not of July 25th, but of 'Saint James' Day', not of August 15th, but of 'our Lady of mid-August.' "

153. L. Voet, "De typographische bedrijvigheid te Antwerpen in de 16e eeuw," *Antwerpen in de XVIe eeuw* (Antwerp, 1975), pp. 233–55 (with bibliography).

154. W. Nijhoff and E. Kronenberg, *Nederlandsche bibliographie van 1500 tot 1540*, p. 1923ff.

155. M. Nauwelaerts, "Humanisme en onderwijs," *Antwerpen in de XVIe eeuw*, pp. 257–300 (with bibliography); Prims, "Cultuurwaarden en cultuurtekorten te Antwerpen in de eerste helft van de zestiende eeuw," p. 15ff.; and "Het ontluiden van het Humanisme te Antwerpen," p. 523ff.

156. L. Voet, "De typographische bedrijvigheid," p. 236.

157. L. Roose, "De Letterkunde," *Antwerpen in de XVIe eeuw*, pp. 321–48; Roose, *Anna Bijns*, p. 1ff.; van Mierlo, pp. 308–45. For religious literature. see Post, *KG*, vol. 1, pp. 367–414.

158. Van Mierlo, pp. 383–85.

159. Ibid. p. 327.

160. L. Debaene, *De nederlandse volksboeken.*

161. G. Duby, "Diffusion of Cultural Patterns in Feudal Society," *The Chivalrous Society* (Berkeley / Los Angeles, 1977), pp. 171–77. An interesting discussion of the diffusion and educational values of chivalric ideals in Tudor England during the era of Massys is A. Ferguson, *The Indian Summer of English Chivalry* (Durham, N.C., 1960). Also, M. Vale, *War and Chivalry* (London, 1981).

162. The carnival atmosphere of mockery is discussed by M. Bakhtin, *Rabelais and His World*, transl. H. Iswolsky (Cambridge, Mass., 1968), and in connection with Erasmus by D. G. Watson, "Erasmus' *Praise of Folly* and the Spirit of Carnival," p. 333ff. On carnival in general, see the fine study by P. Burke, *Popular Culture in Early Modern Europe*, p. 178ff. (with bibliography); E. LeRoy Ladurie, *Carnival in Romans* (New York, 1979), p. 305ff.; and N. Z. Davis, p. 97ff.

163. Debaene, p. 353.

164. A. van Elslander, ed., *Het volksboek Vanden. X. Esels* (Antwerp, 1946).

165. R. Lievens, ed., *Tghevecht van Minnen* (Louvain, 1964).

166. Debaene, pp. 347–51; and "Rederijkers en prozaromans," *Gulden Passer* 27 (1949): 1–23; J. van Mierlo, "Nieuwe

studieën over Anna Bijns en andere opstellen," pp. 329–72. The most reent discussion, a dissent, is L. Roose, *Anna Bijns.* Certainly most of these *prozaromans* were published in Antwerp by Vorsterman, van Hoochstraeten, and van Doesborch.

167. C. Kruyskamp, ed., *De refreinenbundel van Jan van Doesborch* (Leyden, 1940). For related works, K. P. F. Moxey, *"The Ship of Fools* and the Idea of Folly in Sixteenth-Century Netherlandish Literature," in *The Early Illustrated Book Essays in Honor of Lessing J. Rosenwald* (Washington, 1982), pp. 86–102.

168. Roose, *Anna Bijns,* pp. 263–88.

169. For van Doesborch, see Kruyskamp, *Jan van Doesborch;* F. Lyna and W. van Eeghem, eds., *Jan van Styevoorts refreinenbundel Anno 1524;* also A. van Elslander, *Het refrein in de Nederlanden tot 1600;* G. Degroote, "De poezië der Rederijkers," pp. 292ff., 362ff.

170. A. van Elslander, "De Mariavereering bij de rederijkers," p. 57ff., emphasizes the predominance of the cult of the Virgin, in *rederijker* "joyous refrains"—a predictable emphasis in light of the fact that no fewer than 18 of the Chambers of Rhetoric in the Netherlands were dedicated to some aspect of the cult of the Virgin, including the Seven Sorrows of the Virgin cult of the Antwerp De Violieren *rederijkers* within Massys' own St. Luke guild.

171. Roose, *Anna Bijns,* Book 3, pp. 286–87, refrain 6: "De grootste boeven in haer meest gelucxs verserven Dit soude ons met recht."

172. A. van Elslander, *Het refrein,* pp. 95–120 / 146–65. See the following verses: van Doesborch no. 110 ("Against a babbler there's no guard"—*Want tegen een clappart en is er geen wachten);* van Doesborch no. 113 ("What one does in the world stripping worth to the bone"—*Wat doetmen ter werelt ten wert benijt);* van Doesborch no. 118 ("To trust well brings much evil"—*Bi wel betrouwen geschiet veel quaets);* van Doesborch no. 89 ("This seeming virtue is a sin before God"—*Dit duecht schijnt ende sonde voor gode is*); van Doesborch no. 86 ("Society will lack for goods"—*Gheselscap sal voor Goet Ghebreken*); Styevoort no. 160 ("Gold, now most prized in the world"—*Tgelt is nu ter werelt meest ghepresen*); Styevoort no. 182 ("The rich, who are called well-born"—*Die rijke die heet wel gheborene*); Styevoort no. 164 ("To plunder must be wholesome fare"—*Rapen moet wel sijn een ghesonde spijs*); Styevoort no. 83 ("To have most of what costs is Woman's lust"—*Haelt most wat cost tes Vrouwen lost*); van Doesborch no. 94 = Styevoort no. 195 ("Drunkenness, sin, harm, and shame"—*Dronckenscap sonde, schade, en schande*); van Doesborch no. 115 ("The Drink-pot makes many penniless"—*Een drinckpot maect menigen geldeloos*).

173. Van Elslander, *Het refrain,* p. 157ff; Styevoort, nos. 60, 189. Van Doesborch no. 117 ("Let us drink, let us pay / Though money flies with passing day"—*Laet ons drincken, laet ons storten / Al mindert ons goet, ons dagen die corten);* Styevoort no. 17 ("Speak, Scream, Screw [or Sew, a course pun], God Made Women"—*Spreken, scrijen, naijen, heef God den vrouwen beraijen*); Styevoort no. 40 ("Such Hay Horses Follow Today"—*Sulck hoy volcht nu den paerden nae*); Sytevoort no. 236 ("After how the world is going / Girls will fall so much to heat / That, lust or disgust, they'll have the tail"—*Na dat die werelt nu gaet / Soe vallen die meijskens veel te heet / Ist lief of leet / Sie willen den steert hebben*); Van Doesborch no. 152 ("Eat your fill when you're offered your pick"—*Est nu goed alsmen u willeken doet*); van Doesborch no. 149 ("Of Laughter and Artistry Unexpected"—*Van lachen en constic mi niet ghewachten*).

174. K. Renger, *Lockere Gesellschaft* (Berlen, 1970), discusses visual analogs in the Netherlands to this literary tradition as well as the verses themselves, and he includes a fine bibliography. Cf. also the works of D. T. Enklaar, *Varende Luyden (Assen, 1937); and Uit Uilenspiegel's Kring* (Assen, 1940); and the English discussion by H. Waddell, *The Wandering Scholars* (London, 1927). The edition of these "vagrant" verses is *Veelderhande geneuchlijcke dichten, tafelspelen ende refreynen* (Leyden, 1899).

175. Styevoort no. 85 ("The Stone Hidden under the Exposed Lump"—*Die keije verborghen onder die blesse bloot):* "Moria seer hoghe vernaemt." See also van Doesborch no. 91 ("It is a wonder what the deluded heart will endure"—*Tis wonder was verdoolde herten lijen);* no. 116 ("He will suffer who acts with foolish will"—*Wie salt verdragen dat sot wille doet).*

176. Styevoort no. 165 ("All fools and none carry bells"—*Alle sotten en draghen gheen bellen);* no. 16 ("Everyone has a strange spirit that torments him"—*Elc heeft een vreemt geestgen dat hem quelt*).

177. Styevoort no. 39 ("How ill ought to go in that world"—*Hoe sout dan Qualick in die Weerlt gaen*).

178. Kruyskamp, *Jan van Doesborch,* no. xliii. See also van Mierlo, pp. 291-4; van Elslander, *Het refrein* pp. 121-45; Roose, pp. 188-204. For the amorous refrains of van Doesborch, see Kruyskamp, nos. 1-80, divided about equally between pure, sincere love poems and lovesick laments. Styevoort presents a similar blend, e.g., nos. 5, 7, 14, 25, 26, 38, 43, 46, 173 (positive) and nos. 8, 11, 19, 29, 36, 63, 82, 172, 187 (laments). Bijns inclines toward the cynical and plaintive. To this day, the modern Dutch word for marriage, *trouw,* derives from the courtly lover's ideal of faithfulness.

179. On the vast subject of courtly love, the following are useful: O. Lauffer, *Frau Minne in Schrifttum und bildender Kunst des deutschen Mittelalters* (Hamburg, 1947); E. Köhler, *Ideal und Wirklichkeit in der höfischen Epik* (Tübingen, 1956); H. Furstner, *Studien zur Wesenbestimmung der höfischen Minne* (Groningen, 1956); H. Kolb, *Der Begriff der Minne und das Entstehung der höfischen Lyrik* (Tübingen, 1958); D. Wiercinski, *Minne, Herkunft, und Anwendungsschichten eines Wortes* (Cologne, 1964); L. Pollmann, *Liebe in der hochmittelalterlichen Literatur Frankreichs* (Frankfurt, 1966); F. X. Newman, ed., *The Meaning of Courtly Love* (Albany, 1968), with bibliography; and R. H. Bloch, *Medieval French Literature and Law* (Berkeley / Los Angeles, 1977), pp. 215-58. Most recently, see the overview by J. C. Moore, " 'Courtly Love': A Problem with Terminology," *Journal of the History of Ideas* 40 (1979): 621-32, with bibliography. Concerning late medieval art, three recent studies are most useful and full of references: R. S. Favis, "The Garden of Love in Fifteenth-Century Netherlandish and German Engravings" (Ph.D. dissertation, University of Pennsylvania, 1974); S. L. Smith, " 'To Women's Wiles I Fell': The Power of Women Topos and the Development of Medieval Secular Art" (Ph.D. dissertation, University of Pennsylvania, 1978); P. Watson, *The Garden of Love in Tuscan Art of the Early Renaissance* (Philadelphia, 1979).

180. Debaene, *De nederlandse Volksboeken,* pp. 282-86.

181. Roose, *Anna Bijns,* p. 17.

182. Geertz, "Centers, Kings, and Charisma."

183. Roose, *Anna Bijns,* pp. 208-62; Prims, *Geschiedenis,* p. 289.

2

A Tale of Two Triptychs

In terms of documented pictures, Quinten Massys seems to emerge, like Minerva, full-grown when he first appears. The earliest dated pictures by him are two large altarpieces, which followed one another in immediate succession during the period from 1507 to 1511. Together, they reveal the work of a mature artist already capable of working on a grand scale with extraordinary fineness and precision. The two works are also intimately tied to Massys' two home towns. The first, commissioned for the town of his birth, Louvain, was an altarpiece made for a religious confraternity of St. Anne. The second, destined for Massys' adopted city, Antwerp, was dedicated to the two saints John and created for the local shrineworkers' or "joiners" guild.

The striking fact about both altarpieces is that they contain internal visual differences between their component parts and also differ markedly from one another. Indeed, the wings seem almost to be made by separate artists, so different are their stylistic and thematic choices from the forms of the central panel in each case. The Louvain *St. Anne altarpiece* has conservative wing panels, closely patterned on previous Netherlandish painting, but its tranquil centerpiece reveals new forms imported from Italian painting, possibly including the works of Leonardo da Vinci. In contrast, the central panel of the Antwerp altarpiece seems dependent upon previous Flemish models, but the inventive wings show close study of the art of Albrecht Dürer and Leonardo within a crowded kaleidoscope of exotic costumes, grotesque faces, and energetic movement.

The variety of forms and subjects contained within these two altarpieces raises the questions how a single artist could possibly construct such a counterpoint of harmonies at the same moment, and what purposes motivated these visual contrasts. The hypothesis advanced here will be that these separate choices were deliberate and that they were carefully adjusted to the specific depiction of a given subject, to the audience of the work, and to the desired overall religious effect.

Sacred personages embody the values of religious life and serve to organize the relationship between daily life and transcendent reality. Along with ritual, in this case the mass before the altar adorned with these alterpieces, it is art that incorporates the religious figures within images made present within a culture.[1] Like frozen visions, sacred pictures constitute religious relationships between this world and the next, providing images of religious authority and narratives that recreate mythical events basic to the establishment of a community of the faithful. Religious art summons up emotional states of piety and often serves to motivate proper ethical behavior. Religious images, like the imposing altarpieces by Massys, represent the very spiritual foundation on which the confraternity, guild chapel, or other congregation was established.

> Such a work was the emblem of a specific group, ensign of its identity, and this [image], wherever it was located, gestured toward another locale than where it was actually situated; it implies a seat of power, the center from which a society took its measure and its orders.[2]

The *St. Anne altarpiece* (Brussels, Musées royaux), was made between 1507 and 1509 for the religious confraternity of St. Anne in Louvain; the brotherhood's chapel was located in the church of St. Peter.[3] The centerpiece of the Louvain St. Anne triptych is a large panel of the Holy Kinship, the family of St. Anne, mother of the Virgin. The picture focuses on the triad of Anne, Christ, and the Virgin, the group known from German painting and sculpture as the holy *Anna Selbdritt.* Massys' arrangement shows the two women flanking and supporting the Infant, Anne holding a bunch of grapes, Mary grasping a small tether, which restrains the tiny goldfinch perched on Christ's finger. Around the central figures are the other relatives of Christ, the families of Mary's sisters. According to medieval legend, such as the story recounted in the 13th-century compendium the *Golden Legend* of Jacobus da Voragine, St. Anne had three husbands. The first was Joachim, father of the Virgin; two succeeding spouses were named Cleophas and Salome; and St. Anne had two further daughters, each named Mary, by the two later husbands. The Holy Kinship of Massys' panel, then, depicts Christ's grandparents, as well as the aunts and uncles and little cousins his own age who formed the larger family group. The first of Mary's stepsisters, Mary Cleophas, married Alpheus, and she produced the four children seen at the lower left of Massys' composition (St. James the Less, who holds a carnation, St. Simon, St. Jude, and Joseph the Just, the little boy in the corner with the open prayerbook and the devotional woodcuts). The other stepsister, Mary Salome, married Zebedeus and produced James the Great and John the Evangelist; she and her elder son are shown holding figs in the right-hand corner of Massys' work. *Pl. 1*

But the Massys panel is a great deal more than just a line-up of the dramatis personae, for the holy figures are placed within a majestic building, an arcade with three openings, the central one crowned by a dome with an open window. The area of the holy women is a verdant garden of grass and flowers; the husbands—Joachim and the three younger men—stand behind a marble balustrade. Behind and below the open structure lies a vast landscape panorama, a green valley encompassed by hazy blue hills. Behind St. Anne a craggy rock echoes the outline of the women and provides a touch of the exotic, with a large aperture in its side and a castle on its lofty summit.

From the above description, Massys' *Holy Kinship* can be seen to combine genealogical completeness with a richness of setting that sets the saintly figures apart from the run of ordinary humanity. Both effects are essential to the image and serve to link it with a series of Holy Kinship paintings from the late 15th and early 16th centuries.[4]

In general, the setting for the *Holy Kinship* tends to be either the interior of a church (the outstanding Netherlandish example is by Geertgen tot sint Jans) or the sacred precinct of an enclosed garden, as in Massys' foreground. The immediate model for Massys' conception of the scene was a Holy Kinship retable prepared by a colleague in Antwerp, the "Master of Frankfurt," so named because this altarpiece was sent to the Dominican cloister in Frankfurt, where the altarpiece was consecrated in 1492.[5] In the center panel of the Frankfurt *Holy Kinship,* the *Anna Selbdritt* is isolated on a marble throne, set several steps above a lush garden in which the remainder of the family crowds around the central figures. There is no separation of the background landscape from the grassy, flower-covered lawn of the foreground. (The lily in the right corner has long been associated with the Virgin in Netherlandish art.) There are no tall mountains; no building sets off the space. Instead, the entire space looks like an earthly paradise, akin to the innumerable garden images of the Virgin among Virgins so popular in late 15th-century Netherlandish paintings, or to the all-saints image at the bottom of Jan van Eyck's Ghent altarpiece.[6] *Pl. 2*

That Massys knew the work of the Master of Frankfurt is demonstrated by the two stepsisters in the

Pl. 3 corners of their respective altarpieces, particularly the turbaned Mary Cleophas reaching over to her oldest child in the left foreground of both works. The Master of Frankfurt's image is even more densely packed and varied than that of Massys, but both these Antwerp contemporaries evoke a religious world that is filled with detail—detailed knowledge of Christ's genealogy and extended family, plus detailed description of the garments, faces, and settings of the various characters. Both artists share a fascination with a costume: we have the impression that everyone showed up well dressed to have his likeness painted. Only the poses or backdrops are rearranged according to the artist's temperament.

But when Massys was choosing appropriate models for his complicated scene, he did not rely only on a comparable subject by the Master of Frankfurt. He also paid close attention to the forms of the most popular Madonna images in Netherlandish art, the Bruges altarpieces of Hans Memling (d. 1494) and Massys' contemporary Gerard David (d. 1523). Massys literally copied his Madonna and *Pl. 4* Child in the center from a David altarpiece, the *Baptism* made for Jan de Trompes, probably during the period (c. 1502–ca. 1507), just before Massys began work on the Holy Kinship altarpiece.[7] In both type and orientation, Massys' Virgin is borrowed from David's Madonna on the exterior of the *Baptism*; this type is distinguished by her long hair and her smooth facial contour, and Massys has retained the crescent-shaped composition of the overall body. In addition, he has retained the modest smock worn by the infant Christ in David's work, along with the symbolic bunch of grapes in the Child's hand to suggest the true wine of the eucharist and the stem of His lineage.[8] Massys' general type of the Virgin and her family, characterized by soft, almost unmodeled skin, smooth oval faces, high foreheads, and graceful, slender hands, recalls the types of David's famous predecessor at Bruges, Hans Memling. Also related to Memling is the use of architecture, open to a sunny landscape background, to house and to organize the holy figures. Marble columns and balustrades in front of green, tree-filled valleys and occasional houses or castles provide the combination of spaciousness, tranquility, and earthly harmony that is so basic to the image of the Virgin and saints in late 15th-century art.

Massys, we have seen, starts from this Memling/David/Master of Frankfurt foundation and ultimately depends upon it. But then he adds one more unexpected ingredient to the new concoction of the *Holy Kinship*. That ingredient is the element of fantasy in both architecture and landscape. For his forms of fantasy, Massys seems to have turned to the art of Italy. No hard evidence exists to support the idea of a trip by Quinten south of the Alps, and there is a strong possibility that the artist could have encountered Italian art in his own home town. In the previous generation, the art of Hans Memling had been significantly affected by the Italian merchant community in Bruges, and their numbers in Massys' Antwerp were almost as extensive.[9] In any case, Massys surely borrowed from Italian art in creating his *Holy Kinship*.

The architecture of the *Holy Kinship* has frequently been compared to the forms of Italian painting. The square pilaster crowns, the triple-arched opening, the tie rods between supports, and the single point of view, which permits a low vantage point for the ceiling vaults—all are characteristic of the settings in pictures by Pietro Perugino, such as his *Pietà* (ca. 1495, Dublin), his 1491 altar of Giuliano della Rovere (Rome, Villa Albani), or his 1493 *Madonna and Saints* (Florence, Uffizi).[10] But the arcades of Perugino could not have stood alone as a model for Massys, for they do not suggest the dominant form of the architectural space of the *Holy Kinship* panel—the open dome at the center. This kind of central area was unknown in both northern and central Italian art, but it is a pattern found frequently within the tradition of Venetian art. Scholars have also cited a comparison with the works of Cima da Conegliano from the 1490s, featuring an open dome with window very close to Massys' vault.[11]

Only the visual borrowings suggest that Massys ever went to Italy. His knowledge of painted architecture by Perugino or Cima could have come through the Antwerp collections of the Italian merchant community, which comprised a major element of the northern port city. Certainly the Italianisms—*sacra conversazione* formulas, putti, and garland ornament—of Memling seem to have come through the patronage and requests of local Italian merchants in Bruges (e.g., the Portinaris). And Massys could well have been emulating the local Flemish example of Memling (e.g., the

Washington *Virgin and Child*) when he turned for inspiration to the carefully painted architectural forms in Italian painting.[12]

The fact that Massys could have borrowed his unusual architectural forms from Italian art does not fully explain the reasons why he should have chosen to do so. A clue to his meaning is given by the energetic sculpted figure ornaments in the background, just above the heads of the Virgin and St. Anne. Two warlike nudes are shown with lethal weapons poised, the one with a large rock, the other with a bow and arrow. Men in combat also adorn the obviously otherworldly architecture of Petrus Christus' Washington *Nativity*, completed half a century before the Massys *Holy Kinship*.[13] Within the context of Christ's birth, the sculpted warriors appear alongside scenes from Genesis and serve to incorporate a reference to the violent and sinful nature of mankind prior to Christ's mission of redemption. The same message can be inferred for Massys' architectural figures; their nakedness indicates a primitive bestiality that contrasts with Christ's divinity and the saintliness of the relatives who stand beside Him under this shelter. The palace of heavenly beings stands erected upon the former fallibility of man; Christ as new Adam frees humanity from the burden of Original Sin. And the presence of such warlike figures also indicates, like the light through the window of the dome, what a fantasy architecture Massys has created. His building is truly a realm, like the buildings of the Italian pictures which were his models, suitable for the display and habitation of spiritual beings.

Much the same symbolic use of believable settings pertains to Massys' use of landscape in the *Holy Kinship*. An expansive, airy quality of landscape, which extends behind the foreground Madonna and saints, is a commonplace effect in the art of Hans Memling of Bruges, one of the most successful painters from the generation before Massys. In Memling's art, serenity seems to be the outcome of the reign of the Virgin, for the tranquil meadowlands and river valleys are placed directly behind a space where the Virgin is enthroned among kneeling donors, angels, and saints. Much the same image is created by Massys in the landscape background of the *Holy Kinship*.

Once again, however, Massys departs from the precedents of Memling. Instead of the watermills, riversides, and gentle grazing land of Memling, the *Holy Kinship* features blue, distant mountains. These lofty crags seem for the most part to be based in reality, but the towering peak behind St. Anne offers an imaginative departure with its unstable tilt, its cleft, and its castle on the summit. Within the Netherlandish tradition, only the work of Dieric Bouts and his followers in Louvain, such as the Master of the Pearl of Brabant (Munich), were interested in such craggy mountain vistas in their pictures. In those instances, such as the Pearl of Brabant panel of John the Baptist, the formidable background denoted that the setting was a wilderness retreat, a hermitage for the saint. In contrast, the Massys picture combines this formidable environment with a foreground family group, juxtaposing unspoiled nature with a complicated artificial architectural construction.

Within this juxtaposition of the natural and the artificial, between the tranquility of the holy figures and the power of the distant mountains, lies the creative fantasy of Massys' *Holy Kinship*, the new tone that separates his image from the 15th-century garden images of the same subject. Again, the catalyst seems to have come from Italy, in this case from Leonardo da Vinci, although we cannot be certain how Massys came to know the images of Leonardo. Indeed, the most telling comparison between the *Holy Kinship* and the paintings of da Vinci was probably impossible, since the *Madonna with St. Anne* (Paris, Louvre) was probably painted at about the same time as the Louvain altarpiece and may even postdate it.[14] It was the invention of Leonardo to suggest the spiritual majesty of the *Anna Selbdritt* by placing the holy figures against and above a primeval mountain range, untrammeled by human habitation and formed by the mightiest of geological forces. The *Madonna with St. Anne*, however, is not unique in Leonardo's work. Instead, it is the culmination of his developing ideas about how to suggest the otherworldly, spiritual strength of the earthly mother of Christ. Particularly in the two versions of the *Madonna of the Rocks* (London, Paris), Leonardo has developed this contrast, but he also fixed it into images like the early, small *Madonna and Child with Carnation* (Munich), where the two figures are placed within a palatial room, behind which a row of hazy blue mountains serves to demonstrate their religious dominion.

Massys has adopted Leonardo's visual language to achieve the same suggestion of importance and majesty for his *Madonna and St. Anne*. But he also seems to have intended a more specific meaning with the metaphoric juxtaposition of landscape and holy figures. In particular, the jagged crag with a castle on its summit stands out in the center of the composition, as it echoes the silhouette of St. Anne's pose. Traditionally, in Flemish art, the Virgin is symbolized visually by castlelike buildings, both in her role as the *porta coeli* (gateway to heaven) for mankind, and in her identification with the impregnable Tower of David from the Song of Songs (4,12).[15]

Other objects within the *Holy Kinship* panel also carry symbolic significance, because they are held by the holy figures and isolated from any other context. Many of these are commonplace within 15th-century painting, such as the grapes offered by Anne to the young Christ Child. These grapes refer to the eucharistic equation of wine with the blood of Christ, a metaphor made explicit in several biblical verses, such as "I am the true vine" (John 15:1). Moreover, as de Jongh has shown, the prominent stem on the grape cluster itself refers to Mary (and, by extension, St. Anne) as the nurturing vine that made possible the sacrifice of the Passion.[16] The goldfinch on Christ's hand is also a frequent accessory in religious pictures, where its power of flight naturally suggests comparison with the spiritual elevation of the soul or the Resurrection itself.[17] In the case of Massys, however, the finch has been shown fastened with a tether, like a common household pet, as indeed the bird was in Flanders. Aside from the natural ease of showing the bird as a pet rather than an empty attribute in Christ's hand, this tether seems to suggest that the binding of the bird is analogous to the spiritual condition of Christ as the Word made Flesh, the incorporation of divine love into human form. In this case, the finch would be the equivalent of the caged birds that appear in a series of images of the penitent St. Jerome in his study by Joos van Cleve, where the imprisonment of the bird corresponds to the imprisonment of the soul of the saint, who longs for his spiritual release at the Last Judgment.

In the hands of Mary Cleophas and her oldest son, St. James Minor, are carnations. The symbolic aspects of this flower have been discussed at length; basically, its fleshlike color has associated the carnation with the Incarnation, again the Word made Flesh, of the Christ Child.[18] And the fruit held by both Mary Salome and her elder son, St. James Major, also betokens Christ's significance. It is the fig, often considered to be the equivalent of the apple of Paradise.[19] In the context of the Holy Kinship, the fig would represent Christ's redemptive mission as the New Adam, whose sinless earthly life redeems mankind from original sin and restores him to the possibility of grace.[20]

In short, all the symbolic objects amplify a single theme, the earthly mission of Christ and the miracle of His Incarnation. This is, after all, the significance and destiny of the Immaculate Conception, the reason why both Saint Anne and the Virgin were singled out from ordinary women. By using these referential still-life items, Massys has underscored in a symbolic fashion what he also accomplished visually through his composition: he has placed Christ at the center of the image and has shown the way in which Mary and Anne support the Child and contribute to the divine plan. The same could be said of the two cadet branches of the *Holy Kinship*. Mary Cleophas, Mary Salome, and their children pay homage to Christ by their subsidiary positions, by their holding the symbolic attributes (the same attributes, reversed, that they had held in the Master of Frankfurt image), and, in life, by the support given to Christ's mission by the children in their vocations as apostles and missionaries.

One should note, as the discussion of the finch (note 18) makes clear, that the plant and animal possessions of the holy figures are not absolutely definable in any fixed, dictionary fashion. They are, rather, metaphoric attributes, conveying qualities of virtues of the holy figures, and they receive their symbolic effectiveness through their juxtaposition with the holy figures. Inserted into this religious context or even visually juxtaposed with it, like the distant cliff and castle, each item can be understood as partaking of the spiritual values of the principals. The relationship here is one of reflection, where the particular element of the microcosm encapsulates the aspects of the larger cosmic order, or macrocosm, by virtue of their mutual affinities, or "similitudes," which Panofsky, quoting Aquinas, has described as "corporeal metaphors of things spiritual" *(spiritualis sub metaphoris corporalium)*.[21]

A final set of objects provides still another clue to the devotional orientation of the *Holy Kinship* panel. In the lower left corner, beside the youngest child of Mary Cleophas, Joseph the Just (who failed to become an apostle because the lot decided for Barnabas), Massys has placed two woodcut prints that evoke prayers to Christ.[22] The first print shows the Lamb of God with the words "simple, innocent, humble and merciful." The second presents the holy name of Christ and the text "Blessed be the name Jesus and Mary his beloved Mother forever." Devotion to the holy name was promoted first in Italy by the great Franciscan preacher Saint Bernardino of Siena (1380–1444), but it also enjoyed great popularity in the Netherlands and formed the subject of a number of inexpensive devotional prints like the one in the Holy Kinship panel.[23] A third devotional aid in the hands of the precocious child is a book of hours, executed in the contemporary style of manuscript illumination found at Bruges, including the distinctive floral borders of gold. The prayerbook is open to an image of David in prayer, the common pictorial introduction to the Penitential Psalms, so it, too, addresses prayer to God as do the woodcut prints. The fact that the child is unlettered causes the prayerbook, like the prints, to be faced toward the viewer and to invite prayerful address to these painted images, just as the pious would use real examples of such devotional aids in their daily prayer. Once again, the implication is that the young children are already future apostles in their devotion (ironically, the youngest, who has the largest number of aids, is the only child who did not become an apostle later) and that the viewer should follow their example and pay homage to the Christ Child, "simple, innocent, humble, and merciful."

Pl. 5

Taken together, the Massys *Holy Kinship* is actually an assemblage of formal means organized to promote devotion to Saint Anne and to her divine progeny. The conservatism of the basic image of saints in a sacred garden is reinforced by the traditional symbolic attributes referring to Christ and by the literal replications of contemporary aids to devotion in the corner of the painting. These features define the panel as a votive image, organized according to a hierarchy of spirituality that descends from Christ to the youngest child, who has the most contemporary and earthbound objects in his hands. The fullness of the family genealogy combines with this hierarchic organization to provide a sense of completeness and calm, the ordering of the divine plan set in motion by Saint Anne.

Grafted onto this formula is the sense of wonder generated by Massys' additions to the predictable Netherlandish elements, as presented by the Master of Frankfurt. The Italianate architecture, on the one hand, isolates the figures from any suggestion of worldliness or ordinary activity. The extraordinary imported forms of the building serve to create a special zone of sacrality, much as the use of the church architecture in Geertgen's *Holy Kinship* is meant to set those figures apart. Yet Massys' portico also permits him to present the rich, hazy landscape background vista, and this, too, magnifies the significance and isolation of the holy figures. On the one hand, it shows them elevated over the mountains and valleys in a position of dominance like the commanding site of a palace. And visual placement of just such a palace beside the Virgin and Saint Anne in the center of the composition strengthens the association between the Virgin and the celestial castle mentioned in mystical and apochryphal writings. Thus, the mountains and palace add to the symbolic dimension of the objects in the hands of the holy figures, even as they contribute to an air of mystery and cosmic scope in the picture as a whole.

The importance of Saint Anne in the doctrine of the Immaculate Conception is that the mother of the Virgin provided the miraculous exemption from Original Sin that is the perfection and essence of Mary's spirituality Because of the legend that Anne's conception was itself miraculous, the Virgin was untouched by the corruption of flesh and was a fitting vessel for the birth of Christ. The source for this idea is an apocryphal book, the *Protoevangelium of Saint James,* or *Gospel of the Infancy of Christ.*[24] It tells the story of how Joachim and Anne were not blessed by children and grew to old age without a family, in spite of living a righteous life in which they saved a third of their goods for charity and a third of their goods as an offering in the temple. But because of their barrenness, the couple was thought to be under divine wrath, and their offering for the temple was rejected by the high priest. Joachim retreated into the mountains, where he meditated and fasted in humiliation. There, an angel announced to him that his wife had conceived a daughter, who was to be called Mary. This angelic message reveals that the mother of Mary was herself singled out by divine will to ensure the sanctification and purity of the Virgin Mother. The righteous holiness of Saint Anne, then, is the basis of the Immaculate Conception of the Virgin and the wellspring of Anne's increased popularity during the 15th century, when Pope Sixtus IV approved an office for the feast of the Immaculate Conception in 1474.[25]

The fascination during the entire century with Saint Anne and the extended family of Mary points to a pervasive mental habit of late medieval piety: the multiplication of religious details. Within the context of the gospel narratives, we find in this period a striking emphasis on the fullest description of characters, minor events, and the setting. This can be seen in such 14th-century texts as Ludolph of Saxony's *Vita Christi,* the *Revelations* of Bridget of Sweden, or the *Meditations on the Life of Christ* by an anonymous Franciscan. In painting, an example of the same narrative emphasis is the so-called "populous Crucifixion," where accessory characters, such as soldiers, Jews, and onlookers, are added to the mass of figures described in the gospel text and the kinds of texts just mentioned; frequently, other scenes from the Passion are also incorporated into the background of the crowded single panel.[26]

With a proliferation of images celebrating the Holy Kinship, the glorification of Saint Anne has moved from the realm of doctrine, based upon the holiness of the Virgin and of Christ, to a more secular realm of interest in family details that in modern times finds frequent expression in gossip columns and movie magazines. If the extended family of the Virgin is a religious "royal family," then Saint Anne is the queen mother, and all the relatives are the nobility. The activities of the English royal family are followed today with similar zeal by the popular press. Somehow, the production of saintly offspring—not just the perfection of the Virgin and Christ, but also the righteousness of the other grandchildren who were active apostles of Jesus—is the testimony of Anne's own holiness and the appropriate central image for the Louvain confraternity dedicated to her praise.

Massys' symbolic image, therefore, incorporates a hierarchy of holiness whose apex is the figure of Christ and whose first rank of virtue is represented in the center of the image by the Virgin and Saint Anne. Around this nucleus, the periphery of the Holy Kinship is distributed like the ripples from a splash, and the viewer is given the suggestion that the divinity of Christ emanates through the world by stages. Christ's cousins were his disciples and future apostles. Their kinship assures their virtue. For the viewer, too, by extension, the brotherhood of the confraternity is an alliance for mutual support and religious reinforcement. The sponsorship of Saint Anne is particularly appropriate, for her role as the wellspring of the Immaculate Conception gave her particular status as the queen mother of the Church, and her supervision over the Holy Kinship suggests an attentive supervision over the community of faithful in the confraternity dedicated to her honor.

Within the all-embracing protection and dominion of Saint Anne, the Virgin, and Christ, the imagery of Massys includes the natural and architectural scenery. By virtue of the viewer's identification of the figures in the picture as Christian saints enthroned in glory, the surroundings of the figures can be seen to be the province of their sanctity—in short, their domain. This is made explicit in the case of the landscape by the visual juxtaposition of the distinctive mountain with its castle to the central group, but it is all the more clear upon reflection that the distant mountain range, an unfamiliar fantasy creation for a Netherlander, is open to access from the wide spaciousness of the architecture. That building, in turn, has the artificial whimsy and association with saints that results from its importation from Italy, but it also includes symbolic indicators, the warlike naked sculptures, which bracket the central area of both the landscape and the holy figures in order to establish the artifice and sanctity of the building precinct. In short, both the landscape and the architecture are the outgrowth of the presence of the holy figures; they are locations but also attributes that identify the sanctity and prestige of the figures. By their splendor and their extent, they magnify the glory of the Holy Kinship.

The immobility of the figures, their arrangement into ranks and rows, as well as these scenic enhancements contribute to the successful realization of this picture as a cult image. Again, the emphasis of prayer before the image is reinforced by the inclusion of other visual forms of devotional aids at the lowest level of the picture, closest to the viewer. These are the items held by the youngest child: the two symbols of Christ, woodcuts of the Agnus Dei and the Holy Name, and the prayerbook open to the first Penitential Psalm and the traditional concomitant image of King David in Prayer before the Lord. In the same way, the member of the confraternity of Saint Anne is encouraged by all of Massys' pictorial symbols to glorify the patron saint of the brotherhood, even as he keeps the central image of Christ at the heart of his meditation.

The triptych as a whole revolves around the history of Saint Anne and her husband Joachim. Yet it is curious that the central event of their lives within the unfolding religious history is not depicted: the Annunciation to Saint Anne of the Immaculate Conception, which would ordinarily occupy the position between the Annunciation to Joachim (on the left wing) and the Death of Saint Anne (on the right wing), is omitted. In its place, the cult image of the Holy Kinship is substituted. Again, a popular image featuring both Joachim and Anne after their divine revelations is the dramatic scene of their subsequent Meeting at the Golden Gate, which appears only in the distance of the Joachim wing of the triptych. Instead, Massys has chosen to emphasize the theological position of the patron of the confraternity, to underscore her role in God's mission rather than the narrative events of her life in and of themselves. *Pl. 7*

Massys' freedom with conventional arrangement extends to the exterior of the altarpiece, where he begins the story of the two parents of the Virgin. In place of the common 15th-century convention of showing cult images on the exterior of triptychs in the form of imitation sculpture *en grisaille,* Massys arranges complementary narratives that situate the couple's dilemma before the miraculous revelations and the Immaculate Conception. The two scenes are constructed around their crucial offerings in the temple. An early offering is gratefully accepted by the high priest, inasmuch as it comes from one of the most righteous of couples; the charity of Joachim and Anna is displayed in miniature in the background of the scene, where they are shown distributing alms to the needy and crippled. This charity tallies with the description of the Virgin's parents given in the popular handbook of saints, Jacobus da Voragine's *Golden Legend,* which states that the couple gave away two-thirds of their goods to charity and the temple, and kept only one-third for themselves. Indeed, their offering to the temple is presented in a small treasure chest. But since their lack of divine favor was marked by their childlessness, the second depicted offering of Joachim, made years later, was rejected by the high priest. The passage of time since the first donation on the other wing is marked by the whitened beard of the priest and by the addition of a beard for Joachim. The humility of the saint contrasts with the unsympathetic faces surrounding him, which are marked by ugliness and distortion. One face is foreign, dark and swarthy; a second is old, gaunt, and drawn. At the far right is a fat and prosperous man, dressed in fur-trimmed robes and wearing a prominent coin purse on his belt; this man's selfish vanity and display of wealth contrast with the simple dress and generosity of Joachim. The visual language of grotesques used here shows Massys' personal interest in ugly types as the embodiment of moral turpitude (see especially Chap. 7). This particular use seems to have been stimulated by the faces along the background of Dürer's *Martyrdom of St. John* from the 1498 woodcut illustrations of the *Apocalypse.* Massys was later to use this Dürer source for several figures in the wings of his Antwerp *St. John altarpiece* of 1508–11. In particular, the fat man among the onlookers of the Dürer crowd bears a generic resemblance to the plutocrat at the right of Massys' shutter. Other specific parallels are not particularly close in visual terms, but the very idea of contrasting a handsome, unblemished face of a saint with negroid, wrinkled, or unattractive detractors seems to have come to Massys from Dürer. In addition, Dürer's use of a balustrade to separate the less-important figures from the main action is a device that Massys incorporated into the cult image for the center of the triptych in order to surbordinate the lesser figures, the male saints, to the center of attention, the *Anna Selbdritt.* *Pl. 8* *Pl. 9* *Pl. 14*

The exterior of the altarpiece, then, highlights the narrative history of the parents of the Virgin, and its religious focus is on the externalized actions of religion: acts of charity and offerings in the temple. These are public actions, outward signs of piety and acceptance or rejection. Massys even adds a distinctive personal note to the depictions. In the earlier scene on the left, he includes a deed in the hand of Joachim, which possibly reproduces a donation of the artist himself to his children, here presented as one of the charitable gifts of the saint.[27] Massys has also included a local reference to the scene of the first offering by situating the temple in his adopted city of Antwerp, whose nearly finished cathedral spire has been imaginatively completed by the artist and placed in the background of the scene.[28] Whether Massys meant thereby to identify the new Antwerp cathedral as a modern version of the historic temple cannot be answered. But his inclusion in the background of a Louvain picture of a civic monument that would have been as recognizable to his contemporaries as today's Eiffel Tower to Parisians indicated that the location of the scene in Antwerp had particular, personal meaning for Massys. The localization of the scene within his new home town at least indicates that Massys felt such charitable actions as those of the saintly couple to be possible in his own time and place.[29] The presence of his name on the deed in Joachim's hand also attests to that possibility and to the artist's personal profession of piety in the picture. Again in the later scene on the right, Massys includes himself, a literal, self-portrait between the heads of Joachim and the high priest. Not only is his face far more attractive than the other onlookers to the scene, but it is placed in an area separated from them, seemingly at a higher level, at the height of the raised altar. Bare-headed like the saint and confronting the viewer, the artist seems to express his own compassion for the plight of Joachim by his presence at the scene and to elicit the sympathy of the Louvain brothers by his gaze, even though he appears in the company of an ugly assemblage of mankind. With these personal testimonies within the images and with the actions that form the subjects of the panels, Massys presents a religion of participation and externalized profession of belief. We shall see later how much the corporate religiosity of confraternities contributed to this outlook toward religion and how the general shape of religion in Massys' time promoted visible manifestations of personal piety.

The two scenes on the interior shutters of the St. Anne triptych serve to complete the narrative that was begun on the exterior. The action continues to be read book-fashion, from left to right, beginning
Pl. 10 with the Annunciation to Joachim in the wilderness by an angelic messenger of God. Behind this scene
Pl. 7 in the distance is the encounter of Joachim and Anna after their revelations, the Meeting at the Golden Gate, a tiny action in front of the massive city wall within Massys' panel. Once again, as in the case of the charity of Joachim and Anna from the exterior of the triptych, Massys feels free to include the same figures twice in one panel, using the spatial isolation and small scale of the subsidiary scene to indicate that it takes place in a different location and time. The final scene of the narrative is the
Pl. 6 moving Death of St. Anne on the right wing, painted almost entirely in rose tones. Here the viewer is deliberately placed at the foot of the saint's bed, as if in a kneeling position, and is encouraged to peer over the shoulder of the female saint in the foreground toward the prostrate form of St. Anne. The tearful actions of the others in the same position and the open space beside them at the foot of the bed leave no doubt about the empathic emotional role prepared for the viewer. The viewer is not so clearly placed in the Joachim scene, but the panel is divided into the earthly realm of the saint and viewer and an open, airy, celestial realm of the angel, which the viewer, like the saint, must look up to see. Taken together, the two scenes advance and complete the narrative of St. Anne and her husband, counterposing an example of direct visionary contact with the divine with a fixed, emotional address by the frailer, more fleshly aspects of the holy figures. In each case, the intensity of the experience is based upon intimacy, direct contact with either divine revelation or mortal humanity.

Massys in his altarpiece was faced with visual tasks quite unlike the more usual images of the Madonna enthroned. Here again, as in the use of foreign models for his setting of the central cult image, the artist turned to outside models for his organization of the scenes. For the *Annunciation to Joachim*, he borrowed from the great Louvain artist of the previous generation, Dieric Bouts, whose
Pl. 11 *Moses at the Burning Bush* (Philadelphia Museum of Art, Johnson Coll.) offered one of the few examples of an art of revelation within the Flemish tradition. On the one hand, by his repetition of a Boutsian formula, Massys paid homage to the most famous predecessor of painting in his original home town. At the same time, he had recourse to an image that showed not only the appearance of God to man, but one that situated the entire event within an isolated outdoor setting. From the Bouts

image Massys has borrowed the gesture of surprise, expressed by the two raised hands of the hermit, and the posture of genuflection before a small pile of rocks above which the apparition appears. Both Bouts and Massys show the bearded religious figure on two occasions within the same panel, although in Massys' case, the second image is only dimly perceptible in the distance. Numerous differences have arisen because of adaptation of the scene to a narrow, vertical format; but both artists show the same formula of man's reaction to the divine, a formula made even more compatible for Massys by the similarity of setting, a hilly retreat populated by sheep. The derivation from Bouts was accomplished without any adjustment of the orientation of the scene; Massys is content to leave Joachim facing leftward, even though the resulting flow of movement carries outward from the central panel rather than focusing on the center.

Derivation is also essential to the image of Massys' right wing, where the *Death of St. Anne* is based upon the *Death of the Virgin* by Hugo van der Goes. The Master of Frankfurt had already used this model for his own scene of the Death of the Virgin. Owing to the lack of models for the Death of St. Anne and the popularity of the Hugo image, it is not surprising to find Massys turning to this famous precedent for inspiration. Again, he has retained the orientation of the scene toward the left, and he has captured such elements as the pallor of the deceased and the low point of view much more successfully than the adaptation by the Master of Frankfurt. The Hugo scene would have served as a powerful stimulus to the suggestion of religious grief that is so basic to the Massys image. *Pl. 12*

The interior panels of the *Holy Kinship altarpiece* are not literal copies from their recent Flemish models. Instead, they are adaptations, based upon a formula suited to the religious subject of the picture. Massys felt free to include additional elements in the picture, such as the walls of the city of Jerusalem, when they served to specify the location of the depicted events. In the case of the Joachim panel, the presence of the walls was necessary because of the narrative completeness of the entire altarpiece; the walls provided a setting for the diminutive scene of the Meeting at the Golden Gate. In the other instance, Massys retained the outlines of a deathbed scene and successfully communicated the emotional intensity of the event; but by substituting a youthful Virgin with a candle along with the other familiar faces of the kinship from the central panel, he transformed the model into a scene from the life of St. Anne. *The Death of St. Anne* not only continues the cast of characters from the cult image into the narrative flow, but also tailors the scene to the specific needs of the confraternity. In each of these cases, we see the artist working from previous artistic models to create new visual solutions to particular tasks.

In short, it is no assertion of personal inventiveness or stylishness nor striving to be original that determines the forms of Massys' altarpiece panels. Instead, these individual works are tailored to the purpose they served in the religious life of the confraternity. They do not even have an unbroken internal flow. The central cult image disturbs any literal continuity from one scene to the next as part of an unfolding narrative. The interior deathbed scene prevents any suggestion of a continuous outdoor space from the left wing to the right wing. The intrusion of the artist's face and the Antwerp cathedral (significantly placed on the less-prominent, theologically inferior exterior) challenge the separation between the historical and holy world of the religious figures and the modern world of the confraternity.

Habitual organization, like the reading from left to right, shapes the horizontal development and the narrative development of the altarpiece; moreover, the exterior has the most personal references, and its scenes have the least borrowing from previous imagery. The interior subjects closely resemble the picture-making of recent Flemish religious art, both in the narrative scenes, borrowed from artists—Bouts and van der Goes—of the previous generation, and in the cult image, a basic concept, close to Memling but with Italianate overlay and presented only a few years previously by Massys' colleague, the Master of Frankfurt. The choice of the triptych format is itself probably the most traditional aspect, for this is the conventional organization and large-scale presentation favored for 15th-century altarpiece production. In short, any constraints are the result of chosen convention, and the choice lay in the forms that the confraternity felt would provide a proper religious work of art.

The brothers of Louvain wished to honor their patron, St. Anne, with a large-scale altarpiece that would sketch the events of her life and present her religious significance in a cult image that included her essential relationship to Christ and the family of His disciples.

The St. Anne altarpiece formed the religious focus of the confraternity and causes us to inquire what kind of organization would shape its spiritual life around such an image. Such confraternities were a basic form of religious life in 15th-century Europe.[30] During a period when few cathedrals were being built, the confraternities and their chapels were a principal focus of lay attention and collective religious feeling and action. Religious brotherhoods acted together for mutual aid, and they produced a number of ritual activities in concert: masses, feasts, processions, and funerals, often dedicated to the glory of the saintly patron or a particular devotional focus. Some of the confraternities even maintained hospitals, and most of them were involved in various aspects of community service. In short, these groups functioned as a combination of religious affinity groups and service clubs. Massys' Antwerp also offered examples of the same kind of organization. There, brotherhoods were dedicated to the Holy Cross, the Holy Circumcision, the Praise of Our Lady, and the Holy Sacrament. Toussaert, in particular, has stressed the degree to which religion had become in Flanders a collective activity; and although his assessment of this development is that true personal piety had vanished, his careful inspection of the documents demonstrates the importance of group religion, partly through confraternities.[31] More recently, Ozment has taken this instinct for joining as evidence of profound religious insecurity and the need for reassurance through a group, a kind of safety-in-numbers in a period of intense spiritual anxiety.[32]

Whatever their emotional motivation, confraternities provided a collective sense of spiritual community and worth, and the same period that saw them flourish also saw the rise of attention to the cult of the Virgin Mary, particularly as protector of mankind, as intercessor with Christ, and as bestower of grace.[33] A particularly vivid image of this conception of the Madonna Misericordiae is the vision of the Virgin standing with a troupe of the faithful nestled within the outstretched borders of her mantle. It was a religion of maternal consolation and protection. The text of the mass expressed this same sentiment: "Saint Mary, succour the miserable, strengthen the weak, console the grieving, pray for the people, intervene for the clergy, intercede for women." The emphasis on maternal tenderness found expression in a marked interest in the birth and childhood of Christ and a particular emphasis on the developing cult of the purity of the Virgin, which focused on the Immaculate Conception; i.e., the miraculous birth accorded to the barren St. Anne.[34]

Massys' altarpiece for the confraternity of St. Anne incorporates both aspects of the Virgin: her maternal tenderness and her theological purity. The familial compassion of St. Anne and of the Madonna herself can be seen in the center of the picture as the focus of attention. Moreover, the theological suggestion of extended protection is implied by the Holy Kinship itself, where the generations of St. Anne's family become the entourage of Christ; the patron of the confraternity is the matriarch of the Holy Kinship. By extension, the confraternity is an adopted family of charitable Christians. The other importance of St. Anne lies in her relation to the doctrine of Immaculate Conception. The mother of the Virgin thereby provided the miraculous exemption from Original Sin that is the perfection and essence of Mary's sprituality.

Herein lies the significance of the Annunciation to Joachim, as portrayed by Massys on the left wing of the alterpiece. Voragine's text records the angelic message as paying special consideration to the good works of the holy couple: "Thine almsworks have ascended in the sight of the Lord." This again was good news to the brothers of the confraternity, whose corporate charity was one of the hallmarks of their piety; Massys also included the charitable alms of Joachim and Anna in the exterior scene of their further charity in the temple. Thus, the altarpiece stresses not only the events of the life of St. Anne, but also the basis of her theological significance; moreover, it establishes ethical parallels between her piety and that of her confraternity. Their religious image was the very picture of the pious values of the brothers of St. Anne.

The cult of St. Anne was not confined to the Louvain brotherhood. Antwerp had its own brotherhood, founded in 1498, which included the Emperor Maximilian among its members.[35] Flanders also had a special pilgrimage site—Bottelaera, near Ghent—which was dedicated to the veneration of St. Anne. The brotherhood in Louvain was thus part of a flourishing cult, also especially strong in the Rhineland during the late 15th century.[36] Their corporate commission of a St. Anne triptych was not only a focus for their local religious life in the Louvain chapel, but an expressive instance, like the Frankfurt *Holy Kinship altarpiece* of the Master of Frankfurt, of the widespread spiritual importance of the Virgin's mother.

The rich adornment of an altarpiece was the prerogative of a purely religious group, but it was also an outgrowth of other social organizations whose religious inclinations were not the raison d'être but only part of a larger group identity. These retables were frequently commissioned by professional groups as well, brotherhoods organized around a common trade. One such group, the Antwerp guild of the altarpiece joiners, or shrineworkers, commissioned Massys' second great altarpiece, the *St. John altarpiece,* whose centerpiece featured the Lamentation over Christ's body. Originally, the shrine- *Pl. 20* workers' guild had been joined with the coopers of Antwerp since 1428, although the cooperative guild had no alter shrine until 1456.[37] In 1497, the two professions split up, necessitating a new and separate altarpiece for the shrineworkers' altar. They commissioned Massys to paint this altarpiece triptych in 1508, and they specified that it should have the same subject in the central panel that the joint guild had once enjoyed: the Deposition.[38] For the subjects of the wings and the exterior of the altarpiece, however, the shrineworkers paid homage to their own patron saints, the two saints John, the Baptist and the Evangelist; this choice was a deliberate contrast to St. Matthew, who was the patron saint of the coopers after the separation of 1497.

Because of the importance of their own distinctive patron saints, Massys' 1508-11 altarpiece for the shrineworkers places as much emphasis on the two saints John as the triptych for the confraternity of St. Anne had stressed the Virgin's mother. Whereas the Louvain triptych presented a generally traditional appearance derived from the dependence on recent Flemish compositions, the Antwerp altarpiece, in contrast, presents a much more unusual, exotic, and innovative imagery, based in part on the works of Dürer and Leonardo da Vinci, in part on the contemporary styles of local Antwerp retables of sculpture and painting. An observer who did not know that the Louvain and Antwerp triptychs were both by the same artist might fail to recognize the common authorship of Massys in such divergent creations. Here we see how Massys' visual solutions to the symbolic requirements of his patrons resulted in a distinctive combination of thematic parts and expressive treatments.

The immediate impression of Massys' Antwerp altarpiece wings is one of crowding, especially after the spacious open areas of the St. Anne interior. This impression is heightened by the rich variety of colorful costumes, which include a number of overtly foreign elements, such as turbans, or costly materials, such as the ermine cape of Herod, and dazzling patterns of jewelry and brocade. The crowding is magnified by the twisting poses of the figures, who seem to be crammed into tight corners of the narrow vertical wing panels. Out of the welter of heads emerges an emphatic contrast between the beautiful, fair faces of the holy figures and an exaggerated, swarthy ugliness of their tormentors. This note had already been struck on the *Expulsion of Joachim* from the exterior of Massys' *St. Anne altarpiece,* but it marks a considerable departure from the undisturbed beauty and tranquility of the Holy Kinship and the St. Anne wings. In fact, one of the most distinctive qualities of the *St. John* wings is their energetic movement, all the more effective for seeming to be bottled up in the crowded, vertical space.

As previous scholars have noted, several of the exotic elements of these two scenes were borrowed by Massys from other works of art.[39] In particular, the tiny page at the front of the table in the scene of Salome and Herod is borrowed from a black man pouring oil over the body of John the Evangelist in *Pl. 13* Dürer's *Martyrdom of St. John* from the *Apocalypse* woodcut series of 1498. The subject of the St. John *Pl. 14* martyrdom was probably Massys' original reason for consulting the Dürer print, just as he had consulted the Flemish models for his equivalent scenes of Joachim and Anne. We have also seen that he removed some of the spectators from Dürer's scene for the onlookers of the *Expulsion of Joachim,* just as he shifted the black attendant from the martyrdom of one St. John to the martyrdom of the other. In similar fashion, the figure of Herod from the martyrdom of the Baptist has been adapted, complete with his ermine collar, high-crowned turban, and badge of office, from the figure of Emperor Domitian in Dürer's print; Massys has even retained the background brocade and the orientation of the seated ruler. Facing forward, the same figure appears on horseback in Massys' own *Martyrdom of the Evangelist;* in this second instance, the chain and turban crown are copied literally from Dürer rather than being adapted. The row of heads behind the Evangelist has also been transposed by Massys from Dürer's composition, although without the balustrade and clear separation in the woodcut. Obviously, the grotesque and foreign appearances of the Evangelist's tormentors in Dürer's image made an impression on Massys, for he has retained the overall appearance of the crowd of heads in his altarpiece wing. Moreover, Massys has adopted the basic setting of the print for his own background of the Porta Latina and tree, but this is hardly surprising because of the shared theme of the two images.

Pl. 15

For some of the heads of the tormentors, Massys turned to another source: a drawing by Leonardo da Vinci. No documentation survives to establish how Massys could have known it, but his visual borrowing makes certain that the Antwerp artist had access to Leonardo's famous drawing (ca. 1495, now in Windsor Castle) of *Five Grotesque Heads.*[40] That Massys borrowed from Leonardo is important in itself (although not enough evidence to suggest that the artist traveled to Italy); but it is especially interesting because it points out, like the other deriviations of the Louvain and Antwerp altarpieces, that the responsive artist was seeking in such sources some specific quality for his images, a quality tied to his artistic purpose. In the case of the Leonardo grotesques, Massys has inserted the ugly faces into a larger narrative context of a saint's martyrdom, instead of preserving the isolated context of Leonardo's original sheet with just the five heads. For Massys, the faces reflect the ungodly spirits of the tormentors of St. John, just as the ugliness of the bystanders in the *Expulsion of Joachim* had suggested their spiritual inferiority to the father of Mary. What had been a suggestion in the Louvain altarpiece exterior has become a strong assertion in the Antwerp interior. Greater prominence of the grotesques in sheer numbers and in active movement is linked with the greater syntactical significance of placing them more visibly beside the central image of the altarpiece. Massys establishes a symbolic link between the beauty or ugliness of a figure's appearance and the holiness or godlessness inherent in that figure's essence. The unsullied beauty of the entire *Holy Kinship* interior, broken only on the exterior of the Louvain altarpiece, has been powerfully violated in the Antwerp altarpiece, disturbed by the intrusion of the world's moral ugliness in grisly scenes of martyrdom.

Pl. 16

Pl. 17

Just as the ugliness derived from Leonardo (and Dürer) is a meaningful feature of the images, the significance of the larger phenomena—of crowding, of activity, and of colorful richness—commands inspection. This visual expression is the feature of a host of local Antwerp altarpieces, both painted and sculpted, during the first two decades of the 16th century, altarpieces that have been grouped together under the descriptive label "Antwerp Mannerism" or "Netherlandish painters of the Late Gothic style."[41] No firm chronology serves to anchor this group of altarpieces to the 1508–11 dated Antwerp altarpiece of Massys; indeed, most of the surviving altarpieces with these features are by completely anonymous painters and are undistinguished in their execution. Several facts, however, serve to link this visual idiom with the joiner's guild, which commissioned the altarpiece wings from Massys.

Roosval has already demonstrated physical links between the Antwerp Mannerist painters and contemporary Antwerp sculptors.[42] Many of the paintings called "Antwerp Mannerist" were created as wing panels for sculpted centers of altarpiece retables, many of which were part of the lively export trade between the port of Antwerp and outlying cities. Moreover, most of the features described here for the paintings are equally applicable to the small, detachable, wooden sculpted figures that compose the ensembles of the sculpted scenes of the altarpiece.[43] Flowing costume drapery, crowded and active movements, exotic costume (particularly headgear), and frequent colorful painting and gilding characterize the carved figures no less than the painted. Antwerp was not the only center of this kind of retable carving and export; Brussels was perhaps even more active, just as Leyden seems to have vied with Antwerp for the production of these "late Gothic" painted panels.[44] But Antwerp was the site where Massys lived, and Antwerp was the center where the joiners (or shrineworkers, as they were also called) produced the casements, frames, and ornamented housings of the small sculpted figures, as well as the panels for painters. This connection between Massys' visual forms and the forms of carved wooden images is also an adaptation to the circumstances of the commission of the *Saint John altarpiece*. Originally, the joiners' guild had placed an order for a carved retable with two Louvain sculptors, Peterceels and van Kessel; in 1503, they transferred the commission to an Antwerp sculptor, but after a delay of five years it came at last to Massys in September 1508.[45]

While the shrineworkers proudly maintained their distinction and privileges over the sculptors in wood (who, like Massys, were members of the painters' guild of St. Luke), it is clear that both the joiners and their painter were intimately familiar with the expressive carved figures in contemporary Antwerp retables. Thus, it was a natural request for the shrineworkers to encourage Massys to paint martyrdom scenes that evoke comparisons with contemporary sculpted scenes and with the associated "Antwerp Mannerist" painting vocabulary. It is even possible that Massys' own early version of a painted equivalent to sculpture for the shrineworkers in 1508–11 was instrumental in the actual creation and popularization of "Antwerp Mannerism" in the busy port city, even though Quinten did not continue his experiment for the joiners in his later output.

One other important aspect of the choice of "Antwerp Mannerist" pictorial features is the pictorial association of the richness, foreignness, and activity with the agents of evil and ugliness. This association should not surprise us, in light of the traditional Christian ideal of poverty and humility and consequent rejection of worldly ambitions; corruption is particularly pointed in the martyrdom scenes, on one wing with the opulent surroundings (brocades, imperial insignia, wine, page, musicians) of Herod, on the other with the exotic costumes and dense swarm of agents of Domitian. Against this background, Antwerp's prominence in the arena of international trade surely plays a role. In fact, the most popular of all the scenes in Antwerp Mannerist pictures is the Adoration of the Magi, a deliberate emphasis on opulence and wealth in subordination to true, spiritual worth in the humble form of a newborn infant (see Chap. 5). Like the spiritual crossroads in Bethlehem, Antwerp was the financial and commodity crossroads of all Europe in this period, a fact attested to by the motto over the doorway of the magnificent new Bourse, constructed for international exchange in 1531: "For the service of merchants of all nations and languages."[46] Moreover, the emphasis on foreign visitors in Massys' grotesques and the three magi (who were taken to represent the three major continents—Europe, Asia, and Africa) offers analogies to the variety of foreign national trading companies doing business in Antwerp: Portuguese, Spanish, Italian, English, French, South German, Baltic and Hanse German traders. The entire Antwerp commercial operation was carried on under the explicit protection and sponsorship of the Emperor Maximilian, who (as described in Chap. 1) in June 1488 had established Antwerp over Bruges as a free-trade port. It was entirely natural to associate the Holy Roman Empire with the emperors who ordered the martrydoms of Christian saints, but it was equally easy for a resident of Antwerp to associate the current emperor, Maximilian, with foreign traders and the general commercial prosperity that had grown up in the city on the Scheldt. Massys developed his critical outlook toward riches, already suggested in the *Expulsion of Joachim*, in his *Adoration of the Magi* (1526, New York, Metropolitan Museum; F. 8, cat. 40; see Chap. 5); he also developed it in a series of *Pl. 79* secular paintings, beginning with the *Moneychanger and his Wife* (1514, Paris) and continuing through *Pl. 118* the grotesque pair of *Old Man and Old Woman* of around 1520 (see Chap. 7).[47] But it was an antagonism *Pl. 122* expressed first in the presentation of Joachim's charity and unwarranted expulsion and then even *Pl. 123* more forcefully in the decadence surrounding the heathens of the martyrdom scenes of the Antwerp altarpiece.

The reverse of the Antwerp altarpiece is a conventional exterior, presenting imitation sculptures of *Pl. 18* the patron saints of the trade guild in tones of brown and gold, a variation on the grey tones of *Pl. 19* *grisaille*.[48] For the most part, altarpieces remained closed except for Sundays and feast days, and during the 15th century, cult images of saints or anticipatory events like the Annunciation had appeared in reduced color tones to show their reduced significance. Their status as imitation sculpture rather than as living flesh further points to their reduced status within the ensemble of the altarpiece.[49] This reduced significance of the outer wings had previously enabled Massys to include his own portrait and the recognizable landmark of the Antwerp cathedral tower within the context of an otherwise religious narrative on the *St. Anne altarpiece;* nevertheless, the Louvain exterior, with events taken from religious history, is much more tightly connected to the interior of the *St. Anne altarpiece* and much more a product of theological concerns for completeness than are the effigies on the outside of the Antwerp joiners' altarpiece. There, the two saints John, who appear on both the interior and the exterior of the wings, serve as the cult focus of the guild and serve to identify the corporation just as fully as the use of an Antwerp Mannerist style on the interior. A corporate desire for identity and recognition also helps to explain the unusual coincidence of a traditional *brunaille* exterior in conjunction with a crowded, lively, visually striking interior painted in the most novel, fashionable, local style. The shrineworkers ordered a retable with all the traditional components, but they also wanted to stress their patron saints and to present their corporate image in the most vivid and noticeable way—both in the dazzling style, already associated with them as shrineworkers, and in the choice of grisly martyrdom scenes so well suited to the presentation in the idiom of Antwerp Mannerism. Clearly, the needs and requests of the Antwerp shrineworkers were vastly different from those of the Louvain St. Anne confraternity.

The center panel of the Antwerp altarpiece is linked as the martyrdom of Christ to the martyrdom *Pl. 20* scenes of the two saints John on the wings in an analogy of suffering. Massys, however, has presented not the Calvary or the events of suffering during the Passion, but instead the Deposition of the body of Christ after the Crucifixion and the Lamentation over the body by the holy mourners. This image is certainly in keeping with the function of the image as the centerpiece of a retable on an altar, for in stressing the body of Christ, the picture conforms to the liturgical emphasis on the reenactment of Christ's sacrifice in the eucharist. Moreover, in the prominent central position of the altarpiece, the Deposition serves as a vehicle for religious contemplation, a natural outgrowth of devotional worship directed at the altar as focus of attention in the mass. Visually, Massys has emphasized this votive function of his image by placing the body of Christ in the most significant possible position, central in the picture and extended across the front of the scene. This is the position closest to the viewers in the chapel and to the altar below the retable. Christ's body links all the figures of the central image together to serve as a visual focus; Christ, in turn, is tightly framed by them and turned in such a manner that his body is visible to the viewer, as if from above, along its entire length. The body of Christ offers the most suitable image for an altarpiece and cult image.

Moreover, the presence of St. John the Evangelist, offering tender support to the Virgin Mary just above the outstretched arm of Christ, offers additional justification for this *Lamentation* as the central image of the shrineworkers' altarpiece. By putting one of the two patron saints at the pivotal center of all the figures in the image, Massys has reemphasized the saint's historic significance in the Gospels.

The form of Massys' image also reveals purposeful choice in the selection of the scene, for the *Lamentation* itself is an amalgam of several traditional and justly famous Flemish altarpieces, particularly the works of Roger van der Weyden. The principal source was one of the most famous of all 15th-*Pl. 21* century altarpieces, the *Deposition* of van der Weyden (Madrid, Prado), made for the Church of St. Peter's Outside the Walls in Louvain, again the commission of a corporation, the crossbowmen's guild.[50] A copy of the altarpiece had already been made as early as 1443; that copy, the *Edelheer altarpiece,* was in place in Louvain at the time that Massys was active on the *St. Anne altarpiece* for the same city. During the same period, the van der Weyden *Deposition* was one of the most frequently copied images of the 15th-century; during Massys' day, versions of it were produced by Jan Mostaert and Joos van Cleve, to name only two prominent 16th-century artists.[51] Neither their works nor that of Massys are literal copies after the van der Weyden original, however; there is no possibility of deception or mistaking the later versions for the earlier prototype. In Massys' case, the gold background so essential to van der Weyden's image has been completely replaced with a scenic background that includes the peak of Golgotha and the distant skyline of Jerusalem. Massys has retained much of the spirit of the earlier work, in particular the close interweaving of the figures into a clustered composition, as well as several of the principal types and costumes (especially the corpulent, wealthy Joseph of Arimathea in his expensive brocades), yet there is virtually no correspondence between individual details of the respective works. More literal borrowing of motifs came from another van der Weyden *Lamentation* in this case, possibly the very last picture by the 15th-century master (The Hague, Mauritshuis).[52] From this image, Massys took the arrangement of Christ's body on the ground in the front of the picture; he also took the intimate pose of John the Evangelist comforting the Virgin, her hands clasped in prayer and his tenderly poised on her shoulder. Even the relative disposition of figures is similar between the Hague *Lamentation* and Massys' Antwerp centerpiece. Joseph of Arimathea stands behind Christ's head and John and Mary above His outstretched arm, men all on one side, women on the other. The cluster of women from Roger's late work has not been quoted exactly, but one of the gestures has been retained by Massys: the gesture of the woman wringing her hands. In short, Massys has conflated aspects of both famous van der Weyden images for his own version of the *Lamentation.* He might have been guided to this choice of models by a recent image by his colleague, the Master of Frankfurt (Munich, Alte Pinakothek, F. 127).[53] In this case, however, it is not certain which of the two artists made the earlier variation of van der Weyden. In any case, the popularity of the 15th-century images as models for Antwerp altarpiece designs is reconfirmed by the similar replication of the Master of Frankfurt.

Pl. 22

Pl. 23

The conservative nature of Massys' central panel conforms to the traditionalism he had displayed in the exterior wings and suggests that the centerpiece, like the exterior, was specifically designed to contain all the proper ingredients. The sacred importance of the central panel made the choice of a traditional model all the more likely, and the popularity of van der Weyden's precedent for other altarpieces around the time of Massys' retable suggests that the great 15th-century work had become considered a "classic" solution over the course of the intervening half-century. Another important factor in the decision by the shrineworkers must have been the fact that their joint altarpiece, shared with the coopers, also featured a central *Deposition.* Precedent, both in the form of the joiners' previous altarpiece with the coopers' and in the forms of earlier famous Flemish triptychs, exercised a strong role in the decision to have Massys adapt his *Lamentation* from the model of Roger van der Weyden.

Within the limitations imposed by van der Weyden's imagery, Massys has added a number of new features. Unlike the otherworldly, isolated, artificial gold background of the crossbowmen's *Deposition* (which itself resembles nothing more than a guilded shrinebox, come to life), Massys has inserted a complete landscape background. This background physically complements the foreground cluster of figures. For example, the rising peak of Calvary extends the vertical movement in the center of the figural composition, where John's gesture shelters Mary. Other landscape features echo the poses of figures in the foreground. The arched opening of the tomb at the right side of the picture mirrors the bent-over posture of the Magdalene, as she salves the wounds on Christ's feet. On the other side, the gentle fall of the Jerusalem hillside leads into the foreward lean of Joseph of Arimathea, as he bends over to support the head of Christ. But landscape elements are also distracting reminders of an ongoing narrative, in which the grief of the Lamentation is but a crucial moment. On the hill of Calvary, the two thieves still stand on their crosses, even as the man with the ladder, who presumably just provided for the Deposition of Christ, departs from the scene. A number of bystanders seem to have no purpose in the image, including a pair of vagabonds, who seem to have just finished a picnic luncheon and to be in the process of making a departure. Part of the story but accessory to the principal narrative of the foreground is the scene at the right, where a trio of figures prepares the tomb for Christ. None of these elements is necessary to a scene of the Lamentation over Christ's body; but just as the peak of Calvary and the city of Jerusalem serve to situate the event of the Lamentation in a recognizable geographical space, these incidentals serve to situate it within a particular moment in time, firmly placed between the Crucifixion and the Entombment. Even the most incidental figures of the background serve to locate the event, for they point by contrast to the holiness of the holy figures. After all, the followers of Christ had taken themselves out of the world of everyday events in order to answer a spiritual vocation, just as in the image of Massys, the holy figures stand apart from the rest of the world, always close to Christ. Their isolation, like their conversation, is ultimately as encompassing as that of Joachim in the wilderness in the story of St. Anne. The mark of this withdrawal from worldly affairs is graphically manifest in the form of the two figures who support the head and feet of Christ: Joseph of Arimathea, a rich man turning to Christ, and Mary Magdalene, the high-born sensualist who turned to the love of Christ (see Chap. 6). All the followers of Christ truly stand apart from the world of "power and pelf," making the rich costumes of the central panel a vivid contrast to the rich costumes of the wings. The stylistic difference between the traditionalist Flemish style, based upon van der Weyden, in the center panel and the innovative, Antwerp Mannerist idiom of the wings also underscores the contrast between the dominant Christian values of the centerpiece and the dominant pagan ambience of the periphery.

Massys' use of such a wealth of detail creates an impression of elaborate staging and theatricality, which Broadley has noted with criticism as an "air of artifice."[54] This theatricality in late medieval art has often been commented upon, most notably in the assertion by Mâle that art of the period was renewed by contemporary religious drama.[55] This relationship has been challenged, particularly in terms of priority of drama over art, whose manifestation of the realistic *mise-en-scène* seems to begin considerably earlier than the corresponding phenomena in drama.[56] Instead, both the drama and the art of the late Middle Ages should be seen as part of a general interest in the incidentals of religious narratives, in the everyday details about the holy figures of Christianity. Huizinga is the author who has most articulately sketched this kind of mentality; the "intimacy with the saints and the attempt to embody them pictorially."[57] Since the advent of naturalism in Gothic sculpture to describe the holy figures, religious art had been portrayed in terms of earthly characters and settings.[58] This tendency was especially marked during the 15th-century in Flanders, when the pictorial innovations in oil technique of Jan van Eyck and Robert Campin made the fullest possible description feasible.[59] By the time of Massys' altarpieces, this kind of description was the normal way of thinking about religious figures, not an exception, despite the fact that naturalistic description seems antithetical to religious distance and the separation of sacral from the ordinary world of men.[60] For precisely this reason, most of the religious art of other parts of the world has been insistently nonnaturalistic.

Regarded in terms of the Flemish norms of religious painting and of drama, Massys' altarpieces are merely an extension and intensification of the attitudes already firmly established for a century. In both his altarpieces, Massys simply became more specific in detail than some of his predecessors. His use of concrete details, such as the walls of Jerusalem in the *Annunciation to Joachim* and the *Lamentation* or the Porta Latina behind the *Martyrdom of St. John the Evangelist,* is a heightening of the more-generalized interest in background by such predecessors as Bouts, Memling, and van der Goes. The same interest in detail contributes to Massys' meticulous care for the costumes of the holy figures. Moreover, the more exotic twists of Massys' altarpieces are established out of this predilection for naturalism and description: only the use of unfamiliar costumes, movements, riches, and spaces can restore a sense of the otherworldly to an art founded upon the worldliness and familiarity of religious figures. Thus it is that Massys seeks in foreign models the costumes and faces (Dürer and Leonardo) and the buildings and mountainous landscapes (Cima, Perugino, and Leonardo) that will remove his imagery from the familiar Netherlandish conventions dominant in 15th-century Flemish art. (This exotic, foreign quality and otherworldliness may also help to account for the widespread popularity and export trade of the Antwerp Mannerist painting style and its equivalent in sculpture; such interpretations of religious scenes were lively, non-local, and convincingly otherworldly—a clear alternative to the more "native" Flemish school of painting.)

Both the Massys altarpieces were created within the general assumption of religious figures as approachable analogues of the human viewers who commissioned the altarpieces. Both the confraternity of St. Anne and the shrineworkers guild were anxious to present believable and palpable patrons as the central concern of their altarpieces. The very identity of the organizations and their entire religious life were to be focused around the altarpiece retable that Massys created for them; conversely, the naturalistic assumptions underlying the altarpieces are an outgrowth of the striving for religious intimacy that led to the foundation of lay confraternities for corporate religion and the extension of guild membership into guild religion. The richness of detail in costume, in setting, in the sheer number of figures involved in each of the events of the religious story makes the saints and their surroundings vivid and present for the groups of worshippers. Furthermore, the miniature details of the background assume a pervasive knowledge of the religious story by the viewers so that a tiny suggestion is sufficient to recall a scene (e.g., the Meeting at the Golden Gate or Beheading of the Baptist) in its full significance and immediacy.

Yet it is also obvious that the Massys pictures attempt to express a gulf between the human worshippers of his day and the holy figures of Christ's time. The enhancement of costume and setting, as well as the consistent beautification of the holy figures so that all the members of the Holy Kinship and the saints of the Antwerp retable look alike, are factors that contribute together to the idealization of the sacred, to the separation of the sacred from the ordinary and everyday. Massys undoubtedly strove for these effects in order to enhance the glory and prestige of the patron saints of these two religious corporations. But the potential for feeling ever more estranged from the holy figures lay dormant in this new emphasis on the otherworldly. And here again surfaces the religious insecurity and superstition adduced by both Toussaert and Ozment in their discussions of the end of the 15th-century.[61] The insecurity that drove laymen into conformist confraternities also found expression in the increasing distance between ordinary mankind and their sacred ideal, as expressed in art. (This trend, by the way, will continue to characterize Flemish painting throughout the 16th-century—either in artists, like Bruegel, who stress the ordinary realm, or in artists, like Floris and eventually Rubens, who focus on the transcendent religious ideal.)

Looking back at the two major altarpieces painted by Massys during the years 1507–11 prompts several important methodological conclusions. The main point seems to be that Massys adjusts his presentation of each panel and of the two successive altarpieces in order to present the holy figures in an "appropriate" form of expression. His use of sources and his stylistic means of presentation are selections from the range of contemporary possibilities, combined with personal imagination to evoke particular qualities of the images, qualities that communicate basic assumptions about each subject and its importance. This tailoring of stylistic features to the desired content of the picture places principal emphasis on the work of art as an item of visual communication. The altarpiece is a social act to the extent that this communication is successful and the assumptions are shared; normally, the success will depend as much upon the artist's conformity to the locally established visual conventions as it will to his inventiveness, which might well be so individual as to be esoteric or arcane (the case of Bosch is a puzzling example). We can assume from our knowledge of the two religious organizations that Massys' altarpieces were already shaped by the attitudes of the people who commissioned the works. Possibly the images were highly specified by their eventual audience, although no evidence survives. At the very least the contract to produce altarpiece retables implied a specific and significant religious context: a chapel location, a kind of corporate identity with the patron saint who was the main subject of the retable, and a host of other factors that Massys would have understood well from his position inside the culture. Many of these shared assumptions were implicit, although they must be articulated today by historians of that culture as if the works of art had been made for a culture isolated in space rather than in time.

We noted at the outset of this chapter how much the two triptychs of the same period seem to differ from one another in stylistic terms; however, the general remarks about Massys' use of naturalism and exoticism attest to an overriding continuity of attitudes by the artist toward the sacred realm and its visual depictions. Particularities of the individual panels have to do with the specific subjects depicted and the needs of the viewing audience, as well as the conventions of altarpiece arrangements, which provide for descending importance from centerpiece to interior wings to exterior.

Conventions of the triptych format recall the importance for all of this discussion of the specific assignment that Massys fulfilled with both these altarpiece retables. The possibilities as well as the limitations of the triptych structure were the defining conditions of the solutions worked out by Massys. His two great altarpieces were painted retables for chapel altarpieces; in the Netherlands of the early 16th century, that restriction meant that the retables would take the form of triptychs. Within the boundaries of that definition, all the other variables of content—subject matter, formal expression, and the relationship between panels—were worked out in the flexible modal constructions described in this chapter. But Massys worked in a number of alternative pictorial formats, each with a defining set of visual restrictions, each intended for a different pictorial purpose. The artist's other alternatives, and his varied solutions to these individual assignments and restrictive conventions, will be the subject of the remainder of this book.

NOTES

1. This concept of the symbolic interpretation of culture as system is based upon the work of Clifford Geertz, particularly the essays collected in his *The Interpretation of Cultures:* "Thick Description: Toward an Interpretive Theory of Culture," pp. 3–30; "Religion as a Cultural System," pp. 87–125; "Ethos, World View, and the Analysis of Sacred Symbols," pp. 126–41.

2. Harry Rand, "The Modes and Recent Art," *Arts* 55, no. 4 (1980): 78–86, discusses this communal purpose of imagery, "to define the boundaries of a group," as the "Imperial mode" of aesthetic utility. The quotation is from Rand's shorter version of this paper, "The Imperial Mode in Modern Art," a talk presented at the 1980 College Art Association meeting in New Orleans. Rand's use of the term "mode" has a different meaning from the tradition within literary history and theory and means something closer to his own phrase "aesthetic utility," and should not be confused with Northrup Frye's standard discussion or other recent uses of the word.

3. The date of commission is not preserved in documents, nor are any payments recorded. The earlier date is furnished by estimate, given the size of the undertaking, but the terminus is provided by the artist's own inscription on the exterior of the left wing: "QVINTE METSYS SCREEF DIT 1509" (Quinten Metsys wrote this 1509).

4. The Westphalian Master of 1473, whose name work (ca. 1470) is today in Cologne (Wallraf-Richartz Museum), offers an early and complete image of this genealogy set in a church interior (P. Schabacker, "The Holy Kinship in a Church: Geertgen and the Westphalian Master of 1473," *Oud Holland* 89 [1975]: 225–42). The most famous image of the kinship of Christ in the church interior is by Geertgen tot sint Jans of Haarlem (Amsterdam, Rijksmuseum); see J. Snyder, "The Early Haarlem School of Painting II," pp. 128–29, and "Geertgen schildert de voorouders van Christus," *Bulletin van het Rijksmuseum* 5 (1957): 85–94. The popularity of this Holy Kinship theme in the paintings of the School of Cologne (there is also a Master of the Holy Kinship from Cologne, whose name altarpiece dates from around 1500) is an indication of the cult veneration of St. Anne in Cologne, the archdiocese of Louvain. According to F. Prims ("Quinten Massys en de Annadevotie," pp. 64–70), both Cologne and nearby Aachen claimed to possess relics of St. Anne. The basic study of the subject remains B. Kleinschmidt, *Die heilige Anna, Ihre Verehrung in Geschichte, Kunst, und Volkstum.* Also see Toussaert, pp. 288–89.

5. Friedländer, vol. 7, p. 54, no. 129. The details of the commission are given by H. Weizsäcker, *Die Kunstgeschichte des ehemaligen Dominikanerklosters in Frankfurt-am-Main* (Munich, 1923), p. 127.

6. The fullest discussion is L. Brand Phillip, *The Ghent Altarpiece and the Art of Jan van Eyck* (Princeton, 1971).

7. The David *Baptism triptych* is dated on the basis of the vital statistics of the two wives of its donor, Jan de Trompes of Ostende. The first wife, Elizabeth van der Meersch (died 11 March 1502) appears opposite Jan de Trompes on the right interior wing of the triptych; on the reverse of that wing, receiving the benediction of the Madonna and Child, is the second wife of Jan de Trompes, Madeleine Cordier. The fullest discussion is A. Janssens de Bisthoven and R. Parmentier, *Les Primitifs Flamands I. Le Musée Communal de Bruges,* 2nd ed. (Antwerp, 1959), p. 20.

8. E. de Jongh, "Grape Symbolism in Paintings of the 16th and 17th Centuries," pp. 166–91.

9. For the Italian merchant community in Antwerp, see J. Goris, *Etude sur les colonies marchandes méridionales.* A general discussion of Massys and Antwerp's foreign communities is given in Chapter 3, below.

10. A full discussion, reaching negative conclusions concerning Italian influence, is in H. T. Broadley, "The Mature Style of Quinten Massys," pp. 111–19.

11. Cohen, *Studien zu Quinten Metsys,* p. 66; C. Aschenheim, *Der italienische Einfluss in der vlämischen Renaissancemalerei* (Munich, 1909), p. 8; Broadley, "Quinten Massys"; de Bosque, pp. 96–97.

12. No satisfactory study of Memling and Italy has been made to date, but Guy Baumann is preparing a dissertation for Princeton University that will treat this important topic. Also see K. McFarlane, *Hans Memling.*

13. On the Washington Christus, see P. Schabacker, *Petrus Christus* (Utrecht, 1974), pp. 114–16; J. Upton, "Devotional Imagery and Style in the Washington *Nativity* by Petrus Christus," *Studies in the History of Art* 7 (1975): 62, n. 30: "The two pagan warriors in the spandrels complete this image of general disorder in the world 'before the Law.' "

14. Broadley, p. 130, is again negative about any relationship between Massys and the "crystalline Dolomitic vistas of Leonardo da Vinci." On the Louvre *Anna Selbdritt* of Leonardo, see J. Wasserman, "The Dating and Patronage of Leonardo's Burlington House Cartoon," *Art Bulletin* 53 (1971): 312–25, with bibliography.

15. P. Eich, "Empfängnis Maria, unbefleckte," *RDK* V, 242–59.

16. E. de Jongh, "Grape Symbolism," pp. 184–86: "If Christ was the bunch of grapes, Mary was the vine or tendril, a metaphor that occurs in a poem by the medieval Dutch poet Jacob van Maerlant." De Jongh also cites a verse by Massys' fellow

Antwerp *rederijker* Anna Bijns: "Pure body, free of sinful stink, / You have borne / The grape, whose wine, the sweetest drink, / Reconciled the Pharaoh—oh fertile tendril."

17. This symbolic bird has a variety of meanings, but it has been explained as a reference to the spirituality of the soul, as opposed to the earthbound flesh of the body, and to the Resurrection. It can also refer to death and to the sacrifice of the Passion because of the bloodlike spot on the bird's plumage (H. Friedmann, *The Symbolic Goldfinch* [Washington, 1946], p. 7ff.). Friedmann, whose examples are mostly Italian, denies any significance to the tether, asserting (pp. 115–16) that only lesser artists painted the finch as a common household pet. Also R. W. Brednich, "Vogel am Faden: Geschichte und Ikonographie eines vergessenen Kinderspiels," *Festschrift Matthias Zender: Studien zu Volkskultur, Sprache, und Landesgeschichte*, vol. 1 (Bonn, 1972) pp. 573–97.

18. I. Bergström, "Disguised Symbolism in 'Madonna' Pictures and Still Life," pp. 307, n. 13, and 345, n. 31, where he interprets the carnation as meaning "Resurrection through Christ." The flower was introduced to Europe only ca. 1450. Its association with the Incarnation (note the etymological similarities) is on account of the fleshlike red color; the flower's connection with the Passion is its spiky, nail-like shape (*nelke* or *nagelbloem* is the Germanic term for carnation: nail-flower). The fullest discussion is I. Bergström, *Den symboliska nejlikan*, and also his "On religious symbols in European portraiture of the 15th and 16th Centuries," *Umanesimo e Esoterismo*, ed. E. Castelli (Padua, 1960), pp. 335–43; R. Koch, "Flower Symbolism in the Portinari Altarpiece," pp. 70–77.

19. A fig also appears in the Master of Frankfurt's *Holy Kinship* as the equivalent of an apple. For the fig as fruit of Paradise, see L. Behling, *Die Pflanze in der mittelalterlichen Tafelmalerei* (Weimar, 1957), pp. 48, 141. The fig tree, rather than the apple tree, was believed to have been the Tree of Knowledge in Paradise because of the Genesis 3 reference to Adam and Eve covering their nakedness with fig leaves. Thus the fig could be viewed simultaneously as the fruit of Paradise and the fruit of corruption; see O. Goetz, *Der Feigenbaum* (Berlin, 1965).

20. O. Erich, "Adam-Christus (alter and neuer Adam)" *RDK* I: 157–67.

21. E. Panofsky, "Reality and Symbol in Early Flemish Painting: 'Spiritualia sub metaphoris corporalium,' " *ENP*, 131ff. A useful general discussion of the concept of similitudes is given by M. Foucault, "The Prose of the World," *The Order of Things* (New York, 1973), pp. 17–45.

22. Illustrated in K. Smits, *Iconografie van de nederlandsche primitieven* (Amsterdam, 1933), fig. 13. The readings of the inscriptions are cited on p. 38.

23. On the cult of the Holy Name in Antwerp, see Prims, pp. 144–45; on the cult in general in the late Middle Ages, see Delaruelle, Labande, and Ourliac, p. 647.

24. M. R. James, *The Apocryphal New Testament* (Oxford, 1975), p. 40. See also the medieval compendium of religious myths by Jacobus da Voragine, *The Golden Legend*, pp. 521ff.

25. M. Levi d'Ancona, *Iconography of the Immaculate Conception in the Middle Ages and Early Ren.*, p. 3.

26. E. Roth, *Der volkreiche Kalvarienberg*, 2nd ed. (Berlin, 1967).

27. Identified by Marlier with the document preserved in the Antwerp civic archives from the shrineworkers' payments for Massys' altarpiece (15 March 1508; de Bosque Appendix, 424, no. 4). See *De eeuw van Bruegel*, Brussels, exh. cat. (1963), p. 137, no. 162.

28. The source for this civic identification is the painting of Gerard David of Bruges, whose *Judgment of Cambyses* (Bruges, Groeninge Museum) features a background vista that includes the local shrine of the Holy Blood. Since the Cambyses panels were commissioned for the Town Hall of the city of Bruges and displayed there in the Hall of Justice, the presence of a local landmark is hardly surprising; it even serves as a symbolic relocation and reenactment of the virtues depicted in the historical narrative.

29. Bruges painters of the late 15th century, notably the Master of the St. Lucy Legend, often used their native city as the background for religious scenes featuring the Virgin and saints, implying, perhaps, that Bruges held a special position under the protection of the Madonna (much like the position advanced by Siena in Italy, for which see H. van Os, *Marias Demut and Verherrlichung in der sienesicher Malerei 1300–1450).* The anonymous Bruges masters are discussed in Friedländer, vol. 6 (with bibliography), pp. 37 ff., and in the exhibition catalog *Les Primitifs flamands anonymes*, p. 47ff.

30. Delaruelle, Labande, and Ourliac, pp. 666–94; Toussaert, pp. 219f., 261f., 478–83; G. Le Bras, *Etudes de sociologie religieuse*, vol. 2 (Paris, 1955–1956), pp. 423–57; Post, *KG*, pp. 383-86.

31. Toussaert, *passim*.

32. S. Ozment, *The Reformation in the Cities*, pp. 1–46.

33. Toussaert, pp. 280–88; J. A. F. Kronenberg, *Maria's Heerlijkheid in Nederland*, pp. 1903ff.; Post, *KV*, pp. 462–64. For art, H. Aurenhammer, "Marienikone und Marienandachtsbild," pp. 135–49; E. Mâle, *L'Art religieux*, pp. 198–221.

34. Delaruelle, Labande, and Ourliac, pp. 779–86; Levi d'Ancona, *Iconography*. The history of St. Anne is included in the *Golden Legend* under the entry of "8 September. Birth of the Blessed Virgin Mary."

35. Prims, p. 146ff., and "Quinten Massys en de Annadevotie," pp. 64–70; E. Schaumkell, *Der Kultus der heiligen Anna am Ausgang des Mittelalters* (Freiburg / Leipzig, 1893).

36. See above, n. 4. A seminal text of the period was the 1494 publication in Mainz by Abbot Trithemius of Würzburg, formerly of Trier, in praise of St. Anne. This text was translated into Flemish and well circulated (Toussaert, p. 289). Bruges also had a St. Anne confraternity; Ghent claimed to have a relic of St. Anne in the Church of St. Nicholas.

37. Prims, "De schilderijen van het Kuipersaltaar," pp. 296–301.

38. Ibid. According to "tradition," i.e., unsupported allegation beginning in the 18th century, the coopers' *Deposition altarpiece* was also painted by Massys, and it has been identified by several scholars with the large *Lamentation* (F.14), formerly in the Wetzlar collection, Amsterdam (see de Bosque, pp. 164–65). This work is here considered a workshop product of Massys' mature middle period, the "Patinir years," a date also supported by de Bosque ("ca. 1515–16"). The date of the coopers' commission is unknown, although Prims suggests that the likeliest period would have been before the 1497 split of the two guilds. The shrineworkers adopted the previous joint patron, St. John, instead of a more particularized patron saint, like the coopers' St. Matthew, suggesting to Prims that the coopers had already appropriated their own sponsor saint for an altarpiece

prior to 1508. Not only is the Wetzlar work probably later in date than the coopers' commission as well as inferior in quality to the *St. John altarpiece*, but its large size also does not conform well to the 1748 description by Jacob de Wit (*Kerken van Antwerpen*, cited by Prims) of figures "smaller than life" in the coopers' retable.

39. J. Held, *Dürers Wirkung auf die niederländische Kunst seiner Zeit*, pp. 67, 79ff.; J. Bialostocki, "Opus Quinque dierum: Durer's 'Christ among the Doctors' and Its Sources," p. 17ff.; L. Silver, "The *Ill-Matched Pair* of Quinten Massys," p. 109.

40. K. Clark and C. Pedretti, *Drawings by Leonardo da Vinci . . . at Windsor Castle*, vol. 1, p. 84, no. 12495; Silver, "The *Ill-Matched Pair*" and "Power and Pelf," p. 69.

41. Friedländer, vol. 11, remains a basic source: *The Antwerp Mannerists*, Eng. ed. Also see L. von Baldass, "Die niederländischen Maler des spätgotischen Stiles," pp. 120–38.

42. J. Roosval, "Les peintres des retables neérlandais en Suéde," pp. 310–20. Another dated example of the collaboration of painters and sculptors is an altarpiece that remained in Antwerp—the Averbode retable; this altarpiece has even more significance in our context because its sculpted central portion is a *Lamentation* derived from the *St. John altarpiece* (see R. Marijnissen, "Het retable van Averbode uit de verzamelingen van het Museum Vleeshuis," *Antwerpen* 7 [1961]:6–15, showing that the retable was bought in December 1514 by the abbey of Averbode from a certain William Cruypers).

43. J. de Bosschere, *La Sculpture anversoise aux XVe et XVIe siècles*, as well as the vast scholarly corpus by Count J. de Borchgrave d'Altena, particularly *Les retables Brabançons 1450–1550* and *Les retables Brabançons conservés en Suéde.*

44. L. von Baldass, "Die niederländischen Maler"; W. Gibson, *The Paintings of Cornelis Engebrechtsz.* (New York, 1977), p. 83ff. ("Mannerist Influences and the Leyden *Crucifixion*"). Gibson points out (p. 86, n. 12) that the earliest dated Antwerp Mannerist altarpiece is the 1513 Kempen (Westphalia) retable, sculpted with painted wings like the Averbode retable in Antwerp (1514; see n. 44), by the Antwerp artist Adriaen van Overbeke (master in the guild 1508).

45. F. Prims, "Quinten Matsys, een onbegrepen Meteoor," *Antwerpiensia* 22 (1952): 162–63, believing the commission, however, to be that of the *St. Anne altarpiece*. In this supposition, Prims is following E. van Even, *L'Ancienne école de peinture de Louvain*, p. 373, and Hymans, "Quinten Matsys," p. 205. Broadley, however, makes the proper correction (pp. 49-50, n. 1), noting the document (p. 50, n. 2, unrecorded in de Bosque), quoted from the register of the joiners' guild by J. Immerzeel, Jr., *De levens en werken der Hollandsche en Vlaamsche Kunstschilders, beeldhouwers, graveurs en bouwmeesters van het begin der vijftiende eeuw tot heden*, vol. 2 (Amsterdam, 1842–43), p. 216. Prims makes the informed assertion that there were *no* painted retables at all in Antwerp before 1500. In addition to the works of art mentioned in note 42, the dated 1504 Massys-related Antwerp retable of
Pl. 74 painting and sculpture in Valladolid, San Salvador (F.84; see cat. 8 and especially de Bosque, pp. 137–45, figs. 47–48, pp. 116–20) shows an example of collaboration in Antwerp early in the new century. The Valladolid retable has a carved interior with central sculpted cult figure of St. John the Baptist surrounded by sculpted narrative scenes. Prims, (vol. 7.2, pp. 53–55) discusses the shrineworkers in the general economic context of the city and in relation to sculptors and painters.

46. Quoted in J. Murray, *Antwerp in the Age of Plantin and Brueghel* (Norman, Okla., 1970), p. 67. The finest overview of 16th-century Antwerp is L. Voet, *Antwerp the Golden Age*, Brussels, 1973 (with bibliography). See also J. Goris, *Etude sur les colonies marchandes méridionales*; H. van der Wee, *The Growth of the Antwerp Market and the European Economy*; R. Ehrenberg, *Das Zeitalter der Fugger* (Jena, 1896); S.T. Bindoff, "The Greatness of Antwerp," *New Cambridge Modern History II. The Reformation* (Cambridge, 1958), pp. 50–69; J.A. van Houtte, "Anvers aux XVe et XVIe siècles, expansion et apogée," pp. 248–78; W. Brulez, "Brugge en Antwerpen in de 15e en 16e eeuwen: Een tegenstelling?" *Tijdschrift voor Geschiedenis* 83 (1970): 15–37.

47. Silver, "Power and Pelf."

48. The subject of grisailles, especially in terms of liturgical needs and the relationship between painting and sculpture on retables, remains neglected and crucial. For the state of research, see M.T. Smith, "The Use of Grisailles as a Lenten Observance," *Marsyas* 8 (1959): 43–54.

49. P. Philippot, "Les Grisailles et les 'degrés de realité de l'image dans la peinture flamande des XVe et XVIe siècles," pp. 225–42.

50. S.N. Blum, *Early Netherlandish Triptychs*, pp. 49ff.

51. Illustrated in Friedländer, vol. 9, no. 31; vol. 10, no. 1.

52. E. Panofsky, "Two Roger Problems: The Donor of the Hague Lamentation and the Date of the Altarpiece of the Seven Sacraments," *Art Bulletin* 33 (1951): 33ff., and *ENP*, p. 284.

53. Friedländer, vol. 7, p. 75, no. 127, formerly in the Cologne Carthusian church.

54. Broadley, pp. 67–68; see also pp. 48–49 for related but more-favorable comments concerning the *St. Anne altarpiece* exterior.

55. E. Mâle, *L'Art religieux*, pp. 35–84.

56. E. Roth, *Der volkreiche Kalvarienberg*; F.P. Pickering, *Literature and Art in the Middle Ages* (Coral Gables, 1970), pp. 161ff., 234ff., 273ff.

57. J. Huizinga, *Waning of the Middle Ages*, pp. 67–77.

58. M. Dvořak, *Idealism and Naturalism in Gothic Art*, transl. R. Klawiter (South Bend, Ind., 1967); W. Sauerländer, *Gothic Sculpture in France 1140–1270*, English ed. (New York, 1972), pp. 42, 50ff. An analogous phenomenon can be seen in much late medieval mystical literature or legends, e.g., the 14th-century concrete visions of Gospel figures in the *Meditations on the Life of Christ* by the Pseudo-Bonaventura, the *Vita Christi* by Ludolphus the Carthusian, the *Revelations* of St. Bridget of Sweden, or the *Historia Scholastica* of Petrus Comestor (see Delaruelle, Labande, and Ourliac, pp. 709ff.) Useful studies on the topic of literature are the works of H. Vollmer, *Materialen zur Bibelgeschichte und religiösen Volkskunde des Mittelalters* (Hamburg, 1912–1929), and *Bibel und deutsche Kultur*, (Hamburg, 1931–1941).

59. Panofsky, *ENP*, 149ff. ("Ars Nova"); C. de Tolnay, *Le Maitre de Flémalle et les frères van Eyck* (Brussels, 1938).

60. On the demarcation of limits between the holy and the ordinary, see M. Eliade, *Sacred and Profane*, Eng. ed. (New York, 1959); and the work of structural anthropologists as summarized by E. Leach, *Culture and Communication* (Cambridge, 1976), pp. 33–36, 81–93.

61. Toussaert; Ozment, *Reformation in the Cities.*

3

Merchants and Monarchs: Art for Export

The two great triptychs of Louvain and Antwerp that form the cornerstone of Massys' scholarship were made for local consumption in the Netherlands, and they represent the basic collective patronage of this kind of large and expensive chapel ornament: religious and professional confraternities. During the period of the teens, Massys also worked on other altarpiece projects that were destined for foreign sponsors in Portugal and in Germany. These other projects demonstrate the international reputation of the Antwerp painter abroad and also exhibit the extent of Antwerp's international traffic in currency and commodities. Furthermore, the character of the exported art works clarifies some basic attitudes of Massys toward religious art-making.

Earliest of the exported art works was a massive polyptych made for Portugal. Painted for the church of the Convent of Madre de Deus in Xabregas, near Lisbon, the polyptych's subject was the Seven Sorrows of the Virgin. Its component panels are now scattered, but originally the retable featured seven scenes of Mary's grief around a larger, central image of the *Mater Dolorosa,* the mourning Virgin whose grief is made visible by the metaphor of a large sword pricking at her heart.[1] Suffering, in fact, is the keynote of the entire altarpiece. Beginning with the *Presentation in the Temple,* a scene that prefigures Christ's sacrifice on the altar of religion, the images progress through the Gospel narrative to the stirring climax of Mary's Compassion, the *Pietà,* and a final coda of the *Three Maries at the Tomb,* chronologically the last scene and the literal depiction in isolation of the women's grief after the death of Christ. *Pl. 24* *Pl. 25* *Pl. 26* *Pl. 27*

The theme of the Seven Sorrows of the Virgin was an extremely popular one for altarpieces during the period of Massys. An example is the Hoogstraeten altarpiece (F. 103) from the environs of Antwerp (Antwerp, Koninklijk Museum),[2] which depicts the canonical seven scenes along with an additional shutter panel of a donatrix with her patron saint. In this particular case, the scenes of the Passion are depicted in larger size with a tall, narrow panel of the *Mater Dolorosa* instead of Massys' large, almost square central image. Also unlike the Massys retable, two of the seven scenes of the Hoogstraeten altarpiece occur in the background of the larger panels, with other major scenes in the foreground. The Flight into Egypt is visible as a parallel movement across the image behind the major foreground movement of the *Carrying of the Cross;* behind the *Entombment* image is a background view of the antecedent Gospel event, the Lamentation on Calvary. Other examples of the Seven Sorrows theme emphasize the central image of the Mater Dolorosa, the Virgin with her heart pierced with a sword of grief. A number of these images were produced by the Brussels workshop of Bernard van Orley.[3] They feature a central, dominant iconic image of the mournful Virgin, presented at half-length, surrounded by the seven small images from the Gospel narrative. Here, as in the case of the Massys image, the emotional state of the Mater Dolorosa is the true subject of the altarpiece, and the story events are the stimulus of her grief.

A compromise formula for presenting the sorrow of the Virgin along with the canonical seven scenes is the large panel (F. 63; Brussels, Musées Royaux) by a follower of Massys, where the Lamentation, one of the selected Gospel events, has been extracted and presented as the dominant central image.[4] The Lamentation, however, has been condensed from a group mourning on Calvary to an isolated vignette of the Virgin alone mourning for the dead son on her lap—in short, a Pietà. The relics of the Passion—crown of thorns, sponge—appear prominently in the foreground, and the ominous large shape of the cross, which still holds the large nail that bound Christ's feet, looms just to the right of the two figures. The Calvary landscape with Jerusalem in the background is visible behind the *Pietà,* so the event is given its fullest historical setting. At the same time, the crucial Seven Sorrows image of grief—the sword—is introduced to the historical narrative to emphasize the central point of Mary's misery. In small roundels around the large Pietà are the remaining six scenes of the Seven Sorrows of the Virgin: the Presentation in the Temple, Flight into Egypt, Christ among the Doctors, Carrying of the Cross, Crucifixion, and Entombment.

That the Brussels image was not painted by Massys himself, yet allegedly came from the house of the painters' guild of St. Luke in Antwerp, where it was installed in 1505, is consonant with the religious life of Massys' own guild brothers. In the following year, 1506, the St. Luke guild of Antwerp commissioned a sculpted retable with seven tabernacles for each of the moments of sorrow.[5] Their interest in the cult came about through contact with the Windesheim Congregation, the monastic arm of the *devotio moderna* movement in the Netherlands.[6] The cult seems to have been founded by a Windesheim canon, Jan van Coudenberge, secretary and confessor to Philip the Fair and his court in Brussels and prebend to congregations in Abbenbroek, Reymerswaele, and Bruges. Jan van Coudenberge was impressed by a picture in Rome, ascribed to St. Luke, of the Virgin of sorrowful countenance, and he promoted meditation on the sorrows of the Virgin. While there had been a brotherhood dedicated to the Sorrows of the Virgin a century earlier in Utrecht (1380),[7] the first confraternities dedicated to the Seven Sorrows of the Virgin as they were known to Massys and other artists were established only a few years before the pictures. The first of them was founded in 1492 at Reymerswaele, then spread to Bruges, probably under the aegis of Jan van Coudenberge. The link to the Antwerp St. Luke guild was through the Windesheim congregation of nearby Mechelen, whose rector, Petrus Verhoeven, had contact with the "prince" of the Antwerp *rederijkers* guild (a branch of the St. Luke guild), a priest named Jan van Parijs (John of Paris).[8] Verhoeven intervened on behalf of the Antwerp St. Luke's guild, his own house in Mechelen, and a few other adepts of the cult for recognition by the bishop of Cambrai. By 1496 the Antwerp Goudbloem *rederijkers* had already performed an allegorical play, devised by its brethren of the Brussels *rederijkers,* who called themselves the Mary Crown of Seven Sorrows, in honor of the *Violieren* of Antwerp, the *rederijkers* within Antwerp's St. Luke's guild, who now called themselves the "Brotherhood of the 7 Sorrows." Van Coudenberge had also done his job well at the court in the Netherlands; both Philip the Fair and his father, Maximilian, followed by Emperor Charles V, adopted the cult as a kind of family devotion and encouraged local nobility and subjects to adopt it.

The Seven Sorrows altarpiece therefore was created by Massys at a time when that cult enjoyed extensive popularity in the Netherlands. Within his own guild, the *rederijkers* of the chamber *de Violieren* formed their own religious brotherhood and were responsible for the commissioning of an altarpiece retable from the artists of the St. Luke's guild. With so many other Netherlandish confraternities and churches endorsing the cult, and with the support of the highest nobility and the emperor, it is hardly surprising to find numerous 16th-century examples of this popular theme on painted altarpieces.

The theme of the Seven Sorrows of the Virgin is itself a specialized outgrowth of a widespread late medieval orientation toward intensive meditation on the emotional and physical suffering of the Passion. The petition by Verhoeven to the bishop of Cambrai makes its purpose explicit: "dedication to the meditation of the Seven principal sorrows of Our Lady in connection with the Passion of Christ to the end of proceeding in virtue and avoiding all harm."[9] Religious literature of the period beginning in the 14th century had placed great stress on empathic participation in the religious experiences of the Gospel, particularly on Christ and His sufferings.[10] Beginning with books like the *Hundred Articles on Christ's Passion* by Heinrich Suso (d. 1365) or the *Meditations on the Life of Christ* by an anonymous 14th-century Franciscan, this ascetic and reflective trend retained its hold on the community of the faithful until Massys' era. An outgrowth of the late medieval general call for an Imitation of Christ, most familiar from the treatise of that name by Thomas à Kempis, the sufferings of Christ formed a principal theme of the best-selling books of the early 16th century. In itself, this meditative devotion on the Passion was not new; previously the tale of suffering had been divided into seven parts, each to correspond to canonical hours of prayer during the day.[11] But the extent of engagement with the meditation on Christ's suffering can be gauged from some more-specialized variants of devotion during the 14th to 16th centuries, such as the cult of Christ's wounds (usually numbered in the hundreds and each the recipient of dozens of Pater Nosters and Ave Maria prayers), Holy Blood, and tears. In addition, the weapons of martyrdom came to be venerated as the *Arma Christi* and treasured as relics in their own right.[12] The *Arma Christi* became a popular image, especially in inexpensive woodcut editions, because prayers of indulgence before the weapons of martyrdom were supposed to promise many days or years of indulgence.[13]

Along with counting the wounds and weapons of Christ's suffering, the devout worshippers of the late Middle Ages, and the artists who responded to their piety, focused on the more incidental and previously neglected moments of the Passion in the Gospels—such scenes as Christ Saying Farewell to his Mother (notable pictures by David, and Massys' final diptych in the Prado [1529, cat. 49]), Christ on the Stone (Gossaert, a lost composition known from copies), and the Nailing to the Cross (David).[14] Many of these scenes also became important parts of the printed series of engravings and woodcuts by artists throughout northern Europe (Schongauer, Dürer, Israhel van Meckenem, Lucas van Leyden).

With this much emphasis on the physical suffering of Christ and attention to the minutiae of the Passion narrative, the cult of the Seven Sorrows of the Virgin was almost an inevitable consequence. The intense veneration of the Madonna, which was a commonplace in late medieval theology, crystallized around the same kind of Mary-centered personalized Gospel stories and multiple numbers of her emotional states.[15] As early as 1380 an Utrecht brotherhood dedicated to the sorrows of the Virgin had been established. The late 15th century saw the rise of the cult of the rosary, which received a stimulus in the form of its own indulgence from Pope Sixtus IV in 1478 (see Chap. 4).[16] Linked to the prayers with the rosary were 150 mysteries (joyous, sorrowful, glorious, etc.) from the life of Mary and Christ. Another of the contemplative formulas of Mary devotion was the Seven Joys of the Virgin, the subject of religious art, such as the Peter Aertsen altarpiece for the church of St. Leonard of Zoutleeuw (Léau) or the 15th-century panorama of scenes by Memling (Munich).[17]

The most frequent meditative grouping of the veneration of the Virgin during this period was the Seven Sorrows of the Virgin.[18] Mary's Compassion was the theological equivalent to the suffering of her Son: in addition to the sorrowful climax of the Passion, other moments from the Gospel narrative were selected as prefigurations of her sorrow as Stabat Mater, the lamenting mother at the foot of the cross. During the late Middle Ages, the number of sorrowful events varied (12, 15, 27, 50) even as the wounds of Christ were not fixed in any way, but the most usual number of dolors eventually tended to be seven. In the two decades before Massys finished the *Madre de Deus altarpiece,* no fewer than seven separate treatises had been published in Antwerp alone that were dedicated to the Seven Sorrows and their meditation.[19]

An anonymous *rederijker* poem, published in the 1524 anthology of Jan van Styevoort (no. 151), captures the mood of the grieving Virgin at the Crucifixion which was the object of pious meditation:

"In Praise of the Most Sorrowful Mother of Our Lord"

O sweet Maria, how was your courage
When Jesus suffered death before you
Abused, disfigured, wet with blood,
Overflowing tears you bawled.
With heavy heart you said:
'See here a downy lamb without sin
O man, this pain was sent me
By you, so come and aid my wails
Your Creator sees how filled with wounds He is,
With your guilt my child is put to death.
My friends, stand beside my tears
And see my son, your God, abused . . .[20]

This emotional intensity, rather than attention to any particular events, underlay the meditation on the Seven Sorrows and the Lamentation of the Virgin ("Onser Vrouwen Claghen"). In fact, the Massys depiction departs from the usual selection of sorrowful Gospel narratives. In place of the Entombment of Christ, an event which essentially replicated the Lamentation over the Dead Christ in both locale and cast of characters (indeed, the two scenes appeared in a single panel of the Hoogstraeten altar), Massys substituted a later moment from the Gospels: the *Women and St. John at the Tomb* (Lisbon). *Pl. 27* This scene is more specifically focused on the Virgin and her grief, for the corpse of Christ is now absent; moreover, the absence of any action makes the emotion of the holy figures the entire subject of the picture. In this Massys image, the Madonna is the most immobile and prayerful of the figures. Enshrouded in her cool blue mantle, she is surrounded by the hot red of John's garments and by the warm reds and oranges of her other companions. The distant background sky is aglow with the twilight of a setting sun, just visible as it disappears behind a rocky escarpment. Nature echoes the mourners' grief with its own dying glow.

Again, in the Infancy scene within the Seven Sorrows cycle, Massys has made a substitution for the usual Flight into Egypt that emphasizes the emotional state of the Virgin. Rather than showing the Holy Family in flight on a donkey, suffering the privations of fugitive life, Massys has depicted them in the Madre de Deus *Rest on the Flight* (today in Worcester, Mass.) at the edge of a rocky landscape, which *Pl. 28* communicates the hardship of their situation. The direct inspiration of this alteration was the contemporary imagery of Gerard David of Bruges, whose *Rest on the Flight into Egypt* (New York, *Pl. 29* Metropolitan Museum) features a moment of quiet repose with the Virgin in the center of a grassy clearing holding the Child in her lap. In fact, the nursing Madonna by David was a specific source for the Massys image, for the Worcester Massys shows the Virgin offering the Child the edge of her veil with the same gesture as she had offered her breast in the David panel. The meaningless and tentative movement of the Massys version can only be understood as a nursing motif reshaped by a discreet Massys in the interest of propriety and modesty.

Unlike David, Massys has placed St. Joseph prominently in the foreground as an integral member of the family unit. In David's versions of the Rest on the Flight, Joseph is at best relegated to the role of provider in the background, shaking fruit off the trees to feed the Holy Family, and often he is not included at all. In Massys' Worcester *Rest,* Joseph occupies center stage and offers Christ an apple, emblematic of man's redemption from Original Sin but carried naturally by the Holy Family as part of the contents of their humble wicker picnic basket. Like St. Anne and the Holy Kinship, the interest in Joseph and the daily life of the Holy Family is an outgrowth of late medieval fascination with religious detail in the bourgeois urban environment of Massys' Antwerp.[21] This family scene also represents the artist's attempt to provide a cohesive emotional cluster of people, like the *Women at the Tomb.*

Massys attempts to inject a note of informality and spontaneity into the scene by inserting the donkey into the right half of the image; the animal pauses for lunch and refreshment as do the holy figures. Nor have the narrative circumstances of the *Rest on the Flight* been neglected. Massys includes the Massacre of the Innocents as a gloomy background contrast to the scene of family tenderness in the foreground. This immediate peril, added to her foreknowledge of Christ's eventual suffering on the cross, evokes the mournful countenance visible on the face of the Virgin. A poignant little tear on Mary's cheek makes explicit the sorrow that is the theme of the entire altarpiece.

The Seven Sorrows altarpiece, then, corresponds to a peculiar religious temper of the late Middle Ages: a combination of fervent interest in the specific details of the family life and narrative history of Christ and the Virgin along with a desire for empathy with the profound emotions of the holy figures in their suffering and their triumphs.

That such an altarpiece retable should be sent to Iberia was not without precedent. A 1505 altarpiece of the Seven Sorrows of the Virgin attributed to Jan Joest of Calcar was delivered to the cathedral of Palencia from the Netherlands.[22] It had been ordered by the bishop of Palencia, Juan de Fonseca, who carried out political missions to Brussels for the Spanish crown. Like the retable by Massys, the Palencia *Seven Sorrows retable* had a large central image surrounded by the seven Gospel narratives. Instead of the Mater Dolorosa with the painful sword in her bosom, the Palencia centerpiece features a *Pietà* with the Virgin supported by St. John the Evangelist; nearby, the smaller figure of Juan de Fonseca is shown kneeling in prayer. The Palencia retable adheres even more closely than Massys' altarpiece to the standard selection of Mary's sorrows, as it includes a *Flight into Egypt* and an *Entombment* rather than the *Rest on the Flight* and the *Women at the Tomb.*

Another example of a large altarpiece exported from Antwerp to Spain is the ensemble requested by Licentiate Gonzalez of Valladolid (F. 84; cat. 8). Its painted portions were once attributed to Massys *Pl. 74* by Justi but should properly be considered the creation of an Antwerp follower.[23] The Valladolid altarpiece consists of a central sculpted portion dedicated to John the Baptist. The wings, depicting the *Nativity* and *Adoration of the Magi,* are derived from the works of Hugo van der Goes as well as a workshop composition of the *Adoration of the Magi* by Massys (cat. 8). *Pl. 73*

The contacts between the Iberian peninsula and Antwerp were extremely close during Massys' early career, due to Antwerp's role as depot of spices and other exotic imports from the new colonies and the New World. Both Spain and Portugal maintained merchant "colonies" in Antwerp, just as they had in Bruges during the previous century; in fact, the transfer of the Portuguese trading house from its headquarters in Bruges to Antwerp in 1499 signaled the turning point in the economic competition of those two cities, and shifted the balance of economic power from Bruges to Antwerp.[24]

Massys' associations with Portugal were even more direct and personal and predated his contact with the Portuguese merchant colony. Among his apprentices was one Eduart Portugalois, who began his training in 1504, according to guild records, and who attained master's status in 1506.[25] No firmly documented work by Eduart survives, although Reis-Santos has attempted to associate a number of paintings with the Portuguese artist. One of those works, a *Descent from the Cross* triptych (Lisbon, National Museum), was originally in the same Madre de Deus cloister at Xabregas as Massys' *Seven Sorrows altarpiece* and it reveals compositional affinities with the Massys polyptych. Its artist, therefore, whether Eduart or not, had some contact with Massys' work, either in Antwerp or Portugal.

Massys' means of contacting the Portuguese is not certain, but the Madre de Deus monastery, for which the *Seven Sorrows altarpiece* was commissioned, was a royal foundation, established by Queen Leonora in 1509 in Xabregas, near Lisbon.[26] In 1513 King Manuel ordered cloth for a curtain for the altarpiece on the main altar—in all likelihood the *Seven Sorrows altarpiece* of Massys. The protective curtain probably indicates that the retable was already in place or expected shortly, so the date of the altarpiece can be fixed fairly closely to the period of the early teens.

If we may judge from the pattern of patronage for Massys' subsequent altarpiece for Portugal (the Coimbra *Passion altarpiece*), combined with the fact that the Madre de Deus retable was a royal commission, the likeliest procedure for the *Seven Sorrows altarpiece* would have been for the king to contact his local trade representative, or "factor," in Antwerp and to request him to act as agent in finding the most suitable artist for such a large painting. The coincidence that Massys had just trained a Portuguese apprentice surely did not hurt his chances of coming to the attention of the new Portuguese factor in Antwerp, João Brandão (in Antwerp 1509–14 and again 1520–26).[27] Moreover, the royal request from Portugal came at a time when Massys was at the height of his local fame, the period in which he was completing work on his masterpiece, the *St. John altarpiece,* for the Joiners guild.

The uneven quality of painting in the alterpiece probably is the result of the picture's eventual destination, far from any critical eyes familiar with Massys' work or from patrons able to demand his personal handling of large portions of the painting.[28] Since he was also in the process of completing the *St. John altarpiece* in 1511, Massys would not have had the additional time to devote himself with equal intensity to the *Seven Sorrows altarpiece.* From the appearance of the two works as completed, he chose to concentrate on the local product for the joiners rather than on the export. Workshop assistance on the project was probably made easier by the large number of smaller-scale separate panels, which seem in a few cases (most notably the *Pietà*) to have had little or no participation from Massys himself, although in other cases, especially the Worcester *Rest on the Flight,* the results are the equal of Massys' best efforts. Haverkamp-Begemann has pointed out that this multipaneled format is tailored to the Iberian *retablo* arrangement, in contrast to the standard Flemish triptych or polyptych presentation.[29] Like Jan Joest in the *Seven Sorrows retable* exported to Palencia, Massys has produced a Flemish altarpiece in terms of the religious theme and its distinctive details of emotion and setting (including such recent innovations as the *Rest on the Flight* subject); however, he has "packaged" his creation to suit the conventions of his audience in Portugal. And he was not above cutting corners in terms of workshop execution when he knew that the altarpiece would only be seen abroad.

Massys' second commissioned altarpiece for Portugal was also given to a monastery, Santa Clara in
Coimbra, by Manuel I.[30] Its delivery on 11 September 1517 was accomplished through the interven-
Pl. 32 tion of Silvester Nunes, the Portuguese factor in Antwerp between 1513 and 1517. Unlike the *Madre*
Pl. 33 *de Deus altarpiece,* the Coimbra *Passion altarpiece* is a typical Flemish triptych. Its two wings contain the
Pl. 34 *Flagellation* and *Ecce Homo* on the interior side and an *Annunciation* in grisaille on the exterior, in
Pl. 35 accord with conventional 15th-century formulas, like the two saints on the *Saint John altarpiece* (see
Pl. 36 Chap. 2). Unfortunately, the central panel is missing, except for a preserved fragment of the grieving
Pl. 91 Virgin. The Madonna's folded arms and isolation resemble Massys' Ottawa *Crucifixion* (F. 12; cat. 20)
Pl. 94 or his Louvre *Pietà* (F. 16; cat. 17), and the overall theme of the *Passion altarpiece* would doubtless find
its central climax in one of the scenes from Calvary.[31] In the Coimbra altarpiece, moreover, Massys seems to have taken much more personal responsibility for the painting than he had done for the Madre de Deus retable, for, with the exception of several of the less-accomplished grotesque faces in the wings, there is no evidence of work by assistants.

After the greater attention to the holy figures of the *Seven Sorrows altarpiece,* the Coimbra *Passion*
altarpiece develops a much more intense investigation of mankind's role in the torments of Christ. This
concentration on the contrast between the suffering saint and the crowd of grotesque mockers had
Pl. 15 already been a feature of the *Martyrdom of John the Evangelist* wing of the Antwerp altarpiece. Massys
Pl. 86 would later develop this *Ecce Homo* as an independent picture (Madrid; Venice). In each case, a hostile
Pl. 87 jeering crowd contrasts with a battered and stoically resigned Christ, who resembles the image of the
Man of Sorrows, a highly popular object of indulgences and meditation in the late Middle Ages.[32]

In the case of the Coimbra *Passion altarpiece* the viewer is not allowed to meditate dispassionately on the sufferings of Christ. Instead, Massys deliberately includes the viewer within the hostile crowds of the *Flagellation* and *Ecce Homo.* This inclusion is accomplished, first, by placing the observer in a fixed viewpoint. The oblique views of both settings are meant to be seen from a determined central position. In the *Flagellation,* Christ appears at eye level, open and vulnerable to the gaze of the observer, who seems to complete the circle of assailants. In the *Ecce Homo,* Christ is elevated above the direct gaze of the viewer. As if this were not enough to make him feel uncomfortably like a member of the nearly life-sized rabble below, the observer is included directly by members of the crowd who gaze backward at him from within the painting. At the lower right edge of the panel, a hateful participant in the drama turns casually and looks over his shoulder out of the picture, as if to elicit more support.

This is Massys' strongest indictment of ordinary mankind, for it is no longer possible to regard the grotesque tormentors of religious pictures as "them"—historically remote or alien personalities apart from the modern world. Instead, all men, including the viewer of the Coimbra altarpiece, must share the blame for Christ's Passion. It is no longer possible simply to meditate on His wounds or His suffering, as in the case of the *Seven Sorrows retable.* The image of the Mater Dolorosa from the missing central panel offers the fullest possible contrast to this uncomprehending misconduct on the part of mankind. Her absolute compassion, already celebrated in the central image of the *Seven Sorrows altarpiece* and in the Antwerp *Lamentation,* is the heroic example which ordinary men seem either unwilling or unable to follow.

The Coimbra *Passion altarpiece* suggests why Massys was not forthcoming later with many other altarpieces, particularly on the subject of the Passion of Christ. The artist showed himself in the Coimbra altarpiece as intensely aware of his own mortal shortcomings and moral responsibilities, and these inadequacies seemed all the more vivid in contrast with the compassion of the Virgin or the virtue of the saints. Possibly for this reason, his future work in the sphere of religious pictures led to the production of isolated, small-scale works centered on Christ and the Virgin and emphasizing in particular their tender and loving interaction, either as Madonna and Child or as Pietà groups (see Chap. 4 for the late Madonna icons and Chap. 5 for the late religious devotional narratives). Beauty and love become the possession only of the saintly world in Massys' art.

The *Passion altarpiece* incorporates a late medieval theological position that builds on the sufferings of Christ and the consciousness of mankind's guilt: "perpetual Passion."[33] According to this concept, Christ endures continual suffering up to the time of the Last Judgment for the ongoing sins of men. Massys' contrast of evil Jews with the submissive Christ thereby becomes a modern concern that involves the viewer. The same outlook is made specific in the text of Dürer's 1511 frontispiece to the *Large Woodcut Passion* (B.4), another of the print cycles emphasizing the suffering of Christ. An image of the seated Man of Sorrows, located beyond earth above a band of clouds, is confronted by a cruel, sneering adversary. Affixed to the print are verses by Benedictus Chelidonius:

> These cruel wounds I bear for thee, O man,
> And cure thy mortal sickness with my blood
> I take away thy sores with mine, thy death
> With mine—a God who changed to man for thee.
> But thou, ingrate, still stabb'st my wounds with sins,
> I still take the floggings for thy guilty acts.
> It should have been enough to suffer once
> From hostile Jews; now, friend, let there be peace![34]

This address to the viewer is a charge to contemplate the sufferings of Christ with guilt and in the present as an iconic vision that repeats a tragic narrative.

Massys' final exported altarpiece to Portugal does nothing to contradict the meditative and penitent quality in the Coimbra *Passion altarpiece.* The final Portuguese altar export was not made for the king but for Damião de Gois, who began his career in Antwerp in 1523 as secretary to the Portuguese trading company of India House, but who rapidly established contacts with Antwerp intellectuals in the humanist community.[35] In Antwerp, de Gois studied Latin with Cornelius Grapheus, learned city secretary and an early champion of Luther's religious ideas (see Chap. 8 for a possible portrait by Massys of Grapheus: the Frankfurt *Scholar,* F. 46, cat. 61). Eventually de Gois even carried on *Pl. 146* correspondence with Erasmus.[36] Thus, the contacts and affiliations of the Portuguese representative began to overlap those of Massys during the same period of the 1520s (see Chapter 6 on Massys and the humanist community). Moreover, de Gois was a cultivated man who was keenly interested in Flemish art. He ordered a tapestry cycle of the months and illuminated manuscripts for King John III,[37] and he patronized the Bruges illuminator Simon Bening for a volume for Prince Dom

Ferdinand and a second for himself (later given as a gift to Queen Catherine). De Gois also enjoyed the company of João Bandão, the Portuguese factor who had, in all probability, already been the go-between for the Massys *Seven Sorrows altarpiece* during his earlier tenure in Antwerp and who commissioned various works from Dürer during the German artist's visit to Antwerp in 1520–21.[38]

For many reasons, then, both of taste and of common interests, de Gois was led to Massys, who painted him a *Crucifixion polyptych,* presumably commissioned for personal meditation although later presented to the Church of Nossa Senhora de Varzea (Alenquer).[39] This altarpiece, now lost, is the only known Massys retable datable to the period of the 1520s, but it is an exception that richly illustrates the rule. The altarpiece is the product of a special commission by a client whose ties to Massys were probably affinity and friendship rather than business. This assertion would simply be a surmise were it not for the surviving testimonial by Cornelius Grapheus, who wrote three poems in praise of Massys' paintings as an appendix to de Gois's Legation of 1532.[40] These poems not only serve to underscore the close personal affection of the Antwerp humanist for his Portuguese Latin student, but also provide evidence of a friendship, tied to religious and intellectual sympathies and to personal contact, which is analogous to Massys' involvement with Erasmus and Peter Gillis in 1517.[41] The poems also serve as a valuable indication of how such altarpieces would have been experienced by a pious and learned viewer like Grapheus during the period in which such an audience seems to have had special significance for, and influence on, Massys.

The first of the poems, addressed to the image of the crucified Christ on the cross, is a lament by the poet of his own sins and the sorrow that they must cause his redeemer. This poem is in the meditative spirit of late medieval piety, fixed on the suffering of Christ and specifically colored with the sense of a "perpetual Passion." The second verse addresses the crucifix as well, both lamenting the sufferings of Christ and praying for the salvation of the author. The final poem is addressed to Mary weeping under the cross in prayer, like the surviving fragment of the Coimbra *Passion altarpiece;* presumably she had a similar appearance in the de Gois retable.[42]

These poems by Grapheus underscore attitudes that already could be seen in the Coimbra *Passion altarpiece,* attitudes that stress the viewer's intensive personal contemplation of the religious significance of the scene. The phenomenon is not unique to Massys or Grapheus; indeed, it is the essence of the peculiar blend of practical mysticism that is the common thread of so much late medieval religiosity, from Thomas à Kempis and the *devotio moderna* to the Reformers of the 16th century: fervor admixed with guilt and humility (see also Chap. 5).[43] Meditation, like the poetic meditation of Grapheus, was the cornerstone of that approach to devotion, the indispensible approach to the Imitation of Christ. Art, like the literary anthologies (*riparia*), such as the *Rosetum* (or *Rosary of Spiritual Exercises*) of Mombaer (d. 1501), was conceived as a spiritual exercise, an aid to devotion and personal piety. We shall see (Chap. 4, 5) how Massys' religious imagery consistently moves toward a human and accessible image of the Virgin and of Christ and toward an increasingly more votive and isolated presentation of Gospel narratives precisely in order to stimulate a response from his viewers akin to the poems of Grapheus.

With the exception, then, of the *retablo* format of the *Seven Sorrows altarpiece,* which itself was a subject deeply imbedded in the religious life of the Antwerp painters' guild, none of the Massys altarpieces exported to Portugal was accommodated to a different viewing audience. Instead, the altarpieces reveal Massys' own increasingly serious preoccupation with the physical location and pious reactions of his viewers as well as his use of the Flemish triptych format and Passion iconography to evoke spiritual meditation before the images. The final triptych for Damião de Gois was actually made when such large-scale religious works were no longer being painted by Massys, but the artistic and spiritual orientation of that Portuguese client seem to have been close enough to the artist's own to prevail upon him for one last effort.

In smaller-scale art for export, however, Massys seems to have been more eager to please his foreign clients on their own terms, and he accommodated himself to specific requests. The most obvious example of this is a series of iconic portraits of *Saint Bernardino of Siena* (cat. 23), the famous 15th-century Observantine Franciscan preacher (d. 1444).[44] Bernardino was known for his fiery sermons against licentiousness, for his defense of orthodoxy, and for his cult of the Holy Name of Jesus. St. Bernardino was not a frequently invoked holy figure in the Netherlands, in part because he had only recently been canonized, in part because his great triumphs and largest following were in Italy. Where St. Bernardino does appear, along with St. Donatien and St. Martin in a Gerard David wing, he serves as the name saint for another Italian donor, Bernardinus Salviati, canon of the Church of St. Donatien in Bruges (1498–1519) and illegitimate son of a Florentine merchant (London, National Gallery).[45]

Three Massys-related images of *St. Bernardino* survive, all based upon the same basic prototype. Two are clearly by the Massys workshop and are the work of copyists. One is in the Descalzas Reales convent, Madrid, the other in the Civic Museum, Feltre—both localities in Latinate countries where the preaching of St. Bernardino had lasting effect. A third image (Lisbon, Salazar coll.) has the best claim to being a Massys original (although the *Seven Sorrows altarpiece* serves as a reminder that the artist was by no means averse to sending something abroad under his own label that had not been completely created by his own hand).

When Massys went to paint his own *San Bernardino,* he was well prepared. The picture bears a close resemblance to the standardized Italian images, such as the panel by Sano di Pietro (Brussels) and other 15th-century Sienese masters, although in this case, like Massys' use of Leonardo drawings for some of his grotesques, there is no demonstrable link between the Italian models and the Flemish result.[46] But the Massys image has all the essential elements of the model icon of St. Bernardino: bald and wrinkled pate, gaunt and angular features, brown cowl and cassock of the Franciscan order, and the IHS monogram ("Jesus Hominum Salvator") of the Holy Name in a glory, surrounded by curving golden beams of sunlight. This image of St. Bernardino is presented in bust-length format and the monochrome background of portraits, enabling Massys to suggest both the proximity of the saint and the verisimilitude of the depicted likeness.

Unlike Massys' previous exports, however, the *San Bernardino* is a cult image, a protector saint or intercessor for the devout worshipper. Like the role of St. Bernardino as name and patron saint for Bernardinus Salviati in the David panel, the Massys saint and his monogram are intended to be invoked as objects of piety. This Massys panel, then, should be compared not to large altarpieces but rather to votive images of the Madonna and Child or private objects of piety, such as the *Rem altarpiece* (F. 3, cat. 24; see below).

Once again the crucial agent in the creation of the image was a Portuguese royal factor in the Antwerp trading establishment. In this case, the factor was Ruy, or Rodrigo, Fernandes de Almada, who shared duties (after 1517; he had been a clerk since 1512) with the aforementioned João Brandão. Like Brandão, Fernandes also met Dürer during 1521 and received engravings from the German artist.[47] We do not have the specific knowledge of Ruy Fernandes that survives concerning Damião de Gois, but we do know that he worked his way up through the ranks of the Portuguese trading company from clerk to factor and that he eventually became Portuguese ambassador to France in 1537, so his loyalty to the crown and to the Catholic faith is beyond question. We do not know about any special attachment of Fernandes to the Franciscan order of St. Bernardino, but King Manuel is known to have taken an interest in the order; in 1514, he directed Silvester Nunes, the factor responsible for the Coimbra *Passion altarpiece,* to communicate with Antwerp's Franciscans concerning the ambassador to Portugal from the mythic kingdom of Prester John.[48] Devotion to St. Bernardino, then, was certainly readily available to Fernandes, and his picture of the saint toes the line of visual and theological orthodoxy. For this Portuguese factor, Massys created an image of personal piety that is clearly made to order and expressly suited to its recipient.

The other side of the trading connection in Antwerp was supplied by South German merchants, who previously had been based in Venice (the Fondaco dei Tedeschi) to take advantage of the rich Mediterranean trade with the Orient. When the Portuguese made sea contact with the Orient and thereby by-passed the overland trade routes of the Levant, the South Germans shifted their own center of trade to coincide with that of the Portuguese. The main exchange consisted of Portuguese spices for German metals, especially copper, which was the prized and crucial commodity exchanged in West Africa for slaves.[49] Unlike the Portuguese trading establishment, however, the German traders were not the arm of a powerful national effort, headed by a king; instead they were family corporations from independent cities of the Holy Roman Empire, chiefly Augsburg and Nuremberg. The largest and most famous of the South German trading companies was that of the Fuggers of Augsburg, whose financial prominence was chiefly the result of an imperial stake in rich Tyrolean copper and silver mines, and whose notoriety was chiefly an outgrowth of their astronomical loans to Charles V for the bribes he paid in 1519 for election to the crown of Holy Roman Emperor.[50]

Another family trading company in Antwerp was the Welser family of Augsburg, the first South German corporation to establish a trading company in Lisbon, and which, during the period 1505–17, was the leading European dealer in spices.[51] After 1509, the Antwerp representative of the Welsers was Lucas Rem, who also traveled extensively on business to such Welser outposts as Lisbon, Lyons, and Cologne. Rem compiled a diary, which reveals him to have been a deeply religious man; in addition to his business travels, he made several religious pilgrimages, a sign of pious commitment during Massys' period and one which the artist commemorated in one of his early portraits, the
Pl. 138 *Jerusalem Pilgrim* (after 1509; Winterthur, Reinhart coll.; F. 38, cat. 53). Rem also took a serious
Pl. 37 interest in religious art and commissioned works from both Massys (Munich, Alte Pinakothek; F. 3, cat. 24) and from Joachim Patinir (Philadelphia, Johnson coll.) during the teens.[52]

The small triptych that Massys produced for Rem is datable through Rem's own diary. Rem's first visit to Antwerp was 1508, and he resided there periodically between 1511 and 1518. The diary records that in 1516–17, his earnings were converted into "paintings, gems, and fabrics" in Antwerp. The Massys *Rem altarpiece* not only bears the arms of the merchant, but also shows his patron saint, Luke, on its exterior. In addition, the triptych shows the arms of Rem's wife, Anna Ochainen, and her patron saint, Anne, on the outside wing. The couple were married in Augsburg on 17 May 1518, so the commission of the altarpiece took place on one of Rem's returns to Antwerp after his marriage. The diary tells us that those Antwerp visits took place between September 1518 and January 1519, and also between April and July of 1520. In other words, the small personal triptych that Massys made for the Augsburg patrician merchant was situated between the Coimbra *Passion altarpiece,* made on commission for the King of Portugal, and the *Crucifixion altarpiece,* made a few years later for Damião de Gois.

Unlike the two Passion altarpieces for Portugal, however, the triptych for Lucas Rem is small in scale and personally tailored to the specifications of the donor. The central cult figures are the Holy Trinity and the Madonna of the Sun. On the interior wings are Saints Sebastian and Roch; on the exterior, St. Luke and the *Anna Selbdritt.* Instead of religious events, this triptych features favored saints; instead of carefully delineated spaces and a coordinated single point of view, as in the Coimbra *Passion altarpiece,* the *Rem triptych* is entirely visionary and privately subjective, with no attempt to relate the wings to the center. Only the sensibility of the donor and his individual combination of devotions serve to unite the disparate parts of this votive image. The nearest precedent for such a compilation of cult images was the Memling *St. Christopher triptych,* featuring St. Christopher, St. Giles, and St. Maur in the central panel and the Bruges patrician Willem Moreel and his family kneeling in prayerful devotion on the wings (1484, Bruges, Groeninge Museum).[53]

Unlike Moreel, Rem does not appear in his own altarpiece; instead, he and his wife are replaced by their name saints on the exterior wings—a frequent pattern of 15th-century altarpieces, where sometimes the donor is also included alongside the saints (e.g., the Ghent altarpiece of van Eyck, the Beaune altarpiece of van der Weyden, or the *St. Catherine triptych* of Memling). The saints on the interior wings of the *Rem altarpiece,* however, are intercessors rather than personal saints. Saints Roch and Sebastian were very popular saints in the late Middle Ages, for they were invoked as special protectors against the plague. St. Sebastian's healing powers are reported in the *Golden Legend,* the compendium of saints' lives compiled during the 13th century.[54] According to legend, a plague in Pavia was not quelled until an angel revealed that an altar to St. Sebastian would provide a cure. St.

Roch, on the other wing, was a healer of more recent pedigree. He lived in the 14th century and began to be venerated (as was St. Bernardino) only in the second half of the 15th century, when a series of biographies appeared.[55] According to his legend, Roch suffered from the plague and retired into the wilderness, where he was fed by a dog. An angel asked the dying saint what he desired, and he replied that all Christians should be free of the plague. An Antwerp guild to St. Roch was established as early as 1485,[56] and the frequent epidemic outbursts of the 14th and 15th centuries made such guardian saints as Roch and Sebastian the object of fervent cults. In Rem's diary, a prayer for deliverance from the plague is addressed to the very same pair who are depicted on the wings of the Massys triptych.[57] There was reason for the prayer: Antwerp suffered outbreaks of the plague three times while Rem was living there—in 1513, 1515, and 1517.[58]

In the center of the image are two isolated standing figures, images of the Trinity and the Apocalyptic Virgin of the Sun, the Madonna on a Crescent. These two images are traditional images with extensive cults of their own. The image of the Trinity appears substantially unaltered from 15th-century versions, such as the panel by Robert Campin in Louvain or the sculpture of Campin's *Werl altarpiece* wing (1438) in the Prado.[59] In essence, the image of the Trinity is mystical, based on a concept rather than an event of the Gospels. It is essentially a static symbolic image representing a theological doctrine, but at the same time it is laden with emotion: the presentation of the crucified Christ by God the Father. In this respect, the Trinity image borrows from the current meditations on the crucifix and the wounds of Christ. As such, it was a perfect devotional image, suitable for cult worship and strong emotional attachment and retaining its otherworldly, awe-inspiring majesty through the nimbus of warm, glowing light around the figures.

The figure of the Virgin on the Crescent, or *Maria in Sole,* drawn from the vision described in Revelations, was connected more specifically with a recent cult of its own. It was an indulgenced image; that is, it accorded a remission of penitential suffering in the afterlife when it was the object of specified prayers and meditations.[60] The prayer was attributed to Pope Sixtus IV, the same pontiff who endorsed the efficacy of the cult of the rosary in 1478; it was strongly associated with the cult of the Virgin of the Immaculate Conception, which is specifically mentioned in the prayer "You who were conceived without sin, conceived Jesus without sin."[61] Sixtus IV propagated the cult of the Immaculate Conception; in 1476, he introduced an office for the Feast of the Immaculate Conception and supported it with indulgences in papal bulls of the same year. Associated with these indulgences and prayers, the Virgin on the Crescent—crowned, elevated on a sculpted pedestal, bathed in glowing rays of sunlight—is herself the embodiment of godly purity and Christian grace, a visual symbol of doctrine and majesty that forms the fitting complement to Rem's adjacent Trinity.

That Massys has tried conscientiously to harmonize the two images is demonstrated by the extraneous inclusion at the foot of God the Father and the Crucifix. It is a globe that visually supports the Trinity, as the pedestal supports the Apocalyptic Virgin, but that serves also to underscore the cosmic significance and dominion of the Trinity, as the crescent moon reinforces the otherworldliness of the heavenly Madonna and Child of Revelations. The globe also has personal significance for Lucas Rem, for it depicts the newly explored lands of Africa and Asia, which were the essential backbone of the Portuguese trade with Germany in Lisbon and Antwerp. When Rem had been in Lisbon as the representative of the Welsers, he had organized the wondrous expedition to India of 1506–07, which was described by Balthazar Springer and illustrated with woodcuts by Hans Burgkmair of Augsburg (1508).[62] Thus, these new worlds which had recently come to accept the dominion of the Trinity under the auspices of the Portuguese and their Augsburg trading allies were assisted in this missionary enterprise by the very donor of this altarpiece, Lucas Rem, whose arms appear so proudly underneath the figures of the Trinity and the Maria in Sole.

Like St. Luke and St. Anne of the outer wings, the personal protectors of Rem and his new bride, or like the two saints Sebastian and Roch of the interior wings, traditional intercessors against the plague, the Trinity and the Maria in Sole had private significance for the donor and were put into the altarpiece at his specific request. Koch has discovered that the Trinity and the Virgin were specifically addressed in Rem's prayers for his marriage, recorded in his diary.[63] They are the all-powerful foundations of the Christian faith, of course, but at the same time the Trinity and the Immaculate Virgin are also the special protectors of the Augsburg merchant's sacrament of marriage. Rem's entire altarpiece is a personal talisman, tailor-made protection against plague or any other misfortune for himself and his new wife.

The *Rem altarpiece* is the most cult-centered devotional altarpiece made by Massys for foreign export, even as it is the most personal in design. This commission by the Augsburg merchant in Antwerp serves as a reminder of the city's crucial mediation between Portuguese spices and German metals and the currency exchanges that resulted from that trade. The *Rem altarpiece* also recalls the Portuguese factors and merchant representatives who were the real mediators between Massys and Portuguese royalty in his exported altarpieces. Even when his retables came to ornament a royal monastery in distant Portugal, Massys remained unexposed to the trappings of court or even any contact with diplomats or ambassadors from court. His connections resulted from the mercantile character of Antwerp and his early contact with the new Portuguese trading community, perhaps through the intervention of his own former apprentice, the Portuguese named Eduart. Even where personal sympathies may have added an extra dimension to the completion of an altarpiece for export—the case of Damião de Gois—Massys came to meet his patron as much through the Portuguese trading network as through any web of social or intellectual connections.

Massys did not make many concessions to his foreign audience and its idiosyncracies. He knew that, for the most part, the larger altarpieces were going to serve as pious donations in distant monastic churches, so he was willing to engage workshop assistants for much of the work of the export items; this is true not only of the large-scale *Seven Sorrows altarpiece,* made at a particularly busy time for the artist, but also for the small-scale, personal altarpiece of Lucas Rem. In the case of the icons of *St. Bernardino,* no single image has the certain stamp of Massys himself. Moreover, Massys made little attempt to alter the Flemish triptych conventions, with the exception of his employing the *retablo* format for the *Seven Sorrows altarpiece.* For the most part, his subjects remained the topical religious preoccupations of the early 16th century, the cults that were current in his own Antwerp, even in his own guild of St. Luke (although, in the cases of the *St. Bernardino*s and the *Rem altarpiece,* Massys responded to a particular request outside his general artistic pattern or local religious interests). His Passion altarpieces, in fact, were a most common sort of export items; their spectacles of crowds, costumes, and dramatic gestures, their melodramas of religious torment, had already become clichés, especially in the sculpted altarpieces shipped from Antwerp and Brussels to such faraway places as Scandinavia and to such nearby provincial locations as northern France and rural Flanders.[64] Significantly, the Passion scenes of the Coimbra *Passion altarpiece* are the images that compare most closely to both the martyrdom themes and the Antwerp Mannerist formal idiom of the *St. John altarpiece* (1508–11; F. 1, cat. 11; see Chap. 2).

Yet in his export works, Massys managed to inject a personal stamp that distinguishes his work from the standardized formulas that often shaped his commissions. Already in the *Seven Sorrows altarpiece,* the Worcester *Rest on the Flight* reveals the artist's own personal religious sentimentality—overt maternal tenderness, tinged with sorrow, which makes either the *Pietà* or the *Madonna and Child* the quintessential religious image by Massys. In the Coimbra *Passion altarpiece,* the other side of Massys' religious temperament comes through: his profound sense of distance, as a sinner, from the poetic beauty of religious purity. The Passion scenes that were such a commonplace on exported sculpted retables became a stimulus to Massys' sensibility and a vehicle for dramatizing the contrast between the godly, submissive Christ and the brutally ugly tormentors who effect His Passion. As in the case of the
Pl. 15 Antwerp *Martyrdom of St. John the Evangelist,* the delicate beauty of the holy figures is magnified through Massys' contempt for their wicked antagonists in a sinful world. This gulf between the mundane and the holy, between the sinful and the perfect, informs all of Massys' art and is confirmed by the verses by Grapheus in response to Massys' altarpiece for de Gois.

To the best of our current knowledge, the de Gois altarpiece was the last large-scale image produced by Massys. Increasingly, his own religious predilections turned away from the public art of ecclesiastical decoration toward a private realm of intense personal prayer and meditative devotion. At the end of his career, Massys' output was dominated by the votive Madonna images that better served these private religious functions. The personalized altarpiece of Lucas Rem and the religious poetry of Cornelius Grapheus together form the background of piety that led Massys away from the large-scale production of altarpieces and away from art designed for export.

NOTES

1. E.Mâle, *L'art religieux,* p. 123f.; W.H. Gerdts, "The Sword of Sorrow," *Art Quarterly* 17 (1954): 213–24; Toussaert, *Le Sentiment Religieux au Flandre,* pp. 283–85. On the general theme of the grieving Madonna of the Passion, see *Stabat Mater,* exh. cat., Salzburg, 1972, as well as the fine discussion of the Virgin of com-Passion in van der Weyden's Prado *Deposition* by O. von Simson, "*Compassio* and *Co-redemptio* in Roger van der Weyden's *Descent from the Cross,*" p. 9ff.

2. Friedländer, vol. 7, p. 51, no. 103. According to the Antwerp Museum, the altarpiece came from the Church of St. Catherine at Hoogstraeten.

3. Friedländer, vol. 8, pp. 89, 94–95.

4. Friedländer, vol. 7, p. 67, no. 63; de Bosque, *Quentin Massys,* p. 156 (with bibliography). According to the Brussels catalogue, this workshop image was painted before 1505 for the house of the Guild of St. Luke, Antwerp, the very guild of which Massys was a member. Both the figure types and landscape resemble Massys' later Louvre *Pietà* (F. 16, cat. 17), a work of the artist's middle "Patiniresque" period of the teens; therefore, the traditional date of a decade earlier, ca. 1505, is improbable. *Pl. 94*

5. Prims, *Geschiedenis van Antwerpen,* pp. 142–43; idem, "De St. Lucasguilde en de Zeven Weden," *Antwerpiensia* 13 (1939).

6. On Windesheim and the *devotio moderna* in general, see especially R.R. Post, *The Modern Devotion;* R.W. Southern, *Western Society and the Church in the Middle Ages,* pp. 331–58; F. Oakley, *The Western Church in the Late Middle Ages,* pp. 100–113; A. Hyma, *The Christian Renaissance* (Grand Rapids, p. 192); S. Axters, *Geschiedenis van de vroomheid in de Nederlanden III. De Moderne Devotie;* Delaruelle, Labande, and Ourliac, pp. 911–42.

7. J.F. Kronenberg, *Maria's Heerlijkheid in Nederland,* vol. 2, pp. 211–18.

8. Prims, "De St. Lucasgilde," p. 143.

9. Ibid.

10. J. Huizinga, *Waning of the Middle Ages,* pp. xiv, 190–91.

11. Post, *KV,* p. 459.

12. M. Meertens, *De godsvrucht in de Nederlanden naar handschriften van gebenboeken der XVe eeuw,* vol.2 (Louvain, 1930), p. 83.

13. Ibid., p. 86; Ringbom, *Icon to Narrative,* p. 26.

14. Meertens, vol. 1, pp. 135-41.

15. Mâle, *L'art religieux,* pp. 122ff, 205ff; Delaruelle, Labande, and Ourliac, p. 777ff.; Kronenberg, *Maria's Heerlijkheid,* passim.

16. Ringbom, *Icon to Narrative,* pp. 27–28, and "*Maria in Sole* and the Virgin of the Rosary," p. 362ff; Post, *KV,* p. 463.

17. For Aertsen, see Friedländer, vol. 13, no.294; for the Memling work, Friedländer, vol. 6, no. 33, containing the Circumcision and Massacre of the Innocents, so it cannot be considered a canonical sequence of the Joys of Mary. For this cult, see Kronenberg, vol.2, pp. 204–10.

18. Kronenberg, pp. 211–78. See also n. 1, above.

19. Prims, *Geschiedenis,* p. 144, n.1.

20. Van Styevoort, no. 151: *Lof alder bedrueste moeder ons Heren:* O suete Maria, hoe was u te moede / Als ghi Jesum voer u doot hebt gheleijt, / Mismaect, mishandelt, nat van bloede, / Overvloeijende tranen hebodij doen ghescreyt. / Mit bedructer herten hebdij gheseyt: / 'Siet hier donnosel lammken van sonden vrij, / Mensche, dess pijne was my soe bereyt / Duer u, dus coomt doch en helpt claghen mij, / Dijn scepper aensiet, hoe vol wonden is Hij, / Mets u sculde is mijn kint ter doot gheraect. / Mijn vriendekens, staet my doch met tranen bij. / Ende siet mijnen sone uven God mismaect . . .'

See also E.H.F. de Ridder, "De Devotie tot Onze Lieve Vrouw van VII Weën, haar ontstaan," *Handelingen van het vlaamsch Maria-Congres te Brussel,* vol. 2 (Brussels [1922]).

21. Flemish fascination with St. Joseph had found expression a century earlier in Robert Campin's *Merode altarpiece* (New York, Cloisters), for which see M. Schapiro, " 'Muscipula diaboli,' The Symbolism of the Merode Altarpiece," *Art Bulletin* 27 (1945): 182ff; also Huizinga, p. 168f. The cult of Joseph was promoted by Jean Gerson; see Delaruelle, Labande, and Ourliac, p. 857.

22. Friedländer, vol. 9, p. 11, no. 2; *Les Primitifs Flamands I.10 La cathedrale de Palencia* (Brussels, 1967), p. 47; R. Revilla Vieloa, "El triptico de Fonseca en el Trascoro de la Catedral de Palencia," *Publicaciones de la Institucion "Tello Tellez de Meneses"* 2 (1949): 113–28.

23. K. Justi, "Der Altarschrein des licentiaten Gonzalez in San Salvador zu Valladolid," p. 24ff.; de Bosque, pp. 137–45.

24. Miskimin, *Later Renaissance Europe,* pp. 124–30. For foreign colonies in Antwerp, see Goris, *Les colonies marchandes.* A fine survey of international trade and banking in Bruges is R. de Roover, *Money, Banking, and Credit in Medieval Bruges.*

25. Reis-Santos, "Edouard Portugalois," p. 185ff.; van Puyvelde, "Edouard Portugalois," pp. 288–95.

26. L. Reis-Santos, *Masterpieces of Flemish Painting of the XV and XVI Centuries in Portugal,* pp. 83–84 (with bibliography); R. dos Santos, *O Poliptico da Madre de Deus de Quintino Metsys.*

27. For the Portuguese nation in Antwerp, Goris, *Les colonies marchandes;* Prims, vol. 7.2, *Economische Leven,* 166ff.; J. Denucé, *Privilèges commerciaux.* Brandão also commissioned several works from Dürer during his visit to Antwerp in 1520–1521 (Goris and Marlier, *Dürer Diary,* pp. 58, 62).

28. The painting is fully discussed by D.T. Robbins, "Landscape in the Art of Quentin Massys," summarized here under cat. 12. The 1517 contract in Bruges for Albert Cornelisz. (active 1513–32) to paint an altarpiece of angel choirs for the guild of St. Francis specifies clearly that the artist himself—and he alone—is to paint all the nudes and other essential parts in the large panel over a period of two years (Friedländer, vol.11, pp. 54–55; G. Marlier, *Ambrosius Benson,* pp. 50–52). Like the evidence of a law that prohibits an undesired action and thus bears witness to that very action, this contract makes clear how widespread was the practice of delegating tasks to a painting workshop, especially for the larger-scale works like altarpieces. Moreover, in 1519, the council of the guild of St. Francis sued Cornelisz. for breach of contract on this very point!

29. E. Haverkamp-Begemann, *European Paintings in the Collection of the Worcester Art Museum* (Worcester, 1974), pp. 190–97.

30. J. Figueiredo, "Metsys et le Portugal," p. 6; Reis-Santos, *Masterpieces of Flemish Painting,* pp. 85–86.

31. A close comparison to the Coimbra *Virgin* is the Mater Dolorosa in a Massys workshop *Crucifixion triptych* in Brussels (F.58); see de Bosque, p. 198.

32. Ringbom, *Icon to Narrative,* p. 25. A workshop excerpt of the head of the *Suffering Christ,* drawn from the Venice *Ecce Homo* (Antwerp, Koninklijk Museum) would have served a similar devotional function. For the larger issue of images of the Suffering Christ, see E. Panofsky, "Jean Hey's 'Ecce Homo,' " p. 95ff.

33. Panofsky, "Jean Hey" and *Albrecht Dürer,* pp. 138–39.

34. Translated by Panofsky, *Albrecht Dürer.*

35. E.F. Hirsch, *Damião de Gois* (The Hague, 1967); M. Bataillon, "Le Cosmopolitanisme de Damião de Gois," *Etudes sur le Portugal au temps de l'humanisme* (Coimbra, 1952), pp. 149–96; A. Bell, *Un Humanista Portugues: Damião de Gois* (Lisbon, 1942); J. Segurado, "Damião de Goes," *Belas Artes* 28–29 (1975): 133–84.

36. P.S. Allen and H.M. Allen, *Opus epistolarium Desiderius Erasmus Roterodami* (Oxford, 1906–58), nos. 2826, 2914, 3085 (vols. 10, 11; see X, 251–55 for de Gois's life).

37. Hirsch, *de Gois,* pp. 44–45, citing a letter of 1530 to the king.

38. See note 27.

39. Figueiredo, *Metsys et le Portugal,* p. 9f. See also "Documented Lost Works" (Appendix C).

40. I am grateful to Professor Josua Bruyn for calling my attention to this passage; the title page credits "Joann. Grapheus typis excudebat anno MD XXXII mense Septemb. Cum Privilegio Caesareo, ad Triennium."

41. Grapheus was expelled from Antwerp in 1522 for his "Lutheran" sympathies (see Chap. 8; also F. Prims, "Grapheus en Goch," "Het eigen werk van Cornelis Grapheus (1482–1558)," *Antwerpiensia* 12 [1938]: 165–91). By no coincidence at all, de Gois made contacts with several Reformers and even visited Luther's Wittenberg in 1531 (see Hirsch, p. 22ff.).

42. Cited in abbreviated form in Hirsch, p. 47, n.46. The complete text reads as follows:

> Cor.Graphei, senat. Antverpien a Secretis, carmina aliquot in Damianum Goes Lusitanum. / Pro eodem, in imaginem / Herculi auro artificiosissime insculpta / En omnia Hercules domat / Victor, sed illum mox domat Potens Cupido, ergo quid hen Quid irribus multo est minor? / Aliter / Victor hic Alcides victore Cupidine victus / Cedit, quae exiguis ergo Trophaea animis?
>
> Pro eodem, ad crucifixi / Christi imaginem, in caedrina tabella a / Quintino insigni pictore insigniter depictam. / Piget bone o Christe, ah piget / Mea est, mea est culpa haec, scio, / Quod sic relictus ab ominibus, / Quod tam cruentus undique; / Protectus altum in aera / Confixus hac pendes cruce, / Ergo ad tuos supplex pedes / Volutus, en adsum miser / Damianus hic tuus, mihi / Ignoscito, O ignoscito / Qui totius pro orbis malo / Hanc innocens poenam subis.
>
> Pro eodem, ad eam / ipsam imaginem. / Ah Christi, maximi, optime / Servator orbis perdite / Sola, unica, et certissima / Mortalium spes omnium, / Quem haec tua est adflicto? / Eheu quid his miserrimis / Hic cerno te adfectum modis? / Cen nullus aut erres latro / Porrectum in horrendae crucis / Durissimo istoc stipite, / Imo a pede usque ad verticem / Toto cruentum corpore. / Ah Christe nostrum hoc est scelus / Fatemur, ah nos nos sumus / Causa huius, Ipse te Pater / Nostri omnium pro crimine / Sic adfecit, Te ergo obsecro / O Christi, me, me inquam tuum / Damiano hunc, deperditam / Joan hanc ovem, sanctissimo / Tuo repertam sanguine, / Serva, fons, pane, a tuis / Ut nusquam aberrans semitis / Presto tibi adsit jugiter.
>
> Pro eodem in Virginem Mariam sub filii cruci orantem, / pereleganti pictura a Quintino in tabella depictam. / En virgo mater optima / Sub filii plorans cruce, / Utraque protensa manu, / Pro te misere homo piis / Supplex precatur vocibus / Mi nate per durissima / Tua haec rogo te vulnera / O parce, parce simplici / Sinte, tibi usque; credulae, / Nullum imputam ei scelus / Qui cuncta tollis crimina.

43. S. Ozment, *Mysticism and Dissent* (New Haven, 1973), pp. 1–60; D. Knowles, *The English Mystical Tradition* (New York, 1961); Oakley, *The Western Church,* pp. 89–113; Huizinga, *Waning of the Middle Ages.*

44. Canonized by Pope Nicholas V in 1450, his remains are interred at San Francesco in L'Aquila. G. Kaftal, *Iconography of the Saints in Tuscan Painting* (Florence, 1952), cols. 195–200, no. 55; Delaruelle, Labande, and Ourliac, pp. 642–50. For the Observantine reform movement in the Franciscan Order, see Delaruelle, Labande, and Ourliac, pp. 1090–1100 (with bibliography); Oakley, pp. 231–38; I. Origo, *The World of San Bernardino* (New York, 1962). For the sermons of the saint, see D. Pacetti, ed., *San Bernardino da Siena: le predichi volgari inediti* (Siena, 1935). Also O.F.M. Longré, "Saint Bernardin et le nom de Jesus Christ," *Archivium Franciscanum Historicum* 28 (1935): 443–76; 29 (1936): 142–68, 443–77; 30 (1937): 170–92.

45. M. Davies, *The National Gallery: Les Primitifs Flamands I* (London, 1953), p. 82ff., and *Early Netherlandish School National Gallery Catalogues,* pp. 40–41, no.1045. The work is datable to a period after 1501 because of the donor's biography.

46. See Kaftal. L. Reis-Santos, *Le portrait de Saint Bernardin de Sienne par Quentin Metsys,* discusses all of the Massys versions of this image in the context of the artist's *oeuvre;* see also Reis-Santos, *Masterpieces of Flemish Painting,* pp. 87–88, no.49; de Bosque, pp. 170–71, ills. 182–83. The cult of the Holy Name of Jesus also enjoyed a vogue in Antwerp; see Prims, p. 144ff. We have
Pl. 5 already seen the devotional print of the IHS insignia in the hands of the young child of Mary Cleophas within Massys' *Holy*

Kinship of the *St. Anne altarpiece* (see Chapter 2). For the Holy Name and German art, see H. Feldbusch, "Christusmonogramm," *Reallexikon zur deutschen Kunstgeschichte* 3, cols.715–16.

47. Goris and Marlier, *Dürer Diary;* according to Reis-Santos, *Le Portrait de Saint Bernardin,* the Salazar *San Bernardino* can be traced to the legacy of the house of the Almadas, "Provedores da Casa da India" and the eventual collection of D. José Joaquim Lobo da Silveira e Almada, first count of Carvalhais. That collection came into the possession of Dr. Alberto Gomes de Olveira. Eventually, it was given by Dr. Ricardo de Espirito Santo Silva to President Salazar of Portugal.

48. Figueiredo, "Metsys et le Portugal," p. 8.

49. Miskimin, *Later Renaissance Europe,* p. 124ff.

50. Ibid., p. 164; R. Ehrenberg, *Das Zeitalter der Fugger* (Jena, 1896) Eng. trans. H.M. Lucas as *Capital and Finance in the Age of the Renaissance* [New York, 1963], pp. 66–67). "Fugger" was such a well-known synonym for wealth that it had become a common noun, like the modern "Rockefeller" or "Rothschild." An example of such usage is given in Cervantes' *Don Quixote* II, chap. 23, written a full century after this period, where the Don exclaims, "I only wish I were a Fugger that I might cure them."

51. Prims, vol. 7:2, pp. 151ff., discusses Germans in Antwerp, the Welsers in particular on pp. 163–65. For Rem, see the merchant's diary, B. Greiff, *Tagebuch des Lucas Rem* (Augsburg, 1861), as well as the biographical sketch by R. Koch, *Joachim Patinir,* p. 9 ff.

52. Koch, *Joachim Patinir.*

53. S. Blum, *Early Netherlandish Triptychs,* pp. 97–103; Friedländer, vol. 6, no. 12.

54. J. de Voragine, *Golden Legend,* p. 104ff. (Jan. 20).

55. Prims, vol. 7, pp. 147–48.

56. Ibid.; outbreaks of the plague in Antwerp occurred in 1490, 1513, 1515, and 1517.

57. "Gott durch forpitt Maria seinter werden muetter, Sct. Sebastian, Sct. Rochus, aler gotz heyligen hat mich gar wunderperlich behiet." Quoted by Koch, *Joachim Patinir,* p. 11.

58. Prims, vol. 7, pp. 147–48.

59. Friedländer, vol. 2, nos. 71a, 67.

60. Ringbom, *Icon to Narrative,* pp. 23–28.

61. Ibid, p. 26f.; Ringbom, *"Maria in Sole,"* pp. 326–30; M. Levi d'Ancona, *Immaculate Conception,* pp. 20–28. An example of the prayer appears on an Israhel van Meckenem engraving (Geisberg 164) of the *Madonna on a Crescent:* "Ave sanctissima Maria mater dei regina celi porta paradisisdomina mundi pura singularis virgo Tu sine peccato concepta concepisti Jhesum sine macula Tu peperisti creatorum et salvatorem mundi In quo non dubito libera me ab omni malo et ora pro peccato meo Amen. Sixtus papa quartus concessit undecim milia annorum pro qualibet vice."

62. *Hans Burgkmair Das graphische Werk,* exh. cat. (Stuttgart, 1973), nos. 26–7.

63. Koch, *Joachim Patinir,* p. 11.

64. See Chapter 2, note 43; for painted 16th-century scenes of martyrdom, see *Les Primitifs flamands anonymes.*

4

Private Piety: Devotional Icons

Most of Massys' religious paintings were not large, multi-panel images like the triptychs. Instead, they were smaller isolated panels, primarily depicting the Virgin and Child. Several of the panels emphasize elaborate settings or thrones in order to convey the exalted status of the Queen of Heaven. Others offer a much more intimate aspect of the Virgin, concentrating on her maternal tenderness for her Child. In several of the pictures, the presentation of the figures is close-up, bust- or half-length, as in a portrait. The effect of this group of religious pictures is almost always evocative of religious emotion, centered on the rendering of the holy figure, like the cult images at the center of the personal triptych made in 1518 for Lucas Rem (see Chap. 3). This "empathic meditation" lay at the heart of religious icons throughout the history of Christian art and enjoyed a particular importance in the religious art of the Netherlands to which Massys was heir.[1] The special religious emotion devoted to the Virgin, which we have seen in such triptychs as the *St. Anne altarpiece* or the Madre de Deus *Seven Sorrows altarpiece*, led to a proliferation of iconic versions of the Madonna as a major component of Massys' oeuvre. This interest in Madonna icons was a phenomenon of equal importance for Quinten's artistic contemporaries. Such portraitlike iconic images offer the strongest testimony to the religious sensibility of the late Middle Ages, which Huizinga has so vividly characterized as the "Crystallization of thought into Images."[2]

Massys' earliest pictures were iconic images of the Madonna, showing her enthroned with all the trappings of royalty and surrounded by angelic attendants. Probably the earliest of these images is the *Pl. 38* *Virgin Enthroned* of the National Gallery in London (F. 25, cat. 1), where the balance, symmetry, and full-length treatment lend a severity and majesty to the Virgin and Child. A glittering gold throne emphasizes the queenly status; radiating golden beams in a halo emphasize the otherworldly nature of the Madonna. In the Eyckian tradition of rich ornamental accessories, the Virgin's robe is bordered with precious stones, and an elaborate carpet lies at her feet. The presence of angels hovering above her with a golden crown completes the effect of a celestial vision, as do the music-playing angels alongside the throne.[3] Although the Christ Child, who wears a rosary around his neck, is shown in a more relaxed activity, reading precociously from a prayer book, his overall stiffness and frontality do little to disturb the immobile, solemn stillness of the picture as a whole. This image is an icon of the most severe and formal kind, representing the Virgin enthroned as Queen of Heaven and as Queen *in* Heaven. The hieratic qualities of the image recall the motionless enthroned Madonna of the

Byzantine tradition, the *Hodegiatria.*[4] In Netherlandish art, the prototype of the queenly enthroned Madonna was established canonically by Jan van Eyck with such images as the Dresden triptych of 1437 or the *Madonna of Canon van der Paele* of 1434–36 (Bruges, Groeninge Museum).[5] This tradition remained a powerful current in Bruges up to the time of Massys. Particularly influential were the numerous Madonnas Enthroned by Hans Memling (d. 1494), which featured not only the brocades and jewels later adopted by Massys, but also the angelic music-making entourage. Massys' contemporary in Bruges, Gerard David, also maintained the same tradition in his early work, such as the Louvre *Madonna Enthroned,* a triptych made for Jan de Sedano.[6]

These enthroned Madonnas were images clearly intended for adoration by the donor. Van Eyck's *Madonna of Canon van der Paele,* with the donor presented by his patron saint, George, makes this abundantly clear. The Virgin as celestial queen has granted a visionary audience to her pious supplicant.[7] Memling, in particular, continued this Eyckian tradition in both altarpieces and isolated panels that show a donor, kneeling, in prayerful attendance beside the enthroned Madonna. Saints and angels are the attendants of intermediate status. In contrast to the public large-scale imagery of the altarpiece retables, these cult images of the Madonna were pointedly intended for private worship; their reduced scale is also a result of this more personal intentionality.[8]

The personal and intimate aspect of such Madonna images is underscored by Massys' next pair of pictures of the Virgin. Instead of the full-length majesty of the London *Madonna,* these smaller images are presented as half-length icons with distinct overtones of portraits of royalty.[9] Both of Massys' images, the *Madonna and Child with Grapes* (lost) and the half-length *Madonna Enthroned* (Brussels; F. 20, cat. 3), feature elements indicating royalty. In the former case the elaborate gold throne is related to the London full-length *Madonna Enthroned*; in the latter, a brocade with fleurs-de-lis suspended by angels distinguishes the Virgin as queen. Both pictures feature the jeweled dress borders previously favored by van Eyck and Memling. Ringbom has demonstrated that the half-length form itself was a symbolic mode of presentation[10] because it was based on the portraits of emperors used in connection with the Roman Empire's ruler cult of the first centuries A.D. By extension, the half-length "portraits" of Christ or the Virgin were regarded as substitutes for the person of the divine ruler, just as the imperial portraits were intended as surrogates for the emperor.[11]

Pl. 40
Pl. 41
Pl. 39

In Netherlandish art, the half-length format as an object of direct veneration was made popular by Rogier van der Weyden, who frequently combined the form of the Virgin and Child with a second half-length, a portrait from real life of a donor in prayer, facing the icon of the Madonna. Panofsky calls these diptychs "devotional portraits."[12] They can also be seen within larger compositions as objects of private piety, such as the miniature of Philip the Good at mass, where the duke kneels before such a diptych that presumably includes his own portrait in prayer before the half-length *Virgin and Child* on the other wing.[13] Rogier also fathered a whole generation of separate half-length Madonna and Child images whose successors by Memling, David, Bouts and subsequent Netherlandish artists were a major feature of the painting tradition which Massys learned as a young man.[14] Unlike the Madonna half-lengths of Rogier, however, the images of Memling, and later Massys, were presented with indications of background and setting rather than a flat, monochrome, or gold ground.

The timeless or purely ideational vision of the mid-15th century has given way to the emphatic integration of the divine realm with the material world in Massys' images, a phenomenon already discussed for the *St. Anne* and *St. John altarpieces.* The Brussels half-length *Madonna Enthroned* reveals above the luxury brocade held from behind by angels a clear blue sky set off with clouds. The *Madonna with Grapes* goes even further toward establishing a clear spatial environment: it presents an interior with window openings at either side, overlooking a Flemish cityscape. The Madonna, therefore, is not only made manifest, indeed immanent, by the portraitlike presentation of her icon, but she is specifically linked to the experience of the pious beholder through both her maternal qualities of tenderness and her mundane, physical surroundings. Massys does not go as far in this direction as Memling had done, for example, in the diptych of Martin van Nieuwenhove (1487, St. John's Hospital, Bruges), where both the donor and the Virgin appear within the same, unified

Pl. 137

domestic space that overlaps the two panels of the diptych.[15] For one thing, Massys did not couple his images of the Madonna with portraits of individual patrons in the manner of a van der Weyden / Memling devotional diptych. Moreover, Massys' use of the throne and brocade retains the sense of royal distance that Memling had surrendered, except for halo and jewels, to the bourgeois domestic interior setting of his Nieuwenhove panels. Massys is also much more emphatic about the halo of the Virgin in his two images than either Memling or van der Weyden. In short, the Massys panels in half-length still retain many of the iconic aspects of the traditional Byzantine form of the *Hodegiatria*, which appears often in half-length, the Child poised on the arm of the Virgin, as well as in full-length; however, the severity of the *Hodegiatria* type is softened by Massys through his addition of background details of setting and the informal activity of the Christ Child, either with the open book or the grapes.

This addition of naturalism and informality is part of the same process in Massys that appeared in
Pl. 20 the *Lamentation* of the *St. John altarpiece*, where the scenery of Golgotha, the accessory figures, and the narrative details complemented the fundamentally devotional image inherited from van der Weyden. The votive image is thereby extended from its purely contemplative aspects to the more vivid visualizations of an amplified, natural frame of reference. Essentially, Massys begins with the isolated iconic distance of Rogierian Madonna and Child panels and presents the figures with full suggestion of their majesty and holiness through conventional attributes, like haloes, jewels, brocades, and
Pl. 168 thrones or cushions. Yet, like Rogier himself in the *St. Luke Drawing the Madonna* (Boston), Massys limits his figures only to the sacred characters and thereby enables himself to portray them in richly detailed environments separate from earthly realms or donors, such as Memling's Nieuwenhove. The Madonna can thus be a convincing vision to the viewer yet remain uncompromised as a transcendent and holy figure. For Massys' Mary icons, then, the sentiment remains as devout and spiritual as it had been for previous icons, even though the formal means now include all the naturalistic descriptions applied to holy figures by the Flemish traditions of van Eyck and Memling.

Both the portrait aspects of the devotional diptych and the intimacy of its portraitlike half-length convention can be seen in the first of Massys' diptychs with the Virgin, now in Antwerp (Koninklijk
Pl. 42 Museum; F. 5, cat. 5). In this case, however, the *Virgin in Prayer* is paired not with a donor, but with
Pl. 43 Christ himself as the adult *Salvator Mundi.* This is the most otherworldly of Massys' depictions of the holy figures. The Virgin and Christ are shown against a Rogierian monochrome dark blue background, and their haloes are a combination of emanating gold rays and a colored nimbus of rosy light. Distinctions in status are made clear by the frontal position of the blessing Christ, who also holds a cruciform scepter, and the orientation of the Virgin, whose prayers are directed toward Christ, even though she wears her own glowing, gold filigree, bejeweled crown.

This combined image of Christ and the Virgin is emphatically derived from the petitionary status of the worshiper. The image of Christ as Salvator Mundi, the blessing Savior and King of Glory, had already achieved currency within Trecento art in Italy, where it often adorned the apex of altarpieces.[16] The Netherlandish form shows Christ frontally, in regal attire with His right hand raised in blessing and His left hand holding a globe, a combination of the Byzantine Holy Face icons and the Majestas Domini figures with their regal attributes. Massys had previously painted an isolated image of
Pl. 44 Christ Blessing with Globe, a *Salvator Mundi* in a half-length panel (Raleigh, North Carolina Museum of Art).[17]

In Massys' diptych, the *Salvator Mundi* combined with the *Virgin in Prayer* represents Mary's important theological role as intercessor with her son. Such a combination was already implied in the earliest versions of this pairing in Eastern art,[18] where the praying Virgin is shown turned toward her Son either in an isolated diptych or as part of a Deësis; in the latter, the image of John the Baptist or, alternatively, John the Evangelist, completes the heavenly triad. Already by the time of Roger van der Weyden's *Braque triptych* (ca. 1452; Paris, Louvre),[19] the Deësis had been firmly integrated into Netherlandish art, where it was depicted in bust-length, just as in Massys' devotional diptych. The luminous haloes, as well as the orientation of the two figures and their gestures, had also been codified by van der Weyden long before the Massys images. A close comparison of uncertain date is a single-panel version of the diptych made by a follower of Robert Campin (Philadelphia, Johnson Coll.), which shows only the figures of a blessing Christ and a praying Virgin, reversed from the order in which they are presented by Massys. The "shoulder-bust" formula rather than the half-length of Roger's triptych is closer to the Byzantine forms used in decorative roundels; although Massys includes the hands that were omitted from the Byzantine images, he nonetheless remains closer to the original Eastern form of the image type.[20]

Such faithful compliance with prototypes in Netherlandish art is even more manifest in a series of images of the Holy Face of Christ in the same shoulder-bust format. The best surviving copy of van Eyck's *Holy Face* is the version in Newcastle-upon-Tyne.[21] This particular version is important because it was conceived to be an "historically accurate" rendition of the original *sudarium* image of St. Veronica, a careful modern archaism of a treasured relic and likeness, then conserved in Rome.[22] True to the famous model, van Eyck's image appears without the hands later added by van der Weyden and others. Massys' elaboration of the Holy Face in his images of Christ consists of the addition of blessing hands, scepter, and prominent halo. This amplification is really no more than that made by Massys' contemporary Jan Gossaert, within his parchment *Deësis* (Madrid, Prado). For this image, Gossaert has modified not a theologically significant holy relic, but rather a model from recent Netherlandish tradition: the holy triad at the top interior of the Ghent altarpiece by Jan van Eyck.[23] By creating an elaborate shrine around the holy figures, Gossaert uses Flamboyant tracery to indicate the sacral importance of this image, making a new icon, analogous to the elaborately decorated, sculpted, and gilded cult figures of this period. Despite changes from the Eyckian original, such as Gossaert's elimination of the scepter and tiara of the Lord, the choice of subject, physical types, and Eyckian naturalism of technique make it quite clear that the Ghent altarpiece was the model for Gossaert's newer votive image. In fact, the relationship of Gossaert to van Eyck reveals that Massys, too, stands close to both images. Massys has emphasized elements, ultimately derived from van Eyck's great Ghent original, of the royalty and grandeur of Christ and the Virgin. The combination of Christ's rich robes and his gesture of blessing as Salvator Mundi as well as the crown and praying hands of the Virgin can also be found in Gossaert. Although Massys has eliminated the figure of John the Baptist, shared by both van Eyck and Gossaert, his derivation of elements from the Ghent altarpiece overlaps with the van der Weyden/Campin devotional diptych formula in the *Salvator Mundi/Praying Virgin.*

Pl. 45
Pl. 46
Pl. 47

For both 16th-century artists, Gossaert and Massys, we see evidence of an overt emulation of previous models as well as a creativity in combining them within the same devotional context, rather than a slavishly literal copying of them. This process of adaptation of the traditional images which serve as models has been called "reconstruction" by Panofsky.[24] Both Massys and Gossaert produced devotional images that were intended to serve the private pious needs of the worshiper. To produce images properly suited to this votive purpose, the artists insisted upon using the time-tested solutions of their predecessors, those famous traditional images of the same generic type. Dominating the creation of the new art work, this pictorial type has a fairly strict set of associated conventions—in this case, isolated portraitlike images, often half- or bust-length. Because of the private religious purpose of Massys' and Gossaert's images, they were frequently painted on a small scale and were meant to be seen up close.

As we have seen in the examples by Gossaert and Massys, the importance of the personal address of the image to the pious beholder creates a predilection for choosing images whose efficacy or conferred grace have already been established by tradition. This is the reason why not only the generic conventions but also a strong pictorial conservatism dominates the production of the devotional icons of the early 16th century. For this reason both Massys and Gossaert adapt previous images by Jan van Eyck and Roger van der Weyden for their new works, paintings made in an archaizing spirit analogous to the Eyckian versions of the Holy Face.

An archaizing attitude toward an image requires explanation. Underlying it is a concept of the icon as a particular image bestowing grace, a *Gnadenbild*.[25] Here the image is often associated with a particular devotion or is even itself the cult object of a highly developed devotion. A prominent example of the latter phenomenon is the *Holy Face,* copied by van Eyck, which is supposedly derived from the original relic of St. Veronica, a true portrait of Christ from life miraculously recorded on a veil and preserved as a holy treasure in Rome.[26] Here the magical association of the image with the depicted person informs the wonder-working aspect of the image and even its replications.[27] Naturally, in this circumstance, it is hardly surprising that the essential ingredients of the prototype would be retained in all of its replicas, just as a magic spell ought to contain all of the words in their proper order. That the style of the copy might be modernized, even though archaizing, is no different from repeating the spell with a modern accent, as long as the essentials are retained. Thus it is that the Holy Face derived from Veronica's *sudarium* is recognizable as a product of Jan van Eyck but is readily identifiable with the prototype image that was believed to be the Veronican original; the same image can be seen with all the same essential elements as early as the mid-13th century in the works of Matthew Paris.[28]

The link between the conferral of grace and a pictorial conservatism, which may arise out of this functional interest, is further reinforced by the practice of linking religious indulgences to specific formulaic prayers before prescribed images.[29] One of the images connected with a specific indulgence was the *vera icon,* the Veronica *Holy Face.* In 1216 Pope Innocent III had granted remission from penance to a prayer composed by himself and directed toward the image of the Holy Face; later popes repeated this assertion.[30] Such indulgences were a prominent feature of late medieval piety, a fact witnessed by the vehemence of Luther's protest against them.[31] The cult of the rosary was also connected with promises of indulgences, and we have already noted the presence of rosary beads around the neck of Christ in the three earliest Madonna images of Massys, images created only a short time after the institution of the cult of the rosary during the late 1470s.[32] Although images of the Virgin of the Rosary were not connected in any specific way with a particular prayer or indulgence, their association with cult practices and their conformity to the conventions of other indulgenced images points to the extended use of images as the means of supplication and the hope for grace. With such habits of prayer before images and with the increasing fascination with the cult of the Virgin, promoted by the rosary prayers and by the popular doctrine of the Immaculate Conception, it is little wonder that most of the iconic images created by Massys and his contemporaries were mariological.[33]

In the case of the images of Mary, there were other reasons for pictorial conservatism in the production of devotional icons. Beyond the images connected with particular indulgences, such as the *Maria in Sole* image connected with the Immaculate Conception, specific panels were venerated as authentic portraits of the Virgin, the equivalent to the Veronica icon of the *Holy Face.* Unlike the *vera icon,* these images were not particularly connected to specific prayers, but they were believed to have been painted by St. Luke himself after the features of the Madonna.[34] One such image, an Italo-Byzantine work of the 12th century, was brought to Cambrai in 1440 and was copied no fewer than 15 times by the painters Petrus Christus and Hayne de Bruxelles.[35] Similar prototypes were replicated in 14th-century Bohemia, 15th-century Germany, and 17th-century Austria.[36] Once again, the replication of an image is tied to its sacral function, which promotes archaizing conservatism and careful copying of the essential features of the prototype, even though here the conferral of grace is not systematically associated with the image, as it was in the case of the images of indulgence prayers. Frequently, miraculous powers were attributed to such pictures, and they often became the site of pilgrimages. Replicas came to serve as evocative souvenirs and possible objects of veneration in their own right, one step removed from the identification that had originally informed the images of grace with their power.[37] Instead of venerating an image because it was a true portrait and therefore a substitute for the physical presence of Christ or the Virgin, one would venerate a copy of the wonder-working image as a substitute for the image itself, as an aid to devotion and even as an instrument of grace, particularly in the case of the indulgenced image.

From this mentality, it is but a short step to the general conservation of images of a primarily devotional character, the very phenomenon we have seen in the case of Massys and Gossaert. This is the "compulsion of the iconographic tradition" that has been pointed out by Friedländer.[38] It helps to explain why certain pictures by prominent Netherlandish masters served time and again as prototypes for later images used for devotional purposes. The original could well be an extract from a larger context, such as the Dëesis triad at the top of Jan van Eyck's Ghent altarpiece,[39] or it could be an image that itself was originally seen to be an evocative, portraitlike devotional image of the type we have been discussing, such as the *Holy Face* of Jan van Eyck or the *Dëesis* of van der Weyden's *Braque triptych.* That various of these older images were creatively recombined or repainted in a more up-to-date formal idiom does not diminish the basic fact that the newer versions adhere closely to the basic ingredients of their models and to the dictates of an effective devotional icon.

Several important Massys devotional images of the early 16th century draw their direct inspiration from the same Netherlandish heritage, combining elements of mariolatry from both the Campin/van der Weyden icons and the Eyckian versions of the same themes. The first example is the image of the *Virgin Enthroned* (Brussels, F. 17, cat. 9). Massys here has borrowed from a van der Weyden Virgin in a *Pl. 48* Niche, the so-called *Madonna Duran* (Prado, Madrid), as well as from a van Eyck prototype known only *Pl. 49* from copies, the best of which is the so-called *Ince Hall Madonna* (Melbourne).[40] Both these models *Pl. 50* have in common with the Brussels picture a presentation of the Madonna and Child with Christ reading from a book and actually turning the pages. Massys had already introduced this theme into the earlier London and Brussels pictures, although these two images did not evoke specific comparisons to previous images of the 15th century. Massys certainly knew the Roger painting, for he reproduced it in the background of his Brussels picture as a sculpted Madonna and Child in a niche *Pl. 51* above the doorway of the distant building. For his larger foreground image in the Brussels *Madonna Enthroned,* Massys borrowed the Rogerian convention of dressing the Child in a white smock; more general resemblances include the muted color scheme of rose and grey-white tones and the strong assertion in Massys' picture of a stone throne with tracery, equivalent to the masonry niche of van der Weyden's image. From van Eyck, Massys adapted the suggestion of rich dress, such as the jeweled border of the Virgin's dress, and the sumptuous depiction of textures, such as her flowing brown hair. Like van Eyck, Massys has suggested an interior space with windows, where the Madonna is enthroned as a central, regal figure suitable for cult devotion.

Like the example of the *Lamentation* from the central panel of the Antwerp *St. John altarpiece,* the *Madonna Enthroned* from Brussels illustrates Massys' creative combination of a variety of hallowed models to produce his new image in the same pictorial genre. The process of emulation rather than literal imitation is based upon the shared assumption of the purpose of this picture with the original purpose of its model. Moreover, Massys as an artist shows awareness of the works of his predecessors and deference to their pictorial formulas and expressive styles. This combined attitude is not by any means without precedent, although it has not often been discussed for Western painting. But a strong analogy exists with the attitudes current in Chinese Ming and Ching painting toward the achievements of their predecessors, particularly the heritage of artists of the Yüan period; Cahill has discussed the importance of evoking the style of an artist's predecessors as a vital assertion of the continuity of Chinese painting as a tradition and an ethos.[41] What Cahill did not assert, owing to the almost unvarying nature of subject matter in Chinese painting ("Plum blossoms or riverside views") is that these rhetorical invocations of past stylistic languages are themselves tied to the continuity of purpose and the treatment of analogous themes. Even though Chinese pictures do not have the variety of subjects normally associated with Western categories of painting, it is significant that the invocation of the tradition is accomplished within the same subject, format, and medium as the original models. For Massys, as for Shen Mou, the rhetoric of acknowledging tradition is a result of continuing values, a sense of the unbroken chain of connections to the past and its importance as a guide for the present. The very act of making such a "replica" is itself an assertion that the religious or cultural system of which it is a part is unchanging, or at the very least that the artist wishes it to be unchanging; otherwise, neither his model nor his later version of that model would continue to have meaning.[42] In the same way, we should understand Massys to be not only a pictorial but also a religious conservative in his Mary images in this early stage of his painting career. Perhaps that is the underlying reason for the sobriety and regal distance implied by the particular presentation of the *Hodegiatria* variations.

Another example of the same phenomenon is Massys' *Madonna Standing with Angels* (London, *Pl. 52*

Seilern coll., F. 165, cat. 15), singled out by both Friedländer and Baldass as one of the most insistently traditional images of the artist's output.[43] For this image the constituent models are Campin and van Eyck, combined with a dash of Memling. The two models were very much the same kind of devotional *Pl. 54* icon presented by Massys. Campin's original, a work known only through its numerous copies, is an image of the Madonna nursing in an apse. Like Massys' version, the Campin *Madonna in an Apse* is shown central and dominant, standing erect with her robe flowing out to either side of her on the tiled floor. Beside her, a pair of music-playing angels serve to witness her queenliness, which is only subtly indicated through a modest radiant halo of golden rays. Massys' image also includes angels, although only the lute is retained, and the second angel offers a small bunch of cherries, the celestial fruit.

Pl. 55 Massys' Eyckian source is also a tiny work: the *Madonna in a Church* (Berlin-Dahlem). From this image, Massys borrowed the intimate clutching gesture of the very young Christ Child and the entire apparatus of a formal ecclesiastical structure as the location and theological support of the Madonna. In Massys' case, the specific churchly aspect of the scene has been mitigated, for in the background of the image he has included a throne with brocaded labels, which indicate that it will be the holy throne of Jesus and Mary. Moreover, he has included at the right a view out of doors, which would be improbable in any canonical church space; this view seems to be another indication of the immanence of the Virgin and Christ within the world of mankind, the same kind of visual juxtaposition that he *Pl. 1* emphasized with the background landscape of the *St. Anne Holy Kinship altarpiece* (see Chap. 2). Like the exotic architecture of the Holy Kinship, Massys has borrowed from Memling an Italianate element of putti with garland swags about the entablatures at the base of the arch of the vestibule.[44] This unchurchly element also refers to the queenly splendor of the Virgin and her surroundings; it is a motif that David also borrowed from Memling for his early *Jan de Sedano triptych* (Paris, Louvre).[45] But Massys did include references to the theological structures of the Church, including within the Virgin's vestibule a rank of sculptures of Old Testament prophet figures normally associated with church portals. The presence of these figures testifies to the status of the Virgin as the fulfillment of biblical prophecy and as the embodiment of the Church, the idea made explicit in van Eyck's metaphorical image and, for that matter, in Campin's *Madonna in the Apse*.[46]

In adapting elements from both these famous prototypes, Massys has retained the basic elements that made them so influential and significant: the tenderness between Madonna and Child, the association of the pair with both celestial queenliness and with the Church, and the full-length presence of the holy figures in the foreground of a tiny panel for the pious contemplation of the beholder. These elements made the two images among the most popular of all 15th-century panels. The literal copies after Campin have already been mentioned, but during Massys' period, Bernard van Orley made several close adaptations of the original image.[47] Several replications of the van Eyck image were made during the 15th century, such as the left panel of a diptych made for a Carthusian abbot, Christian de Hondt, by the Bruges Master of 1499.[48] Gossaert also made a copy for the Italian diplomat Antonio Siciliano in 1513;[49] presumably in this case the literal repetition of the image was based as much on the desire to have a replica for aesthetic reasons as it was on shared religious assumptions with the original.

Massys, then, participated, as did others of his generation, in a self-conscious pictorial emulation of Netherlandish tradition. This does not mean, however, that he had to choose the works of Campin, van der Weyden, and van Eyck in preference to the works of his own contemporaries or his immediate predecessors. On the contrary, many of these same artists themselves felt the same way about the Flemish painting tradition. David, Gossaert, and van Orley all show reverence for the past despite imposing their own personal stamp upon the models of the previous century. Moreover, artists of the previous generation, such as Hugo van der Goes, Dieric Bouts, and Hans Memling, were themselves extremely conscious of the image-making of the great founders and attempted to emulate their creations. For all these artists, the literal repetition of an image seems to have stood, alongside the creative adaptation of its elements, as an alternative means of realizing the same ends: the re-creation of the religious image in all of the fullness of its original role and pious purpose. For both altarpieces and isolated icons, it seems a mistake to insist, as Brom does, on the originality and decisive change from the early 15th-century "Founders' Heritage." Instead, it is worth reemphasizing the degree to which an artist like Gossaert or van Orley compromised his own personality in order to conform to both the form and the religious content of a Campin or van Eyck prototype. The same applies to Massys in his altarpiece works like the wings of the *St. Anne* triptych or the Lamentation of the *St. John* retable. But it applies even more for this group of Mary icons, which grow out of formulations of the Flemish painting tradition, and which ultimately owe their conservative nature and pictorial outlines to the very nature of icon-making in Christian art, a conservative adherence to the venerable prototype precisely because of its miraculous or ancient connection to its sacred archetype.

The isolated devotional icons of the Virgin by Massys invariably have been loosed from their original private context; they therefore reveal nothing about the individual for whom they were made, and it is difficult to assign them specific dates with any precision. Based, however, upon the artist's use of varying female types for the same subject figure, an approximate dating can be established that can account for this change of types within basic continuity as a kind of artistic "drift" of forms, a parallel phenomenon to the unintentional formal drift of language.[50] By this reckoning, Massys produced very few of the iconic Madonna images during his middle decade of activity, the teens of the 16th century, but he renewed his interest in the theme with an active output during the final decade, the 1520s. Unlike the earlier Madonna images, however, these later works vary considerably as to the aspect of the Virgin that is stressed, and they show less literal adherence to the traditions of Netherlandish painting in their pictorial formulas. In addition, they draw upon the legacy of Leonardo da Vinci, and they present a more emotionally charged, more human figure of the Virgin, who now seems less like the unmoving center of a theological regime than the active expression of compassion and love, whether bestowed in her queenly or in her maternal guise.

This change is particularly evident in panels that share the same basic content. Perhaps closest to the works of the first decade of activity is the *Madonna Enthroned with Two Angels* (formerly in the van Pannwitz collection, F. 26, cat. 38), a full-length work that demands comparison with the early London *Pl. 57* *Madonna Enthroned.* The van Pannwitz *Madonna* sits on a throne that is not the abstract gold or Gothic *Pl. 38* shrine of the London work, but instead a solid marble construction with volutes upon a distinct cornice. Like the architecture of the *St. Anne altarpiece,* the vocabulary of this structure is an outgrowth of Italian forms; also like the *St. Anne altarpiece* is a view over a hazy landscape in the background portico on either side of the massive van Pannwitz throne. Yet within this palatial environment, the van Pannwitz Virgin is much more animated than her counterpart in the early London panel. She bestows flowers on the angel to her left and delicately balances a standing, twisting Child, who turns to receive an apple (signifying his role as the New Adam and redeemer) from the other angel.[51]

Simply put, the van Pannwitz *Madonna* is no longer a traditional icon. Its significance has ceased to derive from its direct relationship to either the holy figures themselves or to any venerable visual prototypes of the icon heritage. Unlike the Seilern *Madonna Standing with Angels,* where the Virgin was presented purely for devotional contemplation under a framing doorway, the van Pannwitz *Madonna* is enlivened, as the holy figures actively respond to their angelic entourage. Certainly the massive throne, featuring God the Father in its crown, contributes to the necessary dignity and majesty of the holy figures. But the garments of the Madonna are quite ordinary, with none of the queenly or heavenly appurtenances (jeweled diadems, haloes) conspicuous in the early works. Of course, there is little danger of mistaking these figures for ordinary mortals (the angelic attendants alone should prevent any confusion), but neither is the van Pannwitz *Madonna* to be taken as an iconic substitute or equivalent for the wonder-working presence of the holy figures themselves. Massys makes the change of status of the image explicit through his subtle choice of framing. The early frontalized icons were self-contained entities that made no attempt to visualize space beyond the margins of the frame. The later Madonna images, in contrast, not only show angels or window views cut off arbitrarily by the frame, but by their livelier movements within the panel imply a larger space than the exposed viewing field. The sacred actors of the van Pannwitz *Madonna* are not visions removed from space and time, but rather credible flesh-and-blood characters who seem to comport themselves in very human fashion and within convincingly material surroundings. Clearly, Massys' attitude toward making images of the Virgin has changed entirely from the forms and attitudes of the early icons and must be spelled out anew for his mature works. Perhaps no other element of the later Mary images offers so revealing an access to his late works as his decision to abandon his previous reliance on traditional visual models for a more modern set of sources: the more current imagery of his younger Antwerp colleague Joos van Cleve and the expressive faces and movements of Leonardo da Vinci Madonnas.

The distinctive van Pannwitz Christ Child, in both His new figure type and his unusual hip-shot pose, is close to the figure of an *Infant Christ Standing on a Globe* (formerly Dortmund, Becker coll.) by Joos van Cleve.[52] Throughout the late period of Massys, van Cleve's Madonna images play part of an ongoing dialogue; it is not possible, in the absence of secure dates, to say which of the two artists was the innovator of some of the pictorial ideas shared in their pictures. General evidence, however, suggests that van Cleve, although the younger of the two artists (his entry into the Antwerp guild was in 1511, 20 full years after Massys), was more often the donor, for Madonna images were the staple of his flourishing career, particularly the isolated images of the Virgin. It was van Cleve who codified the influence of Raphael and also of Leonardo (see Chap. 9), the latter a considerable influence on the late work of Massys. Van Cleve was certainly not himself an innovator; his earlier pictures owed a considerable debt to the art of Massys himself, as well as to Joachim Patinir and Gerard David.[53] On numerous occasions van Cleve also made his own variations on the art of Roger van der Weyden (Philadelphia, Johnson coll. *Deposition in a Landscape*) and Jan van Eyck (New York, Metropolitan
Pl. 161 Museum *Holy Family,* based on the Eyckian *Lucca Madonna*).[54] But van Cleve used Italian models to set the trend of popular Madonna icons during the 1520s, a popularity attested to by the considerable number of replicas and copies after van Cleve's formulations.

Another picture that shows close ties to van Cleve and, ultimately, to the Italian sources behind van
Pl. 58 Cleve's images is Massys' *Madonna with the Cherries* (F. 67, cat. 50), a picture now lost but preserved in
Pl. 59 numerous replicas. A copy after the missing original is the foreground picture in the gallery painting, depicting the collection of Cornelis van der Geest, by Willem van Haecht (Antwerp, Rubenshuis). The van Haecht image records a 1617 visit to van der Geest made by the regents of the southern Netherlands Archduke Albrecht and Isabella; the visit is recorded by Massys' biographer Alexander van Fornenbergh.[55] According to the account, the picture most prized by the regents and proudly owned by van der Geest was none other than the *Madonna of the Cherries,* which is thereby accorded the place of prominence in the foreground of the gallery picture. We may therefore take its appearance there to be carefully copied from the original in the collection. It shows the Virgin and Child within a palatial throne room with a handsome view, out a window to their right, of a hazy but verdant landscape. The depiction is three-quarter length, with the Virgin and Child seated upon an elaborate throne; sculpted figures appear above a capital of the throne, and foliate tracery continues along its back and side. Amid this testimony to her sacred rank, the Virgin is dressed modestly, wearing only a headband rather than a crown and clad in a squared-off dirndle-like frock rather than the jeweled gowns of the earlier icons.

Most striking here and novel in Massys' Madonna images is the intimacy between mother and Child, centered on the kiss that they exchange in a close embrace. This emotion-laden conduct, like most images of the Madonna and Child, has a venerable pedigree in the history of icons. In Byzantine icons, the image of the Virgin with the Child pressed close to her cheek is called the *Eleüsa;*[56] a famous example is the 11th-century icon, dubbed "Our Lady of Valdimir," where the Child clasps the neck of His mother. This emphasis on emotional tenderness is a characteristic feature of late, Paleologan Byzantine icons, and it had already made an appearance in Western art by the 12th century. For Massys, the principal source for the motherly gesture of the Madonna was the local Louvain tradition
Pl. 60 established by Dieric Bouts, who painted several replicas of the same subject in half-length (Florence,
Pl. 61 Bargello; New York; San Francisco).[57] A more contemporary version of the theme was transformed by
Pl. 62 Gerard David into a *Holy Family* through the addition of Joseph to the group (formerly Paris, Leroy coll.); the David picture also includes a window view of a background landscape.[58]

Yet the influence of Italy by way of Joos van Cleve also helped to determine this new presentation of
a Mary icon by Massys. Van Cleve had absorbed the example of Leonardo da Vinci in a composition of
the *Madonna of the Cherries,* which was copied often in the van Cleve workshop during this period.[59]
Particular to the van Cleve *Madonna of the Cherries* is a corner window, a traceried pilaster, and a
swelling marble column that were all later incorporated into Massys' image. Moreover, even the
physical type of the Christ Child, with His tight blonde curls, baby fat, and puffy cheeks, was adopted
by Massys from his younger Antwerp contemporary. (The dour, full face of Massys' Madonna more
closely resembles the types of David.) Both Massys and van Cleve conscientiously include the overtly
symbolic fruits that refer to Christ's mission: the cherries, a celestial fruit; the apple or orange of
Original Sin; and the grapes, included by Massys on the foreground ledge to signal eucharistic
sacrifice.[60] Activity with intimacy, majestic surroundings with informality of behavior, symbolic
attributes within an emotionally appealing, human presentation of the holy figures—these are the
richly varied elements of the complex, late Madonna images of Massys.

The Berlin *Madonna Enthroned* (F. 18, cat. 37) exhibits the same combined ingredients in its *Pl. 63*
composition. Largest of the Massys Madonna panels, the Berlin *Madonna* is approximately life-size
and probably had a more public role than the small intimate panels that were the rule for votive
images. In the 17th century, the panel served as the altarpiece in the oratory of Archduchess
Isabella.[61] This image is laden with even more still-life symbols than in the *Madonna of the Cherries.*
Cherries and an apple lie on the table, alongside a piece of bread, which complements the wine of the
eucharist; a large and prominent mound of butter has not yet been interpreted as a Marian symbol, but
its placement with the other symbolic elements provides identity by association and indicates that its
nourishment and derivation from milk should be considered as part of its relationship to the fostering
mother of Christ. This interpretation might seem gratuitous were it not for the strong association of
milk with the Madonna and Child in other pictures by both Massys and David (see below). Again, the
action is centerd upon the intimate kiss between mother and Child, here rendered more disconcert-
ingly erotic by an older Christ Child, no longer a mere infant, who so firmly clasps the neck of the
Virgin. The interlaced figures, in fact, are an echo of the amorous overtures of the *Ill-matched Pair,* (F.
54, cat. 35), a secular picture that Massys painted at approximately the same period of time; in
particular, the tweaking gesture of the Virgin recalls the similar enticement of the wily harlot (see
Chap. 7). Already the Christ Child type has developed into the blonde, curly-haired child favored by
both Massys and van Cleve during the later 1520s; but just as in the case of the van Pannwitz *Madonna,*
Massys has presented an older, longer Christ figure who offers more interesting opportunities for
complex poses and motions than an infant. Again, the dress of the Madonna is casual and informal,
although she now bears a veil, a favored item of the van Cleve millinery. Her throne is composite, with
traceried elements that recall earlier, more Gothic creations like the full-length Brussels *Madonna
Enthroned;* leafy ornament on the armrests grows out of the lacy trim of the *Rem altarpiece* of 1518–20 *Pl. 48*
(F. 3, cat. 24), Yet the stout little marble columns inserted into the frame of the throne contain little *Pl. 37*
cameo profiles of emperors and recall the nascent Italianisms of van Cleve during the early 1520s
(e.g., the Vienna altarpiece of the *Virgin Enthroned* or even the earlier Modena *Anna Selbdritt;* see Chap.
9).[62]

A striking aspect of the Berlin *Madonna Enthroned* is its assertive presentation of the Virgin and
Child as part of a world order. Behind the elaborate throne, partitioned behind a wall, is a second
zone of activity. This is a realm characterized as a courtly garden, almost resembling the gardens of
love celebrated in allegories such as the *Roman de la Rose,* or transformed in pictures of the early 15th
century into the *hortus conclusus* of the Virgin and her angelic entourage. Dominating this garden zone
is a large Gothic fountain, which again recalls the central features of love gardens and the allied
reference to the Virgin as the fountain of living waters of the Song of Songs.[63] The garden precinct is
bounded by a low fence adorned with lions bearing pennants, which recalls the royal terraces of the
court at Brussels,[64] and is further demarcated by a hedge composed of roses, a Marian flower.[65] Thus,
the combination of courtly and Marian imagery in the garden zone is the sign of the queenly status
and theological importance of the Virgin. But beyond this zone lies an expansive, green landscape that

Pl. 1 recalls the background of the Brussels *Saint Anne altarpiece* image of the *Holy Kinship.* Common to both works is the layering of space, beginning with the foreground throne and architecture and leading back over barriers to an expansive green belt ringed by blue mountains. Here, as there, the cities and the fertile plains are the eventual recipients of the grace of the Virgin, who is deliberately shown as present in the world, even if separate from it in her royal haven. The maternal tenderness of her kiss to the Christ Child embodies the grace that extends to all of mankind who are willing to acknowledge and contemplate the Virgin; in similar fashion, the vision of the picture makes Mary's love accessible for the pious viewer, who also sees that his world is included within the compass of that love.

The Berlin *Madona Enthroned,* therefore, goes even beyond the humanizing actions of the other late Madonna images, where the embrace or interaction of the holy figures implies a new relationship to the world of the viewer. In addition, it now magnifies the message of these actions by including them in an outdoor world—a human setting, which promises that the tenderness and mercy of the Virgin will be open to the entire community of the truly faithful. Smaller images from the later period of *Pl. 64* Massys' activity fulfill this promise. A vivid example is the small *Virgin and Child Outdoors* (Detroit, F. 23, cat. 42), which is the best surviving version of an image that itself prompted several copies. In the Detroit panel, all the barriers and distinctions of the Berlin *Madonna Enthroned* are eliminated. The Virgin, seen at half-length proximity to the viewer, in contrast to the full-length majesty of the Berlin panel, is now completely without markings of her holiness. She wears a simple cloth head-covering and unadorned dress, and she can no longer be distinguished from an ordinary mother. She appears without mediation in front of a broad and open green landscape, containing a small city, a village, and a hillside castle. Her gentle affection toward the Child continues to be a primary element in the action of the picture, and the only recollection of the other late pictures in terms of theology or dignity is a similar presentation of a foreground still-life with apple and grapes, reminding the viewer of the theological significance of the two figures.

Emphasis on maternal care of the Christ Child, like the warmth suggested by the Detroit *Madonna Outdoors,* is manifested in a series of Massys Madonna images showing the nursing or nourishment of *Pl. 65* the Infant. The Rotterdam *Madonna with Milk Soup* (F. 168, cat. 27) is similar to the Detroit panel in layout; the half-length figures are seen before a verdant, tree-filled landscape. On the foreground ledge of the panel is a symbolic piece of bread, accompanied by the milk soup. Previously, this theme *Pl. 66* of feeding the Child with milk soup had been realized by David,[66] whose version of the subject was copied several times. The relic of the Virgin's milk was actually venerated in several centers in the Netherlands,[67] and the image communicates directly the nurturing aspect and tender intimacy of the Virgin's motherhood. The Rotterdam panel features the same curly-haired type of Christ Child common to so many of Massys' late devotional images. Except for the additional intimacy conveyed by Christ's gentle touch of the Virgin's chin, the *Madonna with Milk Soup* repeats the same basic relationship between the two figures as that of the Detroit *Madonna and Child Outdoors.*

The most homespun of all of Massys' images of the Virgin and Child takes place indoors. It is an *Pl. 67* image, lost but preserved in two copies (Munich and Luton Hoo, Wernher coll.) depicting the *Virgin Nursing the Child* inside a humble living room. In the background, a bed and lighted fireplace set the domestic scene, while the holy figures are seen at three-quarter length in the immediate foreground. The type and the dress of the Virgin are most closely related to the Berlin *Madonna Enthroned,* but none of the regal trappings and precincts of that large panel have been carried over into the interior. No indications of the Virgin's lofty significance appear in the lost composition; even the still-life attributes have been eliminated. This scene harks back to a precedent set by Robert Campin in works, such as the *Madonna of the Firescreen* (London, National Gallery), that stress the domestic interior, nursing Virgin, and humble simplicity of the daily life of the holy figures.[68] Within the Netherlandish painting tradition, Campin demonstrates the furthest development of the picturing of spiritual beings in material terms, the fullest assimilation of an otherworldly incarnation into its earthly guise. In general, Massys' later images of Virgin and Child stress the maternal, earthly, and humble qualities of the two figures, in contrast to the regal, celestial, and majestic aspects of the enthroned figures from earlier in his career. Specifically, his most insistent image of the Virgin of Humility is this *Nursing Madonna* in her bourgeois interior.[69]

Probably the earliest Massys image to depart from the majestic isolation of an icon is a work also known only from copies (F. 61; cat. 14), the *Virgin with the Sleeping Christ Child* on her bosom.[70] The Virgin's eyes are downcast and pensive, as if in this quiet moment she is filled with the foreboding and premonition of the loss of her son. Her breast is exposed, indicating that the Child has just suckled, so again the motif of nourishment and maternal care is paramount. Informality in the scene is reinforced by the simple veil the Virgin wears, although her gold-trimmed gown is slightly more ornate than the dress of the Detroit *Madonna Outdoors*. As in the Detroit image, only the foreground grapes and apple underscore theological connotations of the unmarked figures and setting.

Massys continued to explore the human qualities of the Virgin in one of his very last Madonna images, the so-called *Rattier Madonna* (Paris, Louvre; F. 24, cat. 48), initialed and dated on the panel *Pl. 68* 1529, only one year before the artist's death. Once again, the Virgin is seen in a domestic, bedroom setting. Both the surroundings and the costume are humble; the Madonna wears a simple veil and has no royal trappings of wealth. Humble, too, is the intimacy of her kissing the Child, an action consistent with the close-up view of the half-length figures (unlike the discord between the same intimate kiss and the enthroned majesty of full-length figures of the Berlin *Madonna Enthroned*). Even the still-life on a foreground ledge is presented more informally. To be sure, the symbolic grapes are still prominently visible, this time with the unbroken stem indicating the importance of the Madonna as progenitor of Christ,[71] but they are accompanied by objects which seem to have been part of a luncheon. The sliced peach on its metal plate has been half-eaten, and it is accompanied by a small, thick drinking glass of the sort one associates with a bourgeois table. As in the overall configuration of the picture, this still-life arrangement is not clearly distinguishable from the world of ordinary reality. The pious viewer of the *Rattier Madonna* is meant, therefore, to take special note of the worldly, familiar aspects of the holy figures, an impression confirmed by a view out a window. That view, however, depicts a rather elevated vista over a landscape and indicates that this dwelling is situated above the height of ordinary houses, on a level with a distant, hillside castle (which, in turn, recalls the symbolic fortress of the Virgin in the background of the *Holy Kinship* within the *St. Anne altarpiece;* see *Pl. 1* Chap. 2). Within the pervasively bourgeois environment, then, both the bunch of grapes and the palatial vista are subtle reminders of previous Madonna panels, like the Berlin *Madonna Enthroned,* that include references to more regal or theological aspects of the Virgin's identity. In this late work, Massys continues to stress the humbler qualities of the Virgin but manages, nevertheless, to include suggestions about their ultimate significance.

A final image of the Christ Child by Massys (or his workshop) omits the Virgin entirely and presents the *Infants Jesus and John the Baptist* (F. 29; cat. 34) as playmates, kissing. This subject was extremely *Pl. 69* popular in the Netherlands, particularly in the series of workshop variants from the circle of Joos van *Pl. 166* Cleve.[72] Its ultimate source was a design by Leonardo da Vinci, preserved on a drawing in Windsor *Pl. 70* Castle (No. 12564) and included in a variety of images by his own followers.[73] In the van Cleve and Leonardo images, however, the two kissing children were presented in either elevated landscape or royally draped architectural spaces, which clearly marked their status. Massys, in contrast, placed the two infants in a perfectly ordinary bourgeois bedroom interior, very like the setting of the *Madonna Nursing.* Behind the two children an older woman, possibly St. Anne, witnesses the precocious tenderness. This youthful act of the Christ Child toward His cousin mirrors the intimacy of His kiss with His mother, the central action of such late Massys images as the Berlin *Madonna Enthroned,* the lost *Madonna of the Cherries,* and the *Rattier Madonna.* Again, the stress in the late iconic images is on grace, tenderness, warmth—in this case within a completely undifferentiated setting.

Seen in comparison with the earlier Antwerp icon pair of *Christ Blessing* and the *Virgin in Prayer,* the *Pl. 71* final diptych by Massys also marks the shift from early majesty toward later humanity in these works. *Pl. 72* This diptych, which is signed and dated 1529 on its reverse, actually depicts a narrative scene: *Christ Taking Leave of His Mother* (Madrid, Prado; cat. 49).[74] In this late diptych Massys has split the components of Christ Taking Leave of His Mother into two separate panels; he arranges the holy figures to serve as parallels to the earlier Antwerp diptych. Christ on the right wing gestures in benediction toward the Virgin, rather than outward toward the viewer. Meanwhile Mary, on His right in her traditional position of intercession, gestures in prayer with her hands folded. Yet this very analogy to the earlier diptych points out the significant changes that have occurred since Massys' first works. Mary's head is unadorned in the later panel; neither the halo nor the elaborate gilded and jeweled crown of the Antwerp image has been retained. Moreover, the scepter and halo of Christ have been omitted. Also lost is the direct address of the earlier icon, where a frontal Christ stared directly toward the viewer and extended his benediction into the world of the beholder. The later diptych is more of a self-contained interaction, just as the later Madonnas Enthroned are internally active scenes centering on the embrace of the mother and Child, rather than on the frontal presentation for contemplation of a formally posed majesty.

In the contrast between the 1529 Prado diptych and the early Antwerp icons lies the essence of Massys' change of attitude toward the production of devotional images. The artist centers his final creations on physical actions: nursing, embraces, or a tender, final farewell. Most often, the action takes place in appropriate locales: a bedroom or domestic interior, a throne room, an enclosed garden, or a sunny outdoor space. The holy figures interact with one another and cease to address the pious beholder with their gazes and blessings. Indeed, the viewer has become a *voyeur,* visually eavesdropping on their most intimate and private emotional contacts. Instead of presenting the holy figures themselves as cult objects of worship through visual surrogates, the icons, these late Massys images are visions of their lives together, without the haloes and other signs of glory. Paradoxically, the images that portray the sacred actors at their most human, in the most worldly of settings, are the very pictures that establish the least contact or rapport with the ordinary world of the viewer.

The explanation for this paradox lies in its connection to Massys' other late religious works. We have
Pl. 32 already seen in the Coimbra *Passion altarpiece* of 1514–17 and the lost final triptych made for the
Pl. 33 Portuguese Damião de Gois (see Chap. 3) that Massys' later commissions betray an increasing gulf between the sinful, mortal world of the viewers and the faultless spheres of the holy figures. Verses by Cornelius Grapheus in praise of Massys' *de Gois altarpiece* combine personal contrition for his own sinfulness with deep sensitivity for the powerful emotions of the holy figures during the events of the Passion. The same barriers between saints and sinners was already evident in the great altarpieces,
Pl. 9 first in the *Expulsion of Joachim* of the *St. Anne altarpiece,* then in the *Martyrdom of John the Evanglist* in the
Pl. 15 *St. John altarpiece* (see Chap. 2); each of these images had contrasted the scowling, ugly, vicious tormentors with the unblemished, passive, and resigned saints. During the 1520s, Massys continued to
Pl. 86 stress this basic separation of material and spiritual realms in his Gospel presentations: the two *Ecce*
Pl. 87 *Homos* (Madrid, Venice), related to the Coimbra *Ecce Homo* wing and the unusual 1526 New York
Pl. 79 *Adoration of the Magi* (F. 8, cat. 40).

These images suggest collectively that Massys' late works presume an essential incompatibility between humans and sacred figures. In this respect, the earlier direct contact conveyed by icons to prayerful beholders had become a broken circuit. But the stronger barriers between realms simultaneously permitted a new, fuller exploration of each of the two realms separately. On the one hand, the fallible secular realm in all its foibles came to be portrayed against an iconlike isolation, often against a monochrome background (see Chapter 7). The holy figures, now more comfortably insulated from such inferior creatures, needed none of the earlier trappings of holiness from the icons: haloes, jewels, brocades, or attendant angels. In addition, they required none of the sanction of visual tradition for their own authority and could cease to rely on the Flemish heritage for their formulations.

The later Massys Madonna images relied instead on their own beauteous physical perfection to establish their identities and sacred nature. Even without the trappings of royalty, even in the humblest of actions and surroundings, these figures are unambiguously holy. Precisely because of their essential sacrality, the holy family can more fully embody even the most human and intimate relationships. Their perfect forms and exquisitely tender interactions are the fulfillment of the human virtues of love, which are so conspicuously absent from the secular world in Massys' oeuvre; moreover, the very humility of Mary and of Christ's Incarnation as Jesus lay at the core of the Christian faith. Their new holiness derives from their beauty combined with their actions. It is only fitting, therefore, that their forms often derived not from Flemish tradition, but rather from contemporary imagery stressing both beauty and vitality for such holy figures. These sources consisted principally of Madonna and Child images by both Joos van Cleve and Leonardo da Vinci. When Massys did invoke the Flemish heritage in his later works, it was the legacy of Campin, emphasizing the same maternal and domestic qualities and settings.

Later Madonna images of Massys cannot, in truth, be considered icons, but they do present a vision of perfect holiness in action. That they are no longer the instruments of grace results from altered assumptions on the part of the artist, who now perceives the condition of human sinfulness to be a serious barrier to grace. The later devotional works are significantly removed from traditional cult images, and they increasingly show human actions, now perceived to be beyond normal human reach. In this respect, late works, such as the 1529 Prado *Christ Saying Farewell to His Mother,* stand close to the specific Gospel events that were another staple of Massys' final decade. As the generic boundaries between icons and devotional narratives dissolved for Massys, the artist came to intensify both the emotional pitch and the interaction of the selected figures in a scene. In the following chapter, we shall see just how closely the distinctive final Madonna images resemble Massys' innovative Gospel presentations.

NOTES

1. Ringbom, *Icon to Narrative,* pp. 11-17.
2. Huizinga, *The Waning of the Middle Ages,* p. 151ff.
3. On angels as the performers of celestial music, see E. Winternitz, "On Angel Concerts in the Fifteenth Century," *Musical Instruments and Their Symbolism in Western Art,* 2nd ed. (New Haven, 1979), pp. 137-49; R. Hammerstein, *Die Musik der Engel* (Munich, 1962); and A. P. Mirimonde, "Les Anges musiciens chez Memling," pp. 5-55.
4. V. Lasareff, "Studies in the Iconography of the Virgin," *Art Bulletin* 20 (1938): 36ff.; M. Vloberg, "Les Types iconographiques de la Mère de Dieu dans l'art byzantin," *Maria Etudes sur la Sainte Vièrge sous la direction d'Hubert du Manoir,* vol. 2 (Paris, 1952), p. 413ff.; Vloberg, *La Vièrge et l'Enfant dans l'art français* (Grenoble, n.d.); H. Aurenhammer, "Marienikone und Marienandachtsbild. Zur Entstehung des halbfigurigen Marienbildes nördlich der Alpen," p. 135ff. According to legend, the first of these distanced divinities was painted as a portrait by the Evangelist Luke (D. Klein, *St. Lukas als Maler der Maria* [Berlin, 1933]; C. M. Henze, *Lukas der Muttergottesmaler* [Louvain, 1948]). But the original image was probably a fifth-century icon from the Holy Land brought back to Constantinople by Empress Eudokia in 453. Later the image was associated with a miraculous image *(Gnadenbild)* of the Hodegon Church in Constantinople, an icon erected in honor of Emperor Michael III (842–867), from which church the Greek icon type *hodegetria* takes its name. Also useful is R. Fritz, "Das Halbfigurenbild in der westdeutschen Tafelmalerei um 1400," *Zeitschrift für Kunstwissenschaft* 5 (1950): 161ff.
5. For the van Eyck Dresden triptych, see A. Mayer Meintschel, *Niederländische Malerei 15. and 16. Jahrhundert* (Dresden, 1966), pp. 28–31, no. 799. A. Janssens de Bisthoven and R. Parmentier, in *Les Primitifs Flamands,* p. 36ff., analyze the *van der Paele Madonna.*
6. Friedländer, vol. 6, no. 165; H. Adhemar, *La Musee National du Louvre: I Les Primitifs Flamands* (Brussels, 1962), p. 101ff.
7. The relationship between the van Eyck *van der Paele Madonna* and Flemish epitaph images, usually sculpted reliefs in stone, was pointed out by R. Terner, "Bemerkungen zur 'Madonna des Kanonikus van der Paele,' " pp. 83-91 ; and for van Eyck's *Rolin Madonna* by A. H. van Buren, "The Canonical Office in Renaissance Painting, Part II: More About the Rolin *Madonna,*" pp. 625–26.
8. A grey area of such Madonna images is the group of smaller-scale altarpieces with enthroned Madonnas in the central panel and individual donors or their families on the side or in isolation in the wing panels. Memling, in particular, catered to this private demand for Mary images as triptychs for individuals, such as the Englishman John Donne of Kidwelly (London, National Gallery; see Davies, *Early Netherlandish School: National Gallery Catalogues,* pp. 125–28, no. 6275; McFarlane, *Hans Memling,* pp.1-15. Another Memling example is the single panel of the Madonna with the adoring family of Jacob Floreins (Paris, Louvre; Friedländer, vol. 6, no. 66; McFarlane, p. 31, n. 16).
9. Ringbom, pp. 39–52, "The Holy Portrait *en buste;*" on half lengths, B. Völker, *Die Entwicklung in der niederländischen Malerei des 15. und 16. Jahrhunderts,* Ph.D. dissertation (Göttingen, 1968), esp. 99–120 for Massys' religious pictures.
10. Ringbom, ibid.; See E. Kitzinger, "Byzantine Art in the Period between Justinian and Iconoclasm," in *The Art of Byzantium and the Medieval West,* p. 157ff., featuring a full-length icon of the *Madonna Enthroned with Saints* (Mt. Sinai, St. Catherine's; 186). The same article defines "mode" as the functional use of aesthetic features "appropriate to a particular type of object or a particular subject" (pp. 203–4).

11. E. Kitzinger, "The Cult of Images before Iconoclasm," in ibid., pp. 96ff., 127ff.; Ringbom, p. 39ff.; "Christus als König," *RDK* 3, cols. 691–702.
12. Panofsky, *ENP*, p. 294ff.
13. Ringbom, fig. 5. The miniature is by Jean le Tavernier, Brussels, Bibliotheque Royale, ms. 9092, fo. 9r.
14. On the Rogerian progeny, see D. de Vos, "De Madonna-en-Kindtypologie bij Rogier van der Weyden en enkele minder gekende Flemalleske voorlopers," *Jahrbuch der Berliner Museen* 13 (1971): 60–161; R. Koch, "Copies of Roger van der Weyden's Madonna in Red," *Record of the Art Museum Princeton* 26 (1967): 49 ; Panofsky, *ENP*, p. 296ff.
15. McFarlane, p. 13f., n. 64; Friedländer, vol. 6, no. 14.
16. Ringbom, p. 69f., 171ff., with bibliography.
17. S. Ferber, "Quentin Metsys' 'Salvator Mundi,' " *Bulletin of the North Carolina Museum of Art, Raleigh* 9 (1970); 37–41.
18. O. Pächt, "The Ancestry of the Avignon Diptych," p. 402ff.
19. Panofsky, pp. 275–76; Blum, *Early Netherlandish Triptychs*, p. 29ff.
20. Pächt, "The Ancestry of the Avignon Diptych."
21. Panofsky, *ENP*, p. 187, n. 1.; L. Silver, "Fountain and Source: A Rediscovered Eyckian Icon," *Pantheon* 41 (1983): 98–99.
22. Ringbom, p. 23f., citing E. von Dobschütz, *Christusbilder* (Leipzig, 1899), esp. p. 218ff.
23. Panofsky, *ENP*, p. 353, n. 2; *Jan Gossaert genaamd Mabuse*, exh. cat., p. 83f., no. 8; H. Pauwels, "Jan Gossaert en Van Eyck," p. 4ff.
24. Panofsky, *ENP*, p. 353ff.
25. Ringbom, p. 23ff.; Aurenhammer, "Marienkone und Mariendachtsbuild," p. 28ff.
26. See n. 22.
27. This identification with the prototype was held to be true for images of Roman emperors and later, by extension, for images of Christ. See E. Kitzinger, "The Cult of Images"; Ringbom, p. 39ff.
28. Ringbom, fig. 25.
29. Ringbom, p. 23ff.; Aurenhammer, p. 3ff., stressing the phenomenological relationship of mystical or magical religiosity to the images.
30. Ringbom, p. 23ff.; "Ablass," *RDK* I.
31. Post, *KG*, pp. 473–84; Delaruelle, Labande, and Ourliac, p. 810ff.; the standard reference is N. Paulus, *Geschichte des Ablasses* (Paderborn, 1923).
32. Post, *KG*, p. 481; Ringbom, p. 27f.; and *"Maria in Sole,"* p. 326ff.; Delaruelle, Labande and Ourliac, p. 780ff; J. Snyder, "The Early Haarlem School of Painting II: Geertgen tot sint Jans," p. 131. The first brotherhood of the rosary was founded in Douai in 1470, and in 1479 Pope Sixtus IV established the cult in practice throughout Europe.
33. Delaruelle, Labande, and Ourliac, pp. 779–86; Levi d'Ancona, *Immaculate Conception;* Kronenberg, *Maria's Heerlijkheid.* A large list of references on the cult of the Immaculate Conception can be found in H. S. Ettlinger, "The Iconography of the Columns in Titian's Pesaro Altarpiece," *Art Bulletin* 61 (1979): 59ff.
34. Klein, Henze (see n. 4 above).
35. Panofsky, *ENP*, p. 297; Ringbom, p. 30; C. Périer-d'Ieteren, "La Madone de Grâce de Cambrai," *BMRBA*, 1968, pp. 111–14, Silver, "Fountain and Source," p. 100, n. 27.
36. Fritz, "Das Halbfigurenbild," p. 161ff.; E. Wiegand, *Die böhmischen Gnadenbilder* (Würzburg, 1936); Aurenhammer, "Marienikone."
37. Aurenhammer, p. 28ff. A noteworthy pilgrimage site was the chapel on the location of a former synagogue in Regensburg dedicated to the *Schöne Maria;* inside the chapel was a panel of the Virgin and outside a carved stone statue of her on a column. Miracles, such as healing, became quickly associated with both images, and local artists, particularly Albrecht Altdorfer, made replicas of the wondrous *Madonnas.* Altdorfer painted a panel (Budapest) and also made three woodcuts (W. 88–90), one colored as a memorial. His follower Michael Ostendorfer also issued a woodcut of *The Pilgrimage to Mary the Beautiful at Regensburg* (W.245). See F. Winzinger, *Albrecht Altdorfer Graphik* (Munich, 1963), pp. 27ff., 83ff.
38. M. J. Friedländer, "Uber den Zwang der ikonographischen Tradition in der vlämischen Kunst," p. 19ff.
39. In some respects, this is a process like the extraction from a narrative of the Germanic *Andachtsbild* for mystical contemplation; for example, the abstraction of the Christ and Sleeping St. John from the Last Supper context or the Christ Crowned with Thorns from the Ecce Homo. The principal discussion of this phenomenon is E. Panofsky, "Imago Pietatis," p. 261ff.; also idem, "Jean Hey," p. 9ff.; D. Klein, "Andachtsbild," cols. 681-87; Ringbom, p. 51ff., with bibliography.
40. Panofsky, *ENP*, pp. 183–84.
41. J. Cahill, "Style as Idea in Ming-Ching Painting," pp. 137–56.
42. R. Bernheimer, *The Nature of Representation* (New York, 1961), p. 69ff.
43. Friedländer, vol. 7, n. 40; Baldass, p. 153ff.; also O. Benesch, "The Pictorial Unity of Late Gothic and Renaissance," *Art of the Renissance in Northern Europe*, p. 82.
44. The motif of putti-and-swags is a commonplace in Memling's *oeuvre.* See the Vienna and Florence Mary icons, Friedländer, vol. 6, nos. 9, 61.
45. Ibid., no. 165; also included by David in the unusual but grandiose context of his 1498 *Justice of Cambyses* for the Bruges Town Hall (ibid., no. 222; see Janssens de Bisthoven and Parmentier, *Primitifs Flamands*, p. 12ff.). The *Sedano triptych* also transcribes a van Eyck composition, the Virgin and Child of the 1436 *van der Paele Madonna* (Bruges; Janssens de Bisthoven and Parmentier, p. 36ff.)
46. On the interpretation of van Eyck's Berlin *Madonna in a Church* (applicable as well to other images of the Madonna in churchlike surroundings by van Eyck: the *van der Paele Madonna* and *Dresden Madonna*), see Panofsky, *ENP*, p. 144ff.; also C. Purtle, *The Marian Paintings of Jan van Eyck* (Princeton, 1982), esp. pp. 144–56.

47. Friedländer, vol. 8, no. 125; Panofsky, *ENP*, p. 352, n. 12; G. Brom, "Vernieuwing van onze Schilderkunst in de vroege Renaissance," pp. 26–27, stresses not the copy itself but the "modernized" Renaissance architecture and ornament.
48. *Flanders in the Fifteenth Century*, p. 171ff., no. 43; *Primitifs flamands anonymes*, p. 57ff., no. 18. Also, Silver, "Fountain and Source," p. 99.
49. Panofsky, *ENP*, p. 353; Brom, *Vernieuwing*, pp. 28–29; *Jan Gossaert genaamd Mabuse*, pp. 76–80, no. 7. The discovery of the name of the Italian patron was made by J. Duverger, "Nieuwe gegevens betreffende het Breviarium Grimani," *Annuaire des MRBA de Belgique* 1 (1938); 19–30, permitting the dating of the panel to around the year 1513.
50. This concept of "drift" within repeated artistic types is presented by G. Kubler, *The Shape of Time* (New Haven, 1962), p. 60.
51. O. Erich, "Adam-Christus (alter und neuer Adam)," *RDK* I, cols. 157–67.
52. Friedländer, vol. 9, no. 35; R. Fritz, *Sammlung Becker I. Gemälde alte Meister* (Dortmund, 1967), no. 27 ("ca. 1518").
53. See Chapter 9. On Joos van Cleve, see two unpublished dissertations: J. Hand, "Joos van Cleve: The Early and Mature Paintings" (Princeton University, 1978); E. Lanc, "Die religiösen Bilder des Joos van Cleve" (Vienna, 1972). The standard monographs are von Baldass, *Joos van Cleve*, and Friedländer, vol. 9, Eng. ed. On Joos and Leonardo, see G. Marlier, "Joos van Cleve—Fontainbleau and Italy," *Connoisseur* 165 (1967): 25ff.; S. Sulzberger, "L'Influence de Leonard da Vinci et ses repercussions à Anvers," p. 105ff.; J. Hand, "Joos van Cleve," 212ff. Cf. also the discussion of Joos's Kansas City/Cincinnati *Madonna of the Cherries* (Friedländer, vol 9, no. 58) by M. C. Leach, "Michelangelo Invenit, Joos van Cleve explicavit," *Studies in Iconography* 5 (1979): 93–106.
54. Friedländer, vol. 9, no. 65; Panofsky, p. 354; Brom, "Viernieuwing," pp. 24–25.
55. J. Held, "Artis Pictoriae Amator," p. 53ff.; F. Baudouin," 'The Picture Gallery of Cornelis van der Geest' by Willem van Haecht," in *Rubens*, p. 283ff. The visit is mentioned by Fickaert, *Metamorphosis*, p. 15, and by van Forenenbergh. *Die Antwerpschen Protheus*, p. 25.
56. Lazareff, "Iconography of the Virgin," p. 36ff.; Vloberg, "Les Types iconographiques"; Aurenhammer, "Marienikone"; Ringbom, p. 59, n. 25; D. Schorr, *The Christ Child in Devotional Images in Italy during the XIV Century* (New York, 1954), pp. 38–48; K. A. Wirth, "Elëusa," *RDK* IV, cols. 1297–1307; Silver, "Fountain and Source," pp. 99–100. The Eleusa type in its "Glykophilousa" variant formed the image of the Italo-Byzantine icon copied by Petrus Christus and Hayne de Bruxelles in 1454 at Cambrai (see above, n. 35).
57. Friedländer, vol. 3, nos. 9, 9a, add. 115.
58. Friedländer, vol. 6, no. 218.
59. Friedländer, vol. 9, p. 29, no. 63. On Joos van Cleve and Leonardo, see the references above in n. 53, plus the following: G. Glück, "Schicksale einer Komposition Leonardos, der einander küssenden Kinder Jesus and Johannes," p. 502ff.; I. Hecht, "The Infants Christ and John Embracing," pp. 222–29.
60. I. Bergström, "Disguised Symbolism in 'Madonna' Pictures and Still-Life," pp. 303ff., 342ff.; E. de Jongh, "Grape Symbolism in Paintings of the 16th and 17th Centuries," pp. 166–91; H. Friedmann, "The Symbolism of Crivelli's Madonna and Christ Enthroned with Donor in the National Gallery," *Gazette des Beaux-Arts* 32 (1947): 65ff.; J. Snyder, "Jan van Eyck and Adam's Apple," *Art Bulletin* 58 (1976): 511ff.
61. M. Smeyers, "Schilderijen van Kwinten Metsys in het bezit der Aartshertogen Albrecht en Isabella," *Miscellanea Josef Duverger*, vol. 1 (Ghent, 1968) p. 139ff.
62. Friedländer, vol 9, nos. 18, 45. Massys himself had shown such a cameo profile portrait of the Roman emperor against a background brocade and in the spandrels of the *Dance of Salome* wing of the 1508-11 Antwerp *St. John altarpiece* (F. 1, cat. 11). Close in time to the Berlin *Madonna Enthroned*, Quinten inserted similar profiles into the marble throne of the van Pannwitz Madonna.
63. E. Mâle, *L'Art religieux*, pp. 198–221; P. Eich, "Emfängnis Maria, unbefleckte," *RDK* 5, cols. 242–59; H. von Einem, "Die 'Menschenwerdung Christ' des Isenheimer Altares," *Kunstgeschichtliche Studien für Hans Kauffmann* (Berlin, 1956), pp. 152–71; Silver, "Fountain and Source," p. 101.
64. A. Smolar-Meynart, "The Establishment of the Court of Philip the Good and the Institutions of Government in Brussels: A City Becomes a Capital,' " *Rogier van der Weyden*, exh. cat. p. 15ff., esp. 19, with illustrations.
65. R. Koch, "Flower Symbolism in the Portinari Altarpiece," p. 70ff.; L. Behling, *Die Pflanze in der mittelaltarliche Tafelmalerei* (Weimar, 1957).
66. Friedländer, vol. 6, no. 206; T. Musper, "Die Suppenmadonna des Gerard David in den Musées Royaux des Beaux-Arts de Belgique," *Bulletin musées royaux des beaux-arts de Belgique* 17 (1968): 11–14.
67. Post, *KV*, p. 464; Kronenberg, *Maria's Heerlijkheid*, vol. 2, p. 328. Included among these centers was St. Donatien's Church in the Bruges of Gerard David (Toussaert, p. 292).
68. On Campin, see Panofsky, *ENP*, p. 149–77; Friedländer, vol. 2; M. Davies, *Rogier van der Weyden*, p. 253; and the revisionist interpretation by L. Campbell, "Robert Campin, the Master of Flémalle, and the Master of Mérode," *Burlington Magazine* 116 (1974): 634ff. The biographical data are surveyed by T. H. Feder, "A Reexamination through Documents of the First Fifty Years of Roger van der Weyden's Life," *Art Bulletin* 48 (1966): 416ff.; P. Schabacker, "Notes on the Biography of Robert Campin," *Mededelingen van de Koninklijke Academie voor Wetenschappen, Letteren en Schone Kunsten van België* 41 (1980): 3–14.
69. For the Madonna of Humility, M. Meiss, "The Madonna of Humility," p. 434ff., and *Painting in Florence and Siena after the Black Death* (Princeton, 1951), p. 132ff.; H. van Os, *Marias Demut und Verherrlichung*, pp. 79ff., 101ff.
70. De Bosque, pp. 145–48. A later variant by the Massys workshop is the small panel in Tours (ibid., p. 239; also G. Ring, "Additions to the Works of Jan Provost and Quentin Massys," *Burlington Magazine* 80, 1942, p. 71ff.).
71. De Jongh, "Grape Symbolism," pp. 166–91.

72. For van Cleve, see Friedländer, vol. 9, no. 37; E. Lanc, "Die religiösen Bilder," pp. 128–29.

73. For the Leonardo design, see G. Glück, "Schicksale einer Komposition Leonardos," p. 502ff.; Hecht, "Infants Christ and John," pp. 222–29.

74. Gerard David had also portrayed *Christ Taking Leave of His Mother* on a small scale in a pair of late diptychs, pairing the scene with an equivalent scene from the Infancy, an Eleusa-like *Madonna and Child,* showing the intimacy of cheek-to-cheek contact (Friedländer, vol. 6, nos. 168–70; Munich, Basel). For the theme in general, often placed just before the Entry of Christ into Jerusalem in Gospel narrative images, see O. Schmitt, "Abschied Christi von Maria," *RDK* 1, cols. 102–5; J. Breckenridge, " 'Et Prima Vidit': The Iconography of the Appearance of Christ to His Mother," *Art Bulletin* 39 (1957): 9–32, discussing the appearance of the risen Christ to Mary, the other principal moment of their familial farewell. The subject seems to have been a product of late medieval extrapolations on biblical texts, filling in narrative and emotional details in works such as the Pseudo-Bonaventura's 14th-century *Meditations on the Life of Christ,* eds. R. Green and I. Ragusa (Princeton, 1961), where this event appears in its earlier moment as Chap. 72, in its later as Chap. 86.

Pl. 98

Since this chapter went to press, an important new study by Leo Steinberg, *The Sexuality of Christ in Renaissance Art and in Modern Oblivion* (New York, 1983) has confirmed and amplified most of these observations, particularly in the late Madonna panels, concerning the "humanation" of Christ. Indeed, Massys' own development for this genre seems to recapitulate the Renaissance itself in microcosm; here, hieratic Byzantine (-based) icons give way to a new " 'admixture of earthly realism' that was needed to flesh out the icon. . . . Renaissance culture not only advanced an incarnational theology (as the Greek Church had also done) but had evolved representational modes adequate to its expression" (pp. 71–72). This "humanation" was captured perhaps most fully in the lifelike Madonna and Child imagery, later emulated by late Massys, of Campin (and van Eyck). By contrast, the earlier, iconic images of Massys still seem to be steeped in majesty, emphasizing, with medieval Christianity, the divine component of Christ's incarnation. Thus the paradox, articulated above, of the later Madonna images—their (even erotic) humanity, in isolation from their human viewers—is akin to the "special status" Steinberg sees for the body, especially the genitalia, of Christ: a spiritually based, unique "exemption of Christ's nakedness from the mores of Christendom" (p. 72). Through the gulf between Christ's humanity and humankind in Massys' religiosity, the former could more easily find visual expression.

5

Into the Action: Gospel Events

Purely narrative religious art is a rarity except in large-scale cycles, like the frescoes in Italian chapels, capable of giving a chronological description of events in sequence.[1] Illustrated Bibles furnish the best examples of religious narration, but these are relatively rare in the 15th-century, an era of private devotion whose principal illuminated religious books are devotional texts such as the Book of Hours.[2] Smaller, more specific texts, such as the *Apocalypse, Life of Mary,* or *Passion of Christ* as produced by Dürer, are examples of relatively complete illustrated narrative cycles that conform closely with their texts. Printmakers had learned early that a combination of good marketing and piety made cycles of the Life of the Virgin or the Passion into effective, successful series of engravings. Martin Schongauer, Israhel van Meckenem, Lucas van Leyden, and Albrecht Dürer are a selection of engravers whose narrative cycles display this insight. Another fascinating instance of 64 successive narrative events in miniature is the Stein triptych of the Passion (Baltimore, Walters Art Gallery) by the 16th-century Bruges illuminator Simon Bening.[3]

For Massys, on the other hand, none of the images illustrating narrative events from the Gospels is presented as part of a series of images, except in the context of an altarpiece, which already has a dominant liturgical and devotional function.[4] These images are not meant to be read in sequence or to be thought of in terms of their storytelling, but rather must be seen as affective cult images. For example, the Coimbra *Passion altarpiece* (ca. 1514–17; F. 196, cat. 18) contains two scenes from the *Pl. 32* chain of events of Christ's final suffering—the *Flagellation,* unique in Massys' surviving art, and the *Pl. 33* *Ecce Homo,* a subject of several isolated images. But these two Passion scenes surrounded a central, larger Passion event, now destroyed—either a *Crucifixion* or a *Lamentation* (see Chap. 3). The three scenes, then, could not have been read in their proper historical sequence, for the *Flagellation,* the first chronological scene, occurs as the left wing of the triptych (the next event, the *Ecce Homo,* forms the right wing), and the third scene in chronological terms is actually made into the climactic moment, both theologically and emotionally, as the larger, central image. As a result of these other functional priorities, the picture of the *Crucifixion/Lamentation* was shifted out of its proper position within a sequence based on coherent narration. The Coimbra *Passion altarpiece* is the closest of Massys' religious scenes to have any logic based on narrative. It uses three scenes that feature the adult Christ in events from the Gospels, which are closely related in time and space (although here, the interior of the *Flagellation* and the balcony of the *Ecce Homo* are clear changes of scenery). Other Massys altarpieces either break the unity of three related actions (e.g., the *Holy Kinship* centerpiece, a family portrait, surrounded by events from the history of St. Anne) or they have comparable actions involving unrelated individuals (the two saints John martyred alongside the *Lamentation* over the dead Christ in the Antwerp *St. John altarpiece*).

In short, Massys' altarpieces surrender narrative logic to the demands imposed by their liturgical or devotional functions. In this respect, his multi-paneled works fail to convey narrative sequences in the manner of text illustrations or narrative print cycles. Moreover, in isolated religious scenes, where he also uses religious history as the basis for many of his images, Massys frequently reorients the descriptive recounting of events—the who, what, where, when, and how of his textual sources—to the purpose of achieving an expressive image, one more suitable for emotion or devotion. Particularly in his later works, Massys also strives for greater immediacy and intimacy through his half-length presentation of the holy figures in action.

An example of his transformations can be seen in two Massys images of the *Adoration of the Magi*.
Pl. 73 The first, dating from the early part of the artist's career, is reflected in several copies (F. 59; cat. 8); the St. Louis workshop version is illustrated here. The main figures are all repeated exactly in the several versions. Mary, dressed in dark robes, is seated at the right with Christ leaning forward from her lap. Behind stands Joseph, a bearded and humble character only visible in bust-length. The first king, tonsured and beardless, kneels before the Holy Family; behind him, a second, dark-bearded magus stands with a covered golden goblet. After this quartet of figures, the remaining actors vary in the several copies, including the pose of the third king, a black man, who probably was engaged in the process of removing his hat with one hand while presenting his gift with the other. The site of the main action seems to be the Netherlandish commonplace of a stall located within Roman ruins, an image made popular in the mid-15th century by Roger van der Weyden (for instance, the *Bladelin altarpiece,* Berlin).[5] Common to the background of all the copies is a small Flemish village in a green valley. Both in subject and in details of the composition this Massys is closely followed by the Valladolid
Pl. 74 shutter dated 1504 (F. 84) and by an undated *Adoration of the Magi* (F. 87; Philadelphia, Johnson coll.)
Pl. 83 attributed to the Master of the Morrison Triptych.

This Massys *Adoration of the Magi* is expansive in its presentation. All the figures are seen at full-length. Their entire bodies are used in gestures that express intense pious involvement; the kneeling or genuflecting magi incline in forceful profiles toward the Christ Child on the lap of Mary, and the Holy Family, in turn, complements and completes this motion by leaning forward to accept the offerings of the visitors. Compositionally, the scene is a human parenthesis of prayer answered by grace. Except perhaps for the St. Louis workshop vision, the copies do not permit us to reconstruct the precise effects of the setting: the size of the magi's retinue, the expanse of the shed and ruins, the scope of the Netherlandish landscape behind, or even the original physical dimensions. But regardless of scale or particulars of the ambience in the missing original, all the copies of the *Adoration of the Magi* tell us that the image was impressively filled with details. It had a fullness of characters, crowded across the foreground of its slightly vertical dimensions. It also had a fullness of description, from the lavish and exotic costumes of the magi to the details of the environment.

The visual confinement of the Holy Family to the right portion of the composition makes them the passive recipients of the left-to-right movement and of the pious offerings of the three magi, but it also serves to place them in a position of humility, outside the prominent center of the picture. Their humility is underscored, too, by the simple clothing they wear, in marked contrast to the splendor of their regal visitors. Within the picture and within the splendor of worldly power and regalia (particularly the splendid brocade of the kings), the Holy Family shows its true majesty and importance through its modesty and humility.

Massys' *Adoration* is itself a composite of two *Adoration* compositions by one of his most illustrious
Pl. 76 15th-century predecessors, Hugo van der Goes.[6] The first is the *Monforte altarpiece* (Berlin-Dahlem), which features Mary and Christ along a wall and the magi kneeling or standing in the same poses as Massys' figures. In addition, it features the same dress and facial types, including the Goesian black

magus later repeated by Massys. The left background of the *Monforte altarpiece* features buildings and grooms with horses like the background of several of the copies after Massys. The *Monforte altarpiece* was a favorite object of artistic copying during Massys' period. The entire Monforte triptych was copied (Antwerp, Koninklijk Museum) by Massys' Antwerp contemporary the Master of Frankfurt.[7] *Pl. 75* The other 1504 Valladolid panel, a *Nativity,* adapts Hugo's formula from the left wing of the altarpiece, where Mary kneels with angels in adoration of her Child, and Joseph stands beside her and removes his cap. Moreover, the number of adaptive variations on Hugo's inventive composition is legion: to cite only one famous example, Jan Gossaert's early 16th-century *Adoration of the Magi* *Pl. 77* (London).[8]

The other Hugo van der Goes *Adoration of the Magi* is lost but is preserved in a careful copy by Gerard David (Munich, Alte Pinakothek)[9] and other copies by manuscript illuminators. Dubbed the "stall in the hill" *Adoration,* this Goesian composition has the same left-to-right orientation as Massys' *Pl. 78* work, and it also presents the more closely cropped type of Joseph later adopted by Massys.

What the Massys image retains from its antecedents is the decided emphasis on stilled movement and reverential intensity. Hugo's large-scale figures already present the prayerful kneeling and genuflecting poses that figure in Massys' *Adoration.* The rich description present in all 15th-century Flemish pictures was brought to a height of perfection in Hugo's *Monforte altarpiece:* the foreground flowers, the golden gifts, the details of the setting and costume all have existential importance which matches the assertive visual prominence. Partly for this reason, individual still-life elements in Hugo's pictures have been singled out for symbolic readings, usually floral images related to the Virgin and her purity.[10]

The calculatedly derivative nature of Massys' early *Adoration* points to the importance of a "visual pedigree" in Netherlandish art around 1500. We have already seen (Chapter 4) that the portraitlike authenticity of icons led to their being copied—either carefully or freely—from famous established predecessors. The number of copies and variants after Hugo's *Monforte altarpiece* suggests that this work, too, was a highly venerated image whose composition led to numerous reworkings of its "successful" formula. In this respect, the Monforte is one of a select number of "model altarpieces" which spawned copies and imitations well into the 16th century. The *Deposition* by Roger van der Weyden (Madrid, Prado) is probably the most often imitated 15th-century exemplar, along with van *Pl. 21* Eyck's *Ghent altarpiece* and Roger's *Columba altarpiece* (Munich). Modern observers have tended to follow the lead, best expressed in theoretical terms by George Kubler, that certain influential, original, and powerful works of art, called "prime objects," gave rise to a succession of repetitive, derivative, and therefore less-original works that followed.[11] There is no reason, however, to assume that the Netherlands of Massys' early years had anything like the modern aesthetic preference for novelty or for a clearly personalized, recognizable "style" of an individual artist. Indeed, there is evidence to the contrary. The absence of signatures on pictures, coupled with the anonymity of many of the 15th century's painters, demonstrates how little personal identification mattered to most of the makers of pictures in Flanders.[12] For example, not one of the many works ascribed to Roger van der Weyden, including the Prado *Deposition,* is signed by him, and the same applies to Hugo van der Goes. Moreover, the identification of the anonymous masters with a name in documentary records is often a matter of controversy; even when successful, as in the notable case of the identification of the Master of Flemalle with Robert Campin by Hulin de Loo, the process reads like a clever detective story.[13]

Instead of looking for our own modern standards of imagination, originality, and distinctive personality in 15th- and early 16th-century Flemish works, we should rather be looking at the works themselves in order to derive our language of criticism. And in this respect, Massys' early *Adoration of the Magi,* like his early icons, is clearly seeking to ally itself with the art of the previous century. Its archaism is deliberate, and the degree to which it can be confused with the legacy of Hugo van der Goes, as in Winkler's study, is a mark of its success, not of its failure. Massys submerges his own style and artistic identity within the adopted formulas of his great predecessor in the hopes that this pedigree will satisfy the requirements of his artistic commission.

Such archaism and dependence need not be denigrated through the standards of our modern vision. On one extreme, the early 16th-century artist can practice a "knowing and imaginative" borrowing,[14] like Gossaert in his London *Adoration of the Magi,* where the addition of an assertive recession combined with the Goesian hyperrealistic crispness of description adds a new tension and visual richness to Hugo's invention. Massys' image, too, is anything but slavish copying; it borrows the basic figure types and setting of the *Monforte altarpiece* and combines them with the strongly movemented thrust of the adoring magi converging upon the Holy Family at the right, taken from the second, "stall in the hill" *Adoration* by Hugo. There is yet another lesson to be learned by the modern viewer. The very resemblance between Massys' composition and the impressive but anonymous surviving work of 1504, the Valladolid shutter of the *Adoration of the Magi,* serves as a reminder that visual vitality can be reimplanted in each new painting, regardless of whether the compositional ideas are developed "from scratch." Probably no two works could be exact duplicates of one another in any case, and the unintentional deviations by individuals permit modern-day art historians to indulge themselves in the game of guessing the identity of the would-be impersonal copyist.[15]

Massys' *Adoration* is not preserved, except in the St. Louis workshop version, so its specific context and its presentation (scale, frame, possible use of wings) cannot be established. Nevertheless, its insistent monumentality reinforces the impression, suggested by its dependence on previous altarpieces by van der Goes, that its purpose was to adorn a church or chapel altar, or at least to serve a devotional function. All the principal figures are presented in large scale across the foreground of the image; moreover, their own action is that of prayer, making the *Adoration* a fitting subject for liturgical focus and a popular choice for 15th-century altarpieces. Like the veneration of Christ's body in the mass, the Adoration of the Magi theme concentrates attention by the magi (within the image) and by the viewer (from without) upon the figure of the infant Christ. In Massys' case, this focus is underscored strongly by the powerful left-to-right movement across the foreground, culminating in the piled-up composition of the heads of the Child, Mary, and Joseph. In short, this is a frozen, highly significant moment from the continuity of the Gospel story. It is not, as far as we know, part of a continuing narration, although in the case of the *Monforte altarpiece,* the left wing precedes the *Adoration* chronologically with the *Nativity,* and the right wing succeeds the *Adoration* with the *Circumcision.*

Of course, the presence of any Gospel scene on the wing or center of an altarpiece does not preclude its concern with the unfolding story of the Gospels. Even within a single panel, subsidiary spaces can effectively include earlier or later moments of the same story, provided the artist is willing to sacrifice the spatial and temporal unity of his picture. This kind of narration, which Weitzmann calls the "simultaneous method" within a single frame,[16] contrasts with the "monoscenic method" of a single episode in a single space. An extremely full example is the Vienna wing of the Haarlem *St. John altarpiece* by Geertgen tot Sint Jans, which includes in the image of the *Burning of the Bones of John the Baptist* a series of events both before and after that action (burial of the Baptist's head, burial of his body, translation of his relics).[17]

Thus, in terms of time-space considerations, the Massys image is monoscenic, but in terms of its function in the church as an object of liturgical focus and devotion, the scene can be considered to have been chosen more for its devotional elements, built into the story of the Adoration, than for any strictly narrative purpose. Immediate recognition of the principal groups and their contrast in terms of dress, gesture, and location serves as an index of the basic symbolic content of the Adoration as a prototype for the modern mass, taking place below each and every altarpiece.

Medieval theologians distinguished between two broad categories of imagery: *imagines,* or votive pictures, like the icon, and *historiae,* or stories, notably biblical tales in pictures.[18] What is intriguing about the altarpiece subjects based on stories from the Gospels, like the Adoration of the Magi, is that they stand midway between these two traditional distinctions. On the one hand, their clear liturgical function earmarks them for the blend of cult worship and contemplation that was also reserved for iconic likenesses of holy figures. Yet at the same time, their stilled actions, taken from the Christian history, include a multitude of figures in arrested motion within a specific location and a precise moment in time. In the case of Massys' image and its Flemish predecessors, the meticulous description of costumes, setting, and individual characters adds further specificity to the narrative moment, even within the hieratic conventions of a symbolic altarpiece function. For Hugo and his young imitator Massys, altarpiece painting offered the unmatched opportunity for drama and grandeur along with the appropriate Christian devotion.

A 1526 *Adoration of the Magi* (F. 8, cat. 40, New York, Metropolitan Museum), shows that, by the end of Massys' career, some of this balance and grandeur have been altered to produce new effects on the Christian beholder. Gone are the full-length figures of the early, Goesian *Adoration;* in their place, half-length figures crowd into a narrow vertical format. The later work is aggressive, too, in its contrasts, pitting the smooth, white, oval face of the Virgin at the left against the wizened wrinkles and thin grey hair of the oldest magus, or the hirsute ruddiness of the middle magus, or the olive exoticism of the black magus. These contrasts had been present in the earlier *Adoration,* too, but in the 1526 work they are exaggerated, particularly in the splendor of the glittering gilded gifts of the three kings. Gold filigree decorates the foreground scepter and chalice, on a ledge in the immediate purview of the observer, as well as the collars, swords, and trim of the three potentates. The Virgin remains simply dressed in a basic blue mantle and white headdress; she is isolated once more by a visual partition in the form of a hanging cloth behind her and a thick vertical pilaster, itself ornamented with Romanizing grotesques, between the holy figures and their admirers. This later *Adoration* emphasizes still more the humility of the Virgin and Child in comparison to the regal splendor of the magi; in this contrast, the adoration by these opulent worldly potentates of the completely unadorned King of Kings communicates the essential paradox of the Christian mystery. Again, fullness of description is adduced, even enhanced, for the richness of the storytelling. But the artist's decision to present his figures in half-length points to a new conception of the beholder's share in the viewing of Christian narrative. *Pl. 79*

As we have already seen, such half-length images were basic to both the intimacy and the portraitlike authenticity of icons. As such, they were a compelling form for devotion, as Ringbom has magisterially demonstrated.[19] Ringbom goes on to point out that the frontier between *imagines* and *historiae* was further compromised in the course of the 15th century by the development of half-length narrative pictures very like the 1526 *Adoration* by Massys. In both Italy (most notably in the works of Mantegna) and in Flanders (principally Hugo, but possibly also van der Weyden in works now lost), the portraitlike icons that figured in diptychs were fleshed out with figures and transformed into half-length narratives, which retained much of the power and authenticity associated with the original, isolated, bust-length holy figures. Ringbom summarizes the move toward this new, blended image with the phrase "Icon to Narrative." As we have already noted, however, many of the seeds of this transformation were already present in the large narrative scenes of 15th-century Flemish altarpieces, another gray area in time and space between the devotional image and the narrative. The late Madonna images and diptychs by Massys stressed even more action by holy figures (Chap. 4). Is it not equally possible to conceive of Massys' alteration of his late storytelling as a kind of "Narrative to Icon"?

Many of the new elements of the 1526 *Adoration* were grafted onto the Goesian formula from elements which Massys had the opportunity to experience in the active art center of his native Antwerp. For example, the profile head of the aged magus is another of Massys' borrowings from Leonardo da Vinci's drawings of grotesques, in this case the kinds of old men still preserved in two late drawings now at Windsor Castle (Nos. 12499/500). Massys had already used Leonardo heads in his great Antwerp *Lamentation altarpiece* (see Chap. 2) and reused some of the individual studies in such secular works as the *Ill-Matched Pair* (F. 54, cat. 35) and *Grotesque Old Woman* (F. 52, cat. 32; Chap. 7), close in time to the 1526 *Adoration.* The head of the old magus is also not without its precedent in Hugo's work, if we can trust the copy of the *Monforte Altarpiece* made by the Master of Frankfurt. That copy shows the right wing of the Hugo work, the *Circumcision,* with a similar graybeard in the guise of *Pl. 80* *Pl. 17* *Pl. 124* *Pl. 129* *Pl. 81* high priest; like the Leonardo head, his pate is bald, his hair and beard white, his nose aquiline. Of Massys' exposure to both these powerful artists there can be no doubt, and it seems pointless to choose between them as sources for the arresting visage of the old magus. Massys could not have helped noting the Goesian high priest as he reviewed the composition of the *Monforte altarpiece,* the ultimate source for his triad of black, red, and white kings in his *Adoration.* But the intensified emphasis on physiognomy, particularly the stress on age and deformity in the senior magus, points to the impact of Leonardo. The consequences of this use of unattractive and exotic heads within the context of an Adoration emerge when we consider the other Antwerp versions of this subject.

In fact, the Adoration was by far the most-popular visual product of Antwerp painting during the years of Massys' maturity. In particular, the group of anonymous artists commonly referred to by the phrase "Antwerp Mannerists" seems to have flourished during the teens of the 16th century; their *Pl. 82* favorite subject by far was the Adoration of the Magi. The Adoration theme enabled the Antwerp Mannerists to indulge in most of the predilections that are the hallmark of their production: exotic costumes, often with glittering highlights and fluttering draperies; odd figure types, seemingly from every nation, crowded tightly together; and fantastic settings, usually ornate but ravaged ruins opening up onto a luminous background landscape.[20] We have already seen one of the roots of such a style in Massys' work in the Antwerp *St. John Altarpiece,* and the connections of that work to the flourishing Antwerp export trade of sculpted retables is another clue for the explanation of the characteristics of Antwerp Mannerism. In fact, several of these painted scenes are found in combination with the figurated sculpture of Antwerp's carvers, usually as the wing panels adorning a sculpted central interior.[21] While it is less clear that the Antwerp Mannerist paintings were as large an export commodity as the sculpture of Antwerp, the powerful vogue for these pictures and the relative uniformity of their visual conventions point to an assembly-line production responding to high demand.

Aside from its potential for decorative elaboration, there is reason why the subject of the Adoration of the Magi should be especially prominent among the Antwerp Mannerist painters. That reason lay in the very nature of Antwerp during the 1510s. The city of Massys and the Mannerists had become a boom town in terms of incoming trade and visitors from foreign lands. The Portuguese spice trade was the basis of the new prosperity, and along with the Portuguese, a variety of national trading communities, of "nations" (including Spanish, Italians, English, and both Northern and Southern Germans) was established in Antwerp. It is not possible to reconstruct the literal composition of the foreign community at Antwerp, but it is certain that the city acquired a most cosmopolitan flavor during the period in which Antwerp Mannerism was beginning to flourish, shortly after 1510.[22] Both newcomers from the provinces and natives of Antwerp must have been dazzled by the meteoric rise of the city and the sights and sounds of its burgeoning prosperity. Something of this impression has been preserved in the descriptions of Antwerp in Albrecht Dürer's diary of his visit to the Low Countries in 1520–21.[23] It is significant that some of Dürer's strongest alliances during his visit were with the Portuguese community, and he even made a careful silverpoint study (Florence, Uffizi) of Catherina, the Moorish servant of the Portuguese factor Brandão.[24] Precisely these kinds of sights and studies made their way into the numerous Adorations, including the carefully drawn black magus of Massys' own 1526 *Adoration.*

One further document for the association of the magi's visit with Antwerp's own prosperity is the inclusion of the city skyline (including the uncompleted towers of the cathedral) in the background of *Pl. 83* one such *Adoration of the Magi* (F. 87, Philadelphia, Johnson coll.), a variant upon the Goesian formula of the Valladolid shutters by the Master of the Morrison Triptych.[25] Of course, the local chauvinism could simply be a reference to Antwerp as the New Jerusalem, like the presence of Paris as the background to the Meeting of the Magi in Jean de Berry's *Tres Riches Heures,* painted by the Limbourg Brothers a century earlier. But whereas the conceit of the French duke could make his national capital a crossroads for kings, it was actually appropriate in the early 16th century to see Antwerp—a world economic capital and a crossroads for the nations—as the repository of the kings' gifts and their admiration.[26] In this respect the *Adoration* was particularly apt, since tradition held that its three magi were representatives of the three corners of the earth: Europe, Asia, and Africa. Now the Portuguese had linked all three regions into a single trade nexus bound for Antwerp, so the presence of Moors, Indians, or other Asians in Antwerp was a real-life possibility rather than the stuff of imagination.[27]

Even though Antwerp Mannerism had pretty much run its course by 1526, the interest in the three magi remained strong in Antwerp painting. In particular, Massys' younger contemporary Joos van Cleve continued to paint the subject during the 1520s. One van Cleve *Adoration of the Magi*, repeated in *Pl. 84* versions in both Detroit and Naples, probably predates the Massys images by only a year or two.[28] Van Cleve's swarthy, dark-bearded Asiatic king and his black African magus provide figure types that are closer to Massys than to any other Antwerp precedents. Joos's setting, with improvised wood lintels and Italianate pilasters, also reappears in Massys' picture, and the gifts of the magi, most notably the foreground goblet and scepter, are strikingly similar. Also important in both works is the crowded retinue of the kings in the middleground threshold. Joos van Cleve was dean *(dekan)* of the Antwerp painter's guild in 1525 and had occupied that position several times since his admission to membership in 1511, so it is certain that Massys knew his work. Joos's career serves as a kind of weathervane in Antwerp art to local visual fashions—from Bruges-influenced archaisms, to Antwerp Mannerism, to this more-monumental, Italian-influenced work of the 1520s (see Chap. 9)—so the Detroit / Naples composition offers a good point of departure, a kind of artistic *koine* for Antwerp in the mid-1520s, which is basic for our understanding of the later Massys image.

Viewed against the Joos composition, Massys' 1526 half-length again stands out by virtue of its assertive physiognomies and by virtue of its rejection of the traditional altarpiece format of the triptych. The busts and half-lengths also bring the viewer into a more empathic relationship with the magi as a kind of coworshiper, rather than as a detached observer of the actions and gestures of the full-length figures. The Virgin tilts her head downward in the direction of the Child and leans her body forward in the direction of the old magus, but in fact the basic posture of her body faces out of the picture and confronts the viewer directly. Separated by the table on which the goblet and scepter rest, the observer is able to understand himself as an additional participant in the process of adoration.

At this point Massys' choice of the Leonardesque face for the principal magus takes on additional weight. After all, it is an ugly and aged face, yet it is a face to which the Virgin and Child incline as they receive the king's prayerful gesture and intense, adoring gaze. This is not, after all, a solemn and grand ceremony of worshipers, like Hugo's *Monforte altarpiece* or Gossaert's London *Adoration.* Neither is it the spectacular and ornate display of an Antwerp Mannerist composition or the early versions of this subject by Joos van Cleve. Although it adopts elements from both these conceptions, Massys' 1526 *Adoration* nevertheless presents the inescapable impression that these are somehow ugly or strange characters adoring the Infant, and that quite possibly the viewer is to be included among them. Only the 1564 London *Adoration of the Kings* by Peter Bruegel presents so incongruous a set of worshipers (although in that case the element of humor in the faces softens its disturbing aspects), and there the figures are full-length, with less psychological address of the beholder.[29]

The same impression regarding the representatives of mankind emerges from an inspection of the retinue of the magi, crowded behind them in the middleground of Massy's picture. Unlike the dignified and staid followers of Joos van Cleve's composition, Massy's entourage reacts strongly, and they present the same powerfully expressive faces as their leaders in the foreground. Several of them strain eagerly to see the spectacle before them and raise a hand in the profession of amazement or piety, like the magi. But others openly scowl, like the man featured directly between the red and black magi (his face seems to be a modification of an unbearded Leonardo type, like the scowling *Old Man,* *Pl. 85* now in Rome).[30] Others seem to be looking around at their comrades to see what their proper reaction ought to be or to seek some explanation for all the fuss. (This same puzzled reaction reappears in the right figure of the two *Praying Monks,* painted by Massys around the same time). In short, this group of representatives of mankind is a mixed lot. They seem to encompass the usual comprehensive slate of people: not only the three regions of the globe, but also the basic distinction of age, ranging from the youth of the Moor, to the bearded maturity of the Asian, to the withered baldness and white hair of the European. But while the magi, recipients of a miraculous epiphany, are responding with proper reverence, their less-enlightened followers display a variety of emotions.[31] Some, in fact, are openly hostile to the wondrous figures before them. Massys uses the retinue of the magi to present the viewer with a rabble, the same kind of crowd witnessing the Child as will later judge Him and condemn Him to crucifixion.

This, then, is the significance of the choice of half-length and forceful faces in the 1526 *Adoration* by Massys. The viewer is invited by the presentation of the scene to join in with the contemplation of the holy figures, just as he would do for a half-length icon; and it is significant in this respect that the
Pl. 64 figure of the Virgin is virtually identical to the humbly dressed half-length Madonna panels produced
Pl. 68 by Massys in his final years, such as the Detroit *Madonna Outdoors* or the 1529 Paris *Rattier Madonna.*
But at the same time, the nature of the magi and their followers adds a disturbing note to the observer's experience of the picture, for the characters in the story with whom he would most properly identify are presented as either unattractive, unfamiliar, or unresponsive to the religious moment. Massys suggests that true piety is not a natural instinct, common to all men, but rather that it is a response that must result from insight, or even divine instruction (like the vision of grace offered to the magi). With such a picture as the 1526 *Adoration,* the viewer is encouraged to practice precisely the same reverential devotion as the magi within the image process. And in the process of extracting this new, active contemplation of the religious subject, Massys has transformed his 1526 *Adoration of the Magi* from the altarpiece-centered conception of his earlier work into a new, hybrid religious work that combines biblical storytelling with meditative empathy.

The same kind of transformation can be seen in the case of a subject drawn from the Passion
Pl. 33 narrative. Massys' first rendition of the *Ecce Homo,* or Christ Presented to the People, was the altarpiece wing of the Coimbra Passion Altar (1514/17; F. 196, cat. 18; Chap. 3). In that work, the tall, full-length format of the altarpiece led the artist to present his figures at virtually full-length, with Christ and Pilate appearing at half-length on the palace balcony above the jeering crowd. In this instance, the equation, so frequent in Massys' work, of ugliness with spiritual evil (the root cause for finding the magi disturbing within the 1526 *Adoration*) is imposed upon the crowd so that no uncertainty is possible about their malevolence to the Savior. In contrast, Christ is presented as humble, inward-turning, and physically stooped before the abuses of the mob. In the case of the Coimbra image, the viewer can take a relatively distanced and detached look at the biblical event, but already there is some attempt on Massys' part to involve him; in the lower right corner of the wing is a figure, looking much like the sharp-faced skeptic in the 1526 panel, who gazes outward toward the beholder even as he raises both hands in a gesture of refusal, or denial toward Christ. This disturbing glance seems to implicate the viewer in the torments of Christ or at least to seek his assent in the condemnations by the crowd.

Such an impression is heightened in Massys' next version of the Ecce Homo, the Madrid (Prado)
Pl. 86 *Christ Presented to the People* (F. 10, cat. 31). This second picture lowers the horizon line from the approximate mid-point of the picture to somewhere near its lowest reaches. In consequence, the viewer is placed squarely within the crowd, and he must look upward toward Christ and Pilate as if he were an active participant in the judging process. The Prado *Ecce Homo* is even more aggressively ugly in the heads of the mocking crowd; indeed, most of the hostile faces are far worse in appearance than the skeptical followers of the magi in the 1526 *Adoration.* Like those heads, the heads of the Prado
Pl. 16 crowd owe a considerable debt to Leonardo, principally the *Five Grotesque Heads* drawing that Massys
Pl. 17 had previously employed for the tormentors of his *Martyrdom of John the Evangelist.* Massys is careful to
underline the irony of the crowd's ignorance by means of the sculptures that ornament Pilate's palace. Not only are there images of pagan gods and heroes on the facade, which contrast with the humble appearance of the true King of Heaven before the people, but there are also images that offer ironic models of the proper response to Christ. Within the arch is a scene of an enthroned figure receiving homage, like the Adoration of the Magi theme. Alongside it on the front of the palace is an image of

Caritas, a nude young woman nursing a host of small naked children (she, in turn, is observed by an older, bearded man, recalling the protective Joseph behind the Virgin in many Nativities). But only the viewer can locate these alternate visions of right conduct; the crowd is too preoccupied with its abuses and takes no notice of the sculpted scenes. At the lowest level of the palace, on the balustrade behind which Christ and Pilate stand, is a relief scene, almost invisible in photographs of the painting, which is more in keeping with the crowd's attitudes: a painful scene of flagellation. Presumably this distressing image refers to the physical torment Christ has just undergone, the very torment which lay on the other wing of the Coimbra *Passion altarpiece.*

Yet for all his conviction that this scene lies in the past and was the responsibility of the ignorant masses of Christ's day, the viewer cannot escape the process of associating himself as an active persecutor with that very rabble. For the frog's-eye perspective of Massys' picture insistently places the viewer among the rabble, looking directly at the boot of Pilate and up at the balcony where the judgment is taking place. In addition, the device of direct address from within the picture, which Massys had already used in the *Ecce Homo* of the Coimbra *Passion retable,* has been repeated in the Prado picture. At the lower right corner of the panel is another figure, gross and ugly, staring out at the viewer; as in the Coimbra picture, the fat man and his comrades raise their hands defiantly against Christ. In the Prado picture more than in any other of his works, Massys goes out of his way to indict mankind for its failure to acknowledge and revere the unpretentious majesty of Christ. Unlike the *Adoration of the Magi,* where the problem is simply one of recognition and enlightenment, here the crowd fails abjectly even to be Christian, let alone show true piety toward Christ Himself. They condemn Him like a common criminal with an absolute lack of compassion or Christian charity. And Massys suggests visually that this process can easily be repeated today, that it should not be viewed as an isolated or historically distant dilemma of choice, by forcing the beholder of his image to include himself among this odious assembly.

In Massys' final composition of the *Ecce Homo* (Venice, F. 11, cat. 46), the crowd is no longer present as a distinct group. Instead, the ugly and angry faces of malice are alongside Pilate and Christ, and the entire scene is enacted directly before the viewer. This *Ecce Homo* is no longer Christ Presented to the People but rather Christ Presented to the Beholder. Like the iconic images of devotion, the scene is now presented up close, at three-quarter length. Now the image focuses on the spiritual detachment of Pilate, who seems to wash his hands before our eyes with his averted glance and upraised hands, almost like the gestures of denial by the mob in the previous two pictures. And of course it also focuses, like so much of the late medieval piety which we have already discussed in terms of the previous altarpieces, on the figure of the Suffering Savior, the Man of Sorrows. Christ, crowned with thorns and slumping wearily after the blows of his tormentors, is the very heart of this picture, and He stands in need of the viewer's mercy and compassion. The only palace ornament is a capital, which echoes the crown of thorns, on a column base, now devoid of the expected figure sculpture (such as the pagan star-god of the Prado *Ecce Homo*); this single unadorned column may well be an allusion to the Flagellation. *Pl. 87*

That this picture is closely related to the images of Christ as the Man of Sorrows is demonstrated by the several mediocre copies that excerpt the Venice *Ecce Homo* Savior to produce an iconic image of the type called by Ringbom the "Salvator coronatus," a fusion of the Man of Sorrows with the Salvator Mundi (e.g., Dieric Bouts, Hugo van der Goes, or the French painter Jean Hey).[32] Again, the distinction should be drawn between the "subtractive" process of producing a close-up narrative scene with limited figures, cut down from the larger, full-scale altarpiece, and the "additive" method of producing a close-up narrative by supplementing iconic figures with the necessary accomplices to create a proper storytelling. Ringbom and Panofsky suggest that many of the close-up narratives are the result of addition of figures to devotional images like the Man of Sorrows or Madonna and Child; however, the example of Massys shows that the reduced narratives with meditative emphasis, such as the 1526 *Adoration of the Magi* and the Venice *Ecce Homo,* are instead the result of a subtractive concentration of figures and bust-length format from the fuller richness of altarpiece narrative. Yet the controversial nature of the development itself serves to underscore the degree to which the hybrid images by Massys lie halfway between the story-telling and devotional functions of religious pictures, between *historiae* and *imagines*. They are as capable of being further reduced to icons, like the Man of Sorrows, as they are capable of being seen as full-blown religious narratives.

The Venice *Ecce Homo,* then, culminates the rethinking of the religious narrative image that Massys had been developing. It simultaneously presents all the necessary aspects of the story that serve to give it concrete reality: the costumes and props (Pilate's chain of command and his beautiful ermine collar, Christ's wounded skin and crown of thorns), the setting and characters, especially the snarling faces of Pilate's henchmen. But it also forces the Christian viewer to contemplate the fearful spectacle of the injured Christ begging for mercy, as if the issue of crucifixion were still in doubt. Massys' image offers the dilemma of judgment directly and individually to the beholder, who is no longer submerged within a large crowd. Confrontation with the viewer by the holy figures demands response in the form of active involvement with the religious story. Whether a case of Adoration for the Christ Child or mercy for the Man of Sorrows, Massys' half-length narratives offer a call for empathy.

In the case of the Road to Calvary, the transformation to contemplative image is equally compelling. *Pl. 88* When Massys painted *Christ Carrying the Cross* in the *Seven Sorrows polyptych* for the Madre de Deus convent in Portugal (ca. 1510–12; see Chap. 3), he included an entire cast of characters; akin to the *Pl. 15* tormentors of the *Martyrdom of St. John the Evangelist,* completed just before, are the hideous grotesques who suppress Christ and hinder His progress with the cross. Witnesses in the middle ground beside Christ are John and the holy women, including the Virgin, whose grieving compassion is the subject of the entire polytpych. Accessory figures, such as Simon of Cyrene helping Christ with the heavy burden of the cross, and a mounted Roman official, complete the drama, which unfolds *Pl. 89* before the city walls. Only a few years later, the Amsterdam / Hague *Christ Carrying the Cross* (F. 167; cat. 15) modifies the presentation of narrative in order to include elements of direct viewer address. The number of characters and narrative details have been pared down; Mary and the other mourners are absent, and only the tormentors surrounding Christ have been included. While the city walls have been retained in smaller scale and a distant view of Golgotha appended, the real focus of the Amsterdam image is Christ and the cross. The two diagonal beams of the cross dominate the picture, and their intersection at the very center serves to signal the suffering visage of Christ and also to emphasize the massive weight under which His body slumps below. Visually, the cross marks off a pictorial sector in which Christ is isolated; around Him the vexing soldiers seem to swarm like noisy insects. The effect is reminiscent of the powerful half-length image by Bosch of *Christ Carrying the Cross* (Ghent), presumably a late work which was painted around the same time as the Massys image.[33] There, Christ is literally swallowed up within a murky sea of dark and grotesque faces of His persecutors; only the central placement of Christ's face and the diagonal placement of the cross serve as signposts to locate Him.

In psychological power, the Bosch image is even more compelling than Massys' full-length Amsterdam *Road to Calvary.* Indeed, the Bosch image stands as a possible prototype for the later Massys half-lengths, like the New York *Adoration of the Magi* and the Venice *Ecce Homo.* But the Bosch head of Christ is completely introspective, eyes closed and motion stilled. Massys' Christ, in contrast, has fallen under the weight of the cross. He supports His burden during this pause with a hand on a knoll, which helps to brace the upper beam. In the meantime, Christ's body is turned toward the observer, and His pain-wracked gaze casts imploringly outward. The picture literally calls out for assistance, and it is directed toward the beholder. Like the device of eye contact, which he was to use *Pl. 33* during the same period for his Coimbra *Ecce Homo* wing, Massys intensifies the experience of the religious narrative by addressing the viewer. And the consequence of his arrangement is more than an enlivening of the storytelling: it is once again a call to involvement, in this case a cry for help in carrying the cross.

The call to carry the cross with Christ in an empathic way was a commonplace within meditational literature of the late Middle Ages. To cite just a few famous examples which need not have been familiar to Massays, Thomas à Kempis addresses an emotional call to Christian ascetic ideals through this metaphor:

> Man is not by nature inclined to carry the cross, to love the cross, to chasten the body, and to bring it into subjection. . . . But if you trust in the Lord, you will be given strength from Heaven, and the world and flesh will become subject to your will. . . . Resolve, then, as a good and faithful servant of Christ, manfully to bear the cross of your Lord. . . . Christ has gone before you, bearing his cross; He died for you on the cross, that you also may bear your cross and desire to die with Him. For if you die with Him, you will also share His glory.[34]

In his *Handbook of the Militant Christian* (*Enchiridion militis Christiani*, 1503), Erasmus conveys something of the importance of devotion to the cross for Massys' period, even in belittling that devotion:

> There is, however, one remedy that can be applied to any and all temptations, and that is the Cross, which is the example for those who fall, the refuge for those who toil, and the weapon for those in the fray. This is the one weapon you should use against the Devil. The people have the Passion read to them and adore the image of the Cross. They strengthen themselves by hanging crosses about themselves and by keeping parts of the true Cross about their homes. They work themselves into veritable agonies as they meditate on Christ's Passion and cry tears of compassion for Him. The true value of the Cross, however, is in profiting from its many examples. You cannot say that a person loves Christ if he does not follow his example.[35]

The Erasmus passage makes clear how much of a role serious reading and meditation inspired by Christ's Passion played in the religious life of Massys' day. We have already examined testimony to the same effect in the meditative and emotional poems written by Cornelius Grapheus (1530) in response to the Massys *Crucifixion triptych* for Damião de Gois. It is hardly surprising, then, to find a large number of Massys paintings of the Crucifixion. These images also remind us that intensive meditation does not require as powerful a visual expression as the outward gaze or half-length presentation that we have just seen in Massys' mature works.

Besides the de Gois Crucifixion altarpiece of the 1520s and a "Holy Cross panel" destroyed in the Antwerp cathedral during the iconoclastic riots of 1566 (see Appendix, Lost Works),[36] Massys can be credited with a number of other versions of the same subject. One of the earliest images that can be associated with the artist, the *Seilern Crucifixion*, includes a pair of donors kneeling in prayer under the *Pl. 90* cross.[37] Their piety makes them witness to the sorrowful event, and their inclusion makes them perpetual mourners along with the Virgin and St. John, even though they are clearly distinguished from the holy figures by dress, kneeling pose, and distance from the central cross. It is significant that the donor at the right is dressed in the white robes of the Carthusian order, at whose monastic house in Kiel Massys died and was buried in 1530.

During the same period when Massys was finishing the Coimbra *Passion altarpiece* and the Amsterdam *Christ Carrying the Cross*, the artist was also producing a number of impressive *Crucifixions*. A *Crucifixion triptych* from this period, possibly involving considerable workshop assistance, also shows a married couple as donors with their patron saints before a continuous landscape (Antwerp, Mayer van den Bergh Museum; F. 56, cat. 22). That central composition appears to be an expanded version of a single-panel *Crucifixion* (Ottawa; F. 12, cat. 20), which included only the figures of Mary and John *Pl. 91* standing beside the cross and the grieving Magdalene clinging to its base. As in the case of the icons of Christ and the Virgin (see Chap. 4), this *Crucifixion* has archaistic tendencies going back to compositions by Roger van der Weyden and Jan van Eyck. In those 15th-century examples, the grieving Virgin as Stabat Mater appears on the right side of the cross, her head sunk passively downward, shielded by her mournful, dark blue robes;[38] opposite her, in contrast, the anguished John the Evangelist looks upward toward the cross, wringing his hands dramatically against his vivid red garment.

The vertical figure of Christ is borrowed from an Eyckian composition, known from its copies on panel (Venice, Ca d'Oro) and from manuscript illumination (the *Turin-Milan Hours*, fo. 48v.).[39] The *Pl. 92* van der Weyden prototype (which itself may be a variant of the Eyckian formula, since it retains the

Pl. 93 basic figures and layout),[40] is best reflected in a small workshop retable, the *Sforza triptych* (Brussels), which adds the fluttering loincloth of Christ and the more animated gesture of the Evangelist with the more averted pose of the Virgin. The grieving Magdalene is yet another der Weyden trademark in the Netherlands, probably borrowed from the Trecento models Roger had seen in Italy, and first appearing in Roger's work in his Vienna *Crucifixion triptych.*

If one may extrapolate from the conclusions drawn earlier regarding archaisms as essential components of the creation of many icons and altarpieces, it is entirely possible that the borrowed features of Massys' Ottawa *Crucifixion* were adopted precisely in order to make it a "proper" object of meditation. Such an image could thereby partake of the pedigree and perhaps even an associated wonder-working efficacy of its predecessors, just like the superstitious objects of meditation on the cross cited by Erasmus.

Of course, the crucifixion is the central theme of Christianity, but its representations held particular significance within Massys' Antwerp. The city's oldest religious confraternity (established 1375) was dedicated to the Holy Cross and located within the cathedral.[41] Along with the other Antwerp confraternities (and those in other cities, such as the Louvain confraternity of St. Anne), the Brotherhood of the Holy Cross flourished during the late 15th century, and it promoted celebrations of the Invention of the Cross and the Raising of the Cross. The confraternity held Friday masses before its altar, which stood in front of the chapter choir, between the main altar of the choir and the parish altar. The brotherhood also paid for the erection of a new crucifix with John and Mary in front of the high choir in 1500.[42] It is highly possible that the popularity of the Crucifixion as a subject for Massys and his contemporaries, such as Joos van Cleve, was stimulated in part by the local devotion of the Antwerp Holy Cross confraternity.

Essential within the Crucifixion scenes and integral to many other Passion subjects is the figure of the grieving Virgin. We have already seen the mourning Virgin at the very center of Massys' Antwerp
Pl. 20 *Lamentation;* her suffering was the basis of the *Seven Sorrows* polyptych of the same period, a work
Pl. 24 which contained not only the *Crucifixion* but also the *Road to Calvary, Lamentation,* and *Holy Figures at the*
Pl. 26 *Tomb* among its Passion scenes of grief. The cult of the Seven Sorrows has already been mentioned,
Pl. 27 and its local significance was its adoption by Massys' own St. Luke guild. But the idea of the Virgin's suffering in a kind of com-Passion was a widespread 15th-century theological concept, whose significance for art has been beautifully sketched by Otto von Simson in connection with van der
Pl. 21 Weyden's Prado *Deposition.*[43] Thus, it is hardly surprising to find Massys producing imagery of the Lamentation and the special intimacy of the Virgin with her dead Son, the Pietà, as a kind of *exemplum* of pious grief.[44] During the teens, around the same time as the Amsterdam *Way to Calvary* or the
Pl. 94 Ottawa *Crucifixion,* Massys produced a *Pietà* (Paris, Louvre; F. 16, cat. 17) that includes the sorrowful John the Evangelist as a helper with the head of the dead Christ. Like most of the Passion images of the teens, the Louvre *Pietà* is full-length in presentation, and it contains a rather full description of the Calvary landscape. Behind the figures lie the walls and the city of Jerusalem, the rocky mount of Golgotha, and the rock-cut tomb in which figures with candles are preparing to receive Christ's corpse. Yet, like the Ottawa *Crucifixion,* the Louvre *Pietà* looks backward for its visual arrangement. Its three figures are derived in most essentials (including the white cloth held by the Evangelist under the head of Christ) from Massys' great predeccesor in Louvain, Dieric Bouts. Bouts' *Lamentation* (Paris, Louvre) also provided an extensive landscape background, although it featured a grieving Magdalene and situated the mourners directly under the foot of the cross.

Massys returned to the same subject at the end of his career in a *Pietà* composition known only
Pl. 95 through a series of workshop variants and copies, the best of which is now in Brussels (F. 15, cat. 47).[45] As in the case of the other, late, religious narratives, this *Pietà* is in half-length. It features only the Virgin and her dead Son behind a foreground ledge on which are placed the relics of the Passion: crown of thorns and nails. The tender embrace of the Madonna, kissing her Son on the lips, recalls the
Pl. 68 panels of Madonna and Child from this same late period, such as the 1529 *Rattier Madonna* (F. 24; cat.
Pl. 58 48) and the lost *Madonna of the Cherries* (F. 67; cat. 50). The late *Pietà* features a host of landscape

elements that serve both to locate the story in a specific locale and to convey something of its emotional tenor. Golgotha is visible with its three crosses in the right distance, but equally important is the dense, gloomy pall of clouds above the place of martyrdom, broken only by the glowing sunset on the horizon behind the hold figures. Nature herself seems to be mourning the death of Christ, as the Bible describes, and Massys has added an extra feature in the withered tree behind the Madonna to underscore the mood of death.

Just as Bouts's *Lamentation* served as a model for Massys' Louvre *Pietà*, so this later *Pietà* has an archaistic foundation in the works of van der Weyden. Roger and his workshop produced a series of Pietà compositions, usually with a donor witness kneeling prayerfully beside the holy figures (best version, London, National Gallery).[46] The van der Weyden formula also features a tender kiss between Virgin and Christ, although it is presented at full-length. The presence of pious donors within the picture indicates a devotional intent of Roger's images similar to Massys' *Crucifixion* with donors, a use of Gospel narrative as a stimulus to devotion. Other details, such as the red mantle of Mary and her white cloth headcover, seem to be derived by Massys from the Rogerian model. *Pl. 97*

Like his other, late, religious narratives, Massys' *Pietà*, comes close to realizing both story-telling and meditative functions in a single image, although here only the holy figures are presented in a kind of iconic timelessness, extracted from the narrative context, like the German *Andachtsbild*.[47] Not only is the embrace analogous to the more activated late images of Madonna and Child by Massys (see Chap. 4), but the prominent presence of the relics of thorns and nails encourages a kind of stilled contemplation of Christ's sufferings and Mary's cosufferings. No longer is the viewer asked to participate as a potential judge of Christ's verdict or as a needed helper with the burden of the cross. Instead, the pious beholder is meant to go beyond the historical specifics of the narrative to its ultimate message for mankind. Like the many current meditations and readings about the cross and the Passion mentioned by Erasmus, this painting serves as a stimulus to pious reflection, and it centers on both the two holy figures and on the relics that enjoyed such widespread popularity as objects of veneration in the late Middle Ages.[48]

This transformation of narrative to icon is the fullest development by Massys of the reversal of Ringbom's "icon to narrative" process. Yet it cannot be seen completely in isolation from the late images of the holy figures themselves. We have already seen how much Massys was conscious of the mother-child relationship that lies behind the *Pietà*, so much so that his figures of the Virgin kissing the Child and the Virgin kissing her Son in the *Pietà* are virtually interchangeable. Even the diptych figures of Massys' final years approximate the effects of the late *Pietà* and the other late religious narratives. For in a work like the 1529 *Christ Blessing* and the *Madonna in Prayer* (Madrid, Prado), the two halves of the diptych work together as if they were reenacting an interchange from the Gospel story, specifically the apochryphal subject of Christ Bidding Farewell to His Mother. Gerard David had already paired icons of *Madonna and Child* and *Christ Bidding Farewell to His Mother* (New York, Basel, Munich). Massys, then, was able to realize some of the dramatic possibility latent in his Prado diptych of the two adults even as he also perceived the profoundly emotional and spiritual depths possible behind the narrative base of his *Pietà*. At the very point where his iconic images appear most human and dramatically alive, the artist's narratives most closely approach iconic timelessness. Once again, *historiae* and *imagines* fuse. *Pl. 71* *Pl. 72* *Pl. 98*

What remains to be discussed is the theological context in which such an intensive examination of the religious story was encouraged. The emotional character of religiosity in the late Middle Ages is well represented through the vast religious literature that circulated in the late 15th and early 16th centuries.[49] Intensely descriptive retellings of the details of the Gospel stories had crystallized in meditative literature of the 13th century, such as the anonymous Franciscan *Meditations on the Life of Christ* and the widely circulated 14th-century *Vita Christi* by the Carthusian monk Ludolph of Saxony. These books were supplemented by a host of ascetic tracts on true Christian piety, the most famous of which is the *Imitation of Christ* by Thomas à Kempis, a book originally written for the author's fellow canons in the Windesheim congregation of the *devotio moderna*, but which became one of the first "best sellers" for the general public in the early era of printing. In addition to Latin texts, many of these devotional books were published in the Netherlands vernacular. The brief list selected by Post includes the following examples: *A Handbook for the Spiritual Life* by Jan van Baerle, *Epistle to his Sisters for their Evangelism* by Jan van den Berghe, A *Booklet on the Passion of Our Dear Lord* by Sister Bertken, *Book of the Angels, A Devout Book* (Meditation on Christ's wounds), *The Imperial Throne of Our Lord, The Fifteen Gratitudes of the Passion of Our Dear Lord* by Garrit van Gouda, and the like.[50] Many other works were given over to explaining the mysteries of the mass along with tales of wondrous sacramental miracles.[51]

The most popular theme of the literature of this period was the Passion of Christ. The mass of books devoted to retelling or meditating on Christ's sufferings were intended to evoke reader compassion and to lead ultimately to that elusive goal of the "Imitation of Christ." Most of this literature was already several centuries old, at least in inspiration; here again, the example of Ludolph the Carthusian was a basic model. Like the meditations of the day concerning the Virgin and her Sorrows or Joys, the Passion of Christ was generally subdivided into parts suitable for detailed contemplation; the most popular configuration was the number seven, corresponding to the number of canonical hours of prayer in the day. Thus, a popular text in Dutch drew the title *On the Seven Periods of the Passion of Our Lord.*[52] Often prayers were directed specifically toward the Suffering Christ or even to His holy wounds; in fact, the early 16th century was a high-water mark of devotion to the wounds of Christ, each of which (the number was reckoned variously) came to receive Pater Noster prayers, like the rosary devotion of the Virgin. We have already seen the importance of the spread of indulgenced images, which received special prayers and offered a kind of grace in return. One important indulgenced image was the Man of Sorrows, Christ after the Passion, revealed in all His suffering to the devout beholder.[53]

Precisely this combination of prayerfulness and the vivid realization of Christ's painful Passion is found in many of the Massys images from the Gospels. The Ecce Homo subject, in particular, offers the viewer the chance for both contemplation of the suffering Savior and an almost cinematic reenactment of the crucial moment of judgment by the people. Such "pathetic naturalism" (Huizinga) followed by meditation and prayer had been the formulaic presentation of the *Vita Christi* by Ludolph the Carthusian in the *Meditations on the Life of Christ.* Yet behind the images of Massys and the retellings of the Passion lay something more deeply felt than simply a passive viewing of a Gospel drama. We have already seen the emotion expressed in verse by Cornelius Grapheus before the Massys paintings of the Crucifixion. But the presence and modernity of the Passion imagery for a 16th-century viewer is suggested by the curious concept of "perpetual Passion" (see Chapter 3).[54] According to this concept, Christ suffers continual torment for the sins of mankind up to the time of Judgment. The Passion, therefore, is no longer a historically unique and distanced event with only cautionary overtones. Instead, it is the living, modern, unresolved dilemma of active choice, like the pending judgment within Massys' Ecce Homo scenes.

Hence, the meditation upon the body of Christ which appears so frequently in these Passion pictures is the outgrowth of an immediacy of the religious story within the everyday moral and spiritual world of 16th-century viewers. And the grotesque presence of tormenting soldiers and townsmen is a reminder that it was, and is, mankind's burden of sin and ignorance of Christ which caused the Passion and prolongs earthly suffering. Even in an image like the 1526 Massys *Adoration of the Magi,* the charge to the viewer is to recognize and worship Christ instead of spurning Him or ignoring His presence.

Little is known concerning Massys' religious orientation other than what can be gleaned from the pictures themselves. But the significance of the site where he died and was buried—the Carthusian monastery at Kiel, near Antwerp—should not be underestimated. The Carthusians were not a hospital order; therefore, Massys' turning to that brotherhood in a time of anxiety and physical danger (the outbreak of the plague or "sweating sickness") indicates a particular closeness on the artist's part toward the Carthusians. How long such closeness had existed and its specific nature cannot be established with the limited information now available. Yet the assumption of Carthusian religiosity as a component of Massys' beliefs does help to explain some of the changes in the artist's work and some of the distinctive characteristics of his final religious paintings. The Carthusians (established 1084) were an intensely spiritual and disciplined order, whose motto was "never reformed because never deformed" (*nunquam reformata quia nunquam deformata*).[55] The order was founded upon a "theology of solitude" and a "philosophy of solitude"; its strict life of silence and hermitic cloistering included full regulation of all aspects of life. Their ascetic orientation is reflected in an active literature composed by brethren of the order during the 15th century, the most famous of whom was Denys van Rykel (Dionysius the Carthusian) (1402–71). Huizinga quotes Denys as saying that true devotion is a sort of tenderness of the heart, which easily moves the devout to tears of piety, "the daily baptism of tears.[56] Devotional tracts form the fundamental life's work of this pious Carthusian, whose collected works run to 42 volumes in the modern edition. Moreover, in analyzing beauty, the lifeblood of an artist like Massys, Denys concludes that all things earthly are merely attractive, while all true beauty flows from God, like brooks from a source. His title of this treatise summarizes his viewpoint: "On the Loveliness of the World and the Beauty of God" (*De venustate mundi et pulchritudine Dei.*)[57] In paintings, then, the holiness presented is the true beauty, not the picture itself, and the earthly elements of the image are only subordinate manifestations of the divine. Characteristic of Denys and other 15th-century Carthusian writers (e.g., Jacob van Gruitrode, d. 1475) is a kind of practical religious idealism, which instructs the members of various professions in their proper Christian exercise.[58]

Aside from ascetic treatises and theological reflection, Carthusian literature focused upon the life and sufferings of Christ. Here the continuing model for Carthusian piety and preaching was the *Vita Christi* by Ludolph the Carthusian (d. 1378).[59] Although prescribed for reading within the Carthusian refectories, the *Vita Christi* also had a considerable public following through the printing press. In Antwerp alone, six separate editions appeared in Dutch between 1503 and 1536.[60] An indication of the book's impact on the congregation where Massys was buried is given by one of its monks, Jan van Haarlem (d. 1535/6), in his book the *Passio dominica.* After a series of chapters on the sufferings of Christ, the *Passio dominica* simply omits a final chapter and refers the reader instead to the *Vita Christi* text.[61]

Because of its formative influence on so many other devotional tracts based on the Gospels and because of its powerful influence on the Kiel Carthusians, Ludolph's *Vita Christi* must be considered an important framework for Massys' late narrative religious paintings, particularly the Passion pictures. Like those late Massys images of the *Ecce Homo, Adoration,* and *Pietà,* the *Vita Christi* combines the historical narrative in vivid description and physical closeness with a strong meditative component. Its aim is the perfection of the life of a Christian reader through contemplation and imitation of the example of Christ. In keeping with Massys' own predominant interest in the Passion of Christ, the *Vita Christi,* too, devotes its entire second half to the Passion and arranges its meditations on those events according to the canonical hours of prayer. In detail, Ludolph's reflections also parallel the impression in Massys' pictures. About the Calvary he says:

> Accordingly look at the evildoers everywhere striving villainously. Observe what they do to your Lord, what is said, and what happens by and through Him. Vividly imagine yourself present.[62]

Each of the moments of the Passion carries a lesson by Ludolph for the devout reader. The message for the Ecce Homo passages states:

> Let men reflect what terrible things were those clamors of the Jews and let him remember forever the insidious sins of man so that, on the contrary, either everyone cry out together against what is nearest or give out in favor of God.[63]

And the kinds of admonitions or exhortations that seem to be present in Massys' pictures also come out from the pages of the *Vita Christi.* In one section, Ludolph urges every Christian to take up the cross and follow Christ's example;[64] elsewhere, he warns against driving modern nails into Christ with our sins.[65] And he is eloquent about the compassionate sufferings and tenderness of the Virgin Mary for her Son.[66]

While Ludolph the Carthusian cannot conclusively be determined as the inspiration for Massys' late religious imagery, the continued popularity of the 14th-century text of the *Vita Christi* points out the kind of spirituality that pervaded religious life well into the 16th century. It was a meditative and personalized reflection upon the Gospel texts, making them vivid and immediate as moral dilemmas for the modern worshiper. During the course of his career, Massys strove to find the visual analogue to such charged spiritual narratives. After the panoramic plenitude of his earlier works, like the St. Louis *Adoration* or the great altarpieces, his works develop a narrower focus, centered on the figures of Christ and the Virgin, as well as a more charged emotional atmosphere, which strives to absorb the viewer. This kind of change can be compared to the more active, gesturing figures of the later Massys Mary imagery, where expression of emotion is made more immediate and visible through maternal hugs and kisses (see Chap. 4).

Religious narratives, then, reveal as full a transformation over the course of Massys' career as any other category of his work. They show formal and functional kinship with the iconic images examined earlier and suggest that the artist increasingly attempted to address his pious viewers directly and to evoke the same kind of intense contemplative involvement for religious actions as for icons. The hypothesis advanced here is that the artist's developing conception of religious narrative is an essentially devotional image, analogous to the Carthusian presentation of scriptures for meditation and quite possibly connected with Massys' actual contacts with the Carthusians at Kiel. Associated with this more personal and private ideal of piety is the retreat from those massively impressive altarpieces that had been a mainstay of Massys' career in his maturity.

Yet neither the "Carthusian" religiosity of his later years nor the more general forms of late medieval piety sketched here serve to condition the artist's most distinctive and unusual images of saints and sinners. For the background to another group of portraitlike works, featuring the meditative saints resisting temptation and grotesque sinners giving in to it, we must now turn to Massys' documented contact with Erasmus and the likely consequences of that important meeting.

NOTES

1. E. Borsook, *The Mural Painters of Tuscany from Cimabue to Andrea del Sarto* (London, 1960). Giotto's Arena Chapel and Duccio's *Maesta* retable offer early examples of fully illustrated cycles in Italy and may be compared to the mosaic and fresco cycles of later Byzantine art: in particular, the Kariye Djami (St. Savior in Chora, ca. 1315–1321; P. Underwood, *The Kariye Djami* [Princeton, 1966]).

2. On illustrated Bibles, see S. Hindman, "Fifteenth-Century Dutch Bible Illustrations and the Historia Scholastica," *JWCI* 37 (1974): 131–44. Perceptive discussions of pictorial narrative can be found among the following: P. Parshall, "Lucas van Leyden's Narrative Style," pp. 185–237; O.Pächt, *The Rise of Pictorial Narrative in Twelfth-Century England* (Oxford, 1962); K. Weitzmann, *Studies in Roll and Codex* (Princeton, 1970), esp. pp. 12–46; the collected papers on "Narration in Ancient Art," *American Journal of Archaeology* 61 (1957): 44–91; N. Goodman, "Twisted Tales; or Story, Study, and Symphony," *Critical Inquiry* 7 (1980): 103–19. A classic distinction between literary and visual story telling, based upon successive narrative events in texts and stilled, concurrent actions in pictures, is offered by G. E. Lessing, *Laocoon*, trans. E. Frothingham (Boston, 1910). Out of the vast literature on textual narration, the following recent works can be singled out: R. Scholes and R. Kellogg, *The Nature of Narrative* (Oxford, 1976); S. Chatman, *Story and Discourse* (Ithaca, 1978); *On Narrative*, spec. issue of *Critical Inquiry* 7 (1980). The Books of Hours are discussed well in a pair of introductions: J. Harthan, *The Book of Hours* (New York, 1977), esp. pp. 26–29 for religious scenes; L.M.J. Delaissé, "The Importance of Books of Hours for the History of the Medieval Book," *Gatherings in Honor of Dorothy Miner* (Baltimore, 1974), pp. 203–25. See also Delaruelle, Labande and Ourliac, pp. 701–2.

3. Ringbom, *Icon to Narrative*, "The Narrative Close-up in Ghent-Bruges Painting," p. 193ff., esp. p. 205ff. M. Kupfer-Tarasulo, "Innovation and Copy in the Stein Quadriptych of Simon Bening," *Zeitschrift für Kunstgeschichte* 42 (1979): 274–98.

4. See the fine discussion, with bibliography, on devotional images in Ringbom, p. 52 ff. The classic reference work is J. Braun, *Der christliche Altar in seiner geschichtlichen Entwicklung*, vol. 2 (Munich, 1924); the emergence of the Netherlands triptych form for altarpieces is discussed by Blum, p. 1ff.; L.B. Philip, *The Ghent Altarpiece*, 165 ff.

5. Blum, p. 20; a motif also found in the early *Nativity* of Bouts (Madrid) and Petrus Christus (Washington).

6. Friedländer, vol. 4, nos. 20, 17. F. Winkler, *Das Werk des Hugo van der Goes* (Berlin, 1964), pp. 189ff., 9 ff., includes the copies related here to Massys as reflections, instead, of a lost Hugo composition, p. 198ff.

7. Friedländer, vol. 7, no. 123.

8. *Jan Gossaert genaamd Mabuse,* exh. cat., p. 23; Davies, *Early Netherlandish School; National Gallery Catalogues,* pp. 63ff., no. 2790.

9. K. Arndt, "Gerard Davids 'Anbetung der Könige' nach Hugo van der Goes. Ein Beitrag zur Kopienkritik," *Münchner Jahrbuch der bildenden Kunst* 12 (1961): 153–75.

10. Koch, "Flower Symbolism," p. 70ff.

11. G. Kubler, *The Shape of Time* (New Haven, 1962), pp. 39–45.

12. Some signatures, however, might have disappeared with the original frames of the 15th-century images; see J. Folie, "Les oeuvres authentifieés des primitifs flamands," *Bulletin de l'Institut Royal du Patrimoine Artistique* 6 (1963): 183–256.

13. G. Hulin de Loo, "An Authentic Work by Jacques Daret, Painted in 1434," *Burlington Magazine* 15 (1909): 202ff.; Panofsky, *ENP,* p. 157–58; M. Davies, *Rogier van der Weyden,* pp. 191–92.

14. The term is based on Panofsky's discussion, *ENP,* p. 350ff., where the judgment of Gossaert is that his archaism is "non-essential and imperceptive."

15. E. Gombrich, *Art and Illusion* (Princeton, 1960), pp. 73–75, 365–66. The 1494 Dürer drawing after Mantegna's engraving *Battle of the Sea Gods* is a case in point (Panofsky, *Albrecht Dürer,* pp. 31–2), as is the ongoing dialogue of Rubens's copies after Titian. The philosophical problem of "true copies" or "replicas" is discussed by N. Goodman, *Languages of Art* (Indianapolis, Ind., 1968), pp. 115–16, 131ff.; see also p. 99ff on "fakes."

16. K. Weitzmann, *Roll and Codex,* pp. 12–46.

17. Snyder, "The Early Haarlem School of Painting II. Geertgen tot sint Jans," p. 113ff.

18. Ringbom, pp. 11–16.

19. Ibid., p. 39ff.; on northern half-length *Adorations,* see pp. 100–106. Also, B. Völker, *Die Entwicklung des erzählenden Halbfigurenbildes in der niederländischen Malerei des 15. und 16. Jahrhunderts* (Göttingen, 1968), esp. 99–120 for Massys religious works.

20. Friedländer, vol. 11; see also the references in Chapter 2, this volume, esp. n. 41.

21. See Chapter 2, n. 2.

22. Goris, *Les Colonies marchandes méridionales.*

23. Goris and Marlier, *Dürer Diary,* esp. "Introduction," p. 13.

24. Ibid., p. 85, ill. 66.

25. For the Master of the Morrison Triptych, see Friedländer, vol. 7, pp. 41–45. The identity of this anonymous artist has continued to challenge scholars. G. Nieto Gallo, writing about the Valladolid shutters (F. 84), has basically adopted Friedländer's own suggestion (vol. 7, p. 44, n.8) that the Master of the Morrison Triptych should be equated with Quinten's 1495 registered apprentice "Ariaen" (who became master in 1503, the year of the shutters), but chooses rather to assume that Ariaen is none other than Adriaen Skilleman, who attained his master's certificate from the St. Luke's guild in 1499 (G. Nieto Gallo, "El Retablo de San Juan Bautista en la Iglesia del Salvador de Valladolid. ¿ Quentin Metsys o Adriaen Skilleman?" pp. 13–21, 1931–39, pp. 47–70). Valentiner, seconded by Wescher, chose the name of a prominent Antwerp painter, Simon van Herlam, active 1502–1524, whose name implies a Dutch origin near Geertgen tot sint Jans that tallies with some works assigned to the *oeuvre* of the Master of the Morrison Triptych (W. R. Valentiner, "Simon van Herlam, the Master of the Morrison Triptych," pp. 5–10; P. Wescher, "Beiträge zu Simon van Haarlem, dem Meister des Morrison Triptychons," pp. 175–88). Martin Davies has demurred, with his usual skepticism, in discussing the London triptych of Virgin with Saints (F.83, no. 1085); see Davis, *Early Netherlandish School,* p. 122.

26. The use of one's native town as skyline behind holy figures had already been practiced in Bruges in the later 15th century, particularly by the Master of the St. Lucy Legend. This same analogy of Antwerp as a world trade center with the centrality of Christ among the magi persisted into the 17th century in Antwerp, for it resulted in Rubens's first major painting for his home town, the *Adoration of the Magi* (1609; today Madrid, Prado). This 17th-century *Adoration* was placed, significantly enough, in the Chamber of the Nations in Antwerp's City Hall (C. Norris, "Rubens' Adoration of the Kings of 1609," pp. 129–36; Baudouin, "Rubens Altarpieces before 1620," in *Rubens,* pp. 71–72.

27. The major survey is D. Lach, *Asia in the Making of Europe* (Chicago, 1965); on the spice trade, vol. 1, pp. 91–147. On the Portugese, see C. R. Boxer, *The Portugese Seaborne Empire 1415–1825* (Oxford, 1963); and the more recent and synthetic remarks by I. Wallerstein, *The Modern World-System,* esp. pp. 215–25. For imported exotic elements in art-making, there are many discoveries in G. Pochat, *Der Exotismus während des Mittelalters und der Renaissance.*

28. Friedländer, vol. 9, p. 19f., nos. 10, 10a. The Detroit image is signed on the dagger of the senior king with the initials JB for Joos van der Beke, alias van Cleve. Friedländer dates the work ca. 1520; also see Hand, "Joos van Cleve," p. 126, who dates it ca. 1525.

29. F. Grossmann, *Peter Bruegel The Paintings,* 3rd ed. (London, 1975) p. 196. An insightful discussion of this neglected Bruegel masterwork is given by E. H. Schack, "Peter Bruegel's *Christ Carrying the Cross* and other Religious Paintings" (Master's thesis, University of California, Berkeley, 1978), pp. 40–43.

30. A. Popham, *The Drawings of Leonardo da Vinci* (New York, 1945), no. 138A.

31. The *Vision to the Magi,* a literal epiphany, is the subject of a wing of van der Weyden's *Bladelin altarpiece* (Berlin), for which see Blum, 19f.

32. Ringbom, "The Suffering Christ," 142ff.; Panofsky, "Jean Hey," p. 95ff.; G. von der Osten, "Ecce Homo III," *RDK* 4, col. 692.

33. Ringbom, p. 153ff., esp. 168–69, "Hieronymus Bosch's Passion Images." In these Bosch panels, the theme of the "impotence of goodness" in half-length narratives was first expounded as a model for Massys.

34. Thomas à Kempis, *The Imitation of Christ,* trans. L. Sherley-Price (Harmondsworth, 1952), pp. 87 (ii,12), 85.

35. J. P. Dolan, ed., *The Essential Erasmus,* p. 80.

36. Perhaps to be identified with the "Our Savior" seen by Guicciardini in 1561. This could also be the *Lamentation* for the shrineworkers' guild, which also had a chapel in the cathedral. For the reference, from Bertrijn's *Chronijck der Stadt Antwerpen,* *Pl. 20*
pp. 133, 145, see J. Bosschere, *Quinten Metsys,* p. 103 (p. 7 for Guicciardini).

37. *Flemish Paintings and Drawings at 56 Princes Gate London S.W.7, IV Addenda* (London, 1969), pp. 3–4; de Bosque, pp. 135–36.

38. *Stabat Mater,* exh. cat. (Salzburg, 1970).

39. Panofsky, *ENP,* p. 235, n. 2; M. Meiss, "Jan van Eyck and the Italian Renaissance," in *The Painter's Choice,* p. 29f.

40. Davies, *Rogier van der Weyden,* p. 206ff. (with bibliography).

41. Prims, *Geschiedenis* 7, pp. 123–24.

42. Ibid., p. 161. Two other altars lay below the crucifix, which also included the two other crosses when the whole ensemble was finished at last in 1546–47. Perhaps the Massys image was included among this group.

43. O. von Simson, "*Compassio* and *Co-redemptio* in Rogier van der Weyden's *Descent from the Cross,*" p. 9ff.; also Delaruelle, Labande and Ourliac, 759; Toussaert, pp. 283–85: The first theological study on the compassion of the Virgin in Flanders appeared in 1495, the work of a Dominican of Lille, Michel François.

44. On the *Pietà* in general, see Mâle, p. 123f.; E. Reiners-Ernst, "Das freudvolle Vesperbild und die Anfänge der Pieta Vorstellung," *Abhandlungen der bayerischen benediktinischen Akademie,* vol. 2 (Munich, 1939); E. Panofsky, "Reintegration of a Book of Hours Executed in the Workshop of the 'Maître des Grandes Henres de Rohan,' " *Medieval Studies in Memory of A. Kingsley Porter* (Cambridge, Mass., 1939), p. 479ff., esp. p. 491. The specific motif of the last kiss between Mary and the dead Christ is the Byzantine "threnos," for which see K. Weitzmann, "On the Origin of the Threnos," *De Artibus opuscula XL. Essays in Honor of Erwin Panofsky* (New York, 1961), p. 476ff.; M. Meiss, "Italian Primitives at Konopiště," *Art Bulletin* 28 (1946): 1ff.; Ringbom, p. 136ff., speaks of 15th-century half-length Pietàs as the basis for augmented scenes of the Deposition with several figures.

45. For the Brussels image and a lesser version in Madrid, Museo Lazaro-Galdiano, see de Bosque, p. 168.

46. Davies, *Rogier van der Weyden,* p. 221; Davies, *Les Primitifs Flamands: National Gallery London III,* no. 130.

47. Klein, "Andachtsbild," *RDK* I, cols. 681–87; Panofsky, "Imago Pietatis," p. 261ff.; Ringbom, p. 52ff.

48. Toussaert, pp. 291–92; Post, *KV,* p. 396; Delaruelle, Labande, and Ourliac, pp. 781–82 (755–56 on relics of the Passion).

49. Post, *KG,* pp. 367–415; M. Meertens, *De godsvrucht in de Nederlanden naar handschriften van gebenboeken der XVe eeuw* (Louvain, 1930); Delaruelle, Lebande, and Ourliac, pp. 695–722; J. Huizinga, p. 151ff.

50. Post, *KV,* pp. 458–59.

51. Post, *KG,* vol. 1, pp. 409f.

52. Post, *KV,* p. 459. The "mimesis" of this period, i.e., the reenactment or reproduction of the events of the Passion (also signaled by the flowering of religious drama in this same period), also included meditation on the successive "Stations of the Cross" (Delaruelle, Labande, and Ourliac, p. 760), often organized along the successive canonical hours of daily prayer. This assimilation of meditation to the hours of the Church day is reinforced in illuminated Books of Hours (for which, see above, note 2) by the successive depiction of scenes from Christ's Infancy or Passion alongside the progressing texts of the Hours of the Virgin or Hours of the Cross.

53. Ringbom, pp. 25–26; Male, pp. 94–98; R. Bauerreiss, *"Pie Jesu" Das Schmerzensmannbild und sein Einfluss auf die mittelalterliche Frömmigkeit* (Munich, 1931); G. von der Osten, *Der Schmerzensmann Typengeschichte eines deutschen Andachtsbildes von 1300 bis 1600* (Berlin, 1935); W. Mersmann, *Der Schmerzensmann* (Dusseldorf, 1952); also Panofsky, "Imago Pietatis." See also the related theme, taken up by Dürer's frontispiece to the *Large Woodcut Passion* (1511) of "Christus in Elend," for which see *RDK* 3.

54. Panofsky, "Jean Hey," p. 108ff.; also E. Bustenback and T. Hillman, "Die Steinbacher Pieta, ein Beitrag zur Ikonographie des Vesperbildes and des Schmerzensmannes," *Die Christliche Kunst* 33 (1937); 268ff.

55. For the Carthusian order in the Netherlands, see E. de Moreau, *L'Eglise en Belgique,* vol. 4, pp. 275–81, 348–51; S. Axters, *Geschiedenis van de vroomheid in de Nederlanden III. De Moderne Devotie,* pp. 198–224; Delaruelle, Labande, and Ourliac, pp. 1032–34. An apt summary is given by Toussaert, pp. 461–62: "When one would view the highest summit of perfection and asceticism, one should go knock at the gate of the Charterhouse."

56. Huizinga, p. 191; Post, *KG,* vol. 1, pp. 403–4.

57. Huizinga, pp. 266–68.

58. Ibid., p. 215; Post, *KG,* vol. 1, p. 404.

59. See the study by M. Bodenstedt, *The Vita Christi by Ludolphus the Carthusian,* (Washington, 1944).

60. W. Nijhoff and M. E. Kronenberg, *Nederlandsche Bibliographie van 1500 tot 1540,* nos. 1407–12.

61. Prims, 247–48.

62. Ludolphus de Saxonia, *Vita Jesu Christi,* vol. 2 (Paris / Rome, 1870), pp. lxiii, 565.

63. Ibid., pp. lxii, 548.

64. Ibid., pp. lxiii, 549.

65. Ibid., pp. lxiii, 567–8.

66. Ibid., pp. lxiv, 616; lvx, 623; lxvi, 635.

6

Massys and Erasmus

"The better image will his writings show."

On 30 May 1517, Erasmus of Rotterdam wrote to his friend Thomas More in England to tell him that a double portrait was in progress of Erasmus and a mutual friend from Antwerp, Peter Gillis (Petrus *Pl. 99*
Aegidius).[1] The two portraits occupied a single panel, according to the letter, and would be sent to *Pl. 100*
More as a gesture of friendship. Later letters indicate that More was impatient to receive his gift, several times delayed.[2] A 1 August letter to Gillis from Erasmus, then in Louvain, mentions the artist by name: Quinten.[3] By 7 October, More acknowledged receipt of the diptych in letters addressed to both Erasmus and Gillis; moreover, he, too, mentions "our Quinten" by name as part of a long panegyric to the picture and its artist.[4]

These letters are the concrete documentation of Massys' most famous portrait, the 1517 image of *Erasmus* in his study (F. 36, cat. 58), a portrait complemented and completed by the adjacent figure of *Peter Gillis* (F. 37). Numerous copies after the two portraits testify to their popularity among the admirers of both Erasmus and Gillis,[5] and More's own laudatory letter indicates his satisfaction with Massys' work. The More letter also underscores the personal details which the artist infused into the portraits:

> You recognize without doubt their features which you see here, even if you only had seen them once in the past; if not the identify of the first would be revealed to you by the letter which was written to him; the other, to draw you out of ignorance, writes his own name; however, in the event that he is silent, the titles of the books, which by right of their celebrity are read the world over, would tell you who he is.[6]

More even goes so far as to marvel at Massys' success at imitating More's handwriting in the letter from More held in Gillis's hand in the portrait.

The portrait of Gillis survives in the collection of the Earl of Radnor, Longford Castle.[7] The letter in his hand is addressed, as More recounted in his description to Gillis by his Latin name: "Vir literatisimo Petro / Egidio Amico charismo / Antverpiae" (To the most learned Petrus Aegidius, dearest friend, at Antwerp). Behind Gillis in the portrait are books by Erasmus and classical authors, their titles marked on their page-ends: a Latin Plutarch, Seneca, Suetonius, [Quintus] Curtius Rufus, all works edited by the Rotterdam humanist.[8] The books by Erasmus himself are an edition in Greek

Archontopideia) of the just-published *Institution of a Christian Prince* (1516) and, on the table under Gillis's finger, the *Antibarbaron (Antibarbari),* one of Erasmus's earliest writings (ca. 1494–59), penned during his monastic days with the Augustinian canons at Steyn, Holland.[9] The *Institution* (or *Education*) *of a Christian Prince,* addressed to the young, newly crowned Charles V, is Erasmus's most systematic exposition of political theory, characteristically dealing as much with ethics and the training of the mind as with the prince himself.[10] Of course, the *Institutio* would have been selected in part because of its recent appearance, but it also is the work of Erasmus most nearly resembling the work and the writings, including *Utopia,* of More himself, written when Erasmus was briefly in his own right the officially titled counsellor to the young Prince Charles.

What is known of the biography of Gillis (1486–1533) tallies well with this impression gleaned from the Massys portrait.[11] Like Massys, Gillis was an Antwerp native, the secretary of magistrates *(stadsgreffier)* of the city.[12] His Latin learning also led him into service as editor and proofreader for the Antwerp publisher Dirk Maartens, who published a pair of Erasmus's works in 1504; the two friends of the diptych probably met during that period through this literary nexus. Erasmus was Gillis's frequent houseguest in Antwerp between the years 1514–21, and one of those visits furnished the opportunity for the Massys portraits in 1517. Gillis was also a friend of Thomas More in his own right, having helped to see *Utopia* through Maartens's Louvain press during the year prior to the portraits, 1516. The English scholar and Gillis had first met during More's diplomatic embassy to Flanders in 1515, the period of the composition of the *Utopia.*[13]. In fact, the *Utopia* narrator, the ficitious Raphael Hythlodaeus, tells his story to More and Gillis in the latter's garden in Antwerp, and More prefaces the book with a letter to Gillis. The friendship, then, was shared between Erasmus, More, and Gillis, and the combination of Latinity and political history in the image of Gillis was directed toward a man of singular qualifications in the same areas, "the King's good servant," Thomas More.

In addition to his learning, Gillis is revealed in his role as secretary-scribe by both More's letter in his hand and by the sandbox on the table beside his arm, a device used to blot or dry ink on one's correspondence. But the image is made lively, actually activated, by More's letter to Aegidius, which Gillis holds in readiness to read to Erasmus.

The great Rotterdam humanist, too, occupies the same scholarly study as Gillis and sits before books, also entitled on their page-edges, which tell about his scholarly identity. We know of these titles, too, from the encomium for his panel written by More "towards the diptych, where the eminent artist Quintinius has represented Erasmus and Peter Gillis in such a way that at the side of Erasmus, who begins his *Paraphrase of the Letter to the Romans,* there appear painted books which show their titles . . . and Peter holds in his hand a letter of More's addressed to him."[14] Today, only the highly scrubbed portrait version at Hampton Court shows any book with titles, like the Radnor *Gillis;* Margaret Mann Phillips and J. B. Trapp consider this a persuasive argument for the originality of the Hampton Court image as More's own.[15] Whether the Hampton Court image is a faithful replica or, more likely, the long-"missing" original, it faithfully records the message which Erasmus instructed Massys to communicate through the books and their titles. That message is a full tribute both to Erasmus's range of learning and publication and to his close personal friendship and intellectual affinity with Thomas More. In the Hampton Court picture, the painted titles are *Hor (Moria,* for *Moriae encomium* or *Praise of Folly,* 1511), *Loukianos* (a Greek edition of Lucian), *Novum Testament (um),* and *Hieronymus.* The term "moria" serves double duty as a title, for it is at once a pun on the name of Thomas More and the Greek word for folly. Erasmus explained in a prefatory letter to his first edition that it was this pun on his friend's name and their mutual love of wit had led him to reflect on the subject of *moria,* folly.[16] The presence of the *Moria* among the titles of Erasmus not only serves to identify the author of the *Praise of Folly* by his most famous work, but it also serves as a sign of their friendship, first commemorated in the dedication of that very book and in its title and now reinforced by the presentation of this portrait of the Christian humanist to his dear friend More in England. Erasmus and More were also colleagues. They collaborated on translations of the witty satires of Lucian during Erasmus's visit to England in 1506,[17] and both authors went on to make use of Lucianic techniques such as dialogue and irony in their satiric works.[18] Thus, the title *Loukianos,* like *Moria,* is an essential witness to Erasmus's intimacy with More and a *sine qua non* of the portrait's intention as a gift to the Englishman.

The Latin *New Testament* is a tribute to one of the most important of Erasmus's continuing projects: the first modern scholarly editions, in both Latin and Greek, of the Bible. The new Latin translation, begun in England in 1505 during the same visit when the translation of Lucian was undertaken with More, was completed ca. 1506 and incorporated in a manuscript dated 1509. (John Colet of Oxford and St. Paul's, more than More, had encouraged the enterprise, but all three were mutual friends.)[19] Almost a decade later Erasmus began work on a Greek edition of the New Testament, which was published in 1516 by Froben in Basel alongside Erasmus's Latin translation. This publication was a landmark in Erasmus's career and in his campaign for what has since come to be condensed under the heading of "Christian humanism"—the fusion of classical learning, Christian piety, and the combined interest in proper study of the biblical texts and Church fathers. As McConica succinctly terms this program: "It seems clear that for Erasmus 'theology' was, quite simply, the study of Scripture according to his own critical canons."[20] Thus, the presence of the Latin *New Testament* behind Erasmus in the Massys portrait refers at once to the religious goals of the humanist's sojourns in England and to his ongoing mission of religious scholarship, which had just been culminated by the *New Testament's* 1516 publication in both Latin and Greek.

Finally, the *Hieronymus* behind Erasmus speaks profoundly of the humanist's values and of his recent accomplishments. In 1516, Erasmus published in Basel an edition of the letters of St. Jerome in four volumes, part of a nine-volume edition of the saint's works to be published in that year by Froben.[21] This achievement was the culmination of a decade and a half of activity, beginning with Erasmus's first acquaintance with the Jerome letters during his monastic life at Steyn. Scholars have often appreciated the particular affinity between Erasmus and St. Jerome, "the hermit of Bethlehem who translated the scriptures, who cultivated the tongues, who loved the classics, who cared so little for systematic theology, and so much for life [where] he saw the prototype of his own mind and the champion of the 'philosophy of Christ.' "[22] Erasmus's letters expressed his sympathy with Jerome. In a 1501 letter to Anton van Bergen, he contends that he would rather live as a madman with Jerome than as a learned scholar with the mob of modern theologians: "It is my delight to set foot on the path into which Jerome and the splendid host of so many ancients summon me."[23] Even the humanist's personal and piercing epistolary legacy may in part be the outgrowth of his lifelong interest and editing of Jerome's letters. Of that ongoing project, he reports in a letter of 1513 to his friend Ammonius (Allen 273): "My enthusiasm for emending and annotating Jerome is such that I feel as though inspired by some god."[24] Hence *Hieronymus* (Jerome) occupies the most prominent position of any of the books in the Massys portrait, easily visible and closest to the reach of the writing humanist.

Erasmus is at work. The Massys portrait does not simply show a man surrounded by his books, but instead records a scholar writing in his study. Again, the Hampton Court *Erasmus* records for us precisely what the humanist engages himself with. The words proceeding from his pen are the opening lines of Erasmus's *Paraphrase of the Epistle of the Romans,* deciphered from the portrait by Margaret Mann Phillips and depicted, according to her, in a manner extremely close to being a forgery of Erasmus's own more formal manner of handwriting.[25] Such exactitude of copying was also demonstrated in the letter from More held by Gillis, and More himself mentions his recognition that Erasmus's task was the *Paraphrase.* That *Paraphrase,* like More's *Utopia,* was published in Louvain by Dirk Maartens, and was actually Erasmus's current project when the portrait was painted.[26]

Erasmus's *Paraphrases* were an outgrowth of his New Testament translation project. His work as a critic and a Christian thinker did not end with the 1516 publication of the Greek and Latin text edition; in addition, he attempted to bridge the gap between the public and the original texts of Scripture with commentaries on the sources which were becoming available for the contemplation of an educated laity.[27] He expounded this hope for the propagation and reflection on Scripture in an introductory *Paracelsis,* appended in 1516 to the New Testament and subtitled "adhortation to the study of Christian philosophy."[28] During the next seven years, 1517–24, and beginning with the very year of the Massys portrait, Erasmus published his *Paraphrases*—annotations to the text, exposition, and exegesis—consolidated into separable essays from the notes published with the New Testament text. The *Paraphrases* were intended to reach, in Erasmus's own words, "the farmer, the tailor, the mason, prostitutes, pimps, and Turks,"[29] and in his lifetime they were translated into the most important vernacular languages of Europe: English, French, German, and Bohemian.[30] The first of these *Paraphrases*, on the Epistle to Romans, is the one shown in the Massys portrait. Erasmus has asked the artist to depict him at the very onset of his newest and potentially most important religious project to date, an achievement as valuable to posterity as any of the books shown completed on the adjacent shelves.

Massys' portrait diptych represents a marked departure from the artist's previous conception of a likeness. Prior to the Erasmus-Gillis pair, the painter had concentrated exclusively on the features of his sitter, with the posed figure set against a monochrome background of green or blue, as in the
Pl. 138 *Portrait of a Pilgrim* (1509, Reinhart coll., Winterthur, F. 38, cat. 53). In this 1517 commission, however, he represents two characters in action: Erasmus pauses reflectively in his scholarly labors, while Gillis gazes anxiously at his friend, at once wishing to share the newly arrived letter from More but unwilling to interrupt the contemplation of his friend. The interior space they share is a single room extending across both panels. Both the table and the bookshelves link the areas of *Erasmus* and *Gillis* into a unit. And their actions, as well as the specificity of their texts, letter, and *Paraphrase*, also provide a definable moment in time for the diptych of the two friends.

The choice of a study space and figures in action recalls Massys' first known foray into the depiction
Pl. 118 of daily affairs, his 1514 *Moneychanger and his Wife* (Paris, Louvre; F. 53, cat. 16). In that work, sitters appear at half-length behind a table whose front edge, with the same greenish cover and gold tacks, is presented in the Erasmus-Gillis portraits. The moneychanger's interior also comes with a bookshelf, filled with ledgers and other items of importance to that profession. That generic tradesman and his wife are not specific people, nor can the precise period of their business be determined the way it can for Erasmus and Gillis. But the two characters are engaged in their activity just as surely as are the two humanists of 1517, the man weighing coins as his wife is leafing through her prayerbook and watching him. The *Moneychanger and his Wife* is modeled on a preexisting kind of image, the so-called "professional portrait," such as Petrus Christus's 1449 image of the patron saint of goldsmiths working
Pl. 119 at his trade as if in a contemporary Flemish world, the *St. Eloy* (New York, Lehmann coll., Metropolitan Museum; see Chap. 7).[31] For Massys to pattern his *Erasmus-Gillis* so closely upon his previous *Moneychanger* indicates the importance to him of capturing a sense of activity, the distinctive space and work of the scholar in his study.

But the scholar-in-his-study quality of the Erasmus portrait is more than just the desire for verisimilitude. In his *Erasmus,* Massys also evokes a visual tradition of "author portraits" closely akin to the larger category of "professional portraits," which were so formative to the Louvre *Moneychanger.* Beginning with the earliest preserved Christian manuscripts, author pictures of the Christian evangelists, perhaps themselves based upon ancient images of poets or philosophers, adorned the beginnings of their texts in more lavish, illustrated manuscripts.[32] In their more developed form, such author portraits show the scholar seated before a lectern and a writing desk, before him often an open book and other essentials of his profession, such as quills, inkpots, and blotting-sand boxes. Much closer in time to Massys' Erasmus is an Eyckian image of *St. Jerome* (Detroit, Institute of Arts, dated ca.
Pl. 101 1442 and possibly painted or completed by the young Petrus Christus).[33] Panofsky has demonstrated that this particular image found its way into the Medici collections in Florence by 1492,[34] but its existence there could well have been known to Erasmus; the image spawned a host of imitations by artists on both sides of the Alps, in both manuscripts and monumental painting.[35]

Massys' *Erasmus* shares a number of features with the Detroit *St. Jerome,* beginning with the "corner space" interior, a feature of Christus's own portraits,[36] which permitted the artist to show the scholar comfortably lodged within his specific work setting. Along the rear wall, both pictures show piles of books on a shelf. (Christus's image also includes still-life objects on a second shelf, which suggests that

Massys' use of many of the same objects—prayer beads, glass vase, orange—in his 1514 Louvre *Moneychanger* might also be based upon his knowledge of either the Detroit *Jerome* or one of its imitations.) Both panels show their subjects in three-quarter profile, absorbed in thought while in the midst of work; Erasmus, of course, is writing, while St. Jerome is consulting the text of a large Bible.

This visual fusion of the image of *Erasmus* onto a previous *Jerome* image is surely no accident. We have already seen Erasmus's own powerful affinity, even his identification, with the activity and personality of St. Jerome and the prominence accorded to the edition of *Hieronymus* on the shelf of the picture. Moreover, Massys has added to the image of Erasmus an item frequently found in the study of St. Jerome: a pair of scissors, emblem of the editorial selections made by the compiler of the Vulgate.[37]

In short, then, the *Erasmus* of Massys is a knowing evocation in paint of the character and the achievement of the Rotterdam humanist. It is a fulfillment of the image which Erasmus desired to be carried of himself both to his friend in England and, eventually, to posterity. Up-to-the-minute, not only with recently published works *(Hieronymus, New Testament, Institution of a Christian Prince)* from 1516, the picture also records, on the desk of the scholar, uncompleted works in the very process of their being penned *(Paraphrase of Romans)!* Margaret Mann Phillips's scenario of the conversations between Massys and his famous sitter cannot be far off the mark. Erasmus asks to have himself portrayed within the tradition of Christian scholars in "author portraits," and his special fondness for St. Jerome dictates the choice of the Eyckian prototype as a model for Massys. Erasmus must also have selected the books, so carefully arranged in the background of the portrait, and the opening passage of the *Paraphrase,* which Massys went on to copy so minutely. These books represent the breadth of his knowledge of classical sources, of his religious writings and editions, of his satirical works. They also represent the ways in which his personal ties to More and their mutual interests have informed his *curriculum vitae,* his intellectual development and career. The diptych with Gillis is at once a tribute to a three-way friendship, to the absent friend who will receive the portraits (More), and to the unique spirit of Erasmus himself, who is the essential link in this chain of affinity as well as its guiding light.

More's appreciation of the portraits is equally knowing and favorable. To Erasmus, he writes on 7 October 1517:

> Though nothing but sketches with crayon or brush, the images and traits of these men would charm anyone who has not lost all feeling for letters and for virtue. As for me, they had the power to inspire in me an extraordinary emotion, by the recollection of what such friends awaken in me . . . ; and who could translate into words, or better, who could gather into his thoughts, how marvelously I am moved by the portraits of these men, now that they have been drawn and rendered with so much virtuosity that they could easily hurl a defiance to all the painters of antiquity?
> . . . However, to avow the truth, I cannot truly resist this delicious flutter of glory, which the conviction of my being recommended to distant posterity provokes in me by the friendship of Erasmus, witnessed by the letters, the books, the portraits, and so many other signs of his friendship.[38]

His letter to Gillis in gratitude for the gift reveals More's awareness of the pictorial devices of Massys to commemorate his distinguished sitters:

> You will recognize without doubt those features which you see here, even if you have only seen them a single time in the past; if not, the identity of the first will be revealed to you by the letter which has been written to him [Gillis]; the other, to draw you out of ignorance, writes his own name [Erasmus in the title of the *Paraphrase*]; however, if you suppose him to be silent, the titles of the books, which, by reason of their celebrity are read throughout the entire world, would teach you who he is.[39]

The subtlety and thoroughness of Massys' portraits of *Erasmus* and *Gillis,* so well appreciated by Thomas More, point to collaboration between painter and patron. This, of course, does not imply any necessary sympathy between Massys and Erasmus, let alone actual understanding of the humanist's religious work by the artist. But the successful interaction in the production of the diptych helps to explain why Erasmus turned to Massys, the son of a smith, only a couple of years later to produce a second portrait for him, this time a bronze medal (see Appendix A).[40] The letters of Erasmus leave no doubt that Quinten was the creator of this medal. Doubtless, Massys' previous experience in bronze casting, derived from his family's profession at the forge, and his previous successful medals led Erasmus to choose him for this new task. When a second unauthorized portrait medal appeared, Erasmus wrote to a friend in 1528, expressing surprise and wondering where the second artist got his likeness: "I ask myself where your sculptor was able to procure my portrait, lest by chance he should possess that which Quentin cast in bronze in Antwerp."[41] The medal contains, on its obverse, a profile portrait bust of Erasmus, the date, and a pair of inscriptions. The first inscription, in Greek, reads: "The better image will his writings show"; later, this same legend appeared on the engraved portrait of Erasmus, completed by Albrecht Dürer in 1526.[42] Alongside appears a Latin inscription, on both medal and engraving: *Imago ad vivā effigiē expressa* (the image struck from the living model). On the reverse, a profile bust of Erasmus' mascot, Terminus, on a socle,[43] along with the god's device, so much taken to heart by Erasmus, *Concedo nulli* (I yield to none). Above the statue, two more lines in Greek and Latin. The Greek inscription reads, "Consider the end of a long life"; this is a traditional memento mori sentiment, but at the same time it establishes the role of Terminus as the giver of boundaries. The Latin inscription which follows makes this idea explicit: *Mors ultima linea rerū* (Death is the extreme limit of things; Horace, *Epigrams* I, 167a).

In 1528, Erasmus described in detail in a letter to Alfonso Valdes, humanist councillor of Charles V, precisely what the Terminus emblem meant to him:

> There are some who seek to make Terminus, the seal on my ring, an occasion for slander, protesting that the addition of the device *Concedo nulli* shows intolerable arrogance . . . They are dreaming if they think it is Erasmus who says *Concedo nulli.* But if they read my writings they would see that there is none so humble that I rank myself above him, being more liable to yield to all than to none.
>
> Now those who know me intimately from close association will attribute any vice to me sooner than arrogance, and will acknowledge that I am closer to the Socratic utterance, "This alone I know, that I know nothing", than to this, "I yield to none" . . . At least, as they knew that in devices of this kind one actually aims at a certain degree of obscurity in order to exercise the guessing powers of those who look at them . . . they should have inquired of experts in this kind of matter. In former times field boundaries were marked with some sign. This was a stone projecting above the earth, which the laws of the ancients ordered never to be moved; here belongs the Platonic utterance, "Remove not what thou has not planted". The law was enforced with a religious awe, the better to deter the ignorant multitude from daring to remove the stone, by making it believe that to violate the stone was to violate a god in it, whom the Romans call Terminus, and to him was also dedicated a shrine and a festival, the Terminalia. This god Terminus, as the Roman historian has it, was alone in refusing to yield to Jupiter . . .
>
> . . . And so from a heathen god I made myself a device, exhorting me to correct my life. For death is truly a boundary which knows no yielding to any. But on the medal is added in Greek: "Consider the end of a long life", in Latin *Mors ultima linea rerum.*
>
> There is my defence on Terminus, or better say on hair-splitting. And if only they would at least set a *term* to their misrepresentations![44]

The emblem also had a more personal significance for Erasmus, based upon the defiant nature of the god Terminus, who, according to Roman legend, refused to abandon the Capitoline sanctuary area in order to make way for the temple of Jupiter. This truly is the spirit of *Concedo nulli,* independent and critical thought, even to the point of satire on established ideas and institutions, both in religion and contemporary life. The spirit of Terminus lurks behind the satiric mode in Erasmus's fiction, such as the *Praise of Folly* and the *Colloquies,*[45] and the emblem of Terminus is an outgrowth and expression of both Erasmus's classical learning and his *philosophia Christi.*

Again, the inspiration for the 1519 medal surely came from Erasmus himself, particularly this apt and witty symbol of Terminus and the accompanying learned inscriptions. The letters of Erasmus also record numerous occasions where he sent casts of the medal to friends in much the same manner as he had forwarded his painted portrait to More.[46] In fact, it might well have been More's praise for the Massys portrait which suggested the subsequent casting of Erasmus's likeness in metal:

> O, Quintinus, renovator of ancient art, artist no less great than the grand Apelles, you who, thanks to your delicious harmony of colors, are capable of making an inert drawing live, why have you chosen this fragile wood to paint these portraits so ably and laboriously realized, so that I scarcely know if the future shall ever see the like; these portraits which ought to have been entrusted to a more durable matter in order to conserve them for ever?[47]

In both Germany and the Netherlands, the early 16th century saw a revival of the vogue for commemorative portrait medals with the likenesses of military and political leaders and, early on, humanist scholars (Alberti, Guarino, Vittorino da Feltre).[48] Artists in Italy, notably Pisanello, had introduced this revival based on ancient coins, in bronze during the 15th century. Like Erasmus's own image, such medals offered a combination of portrait on the obverse with, frequently, a reverse face with allegorical personages, mottos, or emblems combining word and image. Massys' medals prior to the Erasmus image had been without reverse sides, another testimonial to the importance of the Terminus image in Erasmus's careful supervision of his personal emblem for the medal.

Erasmus's own words illuminate the importance and purpose of such portrait medals in his humanist world of the early 16th century. Writing to Pirckheimer in Nuremberg, 14, March 1525, he opines:

> Portraits are less precious than jewels—I have received from you a medallic and a painted portrait—but at least they bring my Willibald more vividly before me. Alexander the Great would only allow himself to be painted by Apelles' hand [More's own praise for Massys]. You have found your Apelles in Albrecht Dürer, an artist of the first rank and no less to be admired for his remarkable good sense. If only you had found some Lysippus to cast the medal! I have the medal of you on the right-hand wall of my bedroom, the painting on the left; whether writing or walking up and down, I have Willibald before my eyes, so that if I wanted to forget you, I could not . . . There is another very pleasant thing—the portraits often occasion a talk about you when my friends come to visit me . . . You have a medal of me [the Massys medal, alluded to in the previous letters to Pirckheimer; see above]. I should not object to having my portrait painted by Dürer, that great artist.[49]

The advantage of such portrait models for humanists was their reproducibility. Along with their connotations of classical learning and ancient forms, these tributes were available in multiple casts, like an engraving. In fact, it is no coincidence that the 1526 portrait finally made of Erasmus (B. 107) by Dürer was an engraving,[50] which borrowed considerably from both the painted predecessors of Massys and Holbein and from the medal inscriptions of Massys' *Erasmus* of 1519. Drawing upon the rectangular format and the illusionistic possibilities of the painted portraits, Dürer's engraving also shows Erasmus at work in a study. The scholar is writing at a table on a lectern; along the front edge of the print rises a stack of thick books on a projecting shelf. Like the Massys painting for More, Dürer's Erasmus presents the subject in three-quarter profile, rather than the strict profile convention of the medal tradition. The engraving, then, is also a portrait-in-action of the scholar with the attributes of his profession and a suggestion of his location in a proper space for his work. Yet it also contains affinities with the commemorative medals by virtue of its association with printing, and as a result, Dürer has appropriated both the Latin and the Greek inscriptions of the Massys medal for his engraving. In effect, the engraving could also be sent to a host of Erasmus's friends as a memento or a souvenir, like the medals described in the letters to Pirckheimer, even though an engraving was not a unique object, like the More painting, nor nearly as expensive as the bronze medal. *Pl. 104*

Less durable than the portrait desired by More and perhaps less solemn than the sober bronze profile of a medal, the engraved portrait with inscriptions was a suitable alternative to, and compromise between, these media, and in Dürer's case was a favored form of portrait creation during the period in which he completed the 1526 *Erasmus*.[51] Dürer records sending two hundred impressions of his 1519 engraved portrait of *Cardinal Albrecht of Brandenburg,* along with the plate, in return for 200 florins and a measure of damask for a coat. In the same letter, Dürer expresses his desire to make an engraved portrait of Luther:

> God helping me, if I ever meet Dr. Martin Luther, I intend to draw a careful portrait of him from the life and to engrave it on copper, for a lasting remembrance of a Christian man who helped me out of great distress.[52]

Four years later, Dürer made a second, larger engraved portrait for Albrecht of Brandenburg (1523), and he indicates in a letter to the cardinal that he has pulled no fewer than five hundred impressions and sent them along with the plate to his patron.[53] In the years that followed, Dürer produced other engraved portraits of contemporary figures in the nascent Reformation: *Frederick the Wise* (1524; B. 104), his intimate friend *Pirckheimer* (1524; B. 106), and finally, *Philip Melanchthon* (1526, the same year as his *Erasmus;* B. 105). In each of the portraits, Dürer sets a bust effigy above an inscribed tablet, expressing in Latin the same kinds of sentiments as the *Erasmus* print concerning the lasting fame of the sitter for posterity.[54] This combination of bust portrait and mottos, then, is a paper counterfeit of a bronze medal.

Pl. 105

The *raison d'être* for this network of exchanges and these clusters of reproducible images, like medals and prints, lies in the character of the Northern intellectual community. The world of "Christian humanism," of scholars and religious thinkers, was both vast and extended, and the simple roster of countries, let alone individuals, who received Erasmus's ubiquitous letters amounts to virtually all of Europe. Erasmus's residences also testify to the range and extent of his personal contacts: Paris, England, Italy, Belgium, Strasbourg, Basel, Freiburg. Erasmus himself was the linchpin in this community of scholars; his letters were the concrete links between the disparate members of this group. As Huizinga has noted,[55] the community comes to define itself by taking the name of its central figure, as some of the German friends of Erasmus began in 1516 to take the name *Erasmiani.* Panofsky has justly contrasted this extended character of Northern humanism with its Italian counterpart.[56] He characterizes the close personal contact and geographical compactness of Italian scholars within only a few adjacent locales as aristocratic and "centripetal", oriented toward cosmopolitan, definable centers (Florence, Venice, Ferrara, Rome). The northern scholarly world had only Erasmus as its center, and even he was a highly mobile focus of attention, changing his own location every few months. This diffuse environment should then be described as egalitarian and "centrifugal," diffusing out of an ill-defined core toward a constellation of scholars at the perimeters of an intellectual universe. In such an expanse of geographical dispersion, having a tangible sign of absent colleagues takes on special significance and complements their epistolary contact. Erasmus makes precisely this point when he writes to Pirckheimer about enjoying both a painted portrait and a medal as souvenirs of his absent friend and when he talks about the talks occasioned by the portraits when mutual friends behold them. Having reproducible images, like medals or the less-expensive engraved portraits, enabled distant scholars, like Erasmus and Prickheimer, to exchange likenesses as they exchanged letters. For this reason, Thomas More takes Erasmus's generosity in commissioning and sending a unique, painted portrait as a sign of special affection: "I cannot tell you how proud I am to think that by this signal proof you have declared that there is no one by whom you are more loved than me."[57] And to Gillis, he reemphasizes the power that the paintings have to make him feel close to his absent friends: "More regrets to be separated from them by space, him who is linked to both of them by love, as near as anyone can be to himself."[58] Letters carry the sentiments of absent friends; portraits bear their actual features.

Even the paintings of *Erasmus* and *Gillis* by Massys or the subsequent portraits of *Erasmus* by Holbein enjoyed sufficient demand and popularity to be replicated in oil on numerous occasions.[59] The finest surviving replicas of the Massys portraits, probably by Massys himself, are the *Erasmus* in Rome (Galleria Nazionale) and the *Gillis* in Antwerp (Koninklijk Museum); neither of these two works contains the book titles, referred to in More's letter and legible in the Hampton Court *Erasmus* and the Radnor Collection *Gillis.* But a host of lesser copies, particularly of the Erasmus, show that the demand

Pl. 99
Pl. 100

for multiple images enabled lesser, now-unknown artists to earn a living off the famous exemplars of Massys and Holbein.

Massys' masterful assimilation of the Erasmian spirit into his pendant portraits and medal has already been noted. Surely, the inspiration for the conception of the author portrait painting of the Terminus emblem must have come to the artist, like the selected book titles, from the humanist himself. There is, moreover, no necessary reason to think that even a pair of portrait commissions as successfully realized as these should imply any more profound connection between the artist and his sitter. Yet within the career of Massys, the portrait of Erasmus marks a distinct turning-point in his presentation of a human figure, and it also initiates a series of portraits by Massys of other scholarly individuals.

One indication of how great was this change in his conception of portraiture is the contrast of the 1517 *Gillis* pendant with a previous Massys likeness of the same Antwerp humanist (Oldenburg, Museum; F. 49, cat. 56).[60] The dark hair color, strong and uptilted nose, and dimpled chin all strongly *Pl. 102* suggest that both pictures depict Peter Gillis. Unfortunately, the Oldenburg picture is undated, so its place in Massys' chronology depends upon comparison of its manner of handling with the artist's touch on the other dated or datable portrait works (Chap. 8). The closest portrait comparison is the Winterthur *Pilgrim,* dated 1509, which has many of the same conventions of arrangement: the *Pl. 138* avocado green monochrome background, the harsh contrasts of lighting, the oblique gaze of the sitter. (Some of the notable differences are the half-length with hands of the Winterthur *Pilgrim,* which contrast with the bust-length without hands of the Oldenburg *Gillis.*) But these are formulaic habits of representation that accord with traditions of portrait-making; what really defines the time of origin of the Oldenburg *Gillis* is its painterly technique. The heavy-lidded facial types, the linear edges and sharpness of contours and planes, and the contrast of textures between the more roughly modeled, deeply shadowed male figure and his delicately shaded, fine-toned female companion show striking *Pl. 103* parallels with the 1514 *Moneychanger and his Wife* (F. 53, cat. 16) as well as with the undated pair of *Pl. 118* portraits in Badminton.

Comparison of the Oldenburg image with the Longford Castle *Gillis* has led the one scholar who recognized the identity of the sitter to conclude that the Oldenburg painting showed Gillis as an older man; to date a picture, however, on the basis of the apparent difference in age is a risky venture at best (even more so, if two artists painted the man's portrait, as Müller-Wulckow supposes).[61] For one thing, the amount of direct contact between the portraitist and his sitter might vary considerably on the two different occasions. We know nothing about the circumstances surrounding the Oldenburg portrait, but evidence from Erasmus's letters to More makes clear that Gillis was ill during the painting of the *Friendship diptych* and not fully recovered when he sat for Massys.[62] Moreover, the Oldenburg portrait emphasizes a dramatic lighting which would be inappropriate within the scholar's study of the diptych with Erasmus. That lighting also serves to distinguish Gillis from his wife, and it is entirely possible that the formal, commemorative circumstances of a wedding diptych would call for a more forceful and mature visage than the seemingly casual appearance of two friends in the process of work and conversation. Thus, the relative dates of the two Gillis portraits by Massys are not at all well defined, unless we take the formal resemblances to the other dated Massys works, ca. 1509–14, to indicate an earlier creation of the Oldenburg portrait.

The facts about Gillis's life offer no conclusive proof, for the Antwerp humanist had two wives who would qualify as the sitter for the Oldenburg pendant, one on each side of the 1517 date of the *Friendship diptych.* His first marriage did occur at the time assumed here to be approximately correct in formal terms for the period of the Oldenburg portraits. In August 1514 Gillis married Cornelia Sanders, a wedding which was commemorated by Erasmus in his colloquy, "Epithalamium Petri Aegidii," first published in 1524 but already mentioned in letters of 1514.[63] But a second marriage by Gillis took place in August 1526, involving Maria Denis. Massys was still alive in Antwerp and conceivably could have painted the portrait of Gillis and his new bride in 1526 just as easily as in 1514.

Taken together, however, the pattern of contacts between Massys, Gillis, and Erasmus supports the formal arguments for an earlier date of the Oldenburg portraits. Gillis's marriage in 1514, his meeting with Erasmus's friend More in 1515, his supervision of the publication of More's *Utopia* in Louvain in 1516, and finally the *Friendship Diptych* of 1517—all point to the importance of Gillis and Antwerp in the development of the double-portrait commission for Massys. The crucial missing ingredient in the equation is the contact between Gillis and Massys. While the famous Antwerp artist could have been sought out for the first time in 1517 by his fellow-townsman, Gillis, the ca. 1514 wedding portrait would have afforded a convenient prior contact. Social circumstances, then, reinforce the formal evidence to suggest a mid-teen date for Massys' portrait of Gillis and his bride, presumably Cornelia Sanders.

Pl. 153 Whether these dates are correct or not, the departure in the 1517 *Friendship diptych* work from *Pl. 154* Massys' other portrait diptychs, including both the Oldenburg and the Badminton double portraits, is impressive. From the tradition of the author portrait, in particular the overtones of St. Jerome in his study, Massys moves toward an evocation of the work and the environment of his sitter in place of the monochrome background, of his previous portraits (cf. Chap. 8), inherited from Roger van der Weyden. Operating to fulfill the dictates of Erasmus, the artist awoke to new possibilities in his portrait art. After this period, he turned for inspiration to a different predecessor in portraiture, the Bruges artist Hans Memling (d. 1494); in particular, for the tranquil background landscapes and impressive columned interiors, derived from Madonna images, as environments for pious sitters. It also seems to *Pl. 141* be more than coincidence that each of the sitters for Massys' late, Memling-inspired portraits with this *Pl. 144* expanded setting is identified by both costume and attributes as a man of learning. The Frankfurt *Pl. 146* *Man Reading,* datable by costume to around 1520–21 (see Chap. 8) contains spectacles and an open *Pl. 145* book. The Edinburgh *Notary* displays quill pen, inkpot, seal, and wax of a writer at his desk; this professional apparatus is worth noting in light of Gillis's own official post as *stadsgreffier,* or city *Pl. 143* secretary of Antwerp, since 1510. Finally, the Vaduz *Canon* is dressed not only in his ecclesiastical robes but also wears the *biretta* cap of an academic; his scholarly interests are further reinforced by the spectacles and book in his hands.

In the case of the *Canon,* Massys' connection with Gillis might have continued to play an important role. The name of the *Canon* is not known for certain, but good evidence (Chap. 8) supports the hypothesis that the sitter is none other than Peter Gillis's brother, Nicolai Claesz (Egidius). Nicolai had become a canon official *(kanunnik-cantor)* as early as 1510 and was distinguished from the other Antwerp canons as the only doctor of theology among them.[64] Only Nicolai Egidius would qualify to wear the canon's robes and the academic's *biretta* of the Vaduz portrait. With Peter Gillis's brother as a sitter for his portrait, the formal connections with Massys' 1517 characterization of scholars can be seen to be applied to a member of the same social and scholarly circle.

Again the evidence is inconclusive (Chap. 8), but the Frankfurt *Man Reading* could also be a member of the scholarly circle of educated men in Antwerp, the Latinist and secretary of magistrates in Antwerp: Cornelius Grapheus (d. 1558). No secure comparable portrait of Grapheus survives; the *Pl. 148* principal portrait of this scholar shows him as an older man, bearded.[65] But that portrait seems to reveal the same prominent nose, fleshy lower lip, and powerful blocky head as the Frankfurt portrait by Massys. Grapheus could be expected to appear within any cluster of images of Antwerp scholars, for in 1520 he collaborated with Gillis on Antwerp's tribute to the visiting Charles V, penning an *Aggratulatio* for the Emperor.[66] A drawing of Grapheus mentioned in his Antwerp diary entries by Dürer has never been identified; but a search through Dürer's surviving chalk drawings for the same visage is rewarded with a striking match to Massys' *Man Reading;* the charcoal drawing, dated with the *Pl. 147* indispensable year of the diary, 1521, of a *Young Man* (formerly Schlossmuseum, Weimar).[67] Dürer's drawing gives the impression of a younger age for the sitter than Massys' painting, but the face is unmistakably the same—particularly the large, rounded, rosy nose, also the brows and lips. Of course, the apparent age difference must be explained either by the different visions of the two portraitists, or else by a significantly later dating of the Massys picture (far less likely, given the distinctive fashion of the hat in the Massys' painting, a peculiar tied bonnet which also appears in other 1520–21 Dürer portrait drawings).[68]

Even if the Frankfurt *Man Reading* is not Cornelius Grapheus or the Vaduz *Canon* Nicolai Aegidius, the learned character of these two men in these later Massys portraits adds to the picture which we already know of Massys' contacts with Gillis and Erasmus, and creates a solid impression of the artist's continuing affiliation with a scholarly and religiously reflective Antwerp circle. Further evidence of this social environment for Massys is his work for the Portuguese factor Damião de Gois (see Chap. 3). De Gois was a student and, later, a close friend of the same Cornelius Grapheus, and he also corresponded with Erasmus.[69] For de Gois, Massys painted the *Crucifixion altarpiece* for the Church of Our Lady of Varzea; in 1530, Grapheus composed for de Gois the set of three poems in response to his experience of Massys' image. This correspondence among learned friends corresponds to the same kinds of exchanges which we have already seem between Erasmus and his network throughout Europe and to the praise of pictures which More has already demonstrated in his lauding of Massys' portraits.

These contacts and contracts for Massys after the period of his 1517 portraits of Erasmus and Gillis point to more than a casual involvement with the learned circles of Antwerp. Of course, a few portraits and an altarpiece cannot be construed to constitute any major readjustments in Massys' notion of art-making, let alone his religion. Within his artistic output, however, several larger trends become noticeable during Massys' final decade of production, that is, during the ten years after his 1517–19 contact with Erasmus. The first of these is negative; Massys painted virtually no altarpieces after that date, the one exception being the *Crucifixion retable* for de Gois, whose affinity for the humanist circle of Antwerp has already been mentioned. Another change of direction in Massys' *oeuvre* during the later period of his career is the marked increase in his paintings of nonreligious subjects. With the exception of the 1514 Louvre *Moneychanger and his Wife,* a work which lacks the satirical flavor and use of grotesques of the characteristic Massys secular subjects, all these worldly images appear to date from the final decade-and-a-half of the artist's activity. A final peculiarity of Massys' work after his exposure to Erasmus is a handful of pictures that seem to be hybrids poised between secular and sacred themes. For the most part, these are images of religious figures in particularly stressful, emotional, human concerns: saints reflecting on issues of Christian virtue, temptation, and death. Several of these images in particular suggest a connection between Massys' conceptualizations and Erasmus's writings.

The Massys painting that seems to grow out of his experience with Erasmus himself and with the local Antwerp Erasmians is a missing *St. Jerome,* known from various adaptations by Massys' son Jan,[70] *Pl. 106*
and best represented by a copy in Vienna (Kunsthistorisches Museum; F. 70, cat. 28). We have already taken note of Erasmus's special interest in, and identification with, St. Jerome, and the echoes of the saintly author in his study that underlie the conception of Massys' portrait of Erasmus at work. Indeed, Massys' half-length of *St. Jerome* is, in many respects, an adaptation for the historical religious figure of the portrait he had recently made for the living Rotterdam humanist. Like the *Erasmus* or even the 1514 *Moneychanger and his Wife,* Massys' *Jerome* is also featured at bust-length, and close-up *Pl. 118*
like a portrait, although he is distinguished from the ordinary run of mortals by his thick, flowing, white beard. This more intimate conception of the saint in his study marks a departure from the 15th-century Eyckian presentation. The earlier image showed the saint at full-length, accompanied by the lion that is at once his attribute and the companion from his earlier apochryphal adventures. This basically scholarly but fully equipped St. Jerome is the image presented as late as 1514 in Dürer's famous master-engraving (B. 60) of the saint at work;[71] again, the lion ornaments a foreground sill, and the viewer's eye is allowed to wander through the spacious, well-lighted cell. In Dürer's engraving, all of the still-life elements are of a size comparable to the bowed, bald head of the saint, and the viewer takes note of the scholarly ambience surroundings of the philologist rather than any distinctive individual personality.

In the Massys *Jerome,* on the other hand, the character of the saint is expressed differently, and more vividly, through the close-up features of his face. This St. Jerome is lost in profound thought. His right hand crosses his breast in a gesture of contrition, while his left hand is poised delicately on the crown of a skull. Before him lies a Bible, open to a full-page illumination of the Last Judgment. We no longer behold the scholarly activities of St. Jerome; together with his cardinal's hat, the token of his active life within Church affairs, Jerome's books have also been laid upon the shelf. His pen lies inactive beside the skull on the table.

From the skull and the Last Judgment image, we can infer that the reverie in Jerome's eyes is his reflection upon man's ultimate fate. Many of the images in a series of variations upon this Massys original underscore the message with an inscription above the head of the saint: "Respice finem" *Pl. 107* (Look to the end); in these derivations, most of them by Joos van Cleve and his workshop, Jerome is depicted pointing directly at the skull and staring outward, almost in confrontation with the viewer.[72] The van Cleve images, however, adopt a directed, preaching tone quite foreign to the Massys model, where Jerome's touch merely grazes the skull and his look rises obliquely outward above the open prayerbook. The crucial intermediary in the transformation of St. Jerome from a meditative and prayerful recluse into a glaring and forceful sermonizer was Dürer's own painted variant on the Massys picture, a 1521 panel of *St. Jerome* (Lisbon, Museu Nacional), which he gave to "Rodrigo of Portugal."[73] The idea of painting the figure at half-length seems to be Dürer's principal debt to Massys, along with the idea of the skull, but Dürer's interpretation of the saint underscores the more moderate and contemplative tone of the Massys image. Dürer's Jerome is cramped within his pictorial space, and his glowering visage dominates the entire presentation of the picture. In contrast, Massys' saint is framed within a comparatively expansive study, where a variety of books and spaces offer relief from Dürer's insistent bareness and the unmodulated crucifix.

Both saints, then, are concerned with the death's head that lies before them on the study table, but Massys' *St. Jerome* features a religious man in pious reflection concerning man's end, evoked by his prayer and within a context of his studies. In effect, Massys' *St. Jerome* does precisely what Erasmus himself instructs mankind to do on the obverse of his medal, struck by Massys in 1519. With the bust of Terminus and the inscriptions of the medal, the humanist points just as surely as do the *Sts. Jerome* of Dürer and Joos van Cleve, and he exhorts mankind to the same prescription—attention to the end of a long life.

Entire studies have been devoted to the attention in the late Middle Ages to the subject of Death,[74] which is dramatically represented as a universal end of all mankind by the topos of the Dance of Death. The 15th century saw the rise of a popular printed treatise entitled *The Art of Dying (Ars Moriendi),* which served as a kind of handbook or exemplum of how the pious Christian could combat the blandishments of the Devil on a deathbed—the same image preserved in the engraved work of Master E. S. or a panel by Bosch (Washington).[75] These works, however, are profoundly concerned with issues of attachment to worldly goods and with doubts or crisis of Christian faith. They present the macabre, even horrific, aspects of death as the spectre of earthly vanity. Massys' *Jerome,* in contrast, takes a broader view of death, seeing it in the perspective of what the late Middle Ages, following Denis the Carthusian in his *Quattuor Novissima,* called the "four last things": Death, Judgment, Heaven, and Hell.[76] With the vision of the Last Judgment in mind, the devout Christian, like Jerome, is encouraged to live on earth a life truly worthy of salvation. In the *Enchiridion,* Erasmus calls upon the pious Christian to prepare for even a sudden death during life by practicing virtue as a way of life.[77] This message, while hardly a new one in Christian thought, was a principal idea of the *Enchiridion,* which is at once a handbook and a dagger, in short, a "manual of arms" in the "battle of daily life" against the mighty foes of salvation, the temptations of the flesh.[78] The arms of the true Christian, according to Erasmus, are prayer and knowledge.[79] Erasmus was to maintain this basic argument to the end of his life. His treatise *On Preparation for Death* (1533), prepared three years prior to his own decease, repeats the same message: "Meditation on death is meditation on true life."[80]

Prayer and knowledge are very much the subject of Massys' *St. Jerome,* where the saint's erudition serves him in prayer, where his awareness of death combines with his Christian certainty of Judgment to inspire him with true penitence on his pathway of virtue. Massys' picture is not an illustration of the text of an Erasmian treatise, but it is, nevertheless, the embodiment of Erasmus's ideal of the pious Christian scholar. *St. Jerome,* as depicted by Massys, fulfills the religious aim of Erasmus, not only in the

Enchiridion but also in most of his life's work as a theologian. It focuses on death as a subject of meditation in order to promote "an interiorization, a spiritualization of religious practice, a more personal affair between the individual and God."[81] What we witness on the face of, and in the gestures of, Massys' *St. Jerome* is the expression of that interiority, of a deep-seated and informed Christian faith by a saintly exemplar of Christian living.

Nothing indicating the original destination of Massys' *St. Jerome* has survived. And nothing, except the choice of St. Jerome from among all possible saintly models, indicates that the specific ideas of Erasmus inform Massys' picture. Yet in Massys' panel, Erasmus's favorite saint displays Erasmus's ideal of Christian conduct, the turning away "from those things whose appearance is deceptive to those things that are real . . . from the pleasures of the flesh, the honors of the world that are transitory, to those things that are immutable and everlasting."[82]

The Christian ethos practiced by St. Jerome in the panel by Massys does point to an altered concept of religious life and of religious art on the part of the painter. The increased attention toward an interiorized spiritual state, as depicted in the *St. Jerome,* implies that rituals and other outward religious acts assumed reduced importance in the spiritual life of the Christian worshipper. This unsacramental, inner religion is a central message in the works of Erasmus, beginning as early as the *Enchiridion.*[83] In describing the basic components of the Christian moral life, Erasmus devotes an entire section of the *Enchiridion* to "the inner and the outer man," drawing a distinction, based upon the writings of Paul, between the soul, led by the spirit, and the body, subject to restraint under religious law. In drawing this contrast, Erasmus writes of

> those who think that their salvation consists in wearing a blessed medal or carrying an indulgenced relic. If receiving the very sacrament of His body is nothing unless done in a spiritual manner, then I think it is plain enough that all other material things are useless unless they are spiritualized . . . If you believe in what takes place at the altar but fail to enter into the spiritual meaning of it, God will despise your flabby display of religion. . . . To place the whole of religion in external ceremonies is sublime stupidity.[84]

This attitude toward the spiritualization of religion seems to have been shared by Massys after his contact with Erasmus, though again not necessarily on account of that contact. It is, however, a curious fact that Massys virtually ceased to make altarpieces during his final decade of productivity, while other Antwerp artists prospered with commissions for retables. The one exception to this trend truly proves the rule, for we have already noted that Damião de Gois was himself associated with the Erasmian circle of Antwerp.[85] The reason for the absence of late Massys altarpieces, of course, might well be that Massys, who had made impressive altarpiece retables as early as 1507, had already passed from favor in his home town and given way to more fashionable currents in religious paintings on this large scale. But one can also take this abandonment of altarpiece commissions to be the result of more than changing public taste or of the aging artist's disinclination to tackle such major projects. Such a trend would be entirely consonant with Massys' adoption of the Erasmian attitude toward an inner religion, with the inevitable reduced emphasis on sacramental aspects of piety.

Massys' stress on the importance of internalized spirituality can be inferred not only from what he does not do in his later religious pictures, but also from a peculiar subject of human behavior which he painted during his final decade: *Two Praying Monks* (F. 80, cat. 45). The earliest description of the *Pl. 108*
picture suggests that the depicted devotion might not be entirely heartfelt or sincere: "Worshippers *Pl. 109*
from life, appearing to read piously with paternosters in hand."[86] That notice, written by Massys' 17th-century biographer, van Fornenbergh, cannot be taken as definitive concerning the picture, but it does demonstrate another aspect of interest in the subject—the blending of religion and daily life. Massys' choice of two monks "from life" indicates that his concerns with Christian ethics now extend beyond the exemplary conduct displayed by saints such as Jerome. Instead, it is the religious conduct of more ordinary—and contemporary—members of the Church who have become the subject of a painting and the objects of scrutiny.

Close inspection of the painting indicates that Massys makes an internal distinction between the two supplicants. The monk at the left is concentrating intently on his prayers, with head bowed and eyes lowered. In contrast, the second monk peers over the shoulder of the first, as if to discover some object of his companion's deep contemplation. This second monk already possesses the conventional external aid to prayer, the prayerbeads or paternoster, described by van Fornenbergh; yet his puzzled look clearly indicates that he cannot fathom the meditative inaction of his brother monk. This, then, is the visual contrast between what Erasmus had already contrasted so effectively in print, the difference between the "inner and outer man" or the "turning away from visible things to seek the invisible."

Another copy after Massys' original image contains the inscription "it is good to expect to greet the Lord with silence."[87] While no evidence exists that the missing original ever contained any such inscription, this evidence, coupled with the reading of van Fornenbergh, reinforces the interpretation, advanced here, that the image is an instructional presentation of proper and improper prayer. Another, later copy (end of the 16th century) also contains an inscription with a similar message. It is a drawing by Jacob de Gheyn (East Berlin) that states: "Binding faith and good works mean more to God than high churches."[88] Even in the world of de Gheyn's Calvinist Netherlands, almost a century removed from the *Enchiridion,* Massys' image still called up a caption reminiscent of Erasmus' own words:

> There are some people, too, who get a great deal of consolation out of attending divine services, Mass, vespers, and novenas. If they do this merely because they find pleasure in the ceremonies, because it is emotionally pleasurable or because it enhances their reputation, [they are] deceiving themselves. How many are there who, while in the very act of praying, pass judgment on those who are not naturally prayerful . . . Too many feel that whoever does not carry out the same religious practices as they do is spiritually inferior . . . I think there are far too many who count up how many times they attend Mass and rely almost entirely upon this for their salvation. They are convinced that they owe nothing further to Christ. Leaving church, they immediately return to their former habits. I certainly do not hesitate to praise them for getting to Mass but I am forced to condemn them for stopping at this point. They have failed to let what takes place at Mass also take place in their hearts.[89]

Massys' decision to portray monks rather than lay members of the Church goes a step further to underscore the irony of hypocritical outward professions of piety. Such monks by their very garments vow to live truly Christian lives, yet their external appearance is anything but an unqualified guarantee of the Erasmian goal of internalized spirituality. The humanist makes this explicit in his *Enchiridion,* commenting, like Massys' visualization, on the prayers of monks:

> I warn you with the more diligence because I know that this error has confused, not merely the crowd, but also those who in name and in garb claim perfect religion. These people believe that greatest piety is repeating as many psalms as possible every day, though they scarcely understand them. On every side monastic piety grows cold, languishes, and disappears because the monks grow old and gray in the letter of the scriptures rather than maturing to a spiritual understanding.[90]

Erasmus was hardly unique in his criticisms of outward ceremony and hypocrisy in monasticism. For example, a contemporary satire in prose (first published in Antwerp around 1520), *Broeder Russche,* tells the story of the Devil, disguised as a monk, who deceives his fellow monks as well as lay burghers.[91] But the critique of monasticism offered by Erasmus, himself a former monk who never renounced his vows, is particularly impassioned. Even his early tract on *Contempt of the World* in praise of monasticism concludes with a chapter which largely negates all his praise and challenges the value of the cloister in an era of its decline.[92] This same criticism of monasticism forms the final passage of the *Enchiridion,* as Erasmus reminds the reader of the danger of relying only on external signs of piety.[93]

> I wrote this . . . because I was afraid you might fall into the clutches of those superstitious religious who . . . try to drag [one] into the monastic life, as if one were not a Christian without a cowl . . . Monasticism is not holiness but a kind of life that can be useful or useless depending on a person's

> temperament and disposition. I neither recommend it nor do I condemn it. Let me warn you about it, however. Do not let your relationship with God depend on food, or on any visible thing. [93]

Within the *Praise of Folly* Erasmus castigates

> those who are popularly called "Religious" or "Monks". Both names are false, since most of them are a long way removed from religion . . . when they bray like donkeys in church, repeating by rote the psalms they haven't understood, they imagine they are charming the ears of their heavenly audience with infinite delight.[94]

Erasmus is critical in both this passage and in his *Colloquies* of monks as unclean beggars under the protective mantle of their churchly raiments. Monks are often hypocrites who in fact hide their fondness for food and flesh behind ceremonies. Indeed, "many of them work so hard at their labors that they think one heaven hardly enough reward for their labors." In these and other passages, Erasmus makes clear how closely related the *Praise of Folly* is to his ethical directives in the *Enchiridion;* the particular passage about monks reciting psalms without understanding their meaning is almost a literal transcription from the Handbook to the words of Folly. Erasmus admits as much in the defense of his *Praise of Folly* written in a letter to Martin Dorp (1515).[95]

When he returns to the subject of true piety near the conclusion of the *Praise of Folly,* Erasmus speaks no longer in a mocking tone but rather in the rapturous voice of the Christian fool, where the seemingly mad folly of the cross is understood to redeem worldly folly as the true, spiritual wisdom which speaks directly through the mouth of Dame Folly.[96]

The Massys image of Praying Monks combines a vision of prayer with actors who are no longer saintly or even distanced in time from the world of the contemporary beholder. The image has the intimacy of close-up presentation, like a portrait or an icon. This panel invites attention, even though its subjects are neither familiar nor holy individuals, nor are they fully grotesque like the heads featured in many of Massys' secular satires (e.g., the London *Old Woman;* F. 52, cat. 32). Instead, they *Pl. 122* are anonymous, contemporary Christians whose contrasting behavior is instructive. The didactic message about the nature of prayerfulness cannot come out with quick or casual observation of the panel. It is a muted message, almost demanding the captions or epigrams that accompany several of the copies, mentioned above. The Erasmian content of that message might, in part, be responsible for the understated quality of the Massys picture.

The *Praying Monks* is, of course, not a literal illustration of any Erasmian passage. Yet its message, particularly in the contrast of prayerful conducts, is informed by Erasmian values, to be found within both tracts, like the *Enchiridion,* and fiction, like the *Praise of Folly.* What is also intriguingly like the instructive fiction of Erasmus is Massys' contrast of two interacting figures. In his *Colloquies* in particular, Erasmus used dialogue between two (or three) characters as the vehicle for his didactic ends, and the later colloquies were especially oriented toward moral and Christian instruction.[97] The *Colloquies,* like the *Praying Monks,* are preoccupied with the distinction between outward signs and internal spirit, such as the satire on religious pilgrimage in "Rash Vows" and "A Pilgrimage for Religion's Sake," or superstition in "The Shipwreck."[98] Significantly, the targets for both Massys and Erasmus are the same, as Sister Geraldine Thompson has pointed out: the hypocrite and the fool.[99] Both the writer and the painter attempt to prick the consciousness of their audience through ironic demonstration of the absurdity of wrong-headed or uncritical behavior. Yet in most of the *Colloquies,* as in the *Praying Monks,* the proper moral direction is also presented alongside the satire; this positive display reveals the ultimate optimism behind the moral instruction of the works. In the case of the *Praying Monks,* Massys has not had to employ irony, for his didactic point is effectively established through contrast; elsewhere, however, his scornful presentation of grotesque heads in his secular satires also seems to possess the instructive ridicule at the heart of the *Praise of Folly* and many of Erasmus's *Colloquies.*

No information has survived concerning the commission of the *Praying Monks,* so it cannot be established that the panel was intended for an Erasmian audience. Yet its concern with true piety in prayer rather than the mere trappings of ceremony is an Erasmian preoccupation; moreover, its portraitlike presentation of two contrasting characters from everyday life in a morally instructive contrast recalls the humanist's use of everyday characters in his fictional dialogues. These tendencies come at a time, the 1520s, when Massys' portraits suggest his continued association with the learned Erasmians of Antwerp. The unprecendented and unique production of the *Praying Monks* strongly suggests that Massys' art-making and his religiosity were redirected by his contact with that Erasmian circle in Antwerp after 1517. Moreover, the uncaptioned and understated presentation of the two monks raises the possibility that Massys' panel was produced for that same knowledgeable audience as the artist's visual attempt to enact Erasmus's own call for a revival of piety behind religious signs and ceremonies.

Erasmus's own comments on religious art show a severe sense of propriety that borders on censorship. The humanist makes a sharp distinction between what he considers the sacred and the profane, and he becomes incensed when the boundaries between the two become blurred within the sphere of religious painting. The basic issue, as is so often the case with Erasmus, boils down to Christian education and the use of art in the morally uplifting caue of spiritual edification. In fact, some of his most penetrating discussions of the spiritual uses of both art and music occur within the context of education—specifically, the education of women—in his *Instituto christiani matrimonii* (1526).[100]

> What shall I say about the licence so often found in statutes and pictures? We see depicted and exposed to the eyes what would be disgraceful even to mention . . . Let us thank God that our religion has nothing which is not chaste and modest. All the more grievous is the sin of those who inject shamelessness into subjects that are chaste by nature.[101]

In his treatise on prayer from the same period (*Modus orandi Deum,* 1524), Erasmus rails again at the superstitious worship of the saints and the cult of relics in late medieval religious practice ("The saints have become the successors of the gods").[102] And while he did not condemn prayers to the saints, he did draw the line in religious terms, at idolatrous or credulous practices, "vestiges of ancient paganism," which obscure true Christian piety:

> Not all images are to be banished from the churches but the people have to be taught in what way to use them. . . . It would be desirable that in a Christian church nothing be in evidence but that which is worthy of Christ. But now we see there so many fables and childish stories *[fabulas ac naenias depictas]* like the Seven Falls of Christ, the Seven Swords of the Virgin or her Three Vows and other silly human fabrications of this kind. Further the saints are not depicted in a form which is worthy of them—as when a painter, commissioned to portray the Virgin Mary or St. Agatha, occasionally patterns his figure after a lascivious little whore, or when he, commissioned to portray Christ or St. Paul, takes as his model some drunken rascal. For there are images which provoke us to lasciviousness rather than to piety. Yet even these we tolerate because we see more harm in eliminating than in tolerating them.[103]

This issue of images in religious life was hotly contested at the time when Erasmus penned these lines, for the radical reformers, most notably Zwingli, near Erasmus's adopted home of Basel, were attacking the traditional presence of visual imagery within Catholic churches.[104] It was within the field of this theological controversy that Erasmus defined his own position in his final ideological testament, *On Mending the Peace of the Church (Liber de sarcienda Ecclesiae concordia,* 1533), which was a considered response to the hotheads on both sides of the early Reformation debates.[105] Erasmus's definitive discussion of religious images is guardedly tolerant, yet certainly far from iconoclasm:

> Those who rage against the images of saints have perhaps done so with reason, but to my way of thinking they have been a bit immoderate. Idolatry is certainly a terrible sin, and although the worship of images was removed in times past, there is the danger that diabolical devices might facilitate its return for the unwary. Statuary and painting have a place among the liberal arts as a kind of silent poetry . . . The superstitious element should be eliminated; whatever is useful should be

> retained. . . . In courts and parks it would be all right to depict scenes from human events, provided they lead to good morals. Whatever depicts what is foolish or obscene or seditious should be removed not only from churches but also from public places. . . . If you feel that the images of the saints are devoid of any sense and are not to be honored, keep your thoughts to yourself. But do not disturb those who without superstition lovingly cherish images.[106]

Morality, propriety, and the right image of Christ and the saints is the goal of Erasmus's iconophilism. And it is an old theme with him: even in the *Enchiridion* he had argued for the appreciation of the mental portrait of Christ, as conveyed by the words of Scripture, along with the veneration of his physical likeness to be viewed in the pictures of the Church.[107]

The implications of this attitude for Massys are clear enough. In the mid-1520s, Erasmus specifically attacks as a "silly human fabrication" the elaborate cult of the Virgin which had led to the *Seven Sorrows altarpiece* or the extensive genealogical preoccupation of the *St. Anne altarpiece*. Indeed, the only known late altarpiece by Massys for de Gois was extolled by Cornelius Grapheus for precisely those spiritual and moral values that Erasmus finds praiseworthy in the pictorial narration of the story of Christ. And the shift in Massys' rare depictions of saints between the cult figure of *St. Christopher* (Antwerp, Koninklijk Museum, F. 32, cat. 7) from the early period and the exemplary contemplative *Jerome*, meditating on death and the Last Judgment, seems to indicate a reorientation of the artist's conception of the role of saintly exemplars in the religious life of his viewing public. We need not infer from this change that the contact with Erasmian ideas is fundamentally responsible, but the Erasmus of the *Enchiridion* was a harsh critic of what he regarded as superstitious cult worship of the saints and their relics: *Pl. 113* *Pl. 106*

> Now there are not a few who are given over to the veneration of the saints, with elaborate ceremonies. Some, for example, have a great devotion to St. Christopher. Provided his statue is in sight, they pray to him almost every day. Why do they do this? It is because they wish to be preserved from a sudden and unprovided-for death that day. There are others who have a great devotion to St. Roch. Why? Because they believe that Roch can immunize them against certain physical ailments . . . In short, for everything we fear or desire we set up a corresponding deity . . . This kind of piety, since it does not refer either our fears or our desires to Christ, is hardly a Christian practice. As a matter of fact, it is not a great deal different from the superstitions of the ancients.[108]

Almost a decade later, the same message is hammered home by Erasmus in the *Praise of Folly:*

> The same thing happens when certain regions of the country set up their own peculiar saint and attribute peculiar rites and powers to each one. One gives relief from toothache, another helps in childbirth, another restores things that are stolen, another brings help to the shipwrecked, still another guards the flocks, and so it goes down the line. There are some saints who can do many things, like the Blessed Virgin, whom the common folk honor more than they do her Son. And what do people ask from these saints, except what is foolish?[109]

For the humanist, then, not the wonder-working powers of the saints, but their exemplary lives are to be emulated by the Church community. That is the reason why he is scornful of religious narratives which portray the behavior of holy figures in conduct unbecoming of their dignified status, as in the *Institutio Christiani matrimonii,* where he rebukes painters who show John and Martha whispering in a corner together or St. Peter getting drunk.[110] In this vein, the tendency we have already noted in Massys' religious narratives toward a viewer-as-witness, or viewer-as-participant effect (see cf. Chap. 5) is consonant with Erasmus's call for morally instructive religious paintings, even to the point of every dwelling having the life of Christ upon its walls. From the *Christ Carrying the Cross* (Hague, F. 167, cat. 15), probably painted before Massys had had any direct contact that we know of with Erasmus or Erasmian ideas, to the artist's final close-up half-lengths of the 1526 *Adoration of the Magi* (NY, F. 8, cat. 40) or *Christ Presented to the People* (Venice; F. 11, cat. 46), the story-telling function of the images is increasingly overlaid with the additional emphasis of viewer address, the increasing evocation of viewer empathy. Increasingly, Massys' works call the religious observer of the paintings to acknowl- *Pl. 89* *Pl. 79* *Pl. 87* edge and accept the figure of Christ in a spirit of compassion and love. Here, too, there is a correspondence between the religious program of art-making as espoused by Erasmus and the later picture-making by Massys. Again, the *Enchiridion* sets the theme:

> Perhaps you are wont to venerate the relics of the saints, yet at the same time you condemn their greatest legacy, the example of their lives. No veneration of Mary is more beautiful than the imitation of her humility. No devotion to the saints is more acceptable to God than the imitation of their virtues. . . . I have continually emphasized that the only complete example of perfect piety is to be found in the imitation of Christ. Yet I do not condemn the imitation of his saints; emulate them in such a way that each of them prompts you to eradicate one or another vice, and practice their particular virtues.[111]

Erasmus's remarks concerning the Virgin are particularly interesting in juxtaposition with the late Madonna images (Chap. 4) produced by Massys. Often these panels emphasize the humility of the Madonna and her maternal tenderness toward the Child, rather than her otherworldly or miraculous aspects. Erasmus had insisted on Mary's humility as her essential virtue, and Massys stressed that humility in the modest garb, the nursing or kissing gestures, and the domestic locations of his pictures. The humanist further attacks the widespread cult of the Virgin "whom common folk honor more than they do her Son." Like his treatment of other saints, Erasmus urges following the behavior of the Virgin rather than praying to her with "simple and childish superstition." The Colloquy "Concerning the Eating of Fish" expresses these sentiments vividly:

> How many people put more trust in the protection of the Virgin Mary or St. Christopher than in Christ himself? They worship his mother with images, candles, and songs and offend Christ heinously with impious living. . . . Do we say rosaries and salutations to the Holy Virgin? Rather we should recount to her the humiliation of our pride, the suppression of our lust, and the foregiveness of injuries. The mother of Christ takes more delight in songs like these, and they are ways to her and to her son.[112]

Of course, Massys' late Madonna images in no way exemplify Erasmus's own views on the cult of the Virgin; their very number shows the artist to be responding, together with his contemporaries, such as Joos van Cleve (Chapter 9), to the continuing demand for Mary pictures. Yet it is unmistakable how far Massays has come from his early, iconic proxies for the holy mother herself. The later works, as we have seen, are not solemn icons, but have become sentiment-filled visions of virtuous activity, filled with intimate human qualities yet transcendently beautiful. The degree, however, to which these Madonna panels exemplify the Virgin's virtues as a model for imitation (we have also seen the degree to which Massys sees such virtues as beyond the capacities of sinful mankind—another non-Erasmian view) may be, in part, the degree to which Massys absorbed the moral injunctions of the Rotterdam humanist.[113]

The other major images of saintly feminine virtue in Massys' work are a pair of late half-lengths of *Pl. 110* Mary Magdalene. The principal Massys *Mary Magdalene* (Antwerp; F. 35, cat. 29) is pictured, like the artist's late portraits of scholars, under an open portico before a harmonious, hazy, blue-green landscape. The garments the Magdalene wears in the painting are justified by the saint's life, which, according to the Golden Legend and other medieval religious myths, was a life of great luxury as the descendant of a royal family. The same legends go on to tell how the Magdalene "delivered her body so completely over to sensuality that she was known only as the Sinner."[114] In fact, one of the largest and most impressive of the engravings by Lucas van Leyden, produced around the same period *Pl. 111* (1519; B. 122) as Massys' Antwerp painting, depicts the worldly and courtly pleasures of the Magdalene and her retinue. Usually called the *Dance of the Magdalene,* the print actually catalogues a variety of sensual delights open to the well-endowed and sensuous young woman: hunting on horseback, music, courtly amorous dalliance in the park.[115] Only in the most distant background is it revealed that the sinner has become a saint (though her foreground incarnation is singled out from the other pleasure-seekers by a glowing halo); above the faraway mountain, the tiny figure of the

Magdalene can be seen suspended in air by four angels, according to the legend that she converted to Christianity, became a hermit in the wilderness (believed to be the southern French site of Ste. Baume), and was elevated to heaven for sustenance by angels every day.[116]

Massys has chosen to depict a scene from the life of the Magdalene before she became a hermit. The young woman is shown in the process of gently removing the top of an ointment jar. This gesture follows from the medieval legend that tells how the Magdalene encountered Christ in the home of Simon the Leper and, overcome by divine inspiration, showed her devotion to her new Lord by washing His feet with her tears and by salving them with her own expensive unguents. The Massys image does not show this dramatic self-abasement directly (like the Dieric Bouts image, now in Berlin-Dahlem),[117] but instead concentrates directly on the Magdalene as an individual, who is depicted, like the earlier image of *St. Jerome,* absorbed in thought, glancing away from the viewer and lightly fingering her important attribute, the ointment jar.

The portraitlike presentation underscores the immediacy of her decision-making thoughtfulness and brings the Magdalene both physically and empathetically nearer to the viewer. Massys has actually chosen to depict the very moment of her conversion, whose outcome, anachronistically, is underscored by the large jeweled cross that adorns her breast. In the late Middle Ages, the Magdalene had become the incarnation of the sinner, who repented and was saved: "The sinfulness and conversion have become her decisive attributes and are clear in a particular form of the lyric, the folk song."[118]

Massys' second image of *Mary Magdalene* (Paris, private coll., cat. 39)[119] goes still further in terms of encapsulating the entire story of the saint. Not only does it feature the sensuous aristocrat, wearing all of her splendid finery, in the foreground with her open ointment jar, but it also includes her again as a penitent in miniature within the background cave at the right. In retreat, the repentant sinner is shown, kneeling and nude, with only her long, straight hair to protect her. This is essentially the identical image to Massys' *Penitent Magdalene* (Philadelphia, Johnson coll.; F. 7, cat. 21) of a decade *Pl. 112*
earlier. But for all the resemblance of the Paris *Magdalene* to Massys' Antwerp panel, or, for that *Pl. 52*
matter, to images of the Madonna between columns from the *Seilern Madonna* (F. 165; cat. 13) to the *Pl. 63*
Berlin *Madonna Enthroned* (F. 18; cat. 37), it is still closest in type to the later portraits between *Pl. 140*
columns, such as the New York *Woman* (F. 48; cat. 60) or the Edinburgh *Notary* (F. 45; cat. 64). In *Pl. 145*
short, both the Paris and the Antwerp *Magdalenes* use portrait conventions to emphasize precisely the most human and emotional aspects of the saintly figure at her moment of spiritual crisis and conversion.

The conversion of the Magdalene, moreover, was a frequent topic in Netherlandish morality dramas of the 16th century and thus served as an inspiration to sin-conscious Christians of Massys' environment during his lifetime.[120] The pictures of the Magdalene by Massys, then, also present this kind of role-model for a pious and sinful Christian. Mary Magdalene is an *exemplum* of a sinner redeemed, of a convert forgiven her extensive previous record of vice. Erasmus had used the Magdalene for just such an example in the *Enchiridion:*

> I will not be convinced of your sanctity until you begin to hate and to flee these things that you used to love. Mary Magdalene loved much, and many sins were forgiven her. The more you love Christ, the more you will hate your vices, for just as the shadow follows the body the hatred of sin follows the love of godliness.[121]

This *Enchiridion* passage alone would not be sufficient to link Massys' *Magdalenes* to the thoughts of Erasmus or his humanist circle. But the worldly life and conversion of the Magdalene had, indeed, become a burning issue, 'La querelle de la Madeleine," within these humanist circles during this precise period, 1517–21, when Massys' contact was closest to these theologians.[122] In the spirit of humanist text criticism, a number of 16th-century Bible scholars, chiefly in France, began a debate concerning the validity of identifying Mary Magdalene with the brief mentions of Mary as sister of Martha and mourner of Christ in the Gospels. An illustrated *Vie de Saincte Madeleine* (1517) by François du Moulin de Rochefort prompted the controversy, when it was attacked in print the following year by Lefèvre d'Etaples, the eminent French humanist and friend of Erasmus. Essentially, Lefèvre was attempting to strip away the accumulated accretions of medieval legend and to hold fast to the basic biblical text, where there are no connections made between the several Maries mentioned and the sinful convert with an unguent jar (Luke 7: 36–50).[123] Lefèvre himself was attacked immediately by Marc de Grandval (September 1518), by John Fisher, bishop of Rochester (three times in 1519), and by Noel Beda (November 1519); and he was defended by Josse Clichtove (April 1519), by Henry Cornelius Agrippa, bishop of Metz (twice in 1519), by Symphorien Champier (November 1519), and by Willibald Pirckheimer. Erasmus, in typical fashion, vacillated in his letters and evaded the issue, for the scholars on both sides of the issue were his friends, but he did tend to side with traditional, anti-Lefèvre views that already formed the basis of his *Enchiridion* passage.[124] The dispute was finally resolved on 9 November 1521, when the Sorbonne officially condemned Lefèvre's views and reasserted that all of these stories were parts of a single biography, that of Mary Magdalene.

Mary Magdalene, then, was not only the model of the sinner repentant, but her basic identity and character had recently been reaffirmed. The humanist circle of Erasmus has split over the correctness and orthodoxy of these popular legends of the Magdalene, but Erasmus himself had held to tradition and been upheld. When Massys made his two pictures of the Magdalene, he created his own contribution to the question, an affirmative response. His interpretation of the sinner's conversion might have had its roots in the widespread popular concepts of the Magdalene without any intervention from the Erasmians of Antwerp. Yet the formal and psychological resemblances of his *Jerome* already suggest that Massys' choice of this meditative saint, too, may be linked to Erasmian thought.

Pl. 106

The one surviving image of a saint by Massys that can truly be called a cult image is his Antwerp *St. Christopher* (F. 32; cat. 7), painted during his earliest years. This Christopher image appears in the midst of his most characteristic action, as the giant who ferries Christ by night across a raging river.[125] Like many other early paintings by Massys, this image, too, seems to have been based loosely upon a famous prototype, and it is closely related to several works from the circle of Dieric Bouts, the great painter of the later 15th century in Massys' natal town of Louvain.[126] Christopher was an extemely popular saint in late medieval piety, because morning prayer before his image was believed to prevent sudden death during that day.[127] In busy Antwerp, moreover, Christopher would have held special favor as the patron of travelers and seafarers; Charles V, for example, had a picture of St. Christopher painted on a sail of his ship (along with other painted sails with Madonna and Child, Trinity, and Crucifix) en route to Spain in 1517.

Pl. 113

Some two decades later, when Massys (in collaboration with Joachim Patinir) presents an image of another saint undergoing his characteristic ordeal, his version of the Prado *Temptation of St. Anthony* (F. 31, cat. 26) is created in the form of another human dilemma of ethics. The weakness of this saintly protagonist is an important part of the *mise-en-scène*. According to the Golden Legend account of the saint's life and the majority of artistic depictions of Anthony, such as Bosch's *St. Anthony triptych* (Lisbon), the principal trial of the saint consists of a series of attacks by an army of demons; however, the more extensive accounts of Anthony's temptations also mention the Devil assuming seductive female form.[128] This attempted seduction of the saint by the forces of evil is the scene portrayed by Massys in the foreground of his Madrid painting.

Pl. 114

Three beautiful women assail St. Anthony in Massys' version. The alert viewer will detect the devilish nature of their charms beneath their attractive dress; at the far left of the panel, the train of the olive gown tapers into a lizardlike tail. But the principal scene remains beguiling, not only to the viewer but also to the saint. Weakly, Anthony rejects an apple offered by one of the well-dressed latterday Eves. In fact, Massys' interpretation suggests a Judgment of Paris scene in reverse as much as a reenactment of Original Sin. In the Paris story, too, an apple was the prize, and the consequence of its bestowal was the Trojan War. During Massys' period, the story of the Judgment of Paris was recounted in texts like the *Ovide Moralisée,* where Paris's choice of Venus was interpreted as the equivalent of the Fall of Man in Eden.[129] Sensuous sin is further injected into the image of Massys'

Anthony scene by the tiny ape tugging at the clothing of the saint. This ape represents the temptations of the flesh and is often seen as the companion of Venus, as in the woodcut illustration of Sebastian Brant's Venus in the *Ship of Fools*.[130] The consequences of carnality and sin are made explicit by Massys through the hideous old woman behind the three sirens. She is dressed in courtly costume like the younger women, but she serves as a gruesome reminder of the ravages of time, like the more-common presentation of the Quick and the Dead in the 14th and 15th centuries or the increasingly popular Transi-tombs.[131] The use of such a grotesque and incongruous form (like the London *Old Woman*, ultimately modeled upon the grotesque drawings of Leonardo da Vinci) to convey a moral lesson through absurdity and ugliness is the basis of Massys' secular satires from the same general period as the *Temptation of St. Anthony* (see Chapter 7); indeed, this struggle by a most human saint is simply another way of presenting the moral issues of worldly conduct, which Massys confronts in his nonreligious pictures. *Pl. 122*

What is significant about the old woman is that, like the tail of the devilish temptress, she is visible only to the viewer. Massys places these clues within the picture in order to demonstrate the proper ethical resolution to the observer. Perhaps he felt that such commentaries were necessary additions to the image, particularly in light of the weakness being demonstrated by Anthony himself at a time when virtue is most needed. The *Temptation of Anthony* is yet another Massys image involving viewer choice, like the *Ecce Homo* images of his later period (see Chapter 5). Like the images involving mental decision (and ultimate confirmation of Christian identity) by Jerome and Mary Magdalene, Anthony struggles with worldly distractions. The *Anthony*, then, is an externalized, allegorical enactment of the internal, mental struggles of *Jerome* and the *Magdalene*. Massys has deliberately refrained from emphasizing Anthony's role as a healer of disease,[132] and he has downplayed the stuggle with demons which was such a central concern in the Anthony scenes of Bosch and Grünewald. Instead, the Massys interpretation of Anthony reveals the same concentration on ascetic ideals and moral choice that cause saints' lives to provide mankind with models for proper conduct. Again, the painter's (and Erasmus') interest in the virtues of practicing Christian asceticism is expressed through both moral instruction *(Anthony, Magdalene)* and secular ridicule *(Grotesque Old Woman; Ill-Matched Pair)*. Given this similarity of outlook with Erasmus in the artist's late works, it is hardly surprising to note that all trace of cult images of saints disappears from Massys' *oeuvre* after the 1518–20 *Rem altarpiece*. *Pl. 37*

Still, there is no irrefutable way to attribute Massys' new outlook toward religious image-making to his contact with Erasmus and Erasmian ideas. Certainly, none of his pictures depends in any literal way on passages from the famous humanist. No painting can illustrate a text from a theological polemic in any fashion comparable to conventional iconographic analysis. We know, for example, that the idea of the conversion of the Magdalene was current in everyday religous drama, but only the particular turn of pictorial presentation by the artist focuses on moral instruction and decision-making for the viewer. It is this presentation that seems so close to the spirit of Erasmus. The *Enchiridion*, of course, remains a religious tract, not a sourcebook for imagery that would "decode" unexplained details of Massys' pictures. What is important for understanding the relationship between Erasmus's ideas about religous art and the pictures of Massys is the degree to which the final period of the artist's work seems to pick up the instructional, ethical commitment of the humanist's overall program of religious education. Erasmus himself might very well not have been the direct source of this inspiration. After all, he lived much farther down the Rhine, in Basel and Freiburg, during most of this latest period of Massys. The direct contact of a painter or medallist with a sitter for a portrait need not imply any shared ideas or exchange of any kind. Yet during his final period, Massys continued to paint portraits of scholars, and there is some evidence that those scholars can be identified with the Erasmian circles of Antwerp (see Chap. 8). And Massys' religious images definitely show a shift of emphasis, which even involves virtual abandonment of the great altarpieces that contributed to his reputation as a younger artist. That shift of emphasis—in subject matter, in visual formulation, and in the mode of address to the pious viewer—coincides with the period subsequent to Massys' exposure to Erasmus.

But the humanist's spirit of moral education seems to pervade the artist's picture-making most especially in the secular images of Massys, many of which also seem to coincide with the post-Erasmus period. Here, again, the close relationship between Erasmus and the *rederijkers* of Antwerp (see Chapters 1 and 7) blurs the possible sources of Massys' visual ideas. Attitudes toward society and art's role in a culture are shared with others in that society, and we should by all rights expect to find such shared attitudes in multiple manifestations, and in literature as well as art. Precisely because of the overlaps, the strengths of these attitudes can be documented. Yet we have already seen the degree to which the elusive and mute *Two Praying Monks* concretizes visually the Erasmian contrast between true internal and superficial external peity. One other image of a more-descriptive, portraitlike nature seems to incorporate within a single, fully secular face the essence of Erasmus's comic censure. That image, simply a bust-length presentation of a laughing man, represents the ancient philosopher
Pl. 115 Democritus (F. 55, cat. 43) who, along with Terminus, serves as the *alter ego* of the humanist, laughing at the follies of the world.

An engraving from later in the 16th century identifies this otherwise unspecific grinning individual
Pl. 116 as *Democritus*. Cornelius Cort (active 1552–78) has altered some of the contemporary dress of Massys' image, replacing the tiny cap with the unfamiliar broad-brimmed headgear of a foreigner; moreover, the engraving shows a laughing man with long, curly locks and a small beard. The reason for these changes is explained by the inscription on the print, which identifies the subject as Democritus, who "distinguishes and hears whatsoever little trifles" and who "values the vain and ridiculous in the world."[133] Democritus was the epitome of comic scorn, the Greek philosopher who was taken by the Renaissance to be the man who followed a calling of laughing at the follies of the world. Typically, Democritus was paired and contrasted with Heraclitus, the weeping philosopher, who despairs in the face of mankind's follies. Cort's *Democritus,* based on the altered Massys image, is paired with a *Heraclitus,* for which no known Massys prototype survives.[134] Cort is generally known for the fidelity of his prints to their visual models,[135] and his changes in coiffure and millinery largely leave unaltered the features of the Massys *Laughing Man.* In fact, those changes seem to be largely questions of make-up, which would render the subject more convincing as an ancient Greek philosopher, instead of the
Pl. 145 contemporary man (with a hat like that of the Edinburgh *Notary*) depicted by Massys.

Of course, Cort's engraving, which was made after Massys' death, cannot conclusively identify the painting as a *Democritus* (indeed, one other scholar has taken the *Laughing Man* to be the very embodiment of folly, a *Fool*).[136] The situation is made ambiguous by the contemporary dress of the *Laughing Man,* which removes him from any specific interpretive context, either the ancient beard and dress of a Greek philosopher or the pied clothing and donkey's ears of a full-dressed fool. But, again, the very ambiguity, indeed muteness, of this portraitlike presentation points to a knowing and restricted set of viewers for it, like the case of the *Praying Monks.* And the group most likely qualified to supply the interpretive framework for this enigmatic image would have been an Erasmian group.

Images of Democritus are virtually nonexistent before the Massys *Laughing Man.* The earliest *Democritus* appears in a woodcut illustration to Sebastian Brant's 1497 edition of the *Ship of Fools*, a work well-known to Erasmus and his sympathizers; there, the woodcut was concerned with the follies of the entire world and was labeled "De stultitia mundi" (though it pairs Democritus with Diogenes, rather than Heraclitus, and points to the infancy of that tandem tradition).[137] In all likelihood, it was just the same sort of literary and learned background that gave rise to Massys' *Laughing Man,* if indeed that painting can be seen as an early figuration of a "modern" *Democritus.*

The laughing *Democritus* is appropriate to Erasmus not only because, like Terminus, it is a personal symbol evocative of classical learning, but also because the ironical Greek finds his modern-day counterpart in the author of the *Praise of Folly.* Erasmus himself was more than aware of the relationship; in fact, he underlines it throughout the pages of his text. In the introduction to the *Praise of Folly,* Erasmus singles out his friend Thomas More in just these terms, as one who likes "to play the part of a Democritus in the mortal life we all share."[138] Elsewhere in the *Praise,* Erasmus identifies himself and his comic writing with the laughing philosopher: "All this is utterly foolish, and more than one Democritus is needed for these absurdities, everyone agrees."[139] Later, the Greek is honored as the *primus inter pares* of the world's fools: "They abound in so many forms of folly and devise so many new ones every day that a thousand Democrituses wouldn't be enough to laugh at them, and we'd always have to call in one Democritus more."[140] With this final passage in mind, the contemporaneity of the Massys image, as well as its possible identification as a fool rather than a philosopher, fades into insignificance, for it is as a modern satirist, rather than as Cort's historically distant figure, that Erasmus provides both delight and instruction with his *Praise of Folly*. It is equally true that the anagogical beatitude of the final passages in the *Praise of Folly* shows the vision of Christian folly, infused with divine love—a reversal for the text in both rhetorical and spiritual terms, where worldly wisdom is revealed to be eternal folly, and true wisdom appears to the worldly as folly.[141] In fact, the contrast in the *Praise of Folly* is precisely the same as that already found spelled out between the *Praying Monks:*

> The whole of the Christian religion seems to have some kind of relationship with some kind of folly but fails to agree at all with wisdom. If you would like proof of this, take a look at children, old people, women, and fools and see how they, more than others, take great pleasure in the things of religion . . . Because of this contrast between the pious and the vulgar, each appears to the other to be insane, although in my own opinion the insanity is better attributed to the pious. I think that this will be more clear if I, as I promised, will demonstrate that their highest good is in itself a kind of insanity. . . . And this is why those who are permitted to have a foretaste of this, and they are very few, suffer from something akin to madness. They speak in a manner that is not quite coherent, not in the ordinary manner but with meaningless sounds. Their facial expressions change from joy to sorrow, they weep and laugh, and in short are outside themselves. . . . They regret the return to their senses and prefer nothing more than going back to this state of madness. And this is but a small sampling of the future happiness.[142]

Massys' *Laughing Man,* then, reflects a truly Erasmian spiritual state, which is both a Democritean laughter at the folly of the world and a beatific grin by a participant in Christian folly. Both the contemporary costume and the foolish laughter are the very tools of a modernday spiritual Democritus. In this, perhaps final, secular image, Massys has found a fittingly transcendent culmination to his earlier, morally instructive and bitingly comic portraits of human vanity, greed, and folly, just as Erasmus moves from a harsh catalogue of human vice and folly in the middle part of the *Praise of Folly* to his final, ecstatic vision of Christian folly at the end of the same text.

The *Laughing Man,* then, seems to be the fulfillment, represented also by the *Praying Monks,* of a late Erasmian phenomenon in Massys' work. But this small number of explicitly Erasmian ideas had larger ripples within the oeuvre of the Antwerp artist, as we have already seen in the portraitlike, interiorized conceptions of meditative saints, specifically the *Jerome* but also the converted and penitent *Magdalene.* Seen in the context of his total corpus of religious art, the late religious narratives by Massys also have a viewer-participant quality; the examples of the 1526 *Adoration of the Magi* (F. 8, cat. 40) or the later versions of *Christ Presented to the People* (Madrid, Venice) offer unprecedented opportunities for contemplation and ethical choice. Erasmus's own calls for interior piety in the *Colloquies* of the 1520s and, especially, his challenge to Luther in *De Libero Arbitrio* (*Concerning the Freedom of the Will,* 1524) point to much the same assertion of the importance of choice, despite man's basic sinful state, as Massys' images. For both the artist and the author, cooperation with God, especially at crucial moments like those revealed in the *Adoration* and the *Ecce Homo,* is essential to righteous living and spiritual betterment (as espoused in such books as the *Enchiridion* and the *Institution of Christian Marriage,* also written during this same later period, 1526).

Here a cautionary note should be introduced. Erasmus's theology is often inconsistent and rhetorically suited to a specific occasion within the broad spectrum of orthodoxies which he habitually challenged. Again, none of Massys' pictures should be construed as a painted equivalent for book illustration to one of Erasmus's tracts, even though some works, notably the *Praying Monks,* seem to grow directly out of the words of the Christian humanist. We simply do not possess any documentation to link Massys firmly to the Erasmians of Antwerp, and our entire range of religious data on the artist consists of the single (and distinctly non-Erasmian) fact that he died within the walls of a Carthusian monastery.

To sum up, with all of these caveats in mind, it is surely more than coincidental that Massys' career shows a major shift of emphasis after the point of his actual contact with Erasmus in the 1517 portrait commission. Circumstantial evidence—in the form of the subjects for Massys' late portraits—suggests that the artist may, in fact, have increased his contact with the ideas of the great theologian through expanded contact with Erasmus's Antwerp admirers. Massys' increased output of morally instructive painted secular satires, while strongly indebted to the *rederijkers* of Antwerp, often show strong affinities with the pages of the *Praise of Folly* and may also owe some considerable debt as a concept to the previous (1516) marginal illustrations, seen and admired by Erasmus, by Holbein in a Swiss copy of the printed text (see Chap. 7). The very ambiguity and lack of attributes or contextual explanations for pictures like the *Praying Monks* or *Laughing Man* suggest that a knowing and restricted audience, presumably the same Erasmian circle, was looking at these pictures during the very same period as the commissioned scholarly portraits by Massys. Of course, the subject of the *Jerome* did not have to come from an Erasmian orientation by the artist or his patrons, but no other religious figure lay closer to the heart of the Christian humanist, and the Massys image succeeds in a masterful way in fusing both Jerome and Terminus, Erasmus's two alter egos, into a single, contemplative image.

Our conclusions, then, about this relationship are essentially positive, even though Erasmus himself was in Basel during most of the late period when Massys came to draw inspiration from his teachings. Erasmus, and the portrait commission that he gave to Massys, acted on the artist like a catalyst, a chemical substance which causes a major reaction without itself being permanently changed by that effect. Massys' reorientation in his later period can be said in part to have been initiated by the contact with Erasmus and to have been continued by contact with Antwerp's Erasmians long after the original encounter. In terms of logic, Erasmus and his ideas were necessary, but not sufficient, for Massys; that is, they prompted a shift of religious values and artistic purposes in the artist's late work, but they alone could probably not have occasioned this shift. These Erasmian ideas, moreover, were not all-conquering. After all, Massys continued to produce Mary images at the very end of his career, against all expressed preferences of Erasmus. The artist also ended his days within the walls of an ultra-orthodox monastic order, the very reverse of Erasmus's own youthful flight from a monastery.

Massys could not rely entirely on Erasmus for his new views of religion. Only within the context of a larger culture, particularly the distinctive literary world of the Antwerp *rederijkers*, could such Erasmian views be reinforced. Antwerp's literary world complemented and appropriated Erasmian ideas, providing a fertile field and a receptive audience for the growth of new imagery by Massys. Against that larger background, including both the ideas of Erasmus and Antwerp's humanist circle and the writers and artists of the St. Luke guild, Massys was able to develop a new, more personal religion in his later years, to find alternatives to his earlier, dominant, corporate piety of the confraternities and, in consequence, to reshape the character of his art.

NOTES

1. A. Gerlo, *Erasme et ses portraitistes*, p. 9ff.; G. Marlier, *Erasme et la peinture flamande de son temps*, p. 83ff.; Panofsky, "Erasmus and the Visual Arts," p. 214; L. Campbell, M. M. Phillips, H. Schulte-Herbrüggen, and J. B. Trapp, "Quentin Matsys, Desiderius Erasmus, Pieter Gillis, and Thomas More," p. 716ff. The letter is published in P.S. Allen and H.M. Allen, *Opus epistolarium Desiderius Erasmus Roterodami* (Oxford, 1906–58), no. 584.
2. Allen and Allen, no. 601.
3. Ibid., no. 616.
4. Ibid., nos. 683–84.
5. Friedländer, vol. 7, nos. 36–37, a-c. See also the numerous copies after Holbein's Erasmus portraits: H. Brunin, "De Erasmusportretten van en naar Holbein de Jonge," *BMRBA* 17 (1968): 145–60.

6. Allen and Allen, no. 684. See Gerlo, *Erasme et ses portraitistes,* p. 14, n.14, p. 15f., n.19. The words on the letter in the Longford Castle *Gillis* are legible, arguing compellingly that this is truly the Massys original sent to More.

7. J.B. Trapp and H. Schulte Herbrüggen, *Sir Thomas More 1477/8–1535,* p. 42, no. 54 (with bibliography).

8. Campbell, et al., "Quentin Matsys," p. 719, n. 29–30.

9. A. Hyma, *The Youth of Erasmus* (Ann Arbor, Mich.: 1930).

10. Erasmus, *Education of a Christian Prince,* ed. L. K. Born (New York, 1936); J.M. McConica, *English Humanists and Reformation Politics under Henry VIII and Edward VI,* pp. 29–31; R. Bainton, *Erasmus of Christendom,* pp. 147–50; *Erasmus en zijn Tijd,* exh. cat. no. 231; J. Tracy, *The Politics of Erasmus,* p. 52ff.

11. Trapp and Herbrüggen, *Sir Thomas More,* no. 54, gives a sketch of Gillis's biography. Also, M.A. Nauwelaerts, "Pieter Gillis," *Antwerpen* 15 (1969); 38–46, and "Un ami Anversois de More et d'Erasme, Petrus Aegidius," pp. 83–96 *(Festschrift for E.F. Rogers);* J. Jacques, "Les grandes amis: Erasme et Pierre Gillis," ibid., pp. 97–102; F Prims, "Pieter Gillis," *Antwerpiensia* 10 (1936); 176–99.

12. The early 16th-century position of city secretary, requiring as it did both cultivated learning and serious diplomacy, carried much more responsibility, influence, and prestige than the current English terms connote. An enlightening case study is the career of Lazarus Spengler, *Ratsschreiber* of Nuremberg, for whom see H. Grimm, *Lazarus Spengler: A Lay Leader of the Reformation* (Columbus, 1978).

13. Trapp and Herbrüggen, *Sir Thomas More,* no. 48; Campbell, et al., p. 716, n.2.

14. Allen and Allen, no. 684; Gerlo, *Erasme,* p.14; Campbell, et al., p. 717, n.15.

15. Campbell et al.; Trapp and Herbrüggen, no. 53; M. Mann Phillips, "The Mystery of the Matsys Portrait," pp.18–21.

16. Trapp and Herbrüggen, no. 85.

17. Ibid., nos. 83–84.

18. G. Thompson, *Under Pretext of Priase: Satiric Mode in Erasmus' Fiction,* pp. 22–23, 68–69 (with bibliography); McConica, *English Humanists,* p. 117ff.

19. Trapp and Herbrüggen, no. 38; *Erasmus en zijn Tijd,* nos. 104, 112.

20. McConica, *English Humanists,* p. 24.

21. *Erasmus en zijn Tijd,* no. 211.

22. P. Smith, *Erasmus: A Study of His Life, Ideals, and Place in History* (New York, 1923), p. 191; G. Marlier, *Erasme,* pp. 169–86; *Erasmus en zijn Tijd,* no. 203.

23. Allen and Allen, no. 149. Cited in J. Huizinga, *Erasmus and the Age of Reformation,* letter v. p. 203.

24. Allen and Allen, no. 273; cited in ibid., p. 90.

25. Campbell, et al., p. 719; M. Mann Phillips, "Matsys Portrait."

26. Campbell, et al., p. 719, n. 32.

27. McConica, pp. 24–26; Bainton, *Erasmus,* pp. 175–82.

28. For the text, J. C. Olin, ed., *Christian Humanism and the Reformation, Selected Writings of Erasmus* (New York, 1965), pp. 91–106. A fine commentary is M. Mann Phillips, *Erasmus and the Northern Renaissance,* pp. 77–85.

29. *Erasmus,* Bainton, p. 175.

30. In England, the translation was supported by Catherine Parr, widow of Henry VIII; McConica, pp. 231–32, 240–8.

31. Schabacker, "Petrus Christus' *St. Eloy,*" p. 103ff.

32. D. Klein, "Autorenbild," *RDK* 1, cols. 1309–13; A. M. Friend, "Portraits of the Evangelists. Part I," *Art Studies* 5 (1927); 44ff.; "Part II," *Art Studies* 7 (1929): 4ff.; K. Weitzmann, "Book Illustration of the Fourth Century: Tradition and Innovation," *Studies in Classical and Byzantine Manuscript Illumination,* ed. H. Kessler (Chicago, 1971), pp. 112–17.

33. Schabacker, *Petrus Christus,* p. 124ff. (with bibliography), pp. 18–19, 54–55.

34. Panofsky, *ENP,* pp. 189–90, and "A Letter to St. Jerome: A Note on the Relationship between Petrus Christus and Jan van Eyck," *Studies in Art and Literature for Belle da Costa Greene,* ed. D. Miner, (Princeton, 1954), pp. 102–8.

35. Panofsky, *ENP,* p. 189, n.2. Among the copies are several manuscript illuminations from the mid-15th century, including the famous "Turin-Milan Hours" (ibid., p. 232ff., where the St. Jerome figure was transformed into a *St. Thomas Aquinas)* and the large frescos in Florence, Church of the Ognissanti: *St. Jerome* by Ghirlandaio and *St. Augustine* by Botticelli.

36. Ibid., p. 316; Schabacker, *Petrus Christus,* p. 83ff., no. 4; p. 95ff., no. 9.

37. A. Strümpel, "Hieronymus in Gehäus," p. 173ff.; M. Meiss, "Scholarship and Penitence in the Early Renaissance," *The Painter's Choice,* p. 189ff.; O. Pächt, "Zur Entstehung des 'Hieronymus in Gehäus," *Pantheon* 21 (1963): 131ff.; H. Friedmann, *A Bestiary for St. Jerome* (Washington, 1980), p. 29ff.

38. Allen and Allen, no. 683; Gerlo, pp. 12–13.

39. Allen and Allen, no. 684; Gerlo, p. 15; Campbell, et al., p. 717, n. 11.

40. See Appendix A, and for the most recent bibliography, Trapp and Herbrüggen, no. 87.

41. Allen and Allen, no. 1985. To Henricus Botteus from Erasmus in Basel (1528, March 29); Gerlo, p. 18.

42. On Erasmus and Dürer, see Gerlo, pp. 29-44; Panofsky, "Erasmus and the Visual Arts," p. 220 ff., and *Albrecht Dürer,* pp. 239–40.

43. Panofsky, "Erasmus and the Visual Arts," pp. 215–16; McConica, pp. 13–14; J. M. McConica, "The Riddle of Terminus," *Erasmus in English* 2 (1971): 2; E. Wind, "Aenigma Termini," pp. 66–69; J. Bialostocki, "Rembrandt's 'Terminus'," *Wallraf-Richartz Jahrbuch* 28 (1966): 219ff.

44. Huizinga, *Erasmus and the Age of Reformation,* pp. 246–49; McConica, both works cited; Gerlo, p. 25; Allen and Allen, no. 2018.

45. Thompson, *Under Pretext of Praise.*

46. Panofsky, "Erasmus and the Visual Arts," p. 216ff.; Gerlo, pp. 21–24, recording five separate instances: the Lowlands jurist Nicholas Everardi (Allen and Allen, no. 1092; 17 April 1520); Cardinal Albrecht of Brandenburg, who was himself portrayed twice in engravings by Dürer (Allen and Allen, no. 1101; 15 May 1520); German theologian Georg Spalatin (Allen

and Allen, no. 1119; 6 July 1520); Mathis Meyner of Chemnitz (Allen and Allen, no. 1122; 30 July 1520); and Dürer's close friend from Nuremberg, the patrician humanist Willibald Pirckheimer (first letter Allen and Allen, no. 1398; 21 November 1523). Erasmus and Pirckheimer exchanged a series of letters concerning the portrait medal during 1524, indicating that most of the impressions were cast in lead or else in an alloy of copper and tin, i.e., bronze. Erasmus also suggests in his letters that the medal might give a sharper profile in relief if it were cast with only one side, i.e., without the Terminus, whose thick socle prevented firm casting of both sides at once. See L. Smolderen, "Quentin Metsys Medailleur d'Erasme," *Scrinium Erasmianum* (Leyden, 1969), vol. II, p. 513ff.

47. Allen and Allen, no. 684; Gerlo, p. 15.

48. For the Renaissance revival of portrait medals, see J. Pope-Hennessey, *The Portrait in the Renaissance,* pp. 64–71, 208–9; G. F. Hill and G. Pollard, *Renaissance Medals at the National Gallery of Art;* A. Suhle, *Die deutsche Renaissance-Medaille* (Leipzig, 1950).

49. Quoted in Huizinga, *Erasmus,* p. 239f.

50. See note 42, above; also Trapp and Herbrüggen, no. 88; *Albrecht Dürer 1471–1971,* exh. cat., p. 160, no. 278; *Erasmus en zijn Tijd,* no. 277, 351.

51. D. Kuspit, "Durer and the Lutheran Image," *Art in America* 1975, pp. 56–61.

52. M. Conway, *Literary Remains of Albrecht Dürer* (Cambridge, 1889), p. 89f.; M. Rupprich, ed., *Dürer: Schriftlicher Nachlass* (Berlin, 1956–59), vol. I, pp. 85–87, no. 32, citing the artist's letter to Georg Spalatin, secretary to Frederick the Wise of Saxony (see note 46, above).

53. Rupprich, *Dürer,* p. 238; Conway, *Literary Remains,* p. 128.

54. The inscription on *Frederick the Wise* reads "Sacred to Christ. He served the word of God with great piety. Worthy to be revered by posterity forever." On the *Pirckheimer:* "We live by the spirit, the rest belongs to death." And on *Melanchthon:* "Dürer was able to depict Philip's features as if living, but the practiced hand could not portray his soul."

55. Huizinga, *Erasmus,* p. 98f.

56. Panofsky, "Erasmus and the Visual Arts," p. 218.

57. Allen and Allen, no. 683; Gerlo, pp. 12–13.

58. Allen and Allen, no. 684; Gerlo, p. 15.

59. See above, note 5. Also Campbell, et al., pp. 723–24, n. 51; de Bosque, *Quentin Maysys,* p. 250ff.

60. W. Müller-Wulckow, *Vier Bildnisse des Petrus Aegidius,* identified the Oldenburg portrait as Gillis, but incorrectly attributed the work to Hans Holbein the Younger, ca. 1526, on the basis of the sitter's apparent age; this assessment of dating has been followed by subsequent scholars, e.g., de Bosque, p. 258.

61. Ibid. Even if the Oldenburg picture does show an older Gillis than Massys' 1517 portrait with *Erasmus,* the pendant image of his wife might well be his first wife. In short, the painting need not date after 1526, even if it postdates 1517.

62. Allen and Allen, no. 584; Gerlo, p. 10; Campbell et al., p. 716.

63. First published in 1524 but already mentioned in letters of October 1514. C. R. Thompson, *The Colloquies of Erasmus* (Chicago, 1965), p. 223ff.

64. F. Prims, *Geschiedenis,* p. 57. Nicolai Egidius died in 1534. A list of the other thirteen canons in Antwerp in 1517 is given by Prims on p. 48.

65. The portrait by Phillip Galle was not printed until 1572 *(Variorum doctorum effigies,* Antwerp, fo.4); it is reproduced in E. J. Roobaert, "De Seer Wonderlijcke Schoone Trimphelijcke Incompst van de Hooghmogenden Prince Philips in de Stadt van Antwerpen Anno 1549," *BMRBA* 9 (1960); 44f., ill. 1. For more on Grapheus, with Gillis and other Antwerp members of the Erasmus circle, see G. Degroote, "Erasmofilie te Antwerpen in de eerst helft van de zestiende eeuw," pp. 31–51; M. Sabbe, "Erasmus en zijn Antwerpsche vrienden," pp. 61–78.

66. F. Prims, "De 13 Hypothesen van Pieter Gillis 1520," pp. 159–64.

67. Goris and Marlier, *Dürer Diary,* p. 84, fig. 56 (W. 811).

68. Ibid., figs. 13, 49, 53.

69. See Chapter 3, notes 35–36.

70. Friedländer, vol. 13, p. 29, no. 143 (Madrid, Prado); also L. Reis-Santos, "Jan Quinten Massys Discipulo e Colaborador de seu Pai Mestre Quinten Metsys," p. 10ff.; M. J. Friedländer, "Der heilige Hieronymus von Marinus van Reymerswaele," *Pantheon* 13 (1934): 33ff.; F. Winkler, "Dürers Lissaboner Hieronymus," pp. 12, 14; Marlier, pp. 169–86.

71. Panofsky, *Albrecht Dürer,* pp. 154ff.; *Albrecht Dürer 1471–1971,* exh. cat., p. 157, no. 273; Friedmann, *Bestiary for St. Jerome,* p. 101ff.

72. Friedländer, vol. 9, no. 30. A variant showing the saint nude from the waist up beating his breast with a stone is Friedländer, vol. 9, no. 40; it conflates two traditions: one the saint working in his study, the other Jerome chastening himself with the stone in a wilderness retreat (see M. Meiss, "Scholarship and Penitence"; Friedmann, *Bestiary*). This second type of image and related Joos van Cleve *Jeromes* have been well discussed by J. Hand, "The Norton St. Jerome," Norton Gallery, West Palm Beach, 1972.

73. Goris and Marlier, *Dürer Diary,* pp. 21–22; Marlier, *Erasme,* pp. 187–88; Winkler, "Dürer's Hieronymus," *Albert Dürer aux Pays-Bas,* exh. cat., no. 341. Rodrigo Fernandez d'Almada was the new Portugese factor in Antwerp, one of the circle of trade representatives who also patronized Massys (the *St. Bernardino of Siena,* cat. 23; see Chapter 3). Dürer made a chalk drawing of the factor (Berlin; Goris and Marlier, fig. 49).

74. The descriptions by Huizinga, *Waning of the Middle Ages,* pp. 138–51, are still essential. A useful recent survey with bibliography is *Europe in Torment,* exh. cat. (Providence, 1973), p. 71ff.; *Love and Death,* exh. cat. (Ann Arbor, 1975); Delaruelle, *Labande, and Ourliac,* pp. 761–76; A. Tenenti, *La Vie et la mort à travers l'art du XVe siècle* (Paris, 1952); P. Ariès, *Western Attitude Towards Death* (Baltimore, 1974), and *The Hour of Our Death* (New York, 1981). For the Netherlands in particular, Toussaert, pp. 204–24. The Dance of Death theme was a very popular and publicly visible form of the obsessive attention to universal mortality: H. Rosenfeld, *Der mittelalterliche Totentanz* (Münster, 1954); J. M. Clark, *The Dance of Death in the Middle Ages and the Renaissance* (Glasgow, 1950); D. Enklaar, *De Dodendans* (Amsterdam, 1950); *Europe in Torment,* p. 84ff., with bibliography.

75. *Europe in Torment,* p. 79; Delaruelle, *L'Eglise,* p. 769f.; R. Rudolph, *Ars moriendi* (Cologne, 1959). The ES print is discussed along with an *Ars moriendi* blockbook by A. Shestack, *Master ES,* exh. cat. (Philadelphia, 1967), nos. 4–15. On the Washington Bosch, see C. Eisler, *European Schools Excluding Italian* (London, 1977), pp. 66–69, no. K.1848, with extensive bibliography.

76. E. Lachner and K.-A Wirth, "Dinge, die vier letzten," *RDK* 4, cols. 12–22; "Eschatologie," *RDK* 5, cols. 1457–67; L. Malke, "Zur ikonographie der 'Vier letzten Dinge' vom ausgehenden Mittelalter bis zum Rokoko," *Zeitschrift des deutsches Vereins für Kunstwissenschaft* 30 (1976): 44–46. See, in particular, the Prado tabletop of the *Seven Deadly Sins and Four Last Things* by Hieronymus Bosch, well discussed by W. Gibson in "Hieronymus Bosch and the Mirror of Man," p. 205ff., and *Hieronymus Bosch,* p. 33ff.; C. de Tolnay, *Hieronymus Bosch,* p. 33–34, no. 2.

77. J. P. Dolan, *Essential Erasmus,* p. 60.

78. Dolan, *Essential Erasmus,* p. 39; R. Himelick, transl., *The Enchiridion of Erasmus* (Bloomington, 1963).

79. Dolan, *Essential Erasmus,* p. 35.

80. Quoted in Bainton, *Erasmus of Christendom,* p. 325.

81. Dolan, p. 27.

82. Ibid., p. 62f.

83. McConica, op. cit., 21f.

84. Dolan, pp. 65, 68, 51.

85. Lucas Rem, the last recipient before de Gois of a Massys triptych (ca. 1518 / 20; F.3, cat. 24), was, like the Portuguese, a private individual requesting a work of private devotion, rather than a corporate retable for eucharistic liturgical ornament (see Chapter 3).

86. L. Silver, "Prayer and Laughter," p. 19.

87. Ibid., p. 20: "Bonum est prestolari [sic] cum silentio salutare dei" on a replica at Columbia (?) discovered by Friedländer (cited by Marlier, *Erasme,* p. 247, n. 16). I have been unable to find either this painting or the original Friedländer reference.

88. E. Bock and J. Rosenberg, *Die Zeichnungen alter Meister im Kupferstichkabinett Die niederländischen Meister* (Frankfurt, 1931), p. 29, no. 4092. This caption, however, may be colored by a Protestant (Calvinist) viewpoint and should not be read into Massys' painting.

89. Dolan, pp. 51, 65.

90. Ibid., p. 38.

91. L. Debaene, *De Nederlandse Volksboeken,* and *De Historie Broeder Russche* (Antwerp, 1950).

92. R. Bainton, *Erasmus,* pp. 26–32; A. Hyma, *Youth of Erasmus;* R. R. Post, *The Modern Devotion,* pp. 660–70. Whether the final chapter was appended sometime later remains unclear. According to W. J. Hirten, ed., *De Contemptu mundi,* transl. T. Paynell, 1533 (Jacksonville, 1968), p. xiv, the last chapter was added ca. 1521 (for Erasmus's opinions on monasticism, see the remarks on xxxff.). Several of Erasmus's later *Adages* (1517) attack monasticism directly: "As sties stick to the eyes" *(Ut fici oculis incumbunt)* and *Esernius cum Pacidiano,* quoted in M. M. Phillips, ed., *Erasmus on His Times,* pp. 145–52.

93. Dolan, p. 92.

94. Ibid., p. 148.

95. Allen and Allen, no. 337; Olin, *Christian Humanism,* pp. 55–91. The best discussion of Erasmus's didactic humor in the *Praise of Folly* and *Colloquies* is Thompson, *Under Pretext of Praise.*

96. Thompson, *Pretext,* pp. 62, 70, 77f., 82–84; Dolan, pp. 171–2.

97. Thompson, *Pretext,* pp. 103–51; on monks, esp. pp. 105–11, 135. An example from the *Colloquies* is Erasmus's "Well-to-do Beggars" (1524); see C. R. Thompson, *Colloquies,* p. 203ff.

98. Ibid., p. 138ff.

99. G. Thompson, *Pretext,* p. 150, passim.

100. Bainton, 279–85; Panofsky, "Erasmus and the Visual Arts," pp. 207–14; J. Margolin, *Erasme et la musique* (Paris, 1965), pp. 13–18.

101. Panofsky, *Erasmus and the Visual Arts,"* p. 209f., n. 27; p. 211, n. 30.

102. Ibid., p. 208f., n. 25; Bainton, op. cit., 295.

103. Panofsky, "Erasmus and the Visual Arts."

104. C. Garside, *Zwingli and the Arts* (New Haven, 1966); C. Christensen, *Art and the Reformation in Germany* (Athens, Ohio / Detroit, 1979), pp. 79ff., 93ff., n. 184. Basel had convulsive iconoclastic riots in 1529, and the commune joined in January 1530 with Zwingli's Zurich, Bern, and Strassburg in the Christian Civic Alliance. For a discussion of the broader theological issues concerning religious imagery in the sixteenth century, see K. Moxey, *Pieter Aertsen, Joachim Beuckelaer and the Rise of Secular Painting in the Context of the Reformation.*

105. Dolan, pp. 327-88.

106. Ibid., pp. 380–81; Panofsky, "Erasmus and the Visual Arts," pp. 211–12, n. 32.

107. Dolan, pp. 66–67; Panofsky, "Erasmus and the Visual Arts," p. 208, n. 24, who notes the correspondence of this idea with the inscription on the obverse of the 1519 Terminus portrait medal by Massys and the 1526 Dürer *Erasmus* engraving.

108. Dolan. pp. 60, 66. The same idea of these superstitious practices, derived from ancient folk customs is repeated by Erasmus in his treatise on proper prayer; see above, notes 101–3.

109. Dolan, p. 130.

110. Panofsky, "Erasmus and the Visual Arts," p. 211, n. 30; K. Moxey, "Erasmus and the Iconography of Pieter Aertsen's 'Christ in the House of Martha and Mary' in the Boymans-van Beuningen," *JWCI* 34 (1971); 335f.

111. Dolan, p. 66.

112. C. R. Thompson, *Colloquies,* p. 325. The same message is echoed more ironically in yet another colloquy, "A Pilgrimage for Religion's Sake," where a letter from the Virgin catalogues all of the absurd requests demanded of her in the name of prayer: "So am I alone, a woman and a Virgin, to assist those who are sailing, fighting, trading, dicing, marrying, bearing children, to assist governors, kings, and farmers?" (Ibid., p. 289f.). A fine general survey of Erasmus's views on the cult of Mary is H. Düfel, *Luthers Stellung zur Marienverehrung* (Göttingen, 1968), pp. 49–56.

113. As G. Thompson so aptly summarizes: "Indeed, Erasmus is more interested, one thinks, in the imitation of Christ than in the thought of union with him or love for him" (*Pretext,* p. 165ff.).

114. J. da Voragine, *Golden Legend,* p. 356ff. The medieval literature concerning the Magdalene is extensive. See H. M. Garth, *St. Mary Magdalene in Medieval Literature* (Baltimore, 1950), pp. 347–452; M . Malvern, *Venus in Sackcloth: The Magdalen's Origins and Metamorphoses* (Carbondale, Ill., 1975); W. aus der Fünten, *Maria Magdalena in der Lyrik des Mittelalters* (Düsseldorf, Greifswald, 1937), p. 120ff.; J. Szövérffy, " 'Peccatrix quondam femina:' A Survey of Mary Magdalen Hymns," *Traditio* 19 (1963); 79–146; Szövérffy and W. Wynne, "Typology in Medieval Latin Hymns: Notes on Some Features in the Mary Magdalen, Martha, and Lazarus Legends," *Medievalia et Humanistica* 12 (1958), pp. 41–51; R. Bruckberger, *Marie-Madeleine* (Paris, 1952); F. O. Knoll, *Die Rolle der Maria Magdalene im geistlichen Spiel des Mittelalters* (Berlin / Leipzig, 1934); G. Cohen, "Marie Madeleine dans le drame religieux français du moyen-age," *Convivium* 24 (1956); 141–63; G. Doncieux, "Le Cycle de Marie-Madeleine dans la chanson popularie," *Revue des Traditions populaires* 6 (1881): 257–78.

115. P. Parshall, "Lucas van Leyden's Narrative Style," pp. 224–29, n. 64ff., citing the importance of late medieval drama, such as the 15th-century English Digby Plays. For later traditions of the Magdalene's life and conversion, see K. Moxey, "The 'Humanist' Market Scenes of Joachim Beuckelaer: Moralizing Exempla or 'Slices of Life'? *Jaarboek Koninklijk Museum voor Schone Kunsten Antwerpen,* 1976, pp. 147–50.

116. The site in southern France that was alleged to be the Magdalene's retreat became a famous pilgrimage site; see R. Koch, "La Sainte-Baume in Flemish Landscape Painting of the Sixteenth Century," *Gazette des Beaux-Arts* 66 (1975); 273–82; F. Benoit, "Le culte de Marie-Madeleine," *Annales du Midi* 71 (1959): 178–282; V. Saxer, *Le Culte de Marie Madeleine en Occident des origines à la fin du Moyen-Age* (Paris, 1959).

117. Friedländer, vol. 3, no. 16. A comprehensive study is M. Janssen, "Maria Magdalene in der abendländischen Kunst," (dissertation, Freiburg-im-Breisgau, 1962). The best-known 15th-century appearance of the saint is on the right wing of Roger van der Weyden's *Braque Altarpiece* (Louvre; Blum, p. 34f.), where she appears as one of several saintly intercessors for mankind. In the early 16th century, a new emphasis on the beauty, rich attire, and worldly life of the Magdalene prevailed. A group of paintings after the time of Massys, particularly popular in Bruges and Antwerp, show elegantly dressed courtly ladies, associable with the Magdalene because of the unguent vase attribute (see G. Marlier, *Ambrosius Benson* [Damme, 1957], pp. 188–200, plus the Antwerp works of Jan de Hemessen and the Master of the Female Half-Lengths, Friedländer, vol. 12, nos. 25–33, 81–105). These Magdalenes are engaged in a wide variety of worldly activities: reading, writing, playing lute or spinet, even weighing gold. Because of the saint's rich attire and perhaps also because of the associations with her penitence and spirituality, several ruling ladies had themselves painted by Flemish artists in the guise of the Magdalene, i.e. with ointment jars (Bernard van Orley's *Margaret of Austria,* Friedländer, vol. 8, no. 159; or the Detroit *Catherine of Aragon* by Michiel von Sittow; *Flanders in the Fifteenth Century,* exh. cat., p. 198ff., no. 52).

118. W. aus der Fünten, *Maria Magdalene,* p. 212

119. De Bosque, p. 186.

120. C.G.N. de Booys, "De Legende van S. Maria Magdalene bekeringhe," *Tijdschrift Nederlandsche Taal- en Letterkunde* 24 (1905): 16–44, cited by Moxey, *Pieter Aertsen,* p. 146, n. 98; and by Parshall, "Narrative Style," p. 225, n. 69. Also see Knoll, *Die Rolle,* p. 58ff.

121. Dolan, p. 70f. See also R. H. Robbins, "A Middle English Prayer to St. Mary Magdalene," *Traditio* 24 (1968): 458–63.

122. I am most grateful to my student, Dr. Amelia Carr, for discovering this neglected controversy and for sharing her findings with me. See M. Holban, "Francois du Moulin de Rochefort et la querelle de la Madeleine," *Humanisme et Renaissance* 2 (1935): 26–43, 146–71; A. Hufstader, "Lefèvre d'Etaples and the Magdalen," *Studies in the Renaissance* 16 (1969): 31–60, with bibliography; J. P. Massaut, *Critique et tradition à la veille de la Réforme en France* (Paris, 1974), pp. 67ff., 81ff., 96ff.

123. Lefèvre d'Etaples, *De Maria Magdalena, triduo Christi et extribus una Maria, disceptatio,* 2nd ed. (Paris) (Henri Estienne, 1518; 1st ed., 1517), on the legend concerning the three husbands of St. Anne (see Chapter 2).

124. Allen and Allen, nos. 1030, 1130. J. Rouschasse, *Erasmus and Fisher Their Correspondence 1511–1524* (Paris, 1968).

125. E. K. Stahl, *Die Legende vom heiligen Riesen Christophorus* (Munich, 1920).

126. M. J. Friedländer, "Quentin Massys, Reflexions," p. 53f.; S. Sulzberger, "Dieric Bouts et l'enluminure hollandaise," p. 227ff.

127. See the remarks of Erasmus, cited in Dolan, p. 60.

128. C. Cuttler, "The Lisbon *Temptation of St. Anthony* by Jerome Bosch," *Art Bulletin* 39 (1957): 109–26, and "Witchcraft in a Work by Bosch," *Art Quarterly* 20 (1957): 129–40, and "Some Grünewald Sources," *Art Quarterly* 19 (1956); 101–24. Also, J. M. Massing, "Etude iconographique de l'agression de Saint Antoine de Grünewald," *Cahiers alsaciennes de archéologie* 19 (1975–76): 105–26; D. Bax, *Hieronymus Bosch His Picture-Writing Deciphered,* Eng. ed. (Rotterdam, 1979).

129. Composed in the early 14th century (see J. Seznec, *Survival of the Pagan Gods* [New York, 1953], p. 92f.). The Judgment of Paris was interpreted as an allegory of man's choice among the active (Juno), contemplative (Minerva), and carnal (Venus) lives. The 15th-century text edition has been reprinted: *Ovide moralisee en prose,* ed. C. de Boer (Amsterdam, 1954), pp. 286f., xi, 19. An early, nonclassical interpretation of the theme is Lucas Cranach's 1508 woodcut (B.114).

130. The ape could be interpreted as an embodiment of either folly or sensuality (H. W. Janson, *Apes and Ape Lore in the Middle Ages and the Renaissance* [London, 1952], pp. 199ff., 261ff.; for the Brant woodcut, p. 205).

131. See above, notes 74–75. Also K. Cohen, *Metamorphosis of a Death Symbol. The Transi Tomb in the Late Middle Ages and the Renaissance* (Berkeley / Los Angeles, 1973); on the three living and three dead: T. Rotzler, *Die Begegnung der drei Lebenden und die drei Toten* (Winterthur, 1961); F. Deuchler, "Looking at Bonne of Luxembourg's Prayerbook," *Bulletin of Metropolitan Museum* 24 (1971): 276f.

132. St. Anthony was believed to cure diseases, including "St. Anthony's Fire," an acute infectious skin inflammation. A. Hayum, "The Meaning and Function of the Isenheim Altarpiece: The Hospital Context Revisited," *Art Bulletin* 59 (1977): 501–17.

133. L. Silver, "Prayer and Laughter," pp. 20–22; W. Stechow, "Rembrandt-Democritus," *Art Quarterly* 8 (1944): 233–38; A.

Blankert, "Heraclitus en Democritus," p. 31ff., with the Cort engraving, p. 90, cat. 15, ill. 9. Inscribed "Democritus quidquid nugali cernit et audit / In mundo, vanum ridiculumque putat" (Democritus distinguishes and hears whatever little trifles, He values the vain and the ridiculous in the world).

134. Blankert, "Heraclitus and Democritus" ibid.; inscribed: "Flens Heraclitus miserae ludibria vitae / Conspicit, atque hominum perdolet usque vicem" (Weeping Heraclitus perceives the wretched mockeries of life and suffers continually the fate of men).

135. The two prints can be found in J.C.J. Bierens de Haan, *L'Oeuvre graveé de Cornelis Cort* (The Hague, 1948), p. 151, nos. 151–52. On Cort's accuracy, see also F. Bayer, "On the Relations of the Engraved Works of Cornelis Cort (1552–1578) to the Chronology of the Artists and Works Reproduced," (Master's thesis, University of Toronto, 1975).

136. Von Baldass, "Gotik und Renaissance," p. 97.

137. Blankert, "Heraclitus en Democritus," cat. 6, ill. 3.

138. Dolan, p. 99.

139. Ibid. p. 117: For the spiritual identification of Erasmus with the laughing Greek, see E. Wind, "The Christian Democritus," p. 180ff.

140. Dolan, p. 136.

141. See above, note 96.

142. Dolan, pp. 171–73.

7

Lectures and Laughter: Massys' Secular Images

Massys was certainly not the first painter, even in the Netherlands, to produce pictures other than religious pictures or portraits. Bosch, for example, had already devoted a major portion of his creative output to the development of secular allegories, such as the *Ship of Fools* (Paris, Louvre) or the *Gluttony* fragment (New Haven).[1] Bosch had also "elevated" into paintings themes which had previously been found only in prints, for example the *Ars Moriendi* theme, found in engravings, such as the one by the mid-15th-century Master E. S., and then transmitted as the subject of Bosch's *Death and the Miser* (Washington, National Gallery of Art).[2] Moreover, secular allegory became the subject even of triptychs by Bosch, most notably the *Haywain triptych* (Madrid, Prado),[3] where all the world, including pope and emperor, clutch greedily at a large stack of hay in order to grab a share.

Bosch's secular paintings, however, generally have the character revealed most vividly in the *Haywain:* they are clearly linked to a religious viewpoint that condemns the pleasures of the world as vicious and sinful. In the *Haywain,* in particular, the wagonload of straw is led directly into Hell, and the unfortunate persons in the vanguard begin to transmute into monstrous hybrids, half-human and half-animal. A similar message is conveyed by the Prado tabletop, the *Seven Deadly Sins,* where the secular subjects of the painting are arranged along the perimeter of a giant oculus, at whose center is the suffering Christ, with the words: "Beware, Beware, God Is Watching" *(Cave, cave, deus videt).*[4] Included at the four corners of the tabletop are additional images to put the sinful secular events into perspective: the Four Last Things of late medieval handbooks.[5] The first of the Four Last Things is Death, and again, Bosch turns to the *Ars Moriendi* tradition to illustrate the conflict between things of this world and the need to care for the next world. The remaining three events, Final Judgment, Heaven, and Hell, serve to remind the viewer of the importance of keeping worldly interests in relation to religious concerns. In other words, for Bosch, most activities involving earthly pleasures are the prelude to the torments of Hell; in fact, his Hell scene from the *Seven Deadly Sins* includes labels for the specific torments linked to each of the seven secular vices around the oculus. A religious view overlays all of Bosch's images of worldly activity, and the religious message is that mankind will pay for its sins.

For Massys, on the other hand, the secular subjects appear completely without any of the supernatural or overtly religious accompaniment of Bosch's pictures. They also eliminate the panoramic overview so frequent in Bosch's images, the high vantage point with tiny figures that suggests an omniscient author of the painting, as well as an encyclopedic comprehensiveness for the groups of tiny figures. Massys' secular images almost always include only one or two figures, seen close-up and at half-length. In fact, several of the Massys secular pictures have been mistaken for portraits, a sign of their specifically descriptive and isolated individuality as worldly figures. But Massys, too, created his secular images out of a background of religiosity—in this case a spirit of religious satire informed in part by the outlook of Erasmus, whose contact with Massys we have observed in the previous chapter. Instruction through ridicule—lectures and laughter—formed the basic intention of Massys in his secular pictures, just as they formed the goal of Erasmus's satirical fiction, most especially the *Praise of Folly*.[6]

The didactic ends of Massys' images, then, were also an outgrowth of a religious tone like Bosch's secular subjects, except for the crucial distinction that the theology was different for the two artists. In place of Bosch's preoccupation with sinfulness and its punishment in Hell, Massys substituted a measure of Christian faith and hope along with his condemnation of mankind's follies and sinfulness. For Massys, as well as for Erasmus, the moral dimension of religion is revealed through satire in the secular realm. We have already seen (Chap. 3, 5), how Massys used grotesque features in the context of the Passion pictures to convey the baseness of the tormentors of Christ. Often, he used a defined point of view or a grotesque figure looking out of the picture to implicate the viewer directly and associate him with the crowd of Christ's mockers. The secular pictures do not implicate the viewer so directly; in fact, their portraitlike presentation offers a distanced, objectified *persona* for contemplation by the viewer.[7] But the fact that the pious beholder views this isolated moral anathema instead of being grouped with it, like a scorner of Christ, indicates the new, positive direction of Massys' imagery. The vision of moral ugliness is both an admonition and an exhortation to proper Christian conduct. To regard the foolish, the sinful, and the unholy should stimulate new regard for the good and the holy as practiced and as preached by Christ. Massys' secular pictures are, first, morally instructive, although the same could also be said of Bosch. But they are also instruments toward a more righteous life, because they use a negative yet distanced image to suggest the ugliness and foolishness of the sinful path. Unlike Bosch's godlike viewer, who can see from above only the inevitable path from sinful worldliness to damnation, Massys' viewer confronts within this world an alien, foolish presence, whose very grotesqueness should lead him to a better conduct.

For this reason, Massys' secular images frequently have outlandish and outmoded costumes, generally borrowed from images of the previous century. By presenting the characters of the secular pictures as historically distant as well as morally distant, Massys provides still more separation between the viewer and the moral turpitude of the pictures. This effect also pertains to the use of grotesque features, generally borrowed from the drawings of Leonardo da Vinci, for the secular subjects. These figures, with their funny costumes and hideous faces, cannot be like ourselves. Surely we can, and must, behave better than the figures we see in the images of folly.

Massys thus provides a moral middle-ground for his viewers, a position not available to Bosch's audience. For Bosch, mankind in general was simply steeped in evil, and only the suffering saints, like St. Anthony, who removed himself from the world, were able to rise above their sinful frailty and the legacy of Original Sin.[8] For Bosch, the same grotesque faces who torment Christ in the Passion pictures were also the figures grasping for straw in the *Haywain*. The same overlap of human evil applies to Massys, but in his secular pictures the emphasis is now on *this* world and on a moral dimension of behavior apart from its hellish consequences. While Massys cannot help feeling culpable about the Passion of Christ and mankind's inadequacy to live up to the perfect example of Jesus, he and his viewers can still feel superior to the grotesque and comical figures of the secular half-lengths, figures which by their very portraitlike representation are made analogous to ordinary mortals yet stand apart from them in both formal and moral terms. This gray middle-ground of the human condition is the moral dimension of mankind. It is an arena poised between Heaven and Hell, between pure good and pure evil in spiritual terms. It is an area of free will and potential betterment, just as these moral lessons were preached by Erasmus both in his treatises, such as the *Enchiridion militis christiani*, and in his secular satires, such as the *Praise of Folly*. Godliness begins with good living for Erasmus, and the same message emerges from Massys' secular pictures.

That Massys believed man to be capable of righteous conduct, despite temptation, is evident from *Pl. 118* his very first surviving secular picture, the *Moneychanger and his Wife* (1514; F. 53, cat. 16). Here, unlike the majority of the secular paintings, there is no emphasis on the grotesque, nor any foolish or sinful activity clearly taking place. In fact, at the outset of his worldly images, Massys is not explicitly castigating anything, and his subjects, despite their 15th-century costumes (e.g., the man's red turban) are handsome figures, intent on their work. This image preaches less than any of the secular images to succeed it, yet it, too, proposes a moral situation for its principal characters, and it places the viewer in a privileged position to make his own decision as to the outcome of the dilemma.

The situation of the moneychanger is a professional act: he is in the process of using the scales of his profession, checking the weight and content of coins on his table. His wife watches the scales swing into balance, pausing from her other activity, contemplation of an open prayerbook, of which a page is still poised at the end of her finger. In visual counterpoint (reinforced by a coloristic counterpoint in the clothing of the couple), the active life of commerce and the contemplative life of prayer are intermingled here by the actions of husband and wife. Yet Massys does not satirize or preach. He does not declare that the husband's monetary involvement is inherently sinful and the wife's prayer righteous. Both appear subdued and serious. If anything, the moneychanger rather than his wife seems intent and reverential. According to Massys' 17th-century biographer, Alexander van Fornenbergh, such an impression is not simply an illusion of the modern eye, for the picture had an inscription on its frame (when van Fornenbergh saw it) which quoted Leviticus 19.36, "Let the balance be just and the weights equal."[9] In other words, the care and scrutiny of the weighing obey a biblical injunction and are a form of godly behavior even in a worldly profession. The passage is also an admonition to keep faith with one's fellow man as a way of keeping faith with God, for the Last Judgment will one day hold all men in the scales of divine Justice. This message was literally repeated during the 17th century by Vermeer in his *Woman with Scales* (National Gallery of Art, Washington), where the woman is actually checking the balance of her scales rather than weighing the pearls and gold lying before her on the table.[10] In the background appears a large painting of the Last Judgment—not a signal that the worldly woman is in danger of damnation (à la Bosch) or that she is a literal equivalent of St. Michael with his scales, but instead that she, like Massys' Moneychanger, is enjoined to perform earthly justice with her scales in microcosmic and metaphoric imitation of the divine Justice. Otherwise, the weighers will fall prey to deadly sins, like greed, and themselves be found wanting in the balance.

The wife of the moneychanger, then, is not necessarily abandoning the realm of prayer to concern herself with materialistic interests. She might just as well be superintending the accuracy of the balance which her husband is so carefully measuring. But she runs the risk of losing sight of her prayers amid the worldly concerns of the moneychanger's booth. That both the moneychanger and his wife occupy an intermediate position, akin to the one described for Massys' viewers in general, is revealed by two additional vignettes of the picture completing the poles within which the two figures are poised. These vignettes are visible only to the viewer of the picture, not to the couple themselves.[11] On the one hand is the world of idleness and foolish chatter, represented by an old man (a prefiguration in miniature of the grotesque faces Massys will later use as the central figures of his secular satires), prattling on the street with a younger man in a hat. This scene is behind the moneychanger and his wife, and it fails to disturb their intense concentration on the act of weighing. But a more admirable alternative is also presented within the picture; it appears within the reflection of the mirror at the front of the stall. Visible to the viewer, though unperceived by the couple, is another man in a turban, who is clearly shown in the act of reading a book with a familiar and worn cover, presumably a Bible or a prayerbook. Behind the man rises a church steeple, which is visible out a window (itself presenting an evocative, cross-shaped frame). This is an example of pure contemplation and devotion to God's word, rather than the hybrid mixture of worldly justice practiced by the couple. The message of Massys' picture, then, is poised between these poles, hovering like the elements of the scales themselves. Like the passage from Leviticus, the picture is an injunction and a challenge to live a righteous life within the world. Massys realizes that his moneychanger will never practice the withdrawal and contemplation of the praying man as a way of life, but he cautions against succumbing to the attractions of indolence in the street and the abandonment of a life informed by religion. The picture turns upon a moral tension which is appropriate to the situations of most viewers (especially in urban, prosperous Antwerp), and which, like life itself, remains unresolved yet essential.

Most of the critical commentary on this picture has centered on its potential satire of moneychanging as a reprehensible occupation and on the significance of the wife's turning away from prayer to the lure of the coins. Yet, in contrast to the subsequent images by Massys on secular themes, the figures lack ugly features. They are neither comical nor grotesque. Moreover, the passage from Leviticus provides a check on the moral valence of the picture, although we cannot be sure that the inscription was not added between the completion of the painting and its viewing by van Fornenbergh more than a century later. Many of the objects scattered throughout the painting come out of religious images, in particular Mary pictures. For example, the crystal carafe, filled with water, in the upper left-hand corner of the picture, is a frequent image of Mary's purity in the 15th-century *Annunciations,*[12] and the candlestick, while a symbol during the 17th century for the transience of life, was in the 15th century frequently associated with the Virgin as a metaphor for her bearing the Light of the World.[13] Two other background objects appear in the famous Jan van Eyck *Marriage Portrait* (Giovanni Arnolfini[?]; London, National Gallery, 1434), which itself is one of the images that surely contributed to the air of sanctity amid worldly surroundings that informs Massys' painting.[14] Both the orange, the fruit of Original Sin,[15] and the prayerbeads (beneath the carafe in Massys' image) appear earlier in the van Eyck picture and suggest a religious consciousness and atmosphere that would be inconsistent with a purely satirical reading of the picture.

Massys' image, then, is more of a sermon than a satire, and it is still imbued with religious sentiment, despite its worldly subject. The fact that it still is filled with items more appropriate to a religious context and that it depends on them for its sanctity, much in the manner of van Eyck's unique double portrait, points to the degree to which the *Moneychanger and his Wife* is still a pictorial experiment. Massys seems to have been searching for a new formula to express the sense of moral alternatives amid a worldly situation. In no other Massys secular picture do so many accessories appear; in no other Massys secular picture are subsidiary vignettes used to point up the central tension. Some of these elements are an outgrowth of another important source for the new image: the "sacred portrait" of a saint, *St. Eloy* (1449; New York, Metropolitan Museum of Art, Lehmann coll.), made originally for *Pl. 119* the goldsmiths' guild of Antwerp by Petrus Christus.[16] Like the Christus image, Massys' *Moneychanger* features a mirror,[17] a half-length man with weighing scales and precious objects around him, and a full selection of still-life objects in a booth, which is appropriate to his profession. Although Massys is depicting a man who is emphatically not a saint, he borrows from the 15th-century Christus image a solemn tone appropriate to a devotional image. *St. Eloy* also offered the positive presentation of worldly activity beyond censure because of the presence of the saint, identified by a halo. His use of such a model shows Massys to be experimenting with a new kind of secular image, one without the built-in moral censure that Bosch invariably provided.[18]

Already built into the *Moneychanger and his Wife* are several of the features Massys would emphasize throughout his subsequent secular pictures. The use of 15th-century costumes, borrowed from van Eyck and Christus, serves to remove the figures from the realm of contemporary portraiture. At the same time, the half-length presentation, borrowed from portraiture, serves to personalize the figures and to provide a concrete secular model of behavior.[19] Yet the moral balance and ambiguity of the *Moneychanger* is a unique event in Massys' art—all his later images with secular themes provide a distinctly satirical tone. In these later works, contrasting pairs of figures, grotesque extremes of age or ugliness, and elimination of all incidentals from the visual field enables Massys to concentrate his message and to provide unambiguously critical visions of human vice and folly.

Pl. 120 A long stride toward the final formulation of secular pictures was taken by Massys a few years after the *Moneychanger* in a picture now lost but preserved in numerous copies: the *Banker and his Client* (cat. 19)[20] Whereas the major interest of the moneychanger picture had been the element of choice, both for the couple and for the viewer, the *Banker and his Client* instead depicts an action without alternatives. The two figures crowded into the narrow booth are conducting a business transaction—either a banking entry on the client's account books or a tax payment[20]—and their full concentration, including the client's pointing finger, is devoted to the task at hand; moreover, no other characters or vignettes are visible in the picture. Massys has retained the coloristic interplay between reds and greens and the archaic costumes of his earlier work. Once more, he has probably borrowed from Jan van Eyck, who painted a lost half-length *Banker and Client* (1440).[22] What is profoundly different about the *Banker* after the 1514 *Moneychanger* is Massys' introduction of grotesque faces into the business scene. The ears of the banker are twisted and misshapen, even gnomelike, and the expresion of the client—who now stares directly out of the picture to confront the viewer—is a grimacing rictus. The smooth, handsome faces of the 1514 picture have given way to stern, fearsome looks. All attention of the picture revolves around an account book, and all of the clues of the picture, particularly the facial distortions, contribute to making the transaction appear odious.

Pl. 121 One of the copies (Paris, Cailleux coll.) has an inscription in the accounts ledger in French, a different language from the Flemish Massys spoke, but it might provide a clue to the meaning of the picture. The inscription paraphrases Luke 12:15–21, "The greedy man is never full of money . . . Have no care for unjust riches because they will gain you nothing at the Second Coming and Day of Wrath. Be then without avarice."[23] Without the original picture, we cannot be certain whether Massys used such an inscription in the ledger or on the frame of the picture, but from the subsequent exaggerations of the image by Marinus van Reymerswaele (see the example in London, National Gallery),[24] we can infer that the theme was understood later to involve serious criticism of the vice of avarice, personified by the banker.

Reymerswaele exaggerated still further the Massys elements of archaic and outlandish costume, of coins and papers on a cluttered desk, of wrinkled ugliness and painful grimacing. Like Massys, in the *Banker and his Client,* Reymerswaele has eliminated all traces of religious imagery from the environment of his banking stall and left the impression that the client is a victim of the powerful forces of finance.

Between the two pictures, Massys has completely altered the effects of his secular pictures. His first effort in the category of worldly themes asked the viewer to make a moral choice like that presented to the two protagonists of the Louvre picture, and the neutral, even attractive faces of the *Moneychanger and his Wife* left the outcome of the situation positive, if unresolved. But a few years later, the moral options have been excluded. The faces of the *Banker and his Client* are aggressively ugly, and the artist's ethical posture decidely negative about their fiscal transactions. Many of the same devices have been retained in the second picture: the half-length format, the outmoded costumes, the use of previous Eyckian models as a framework for the new pictorial formula. Massys' tone has changed from cautionary free election to a castigation through visual ridicule. Secular satire has become the new form of sermonizing, where instruction in the good emerges from the hostile presentation of the vicious.

Closely related in tone to this satirical image of the *Banker and his Client* are the biting, didactic poems of Massys' Antwerp colleagues in the St. Luke guild, the *rederijkers.* These essentially bourgeois critics of social ills represent a point of view encapsulated by the Flemish proverb "a usurer, a miller, a moneychanger, and a tax-collector are the Devil's four evangelists."[25] Greed, then, is severely reproached by *rederijker* poets. A powerful example is the poem "Society will lack for goods," which indicts the grasping cruelty of creditors:

Society will still lack for goods
But why do we grieve so over goods?
What good the piece gotten with greed,
When everyone knows he must die?
If I have no coin, I deserve credit.
People are strangled to a husk
Who boldly speak up for their freedom.[26]

These words recall the inscription on the Paris copy of the *Banker and His Client,* and the grimace on the patron's face would probably be over matters of credit.

Other *rederijker* titles show the same concern over finances: "Gold is now most praised in the world," "The rich who are called high-born," and "To plunder must be wholesome fare."[27] Suggesting women's susceptibility to the lure of coins, like the vacillating wife in Massys' Louvre *Moneychanger,* is the poem "To have most of what costs is Woman's lust."[28]

Literature with a more Europe-wide circulation also attacked usury and moneylending. Sebastian Brant's *Ship of Fools,* which first appeared in 1494 and was translated into Dutch in 1504, speaks angrily "Of Greed" (in chapter 3) and "Of Useless Riches" (in chapter 17).[29] Brant, too, is most strident in attacking "Usury and Profiteering," the practice of merchant-bankers, who combine both usurious lending of money and price-fixing of necessities—two of the four devilish acts of that Flemish proverb.[30] All these criticisms are made against a background of eschatological consciousness and the fear of Judgment akin to Bosch's visual presentation of mankind's folly.[31]

Erasmus, too, censured the sinfulness of wealth, beginning with 1511 *Praise of Folly:* "If a merchant wishes to be wealthy, how could he meet with success if he feels a distaste for perjury, if he becomes embarrassed when caught in a lie, or if he is in any way scrupulous concerning larceny or usury."[32] In his 1515 edition of the Latin Adages, under the phrase "To exact dues from the dead" *(A mortuo tributum exigere)* he resumes the attack:

> And indeed it is against nature, as Aristotle said in his *Politics,* for money to breed money. But now this thing is so widely accepted among Christians that while tillers of the soil are despised . . . usurers, on the other hand, are considered to be among the pillars of the Church. And yet usury was condemned by the earliest of the human race, regulated and controlled by the laws of the Gentiles, absolutely banned by those of the Jews, fulminated against in the decrees of the Popes, and censured by them in every way. Not that I am particularly against usuers, whose skill I can see some reason for defending, if it had not been condemned by the authority of the Fathers.[33]

Thomas More's *Utopia,* dedicated to Peter Gillis of Antwerp (see Chap. 6), echoes these admonitory sentiments through his spokesman, Raphael Hythlodaeus:

> We'll never get human behavior in line with Christian ethics [say the preachers] . . . so let's adapt Christian ethics to human behavior . . . Though, to tell you the truth, my dear More, I don't see how you can get any real justice or prosperity, so long as there's private property, and everything's judged in terms of money—unless you consider it just for the worst sort of people to have the best living conditions, or unless you're prepared to call a country prosperous, in which all the wealth is owned by a tiny minority—who aren't entirely happy even so, while everyone else is simply miserable . . . For when everyone's entitled to get as much for himself as he can, all available property, however much there is of it, is bound to fall into the hands of a small minority, which means that everyone else is poor. And wealth will tend to vary in inverse proportion to merit. The rich will be greedy, unscrupulous, and totally useless characters, while the poor will be simple, unassuming people whose daily work is far more profitable to the community than it is to them.[34]

Surely, Massys' *Banker and his Client* is anything but an "illustration" of the preceding texts. Nevertheless, communal feelings of the citizens in late medieval Flemish cities (see Chapter 1's discussion of confraternities and other forms of small-group solidarity) emerges not only in the *rederijker* verses but even in the prose of a sensitive English humanist. The issues of usury and profit, moreover, were hardly confined to prosperous Antwerp, but were a universal dilemma for all men of the late Middle Ages. Beginning with the rise of cities and of a money economy, together with the concomitant reformatory responses of institutions like the Franciscan order, usury had been a live issue in both economic and intellectual life.[35] Theologians, too, debated the spiritual aspects of banking and profit. One leading critic of usury was San Bernardino of Siena, the subject of one of Massys' portraitlike devotional images (see Chap. 3.)[36] The idealized arguments were usually similar to those we have read: the worldly Christian, whose professional activities are regulated by guilds, is entitled to provide for himself and his family as well as the common good, but he may not, according to Church teaching, confuse means with ends and work solely for the purpose of amassing riches. Only labor should be paid; money could not make money. Hence, interest was originally prohibited by strict canon law except as compensation for losses by a creditor.[37] A deep, disturbing split of conscience arose between an emerging awareness of private interests and the professed communal interests of society. This crisis still persisted at the time of Erasmus, More, and Massys. The merchant class was at once distrusted by the less fortunate, more traditional groups, like the *rederijkers,* as well as by the learned, elitist intellectuals, like Erasmus and More. In the common ground of their joint suspicions lay the image of the *Banker and his Client.*

Neither the date nor any other specific circumstances about the *Banker and his Client* can be determined from the surviving copies other than its continuing similarities to the *Moneychanger and his Wife* in both form and subject. But the next pair of secular figures by Massys carries on the image of sin as grotesque. Moreover, these pendants point specifically to the role of Erasmus and his associates in Antwerp as the influential agents who helped to produce the shift of effect in Massys' secular pictures.

The grotesque pair of worldly figures was followed by an aged couple, again in outdated and
Pl. 122 comical costumes: an *Old Woman* (London, National Gallery) and an *Old Man* (New York, Private coll.).
Pl. 123 In this instance, the pictorial sources were separate, like the separate panels on which the two figures appear. In the case of the *Old Woman,* the model was a drawing by Leonardo da Vinci, of which a copy
Pl. 124 still survives in Windsor Castle (no. 12492),[38] without the hands and balustrade of the Massys image, but with the same fantastic wimple headdress and revealing low-cut dress. Massys' London panel maintains the same orientation of the original Leonardo drawing. As for the *Old Man,* no surviving Leonardo model has yet been found, although the picture bears what Panofsky has called a "family
Pl. 125 likeness" to Leonardo's grotesque drawings.[39] Moreover, the painting bears a strong likeness to the Italian Medici patriarch and head of the powerful Medici Bank throughout Europe: Cosimo de'Medici (d. 1464), whose features Massys, the medal-caster, could have known from a commemorative medallion.[40] The artist had already recorded these same features in a 1513 portrait (F. 51, cat. 54;
Pl. 157 Paris, Jacquemart-André Museum; see Chap. 8). A lost Leonardo drawing of Cosimo cannot be ruled out, since the Florentine artist produced a caricature of "Dante," which survives in several versions (for
Pl. 126 example, the copy now in Windsor Castle, no. 12493);[41] however, like the 1513 portrait, little emphasis on caricature or even on grotesque elements of Cosimo's features emerges from Massys' *Old Man.* In contrast, the *Old Woman* offers nothing but monstrous features and comic incongruity of costume and aged sitter. These two pendants, then, appear to have been artificially associated with each other, since they are visually disunified. This disparity suggests some prior conception, some extra-artistic motivation for their pairing.

The main clue for understanding the pendants is the identity of Cosimo de'Medici himself. Cosimo was the 15th century model of the merchant-banker, a man whose fortune was sufficient to establish him, like the Rothschilds or Rockefellers of more recent times, as a European-wide emblem of wealth.[42] The Medici Bank had once been a major factor in the economy and politics in the Netherlands, based at its branch in Bruges, which closed in 1480 because of massive outstanding debts to Charles the Bold and Maximilian of Austria.[43] The bank had also been a potent influence on the artistic life of the Netherlands through commissions by its managers from such Flemish masters as Hans Memling and Hugo van der Goes.[44] At the head of this vast enterprise, Cosimo was both wealthy and powerful, the uncrowned head of Florence.

The New York Massys image of Cosimo portrays him in this light. It enhances the costume to be found on the medal by adding an extensive fur trim that clearly connotes wealth.[45] Moreover, the hands of the *Old Man* display two gold rings, the second of which, a thumb-ring on the upraised right hand, is a mark of distinction and local office, such as alderman.[46] Thus both wealth and power, associated in real life with the figure of Cosimo de'Medici, were assigned to him along with a portrait likeness in the form of Massys' *Old Man.*

Most of the remarks, therefore, that here described the communal transactions of the *Banker and his Client* apply equally well to the prosperous figure of the New York *Old Man.* This is particularly true in light of the fact that in the 15th century, the term "merchant-banker" gave equal prominence to both components, for most international credit transactions were transmitted not by bankers in loans, but by merchants in sales.[47] Commodity speculation became the basis of windfall fortunes for individuals as well as basic international finance. Indeed, these manipulations of staples and currencies were the abuses condemned in the figures of both the miller and the moneychanger mentioned as the "evangelists of Lucifer" in the Flemish proverb, above.

Erasmus's own invective against usurers is equally interchangeable with merchants. The 1515 adage "To exact dues from the dead" even finds usurers preferable to merchants:

> Especially if one considers the morals of our own time, I would sooner approve of a usurer than of this niggardly class of dealers, who are on the hunt for profits from every possible source, by trickery, by lies, by fraud, by cheating, buying up here what they will sell for more than double there, and robbing the wretched poor with their monopolies—and yet these people, who never do anything else than this in their lives, are the ones we think almost the only people worthy of honor.[48]

More, too, castigates these practices in the *Utopia,* issuing a call to "stop the rich from cornering markets and establishing virtual monopolies."[49]

The source of wealth, status, and power for the New York *Old Man* cannot be determined from the painting, but the negative connotations of his prideful pose and aged, sagging flesh are as clear in the picture as are these verbal gibes by Erasmus in the *Praise of Folly:*

> Wisdom commonly makes men scrupulous, which explains why these men are usually to be found in hunger, proverty, and smoke . . . The fool, on the other hand, seems to live in a profusion of wealth and sometimes as head of state.[50]

The Massys *Old Man* is paired with the grotesque figure of the *Old Woman.* Their association was already recorded in the 17th century (where the two figures were mistakenly, if understandably, attributed to Leonardo himself) in an etching by Wenzel Hollar, entitled *King and Queen of Tunis* (Parthey 1603).[51] That the figures are borrowed from Massys is unmistakable, because both the balustrade and the action and response of their gesturing hands is repeated in the engraving, and the Leonardo drawing which served as a model has neither of these devices. The two Massys panels have identical dimensions, avocado-green background, and marble strip; moreover, the raised hands of the *Old Man* cannot be understood without reference to the gesture of the *Old Woman,* who offers him a tiny rosebud. When they are seen together, he is in the process of rejecting her advances. This woman is the epitome of egotism; her self-love blinds her to the fact that her aged and wrinkled body is shown to its worst advantage by the expensive clothing and the archaic, revealing, low-cut gown.[52] The withered rosebud, like the dessicated yet hopeful woman, betokens the "faint desire" she hopes to elicit from her companion. More than in the *Old Man* or any previous Massys secular pictures, the inspiration for the *Old Woman* is literary; this grotesque image comes from Erasmus' *Praise of Folly:*

Pl. 127

> However, it is even more hilarious to watch the old woman, almost dead with age and so like corpses that they seem to have returned from the dead. . . . They painstakingly make up their faces. They can hardly pull themselves away from the mirror. They pluck out hairs from the strangest places. They show their withered and flabby breasts. And, with a quivering voice, they try to stir up a faint desire.[53]

The *Old Woman* is the embodiment of foolish pride, and Massys' use of the Leonardo drawing continues a visual type already presented by Bosch in the *Seven Deadly Sins* tabletop (Madrid, Prado).[54] There, the image of *Superbia* (Pride) was just such a woman, preening before a mirror in her expensive and comical wimple headdress. The mirror is held by a devil who wears exactly the samt hat. Like Bosch, Massys has once again used archaic costume to show figures removed from the world of his viewers, but in the case of the *Old Woman,* such costume now serves a dual function, as it underscores the vanity and the absurdity of the woman's pride.

With one-half of the image embodying deadly sins of pride and luxury, the message of the more portraitlike *Old Man* becomes clearer, and the importance of the underlying identity of Cosimo de'Medici becomes significant. The association of the Medici name with wealth and power points to the danger of another kind of sin: pride in association with avarice. Again, the *Seven Deadly Sins*
Pl. 128 picture by Bosch provides a precedent. Bosch's embodiment of *Avarice* is a public official, identifiable by his baton, the equivalent of the *Old Man's* thumb-ring; the official also wears a large black hat with an oval badge (like the signet on rings) and carries a large purse upon his belt. What marks him as avaricious is his surreptitious acceptance of a bribe from one litigant even as he hears the case of another. Massys' image carries this kind of explicit venality only in conjunction with the obvious grotesqueness of the *Old Woman.* The thumb-ring points to power and political office, whereas the other gold ring is more of a general indication of wealth, like the fur-trimmed garment. In the *Praise of Folly,* Erasmus specifically identifies these outward signs of wealth and their inevitable connection with sinfulness:

> But the most foolish and sordid of all are your merchants in that they partake in the most illicit business by the most illegal means they can find. Sometimes they lie, they perjure themselves, they steal and cheat, and they impose themselves upon the public. Yet they consider themselves important men because they have gold rings on their fingers.[55]

In contrast to the grotesque face of the *Old Woman,* the portraitlike appearance of the *Old Man* is not simply a matter of the particular source Massys had at his disposal, for he could have borrowed the grotesque male heads of Leonardo (as he did on several other occasions). We must conclude that his choice of the features of Cosimo de'Medici was calculated on the basis of the man's merchant-banking background, a background which is reinforced by a few of the accessories of his costume. The fact that knowing the identity and connotations of Cosimo plays a role in the understanding of the picture suggests that Massys produced these dissimilar pendants of *Old Woman* and *Old Man* for a knowledgeable audience, presumably a group of the artist's acquaintances, who could be informed about the Medici identity if they did not already know it. Unlike the paired figures in specific locations and actions of the *Moneychanger* or the subsequent *Banker,* these secular pendants by Massys are arbitrarily coupled. They are not natural companions, nor are they placed in any natural or recognizable locale. Instead, they have been brought together artificially, even borrowed from entirely separate visual sources, and joined through the contrivances of uniform backgrounds, balustrade, and the common gestures around the pathetic rosebud. Once again, the constructed quality of the pictures suggests that a prior conception, satirical in intent and presumably known (if not specified) by a select audience, underlies the creation of the two pictures. The image of the *Old Woman* could, in fact, be understood without any literary background, but it is difficult to ignore the close correspondence between the image and the words of Erasmus, cited above. For the *Old Man,* the use of an Erasmian background is not as specific and also seems to be just one element in a generalized cultural mistrust of merchants' wealth.

Even for the figure of the *Old Woman,* corresponding satirical passages other than Erasmus can be found from Massys' period, particularly from *rederijker* verses. According to one poem, all women are unchaste and fallen in these immoral times:

> After how the world is going
> Girls will fall so much to heat
> That, lust or disgust, they'll have the tail.[56]

A suggestion that young women are inclined toward frivolity and loose living is as insistent about luxurious but inappropriate clothing as Massys' *Old Woman:*

> Observe these girls of merry heart
> Who are believed to be so clever
> Youth hints about the rusty coin
> What's prettily displayed is half-sold.
> They carry their baubles prettily tied
> Their ring cords and needlework, latest fancy,
> A scarf made with golden *manille,*
> And breasts showing through the scarf.[57]

Massys' next secular work, the *Ill-Matched Pair* (Washington, National Gallery),[58] continues the attack of human folly through grotesque figures in action. Like the London *Old Woman,* the *Ill-Matched Pair* requires no background text or reference to be understood. It is the folly of lustful old age seeking youthful beauty, where the folly of the lecherous old man matches the grotesque wrinkled vanity of the London *Old Woman.* Moreover, it is a folly that is matched by the baseness of the pretty young girl, who not only leads the old fool on but has base and greedy intentions on his purse—avaricious thoughts and use of her powers which are an ample match for the New York *Old Man.* Again, the situation is generalized and set against a monochrome background, although Massys no longer relies upon outmoded or comical costumes for his social distancing from contemporary reality. Massys has also maintained the bust-length presentation of his figures in the manner of portraiture, and he has intensified their dynamic interaction with a tightly interlaced crisscross of arms and a complementary tilt of the two heads. *Pl. 129*

Once more, Leonardo da Vinci provides the inspiration for the grotesque leer of Massys' old lecher; the leftmost figure of Leonardo's famous *Five Grotesque Heads* (Windsor Castle, no. 12495), a drawing *Pl. 16* which had previously served for the heads of the tormentors in the *Martyrdom of St. John the Evangelist* *Pl. 17* (1508–11), has simply been reversed and reused for the *Ill-Matched Pair.* The cunning harlot of the picture has still another source, the coquettish woman in the *Tavern Scene* by Lucas van Leyden, a large *Pl. 130* woodcut from around 1520 that has been interpreted by some scholars as an image of the Prodigal Son.[59] In Lucas's woodcut, however, the victim of the woman's wiles is not an old man but a young one; nevertheless, the outcome is the same as in Massys' painting—the cunning wench manages to pick the purse of her paramour in each case. Massys has retained the pose and the costume of Lucas's female *Pl. 131* almost exactly, including the inviting tilt of her oval head and the tweaking gesture on her partner's chin; he has also adopted Lucas's pose for the man, who reaches forward to touch his companion as he places his other hand around her head to draw her still closer.

Also included in both the Lucas print and the Massys painting is a third figure, a fool, dressed in his distinctive garment with bells and asses' ears. In Lucas's print, the fool is a dispassionate observer, distanced from the scene, who stares outward at the viewer of the woodcut and offers a timely warning in the form of an inscription: "Look at how it will turn out" *(Wacht hoet varen sal).* In the Massys picture, the fool appears crowded into the left-hand corner, but he is very much an active participant in the scene, the accomplice who receives the purloined purse. Licking his lips greedily and focusing his crossed eyes on the booty, this fool is an embodiment of the vices that are acted out in the *Ill-Matched Pair.* In this respect, he more closely resembles the courtly fool who accompanies the pleasure-seekers in the pavilion of Luxuria on Bosch's *Seven Deadly Sins* than the fool who is truth-teller, as in the case of Lucas's print.[60] Like the idlers on the street in Massys' *Moneychanger,* the fool of the *Ill-Matched Pair* is visible to the viewer but not to the two other participants in the scene; he also plays a role, serving to label the scene as folly because he is an accomplice.

The *Ill-Matched Pair* appeared frequently in prints and paintings of the late 15th and early 16th centuries, especially in Germany.[61] One of the earliest representations of the theme of mixed lovers was the pair of drypoint engravings by the Housebook Master during the 1480s; one print paired the *Pl. 132* same couple as Massys, i.e., an old man with a young woman; the second print reversed the roles, featuring an old woman with a young man.[62] In both cases, the half-length figures are entwined with one another, the cause of the attraction, a large bag of coins, clearly displayed in the foreground. The Housebook Master's images have some greater importance as background to Massys' creation, because they were copied in the late 15th century by Israhel van Meckenem and also viewed and adapted in Italy by none other than Leonardo da Vinci, whose drawing of the young man with the old woman is now lost but preserved in a copy.[63] Evidence suggests that the Leonardo image found its way to Antwerp along with the *Five Grotesque Heads* drawing, for figures from both of these da Vinci drawings appear in a *pastiche* made by a follower of Massys, who imitated the grotesque heads so basic to the secular satires.[64] At the center of the composite image is the young man with old woman derived ultimately from the German prints, while other Leonardo-derived grotesque heads arranged around the pair are deriding them.

Pl. 133

Pl. 134

The Massys painting, then, has some artistic pedigree in recent images of the *Ill-Matched Pair* as well as in related images of debauchery, such as the Lucas van Leyden woodcut. Yet the assembled quality of the Massys picture, drawing as it does upon both Leonardo and Lucas models rather than on a previous Ill-Matched Pair composition, suggests that the artist was prompted to create his painting from some other kind of inspiration—presumably a literary inspiration. The Ill-Matched Pair was a *topos* in satirical literature of the period.[65] For example, Brant's *Ship of Fools* includes among its numerous examples of folly the situation of the Ill-Matched Pair, where a young man marries an old woman for gain ("Marrying for the Sake of Goods," chap. 52), as well as related chapters: "Of Amours" (chap. 13) and "Of Sensual Pleasure" (chap. 50).[66] Because of its emphasis on marriage for gain and its reversal of the sexes of Massys' pairing, Brant's text cannot have served as the inspiration for the Antwerp artist, but it does demonstrate that his critical concern over the combined problems of sensuality and greed was not confined to the visual arts.

In fact, Erasmus includes the Ill-Matched Pair among the follies he attacks in the *Praise of Folly:*

> Some decide to most conveniently attain wealth by hypocritically catering to childless old men. There are even those [who] would prefer this same procedure with rich old women. Both of these furnish a rare entertainment to these onlooking gods, because they are usually cheated by the people whom they set out to deceive.[67]

Elsewhere, Erasmus chides the foolish pride of old men, a vanity that might apply equally well to the New York *Old Man* or the lustful suitor of the *Ill-Matched Pair:*

> Certainly it is because of my gift that you see those old men of Nestor's age whose appearance is hardly human: dirty, stooped, wrinkled, bald, toothless, and toolless. Yet they are so delighted with life and desire so much to be young again that one dyes his hoary hair, another covers his bald spot with a toupee, another uses false teeth he obtained from heaven knows where, and still another is desperately in love with some young girl and acts sillier than any adolescent.[68]

Women are the cause of much of the temptation and sensuality in the world, according to Erasmus, who contrasts their beauty with the roughness of men as effectively in print as Massys does in paint:

> First, they have the gift of beauty, which they rightly prize above everything else and by whose power they can be tyrannical with tyrants themselves. Where do men acquire that dreadful appearance, rough skin, forest of whiskers, and senility except from the defects of prudence? The cheeks of women, on the other hand, are always smooth, their voices gentle, and their skin soft as if taking part in eternal youth. Besides, what more do they want in life than to please men? . . . Than under what better patron than Folly could they be better recommended to men? For what is there that men will deny to women? And for what return other than pleasure?[69]

But just as the theme of the Ill-Matched Pair had a widespread success beyond the image of Massys, so the literary theme also enjoyed popularity, even within Antwerp, beyond the words of Erasmus. In particular, the local *rederijkers* delighted in mocking both avarice and the cunning wiles of women in their prose and verse. The critical *rederijker* poems on women, mentioned above, could also apply to both the cunning greed and the loose living of Massys' young harlot. Quite a few of the verses in each *rederijker* anthology inveigh specifically against whores, both for their sensuality and their love of money.[70] Foolish male lovers *(Venus janckerkens),* young and old, especially those foolish enough to spend money on women,[71] are warned by *rederijkers.*[72]

Closest to the Massys *Ill-Matched Pair* is a *rederijker* poem, written earlier but first published in the anthology (ca. 1530) by Jan van Doesborch, a printer-writer who had entered the guild of St. Luke as early as 1508 as a master illuminator *(verlichtere),* and who thus was a colleague of Massys.[73] The poem tells of a wily harlot who fleeces an old client of his money. Also relevant to the Massys *Ill-Matched Pair* is the poem's description of the odd couple playing a card game, "spoilsport" *(bot uut roelken).* The association of card-playing with amorous activity or with the war between the sexes was a commonplace in prints and paintings of the period,[74] and in the corner of the Massys picture a deck of cards appears beside the woman's hand and a cluster of coins; appropriately enough, the uppermost card is in the suit of hearts. The poem, "Eat your fill when you're offered your pick," is as derisive a satire as Massys' own *Ill-Matched Pair:*

> A rover—short, old, and free, / With a purse running over with gold,
> Took a Venusberg lass for a spree / Who took clients like him in her hold.
> That lass has her loose, lowly wiles, / Undoing his purse with its glut,
> While showing a face full of smiles, / Like the grin of a flat halibut.
> And she wouldn't arrange place or date, / For she had to sit home in her chair,
> Though she'd whispered before it got late.
> In love's stead, she taught "spoilsport" for pairs, / So he had to go seeking elsewheres.
> He's no wiser, despite this mean trick; / Eat your fill when you're offered your pick.[75]

Another poem in the same vein tells of an old rake plucked by two girls and an old procuress with the help of wine.[76]

Isolated poems are not the only form of *rederijker* literature devoted to the moral criticism of worldly behavior. For example, a collection of verse and prose selections also published by van Doesborch, entitled *Vanden. X. Esels (Ten Asses),* which is roughly contemporary (ca. 1530?) with Massys' *Ill-Matched Pair,* describes "ten kinds of men who by their desperate lives are worthy of wearing asses' ears."[77] Examples of these fools are the married man who, leaving his wife, squanders his money in bordellos with loose women (no. 1), the men who allow their wives to dominate them (no. 2), the men who suffer from unrequited love (no. 3), the men who own whorehouses and offer places for sin (no. 4), the men who live off their wives' prostitution (no. 5), the men who jealously mistrust their wives (no. 6), the merchants who connive for more wealth and boast of it (no. 7), the misers obsessed by avarice whose legacies will be squandered by their heirs (no. 8), the men who boast of their success with women (no. 9), and the pimps who seduce young girls into prostitution (no. 10). Those themes which are not sexual and mercenary in *Vanden. X. Esels* involve at least one of these vices, incorporating the very subjects of Massys' own secular satires.

Within prose tales of the *rederijkers,* other instances of moralizing critiques can be found, such as these passages, cited by Debaene: "This is the way of men, who when they have had their way with women thus no longer pay them any attention" *(Turcas ende Floreta),* or, "Because whene'er their will's been done/Thus the thrills of love all gone" *(Lanseloet).*[78]

Surely Massys never sat down to "illustrate" any of these texts, even with his likely connections with the *rederijkers.* It is all too easy for art historians, so accustomed in their training to seeking out "iconography" in the pictures they study, to look for textual "sources" for imagery, particularly for the images with a narrative content, like religious stories or classical myths. Yet in the case of a picture like the *Ill-Matched Pair*—or still more so with secular images like the *Old Man/Old Woman* pendants, where no significant action takes place between the main figures—the artist's creations should be seen instead as visual analogues to the verbal attacks of the grotesqueness of immorality. Massys shares with his colleagues, the *rederijkers,* what Roose calls

> a *petit bourgeois* vision of life, noticeable in the interest in material repercussions of events in daily life, in the criticism of institutions through their representatives, the sharp attention to human weaknesses and defects, an alert sense of justice, the experience of love as either the basis of domesticity or as the

> playful sensuous gratification (already far removed from the courtly love lyric, of which the refrains "int amoreus" seem nevertheless to be a continuation), in search of instruction and learning, in bold religiosity, along with complete denial of mystical aspirations. There are indeed exceptions here: several poets give evidence of their having read Erasmus, and they show interest in, and knowledge of, theological questions; but even those poets are not peaks but only slopes in a generally rather flat spiritual landscape.[79]

Most of the *rederijkers* came from the same middle-class background as Massys and his family, and their viewpoints were forcefully conservative. They condemned what they regarded as the decline of morality and the spread of vice. A typical pessimistic poem proclaims "It seems to me that all's ill once more" *(Mij dunct tis al mal een mal andere);* here the author proceeds in succession to level his criticism at the universal reign of falsehood, the self-seeking, the lack of justice, the loss of religiosity, the rebellious younger generation, and the widespread adultery and whoremongering.[80] Another, equally bitter poem speaks of golden days gone by, when honesty prevailed in daily life and tradesmen thought more of their customers than of their profit: "How should evil go into that world" *(Hoe sout dan Qualick in die weerlt gaen)*.[81] Those *rederijkers* who were in the De Violieren chamber shared guild membership with Massys in the Antwerp St. Luke guild,[82] and their general cynicism in the "folly poems" sees mankind's daily conduct in terms just as sordid and grotesque as the artist's secular paintings.

To consider *rederijker* poems in this light, as a possibly formative influence on Massys, need not rule out the impact of Erasmus's secular satire on the artist. On the contrary, several of the *rederijker* verses themselves give evidence that the local authors as well as the Antwerp humanists were aware of the spirit, perhaps even the letter, of the *Praise of Folly*. Among the "spiritual poems" *(int vroede),* for example, several follow Erasmus in directly condemning self-delusion or folly: "It is a wonder what the deluded heart will endure," or "He will suffer who acts with foolish will."[83] Hypocrisy in the form of false saintliness is expressly condemned, echoing not only Erasmus's words, but also Massys' image
Pl. 108 of *Two Praying Monks* (F. 80, cat. 45): "This seeming virtue is a sin before God."[84] Yet the group of
Pl. 109 poems most like Erasmus's witty treatise are the poems "in folly" *(int sotte),* which criticize greed, drunkenness, or self-delusion directly and also, like the *Praise of Folly,* offer ironic praise of foolish pleasures. Included among these foolish refrains are the so-called "lying verses" *(leugen-refreinen),* which adopt the assertive *personas* of fools or hedonists. By their immoral or amoral displays, they, like Massys' secular works, evoke revulsion and conversion to their own basic, high moral standards. They are "not sheer nonsense out of some compulsion for the ugly, vulgar, or profane but arise out of the—unconscious—desire for leveling."[85] Often they are scatological or obscene, admixed with sensual vitality and grotesque comedy. One such poem speaks of the stone of folly and begins, "O Moria well-renowned," in echo of Erasmus' words.[86] Still closer to the *Praise of Folly* is a poem "All fools and none carry bells," which comments on the universal folly of mankind. Like Erasmus' opus, the refrain includes a catalogue of the world's fools: court fools, lovers, combattants, stay-at-homes, spiritual prelates, and those "without time" *(tijelooskens):*

> In all tournaments or merry hunts
> In shooting matches or rhetoric feats
> There you'll find numerous fools a-sporting
> With glittering bells for each to behold . . .
> Noble guild brothers, you must note
> How one never remarks on all the fools
> Or sees a sign of bells that shine
> That the wearers aren't the only fools.[87]

The *rederijkers* contend, too, that in every man there dwells a bit of folly, for "Everyone has a strange spirit which torments him."[88]

In his final secular works, Massys seems to have tried to express this kind of universal tendency
Pl. 135 toward folly. A small panel, which seems to date from the mid-1520s, shows only a *Fool* (cat. 44; Old

Bennington, J. Held coll.) dressed in the typical costume of the role, which includes bells and a cowl with asses' ears.[89] Instead of Erasmus's female personification, Dame Folly (or Moria), Massys' fool is a male with grotesque features and leathery brown skin. Like the images of the *Old Man/Old Woman,* the background of the image is a monochrome color, here olive green, and the costume and features of *Folly* are used to convey the picture's message. Another attribute of the fool is his stone of folly, visible as a protuberance on his forehead. Cutting out this stone of folly from the head of a foolish man served as the subject of several Netherlandish paintings during the early 16th century, including works by both Bosch and Jan Sanders de Hemessen; moreover, the stone of folly was the subject of one of the *rederijker* verses, "The Stone Hidden under the Exposed Lump."

> . . . Yet there grows a great mass
> the older the siller is a famous phrase / So the stone's increased and great
> But invisible in its usual state / Otherwise grown to too big a shape.[90]

From the look on the fool's face, the stone does indeed "free his spirit from care." The fool's most important attribute is the strange stick with a figure at the end. Called a marot, this stick was Folly's equivalent to a sceptre.[91] Sometimes the marot had a mirror, emblematic of the fool's role as purveyor of truth, holding a mirror up to the follies of the world.[92] Often the marot had a grinning head with a mouth that could open like a ventriloquist's dummy; in this way, the fool could delegate responsibility for unpleasant truths to his marot. The obscene gesture on Massys' marot was clearly understood as an insult associated with fools, though here seemingly not the direct expression of the Fool, himself.[93]

When Erasmus discusses fools in the *Praise of Folly,* he emphasizes their dedication as unshakable truth-tellers:

> Fools alone have this not insignificant virtue: they alone are candid and truthful. What is more praiseworthy than truth? . . . Whatever a fool has in his heart shows itself in his expression and speech . . . Someone might say that kings hate wise men and avoid them because they fear that one of them might dare to speak the truth rather than what is pleasant; and this is true, kings hate the truth. It is quite admirable, then, that kings will listen with relish to not only a truth but quite a sharp truth from my fools . . . But coming from a fool, it gives great pleasure.[94]

Fools appeared in this same uninhibited role in contemporary *rederijker* morality plays, some of which were called *sotties,* after *sot,* or fool.[95] An example of such a fool in a drama appears in the background of Peter Bruegel's drawing of the virtue *Temperancia,* and we have already seen the fool-as-commentator on the edge of Lucas van Leyden's woodcut of the tavern scene.[96] In literature, the fool became a literary commonplace, particularly after the 1494 publication of Brant's *Ship of Fools.* Both as the embodiment of folly and as the critic of folly in society, fools remained a part of everyday life in town at festivals (cf. the 1493 *Archers' Festival* by the Master of Frankfurt, F. 164) and in mock societies or carnivals.[97] *Pl. 130*

In the case of Massys' *Fool,* the grinning main figure is not speaking; on the contrary, his lips are sealed, and the original inscription on the picture's surface actually instructs the figure to keep his mouth shut *(Mondeken toe).* But, as in the case of the independent minded marot, this fool's message is being broadcast against his will by the crowing cock on his headpiece. Massys' *Fool,* then, is not an active agent, even through his speech; he attempts to remain aloof from the world and its follies, unlike the fool of the *Ill-Matched Pair,* who is an accomplice in the misdeeds. Yet the dramatic tension of the panel is that, even though the *Fool* tries to keep silent, the truth will out, either through the gestures of his marot or through the crowing of his cock. The *Fool* is an outsider of the social fabric,[98] although he tries, unsuccessfully, to observe its proprieties by maintaining discreet silence. His outlandish costume serves to point out his estrangement and, in this case, by revealing the truth; his costume also fulfills this fool's isolation and establishes him as society's critic. The Fool is the 16th-century alienated man and, in his detachment, he can laugh at society and its foolish conventions, even as society laughs at him for failing to observe those same conventions.

Massys makes his *Fool* a laughable character in just the same ways as he had ridiculed the London

Old Woman; both figures are grotesque, detached, outside of any context. Yet the *Fool* glances outward with a silly, sly grin on his face; both marot and cock signal his abusive laughter at the very audience which laughs at him. Here is an ironic reversal, unlike the previous secular satires. Now the grotesque image of the Massys picture laughs back at its beholder, calling the moral position of the viewer into question, just as the ugly crowds in the *Ecce Homo* images had undermined any moral superiority on the part of their beholders. This is truly the role of the fool as expressed by Erasmus' Moria: sharp truth with comic pleasure; and, in a visual detail that adds irony to the scholarly pursuits of Erasmus and the community of humanists, Massys' *Fool* also pursues learning, carrying a book around with him in a pouch at his waist.

Pl. 115 The same meaning pertains to Massys' *Democritus* (F. 55, cat. 43; see Chap. 6) also painted during the artist's final years of activity. Again, the figure does not stare directly at the viewer, but he still involves the beholder, for in this case his costume is contemporary, not alien or ancient like most of Massys'
Pl. 145 secular garb. The short-brimmed cap, in particular, recalls the fashionable headgear of the Edinburgh
Pl. 182 *Notary* or the 1527 Windsor Castle *Man.* More than any other secular picture, the *Democritus* resembles
Pl. 102 a portrait; indeed it employs the same formulas as the portrait of *Peter Gillis* (F. 49, cat. 56) which also has a neutral, colored background with strong lighting and a shadow of the frame on the picture surface. And the *Democritus* is painted without any attributes to reveal his identity. Only the toothy smile identifies the subject as the philosopher who laughs at the world and its follies.

Not only does the classical identity of the image point to its production for a specifically Erasmian audience, as we saw in the last chapter, but the *Democritus* also presents an Erasmian attitude toward the world. Just as Erasmus had singled out Thomas More for praise in the Introduction to the *Praise of Folly* as a "sort of Democritus amid the common run of mortals,"[99] this *Democritus* is singled out only by his smile from the range of portraits by Massys. The contemporary costume indicates that the viewer is not intended to be distanced from *Democritus;* on the contrary, it demonstrates that he can be like Democritus, if only he adopts the same spiritual attitude toward worldly concerns as the author of the *Praise of Folly.*

The *Democritus* reminds us of the crucial and formative role of Erasmus in the development of Massys' secular pictures. Like the *Moneychanger and his Wife* of 1514, the *Democritus* is not a satirical picture, nor is it a morally neutral, cautionary picture like the earliest Massys secular subject. Instead, it is a product of a decade of satire, of spiritual instruction through ridicule. It is a call for the same scornful laughter on the part of the viewer, presumably now a sympathetic and informed viewer, who knows the identity of Democritus and does not need the visual and moral cues of the *Moneychanger's* stall in order to understand the message of the philosopher's laughter: "These things are all very foolish, and one Democritus is not enough to laugh at them."[100] We have already seen in Chapter 6 that the final secular works by Massys, the *Praying Monks* and *Democritus,* are unintelligible without a knowledge of the *Praise of Folly.* The evidence, then, is circumstantial but substantial that, in addition to *rederijker* culture, direct contact with the person and the thought of Erasmus helped to alter the course of Massys' secular pictures during the period following 1517. In effect, Massys' images, like the literary works of Erasmus, are visions of the world colored by a religious sensibility. In effect, the act of painting this kind of secular satire was akin to Erasmus's act of creating everyday verbal dialogues in Latin prose in the *Colloquies,* which the humanist defended in the following manner in an address to the reader of the 1526 edition:

> As physicians do not always prescribe the most efficacious remedies for patients but make some allowance for their cravings, so likewise I thought it well to allure the young—who respond more readily to pleasing than to strict or harsh treatment—with this kind of bait. Accordingly I revised what was published, then added what might help to develop manners also; stealing into the minds of youngfolk, who, as Aristotle truly wrote, are unsuitable hearers of moral philosophy, at least of the sort that is taught by formal rules. Now, if someone protests that it is undignified for an old man to play in this childish fashion, my answer is: "I don't care how childish, if only it's useful" . . . Well, if I had only been joking in their affair, my critics would apparently have put up with it. But now, since in

> addition to dealing with refinement of language I have added here and there some passages to direct the mind toward religion, they slander me.[101]

The humanist made an almost identical defense of his *Praise of Folly* in a 1515 letter to one of the critics of the work, Martin Dorp:

> In this respect I had exactly the same principles in the *Praise of Folly* as in my other works, although my method was different. In the *Enchiridion* I have a straightforward pattern for the Christian life. In the *Praise of Folly* I did in a jesting fashion exactly what I had done in the *Enchiridion.* I wanted to admonish and not to carp; to do good, not harm; to have regard to men's character and not to be a stumbling block.[102]

Erasmus had devised a new form of instructive moral satire, based upon familiarity with classical models of satire like Lucian[103] and the formal rules of classical rhetoric, such as oration and *encomium.*[104] These classical models offered Erasmus a precedent for handling nonreligious subjects in a way suitable for both wit and instruction.[105] In similar fashion, Massys constructed his own secular satire out of heterogeneous sources—borrowing the grotesque faces underlying his own goal of instruction through ridicule from the drawings of Leonardo da Vinci, his critical tone toward social behavior from Bosch, and his formal seriousness of presentation from 15th-century Flemish (especially Eyckian) portraiture. For Massys, too, these disparate elements provided both a satirical bite and a secular precedent of serious subjects.

Massys was not even the first artist to develop visual analogues to the *Praise of Folly.* By early in 1516, Hans Holbein the Younger had made marginal illustrations within a copy of the printed text, the volume owned by a friend of Erasmus in Basel named Oswald Myconius (1488–1532).[106] Like the isolated figures of Massys' *Old Man/Old Woman,* the Holbein drawings are one- or two-person vignettes with a minimum of background scenery or explanation. The placement of the Holbein figures close to the appropriate text passages of the *Praise of Folly* makes the understanding of the images a simpler matter than the contextual reading of an image like Massys' *Old Man.* A number of images, moreover, provide close comparisons between the interpretations of the two artists: Holbein's illustrations 18 and 19 (fo. 27: "the eternal suitor" and the "eager old woman") and illustration 78 (fo. 83, where the true Christian, giving away his wealth, is contrasted with a greedy well-dressed man at table). One of the drawings contains evidence that Erasmus himself saw these drawings; on illustration 64 (fo. 72), the humanist added a written exclamation to an imaginary portrait of himself as scholar at work in his study on the *Adages.* "O, if Erasmus looked like that today, he would at once find himself a wife." Thus it is possible that Erasmus made kind remarks about Holbein's project to his Antwerp friends,[107] whom he visited later during the same year (1516). Even though Massys could never have seen the Holbein drawings in Switzerland, his own visual analogues to the satirical grotesques in the *Praise of Folly* text, which began to develop after his own 1517 contact with Erasmus, could well have found their genesis in the impact of Holbein's caprices on the humanist and his friends.

To connect Massys' secular pictures with Erasmus's texts is certainly not to assert that the artist consciously chose to "illustrate" the early satirical fiction of the humanist. Lucianic irony, classical learning, and verbal pyrotechnics of Erasmus could never be translated into paint in any case, despite the best efforts of Holbein in the very margins of the text. Yet the varying voices and textual complexities of Moria, so often and correctly stressed by analysts of the *Praise of Folly,* should not blind us to the degree to which that learned Latin treatise shared aspirations with its more vulgar and vernacular environment. We have already seen evidence in *rederijker* verses of common cultural symbols, like the fool, and specific Erasmian references, like Moria, which show the diffusion of the *Praise of Folly* into the *rederijker* cultural store.[108] Moreover, several of Massys' secular images—the *Old Man* and, especially, *Two Praying Monks* and *Democritus*—are mute and nearly incomprehensible without some Erasmian caption alongside.[109] The limited, knowledgeable audience for such pictures need not inevitably have been Antwerp's Erasmian humanist circle, but the close correspondences between Erasmus's words and these elusive subjects indicate that whoever viewed these works comprehendingly was conversant with at least the outlooks of the *Enchiridion* and *Praise of Folly.* Massys' secular images may have had more of the vitriolic sermonizing and pessimism of Brant and the *rederijkers* (or of Bosch) than of the rational paradox and optimism to be found in Erasmus's satires.[110] Yet Geraldine Thompson makes clear their basic common ground: "Erasmus' satires are often a form of preaching and always geared to education."[111]

Ultimately, satirical performances in print or in paint draw upon their common experience of satirical behavior in public: the "spirit of Carnival."[112] Most comparable to the *Praise of Folly* and *rederijker* verses as well as to the Massys grotesques is the *topos* of Carnival festivity: the "world turned upside down."[113] This festive ritual inversion was an annual opportunity for communal renewal and reinforcement through a serious and purgative play on status reversal or egalitarianism.[114] As Natalie Davis concludes about village (and civic) misrule in the French countryside of the late Middle Ages and 16th century:

> The use of the imagery of "Kingdoms" and especially of "Abbeys" not only provided a carnival reversal of status in regard to a faraway king or a nearby monastry, to whom peasants might owe services and dues, but—more important—provided a *rule* that the youth had over others and perhaps too a brotherhood existing among themselves, and it gave enormous scope to mockery and derision. But license was not rebellious. It was very much in the service of the village community, dramatizing the differences between different stages of life, clarifying the responsibilities that youth would have when they were married men and fathers, helping to maintain proper order within marriage, and to sustain the biological continuity of the village . . . The characteristic abbeys of misrule in the large sixteenth century city were professional or more likely neighborhood groupings, which encompassed men both young and old.[115]

Carnival is an alternative world with rules reversed, a mocking folk humor that "denies but it revives and renews at the same time."[116]

The entire *Praise of Folly* text is premised on the idea of a mock-performance, the oration of Moria, Dame Folly. Indeed, the opening lines of the "sermon" are addressed to a fictive audience characterized as the intoxicated and devoted following of Folly, like the revelers at Carnival and the targets of the *rederijkers.* Dame Folly has been compared by scholars to Mère Sotte or Mère Folle of the carnival *sotties.*[117] Erasmus shows himself to have been fully aware of carnival behavior, though prudish about its moral consequences. Discussing the nature of carnival holidays in the adage "For the lazy it is always holiday" *(Ignavis semper feriae sunt),* Erasmus reverses the words, but not the thought, of conventional proverbial wisdom that " 'tis not a kermess every day":

> Nowadays, however, the Christian multitude spends those "holy days," which were instituted of old for piety's sake, in drinking, lechery, dicing, quarreling, and fighting. There's no time when more offenses are committed, than on these days when people ought specially to abstain from offending. . . . For to the true Christian, everyday is a feast-day; but to the wrong sort (the great majority) holidays are profane rather than holy.[118]

Erasmus, too, is perfectly capable in his satirical passages of living up to the insults and mock-beatings meted out in *charivari* and *chévauchée* at carnival-time.[119] Furthermore, many of Erasmus's images, as well as Massys', are drawn from the stock farce situations of carnival comedy *(sotternieën)* and popular tradition: the cuckold, the unfaithful wife, the lecherous old woman, the drunkard.[120] Castigating these vicious types, carnival displayed the same message we have heard before: folly is the universal condition of man or, as Moria says, quoting Ecclesiastes, *"Stultorum infinitus est numerus."*[121]

Erasmus's consciousness of the theater is also explicit in Moria's oration,[122] where the metaphor of disguise and miscasting dominates the picture of life:

> If someone should attempt to take off the masks and costumes of the actors in a play and show to the audience their real appearances, would he not ruin the whole play? . . . To destroy the illusion, then, is to destroy the whole play. The masks and costumes are what hold the audience's eye. For what else is the life of man but a kind of play in which men in various costumes perform until the director

> motions them off the stage . . . Everything is done under pretense, . . . but this play could not be performed in any other way.
>
> Suppose at this point some wise man, suddenly dropped from heaven, should confront me and exclaim that the person whom everyone looks up to as a god and master is not even a man because he is ruled by the passions of brute beasts . . . If he continued in this vein, what else would happen, I ask you, except that he would be considered crazy and insane by everyone. Therefore, as nothing is more foolish than an absurd kind of wisdom, so nothing is more imprudent than an untimely prudence. He is all awry, therefore, who does not acclimate himself to the surrounding conditions, who does not follow the crowd, who does not keep in mind that law of conviviality—"Either drink or get out"—and, in short, who asks that the play no longer be a play. On the other hand, he is truly prudent who wishes to have no greater share of wisdom than is fitting for a mortal, who with the rest of the crowd is willing to let things go, or who sociably errs along with them. But that, they say, is folly itself. Indeed, I would scarcely disagree with them, but let them, in turn, admit that this is only acting out the play of life.[123]

The folly of life's play-actors, then, is a mask they have deliberately chosen; Erasmus mentions dignity, noble ancestry, and mourning as theatrical poses. In typical Erasmian fashion, this passage is truly ironic and ambivalent, mock-praising both folly and "wisdom." This seeming wisdom is the Christian critic's eye, seeing through society's shams yet incapable of laughing at the absurdity of the spectacle in order to transcend and enjoy the performance. The paradox here is resolved in the central image of the fool. The fool obeys the "law of conviviality" as an embodiment of, and as an active participant in, worldly foibles. Yet he is also the truth-teller who criticizes those very ailments either directly or through his marot and in the indirect discourse of a jester's humor: "A fool, however, reaps true prudence, unless I am deceived, from experiencing things at close range."[124]

In still another Erasmian inversion, final and anagogic, true wisdom is permitted only to the Christian fool, who, like Democritus, can sufficiently transcend worldly affairs to laugh at the whole foolish lot of them:

> Everywhere they throng in so many forms of folly and fabrication each day that a thousand Democrituses would not be sufficient for laughing at them, and even then there would be work for one more Democritus, to laugh at those who are laughing.[125]

It is as if Massys' own development in his secular subjects recapitulates the progression in the text of Erasmus's *Praise of Folly.* The prudent carefulness and dignity of the Louvre *Moneychanger and his Wife* give way to a sharper moral and critical vision in the later satirical grotesques. The *Banker and Client, Old Man/Old Woman,* or *Ill-Matched Pair* offer a "world upside down," a hideous unmasking of life's players and their true, baser nature of passions, pretenses, and vices. Only in a return to loftier spiritual concerns in the *Praying Monks,* the acknowledgment of the inherent paradox of actor-commentator in the *Fool,* and the final laughter of *Democritus* does Massys begin to realize the final beatific vision of Moria and Erasmus. With the *Fool* and *Democritus,* Massys could lay to rest his guilt-ridden anxieties about worldly sinfulness and inadequacy before the lofty example of the saints and transcend his own pseudo-wisdom of moral superiority to his fellows. Like *Democritus,* dressed in significantly modern costume, the artist, too, in his later years could laugh at human folly and be mindful of the very folly of his own laughter.

The Massys who could laugh at the world's follies with Democritus, with Erasmus, and with the *rederijkers* is the same Massys who could contrast this world's ugliness and diversity with the beauty and purity of the Madonna and Child or the Man of Sorrows (e.g., New York *Adoration of the Magi,* 1526; *Pl. 79*
Venice *Ecce Homo).* Like the late, half-length, religious pictures, Massys' secular satires are based upon *Pl. 87*
feeling and spirit rather than on theological doctrine; now, behavior and choice are the expression of true faith. In this respect, Massys' self-centered secular figures are the opposite pole from the selflessness and compassion of his religious figures, but saint and sinner are both part of the artist's unified moral vision. The grotesque London *Old Woman* with her overdressed vanity is the perversion of the humble and beautiful Madonna, who is simply dressed even when she sits upon an elaborate

throne (van Pannwitz, London, Berlin *Madonnas*). For Massys, like Erasmus, good living and firm faith are inseparable,[126] and truly good living will condition firm faith.

Just as his colleagues, the *rederijkers*, created "folly poems" to go with their chivalric "love poems" and religious "wise poems" (see Chapter 1), Massys' secular pictures, in spite of their apparent differences in subject and presentation, form a didactic outgrowth of his later religious imagery. Satires intended to delight as well as to instruct, the secular subjects bring the artist closest to the popular carnival culture of his day as well as to the shared attitudes of the *rederijkers* and Erasmus.

NOTES

1. On Bosch's secular pictures, see most recently W. Gibson, *Hieronymus Bosch*, pp. 33–47; full catalogue descriptions and bibliographies of the Paris *Ship of Fools* and the New Haven fragment are given by C. de Tolnay in *Hieronymus Bosch*, pp. 347f. (no. 8) and 349 (no. 9); also C. Cuttler, "Bosch and the *Narrenschiff*: A Problem in Relationships," *Art Bulletin* 51 (1969): 272ff.

2. See the references cited in Chapter 6, note 75.

3. Gibson, *Hieronymous Bosch*, pp. 69–77; de Tolnay, *Hieronymous Bosch*, p. 355f., no. 17.

4. Gibson, p. 33ff.; de Tolnay, p. 338f., no. 2; W. Gibson, "Hieronymus Bosch and the Mirror of Man," p. 205ff.

5. See the references cited in Chapter 6, note 76.

6. G. Thompson, *Pretext of Praise;* D. G. Watson, "Erasmus' *Praise of Folly* and the Spirit of Carnival," p. 333ff.

7. On the Massys secular half-lengths, B. Völker, pp. 175–203.

Pl. 114 8. On St. Anthony, including Massys' own *Temptation of St. Anthony* (Prado, F. 31, cat. 26) made in collaboration with Patinir, see Chapter 6. The Massys *St. Anthony* still provides Bosch-like demonic elements in the background scenes, but its foreground image shows a weak and vacillating saint assailed by worldly sirens who attempt to arouse his lustful impulses. By offering the viewer an unresolved choice between good and evil as well as a moment of fallibility, even for a saint, this Massys *Anthony* performs many of the functions of the artist's secular subjects, made during the same period of his career.

9. Van Fornenbergh, *Den Antwerpschen Protheus*, pp. 26-27. (It can no longer be determined whether this inscription was originally on the frame). This suggestion of balance as the theme of the Louvre *Moneychanger* is at odds with the usual scholarly assessment (for instance, by Marlier) that sees it as a severe criticism of fiscal affairs, as in the recent article by G. Vlam, "The Calling of St. Matthew in Sixteenth Century Flemish Painting," *Art Bulletin* 59 (1977): 561ff. Discussing the Louvre *Moneychanger* in light of later, much more vitriolic images of money-handling by Marinus van Reymerswaele and Jan de Hemessen, she states:

> Already there is a clear juxtaposition of objects carrying a moral: jewelry scale versus prayerbook, Mammon versus God, or avarice versus concern for salvation. Although these elements (and ideas) are fairly equally balanced in Quinten's painting, Avarice is winning out in a similar composition by Marinus van Reymerswael, the prayerbook being obscured by the grasping gesture of the woman's hand" [566].

In my opinion, the later Massys secular works give rise to Reymerswaele, et al., but to see the 1514 Louvre *Moneychanger* through the lens of its grotesque successors is to distort it with anachronistic hindsight.

10. Observed independently by E. Snow, *A Study of Vermeer* (Berkeley, 1979), pp. 34, 132ff. Cf. also A. Blankert, *Vermeer of Delft,* Oxford, 1978, 161f., no. 15 and *Masters of Seventeenth Century Dutch Genre Painting,* exh. cat. (Philadelphia, 1984), p. 342–3, no. 118.

11. Again, Massys' later *St. Anthony* offers an analogy in the form of an old, monstrous hag in outlandish, outmoded costume, who points to her own grotesque features as a warning against the temporary charms of the foreground sirens. She, too, is visible to the viewer but not to the beleaguered saint.

12. Panofsky, *ENP,* p. 144.

13. I. Bergström, *Dutch Still-Life Painting in the Seventeenth Century,* p. 154ff.; Bergström, "Disguised Symbolism in 'Madonna' Pictures and Still Life," pp. 303ff., 342ff. A striking early 15th-century instance of the Marian association of a candlestick is in Campin's *Merode altarpiece* (New York, Cloisters), see Panofsky, p. 143; C. I. Minott, "The Theme of the Merode Altarpiece," *Art Bulletin* 51 (1969): 270.

14. The traditional identification of these sitters as Giovanni Arnolfini and his bride Giovanna Cenami has been challenged recently by P. Schabacker, "*De Matrimonio ad morganaticum contracto*: Jan van Eyck's 'Arnoldini' Portrait Reconsidered," *Art Quarterly* 36 (1972): 375–98. The classic study is Panofsky, p. 201ff. Panofsky's "Jan van Eyck's Arnolfini Portrait," *Burlington Magazine* 64 (1934): 117ff., shows that the objects scattered throughout the room are actually objects bearing a "symbolic significance" in what is "in reality a nuptial chamber, hallowed by sacramental associations." See also *Early Netherlandish Painting,* p. 203, and S. Ringbom, "Nuptial Symbolism in Some Fifteenth Century Reflections of Roman Sepulchral Portraiture," p. 68ff.

15. J. Snyder, "Jan van Eyck and Adam's Apple," *Art Bulletin* 58 (1976); 511–15; Ringbom, "Nuptial Symbolism," however, sees the fruit as a sign of nuptial fertility, akin to the frequent wedding diptychs with flowers (see E. Wolffhardt, "Beiträge zur Pflanzensymbolik," p. 190ff.), in the context of van Eyck's wedding portrait.

16. P. Schabacker, "Petrus Christus' *St. Eloy,*" p. 103ff.

17. The simplest explanation of the mirror in Christus's *St. Eloy* and Massys' *Moneychanger* is that this tradesman used the device, like modern mirrors in stores, as a protection against theft (H. Schwarz, "The Mirror in Art," p. 103). A variety of meanings, however, have been associated with mirrors in other contexts and can help to explain the significance of Massys' mirror, with its reflection of the man reading. One principal symbolic interpretation grows out of religious contexts, like the 1434 van Eyck *Marriage Portrait* (Panofsky, p. 203). As a religious symbol, the mirror would thus be the *speculum sine macula* of

Mary's virginity and purity (Wisdom 7, 26); as such, it appears in representations of the Immaculate Conception (P. Eich, "Empfängnis Maria, unbefleckte," *RDK* 5, col. 253f.; G. Hartlaub, *Zauber des Spiegels*, p. 147f.; Schwarz, "The Mirror in Art," p. 97ff.).

Mirrors were also frequently associated with a number of allegorical personifications, both good and bad. Among the virtues, Prudence holds a mirror because of the same scriptural passage from Wisdom: "For she [Wisdom] is the unspotted mirror of the power of God, and the image of his goodness" (see Hartlaub, *Zauber des Spiegels*, p. 158ff.; Schwarz, p. 104; also R. van Marle, *Iconographie de l'art profane au Moyen-age et à la Renaissance*, p. 43, ills. 51, 77–79). Peter Bruegel's engraving of *Prudentia* (B. 136) shows the female allegorical figure carrying a mirror as well as a coffin, for the wise and prudent man continually keeps death in view (see the outstanding recent catalogue for a summary of bibliography and scholarship: *Pieter Bruegel d. Ä. als Zeichner*, exh. cat. [Berlin, 1975], p. 68, no. 72).

The background of death is even more prominent in the mirror held by Pride or Vanity. Both Bosch's *Seven Deadly Sins* (see above, note 4) and Bruegel's *Superbia (*B. 127; *Peter Bruegel d. Ä. als Zeichner*, p. 59f., no. 65) feature the mirror as the attribute of this vice (Hartlaub, p. 149ff., Schwarz, p. 106, ills. 160–61). Hans Memling also portrayed *Vanity* as a nude woman holding a mirror (Friedländer, vol. 6, no. 21; Hartlaub, ill. 151; see also van Marle, *Iconographie*, ills. 94–95). The folly of vanity is often contrasted with death, particularly in German painting of the 16th-century, such as the work of Hans Baldung Grien (Hartlaub, ills. 160–61; also ills. 152–53, 156–57, 162, 175; Schwarz, p. 109). In Honthorst's 17th-century *Vanitas* (Hartlaub, ill. 152), the mirror and the skull are combined with measuring scales akin to those in Massys' *Moneychanger.*

Though Massys' mirror is held by no figure, its resonances from these other contexts provide a background for understanding the painting. A contemplative life and regard for man's mortality is the most prudent course for a Christian, because the approach of death means an end to the vanity of worldly goods and pleasures. Thus the mirror reflection, visible to neither the moneychanger nor his wife, provides the viewer with moral guidance, as well as an example of righteous conduct. As such, the reading man and the church spire serve the same didactic end as Massys' *St. Jerome*, painted a few years later, where the *Pl. 106* extinguished candle on a shelf serves as a *vanitas* image. Within the context of the Louvre *Moneychanger*, the mirror itself could be the final item of Vanity among the coins and riches (Schwarz, p. 103), or else it could be the voice of Prudence (here, however, turned away from the owner), recalling prayer and the Church, like the prayerbeads and other still-life elements. The ambiguity of the mirror-as-symbol is a product of the panel's ambiguity, for the delicate balance between vanity and prudence, between activity and contemplation, between profit and prayer, pervades the Louvre *Moneychanger* and focuses, finally, on the scales.

The mirror of Massys' *Moneychanger* has also been interpreted as a more generalized symbol, owing to its convex shape and resemblance to an eye. Its reflection thus corresponds to the eye of the artist, its imagery to the vision of painting as the *speculum mundi* (J. Bialostocki, "The Eye and the Window," p. 171). Similar round mirrors were standard equipment in painters' studios and appear in the background of numerous 15th-century painted interiors (H. Schwarz, "The Mirror of the Artist and the Mirror of the Devout," pp. 90–105). The window reflection seems, therefore, to derive from workshop observation with actual mirrors, though it may also have had the 15th-century symbolic association of light with the divine, especially in view of the church spire seen in the Massys reflection (Bialostocki, "The Eye and the Window," p. 170f.; M. Meiss, "Light as Form and Symbol in Some Fifteenth-Century Paintings," in *The Painter's Choice*, p. 3ff.; Panofsky, *ENP*, p. 147f.). According to Carla Gottlieb, "The Mystical Window in Paintings of the Salvator Mundi," *Gazette des Beaux-Arts* 56 (1960): 313–32, the reflected window has a narrower meaning, derived from Christ's words, "Ego sum lux mundi" (John 8:12). This more-mystical interpretation would see the whole mirror reflection as the eye of God, a late medieval *topos* found in Bosch's Prado tabletop and numerous texts (for which, see Gibson, "Hieronymus Bosch," p. 215ff.). One central text is Nicholas of Cusa's *De Visione dei* (ca. 1453), identifying God as both witness and mirror of mankind's actions (Gibson, ibid., 217f.; Bialostocki, p. 172f., also citing another Cusanus text, *De Ludo globi* [1463]; S. Sulzberger, "Observations sur le chef-d'oeuvre de Quentin Metsys," pp. 27-34). A similar view had already been advanced for the mirror of the van Eyck *Marriage Portrait* (Panofsky, *ENP*, p. 203; Schwarz, "The Mirror in Art," pp. 97–99). Concerning van Eyck, W. M. Zucker, "Reflections on Reflections," p. 239ff., has described the mirror as representing "omniscience and omnipotence of God" and "also the symbol of the truth of art." But both Zucker (p. 242f.) and Schabacker ("Petrus Christus," p. 112f.) demur from interpreting *St. Eloy's* mirror in these terms, for it is not immaculate and has a large crack in its surface, reflecting "the sinful state of man's world." In Massys' *Moneychanger*, however, the mirror reveals not the bull's-eye vision of the same space, but rather an extension of space outside the realm of the painting. It provides, instead, an alternative world rather than the omniscient inclusion of the entire pictorial world.

18. Another contemporary image which shows moneylending to be morally reprehensible in the spirit of Bosch is Jan Provost's *Death and the Miser* (Bruges; Friedländer, vol. 9, no. 133), where the skeletal allegory returns with his pawn ticket to "redeem" the fat broker himself (see Marlier, p. 351; also H. Pauwels, *Catalogue Musée Groeninge*, p. 64, no. 32, who claims that the scene represents a legend of one J. Lanckart, who sold his soul to the devil).

19. L. van Puyvelde, "Un portrait de marchand par Quentin Metsys et les percepteurs d'impôts par Marin van Reymerswale," p. 3ff., actually takes the Louvre *Moneychanger* to be a portrait.

20. Ibid.; Marlier, p. 251ff.; L. Silver, "Power and Pelf," p. 85f.

21. Seventeenth-century inventories referring to either this picture or its copies make the same association of trades: "A painting on panel of a tax-collector or moneychanger made by Master Quinten" (1616) or "a painting, painted by Master Quinten Metsys, showing the tax-collectors" (1652), cited by Puyvelde, "Portrait de marchand," from J. Denucé, *De Konstkamers van Antwerpen in de 16e en 17e eeuwen: inventarissen van kunstverzamelingen*, pp. 28, 133. The 17th-century (1642) Spanish inventory of the Marquis of Leganés also includes a reference (no. 31) to "otra pintur del mro. Quintin, de un banquero contando getones sobre una mesa, y en ella y en el almario diferentes libros y papeles con sellos de letras y un beconquin en la caveça con orejas" (J. L. Navio, "La gran colección de pinturas del Marqués de Leganés, *Analecta Calasanctiana* 8 [1962]: 271; also, M. Volk, "New Light on a Seventeenth-Century Collector: The Marquis of Leganés," *Art Bulletin* 62 [1980]: 267). The ambiguity of profession is even conveyed by the article on this composition by a noted economic historian, H. van Werveke, "Aantekeningen bij de zogenaamde *Belastingpachters* en Wisselaers van Reymerswaele," p. 43ff. Part of the reason for the

confusion is explained by R. de Roover in discussing the trade background of Reymerswaele's copies of the composition (*Money, Banking, and Credit in Medieval Bruges*, pp. 201, 247, 262): during the 16th century, credit transactions—the equivalent of modern checking accounts—were carried out orally between the banker and the individual client. These same bankers also took deposits and made currency exchanges, the very role performed by the Louvre *Moneychanger.* The London variant of the Massys composition by Reymerswaele contains an account from municipal commodity taxes (M. Davies, *Early Netherlandish School: National Gallery Catalogues*, p. 84), while the Windsor Castle replica displays a careful transcription of a moneychanger's accounts (van Werveke, p. 43).

22. "A panel in half-length of a patron who makes accounts with a factor by the hand of Zuan Heic [Eyck], I think Memelino [Memling] made in 1440." This description (ca. 1530) was made in Italy by Marcantonio Michiel, and the aptness of the date suggests that the picture was, indeed, an Eyckian original with an inscribed frame. Cited by Schabacker, "Petrus Christus", p. 108, n. 35, there considered as a possible source for Christus's 1449 *St. Eloy.*

23. Marlier, p. 276; Puyvelde, "Portrait de marchande": "L'avaricieux n'est jamais rempli d'argent—N'avez point souci des richesses injustes car elles ne vous profiteront en rien au jour de la visitation et la vengeance. Soyez donc sans avarice." A restatement of Luke 12: 15–21, "And thus does the person fare who stores up treasure for himself but is not rich in relation to God . . . Be on guard against all greed, for one's life is not made up of the abundance of his possessions."

24. Davies, *Early Netherlandish School*; Reymerswaele also made caricatural variants on the 1514 Louvre *Moneychanger*, like the 1538 *Banker and his Wife* (Munich, Alte Pinakothek), illustrated in Vlam "Calling of Matthew," p. 644, n. 8.

25. Quoted by I. Bergström, *Dutch Still-Life Painting*, p. 7: "Een wockeraar, een molenaar, een wisselaar, en een tollenaar zijn de vier evangelisten van Lucifaar." Also mentioned by Vlam, p. 565. On the middle-class viewpoint of rederijkers, see Chapter 1, this volume, note 182.

26. Van Doesborch, no. 86 (C. Kruyskamp, ed., *De refreinenbundel van Jan van Doesborch*). "Gheselscap sal voor Goet ghebreken":

> Gheselscap sal voor goet doch falen
> Waer om so willen wi truren om goet?
> Wat bat ghierich gheerighen oft halen
> Elc is doch seker dat hi sterven moet . . .
> Heb ic gheen gelt, men sal mi borgen
> Aen eenen bast moet mense verworgen
> Die coen op haerder vreiheyt spreken.

27. "Tgelt is nu ter werelt meest ghepresen" (*Jan van Styevoorts Refreinenbundel Anno 1524*, no. 160); "Die rijke die heet wel gheborene" (ibid., no. 182); "Rapen moet wel sijn een ghesonde spijs" (ibid., no. 164). All from edition edited by F. Lyna and W. van Eeghem.

28. "Haelt most wat cost tes Vrouwen lost" (ibid., no. 83).

29. L. Debaene, *De Nederlandse volksboeken*, p. 261. The modern English edition is Sebastian Brant, *The Ship of Fools*, transl. E. H. Zeydel, pp. 66, 100.

30. Brant, ibid., p. 302.

31. Useful studies of Brant in a larger context include: B. Swain, *Fools and Folly during the Middle Ages and the Renaissance*; B. Könneker, *Wesen und Wandlung der Narrenidee im Zeitalter des Humanismus Brant, Murner, Erasmus* (Wiesbaden, 1966); J. Lefebvre, *Les fols et la folie.*

32. Dolan, *Essential Erasmus*, p. 160.

33. Mann Phillips, *Erasmus on His Times*, pp. 44, 34ff. See also the adage "Bad money, equal in cost / loss" *(Lucrum malum, aequale dispendio)*, or "Happy the man who owes nothing" *(Felix qui nihil debet)*.

34. Thomas More, *Utopia*, transl. P. Turner (Harmondsworth, 1965), pp. 64–66.

35. J. Noonan, *The Scholastic Analysis of Usury* (Cambridge, Mass., 1958); R. de Roover, *L'Evolution de la lettre de change* (Paris, 1953), pp. 170–206, and "The Concept of the Just Price: Theory and Economic Policy," *Journal of Economic History* (1958): 418–34, and *Money, Banking, and Credit*, p. 150ff.; B.N. Nelson, *The Idea of Usury* (Princeton, 1949); G. Le Bras, "Usure," *Dictionnaire de Théologie catholique*, vol. 15, pp. 2336–72; R. Aubenas and R. Ricard, *L'Eglise et la Renaissance* (Paris, 1951), pp. 334–36 (with bibliography); L.Little, *Religious Poverty and Profit Economy in Medieval Europe* (Ithaca, 1978.). A classic study by R.H. Tawney, *Religion and the Rise of Capitalism* (New York, 1926), deals broadly with this issue.

36. M. Pacaut, "Saint Bernardin de Sienne et l'usure," *Le Moyen Age* (1963): 743–52.

37. Noonan, *Scholastic Analysis*, p. 105; see p. 199ff. for the manipulations of the concept of interest after 1450.

38. Clark and Pedretti, *The Drawings of Leonardo da Vinci*, p. 83; also K. Clark, "Francesco Melzi as Preserver of Leonardo da Vinci's Drawings," *Studies in Renaissance and Baroque Art Presented to Anthony Blunt on his 60th Birthday* (London, 1967), p. 24f., arguing that the Windsor drawing is a workshop replica made by Leonardo's pupil Melzi.

39. Panofsky, *ENP*, p. 355; Clark and Pedretti, *Drawings*, p. 83, no. 12491; see also Windsor no. 12458 for a very close parallel, which Clark cites as "having a look of Cosimo de'Medici, Pater Patriae" (p. 75).

Pl. 158 40. For illustrations of several Cosimo medals, see Hill and Pollard, *Renaissance Medals at the National Gallery of Art*, nos. 245–47. Both the Jacquemart-André *Cosimo* and the New York *Old Man* are presented in strict profile oriented to the left, like the medals. The 1513 portrait also features careful, formal lettering based upon the orthography of Massys' own medals (see Chapter 8 and Appendix A).

41. Windsor Castle, no. 12493 (Clark and Pedretti, *Drawings*, p. 83f.). The basic studies of Leonardo's grotesques are Clark and Pedretti; Gombrich, "Leonardo's Grotesque Heads," in *The Heritage of Apelles*, p. 57ff.; A.E. Popham, *The Drawings of Leonardo da Vinci* (New York, 1945), p. 39ff. See also L. Silver, "Power and Pelf," pp. 73–75.

42. Silver, p. 76f.; F. Schevill, *The Medici* (New York, 1949), p. 104ff.; R. de Roover, *The Rise and Decline of the Medici Bank.*

43. De Roover, *Medici Bank*, p. 317, and *Money, Banking, and Credit*, pp. 34, 86.

44. See Chapter 1, this volume, note 57.

45. S. Sullivan, "Rembrandt's *Self Portrait with a Dead Bittern,*" *Art Bulletin* 62 (1980); 238f., discusses fur trim as a mark of social distinction, along with the aristocratic bearing of portraits by Raphael, Titian, and Rembrandt that, like the New York *Old Man*, also feature a balustrade in addition to the sumptuous costume. Massys' knowledge of these Italian prototypes cannot be established with certainty, but his sense of parody in the pendants depends on an established notion of conventions for depicting nobility. For the relationship between kings and icons at half-length, as if appearing at a balcony, see Ringbom, p. 39ff.

46. Silver, p. 76, notes 45–46. Massys shows only one other thumb-ring in his *oeuvre*: on the hand of Pontius Pilate in the Madrid *Ecce Homo* (F.10, cat. 31). Erasmus's *Praise of Folly* alludes to such rings in castigating merchants:

> But the most foolish and sordid of all are your merchants in that they partake in the most illicit business by the most illegal means they can find. Sometimes they lie, they perjure themselves, they steal and cheat, and they impose themselves upon the public. Yet they consider themselves important men because they have gold rings on their fingers [Dolan, *Essential Erasmus*, p. 137].

Shakespeare's Falstaff attests to thumb-rings' prestige and civic rank: "When I was about thy years, Hal, I could have crept into any alderman's ring" [*Henry IV*, Part 1, II, iv, 329].

47. R. de Roover, *Money, Banking and Credit*, pp. 34, 86, and who states that "although the Medici were the greatest foreign bankers of their time, the emphasis in their business was on trade rather than on banking" (p. 90). On the larger context of international merchants, I. Wallerstein, *The Modern World-System: Capitalist Agriculture and the Origins of the European World-Economy in the Sixteenth Century:*

> Indeed it would not be extreme to talk of a system of international debt peonage . . . it involved the purchase of goods in advance of their production, that is payments in advance for supplies to be delivered in the future. This prevented sale on an open market . . . In theory forbidden by law [like usury], this system could only be applied by merchants who had the means and influence to be able to sustain the practice, that is "foreign merchants, or rich merchants who had easy access to foreign markets." These merchants could thereby take the profits of the price revolution and multiply them [84–86].

See also P. Chaunu, *Conquête et exploitation des nouveaux mondes* (Paris, 1969); M. Dobb, *Studies in the Development of Capitalism*, rev. ed. (New York, 1964); R. Ehrenberg, *Capital and Finance in the Age of the Renaissance*, transl. H.M. Lucas (New York, 1963), concentrating on the Fuggers, an Augsburg family house that succeeded the Medici in the 16th century as the leading merchant-bankers and financiers of Europe as well as the "household word" synonymous with "wealth". More generally, see the *Cambridge Economic History of Europe*, eds. E.E. Rich and C.H. Wilson (Cambridge, 1967); H.A. Miskimin, *The Economy of Later Renaissance Europe*, pp. 123–79.

48. M. Mann Phillips, *Erasmus on His Times*, p. 45. Other adages from 1515 with similar sentiments include *Simul et da et accipe:*

> The merchant class hold nothing sacred except financial profit to which they devote themselves entirely as if to God. By this alone they assess godliness, friendship, honour, reputation, everything either in heaven or earth. The rest is nonsense [ibid, p. 34].

See also *Lucrum malum, aequale dispendio:*

> Would that all mortals, and especially merchants, would inscribe this maxim not only on their boxes but on their hearts, and would think that profit no profit at all which is gained by the loss of a good conscience; and nothing useful that is not honest [ibid., p. 35].

49. More, *Utopia*, p. 49. Brant, too, links "Usury and Profiteering" in his chapter 93 (*Ship of Fools*, p. 302f.), and he makes a link between riches and public office, like that of the Medici or Massys' *Old Man* with his thumb ring: "Such councilmen one fain would choose / As have the greatest wealth to loose" ("Of Useless Riches," ibid., p. 100). See also the *rederijker* verses, cited above, notes 26–27.

50. Dolan, *Essential Erasmus*, p. 160. Again, the ring of office on the thumb of the *Old Man* makes the connection between riches and public office.

51. M.J. Friedländer, "Neues zu Quentin Massys," p. 1ff.; Silver, p. 66f.

52. Davies, *Early Netherlandish School*, p. 95, n. 21, has identified the headdress as a northern European fashion from the second half of the 15th century and the low-cut dress, in contrast, as an Italian costume from the 1480s.

53. Panofsky, *ENP*, p. 355f., and "Erasmus and the Visual Arts," p. 214; Marlier, p. 223. The passage is in Dolan, p. 121f.

54. See above, note 4. The wimpled headdress and mirror of Pride are retained in Peter Bruegel's *Superbia*, mentioned above, note 17.

55. Dolan, p. 137; Silver, p. 78, ill. 17.

56. Styevoort, no. 236. "For that I had but Small Concern"—*Daer het ic luttel sorgen voere:* Na dat die werelt nu gaet / Soe vallen die meijskens veel to heet / Ist lief of leet / Sij willen den steert hebben.

57. Ibid., no. 40. "Such Hay Horses Follow Today"—*Sulck hoy volcht nu den paerden nae:* Besiet dese meyskens van herten lustich / Die net van ghewate sijn bedocht / Juecht geeft te kennen den mont seer rustich / Dat Schoon voort ghedaen is al half vercocht / Sy draghen haer scornkens so gent gheknocht / Syen stertelen ringhen en neelden is hen dincken / Een halsdoicksken met gulden maelkens gewrocht / Ende die borstkens duer die doixkens blinking. Other *rederijker* verses imply that the only virgins are maidens out of fear (Jan van Doesborch, no. 150), while some attack women in general (Styevoort, no.17). "Speak, Scream, Sew, God Made Women":

> God made all things very well
> We thank Him always for our luck
> But in the women He got stuck.

(*Spreken, screijen, naijen heeft God den vrouwen berayen:*

> God heeft all dinghen wel ghemaect,
> Dies moghen wij hem ewich weten dank,
> Mer enden vrouwen heeft Hij ghestaecht.)

For other references to *rederijker* poems attacking women, see A. van Elslander, *Het Refrein,* p. 152ff.

58. L. Silver, "The *Ill-Matched Pair,*" p. 104ff.

59. Ibid.; M. Kahr, "Rembrandt and Delilah," *Art Bulletin* 55 (1973): 254f., with other examples of the wiles of women; K. Renger, *Lockere Gesellschaft* (Berlin, 1970), p. 24f.

60. For Bosch, see above, note 1. A new discussion of both the courtly and the moralizing fool is K. Moxey, "Master ES and the 'Fool of Love,' " *Simiolus* 11 (1980), pp. 125ff. (I am grateful to Professor Moxey for sharing his work with me prior to its publication). See also the literature on fools and folly cited above, note 31, and the following: E. Welsford, *The Fool;* E. Tietze-Conrat, *Dwarfs and Jesters in Art* (London, 1957); W. Willesford, *The Fool and His Scepter* (Evanston, Ill., 1969); G. Bebermeyer, "Narrenliteratur," *Reallexikon der deutschen Literaturgeschichte,* vol. 2, 2nd, ed. (Berlin, 1965), p. 592ff.; W. Deufert, *Narr, Moral, und Gesellschaft* (Frankfurt, 1975).

61. Silver, *Ill-Matched Pair;* P. Wescher, "Ein 'ungleiches Liebespaar' von Hans von Kulmbach," *Pantheon* 22 (1938): 376–79; A. Stewart, *Unequal Lovers,* p. 13ff. For some literary parallels, see W.A. Coupe, "Ungleiche Liebe: a Sixteenth-Century Topos," pp. 661–71.

62. Lehrs, nos. 73, 74; Silver, *Ill-Matched Pair,* p. 107f.; Stewart, *Unequal Lovers,* pp. 41f., 139f.

63. The Leonardo copy (Vienna, Albertina) is attributed to Jacob Hoefnagel, ca. 1630; see Silver, *Ill-Matched Pair,* p. 111; it was copied by Hollar in an engraving (Parthey 1604), like the "Rex et Regina de Tunis" (see above, note 51).

64. Silver, *Ill-Matched Pair,* p. 110f., n. 20; Friedländer, "Quentin Massys as a Painter of Genre Pictures," pp. 115–19; E. Larsen, "Un Quentin Massys inconnu à New York," pp. 171–74. Along with the *Five Grotesque Heads,* the woman at the left with her low-cut dress, snub nose, and wimple (reminiscent of Massys' London *Old Woman* and its source, Leonardo's Windsor drawing, no. 12492) is taken from da Vinci's Windsor drawing, no. 12447.

65. See above, note 61.

66. Brant, *Ship of Fools,* pp. 182f., 88ff., 178ff.

67. Dolan, p. 137.

68. Ibid. p. 121.

69. Ibid., p. 111.

70. Van Doesborch, no. 152 (greed), 144, 151; Styevoort, no. 244 (sensuality).

71. Van Doesborch, no. 108: "The profit is thine, the loss is mine" *(Die bate is syne—Die scaye is myne).*

72. Styevoort, no. 86, calls them unduly mistrustful and jealous, and in no. 35, "sleepers on blocks."

73. R. Proctor, *Jan van Doesborch Printer at Antwerp* (London, 1894).

74. Silver, *Ill-matched Pair,* p. 113f., notes 26-27. The Housebook Master's drawing of the Children of the Planet Venus (J. Graf Waldburg-Wolfegg, *Das mittelalterliche Hausbuch* [Munich, 1957], ill. 17) shows couples playing cards among other amorous activities. Card games, like the more popular chess matches, often appear in images between couples in gardens of love during the 15th-century in various media (ivory caskets, manuscripts, engravings, tapestries). See R. S. Favis, "The Garden of Love in Fifteenth Century Netherlandish and German Engravings: Some Studies in Secular Iconography in the Late Middle Ages and Early Renaissance," (Ph.D. dissertation, University of Pennsylvania, 1974), p. 126ff. A late 15th-century engraving by Israhel van Meckenem (ill. 13) in Silver, *Ill-Matched Pair,* shows a young man defeated at cards by a woman. Perhaps the most frequent use of the theme of cards and chess between lovers is the series of paintings by Lucas van Leyden (Friedländer, vol. 10, nos. 140–43, 171–72, p. 181), for which see P. Parshall, "Lucas van Leyden and the Rise of Pictorial Narrative." (Ph.D. dissertation, University of Chicago, 1974), p. 112ff.

75. Van Doesborch, no. 152: *Eest nu goed alsmen u willeken doet:* Een ruyterken, een alte vrijen deverch / Dat had een borse vol gelts gheswollen / Dat vernam een vrouken wt Venus berch Die sulcken calantkens wel conde pollen . . . / Dat vrouken hadde alte loosen grondeken / Doense syn borse ha ende alle sijn ghelt / Si ghinc hem tonen een lachende mondeken / Ghelijc den pladdijs sijn muylken stelt / Si en sette hem niet meer dach en velt / Om datse thuys sou sitten op haer stoelken / Al hadse hem te voren wat soets ghereIt. / Si leerde hem speelen bot uut toelken / Hit moste gaan soeken een ander boelken / Dit doende en is hi devoort self niet vroet / Eest nu goet alsmen u willeken doet.

75. Ibid., no. 149 ("Of Laughter and Artistry Unexpected"—*Van lachen en constic mi niet ghewachten).*

77. Asses' ears were a frequent mark of the fools' costumes in illustrations to Brant and other images. *Vanden. X. Esels* was edited by A. van Elslander [Antwerp], 1946. For additional commentary, see Debaene, *Nederlandse volksboekeu,* p. 247, L. Roose, *Anna Bijns,* pp. 142–58. I have also made use of K. Moxey, "The *Ship of Fools* and the Idea of Folly in Netherlandish Literature of the Sixteenth Century," in *The Early Illustrated Book Essays in Honor of Lessing J. Rosenwald.* Edited by S. Hindman (Washington, 1982), p. 86–102.

78. Debaene, p. 342, or the passage from *De Historie van Broeder Russche* (ca. 1519–20), primarily a satire on the Church: Women are for sale, they want to be undressed / Because they know what to wear, though for dishonor / They think that prettily done up means half sold / And they wear clasps flecked with gold / The girls say they learn from whores / To arrange their crosses, to enliven their collars / So their neck and their breasts can be seen. / Everyone must beware who comes into danger [ibid. p. 341].

79. L. Roose, *Anna Bijns,* p. 17; also, G. Degroote, "De poezië der rederijkers," pp. 296–98.

80. Styevoort, no. 9 (author's translation): The world's now reversed, falsehood reigns now / Everyone wants his own profit / He swears, he curses, justice falls short. / And no one honors piety, / Virtue is scorned by the devil's counsel / Who now does evil, then advances / Who hates another, thus goes the world / On skates, mate, 'tis all discord now / To speak a word now, other than knavery / Murders words now for false parties / Her company is folly [*sotternie*], be it Fleming or Hollander / It seems to me that all's ill once more.

Because of that discord in every society / Poverty, pestilence, comes with dispatch / We make no mention of contrition / As for conscience, gold suffices / I am well aware that stupidity thrives / Is treasured, brooks no regrets / Serves the body with wicked means / Though here it is sweet, you may well shudder / These sheriffs and bailiffs oppressing the poor / Renewing the taxes in this early vale / Trample on justice, like birds of prey / Seizing the wounded on a claw / Neither lock nor wall, large stockade or small, / They hold balls for one another / It seems to me that all's ill once more.

We live like dogs, that's well established / From out of two mouths we speak with signs [flags] / With which our sins in every hour / Renew God's wounds and cause us grief / And we've no tears, because we carry / Our friends, our kin, our hate and envy / 'Tis great distress, and I renounce my days / More to banish or exile than now / When the one rejoices, the other shows regret / Or each runs to conflict to secure an office / One cuts a purse, worth chastising, / The more he has money, the more he's unburdened / Non potest dici / Die repetice es, sunt amici / Scarcely does justice to an arsonist / It seems to me that all's ill once more.
Faith is blind, no faith to find / The world begins all o'er to wander / No bread is found, fully cautionary / Against the father, the child revolts / Popes, cardinals, clergy and commercials / Germans, Walloons, and the lot / Begin to stray, for virtue they hate / Papal subjects get indulgenced / For two ducats, hardly cheap / His legates, ruffians, soldiers / Who eat gladly with Roman syrup / The mess sups a soup / Where e'er I wander or roam / It seems to me that all's ill once more.
Prince: It's all to rebel, that's clear as well / Adultery is comfortable now / Venus torments take many to Hell / For everyone hurries into a bordell' / Now there's no rank, each man's a noble / They're wearing velvet, the peasants dull / Who dye their hair to make a display / Set with flour, now they must thrive / The more they cover up, the more they must scour / Lining a sack full of small lumps / Because they embroider and paint up / Their socks in strange figures and with diamonds / They must contrast with outsiders / But at the close they still have more ills / Than the sweet Brabander / It seems to me that all's ill once more.

81. Styevoort, no. 39: One sees the world become ever more evil / And I say no and that by these / Although they say, interpreters grow ever falser / You'll hear different tales from me / For I find no one praised in countries / Of princes, knights, *junkers,* or lords / But upright, strong, true, and improving / No one pushed aside or offense taken by any / They only want their subjects to flourish / Not to extort or alarm widows or creatures / Only to do right righteously, to learn from the Scriptures / To win for them heaven and the fear of Hell. / Piety wishes neither robbery nor seizure / Of the means of the common folk / How should evil go into that world.
Behold attorneys, or lawyers / Where they live in corners / Off in Brussels or here in the streets / Where they banish or curse someone. / They locate every legal path in books / And yet desire but simple fees / No craftiness and wills they seek / For they Fear God and Heaven's throne / Because He is just in the Coming Day / The servant, be he Claus or Devil / Serves his master willingly / Like the girl I take my joy in / Everyone follows the Golden Rule / How should evil go into that world.
A horsetrader in a golden world / Would never fool his fellow man / If he sells a horse, it isn't the worse [fig. blind, "with pearly eye"] / He'd give no cunning for xx flies / And even in church or dwelling in cloisters / These mouthers who make money suit / They don't lie and swing a word for x guilders / It all goes, they say, for holy shrines / Clerks, too, increase in virtue / They write no letter out of the way / And thereby may properly be deceived / Girls also have the triumph of God / So they'll be kept 'til after marriage / How should evil go into that world.
Cobblers make thick shoes / Though stretching leather with their teeth / Bakers baking full, big loaves / For 'tis large enough in every land / The tailor's hand is more correct than a round hay-bale / He wouldn't steal two odd swatches / Even though no one stood beside him, / And then the miller, I'll warrant / Is the most upright of all / He wouldn't wish, for 90 pounds, / To dip too deep in someone's sack / Or go past fairness, no matter what they say / He is all just, though he sometimes errs. / How should evil go into that world.
Prince: Whoever we see selling foam for beer / Or doesn't measure full and true / Wherever drunkards roam the streets / Or tricksters, secretly placed somewhere / Where herring-sellers are reproved / For selling freight as the goods / Wherever was seen milkwives, progressive folks, / Bound up with their buttermilk / Or old wives turning to pandering / Where women live who wait for lads / And let them pay for half a stuiver / Where one would find tattlers tattling / One finds in that land none but warnings of virtue. / How should evil go into that world.

82. The history of the *rederijker* chambers in Antwerp, in particular De Violieren, is sketched by L. Roose, "De Letterkunde," *Antwerpen in de XVI eeuw* (Antwerp, 1975), p. 321ff. (with bibliography). Among the basic sources are: J. van Ertborn, *Geschiedkundige aenteekening aengaende de Ste. Lucas Gilde en de Rederyk-Kamers, gezegt van den Olijftak, de Violieren, en de Goudbloem,* 2nd ed. (Antwerp, 1822); J. B. van der Straelen, *Geschiedenis der Antwerpoche Rederijkerskamers* (Antwerp, 1863); F. Donnet, *Het jonstich versaem der Violieren* (Antwerp, 1907); E. de Bock, *Opstellen over Colijn van Rijssele en andere Rederijkers* (Antwerp, 1958), p. 55ff. A good, recent comparison is E. van Autenboer, *Volksfeesten en rederijkers te Mechelen (1400–1600)* (Ghent, 1962).

83. Van Doesborch, nos. 91, 116 *(Tis wonder was verdoolde herten lijen; Wie salt verdragen dat sot wille doet).* On verses *int vroede* in general, see van Elslander, *Het Refrein,* pp. 95–120, esp. p. 118ff., and the references mentioned in Chapter 1. Other "serious" refrains attack scandal (Van Doesborch, no. 110: "Against a babbler there's no Guard"—*Want tegen een clappart en is er geen wachten),* envy (Van Doesborch, no. 113: "What does one do in this World Worth Envying"—*Wat doetmen ter werelt ten wert benijt),* infidelity (Van Doesborch, no. 118: "To Trust Well Brings Much Trouble"—*Bi wel betrouwen geschiet veel quaets).*

84. Van Doesborch, no. 89 *(Dit duecht schijnt ende sonde voor gode is).* The first verse begins: He seems pained and of great virtues / With work(s) of apparent strong devotion / But after great laughter, they are exposed / They lie and deceive friends in need. (Sulc schijnt hi pijnt en deuchden groot / Het werk schijnt sterk na devocien schijn, / Mer achter groot lachter doen si bloot / Si liegen, bedriegen vrienden ter noot).

85. P. Schröder, *Parodieën in de Nederlandse Letterkunde* (Haarlem, 1932), p. 21; van Elslander, *Het Refrein,* p. 146ff., for the refrains *int sotte.*

86. Styevoort, no. 85: "The Stone [of Folly] Hidden under the Exposed Wound": Yet there grows a great mass / The older the sillier is a famous line / So the stone's well-grown and great / But unseen while all's well in season / Else 't would be too large a ball. (*Die Keije verborghen onder die blesse bloot:* Moria seer hoghe vernaemt . . . / Nochtans die keye wast mit gorrten tasse / Hoe ouder hoe sotter dats een woort vermaert / Soe is die keye wel groot van wassen / Mer hy is onsienliec soe is hy te passe / Ander soe waert te groot een cloot).

The subject of the Operation on the Stone of Folly appears in the works of several artists, including especially Bosch (Madrid, Prado, de Tolnay, 337, no. 1) and Jan de Hemessen (Friedländer, vol. 12, no. 217); see also Marlier, p. 285f. The proverbial saying "The older the sillier" *(Hoe ouder hoe sotter)* compares closely to Erasmus's barbs about foolish old men in the *Praise of Folly,* cited above, and to Massys' dotard in the *Ill-Matched Pair.*

87. Styevoort, no. 165: *Alle sotten en draghen gheen bellen:* In alle tornoyen oft vrolyke foreesten / In alle schietspelen of feesten

van rethoryken, / Daer vintmen viel diversche sotten ter feesten, / Mit bellen blinckende om elcx bekyken / Ende lopen ter straten, / Van wycke te wijken, . . . / Mer edel gildebroeders, ghi moet versinnen / Datment alle sotten niet en mach bemercken / Aent blinken der bellen wilt dat bekinnen, / Sy en dragense niet allen die den sot verstercken . . .

88. Styevoort, no. 16 *(Elc heeft een vreemt geestgen dat hem quelt).* Part of the spirit of wild abandon is the frequent mention in folly refrains of the pleasures of drink (see Styevoort, nos. 69, 189; van Elsldander, p. 157ff.). This very vice of drunkenness is condemned in wise verses, such as "Drunkenness, sin, harm, and shame" *(Dronckenscap, sonde, schade, en schande,* to be found in both van Doesborch, no. 94, and Styevoort, no. 195), or "A Drink-pot Makes Many Penniless" *(Een drinckpot maect menigen geldeloos;* van Doesborch, no. 115). Massys' secular pictures refer to this vice on only one occasion, an odd work on paper, the *Drinker* (F. 191, cat. 30), whose attribution to Quinten, rather than an imitator, is not very secure. This subject, however, remained a popular one in 15th-century Netherlandish prints and paintings; see K. Renger, *Lockere Gesellschaft Zur Ikonographie des Verloren Sohnes und von Wirthausszenen in der niederländischen Malerei* (Berlin, 1970), pp. 17ff., 71ff. Also see the loose-living characters in art and literature cited by W. Gibson, "Some Flemish Popular Prints from Hieronymus Cock and his Contemporaries," *Art Bulletin* 60 (1978): 673ff. Fictitious "drinkers' guilds" or "merry companies" in the Netherlands and their parodistic verses can be compared to these lying refrains and praises of drink by the *rederijkers* (see Chapter 1, note 175, plus the anthology of these verses, *Veelderhande geneuchlijcke dichten, tafelspelen ende refereynen* [Leyden, 1899]). These groups are truly the "timeless ones" *(tijelooskens)* referred to in "All Fools and None Carry Bells." This concept of the absence of time is discussed as "The Permanence of the Fool" by W. Willeford, *The Fool and His Scepter* (Evanston, Ill., 1969), pp. 60–72.

89. See the studies on fools above, noted 31 and 60, especially E. Welsford, *The Fool,* p. 121ff. The Massys image is in Tietze-Conrat, p. 94, no. 21, and in Willesford, p. 29, plate 2. Images of fools at festival show the same costume. Particularly striking is the comparison to the fools in the *Archers Festival* (1493; Antwerp; Friedländer, vol. 7, no. 164) by the Master of Frankfurt, an Antwerp contemporary of Massys. In that painting, the fool at the right has the same coxcomb crowned by a rooster (literally a "cock's-comb") as the Held *Fool.* Similar costumes are depicted in abundance in the engravings *Fools at Carnival* by Peter Bruegel (B. 225–26, Lebeer 94–95). Brant's *Ship of Fools* verses, such as in his final Apology, constantly mention (and illustrate) the fool's cap:

> I've joined the fool's fraternity
> I pull the cap which I would fain doff,
> Yet my fool's cap will not come off [Brant, *Ship of Fools,* p. 362].

And of course the Ten Donkeys of *Vanden. X. Esels* are fools with asses' ears (see above, n. 76).

90. See above, n. 86.

91. F. Kerdijk, *Alle Gekheid op 'n Stokje* (The Hague, 1970); Willesford, pp. 33–37; J. J. Mak, *De Rederijkers,* p. 68f., cites a play by Cornelis Everaert of Bruges entitled *Nyeuwen Priestere* ("New Priest"), where the fool is named "Doubtful Sense" *(Twyffelic zin)* and his marot is called "Sick Faith" *(Cranc Gelove).*

92. On the mirror in general, see above, note 17. Again, the marot, like the mirror, is an ambiguous depiction of self-knowledge *(Prudentia)* or of the world's transience and folly *(Vanitas).* In either case, it is a truth-teller. Han Holbein's 1515 marginal illustrations to Erasmus's *Praise of Folly* (for which, see below, n. 106) include an image of a fool staring at himself in a mirror (illustrated in Willesford, p. 33f., plate 9, with commentary; also E. Teitze-Conrat, p. 57, n. 59, fig. 62). For the fool and the mirror, see Hartlaub, ill. 176.

93. Tietze-Conrat, p. 94; J. Gessler, "A Propos d'un acteur dans le Jeu de Sainte Apolline," *Miscellanea Leo van Puyvelde* (Brussels, 1949), p. 269ff. This unambiguous and scatalogical insult is found within several Peter Bruegel images, most prominently in the 1559 Berlin *Netherlandish Proverbs,* where folk sayings like "He shits on the gallows" *(Hij beschijt de galg)* or "He shits on the whole world" *(Hij beschijt de geheele wereld)* are synecdoches for the general satirical contempt expressed in the painting as a whole (J. Grauls, *Volkstaal en Volkleven in het werk van Pieter Bruegel* [Antwerp / Amsterdam, 1957]). I am grateful to Professor Alan Dundes for discussing this complex picture with me and for sharing his subtle analysis, currently unpublished, of the picture: A. Dundes and C. Stibbe, "The Art of Mixing Metaphors: A Folkloristic Interpretation of the *Netherlandish Proverbs* by Pieter Bruegel the Elder."

94. Dolan, p. 125f.

95. W. M. H. Hummelen, *De sinnekens in het Rederijkersdrama,* p. 380ff.

96. See also the fool at the left edge of Lucas's 1519 engraving (B.122) *The Dance of the Magdalene,* whose prominence in this scene clearly involves him in the role of social commentator and veridist, although he, like the Magdalene's entourage, is also a courtly figure (see Moxey, "Master ES"). In the background of Bruegel's 1560 *Temperancia* drawing and print a fool is shown as part of the staging of a morality play (see J. J. Mak, "De Wachter in het Rederijkersdrama," *Oud Holland* 64 [1949] : 162ff.; on the drawing see *Pieter Bruegel d.Ä. als Zeichner,* exh. cat., p. 69f., no. 74, with bibliography).

97. On mock societies, see Chapter 1, n. 181, and the fine examples from 16th-century France discussed by N. Davis, "The Reasons of Misrule," *Society and Culture in Early Modery France* (Stanford, 1975), p. 97ff. On comic plays by the *rederijkers,* called *esbattements* or "farces" *(cluchten)* unless they were only dialogues ("table plays," *tafelspelen),* see Mak, *Die Rederijkers,* p. 79ff. See also Moxey, *"Ship of Fools"* of n.77). Welsford, *The Fool,* p. 238, underscores the importance of Festivals of Fools *(sotties)* from France (they also existed in the Netherlands) on Erasmus. For more on the connections between such *societés joyeuses* and Erasmus, see D. Watson, "Erasmus" *Praise of Folly,"* p. 336ff., n. 10.

98. G. Ladner, *"Homo Viator:* Medieval Ideas on Alienation and Order," *Speculum* 42 (1967): 257–59; Deufert, *Narr, Moral,* p. 122ff.; Hummelen, *Die Sinnekens.*

99. Dolan, p. 99.

100. Ibid., p. 117. The identification of Erasmus with the laughing Greek is articulated by E. Wind, "The Christian Democritis,": p. 180ff. See also Chapter 6.

101. C. R. Thompson, *Colloquies of Erasmus,* p. 625; also Thompson, *Pretext of Praise,* pp. 104–37.

102. Allen and Allen, no. 337; quoted in G. Thompson, p. 23, n.29.

103. Thompson, p. 22f., notes 26–27.

104. Ibid., p. 57, n. 10; Watson, p. 34ff., n. 10. See also W. Kaiser, *Praisers of Folly* (Cambridge, Mass., 1963).

105. A recent survey of the history of this rhetorical idea is P. Salman, "Instruction and Delight in Medieval and Renaissance Criticism," *Renaissance Quarterly* 32 (1979): 303ff.

106. The facsimile edition is H. A. Schmid, ed., *Erasmi Roterodami Encomium Moriae, i.e. Stultitia Laus.* Also, F. Saxl, "Holbein's Illustrations to the *Praise of Folly* by Erasmus," p. 275f. The date of the illustrations is determined by Myconius's 1516 departure from Basel to Zurich and by Erasmus's move to the Netherlands in the spring of the same year.

107. On Gillis, Grapheus, and the other Antwerp friends and colleagues of Erasmus, see Chapter 6, note 65.

108. See note 86, above. The detailed studies by Degroote make explicit this reception and emulation of Erasmus by the *rederijkers.* G. Degroote, "Erasmiana," *De Nieuwe Taalgids* 48 (1948): 145ff., and "De 'Moriae Encomium' in het Nederlands," *De Nieuwe Taalgids* 51 (1951): 160ff., and "Nederlandse Moria-Waardering," *Brabantse Folklore* 22 (Sept. 1950): 3ff., and "Erasmus en de Rederijkers van de XVIe Eeuw," pp. 389 ff., 1029ff., and "Erasmus en de Bourgondische Nederlanden," *Brabantse Folklore* 22 (May 1950): 3ff., and "Erasmus' *Colloquia* in het Nederlands," *Koninklijke Zuidnederlandse Maatschappij voor Taal- en Letterkunde en Geschiedenis* 4 (1950): 76ff., and, last, "In Erasmus' Lichtkring," ibid. 16 (1962): 83ff. Also see H. A. Enno van Gelder, *Erasmus Schilders en Rederijkers.*

109. Silver, "Prayer and Laughter," pp. 17–23.

110. This is the contrast articulated by Swain, Könneker, and Lefebvre in the references cited in n. 30.

111. Thompson, *Pretext of Praise,* p. 44. In discussing the nature of satire, she makes observations that may well have applicability for Massys' secular satires:

> This interposition of an artistic medium between the satirist and his victim creates around the writer a semblance of aloofness or detachment. Semblance only, for the ideal satirist is not actually detached or without sensitivity about his subject. Neither cynical nor skeptical, he is a man of humane spirit, with a modicum of love for his fellows and a basic belief, however submerged, that man is not beyond redemption. . . . The quality of optimism is not lacking in the best satirists—certainly not in Erasmus, but it is perhaps not vested in a hope for amendment on the part of the victim. The ridicule may indeed be directed to someone dead or to a by-gone institution [see Massys' deliberate archaic costumes]; the past is past, but the writer shows his belief in humanity by recognizing that there are those who will contrive a better future . . . its author count[s] on sympathetic readers who would share his repugnance. Ridicule, directed against what cannot be mended because it is no fault of man or society, is hardly satire . . . If the dream of censure is utterly lacking the ridicule is without moral purpose . . . In its finished form, however, the satire must be directed to the correction of some folly or vice grave in character and becoming lampoon or caricature [46ff].

112. Watson, "Erasmus' *Praise of Folly*"; also R. Klein, "Le thème du fou et l'ironie humaniste," *La Forme et l'intelligible* (Paris, 1969), pp. 433–50; P. Burke, *Popular Culture in Early Modern Europe,* p. 178ff., has the most synthetic discussion of "The World of Carnival" with extensive bibliography. Also C. Gaignebet, *Le Carneval* (Paris, 1974).

113. Burke, *Popular Culture,* p. 185ff., with references. Also on the general topic, N. Davis, "The Reasons of Misrule," "Women on Top," *Society and Culture in Early Modern France* (Stanford, 1975), pp. 97ff., 124ff.; G. Cocchiara, *Il Mondo all Roviscia* (Turin, 1963). This *topos* was important in the literature and language of a succeeding epoch: I. Donaldson, *The World Upside-Down: Comedy from Jonson to Fielding* (Oxford, 1970); C. Hill, *The World Turned Upside Down: Radical Ideas during the English Revolution* (London, 1972); E. Le Roy Ladurie, *Carnival in Romans* (New York, 1979). The title "World Upside Down" has been given at times to the Berlin *Netherlandish Proverbs* of Peter Bruegel, mentioned above, note 93; e.g., by D. Kunzle, "Bruegel's Proverb Painting and the World Upside Down," *Art Bulletin* 59 (1977): 197–202; Kunzle, in B. Babcock-Abrams, ed., *The Reversible World Essays in Symbolic Inversion* (Ithaca), pp. 39–94.

114. Burke, p. 199ff. See also the anthropological studies by Victor Turner, et al., cited by Davis in *Society and Culture:* p. 103, n. 24; p. 130, n. 12.

115. Davis, 107, 114; J. C. Margolin, "Charivari et mariage ridicule au temps de la Renaissance," *Les Fêtes de la Renaissance III,* ed. J. Jacquot and E. Konigson (Paris, 1975).

116. Davis., 97: "rather than being a mere 'safety valve,' deflecting attention from social reality, festive life can on the one hand perpetuate certain values of the community (even guarantee its survival), and on the other hand criticize political order." See also Burke, p. 199ff.: "Some functions of popular festivals seem obvious enough. They were entertainment, a welcome respite from the daily struggle to earn a living; they gave people something to look forward to. They celebrated the community itself, displaying its ability to put on a good show; and perhaps the mocking of outsiders . . .

The ritual of charivari seems to have served the functions of social control in the sense that it was the means for a community, a village or urban parish, to express its hostility to individuals who stepped out of line and so to discourage other breaches of custom . . .

These examples are obvious enough. Functional analysis is more interesting when it is more paradoxical, in other words when rituals which apparently express protest against the social order are interpreted as contributions to that order . . . The safety valve theory of festivals has much to recommend it. It draws attention to a number of features of Carnival which have received too little emphasis . . . For example, it helps explain the importance of violence, which, unlike food and sex, was not about to be restricted during Lent. Again, young men could openly express their desire for ladies of higher social status, and respectable ladies could walk the streets. Wearing masks helped liberate people from their everyday selves, conferring a sense of impunity like the cloak of invisibility in folktales . . . Another point in favour of the theory is its suggestion of a controlled escape of steam. The expression of sexual and aggressive impulses was stereotyped and so channelled." See also the important, controversial study by M. Bakhtin, *Rabelais and His World,* trans. H. Iswolsky (Cambridge, Mass., 1968).

117. Watson, p. 338f., n. 19.

118. M. Mann Phillips, *Erasmus on His Times,* p. 76–77. See the dialogue concerning images and inscriptions about kermis holidays in Netherlandish art from Bruegel to van Mander in S. Alpers, "Bruegel's Festive Peasants," *Simiolus* 6 (1972/3): 163–

76; "Realism as a Comic Mode," *Simiolus* 8 (1975/6): 122ff.; H. Miedema, "Realism as Comic Mode: The Peasant," *Simiolus* 9 (1977): 205–19.

119. Watson, p. 345.

120. Ibid., p. 336ff.; Davis, "Reason of Misrule" also, Margolin, "Charivari"; M. Grinberg, "Carnaval et societé à la fin du XVIe siècle," *Les Fêtes de la Renaisance III* (Paris, 1975), p. 550ff.

121. Dolan, p. 162. See also the omniscient criticism earlier in the *Praise of Folly* (ibid., p. 138):

> In short, if you were to look down from the moon, as Menippus used to do, you would think you were seeing a swarm of flies or gnats, quarrelling among themselves, fighting, robbing, sporting, laying traps for each other, indulging in wanton practices, being born, growing old, and dying. One can hardly believe what commotions and tragedies this insignificant being, minute as he is and so soon to die, instigates.

This godlike and satiric viewpoint is precisely analogous to the great Bruegel paintings and prints of 1559–60, like the *Netherlandish Proverbs* or *Carnival and Lent.* See H. Sedlmayr, "Die'macchia' Bruegels," *JKSW* 8 (1934): 137–59.

122. Thompson, *Pretext of Praise,* pp. 58f., 65ff.

123. Dolan, p. 118f.

124. Ibid., p. 118. Also see the extended remarks on the nature of fools later in the text (pp. 125–26), where both aspects are enumerated:

> They are not troubled by the thousand cares this life brings to all men. They feel no shame, fear, ambition, envy, or love . . . They are certainly sacred to the gods, especially to me [Moria], and therefore everyone honors them. Why, kings cannot eat or travel or endure an hour without their fools who give them the greatest delight . . . Fools present only what rulers want: Jokes, laughter, scoffing, and other delights.
>
> Fools also have this not insignificant virtue: they alone are candid and truthful. What is more praiseworthy than truth? Someone might say that kings hate wise men and avoid them because they fear that one of them might dare to speak the truth rather than what is pleasant; and this is true, kings hate the truth. It is quite admirable, then, that kings will listen with relish to not only a truth but quite a sharp truth from my fools.

125. Ibid., p. 136.

126. Thompson, *Pretext of Praise,* pp. 30, 81ff., 153ff.

8

Portraits and Patrons

Massys was not a portrait specialist in the sense of later artists such as Hans Holbein, Antonis Mor, or Frans Hals. Instead, he combined his work on likenesses of individuals with the religious-devotional pictures and secular images that have been studied in earlier chapters. Another striking feature about the portraits by Massys is that they do not depict people of rank or great wealth. In this respect, they differ considerably from the 15th-century portraits of van Eyck or van der Weyden that generally focus upon figures in the court of Burgundy.[1] They most resemble, and indeed they draw upon the pictorial formulas of, the portraits of Hans Memling, whose sitters, when they are known, were members of the urban patriciate of Bruges, but who often have come down to posterity without any identification whatsoever. Proper investigation of Massys' portraits, then, will involve consideration of the kinds of sitters who asked for their own likenesses, but it will also have to consider the pictorial purpose of the category of picture-making we now call portraiture.

In a culture where picture-making normally involved an image of transcendent religious figures, portraiture could not simply evolve out of a desire for a likeness of some ordinary mortal. A portrait had to *say* something; it had to be assertive, to communicate something about the individual depicted. The very act of making a portrait in such a culture already says something important about the worth of that individual, but the portrait image also had to contain some message about that significance within its formulations. Netherlandish portraits, therefore, are not mere likenesses, but are statements, even assertions, about dignity and the worthiness of the individuals portrayed. Whether in association with religious figures or isolated with only their own badges of office or personal attributes, the individuals painted were memorialized. Like a tombstone or another constructed memorial, the paintings focus on the positive, the distinctive, and the characteristic aspects of a person.[2]

The early 15th-century portraits by Jan van Eyck may be regarded as already presenting these kinds of assertions. Of course, the most assertive of all van Eyck portraits was the pair of donors of the Ghent altarpiece: Joos Vydt and his wife, Elizabeth Borluut. They are shown not only as the sponsors of the magnificent altarpiece ensemble, but they are also given a place within that ensemble, albeit a minor place on the exterior wings of the altarpiece.[3] The donors are shown kneeling, their hands clasped in prayer, before the sculpted grisaille patrons of the church and the chapel. They also are given eternal remembrance by their position in the nichelike space they occupy, a shrinelike isolation that was also reserved for the sculptures they pray to and originally was also to be the setting for the

Annunciation that takes place above their heads.[4] Thus, like the prayers to be performed in perpetuity by monks before the altarpiece as a memorial to the donors, the portraits by van Eyck within the altarpiece itself were to serve as memorials to the piety and generosity of Vydt and his wife.

Pl. 136 Van Eyck makes this role or portrait-making explicit on another work, the so-called *Tymotheos*, dated to the same year as the Ghent altarpiece: 1432 (London). Panofsky has brilliantly deduced the identity of the sitter of this portrait to be a court musician of Burgundy, possibly Gilles Binchois, although this identification has not gone unchallenged.[5] Equally memorable is the construction for the portrait, featuring the French inscription "LEAL SOVVENIR" engraved on a stone parapet in front of the figure. The meaning of this phrase, "loyal remembrance," is confirmed by the age of the crumbling stone on which it is carved. The model of this pictorial formula is the portrait bust of Roman funerary monuments.[6] As for the figure who looks out from behind this memorial parapet, he is a young man holding a letter whose dress reflects his modest but fashionable wealth and status. More assertive, in contrast, is the baton of office and the rich costume worn in Van Eyck's portrait of *Baudouin de Lannoy* (Berlin), governor of Lille and chamberlain of the Duke of Burgundy. Moreover, the figure of Baudouin wears one of the most exclusive badges of privilege, the chain and pendant of the Order of the Golden Fleece, the knightly order founded in 1430 by Philip the Good; he is also dressed in a costly brocade given him as a present by Philip in 1427.[7] While this picture is not commemorative in the same sense as the Vydt portrait or the *Tymotheos*, it is equally assertive of the position and dignity of the sitter. We perceive Baudouin de Lannoy in much the same way as we perceive the portraits by Roger van der Weyden, which Panofsky has described "as studies in character rather than studies in individuality . . . as 'products of society' . . . almost as members of one aristocratic family."[8] Wealth, status, and power are all asserted in the *Baudouin de Lannoy*, and the social conventions that indicate those qualities are the very accessories—baton, Golden Fleece insignia—that are singled out in the costume presented by the picture.

In short, the portraits of the early 15th-century masters are meant to be understood as assertions of some kind of power and importance, whether the context of their commemoration was political or religious. This is so much clearer in the small "devotional diptychs" of Roger, which paired the portrait of the prestigious donor with an icon of equal size of the Madonna and Child.[9] We have already investigated (in Chap. 4) the portrait implications of this choice of format and presentation of the Madonna images, but it is a dialogue of equal importance to the new portraits of Roger's court patrons. In place of the wife of a wedding portrait diptych, these wealthy donors directly confront the Virgin to emphasize both their piety and their worldly importance by showing them as suppliants at a celestial audience. Van Eyck, of course, had provided the same line of thought in the mid-1430s on a monumental scale with his *Madonna of Chancellor Rolin* (Paris, Louvre).[10]

With Hans Memling, much of the world of assertion that had been developed within the courtly or patrician world of van Eyck and van der Weyden was diffused into the portraits that grew out of the urban setting of Bruges. In what is probably the most famous of Memling's devotional diptychs, *cf. Pl. 137* *Martin van Nieuwenhove* (1487, Bruges, St. John's Hospital)[11] confronts the Virgin directly across the space of a single room, a bourgeois domestic interior marked by attractive stained glass windows and a view out a window of both a bridge and a flat meadowland. The sitter is subtly distinguished from the holy figures by being turned at an angle while they remain frontal, by being placed within a separate wing of the diptych, and by being shown in prayerful attitude while the Virgin and Child remain impassive. Within the background of the picture, however, a rounded mirror reasserts the common space in which the figures reside. The presence of the Virgin within what is clearly an ordinary, earthly dwelling also eliminates the abstract gold or monochrome backgrounds of the earlier devotional diptychs, and it resolves the debate among art historians about whether the Virgin appears as a vision within Rolin's chateau or whether Rolin has been granted an audience within the celestial palace of the Madonna.[12] In the case of Memling's diptych, the Virgin is clearly manifest and immanent on earth. The implication of such a development is that the Virgin is approachable by, even nearby to, mortal men, and her grace pervades a tranquil world, like the view seen through the window of the *Nieuwenhove diptych.* Roger had already introduced this idea in the dramatic outdoor background of his *Braque triptych.*[13] But in Memling the idea of immanence is extended from van der Weyden's group, consisting exclusively of holy figures, to a combination of the divine and the earthly within the same framework.

Of course, by the inclusion of Nieuwenhove in the company of the Virgin, Memling was using traditional combinations to assert the importance of the young patrician; but in other pictures without the Virgin, with either husband and wife combinations in a diptych or even with isolated single individuals, he continued to employ architectural space or landscape background to underscore the assertion implicit in the very act of creating a portrait.[14] An example of this formula is the *Portrait of an Italian* in Antwerp, where the young sitter holds up a Roman coin of Nero, indicating in all probability that he was a numismatist.[15] Both the features of the man and the presence of a palm tree in the landscape behind him have been taken as evidence that he was an Italian; certainly his presence in front of the landscape suggests a state of harmony with his environment and, by virtue of his visual prominence in front of it, a certain dominance over the landscape. The sunny skies, green fields, and soft atmospheric haze suggest the same tranquility that appeared behind the Virgin in the 1487 *Nieuwenhove diptych.* Even in pictures where the identity is completely unknown and unmarked by attributes like the coin and the palm of the gentleman in the Antwerp portrait, Memling's sitters can *Pl. 144*
be seen to be persons of importance because of their presence in front of a landscape vista or within solid architectural spaces. A noteworthy example is the handsome young man with aristocratic bearing who appears beside a column that opens onto such a grove-filled background (New York, Lehman coll.), or the aged couple beside similar columns and in front of a unified landscape valley that is now split, together with the component panels of this marriage diptych, between Paris and Berlin.[16]

Massys was heir to these portrait formulas from the 15th century, and the portraits he made during the course of his career explore the variety of individual assertions that had been advanced by such pioneers as van Eyck, van der Weyden, and Memling. Unlike some contemporaries, such as Gossaert, who continued to present the sitters as part of a devotional diptych with the Madonna and Child (see Gossaert's *Carondelet diptych,* Paris, Louvre),[17] Massys seems to have presented humans only in isolation or in each other's company. Images of the Virgin or of Christ were always strictly separated from the world of men, even though the holy figures might well be presented, particularly in the later works, within a landscape or other earthly environment. While his sitters were never given dignity by directly meeting holy figures, they were always given some kind of personal, distinguishing attribute or trait that served to confer the same kind of assertion that we have already seen within the court portraits of van Eyck and van der Weyden and the urban world of Memling. Massys also presented his figures within impressive architectural spaces or in front of expansive landscapes. Frequently, he inserted attributes to facilitate indentification or the significance of his figures. Throughout his portraits, Massys remained as attentive to costume for his contemporary subjects as he had been to the archaic clothing of the grotesques in his secular satires.

What is impressive about the pendant portraits of *Erasmus* and *Gillis* is that two sitters are depicted *Pl. 99*
within a spatial environment, engaged in the work that defines their life and significance. Unlike the *Pl. 100*
world of Hans Memling's *Nieuwenhove,* the two figures depend only upon themselves, not upon contact with some transcendant reality or deity, for that significance. Human achievement (albeit often of a religious nature, as the labeled titles of Erasmus reveal)[18] in a human environment is now free-standing and independent. The two men are not noblemen, they are not shown in prayer, and they are not related except by friendship, unlike the previous pendant portraits that bear witness to the sacramental, lasting fidelity of husband and wife. Part of the intimacy and the specificity of the portrait occasion for *Erasmus* and *Gillis* is the result of the diptych's ownership by a mutual friend and fellow humanist, Thomas More. All these men would find lasting merit in such humanistic literary activity, a merit equivalent to the more conventional prayerful poses, meaningful attributes, or tranquil background landscapes of other contemporary portraits. In terms of definable action, circumscribed setting, and specific moment, the portraits of Erasmus and Gillis, then, mark a point of

furthest departure for Massys' work within this pictorial category. Other examples of his portraiture must be defined within the conventions circumscribing this very special case.

Pl. 138 In the first datable picture made by Massys (1509; F. 38, cat. 53), a work from the period of the two great altarpieces, the viewer is offered a vivid example of the assertion of an individual in terms of attributes crammed into the limits of a frame. A well-dressed man, wearing rings and fur-trimmed coat, is visible at half-length, spotlighted against a neutral, dark-green background. The dark clothes and the absence of any specific setting mean that the entire emphasis of the picture is on his face and his hands. He holds a piece of paper with an inscription which is meant to be read: "ETAS MEA 51 DUM SCRIBERETUR 1.5.0.9/FUI IN TERRA SANCTA." The sitter, then, who is not identified by name, is distinguished by the fact that he was a pilgrim to the Holy Land, a fact Massys underscores by the addition of a Jerusalem cross like a notary's seal, to the bottom of the *cartellino.* The man's age and the date (which possibly refers to the date of the pilgrimage, instead of the date of the painting) are the only other facts about him that the picture reveals.

Massys' image, then, is as much a religious document as a likeness. It testifies to the holy activity of the man in question at a time when going on pilgrimage was a sign of religious devotion (see the 1526 colloquy by Erasmus, "A Pilgrimage for Religion's Sake," which criticizes this practice) and was often connected with plenary indulgence.[19] Not only the pilgrimages, but also the records and descriptions of these pilgrimages were popular in the 15th and 16th centuries; the most widespread example is Bernhard von Breydenbach's *Peregrenationes in terram sanctam,* published in Mainz in 1486 and illustrated by Erhard Reuwich.[20] Thus, the distinction of having made such a pilgrimage was a badge of true honor for the sitter of Massys' portrait. In a portrait world where the sitter no longer was allowed the audiences with the Virgin and Child enjoyed by Memling's Bruges patrons, no more powerful a sign of piety could be presented, and it is likely that Massys' sitter insisted on his painted paper certificate for the record of his pilgrimage. Among Netherlandish portraits, the paper's formal inscription most resembles the *Wedding Portrait* (London) where Jan van Eyck inscribed his name as a witness to the sacramental proceedings in 1434: "JAN VAN EYCK FUIT HIC 1434."[21] Visually, too,
Pl. 139 the 1509 portrait depends most upon the example of Eyckian portraits, such as the *Jan de Leeuw* (1436; Vienna, Kunsthistorisches Museum), where the heavy shadows, neutral colored background, three-quarter turn of the head, and prominent hands in the bottom center of the panel all contribute to the continuity of a pictorial formula. Massys, like van Eyck, has not suppressed the wrinkles and imperfections in the face of the pilgrim; however, unlike van Eyck's figures, the *Pilgrim* glances obliquely rather than directly out at the viewer. The effect of this averted glance is a suggestion of a reflective mind which lacks the intensity and boldness of a van Eyck figure. Eyckian naturalism offered Massys a model of uncompromising starkness of presentation, combined here with an inscription to communicate the essential religious message of the portrait.

Other Massys portraits managed to communicate the aspects of religiosity so vital in the commemo-
Pl. 140 rative aspects of portraits. The most beautiful of these is the *Portrait of a Woman* (F. 48, cat. 60; New York), who appears at bust-length within an ornate columnar opening, holding a prayerbook. Details of the book indicate that it is one of the more expensive illuminated books of early 16th-century Bruges, part of the so-called Ghent-Bruges School of illumination headed by Simon Bening;[22] the gilded margins filled with naturalistic floral decoration are characteristic of Bening and his workshop. Paired with the New York *Woman* is her husband, a *Man* (F. 169, cat. 60), whose hand, barely visible over the lower edge of the picture, can be seen fingering the beads of a rosary. The rosary was a principal form of devotion to the Virgin, a cult which had first spread in the Netherlands in the 1470s, encouraged by Alain de la Roche and the Dominican Order.[23] Massys featured the rosary within two
Pl. 38 of his earliest Madonna icons, the London *Madonna and Child* (F. 25, cat. 1) and the Brussels half-
Pl. 39 length icon (F. 20, cat. 3), where the beads lie around the neck of the infant Christ. This rosary devotion was spread in literature and in painting during the last quarter of the 15th century,[24] and serves in the portrait as a mark of piety fully as distinctive as the prayerbook held alongside it.

The custom of juxtaposing husbands and wives in pendant portraits has its own tradition in the Netherlands. Many of the elements of Massys' pair find a precedent in the work of Hans Memling, most notably the portraits, hands clasped in prayer, of *Willem and Barbara Moreel* (Brussels).[25] The *Pl. 141* Moreel portraits feature complementary marble columns surmounting a parapet, which, in the case *Pl. 142* of Memling, runs visually along the neckline of the sitters rather than at their bustlines, as with Massys. Memling also features a harmonious green landscape, dotted with leafy round trees and distant castles, behind the Moreels; Massys will employ this same feature in a number of his late portraits. It is the same tranquil vista that Memling and, later, Massys employed as a complement to the images of the Madonna Enthroned. Extended to the portraits, this landscape provides a realm of prosperity and peacefulness for the pious, praying sitters. The Massys pendants of Schloss Au and New York use only the marble columns to suggest the exalted realm that will be the reward of the devout donors, but something of the landscape's lovely greenness is suggested by Massys in the fantastic vegetal ornament in stone adorning the span between the capitals. Such marble columns, together with rich stone carving, were also a feature of Madonna images by Massys, including the central structure of the *Holy* *Pl. 1* *Kinship* of the *St. Anne altarpiece* (Chap. 2), the Seilern *Madonna Standing* (F. 165/27; cat. 13), and the *Pl. 52* mighty throne of the Berlin *Madonna Enthroned* (F. 18, cat. 37; Chap. 4). In short, then, the Schloss *Pl. 63* Au–New York pendants suggest not only the piety of the husband and wife but also, perhaps, their eventual heavenly reward for that faith.

The suggestive landscape that was such a staple background element of Memling's mature portraits appears in a trio of Massys portraits from the 1520s: the Vaduz *Canon* (F. 39, cat. 65), the Edinburgh *Pl. 143* *Notary* (F. 45, cat. 64), and the Frankfurt *Man Reading* (F. 46, cat. 61). The identity of the *Canon* is not known, although there are tempting reasons to associate the image with the brother of Peter Gillis, Nicolai Claesz (Egidius). Nicolai was the only Antwerp canon listed during Massys' later years who was also a doctor of theology.[26] Dressed in the robes of his ecclesiastical office, the *Canon* is also identified as an academic by the biretta (cap) he wears.[27] The book in his hand and his reading spectacles reaffirm his scholarly-religious predilections. A signet ring on his finger points to a sense of family identity and some prosperity; it is worn on the same right forefinger as the signet on Peter Gillis's hand in the 1517 portrait by Massys (coll. Earl of Radnor, Longford Castle), and the shape and red color of the two rings appear to be quite similar. Although no firmer conclusions can be drawn from the visual evidence, the ring and the biretta together strongly suggest that the Vaduz *Canon* is none other than Nicolai Egidius.

Massys has used the spectacles and book to complement the seriousness of his sitter, already conveyed by the vestments and biretta. Unlike the New York *Woman,* who also holds a book but is portrayed in an animated temporary turn and glance, the *Canon* is a massive and stable visual pyramid within the frame of the portrait. Beside him, two slender trees serve further to balance the composition, reinforcing the air of stability and tranquility. The gaze of the *Canon* is also steady and direct, though calm. The gently rolling landscape dips slightly at its center to focus attention on the sitter. The hazy horizon and wispy clouds and the greenness of the setting suggest a warm, summery day and a relaxed and tranquil environment. The *Canon* clearly is within this landscape, even though he stands at its edge behind a balustrade. Whether this Elysium is an earthly realm of the pastor or whether it is meant to evoke his eternal reward is not made explicit, but the landscape is a fitting complement to the calm majesty of the Canon himself, a realm at once "peaceful, decorative, poetic, civilized."[28]

A landscape also appears behind the Massys Edinburgh *Notary.* The sitter appears here under an *Pl. 145* arcade; landscape appears through the openings between marble columns. This landscape is marked by framing hills, which focus attention on the features of the sitter. In the foreground of the landscape, a number of tiny figures in a village carry on peasant activities: milking, chopping, and dancing. This active country life is a departure from the almost unpopulated background of the Vaduz *Canon*—and its meaning is unclear, particularly in the absence of any information about the

sitter's identity. The Notary is clearly not located within the landscape, but instead is situated in a position to overlook it from his elevated viewpoint, as if it were his dominion.[29] This is a motif in some
Pl. 63 of Massys' Madonna pictures from the same general period (Berlin *Madonna Enthroned;* Paris *Rattier*
Pl. 68 *Madonna*) to show the regal status of the Virgin, despite her humble appearance. In the case of the *Notary,* such a commanding view over the background landscape could point to extensive property holdings and a literal landlord status over the countrylike area surveyed. But it could equally well be understood metaphorically as an image of a special harmony with nature reserved for the faithful servants of the Lord.[30] The landscape behind the Edinburgh *Notary* would then be a vision analogous to the pastoral world of the Vaduz *Canon,* except adjusted to a more active, less contemplative profession. While this interpretation cannot be demonstrated with certainty, one should note, once again, the importance of the transfer of relational imagery between the subject and the setting of a picture from the religious images of the Madonna to a commemorative image of a mortal individual. The problem of interpreting the landscape is complicated by the fact that the Notary is depicted with a halo above his head in the picture's current condition; while this halo is in all probability an even later addition, it could have been added to the portrait shortly after its completion to note the decease of the sitter.

Also contributing to the mystery about the *Notary* is the combination of elements he holds in his hand: a rose and a cross, in addition to the quill pen that is one of the essentials of his clerical trade. In all likelihood, however, the cross associates the Notary with a religious confraternity in Antwerp, rather than marking his death. The most-prominent and the oldest (founded in 1375) of the local Antwerp religious associations was, in fact, dedicated to the Holy Cross (see Chapter 1). Its select membership consisted of the "spiritual and secular aristocracy,"[31] and usually its treasurer was one of the city's secretaries. Another of the principal confraternities, the Guild in Praise of Our Lady (Gilde van Onze Lieve Vrouw Lof), also numbered the richest citizens among its members,[32] and could have prompted the gesture of piety by the Notary; his small rose is a traditional symbol of the Virgin, especially when viewed, as here, in the company of a cross. In short, the two symbols are as much a profession of piety on the part of the Notary as was the text describing his trip to the Holy Land by the *Pilgrim* in 1509. Unfortunately, the *Notary* has left behind an emblem without any explanatory text; his visual symbols can be read only on the most general level, without the specific significance that their juxtaposition or local connotation could arouse for the contemporary beholder.[33]

Very little else can be determined about the Notary. The two rings on his fingers indicate prosperity. The inkpot, quill-holder and paring-knife, wax box, and seal press serve together with the quill in his hand to identify him as an official scribe, but none of the elements of his costume reveals any further specific information. The Edinburgh portrait commemorates both the occupation and the piety of the *Notary*—it is in both senses a "profession" of his identity—but all further meaning of the picture (as is so often the case with portraits) has been lost along with the name of the sitter.

The final Massys image with a background landscape seems also to have been a portrait of a man of
Pl. 146 learning: the Frankfurt *Man Reading.* Distinctive millinery in the form of a broad-brimmed hat with flaps tied in front indicates that the Frankfurt picture is earlier than the Edinburgh *Notary,* as comparison with Dürer's drawings of the fashions of 1520-21 in Antwerp confirm.[34] Frankfurt's *Man Reading* shares with the Edinburgh *Notary* the same columnar arcade and elevated viewpoint over a handsome background scenery. In this case, the landscape is unpopulated, but it does feature a dominant castle on a hillside in the right half of the picture. On the left side is a tranquil river valley. Again, the meaning of this Frankfurt scenery cannot be assessed with certainty, but what is striking in this case is the contrast between the two halves of the picture: a mighty fortress on one side, a gentle expanse on the other. The most mundane explanation would find in this castle the patrician dwelling of the sitter, but this contrast of elements reinforces the basic movement within the picture, a decisive turn and gesture by the *Man Reading* in response to someone outside the frame of the picture. The line of the river follows the line of sight of his eyes and also helps to direct the viewer's attention outward. It is conceivable that the landscape could suggest contrasting aspects of the character of the

sitter. Regardless of specific interpretation of its images, the *Man Reading*, like the *Notary* and the *Canon*, is presented in a kind of *Stimmungsporträt*, to borrow Panofsky's term, a portrait "in which the borderline between the figure and its surroundings, . . . between the indoors and the outdoors has become fluid and all particulars are submerged in soft luminosity, the mind is no longer distracted by a multiplicity of equally compelling details but relaxes in a sense of all-enveloping unity."[35] Unlike the other two portraits with landscape, however, the contrasting portions of the background, together with the emphatic action of the sitter, infuse a disquieting tension and imbalance into the image.

The character of the *Man Reading* is revealed through many of the same attributes as other portraits by Massys. His gown appears to be an academic robe, or *cappa clausa*.[36] The open book on the table and the spectacles also reveal the sitter as a reader, like Massys' *Erasmus* or the New York *Woman* and like *Pl. 99* the later Vaduz *Canon*. Also like the *Man Reading*, the New York *Woman* glanced up from her reading *Pl. 140* and turned outward toward some visitor beyond the frame of the portrait. The 1517 *Peter Gillis* had *Pl. 100* created a precedent for the active scholar gesturing and looking sympathetically outward as if to speak. This suggestion of speech is heightened in the Frankfurt *Man Reading* by the rhetorical gesture of his right hand, lifted as if in protest or argument. No other Massys portrait has such energetic movement or such a suggestion of power as his massive figure, roused into movement and staring intently at his objective.

Peculiarities in the forms of the *Man Reading* become more comprehensible when we discover the name of the sitter. The distinctive blocky head of the Frankfurt portrait matches the features of Peter Gillis's close friend and humanist associate, Cornelius Grapheus (d. 1558).[37] Grapheus was an Antwerp city secretary as well as a Latin scholar who had helped to establish a Latin school in the city.[38] Together with Gillis, he had composed the tributes for the Antwerp 1520 reception of the young Emperor Charles V.[39] Dürer befriended Grapheus during his visit to Antwerp in 1521; his diary of those years also mentions a sketch in hard chalk of Grapheus, but unfortunately the drawing has not until now been identified. Research through the Dürer *corpus* of drawings, however, does reveal a now-lost portrait (formerly Schlossmuseum, Weimar) that bears a striking resemblance to the *Pl. 147* Frankfurt *Man Reading*.[40] To make the leap for identifying this common sitter as Grapheus, however, is a more difficult task. The only certain extant portrait of Grapheus shows him as a considerably older man, bearded after the fashion introduced by Charles V during the 1520s. That portrait is an engraving by P. Galle for the volume *Virorum doctorum effigies*.[41] In spite of the beard, however, and the *Pl. 148* passage of well over a decade since the Massys and Dürer portraits, this engraved likeness of Grapheus has features in common with both earlier works: the same prominent nose, fleshy lower lip, and massive head. Another curious correspondence between the two images is that both Galle and Massys feature the same intent gaze and similarly active responses in the abrupt turn of head and body. Perhaps something of the energy and power of Grapheus is expressed through these common means.

Strongly attracted by Erasmus's suggestions of Church reform, Grapheus had published his own zealous ideas as the preface to a book, *De libertate christiana* by Johann Pupper van Goch. On 22 April, 1522, Grapheus was forced to recant his ideas publicly in the Antwerp cathedral after a strong reaction against "Lutheran" sympathizers, and he even fled the city for a time. Eventually, Grapheus returned to Antwerp and again became city secretary and the designer of future civic pageants.[42] But his portrait by Massys could not have been possible in the years immediately following the 1522 stigma of heresy. Judging by both the clothing fashions and the stylistic features of the image within Massys' development, the picture was painted at the height of Grapheus's fame in Antwerp, in other words just before 1522. Both the scholarly inclinations and the strong personal convictions that we know of the historical Grapheus are conveyed by the portrait, and the association of Grapheus with Gillis also lends weight to the identification of the Frankfurt *Man Reading* with the name Cornelius Grapheus.

All three of the Massys portraits with landscape background seem to have some connection with the world of scholarship and learning; in particular, two of the sitters (Nicolai Egidius, Cornelius Grapheus) appear to have had personal ties to Peter Gillis, whom Massys also portrayed on two separate occasions (1517 in the diptych with Erasmus; with his wife in the Oldenburg pendants).

Moreover, each of the sitters has expressed piety through the object in his hands, whether prayerbook or cross and rose. As a group, then, the portraits with landscape background attest to a contact that had seemed evident from the evidence of the secular satires: a contact with Gillis and other Antwerp friends of Erasmus. Even if we knew nothing of the identities of these three men (and the evidence for their identities remains far from certain), we could still discern Massys' sympathy for their piety simply by the visual transposition of the warm and sunny background settings from his late Madonna images (e.g., Berlin, Detroit, Rotterdam, and *Rattier Madonnas*—see Chap. 4) into the realm of portraiture.

In contrast with the earliest of Massys' portraits, this use of background landscape or even framing marble columns is startling. Massys' first essays into portraiture were conventionalized effigies without much attempt to convey animation. The finest example of the early portraits, the Chicago *Man with a*
Pl. 149 *Flower* (F. 47, cat. 52), features a subject against a neutral, pastel-colored background. Despite the delicate placement of the hands of the sitter on the bottom edge of the picture, his three-quarter profile pose and fixed expression contribute to a static and timeless portrayal. In the generalized softness of description, in the absence of any background setting, and in the conventionalized pose, this Massys portrait strongly recalls the formulaic court portraits made by Roger van der Weyden in Brussels half a century earlier. Panofsky's masterful characterization of the van der Weyden portraits[43] could as easily stand for Massys' *Man with a Flower:* concentration on salient features of both physiognomy and psychology, use of linear modeling with less-intense lighting for a two-dimensional effect, and a tendency toward abstract elegance and the expression of general qualities. This tendency
Pl. 138 is particularly striking in contrast to the Winterthur *Pilgrim* of only a few years later (1509), where powerful lighting contrasts on both figure and background and the momentary averted glance of the sitter suggest both activity and thought plus a lively expression of both space and time.

Massys' *Man with a Flower* is another painted assertion of piety, expressed through the small bloom held in the man's hand. Although its blue color is unusual, the shape of the flower resembles a carnation. Carnations appear in the *Seilern Madonna* and in the *Holy Kinship,* where they refer to the Incarnation of Christ and to the Passion.[44] The Incarnation association results from the pink, fleshlike tones of the flower, reflected in its English name; the connection with the Passion in its spiky, nail-like shape, which gives rise to the Germanic name for the bloom: nail-flower *(nelke* or *nagelboem).* Thus, the presence of the carnation within the Madonna images results from the association of the flower with Christ, but in portraits it seems to have had different overtones.[45] Within portraits in general, the carnation seems to have connoted pious hopes for salvation, as in the tiny triptych of donors, saints, and Madonna and Child by Hugo van der Goes in Frankfurt with its inscription "En esperance" (In hope);[46] there, Christ still holds the carnation, but He extends it outward toward the viewer and brandishes it like a trophy of reward for the faithful. A later portrait with a carnation, *Petrus van Clapis* (1537; Cologne, Wallraf-Richartz Museum) by Bartel Bruyn the Elder bears the inscription "Dum spiro spero" (While I breathe, I hope).[47] Flowers are also a traditional sign of betrothal,[48] suggesting that the commitment implied by Christ to the worshipper in a portrait is sealed by His floral offering. Like the combination of rose and cross held by the Edinburgh *Notary,* the carnation of the Chicago *Man with a Flower* is both a conventionalized symbolic commemoration of the piety of the sitter and an expression of his hope for the divine reward for his faith.

The immediate source for Massys' *Man with a Flower* need not have been van der Weyden, but again seems to have come through the intervention of the painters of Bruges. A similar visual formula from
Pl. 150 Bruges in Massys' own day was the portrait by Gerard David, the *Goldsmith* (Vienna, Kunsthistorisches Museum), where the figure, against a soft green background, clasps the cylinder of rings which is the attribute of his profession. But once again, the principal source seems to have been Hans Memling, whose portraits were far more numerous than those of David and also frequently featured the linear description and monochrome backgrounds adopted by Massys in the *Man with a Flower.* Strikingly close to the Chicago portrait is a Memling *Man with a Carnation* (New York, Morgan Library), where the only major difference from Massys is the direction of the sitter's gaze.

The social rank of the *Man with a Flower* is not particularly lofty. He wears a simple tunic without the fur trim which characterizes even the scholars, such as Gillis, among Massys' sitters. But other Massys portraits reveal a less-modest cast of characters, particularly during the period in which the artist was working on the great altarpieces and establishing himself as Antwerp's leading painter. Another of Massys' earlier portraits is the *Wealthy Man* in New York (F. 41, cat. 51), who is dressed in an extravagant costume of embroidered gilt brocade with fur trim. His sporty cap bears an insignia medallion, and he also carries a sword, the prerogative of a nobleman. This portrait, too, is an assertion of more than the wealth and status of the sitter, for he carries in his hand a blue flower, which has been identified as a sprig of borage, a sign of betrothal.[49] From a later period than the *Wealthy Man* (close in time to the dated 1517 Karlsruhe *Man,* F. 194, cat. 57) comes a pair of portraits of husband and wife (cat. 55; Badminton, coll. Lady Altrincham) which also seems to suggest a higher social rank than most of Massys' portrait sitters. What is distinctive about the dress of the Badminton pair are the fine gold chains around the necks of both husband and wife. Chains were a badge of office and rank during Massys' day,[50] and the artist used chains in another context to demonstrate the official status of Pontius Pilate as procurator—in the Coimbra, Prado, and Venice *Ecce Homo* pictures. The bit of folded paper in the man's hand may pertain to his office, but it also affords the opportunity for the artist to sign his name—a signature unique among his painted portraits. Both the social prominence of the sitters and the presence of a signature suggest that Massys was proud of his accomplishment in these Badminton pendants, at least insofar as he commemorated his own work as well as the character of his worthy sitters.

Pl. 151

Pl. 152
Pl. 153
Pl. 154

Pl. 86
Pl. 87

After these two more opulent examples, the dress and the other identifying marks of Massys' sitters remain fairly constant. Most of the portraits feature men of prosperous appearance in fur-trimmed gowns but without the obvious fortune of the *Wealthy Man,* who appears like a dandy of the court in contrast to the solid, sober cluster of Massys' other portraits. Very little can be determined about the Massys sitters, particularly from the pictures with monochrome backgrounds. Except for the ecclesiastical garb of the *Canon,* the academic robes of *Erasmus* and the *Man Reading,* and the gold chains of the Badminton couple, no distinguishing features of costume single out the individuals according to profession or social rank, although Massys uses attributes, like the accessories of the *Notary* and the book and spectacles of the *Man Reading,* to describe their occupations. In the case of *Erasmus* and *Gillis,* of course, the identity and the professions of the two famous sitters were the entire reason for the picture, and Massys has not only managed to show the two scholars engaged in their typical daily activities, but has managed to convey specifics of their common setting, including Erasmus's book titles. By including even a legible letter from their mutual friend, Thomas More, who was to be the recipient of the "Friendship Diptych," Massys, indirectly, could also memorialize the English humanist. Aside from professional and personal attributes, however, other Massys sitters display only signs of their piety: prayerbooks, rosaries, flowers, pilgrimage souvenirs. Women never appear in Massys portraits except in the company of their husbands.

The unusual images of famous men by Massys deserve attention as exceptions to the general anonymity and local middle-class origin of his sitters. The first of these is a portrait of an exiled king, *Christian II of Denmark* (F. 172, cat. 42; Kroměřice). The husband of Isabella of Austria, sister of Emperor Charles V, Christian II (1481–1559) first visited Antwerp in 1521.[51] At that time, Dürer recorded meeting and sketching him in the diary of his own visit to the Lowlands (2 July 1521); ten days later, Dürer completed an oil portrait, now lost, of the monarch at the court of Brussels.[52] Christian II sought out works of art by other painters besides Dürer.[53] Two years later, while the king was in exile in Brussels, Jan Gossaert drew his portrait (Paris, Institut Néerlandais) in a sumptuous and regal manner.[54] Before a triumphal, Roman-style arch blazoned with heraldry of the provinces ruled by the king, Christian sits in a majestic half-length pose as if he were at a balcony giving an audience.[55] His thick beard and massively posed figure fill the frame of the arch and visually assert the dominion that is proclaimed by the arms behind him. It is ironic that the drawing was composed at a time when Christian no longer had power over the areas claimed by the image.[56] He had sought sanctuary under the protection of his Habsburg relatives in Brussels from his usurping uncle,

Pl. 155

Pl. 156

Frederick. The Gossaert drawing was intended for an engraving that would have served as a kind of royal propaganda, a claim from exile to both the territory and the trappings of the Danish throne.

In contrast to the splendor and majesty of the Gossaert *Christian II,* Massys' portrait barely asserts his power or prestige. The king is seated at a table, holding his own symbolic carnation and glancing outward to the side, like the Massys image of the *Man with a Flower,* rather than staring directly at the viewer, as in the Gossaert drawing. Also like the *Man with a Flower,* Massys' *Christian II* holds a symbol of his piety, a carnation, in his right hand. This was by no means an unprecedented portrayal of a prince; for example, the portrait of Emperor Maximilian (Vienna; 1510 or earlier) by Joos van Cleve[57] has much the same formula, although there the Emperor dominates the entire picture surface and is dressed in royal robes, which quickly distinguish him from Massys' more humble *Man with a Flower* of the same approximate date. What is most striking about the Massys image is the degree to which the portrait formula chosen by the artist could pertain equally well to any individual and seems, therefore, hardly distinctive enough as a form of presentation for a monarch. The insignia of the Order of the Golden Fleece (which the King had received two years earlier, in 1519),[58] climaxes a fashionable tunic with slashed openings; but in contrast with the sumptuous display of furs and stuffs in the Gossaert drawing, Christian's costume in the Massys portrait is modest. We are more likely to identify the New York *Wealthy Man* as a rich and powerful figure than to do the same for Massys' *Christian II.*

Pl. 149

In part, the propaganda purpose of the Gossaert image must have encouraged the intensified majesty and pomp of that drawing. Massys' image was commissioned in 1521, according to the records of payment in the King's accounts;[59] it was made, therefore, at a time when the king's office and status were not cast into doubt, as they had been during the period of exile in 1523, when Gossaert made his portrait. Gossaert, however, was a court painter in Brussels for Margaret of Austria, and he had previously served in the same role as portrayer of nobility when he worked in the service of Philip of Burgundy.[60] Unlike Massys, Gossaert was habituated to depictions of this eminent rank of sitter and to the concomitant emphasis on the richness of costume and majesty of bearing that go with that rank. Massys, the civic painter of the middle class, relied most strongly for his model of portraits of nobility on the elegant aristocratic images of members of the Burgundian court around Philip the Good by Roger van der Weyden more than half a century earlier. As we have seen, however, in the case of the *Man with a Flower,* Massys had already adopted the van der Weyden portrait formula for less-noble sitters, so the resemblances between *Christian II* and the *Man with a Flower*—monochrome background, linear description, averted pose and gaze, and elegant, yet generalized attitude—are as much a result of the readoption of a 15th-century portrait formula as a product of details like the hands with a flower. The devotional character of most of Roger's portraits of nobility had been used by Massys for devotional images of both the urban bourgeoisie and for the one example of nobility he was ever called upon to paint. *Christian II* is the exception in Massys' career which proves the rule that he was truly a painter of the urban middle class.

Pl. 157

One other exceptional picture in Massys' *oeuvre* deserves mention in the context of portraiture. Painted originally on paper, the bust portrait of an *Old Man* (1513; Paris, Musée Jacquemart-André, F. 51, cat. 54) is the only portrait other than the Badminton pendants to have been signed by the artist: "Quintinus Metsys Pingebat ANNO 1513."[61] The use of a Latin inscription and the block letters (in contrast to the Gothic script of his Badminton signature) are a unique feature in Massys' *oeuvre* which, together with the paper support, point to some extraordinary circumstances surrounding the creation of the *Old Man* portrait. In Massys' medal work (see Appendix A), however, such inscriptions are a more common feature, and the bust profile, facing left, of the *Old Man* also corresponds to the formula employed in portrait medals.[62] Massys' 1519 portrait medal of Erasmus is well documented by the letters of the humanist (see Chap. 6)[63] and has served as the basis of the attribution of several other portrait medals to Massys, most of them from the 1490s, a time when the young Antwerp artist was less-distant from the family forge. Certain of the letters in the inscription of the *Old Man* (S,T,E) suggest the particular graphic style of the medallion inscriptions, as if the portrait were a study for a portrait medal or an imitation of such a medal.

The identity of the *Old Man* was first established by Hymans as Cosimo de' Medici (d. 1464), unproclaimed ruler and official "Pater patriae" of Florence and the man who brought the Medici Bank to the zenith of mercantile dominion during the second quarter of the 15th century.[64] Images of Cosimo were available because of portrait medallions struck in Florence shortly after his death;[65] in all likelihood, Massys the medallist borrowed his own image of Cosimo from such a portrait medal, *Pl. 158* although there is some possibility that a Leonardo da Vinci drawing of Cosimo might also have intervened in the creation of the *Old Man* image.[66] From the image of Cosimo in the medal, Massys borrowed not only Cosimo's face, but also his peculiar hat, though the Antwerp artist altered it by raising its crown and giving it a soft, puffy, crushed-velvet appearance. In accordance with Antwerp fashion and the costumes of his own portraits, Massys also gave his Cosimo figure a fur-trimmed robe as a demonstration of his prosperity.

Confirmation of the identity of the sitter as Cosimo de' Medici is given by another posthumous portrait of the Florentine (Florence, Uffizi), this time made for the Medici family by Pontormo, so its canonical accuracy is assured.[67] Pontormo's *Cosimo* has the same features as Massys' *Old Man:* *Pl. 159* pendulous lower lip, deep-set eyes, and sloping brow. In addition, the Pontormo portrait features a hat that is more like the soft, high-topped bonnet of Massys than the hard, low-topped headgear of the Cosimo medals. (Of course, the two works may well have had a common model, now unknown or lost, such as the hypothetical Leonardo drawing.)

Not only do similar heads appear in Leonardo's drawings, such as Windsor Castle images singled out by Kenneth Clark as having "a look of Cosimo de' Medici, Pater Patriae,"[68] but there are also several examples in Leonardo's grotesque drawings of similar hats (Windsor Castle, nos. 12458, *Pl. 125* 12475, 12478). Since the profile head is a characteristic form of a Leonardo study of a head, whether grotesque or ideal,[69] Leonardo might well have served, in addition to a portrait medal, as a source for Massys' *Cosimo.* As we have seen (Chap. 7), Cosimo's features are basic to the meaning of the secular image of the prosperous *Old Man* (New York) which is paired with the Leonardo-inspired grotesque *Pl. 123* *Old Woman.* Indeed, the New York *Old Man* and the Jacquemart-André *Old Man* of 1513 are identical, except for the fact that Massys added hands and a marble balustrade to his earlier portrait likeness in order to produce his secular half-length. In the case of the secular satire, knowing the identity of Cosimo is crucial to understanding the picture as a castigation of greed and pride. In the case of the 1513 portrait, however, no such satirical intent is evident, and the elaborate Latin signature suggests that quite an opposite effect was intended—the commemoration of the deceased Cosimo in a pictorial equivalent of a portrait medal.

The Pontormo image helps to suggest why Massys should have painted a portrait of Cosimo de' Medici in the first place. The year 1513 marked the accession of Giovanni de' Medici to the papacy as Leo X, an event eagerly awaited as the advent of a golden age in arts and letters under enlightened papal sponsorship.[70] Reís-Santos, who was the first to note this relationship between the Cosimo identity of the *Old Man* and the significance for the Medici of the year 1513 when Massys painted the posthumous portrait,[71] suggested that the use of the Medici patriarch as a subject was a deliberate tribute to the new pope and his family. This would explain the anomaly of the Latin inscription combined with the informal but easily portable paper support, unique among surviving Massys portraits.

This hypothesis of Massys' promotional tribute to the Medici merits consideration not only because it accounts for the peculiarities of the Paris painting, but also because it suggests a further possible explanation for the links between the Pontormo painting and the Massys image. Portormo's picture postdates the Massys[72] and offers the only analogy to the alterations of headgear made by the Antwerp artist. If the Massys image was integrated into the collections of the Medici family, then Pontormo could have seen it there and used it as a model for the posthumous portrait of Cosimo that he later presented to the Medici family. Once again, the two artists could well have used common sources—Cosimo portrait medals and/or a lost Leonardo drawing—for their common features. Nevertheless, the use of the features of the founding father of the Medici dynasty remains the common interest of both artists, and this distinctive, deceased Italian sitter helps to account for the unusual inscription and profile treatment of the *Cosimo de' Medici* among the Massys portrait *corpus*.

The *Cosimo*, even more than Massys' *Christian II*, resulted from an exceptional situation. The images of these two famous men, one of them a posthumous image, serve as a reminder that Massys was *not* principally a painter of famous men. Neither was he very often the painter even of wealthy men. Coats-of-arms, expensive costumes, inscriptions—for the most part, all the trappings of wealth, status, and power—are missing from the world of Massys' portraits, replaced only by the signs of piety or profession, the most basic assertions of identity.

Over the course of his career, Massys developed imaginative formulas for portraying the men of his time. From the simple monochrome background of early pictures such as the *Man with a Flower* and the *Pilgrim*, he developed images with additional suggestiveness and informative detail. Borrowing chiefly from the portrait precedent of Hans Memling of Bruges, Massys began to include either the interior setting of a man's occupation and interest or the sunny background landscapes that formed a complement to his spirit. In some cases, like the Frankfurt *Man Reading* or the Edinburgh *Notary*, he used a mixture of interior and exterior environments.

For the most part, however, these portraits with context are themselves exceptional in Massys' *oeuvre*, and they serve to mark the same kind of change we have already noted within his late religious works, the paintings which include the same kind of increased interest in the surroundings of the Madonna (landscape or interior) as these late portraits show for their sitters. The environments are, in fact, inspired by the analogy with the Madonna pictures and seem to be a special testimonial to the sanctity and importance of these particular men. They are, in fact, a definable group of scholarly and educated men, associated (when we can recover something specific about them despite the losses of time) with Erasmus and Peter Gillis. At a time when Massys is still content to use Rogerian 15th-century portrait formulas for other sitters and even repeats such a convention for the portrait of the King of Denmark, it is all the more noteworthy that his most colorful and detailed renditions of setting and his liveliest evocations of character are reserved for this small number of scholarly sitters and humanists. Beginning with the *Friendship Diptych* of *Erasmus* and *Gillis* and concluding with the outdoors image of Gillis's brother, Nicolai Egidius, the Vaduz *Canon*, Massys singles out this local intellectual elite for distinctive and favored treatment, clearly the expression of special admiration and sympathy.

In portraiture, therefore, the pattern of Massys' creative development parallels the changes that are also to be seen in both his religious images and his secular pictures. After some early contact with men of wealth and influence (the New York *Wealthy Man;* the Badminton pendants with the artist's signature), his principal clientele remained the well-to-do urban middle classes whose names are unknown today. But during the period initiated by the *Friendship Diptych*, Massys' contact with the Antwerp humanist community made a particularly vivid impression on him and transformed aspects of his portraiture, just as it had transformed his views on the sacred and the secular.

NOTES

1. Portraiture is still a neglected field in the Netherlands and in general. The basic work on Early Netherlandish portraits remains G. Ring, *Beiträge zur Geschichte niederländischer Bildnismalerei im 15. und 16. Jahrhundert*. On van Eyck and Roger portraits, see the perceptive summaries by Panofsky, *Early Netherlandish Painting*, pp. 194–201, 289–92, and more recently, L. Campbell, "The Portrait Art in the Work of van der Weyden," *Rogier van der Weyden*, exh. cat. (Brussels, 1979), p. 56ff. For general remarks, see M. J. Friedländer, *Landscape, Portrait, Still-Life* (New York, 1963). Also useful are some specialized studies of different regions or periods: J. Pope-Hennessey, *The Portrait in the Renaissance*; L. M. Sleptzoff, *Men or Supermen? The Italian Portrait in the Fifteenth Century* (Jerusalem, 1978); H. Gerson, "Hollandse portretschilders van de zeventiende eeuw," valedictory lecture, Groningen University, 1975.

2. The role of painted portraits as epitaphs or ex-votos should not be underestimated and will be found to be paralleled by sculpted memorials, from the familiar stones and brasses of European medieval pavements to the wall epitaph reliefs of mortals

and saints before the holy throne. For an analogy between such stone reliefs in Tournai and van Eyck's 1436 *van der Paele Madonna* (Bruges), see R. Terner, "Bemerkungen zur 'Madonna des Kanonikus van der Paele," pp. 83–91; for van Eyck's *Rolin Madonna* (Louvre), see A. H. van Buren, "The Canonical Office in Renaissance Painting, Part II: More about the Rolin *Madonna*," pp. 625–26; on epitaphs in general, see P. Schoenen, "Epitaph," *RDK* 5, cols. 872–921; H. Weckwerth, "Der Ursprung des Bildepitaphs," *Zeitschrift für Kunstgeschichte* 20 (1957): 150–55. On donor portraits in the Netherlands, see E. Heller, *Das altniederländische Stifterbild* (Munich, 1976). For the Tournai reliefs in particular, G. Ring, "Beiträge zur Plastik von Tournai im 15. Jahrhundert," *Belgische Kunstdenkmäler*, ed. P. Clemen (Munich, 1923) vol. 1, p. 269ff.; E. Panofsky, *Tomb Sculpture* (New York, 1964), p. 58. A stimulating survey of the relationship between Italian Renaissance bust portraits, ancient ancestor memorials, and medieval saints' reliquaries is provided by I. Lavin, "On the Sources and Meaning of the Renaissance Portrait Bust," *Art Quarterly* 33 (1970): 207ff.

3. E. Dhanens, *Van Eyck: The Ghent Altarpiece* (New York, 1973), p. 37ff. Blum, p. 13ff.

4. Dhanens, *Van Eyck*, p. 117ff. (with bibliography). Also see the infrared photographs of the *Annunciation*, published by P. Coremans, *L'Agneau Mystique au Laboratoire* (Antwerp, 1953), pp. 119–20, plate LXII.

5. Panofsky, p. 196ff., and "Who Is Jan van Eyck's 'Timotheos'?" *JWCI* 12 (1949): 80ff. Recently, the identity of the sitter as a Burgundian court musician has been challenged and replaced with the hypothesis that he is a sculptor instead: W. Wood, "A New Identification of the Sitter in Jan van Eyck's *Timotheus* Portrait," *Art Bulletin* 60 (1978): 650–54.

6. Panofsky, " 'Timotheos'," p. 80; Wood, "New Identification"; I. Lavin, "Renaissance Portrait Bust," p. 210, fig. 7; S. Ringbom, "Nuptial Symbolism in some Fifteenth Century Reflections of Roman Sepulchral Portraiture," p. 68ff.; N. de Grummond, "VV and Related Inscriptions in Giorgione, Titian, and Dürer," *Art Bulletin* 57 (1975): 346f.

7. Panofsky, *ENP*, pp. 198–99.

8. Ibid., pp. 290–91.

9. Ibid., p. 294ff.; K. A. Wirth, "Diptychon," *RDK* 4, cols. 64–74; Ringbom, pp. 45–46.

10. See note 2, above, especially van Buren; Blum, *Early Netherlandish Triptychs*, p. 2; J. Snyder, "Jan van Eyck and the Madonna of Chancellor Nicolas Rolin," *Oud Holland* 82 (1967): 163–71; Philip, *The Ghent Altarpiece*, pp. 190–92, 198–200.

11. Friedländer, vol. 6, no. 14; McFarlane, *Hans Memling*, pp. 13, 31.

12. Most recently discussed by Philip, *Ghent Altarpiece*.

13. Blum, pp. 29–36.

14. Panofsky, *ENP*, p. 349; McFarlane, p. 41.

15. Friedländer, vol. 6, no. 71; Panofsky, *ENP*, p. 349, n. 8; McFarlane, p. 14.

16. Friedländer, vol. 6, no. 74–75.

17. *Jan Gossaert genaamd Mabuse*, exh. cat., pp. 98–104, no. 11.

18. Trapp and Herbrüggen, *Sir Thomas More 1477 / 8-1535*, p. 41, no. 53; M. Mann Phillips, "The Mystery of the Matsys Portrait," pp. 18–21; Campbell, Phillips, Herbrüggen, and Trapp, "Quentin Matsys, Desiderius Erasmus, Pieter Gillis, and Thomas More," pp. 719–20. The heritage of author portraits in illuminated Christian manuscripts lies behind the forms and the content of the *Erasmus*; see D. Klein, "Autorenbild," *RDK* 1, cols. 1309–13.

19. Thompson, *Colloquies of Erasmus*, p. 285ff. On the practice of pilgrimage, see Chapter 1, this volume, no. 147.

20. On Breydenbach, R. W. Fuchs, "Die Mainzer Frühdrucke mit Buchholzschnitten 1480–1500," *Archiv für Geschichte des Buchwesens* 11 (1958–60): 31–71; *Albrecht Dürer 1471–1971*, exh. cat., p. 81, n. 136; p. 197, n. 377 (with bibliography). For depictions of the city of Jerusalem, C. H. Krinsky, "Representations of the Temple of Jerusalem before 1500," *JWCI* 33 (1970): 1–19.

21. The traditional identification of these sitters as Giovanni Arnolfini and his bride Jeanne Cenami has been challenged by P. Schabacker, "De Matrimonio ad morganiticum contracto," pp. 375–98. The classic study is by Panofsky, "Jan van Eyck's Arnolfini Portrait," p. 117ff. Also see his *ENP*, p. 201ff.

22. By F. Winkler, are four studies: "Studien zur Geschichte der niederländischen Miniatur-malerei," *JKSK* 32 (1915), 279ff.; *Die flämische Buchmalerei des XV. und XVI. Jahrhunderts* (Leipzig, 1925), p. 103ff; "Neudentdeckte Niederländer, I. Sanders Bening," *Pantheon* (1942): 261ff.; and "Sanders and Simon Bening and Gerard Horenbout," *Art Quarterly* (1946): 191ff. Also see O. Pächt, *The Master of Mary of Burgundy* (London, 1948); *Bibliothèque Nationale d'Autriche: Manuscrits et Livres Imprimés concernant l'histoire des Pays-Bas 1475–1600*, exh. cat. (Brussels, 1962). Ringbom, p. 193ff., discusses a group of miniature Passion narratives by Simon Bening: the Stein Triptych (Baltimore). Recently T. Kren, *Renaissance Paintings in Manuscripts*, exh. cat. (Malibu, 1983), pp. 3–85.

23. Prims, p. 140–41. See also Ringbom, p. 28; J. Snyder, "The Early Haarlem School of Painting II. Geertgen tot sint Jans," p. 131; Delaruelle, Labaude, and Ourliac, pp. 780–82; Toussaert, pp. 285–86. R. Flahault, *Le Rosaire et ses confréries dans la Flandre maritime XIII–XIXe siècle* (Dunkerque, 1896), claims to have found a record of a confraternity of the rosary as early as 1430 in Houdeghem, confirmed by indulgence by Pope Eugenius IV in 1444, but his claims of 13th- and 14th-century devotions are highly suspect (cited by Toussaert, notes 25–26). The first brotherhood of the rosary is usually cited as that founded in Douai in 1470. In 1479 Pope Sixtus IV established the cult practice throughout Europe.

24. Ringbom, "*Maria in Sole*," pp. 326–30; for woodcuts of the rosary cult, see R. Field, *Fifteenth Century Woodcuts and Metalcuts*, exh. cat., (Washington, 1965), nos. 169, 173.

25. Friedländer, vol. 6, no. 68; on Memling's *Moreel triptych*, see Blum, p. 97ff.

26. Prims, p. 57. Nicolai Egidius died in 1534. A list of the other thirteen canons of 1517 is given by Prims, p. 48.

27. W. N. Hargreaves-Mawdsley, *A History of Academic Dress in Europe* (Oxford, 1963), p. 175ff.; J. Braun, "Biretta," *RDK* 2, cols. 745–50.

28. The description of Memling's portrait landscapes is given by K. MacFarlane, p. 41.

29. The vineyards behind Nicolas Rolin in van Eyck's *Rolin Madonna* have been associated with the actual possessions of the donor by J. Snyder, "Jan van Eyck."

30. This is essentially the interpretation advanced by van Buren, "Canonical office," pp. 620–22, for the *Rolin Madonna,*

where the vineyard is advanced as a metaphor for spiritual husbandry. L. B. Philip, "Ghent Altarpiece," p. 192ff., discusses the natural landscapes in the backgrounds of Eyckian paintings as the metaphor for Heaven itself, and it is quite possible that the extension of these naturalistic images from religious art to portraiture was intended to be part of the act of pious prayer for the sitters' souls.

31. Prims, p. 124. On confraternities in general, see Chapter 2, note 32.

32. Prims, pp. 127–34, esp. 130.

33. They have even been seen in conjunction by some writers as indicating a "rosy cross" or Rosicrucianism, but to invoke this mysterious early 17th-century movement (which, if it ever really existed, was centered in the Rhineland) is anachronistic and unwarranted. Just how inappropriate such an association is can be discovered by consulting F. Yates, *The Rosicrucian Enlightenment* (London, 1972); also R. S. Westman, "Magical Reform and Astronomical Reform: The Yates Thesis Reconsidered," *Hermeticism and the Scientific Revolution* (Los Angeles, 1977), pp. 1–91.

34. Men's hats and caps seem to have shifted in fashion rapidly during this period and can be traced in J. H. der Kinderen-Besier, *Mode Metamorphosen De Kleedij onzer voorouders in de zestiende eeuw* (Amsterdam, 1933), esp. p. 71ff. Comparison with the
Pl. 100 caps of *Peter Gillis* (cat. 58, F. 37) and the Karlsruhe *Man* (F. 194, cat. 57), both by Massys and dated 1517, will establish the
Pl. 152 nature of the millinery changes. The peculiar hat of the Frankfurt *Man Reading* finds its closest comparisons in drawings made by Dürer during his 1520–21 visit to Antwerp and the Netherlands (Goris and Marlier, *Dürer Diary,* nos. 13 [Lazarus Ravensburger], p. 49 [Rodrigo Fernandez d'Almada], p. 53).

35. Panofsky, *ENP,* pp. 316–17.

36. Hargreaves-Mawdsley, *Academic Dress,* p. 175ff.

37. A biographical sketch is provided by E. J. Roobaert, "De Seer Wonderlijcke Schoone Triumphelijcke Incompst van de Hooghmogenden Prince Philips in de Stadt van Antwerpen Anno 1549," *BMRBA* 9 (1960): 44f., n. 63; F. Prims, "Grapheus en Goch," "Het eigen Werk van Cornelius Grapheus," *Antwerpiensia* 12 (1938): 165–84. On Gillis, Grapheus, and other members of the Erasmus circle in Antwerp, see G. Degroote, "Erasmofilie te Antwerpen in de eerst helft van de zestiende eeuw," pp. 31–51; M. Sabbe, "Erasmus en zijn Antwerpsche vrienden," pp. 61–78.

38. F. Prims, "Het ontluiken van het Humanisme te Antwerpen," p. 523ff.

39. F. Prims, "De 13 Hypothesen van Pieter Gillis 1520," pp. 159–64.

40. Goris and Marlier, *Dürer Diary,* 84, 98, fig. 56 (W.811); see also W. Strauss, *Complete Drawings of Albrecht Dürer,* vol. 4 (New York, 1974), pp. 2056–57, no. 1521 / 32.

41. Roobaert, "Seer Wonderlijke Schoone," ill. 1. Published in Antwerp, 1572, fo. 4.

42. Ibid. and the other references cited in note 37.

43. Panofsky, *ENP,* p. 290ff. See also the essay by L. Campbell, "Work of Van der Weyden," p. 56ff.

44. I. Bergström, "Disguised Symbolism," pp. 303ff., 342ff., esp. 307, n. 13. On p. 345, n. 31, Bergström interprets the carnation as meaning "Resurrection through Christ." The flower was introduced to Europe only ca. 1450. The fullest discussion of the symbolic carnation is I. Bergström, *Den symboliska nejlikan.* Disputation by G. Stridbeck, "Den gatfulla nejlikan," p. 81ff. "Nejliksymbolen än en gang," *Kunsthistorisk Tidskrift* 30 (1961), 30ff. Discussion of carnations and other symbolic flowers is R. Koch, "Flower Symbolism in the Portinari Altarpiece," pp. 70–77. Most recently, see M. C. Leach, "Michelangelo Invenit, Joos van Cleve Explicavit," *Studies in Iconography* 5 (1979): 93–106.

45. Bergström, *Den Symboliska Nejlikan,* pp. 87–162.

46. Friedländer, vol. 9, no. 5; Panofsky, *ENP,* p. 338, n. 3. The triptych was donated by William van Overbeke and Johanna de Keysere, who were married on 5 February 1478; in all likelihood, the marriage sacrament prompted their pious donation, as
Pl. 37 the 1518 marriage of Lucas Rem was to stimulate a later commission from Massys (F. 3, cat. 24; see Chapter 3). Flowers, like fruit, are a traditional sign of betrothal, suggesting in this panel that the commitment between the partners is sanctioned by Christ through the marriage sacrament (see Ringbom, "Nuptial Symbolism").

47. Bergström, *Den Symboliska Nejlikan,* pp. 105–6, n. 1. In isolated portraits, then, the contract sealed by the flower is between the pious donor and Christ.

48. Ringbom, "Nuptial Symbolism:" E. Wolffhardt, "Beiträge zur Pflanzensymbolik," p. 190ff.

49. H. Wehle and M. Salinger, *Catalogue of the Early Flemish, Dutch, and German Paintings,* p. 106.

50. J. Held, *Rembrandt's Aristotle and other Rembrandt Studies* (Princeton, 1969), pp. 32–38; Z. Filipczak, "The Golden Chain in the Self Portraits of Rubens and Van Dyck," lecture, College Art Assn., 1978. See S. Sullivan, "Rembrandt's Self-Portrait with a Dead Bittern," *Art Bulletin* 62 (1980): 238, n. 16–18.

51. Married to Isabella of Austria, sister of Charles V, he sought sanctuary under Hapsburg protection from his usurping uncle, Frederick, after attempting to install the nascent Lutheran faith in Denmark. During his exile, Christian II had his portrait drawn by Jan Gossaert and then engraved. This beautiful drawing is in the Lugt collection, Institut Néerlandais, Paris (see *Jan Gossaert genaamd Mabuse,* exh. cat. p. 325ff., no. 65). A painting of the king's children, also by Gossaert, is at Hampton Court. For other portraits of Christian II, see M. J. Friedländer, "Bildnisse des Dänenkönigs Christian II," pp. 89–97; G. Glück, "Portraetter af Christian II og Hans Hustru Isabella," p. 15ff.

52. Goris and Marlier, *Dürer Diary,* pp. 99–100.

53. See Friedländer and Glück, in note 51; for Lucas Cranach's portraits of Christian II, see D. Koepplin and T. Falk, *Lukas Cranach,* exh. cat. (Basel, 1974), vol. 1, pp. 251, 351–52, nos. 160, 238.

54. *Jan Gossaert genaamd Mabuse,* p. 325ff., n. 65.

55. The significance of this pose for icons of Christ as King has been discussed by Ringbom, p. 39ff.

56. For the Hampton Court group portrait of Christian II's young children, see Friedländer, vol. 8, no. 79; *De eeuw van Bruegel,* exh. cat., pp. 111–12, no. 113; S. F. Christensen, "Portraetter af den Danske Princesse Dorothea, Pfalzgräfin der Rhein," *Kunstmuseets Aarskrift* 24 (1937): 130–44.

57. Friedländer, vol. 9, no. 71; L. von Baldass, "Die Bildnisse Maximilians I," *JKSW* 31 (1913/14): 295ff.; J. Hand, "Joos van Cleve," p. 37ff. The *terminus ante quem* is provided by the dated (1510) replica in the Musée Jacquemart-André, Paris.

58. Providing a *terminus post quem* for the Massys picture and virtually all other images of the king. On the knightly order of the Golden Fleece, founded in 1430 by Phillip the Good of Burgundy and later adopted by the Hapsburg relatives of Christian II, see *Het gulden Vlies,* exh. cat., (Bruges, 1962), p. 134, no. 54.

59. Glück, p. 15, n. 21a, citing C. F. Allen, *Breve og Aktskykken til Christian II's og Frederick's Historie* (Copenhagen, 1854), vol. 1, p. 210, n. 1: "meer betalt meester Quintyn die maler t'Antwerpen van meyns g.h.k. ansicht tho conterfiejten, als ich anders niet weet, 20 gulden."

60. *Jan Gossaert genaamd Mabuse* examines other instances of Gossaert's portraits of nobles, such as *Floris van Egmond* (pp. 129–30, no. 17) or the alleged *Baudouin of Burgundy* (pp. 215–16, no. 38); also P. Wescher, "The Departure of King Charles for Spain and Jan Gossaert," *Art Quarterly* 28 (1965): 155–66: G. von der Osten, "Studien zu Jan Gossaert," p. 465ff.

61. L. Silver, "Power and Pelf;" p. 70ff.; *De eeuw van Bruegel* exh. cat. (Brussels, 1963) p. 138, no. 165 (with bibliography). Broadley, "Quentin Matsys, p. 142ff., believes that the signature on the picture is a later addition, possibly in the 17th century, and at the same time he notes its anomalous quality compared to other Massys works. But he is also the only previous author to associate the Jacquemart *Old Man* with portrait medals (p. 146).

62. Broadley, "Quentin Matsys."

63. Gerlo, p. 18, and other references cited in Chapter 6.

64. H. Hymans, "L'Exposition des primitifs flamands à Bruges," *Gazette des Beaux-Arts* 27 (1902): 82; on Cosimo, see Silver, "Power and Pelf," p. 75ff. ; de Roover, *The Medici Bank.*

65. Silver, "Power and Pelf," p. 72; Hill and Pollard, *Renaissance Medals,* nos. 245–47.

66. Silver, pp. 69f., 72ff., on the hypothesis that Leonardo might have created a caricature profile portrait of Cosimo de' Medici, similar to his caricature of another Florentine patriarch, Dante (Windsor Castle, no. 12493), for the entertainment of his Milanese patrons of the 1490s.

67. The date of the Florence *Cosimo* by Pontormo and, consequently, its patron are currently in dispute. According to Vasari, who was in a good position to have accurate data for a 16th-century Medici portrait, the *Cosimo* was made for Goro da Pistoia, secretary of Lorenzo de' Medici, Duke of Urbino, who died in April 1519 (F.M. Clapp, *Jacopo Carucci da Pontormo* [New Haven, 1916], p. 47; K. Forster, *Pontormo* [Munich, 1966], 134–35). Recently, however, the inscription and heraldry on the portrait have been used to support a date of ca. 1537 for the powerful patron Cosimo I Medici (Vasari's own patron; J. Sparrow, "Pontormo's *Cosimo il Vecchio,*" *JWCI* 30 [1967]: 163).

68. Clark and Pedretti, *Drawings of Leonardo da Vinci,* p. 75, no. 12458; p. 83, no. 12491.

69. Gombrich, "Leonardo's Grotesque Heads," p. 57ff. L. von Heydenreich, *Leonardo da Vinci* (London/Basel, 1954), p. 112; Popham, *Drawings of Leonardo da Vinci,* p. 39ff.

70. The anticipation and optimism can be found in Erasmus's letters of the period: "this Julius . . . succeeded in rousing this hurricane of wars. Cannot Leo, who is scholarly, honourable, and devout, succeed in quieting it?" Allen and Allen, no. 288, to Antoon van Bergen, London, 14 March 1514; see also Erasmus's letter of 21 May 1515 from London to Pope Leo X himself: "When Pope Leo was placed at the helm, the world was conscious that by a sudden revolution a worse than iron age had become a golden one." The entire letter (Allen and Allen, p. 335) is an extended panegyric. See H. J. Hillerbrand, ed., *Erasmus and his Age* (New York, 1970), pp. 65ff., 80ff. The first quotation is taken from *Collected Works of Erasmus: The Correspondence of Erasmus* (Toronto, 1974–77), vol. 2, p. 282.

71. L. Réis-Santos, "Preface" to G. Marlier, *Erasme et la peinture flamande,* p. xii. His argument suggested without exposition or documentary support that it was Erasmus himself who commissioned the *Cosimo* from Massys.

72. Dating in all probability ca. 1518–19, but see above, note 67.

9

Conclusions: Contemporaries and Culture

Evaluating the accomplishment of a painter in isolation is a perilous task. On the one hand, to use the works of one man to suggest an image of an entire epoch or even to overstress fascinating oddities at the expense of more frequent, repeated—hence typical and informative—tasks raises numerous possibilities for distortion. Another danger of a monographic focus is that it almost inevitably leads to what Delaissé has characterized as "the aristocratic approach" to art criticism, the assumption that

> the artistic production of a milieu or epoch is entirely explained by the most important creators of the period, and they, in turn, are explained by each other as if they were transmitting the exclusive gift of artistic creation from one to the other.[1]

From this vantage point, which also divides "provinces" from "centers" of art, the creative "genius" of a seminal individual launches major new epochs of visual achievement. That creative spark is transmitted like a sacred flame to worthy successors, and thus the growth or development of a "style" is realized. This model has prevailed since the time of the archetypal art historian Vasari, in the 16th century. It was Vasari who spoke of the pioneers and promulgators of the Renaissance vision in Italy in terms of the lives of great artists, climaxing with the pinnacle of Michelangelo as *ne plus ultra*. In our own day, Renaissance historiography still clings to the structures of Vasari, e.g., in books which credit Leonardo da Vinci with the almost literal "birth" of the High Renaissance style.[2]

Massys, too, has been singled out by history as a creator-patriarch. In Ruben's day, a century after his own career, Quinten was considered as the founder of the Antwerp School of painting.[3] Modern art historians have seen him as a Janus figure, standing astride the threshold of the 16th century, midway between the visual worlds of "Gothic" and "Renaissance."[4] But there are plenty of good reasons for trying to see Massys in a larger artistic company, in what Delaissé calls the "more anonymous and shared participation in the innovations of late medieval art." Not the least of those reasons is the drive, especially in Massys' earlier works (but still present in retrospective late works, like the 1529 *Rattier Madonna*), not to create striking new works of genius, but instead to remake the famous models of 15th-century masters, according to what Friedlander has dubbed the "compulsion of the iconographic tradition."[5]

To establish a visual benchmark for Massys, we can turn our attention to a sensitive barometer for Antwerp art of the period between 1510 and 1530 in the form of a central individual: Massys' younger colleague and contemporary Joos van Cleve.[6] Joos's career swings like a weathervane with each successive stylistic fashion, so a recapitulation of his development can serve as a concise overview of major artistic currents in Antwerp. Following Delaissé, the issue for us is not merely to include another monograph within a monograph, to debate who initiated the visual formulas to be discussed, nor to promote Joos van Cleve as an artistic figure of genius. Instead, Joos's *oeuvre* will serve as a normative check on Massys' own career and as a means of ascertaining the purposeful choices and interpretations of subjects by each artist.

Joos van Cleve (d. 1540) was admitted as a master in the Antwerp St. Luke's guild in 1511, the same year in which Massys completed his St. John or *Lamentation altarpiece* for the shrineworkers' guild. Although van Cleve is two decades younger than Massys, his early career is strikingly similar in orientation, strongly reflecting the Madonna imagery of Bruges. Hand has argued that Joos was active in Burges prior to his arrival in Antwerp, i.e., roughly during the period 1508/09 and 1511.[7] Joos's earliest Madonna picture, a half-length of the *Virgin and Child Adored by St. Bernard* (Paris, Louvre) with a background cloth of honor and a vista into tranquil scenery, owes much to the devotional diptychs of Hans Memling in Bruges, such as the 1487 *Virgin and Martin van Nieuwenhove* (Bruges, Hospital St. Jean). Many of the youthful van Cleve Madonna images display the more relaxed maternal intimacy that Massys only fully realized in his mature works of the 1520s. Much copied, the van Cleve formulas in half-length included a *Virgin with Sleeping Christ Child* (Friedländer 9, no. 52–53);[8] a *Virgin Offering a Wineglass* (F. 54), and a *Virgin Offering a Pear* (F. 60). One early van Cleve half-length, the *Madonna Nursing Christ* (F. 55), is extracted from Bruges, specifically from Gerard David's *Rest on the Flight*, and made into an *Andachtsbild* for votive contemplation;[9] to judge by its numerous copies, this was one of Joos's most popular icons. The full length Joos van Cleve *Rest on the Flight* (Brussels, F. 49) depends just as surely on David, even down to its details like the wicker basket in the foreground, but it also takes place in an expansive Patinir-like landscape (Patinir enrolled in the Antwerp painters' guild in 1515 along with a "Gerard of Bruges," often considered to be David himself).[10] During the period, then, when Massys was completing his own *Rest on the Flight* (ca. 1509–12) as part of the *Seven Sorrows altarpiece*, van Cleve had already begun a veritable industry of Madonna image production, achieving a lifelike warmth and tenderness equaled only rarely by David in Bruges (in the numerous *Rest* scenes and especially in the *Madonna of Milk Soup*) and only a decade later by Massys himself (e.g., the Rotterdam *Madonna with Milk Soup* or Detroit *Madonna Outdoors*). Within the Antwerp market for religious art, the two artists seem to have practiced a kind of division of labor in producing different kinds of images.

Pl. 29
Pl. 160
Pl. 28
Pl. 66

Both Massys and van Cleve made creative use of hallowed Netherlandish Madonna imagery. Massys turned to van Eyck and van der Weyden for his Brussels *Madonna Enthroned* and to van Eyck and Campin for his *Seilern Madonna;* van Cleve adopted van Eyck's *Lucca Madonna* (ca. 1435, Frankfurt, Staedel Inst.) for his own *Holy Family* (F. 65, New York, Metropolitan Museum). Van Eyck's quiet, nursing Madonna has been modified into Joos's standard half-length and amplified with the addition of a markedly aged St. Joseph and a host of symbolic still-life comestibles,[11] most of them already staples of van Cleve Madonna icons. St. Joseph most closely resembles the physical type of van der Weyden, as in the Granada-Miraflores *Nativity;* so he, too, is a borrowing, but his presence in the nursing scene adds a domestic, familial note. Another van Cleve *Holy Family* (F. 66) is derived from the Campin *Virgin and Child* in Frankfurt.

Pl. 48
Pl. 52
Pl. 161

To a certain extent, this fullness of depiction is related to the genealogical wholeness already encountered in Massys' *Holy Kinship altarpiece* (F. 1, 1507–09). Indeed, the Holy Family icon in several variants (F. 64, 66) was Joos's most popular and often-copied image. Seen at half-length, it features an older Joseph in a straw hat, reading behind a humbly dressed Madonna nursing (or, alternatively, holding a playful Child in her lap); rosary and symbolic still-life are often featured. The Holy Family was a major interest of Joos van Cleve, as his own *Anna Selbdritt* (F. 45, Modena, Galleria Estense) or

Pl. 1
Pl. 166

Holy Family with St. Anne (F. 46–7) attest. That these themes were a commonplace in Antwerp painting of the day can be observed in the many outdoor *Anna Selbdritts* (F. 130, 153) or Holy Family scenes (F. 131, 136, 137, 150, 152) by the Master of Frankfurt, possibly to be identified with an important Antwerp painter, Hendrik van Wueluwe (active 1483–1533).[12] Clearly, the domestic reality of parent-child contacts was an important concern in Antwerp's religious art, and Joos van Cleve, among others, provided those kinds of images in both his Madonna icons and his Holy Family scenes.

A key to understanding these half-length images is the prominent foreground still-life arrangement. Directly confronting the viewer, these fruits, flowers (especially the lily), and crystal wine beakers are ordinary objects but are simultaneously symbolic references from the Flemish visual heritage to the purity of the Virgin and the mission of Christ. They derive their additional meaning from their proximity to the holy figures, who are themselves a combination of ordinary, humble appearances disguising spiritual magnitude. The prominent still-life alerts a knowledgeable Christian viewer to the mystery behind appearances and to the analogy, or "similitude," between these earthly symbolic attributes and the holy figures.[13]

Joos van Cleve's half-length icons, which seem to have spawned a renewed, 16th-century interest in symbolic still-life, are thus a sympathetic revival of the mixture of spirit and earthliness that was so basic to the great tradition of Flemish painting from the 15th-century. This detente with the past is the
Pl. 94 goal of much of Massys' earlier art, including his Passion pictures (Paris *Pièta,* Ottawa *Crucifixion*) of
Pl. 91 the teens. And this is precisely the phenomenon that Panofsky terms "peripheral and comprehending reconstruction,"[14] a creatively synthetic archaism, in discussing both Joos van Cleve and Massys.

Yet the urge to transcend banality in presenting such lofty themes and such transcendent figures must have been a major tension in the midst of the Flemish blend of heaven and earth. In the 15th-century, Roger van der Weyden had resorted to artificial frames and devices like the "arch motif" to remind viewers of the sacrality lying behind the earthly appearances of his holy figures (e.g., the
Pl. 49 *Madonna Duran,* Madrid).[15] By the time of Joos van Cleve, the redress of the imbalance toward earthliness was achieved through the figures themselves—either through a dazzling display of drama, costumes, and scenery (the trend usually labeled "Antwerp Mannerism"), or through heroization and idealization of the holy figures themselves (a trend usually labeled "Romanism"). In both these successive and overlapping visual fashions, Joos van Cleve was an important practitioner.

Antwerp Mannerism seems to be a phenomenon closely linked to Antwerp's altarpiece production for export. We have already seen the importance of links between Antwerp painters and sculptors in
Pl. 13 discussing Massys' *Lamentation triptych* (1508–11) for the shrineworkers' guild; various elements
Pl. 15 featured in that work formed the ingredients for Antwerp Mannerism, as developed in the early teens. The same features had become commonplace in Antwerp sculpture a decade earlier and hence were more than appropriate for Massys' martydom scenes offered to the joiners. But they soon came to be seen as widely applicable for Antwerp painting in general and thus crystallized into the conventions of "Antwerp Mannerism": scenic, ruined architecture, exotic Renaissance scrollwork ornament, crowded groups of accessory figures, colorful foreign costumes and figure types, and emphatic gestures and poses all contribute to heighten the drama and spectacle of religious narratives. Particularly favored subjects were the Adoration of the Magi or the Martyrdom of Christ or a saint. The earliest altarpiece painted in this style-formula to be dated is from 1513 (by Adriaen van Overbeke),[16] but many of the early examples are anonymous and undated; frequently, panels of the Antwerp Mannerist idiom appear as wings of altarpieces with sculpted centers (as in the case of the retable, dated 1516, exported to Västerås, Sweden)[17]

Pl. 162 In Joos van Cleve's career a major monument is his *St. Reinhold altarpiece* (F. 20, now Warsaw), consecrated in 1516 in the chapel of the confraternity of St. Reinhold of the Church of Our Lady,
Pl. 24 Gdansk (Danzig). Like Massys' *Seven Sorrows altarpiece* for Portugal, this Passion cycle by van Cleve was an export item, its execution largely shared with workshop assistants and sent out along the trading network of the Hanseatic League. The *St. Reinhold altarpiece* had a carved central core with scenes from the life of the Virgin; van Cleve's painted scenes completed the cycle on the retable's exterior. Joos's sources for his imagery here are as diverse as Massys' earlier altarpiece borrowings.[18] The *Ecce*

Homo draws on Dürer's *Small Passion* of ca. 1511; the *Baptism* depends upon Gerard David's triptych for Jan de Trompes in Bruges; individual features of tormentors can be compared to Massys' own use of the grotesques by Leonardo da Vinci.[19] This amalgam of models contributes to the new effects of drama and spectacle of Antwerp Mannerism, and once again this distinctive *mise-en-scène* arises in association with the elaborate narratives of Antwerp's religious woodcarvers. It is significant that the shrinework of this *St. Reinhold altarpiece* houses its panels in the same framework as Massys' *Lamentation altarpiece:* the characteristic, early 16th-century, bell-shaped format of Antwerp's joiners.

Indeed, Joos seems to have been a lively proponent of the emerging Antwerp Mannerist idiom, as his own bell-shaped Dresden *Adoration of the Magi* (F. 27) attests. The date of this altarpiece is *Pl. 163* uncertain (though Friedländer places it as early as ca. 1512, based on the estimated age of an alleged self-portrait included in the background.)[20] In this *Adoration,* as in the many other Adorations in the Antwerp Mannerist formula, the basic visual effect is one of abundance. Excessive adornment in costumes and architectural ornament contributes to the sense of splendor and exuberance. Urgency and energy by the magi in their devotion to Christ restore the importance of the Gospel narrative, even as their pageantry removes it from the sphere of the ordinary viewer. The African, Asian, and European magi join their riches together into a single activity, analogous to the hosts of worldwide trading representatives who met together for trade in Europe's new queen city: Antwerp.[21] Even where he draws upon a Massys composition (e.g., the Antwerp Mayer van den Bergh *Crucifixion triptych)* in his own *Crucifixion triptychs* (F. 11, 12, or the single panel in Boston, F. 30), van Cleve's *Pl. 164* rendition is theatrical and agitated, even melodramatic, in its expression of grief. At the same time, his imagery retains Massys' use of traditional characters and composition as well as his panoramic staging of the event within a broad, Patinir-inspired landscape.

Joos van Cleve's career is marked by the artist's later modifications of his own formulas. Another *Adoration in Dresden* (F. 28), dated a full decade later by Friedländer and Lanc, has most of the same *Pl. 165* features of composition, characters, architecture, and landscape, but the level of energy and theatricality has changed. Dignity and tranquility inform his cluster of larger, more stately figures. All the individuals are modeled with a new attention to their mass and solidity; this modeling is especially evident in the deeply shadowed face of the Virgin. Scholars have seen influence of Leonardo da Vinci's fabled *sfumato* on these shadowy, solid forms; indeed, the reported original destination of this *Adoration* was a north Italian church, San Luca d'Erba, near Genoa and Leonardo's own center of activity in Milan. In fact, several of Joos's commissioned altarpieces were intended for Genoa: a *Lamentation triptych* (F. 19, with a predella based on Leonardo's Milan *Last Supper*) for Santa Maria della Pace, Genoa, and another *Adoration triptych* (F. 9) even now in the church of San Donato, Genoa. These commissions were probably the result of intervention of local Genoese financiers in Antwerp rather than any necessary trip to Italy by van Cleve.[22] But Joos's Italian connection attests to his continued involvement in Antwerp's art export trade at a time when Massys had already abandoned altarpiece production altogether; moreover, Joos's contacts with Italy provided extensive exposure to the Leonardo elements which Massys had already begun to take up by the time the younger artist began to paint.

During the 1520s, Joos van Cleve was a more public artistic figure than Massys in Antwerp. Joos was dean of the painters' guild—a title Massys never held—in 1519, 1520, and 1525; he registered apprentices in 1516, 1523, 1535, and 1536. Nevertheless, in the 1520s the two artists shared many features, though van Cleve's creations dominated the art of the city. The example of Madonna icons of the 1520s already shows how much the two artists drew together in their formulations. As mentioned above, Massys adopted Joos's foreground still-life for his own mature works: the *Berlin Madonna,* the *Pl. 63* Detroit *Madonna Outdoors,* the *Rattier Madonna,* and the lost *Madonna of the Cherries.* Both artists *Pl. 64* increasingly feature the architectural vocabulary of Italy in the thrones of their Madonnas, even as the *Pl. 68* costumes and actions of the Madonna are more intimate, maternal, and casual (see Chap. 4). In Joos's *Pl. 58* icons, the Christ Child sleeps, nurses, or squirms energetically within the grasp of the Virgin, whereas the most memorable repeated image of Massys is the kiss between Madonna and Child.

The models of Leonardo da Vinci and his disciples hover in the background of both Joos and

Quinten. Many of the gestures featured, particularly on the part of the robust Christ Child, are borrowed from compositions of the Leonardo school (e.g., Giampetrino, Solario).[23] Joos produced numerous replicas of a composition believed to have been invented by Leonardo: a *Madonna of the Cherries* (F. 63), featuring an active, pudgy, and curly-haired Christ Child, plus an Italianate throne with scrollwork, a corner vista over a sunny landscape, a fruit on a corner ledge, and a Madonna with a softly shaded face and a diaphanous veil over her glistening hair. These elements are the very features
Pl. 58 of Massys' own late *Madonna of the Cherries* (lost, F. 67). Another more-literal instance of Massys
Pl. 69 sharing a Leonardo motif with Joos van Cleve is the embracing *Infants Christ and John the Baptist.*[24]
Pl. 166 Here, too, van Cleve and his workshop turned out numerous replicas of the theme (F. 37, with a host of differing backgrounds), while Massys (or his shop) produced only a single version (Chatsworth, Devonshire collection, F. 29), in a bedroom of a bourgeois household. The Joos van Cleve images consistently evoke the royal status behind these most intimate infants; canopies, cushion-pedestals, and nichelike Italianate architectural frames serve to isolate and dignify the holy figures. Here again, Massys seems to have followed the lead of Joos van Cleve in adopting Leonardo's vigorous yet ideal forms for religious figures.

At issue, however, in this ultimate phase of Massys' art and full maturity of Joos van Cleve is not *which* artist originated these pictorial images of divinity, but the reason for their aptness—the formulation of a new religious conception of divinity. Scholars—particularly those viewing Europe from an Italian perspective—assume somehow that the diffusion of Italian Renaissance forms in northern Europe was inevitable, possibly because of some unstated assumption of cultural superiority.[25] Even Panofsky's sympathetic treatment of Albrecht Dürer presumes this vision of Italian superiority, especially in according special emphasis to art theory ("Dürer was the first artist who, brought up in late-medieval workshops of the North, fell under the spell of art theory as it had evolved in Italy");[26] Dürer thus becomes an importing agent, replacing "errors in design" with "right grounding" learned in Italy. But with the exception of Dürer's own treatises, no major discussion of art theory developed in 16th-century northern Europe before van Mander in Haarlem in 1604. Despite the wealth of visual evidence of Italy's impact of Massys' Antwerp, no corresponding verbal borrowing of Italian theory can be traced in Flemish. The reasons for Italy's cultural prestige or influence in Flanders remain to be established.

For Massys and for Joos van Cleve, verisimilitude was not a problematic issue as a basis of image-making, even of religious art. Dürer's theory, too, rests upon the axiom that the best art "more accurately . . . approaches nature by way of imitation."[27] But the Flemish countrymen of Jan van Eyck did not depend upon either Italy or Dürer or even explicit art theory for such principles. Instead, they were fascinated by Italy's quest for "beauty" in art. Dürer's own explorations of beauty (and ugliness) found written, theoretical expression in his *Four Books of Human Proportion* of 1528.[28] In this connection, it is worth recalling that Massys' own fairest creations of religious figures, like Christ in the
Pl. 86 Prado *Ecce Homo* or the Madonna in the 1526 New York *Adoration,* are often set out against a cluster of
Pl. 79 abominable grotesques. While in Madonna icons of Massys or Joos van Cleve the pretty figures are not balanced by ugly, mundane counterparts, it is clear that the equation of beauty with virtue and moral dignity forms the basis of both artists' conception of painted spirituality. Elevated subjects demand an elevated style. This view, incidentally, is also espoused by Dürer's eulogistic biographer (indeed, the first modern biographer of *any* artist—a generation before Vasari) Joachim Camerarius, in the preface to Camerarius' Latin translation of Dürer's *Vier Bücher:*

> No one could believe them virtuous whose minds and hands composed such [illicit] works . . . Albrecht, therefore, we most justly admire as an earnest guardian of piety and modesty, and as one who showed, by the grandness of his pictures, that he was conscious of his own powers.[29]

Camerarius is here praising Dürer's technique and exactitude rather than his subject per se, but these remarks may be extended by analogy to the rhetorical "high-style oration" as a parallel to "noble" or "grand" picturing. The reservation of ultimate beauty for the Madonna and saints could hardly be called a novelty in the art of Massys and van Cleve. Similar remarks could have been made about the leading Bruges master of the previous generation, Hans Memling (himself possibly receptive to Italian modes of beauty as the basis of religious art).[30] Nonetheless, it is also true that Memling, following his mentor Roger van der Weyden (who himself probably visited Italy during the jubilee year of 1450),[31] increasingly refined the features and enhanced the attractiveness of his Madonnas after the humbler, homelier, fleshier, 15th-century precedents of Campin, Christus, and Bouts. With Memling, moreover, began the pictorial importation of Italian Renaissance architectural elements into the transcendent royal pavilions of the Madonnas in Flemish art. We have already noted that both Massys and Joos van Cleve picked up the architectural Italianism within their works, although they, like the anonymous Antwerp Mannerist masters, often emphasized its exotic and decorative qualities through an exaggerated application of "grotesque" ornament.[32] *cf. Pl. 167*

This combination of Renaissance architectural elements and an Italy-based concept of beauty lies at the heart of the Antwerp borrowings from the south. Building upon the foundations of Memling, Massys and then Joos van Cleve attempted to elevate the Madonna further from the ordinary characters and surroundings which had been the very hallmark of 15th-century Flemish paintings. This shift in mentality is actually less extreme than the contrast between two centuries of northern art offered by Roger van der Weyden's *St. Luke Drawing the Madonna* (Boston, ca. 1435) and Maerten van Heemskerck's Italianate *St. Luke Painting the Virgin* (Haarlem, Frans Hals Museum, 1532). But the shift is nonetheless the same for the Antwerp painters, whose assertively beautiful and preternaturally elegant figures dwell among angels in distinctly nonmundane environments. They replace the 15th-century type of nursing mother in her domestic interior before a typical Flemish townscape. In the process both the painter and the viewer are increasingly estranged and separated physically from the holy figures. Whereas Roger van der Weyden's St. Luke appears unaccompanied on eye level with the Virgin and in a (seemingly) earthly setting appropriate to his status,[33] Heemskerck's proto-painter finds himself in an unspecified but doubtless heavenly location (again suggested by the exotic, classical ornamental forms), seated below the Madonna on a thronelike chair bearing a relief based on Europa, symbol of divine rapture.[34] This divinely inspired artist has his brush guided by a bearded Bacchic intermediary who gives counsel over Luke's shoulder. Even the appearance of the saint has altered from the youthful portraitlike model of van der Weyden to Heemskerck's emphatically bespectacled and aged painter, who contrasts with the youthful and beautiful Virgin as fully as van Cleve's senile St. Joseph, and who seems to rise to this solemn occasion only through supernatural assistance. The enlarged gap of status between the spiritual nature of the Madonna and her portraitist is now firmly established by the contrast between her timeless beauty and his underlined mortality. Gone is the easy access of painters and patrons to the Madonna, perhaps nowhere more informal and natural than in the devotional diptychs of Hans Memling (e.g., the 1487 *Nieuwenhove diptych* or the Art Institute of Chicago diptych). Perhaps, in this respect, it is significant that Massys, a generation after Memling, does not combine portraits of sitters with holy figures.[35] *Pl. 168* *Pl. 169* *Pl. 137*

Closer to Antwerp and Massys are a pair of St. Luke images by Jan Gossaert. Both reveal extensive Italian influence, stimulated by Gossaert's visit to Rome in 1508 and by his continued and profound interest in the Italian elements in Dürer's prints. The first Gossaert *St. Luke* (ca. 1513, Prague), originally in the church of St. Rombauts, Malines, takes place in a forest of Renaissance architectural forms and ornamental sculpture. The forms of Luke and the nursing Madonna are clearly derived from the Boston van der Weyden painting, but the foreign architecture designates an isolated, extraordinary and, in this case, celestial setting. The artifice of its layout is manifest in the ornament that lies behind, and corresponds with, each of the foreground figures. Luke's side, being sacred but more earthbound, contains seated prophets or saints,[36] also seated like the evangelist-painter, in lacy, Late Gothic ornament corresponding to the most fanciful decorative elements in contemporary churches. In contrast, the Virgin's side offers standing figures, for the most part, and classically inspired sculptures (a corresponding section on Luke's side is cut off by the frame and invisible). A Hercules sculpture above the Virgin may be taken, like the figure in Nicola Pisano's Pisa pulpit, to *Pl. 170* signify Fortitudo in a repetition of the 13th-century renascent phenomenon described by Panofsky.[37] The owl in a classical setting usually refers to Wisdom in the guise of the bird of Minerva; in this instance the bird of Wisdom is also appropriate to the Virgin as *sedes sapientiae,* the Christian Throne of Wisdom.[38] The putto with a bird has been cited as a borrowing from a classical model, the boy with a goose, but de Jongh has interpreted this sculpture, too, in the Christian context of the Madonna as an angel with an eagle, or the restraint of earthly pride by a heavenly agent.[39]

The remarkable aspect in this welter of classical allusions and nonnative architecture is the absolute assertion of the Virgin's humility and human qualities, even in comparison to van der Weyden.[40] Like Roger's Madonna, Gossaert's Holy Mother is nursing with the Child in her lap, and she is seated at an even lower, more earthly level than the saint-artist. In his figures, Gossaert revives the Rogerian models of the previous century as fully as Massys had done in his early works (e.g., the Brussels
Pl. 48 *Madonna Enthroned,* F. 17, cat. 9) and in line with his own consistent revival of van der Goes and, especially, van Eyck.[41]

The paradox of archaic Flemish figures combined with imported, unfamiliar architecture and ornament is central to the content of the Prague *St. Luke:* because the figures are hallowed by tradition, they can be seen in their most informal and humble activities; because they are in an ornate and exotic—hence, unearthly—environment, they can be witnessed without the celestial paraphernalia of halos or angelic attendants. Yet in the final analysis, they are much more fully estranged from our earthly world than Roger's figures or any of the illusionistic figures and settings of the 15th century. Seen in this conjunction, both revival and Renaissance form part of a common artistic striving, separate but complementary visual idioms that serve to create a more sanctified and distanced image of holy figures in Flemish art. In this respect, the distinctive yet equally exotic costumes and buildings associated with Antwerp Mannerism can be seen to be related strivings for the unfamiliar as a means of alienating the holy figures and Gospel stories from ordinary experience and from the visual illusionism which had so closely linked art and life in 15th-century Flanders.

A peculiar detail in the background of Gossaert's Prague *St. Luke Madonna* adds an instructive footnote to this trend. Visible through the Renaissance vault of the foreground architecture is an open courtyard with a second, pavilionlike building and a fountain, each in the most ornate Flamboyant, Late Gothic style. Within the pavilion, the Virgin and St. Luke appear for a second time—he seated at a writing desk, she standing alongside dictating. De Jongh has determined that the vanishing point of the picture's perspective converges on this second image of the Virgin (he says that their single point of convergence is her womb),[42] so Gossaert clearly wanted the viewer to note this second environment and repetition of the protagonists. This hybrid and arbitrary second architectural style and a second role of the holy figures is consistent with Gossaert's combinations elsewhere in the painting. Already this kind of lacy ornament had been seen behind the more earthbound figure of St. Luke. These Late Gothic forms are used for fundamentally decorative, highly complex visual displays, rather than for clearly structured buildings; as such, their ornateness was deemed especially appropriate for the most visionary or mysterious elements within the Late Gothic church. For example, the fantastic and towering structures that housed the eucharist in 15th-century Flemish churches (a staggering example is the tower by Matthieu van Layen in St. Peter's, Louvain)[43] were constructed with a maximum of this Late Gothic decoration; in addition, tracery for stained glass, vaults, church porches, and towers were major areas for this "flamboyant" architecture.[44] In contemporary Flemish art, the Late Gothic structures most often served as visions of paradisical settings. For example, Gossaert's *Malvagna triptych* (Palermo) features a similar lacy Fountain of Life and lodge behind the Madonna and female saints and an even more fantastic set of consoles and canopies in the Flamboyant style above their heads. The ornate and mystical are again related, making Mary into a "jewel in a very detailed-work setting" (the same kind of foreground embellishment can be seen in the Chicago version of Joos van
Pl. 166 Cleve's *Embracing Infants Christ and St. John).*[45] Thus, the background setting with St. Luke and the Madonna is at once closer to the contemporary architecture of Flanders but also to a visionary fantasy of a realm reserved only for the Madonna and saints. That St. Luke is writing may indicate that he is

composing the Gospels in a moment of inspiration from the Virgin and Child, a *furor poeticus* similar to Moses' authorship of the inspired words of the Pentateuch.[46] In distinction to the celestial palace of the Virgin of the foreground, Gossaert's Gothic background seems to be a specifically religious or church-related realm, where the presence of Gospels-in-composition and of a more nearly earthly architecture offers a link to the human world from the kingdom of Heaven. Yet the entire Gossaert painting retains its distanced and celestial character, even in its separate background, and underscores the profound, essential gulf between holy figures and the community of the faithful.

Gossaert's later *St. Luke Madonna* (Vienna, Kunsthistorisches Museum), usually dated ca. 1520, *Pl. 171* makes an even more emphatic split between its own internal levels of holiness, for the Madonna appears to St. Luke enshrouded in a glowing cloud. Suspended above the ground, the Virgin is surrounded by tiny, colorful angels who carry the Crown of Heaven over her head. In this image, Luke is kept separate from the vision and given access to it through an intermediary, an angel, who guides his drawing by holding the saint's right hand. Luke has removed his shoes—a sign of consecrated ground already seen in the Prague picture. Once again, the setting is sharply delineated with Renaissance vocabulary: rounded arches, pilasters, and elaborate "grotesque" ornament with medallions.[47] This kind of ornament and pilaster system was a commonplace in paintings associated with the Antwerp Mannerists and in related images of the Adoration by Massys (1526; New York) and *Pl. 79* Joos van Cleve. In the Adoration scenes, the ornament can be taken to be a historicizing tendency on *Pl. 165* the part of artists to add a note of archaeological accuracy or architectural antiquarianism akin to what Mantegna had employed in Quattrocento Italy.[48] The pilasters would thus be ruins of the pagan world on which the humble yet triumphant Church of Christ would be erected. Something of the same historicism carries over to Gossaert's Vienna *St. Luke,* which features bearded heads in profile, like Roman emperors, in its ornamental medallions. Yet the site of Luke's vision cannot simply be taken to be a pagan temple, for a seated figure of Moses, with decalogue and horns, fills the aedicula over the saint. The building thus fuses the Old Testament religion under Mosaic law with the pagan forms and decoration of the sanctuary. Into this environment of pre-Christian religion, the promise of the Madonna and Child appears as a vision, like the revelation to the Tiburtine Sibyl and Emperor Augustus,[49] or to an Old Testament prophet. A similar vision of the Madonna in clouds is the tradition of the Madonna in the Sun appearing as part of the Revelations to St. John the Evangelist, as in the frontispiece to Dürer's *Apocalypse* (1511 edition) or *Life of the Virgin* (1511). Gossaert's own isolated icon of the celestial Virgin with radiant sunbeams and glowing aureole (Chicago, Art Institute) indicates *Pl. 172* how otherworldly and alien the vision of holy figures has become, particularly when compared to Memling's half-length Virgins in domestic interiors. From the distance of realities between Madonna *Pl. 137* and Luke, patron saint of painters and contemporary of the Virgin Mary, in Gossaert's Vienna picture, we can easily perceive how vast a gulf of holiness separates the painter himself and his pious audience from the sacred realm of the image.

What both the Chicago icon and the Vienna *St. Luke* by Gossaert reveal is a new aesthetic for the holy figures themselves—a Renaissance-based aesthetic. The Christ Child resembles a youthful version of the Hercules in the Prague *St. Luke;* his powerful muscles are strikingly incongruous on so young an infant, and they are only slightly more powerful than those of the attending angels. The Madonna—youthful, full-bodied, and delicate-featured—also reveals a physical perfection that can only be described as supernatural. The Madonna and Child had smooth, beautiful features in earlier Flemish art, particularly in Van Eyck, van der Goes, and Memling. But compared to the coarser, more ordinary appearance of the Campin–van der Weyden tradition, still dominant in the Madonna of the Prague *St. Luke,* the Vienna *St. Luke* uses its Italianate forms in the same way it uses the radiant cloud: to isolate and elevate the holy figures into a realm of supernatural sanctity. This beautifying trend continued and intensified the previous experiments in Italianate architecture of the Prague *St. Luke.*

Less extreme in his transformations than Gossaert, Joos van Cleve slowly adopted Renaissance forms into his Madonna images. Van Cleve's model was less the full-bodied herculean image adopted by Gossaert than the softly shaded, oval faces stemming from Leonardo's *chiaroscuro* figures. An inspection of Joos's sequence of *Adorations* or Madonna icons reveals an analogous introduction of Italianate architecture during the early teens followed by the adoption of Leonardesque Madonna types and specific Leonardo figure groups.[50]

The late, Italianate Madonnas of Massys take their place alongside the creations of artists like Gossaert and van Cleve. These images also combine both Renaissance architectural forms and the smooth oval faces and delicate limbs favored by Massys. After the slender and angular faces in his small-figure scenes of the teens, Massys' Madonnas of the twenties offer rounded yet fine-featured
Pl. 63 beauty. The Christ Child is often startlingly long-limbed and mature for an infant (Berlin and *Rattier*
Pl. 68 *Madonnas),* making His intimate kiss with the Madonna nearly adult and more unsettling (Gossaert's later full-bodied figures, e.g., the Prado *Madonna and Child,* are almost aggressively erotic in their embrace).[51] Another Christ Child type by Massys accentuates the fleshy baby fat of the infant after the model of Leonardo. The definitive image of this beautiful and Italianate Madonna and Child in a
Pl. 58 sumptuous and Italianate throne is the *Madonna of the Cherries.*

Surprising and seemingly anomalous characteristics of these Massys images—their intimacy, their frequent domesticity, and their human qualities—betray fewer of the celestial attributes of the earliest icons (see Chap. 4). The ultimate step in this direction is the *Rattier Madonna* (Paris), where a crownless, halo-less Virgin embraces her Child in an unadorned bedroom. Yet the physical development of the Italianate features and the new body type of the child confirm the identities and otherworldliness of the Madonna and Child, even in so unexceptional a setting as a bedroom. Because these figures are preternatural, they can interact in a more human and less formal manner. Just like Gossaert's Prague *St. Luke Madonna,* the holy figures of Massys no longer need to sit stiffly on a throne, for they are now creatures innately different from ourselves and not to be confused with ordinary people.

The later religious scenes of Massys underscore the gulf between divine and earthly characters. The
Pl. 86 Prado and Venice *Ecce Homos* contrast the physically beautiful but battered figure of a resigned Christ
Pl. 87 with the Leonardo-inspired grotesques of his human tormentors. Even in a scene like the 1526 New
Pl. 79 York *Adoration of the Magi,* where no torment occurs and no contrast is necessary, the same polarization occurs between a pair of beautiful, unadorned holy figures separated by an Italianate pilaster from aggressively ugly, yet ostentatiously dressed mortals. Indeed, the very humility and beauty of the Madonna and Child are the distinguishing marks of their divinity.

As in the case of Hieronymus Bosch's holy figures within a pernicious earthly setting (the Prado *Adoration triptych* or the Ghent *Christ Carrying the Cross*), the human community in Massys' art has become estranged from its saints and mired in its own sin. For Massys, that sin reveals itself through the grotesque faces that contrast with the beauty of divinity. Gossaert and van Cleve rarely chose to represent ordinary human society at all; hence, their beautified and unruffled worlds remained models of heroic power and delicate grace. But for Massys, the associate of Erasmus and colleague of *rederijkers,* secular pictures had become a pictorial staple, and secular subjects demanded earthly settings as well as unattractive characters. Massys' religious scenes accentuated the moral alienation from the holy which Gossaert, in his second *St. Luke,* made even more distinct between the Madonna and her saintly portraitist.

Both Gossaert's *St. Lukes* and Massys' religious scenes reveal a hierarchical system of relationships that can be extended (as in Massys' Passion scenes) to include the viewer. By implication, those relationships offer a view of the world (as defined within the limits of the pictures' subjects) and of religion which must be deduced for Massys from his art alone. His later works reveal a crisis of confidence in mankind's basic goodness and in the approachability of holy figures. The almost casual,
Pl. 137 easy interaction of Memling's Madonnas and prayerful donors, so influential during Massys' youth and in his portraits, has disintegrated into separate groups of holy figures and sinful mankind.

This uneasiness and lack of confidence in late medieval religion has been the subject of much recent scholarship, particularly in the work of Delaruelle, Labande and Ourliac, and Ozment.[52] The surge of pious practices by the laity—pilgrimages, cults of saints, relics, indulgences—has been tied to a "need for security," a religious "anguish."[53] Institutional organizations, such as the lay confraternities which sponsored one Massys retable (the Louvain St. Anne *Holy Kinship altarpiece,* 1507–09) or the religious branches of corporate guilds (Massys' *St. John altarpiece* for the Antwerp joiners' guild, 1508–11), provided pious solidarity and reinforcement in addition to the sacraments administered by the regular clergy. Indeed, Ozment's analysis of confessional manuals and catechisms from the late 15th century (e.g., the *Mirror of a Sinner,* 1474, or the *Mirror of a Christian Man*) pictures a religiosity filled with anxiety, acutely conscious of sin and human unworthiness.[54] Like Thomas à Kempis' *Imitation of Christ* and other writings of the 15th century, these works impose the rigors of monastic ideals onto laymen. Spiritual preparation to receive the eucharist becomes almost daunting in these manuals as preparation for death and penitence is the constant watchword.

One can note in this context the widespread popularity during the later 15th century—and in prints by Master ES and paintings by Bosch—of the theme of the *Art of Dying Well,* or *Ars moriendi.*[55] Sinfulness and temptation persist even to the deathbed in these images. For Massys, the same kinds of struggles are exemplified in his depictions of saints: Anthony and the Magdalene renouncing sensuality, and Jerome meditating on a skull, the emblem of death. For Massys' nonsaintly or secular characters, in contrast, sinfulness is all-pervasive: luxuriating men and women, wracked by lust, greed, and pride. Once again, a consistent hierarchy of moral worth is established in Massys, as in Bosch; this scale of ethical values finds its analogue in the visible scale that runs from ugliness to ideal beauty.

Most enigmatic of all the Massys images, however, are those of the portraits, neither ugly nor truly beautiful, which seem specifically to exist apart from the artist's vision of the spiritual world. In their half-length format, portraits bear kinship with the meditating saints (Jerome, Mary Magdalene) as well as the lesser mortals of the secular works; however, unlike the grinning *Democritus,* they are often *Pl. 115* mute. The purposes of Massys' portraits, indeed of most early portraits, has yet to be established and may often depend on the identification of the anonymous sitters. Yet Massys' own total *oeuvre* and the attributes within his portraits strongly suggest a spiritual objective, akin to prayer (see Chap. 8), alongside their apparent commemorative purpose. If this were not the case, it is doubtful that Massys would have so conspicuously altered his secular depictions from the handsome and portraitlike figures of the 1514 Louvre *Moneychanger and his Wife* to the emphatic ugliness and repulsiveness of the *Pl. 118* subsequent grotesques. The portraits, moreover, usually contain their own votive implements: open prayerbooks, crosses, prayerbeads, symbolic flowers, and even a certificate of pilgrimage (Winterthur, 1509). The prayerful disposition of portraits is a feature, too, in Gossaert's *oeuvre,* including the *Pl. 138* archaistic diptych (1517; Paris, Louvre) based on the devotional diptychs of van der Weyden, of *Jean Carondelet Adoring the Virgin.*[56] Even the portrait pendants of husbands and wives (parodied by Massys in the *Grotesque Old Couple*) suggest a seriousness accorded to the sacramental nature of matrimony, *Pl. 122* emphasized particularly by the prayerful New York–Schloss Au pair, in addition to their obvious *Pl. 123* memorial function. Also impressive as an ingredient in the later Massys portraits (though equally *Pl. 140* elusive) is the calm and grand background landscape vista extending behind the sitter. The analogy of such scenery to Madonna images, such as Massys' own Detroit *Madonna Outdoors,* is clear, even if its *Pl. 64* meaning remains obscure. Perhaps these settings, too, imply spiritual hopes for the sitters in much the same manner as the symbolic objects in the other portraits. What is particularly striking about Massys' portraits, however, is how overwhelmingly bourgeois his sitters seem to be, in contrast to the prevailing images of noble or royal subjects and their badges of office or recondite attributes to be found so often in Renaissance Italy,[57] or in northern courts. Massys' portraits of Antwerp's citizenry are nowhere as distinctively delimited as is his exceptional departure into an image of nobility, the Kroměřice *Christian II;* even here, the unadorned, restrained Massys image pales before the pomp of *Pl. 155* Gossaert's masterful drawing of the same ruler (Paris, Institut Néerlandais) amid a triumphal arch, *Pl. 156* balcony, and panoply of heraldic coats-of-arms.[58]

As the comparisons to Bosch, van Cleve, and even Gossaert imply, study of Quinten Massys is often valuable less for what that artist minted anew than for the fact that he circulated widely and used the common coin. Even in the case of his innovative secular pictures, which helped open a new kind of pictorial type and also had a lasting influence on the history of painting, our interests lie not with these works simply as a "beginning," but rather with their place in Massys' total *oeuvre.* Here the pole of ugliness of his spiritual vision isolated itself from previous images to form a category in its own right. We have seen how the artist synthesized essentially literary impulses from both the Antwerp *rederijkers* and the local Erasmian circles, and how he also fused the grotesque faces of Leonardo da Vinci (possibly seconded by the examples of both Dürer and Bosch) with the format of portraiture to create his new satiric hybrid. Yet the purpose of that hybrid lay in its reinforcement of a coherent spiritual picture—itself something of a novelty after the more confident urban optimism of 15th-century Flanders—which saw sinful mankind as alienated from true spirituality. Unlike Erasmus, whose doctrine of satire on human folly was simply the obverse of a confident view of mankind's basic teachability,[59] of improvement toward reason and virtuous action, Massys seems to have viewed men's vices more in the manner of Sebastian Brant or the *rederijkers*—i.e., as an essential part of a baser human nature, written on men's ugly faces. Massys' 16th-century artistic vision balked at the confident analogy between this world and the divine that had governed earlier art (the "similitudes" mentioned above). Instead, he saw only the problem of the negation of divine Word in the actions of men. Only in Madonna images did the microcosmic concord between earth and heaven still pertain for Massys, for example in the symbolic fruit and flowers adorning the holy figures.

The issue of this study, then, is just such a 16th-century cultural reading within the (considerable) limits of what Massys himself and his Antwerp culture will allow us to discover. Its interest is not whether Massys ever traveled to Italy (a topic of speculation in many previous studies), but how he exploited for his own purposes the Italian forms that came his way. Its interest lies not in whether Massys was the last of the "Flemish Primitives" of the 15th century (Panofsky uses Massys to conclude his chapter on the "Founders' Heritage," but the Brussels *corpus* of *Les Primitifs Flamands* includes only Gerard David and Bosch, while excluding any artist of Antwerp). Neither is it concerned with whether Massys inaugurated a new epoch in Antwerp and the Netherlands in general, as Friedländer implies in his extensive survey of Netherlandish painting.[60]

Instead, this chapter and indeed this entire book have attempted to view Massys as something other than a traditionalist or an innovator—hardly any artist can be said to be anything other than *both* of these. All art is created out of earlier art and contemporary art as filtered through unique individuals and new sensibilities. All periods are "transitional." So it will explain nothing to label this (or any) artist or to measure his work simply in relation to other individuals or periods. Since no artist's work is a system, we have attempted to respond to the varieties of constraints and particularities of Massys' individual creations and to be sensitive to his "development" of types over the course of his career. Technical discussions concerning opinions of authorship and date have provided an indispensable foundation of this study; these considerations of the *corpus,* however, will be found in the appended Catalogue.

Quinten Massys was a citizen of Europe's fastest-growing city in terms of population, trade, and artistic opportunity. As a leading master of painting in that city, he surely also experienced contact with other, non-local but important artists mentioned in this chapter: Bosch, Dürer, Gossaert, Leonardo. He met foreign trade representatives and supplied pictures on their commissions. He was a colleague of the energetic and outspoken Chamber of Rhetoric "Die Violieren," the Antwerp *rederijkers,* and he met Erasmus and Peter Gillis, the fountainheads of a local humanist movement for educational and religious reform. Massys lived long enough to witness the first manifestations of "Lutheranism" in his city during the 1520s and the first religious persecutions of dissent that followed. As he continued to prosper financially, he increasingly withdrew from large-scale, publicly visible commissions, like altarpieces, and active training of apprentices within the guild system. His later works, whether icons, religious narratives, portraits, or secular satires, are usually presented in a close-up, half-length intimacy that seems consonant with a life of increasing privacy.

Within this range of subcultures and this network of divergent professions and intellects, Massys fashioned his life and art. The aim of this study has been to represent the consistency and outline of that life and thought, largely as revealed through that art. The analysis of Massys' art has also attempted to determine the purposes and audiences for which that art was created: the cultural system of meanings it both helps to define and, in turn, takes for its patterns. Massys' paintings are a form of specific social behavior and, as symbolic presentations of conceptions, are cultural acts. To define those cultural acts, to interpret those meanings, has been the goal of this book.

It is ironic that Massys was not long dead before he had become a symbol of a completely different art. The biographical legends about his life that had sprung up to be recorded in several eulogies 40 years later (see Chapter 1) were perpetuated by van Mander in 1604 and by the chauvinistic biographers of mid-17th-century Antwerp, Fickaert and van Fornenbergh. Massys at this point was revered not for the qualities of his artistic achievement but for his founder's role in the development of an Antwerp School of Painting, then at a climax with figures like Rubens, van Dyck, and Jordaens.[61] This role is what Said calls "authority": "any beginning that involves reversal, change of direction, the institution of a durable movement that increasingly engages our interest [and] constitutes an authorization from what follows from it."[62] Confirming the importance of Massys as a founder is the legend that he was a "natural" artist, untrained and thus untainted by the values of previous artists and centers. Of course, we have seen that Massys' art, like all art,[63] is created out of the received images of his own culture and gives the lie to these biographical legends. But the image of a "masterless master" is a *topos* of its own: Pliny's *Natural History* uses testimony by Duris of Samos that Lysippos was untrained.[64] This image of Massys is also a complement to a new notion of the artist in the 17th century, a new suggestion that the artist is a genius, inspired and creative, instead of a guild-based craftsman. This newer concept of artistry is closer to Dürer's theories than to the practices Dürer was attempting to transform within the German workshops. Fickaert (1648) stresses how Massys rose above his poverty-ridden, tradesman origins on the basis of his talents, exclaiming:

> A wondrous thing of Quinten Matsijs, that even still today/when anyone will be astonished by any work/then says these words: Ay, Masys! Though often one would rather say: Ay friend, just imagine such a thing as a man like Matsijs/—your soul [gheest] is too flat [flecht]; you understand far too little.[65]

By reading back from its own artistic culture and sense of history, 17th-century Antwerp celebrated Massys as founding father, "incomparabilis artis pictor." The very strangeness and inappropriateness of this later conception to the Massys we have met is sufficient to suggest how much more foreign and remote was the culture, examined here, that was the artist's own.

NOTES

1. L. M. J. Delaissé, review of M. Meiss, *French Painting in the Time of Jean de Berry, Art Bulletin* 52 (1970): 209.
2. Exemplified by S. J. Freedberg, *Painting in the High Renaissance in Florence and Rome* (Cambridge, 1961), p. 3ff.; see also his *Painting in Italy 1500—1600* (Harmondsworth, 1970), p. 5: "Leonardo's invention of the idea of style that was to shape so much of the history of the Cinquecento occurred more than two decades before the century began."
3. This concept still controlled the writing of the classic study of Antwerp painting by van den Branden. For the 17th-century view, see F. Baudouin, *Rubens*, Eng. ed. (New York, 1977), pp. 28, 297.
4. A view particularly well presented by Baldass, "Gotik und Renaissance im Werke des Quinten Massys," p. 137ff.
5. M. J. Friedländer "Über den Zwang der ikonographischen Tradition in der vlämischen Kunst," p. 19ff.
6. In addition to the basic studies by von Baldass (*Joos van Cleve Der Meister des Todes Maria*) and Friedländer (Vol. 9, Eng. ed., Leyden, 1972), there are dissertations on van Cleve by E. Lanc (*Die Religiösen Bilder des Joos van Cleve*) and J. Hand ("Joos van Cleve").
7. Hand, "Joos van Cleve," pp. 42, 51f.
8. For a comparable formula by the Massys workshop, of which no authentic original is known, see F.69, cat. 14.
9. For *Andachtsbilder*, see S. Ringbom, pp. 1–71.
10. K. G. Boon, *Gerard David*.
11. Bergström, "Disguised Symbolism in 'Madonna' Pictures," pp. 303–8, 342–49; de Jongh, "Grape Symbolism," pp. 184–86.

12. A. J. J. Delen, "Wie was de 'Meester van Frankfort'?" pp. 74–85. An alternative identification, advanced by W. R. Valentiner, suggests Jan de Vos (active in Antwerp 1489–1533, when he died in Cologne): W. R. Valentiner, "Jan de Vos, the Master of Frankfort," *Art Quarterly* 8 (1945): 195–215.

13. See the references in note 11, above. For a discussion of the intellectual dimension of this metaphoric relationship, see M. Foucault, *The Order of Things*, Eng. ed. (New York, 1970), pp. 17–45. Many of the elements of Panofsky's "hidden symbolism," discussed in *ENP*, pp. 131–48, can be understood via "similitudes."

14. Panofsky, *ENP*, pp. 353–54, yet Panofsky presupposes a microcosmic equivalent of his own theory of the Italian Renaissance, i.e., a distance, and therefore a renascence or revival of the Flemish "Founder's Heritage" of the earlier 15th century. Here the view is proposed that there is more of a continuity in Massys' work with prior Flemish masters, particularly through the powerful influence of Memling on the youthful Quinten.

15. K. Birkmeyer, "The Arch Motif in Netherlandish Painting of the Fifteenth Century," *Art Bulletin* 43 (1961): 1–20.

16. W. Gibson, *The Paintings of Cornelis Engebrechtsz.* (New York, 1977), p. 86, n.12, citing P. Clemen, ed., *Die Kunstdenkmäler des Kreises Kempens* (Düsseldorf, 1891), pp. 62–65.

17. See Friedländer, Vol. II, p. 28.

18. For the *St. Reinhold altarpiece*, see Hand, "Joos van Cleve," pp. 67–72.

19. The general question of the diffusion of Leonardo's grotesques is discussed in J. Bialostocki, "Opus quinque dierum: Dürer's 'Christ among the Doctors' and Its Sources," p. 17ff.

20. Friedländer, Vol. 9, pp. 22–23; more particularly, see J. Bialostocki, "New Observations on Joos van Cleef," *Oud Holland* 70 (1955): 121–29.

21. That this local significance persisted until the early 17th century is witnessed by the city's commission to Rubens in 1609 to paint an *Adoration of the Magi* (now in Madrid, Prado) for a Chamber of the Nations in the Antwerp City Hall. See C. Norris, "Rubens's *Adoration of the Kings* of 1609," pp. 129–36. On the Antwerp trade community and its international "colonies", see Chapter 3, this volume.

22. Hand, "Joos van Cleve," pp. 127–28; Lanc, *Die Religiösen Bilder*, pp. 144ff. The Genoese role in Antwerp's trading community is discussed by Goris, *Les Colonies marchandes meridionales*.

23. W. Suida, *Leonardo und sein Kreis*, p. 197ff.; K. Badt, *Andrea Solario* (Leipzig, 1914), p. 157; S. Sulzberger, "L'Influence de Léonard de Vinci et ses répercussions à Anvers," pp. 105–11; J. Bialostocki, "Leonardo i Nederlandczycy," *Biuletyn Historii Sztuki* 17 (1955): 369–70; G. Marlier, "Joos van Cleve—Fontainebleau and Italy," *Connoisseur* 165 (1967): 24–27.

24. G. Glück, "Schicksale einer Komposition Leonardos: der einander küssenden Kinder Jesus und Johannes," p. 502ff. The Chicago version of the Joos van Cleve composition has been determined to be from the collection of the prosperous Amsterdam banker Pompejus Occo by I. Hecht, "The Infants Christ and John Embracing," pp. 222–29.

25. An analogous assumption of cultural osmosis from "superior" to "backward" cultures is often made in archaeology, which credits Egypt and the Fertile Crescent with priority for most visual inventions in art and architecture. This credit comes by virtue of the greater information we possess about these "cradles of civilization" owing to their early literacy. In recent years, however, this assumption has been challenged on the grounds that literacy does not necessarily assure dominance in all cultural matters or eliminate the possibility of independent invention by a "lesser" culture with different priorities and interests. Such a model eliminates the need for direct contact and influence unless proven otherwise. See C. Renfrew, *Before Civilization* (London, 1973).

26. Panofsky, *Albrecht Dürer*, pp. 80, 244.

27. Ibid., p. 243. But the distinction of means between northern and southern art, so rigidly polarized by art historians (e.g., E. Gombrich, "Light, Form, and Texture in Fifteenth Century Painting," in *The Heritage of Apelles*, p. 19ff.) may still be seen to be part of a greater common impulse, viz. "the depiction of objects established by perception." See the stimulating article on both Alberti and the camera by Joel Snyder, "Picturing Vision," *Critical Inquiry* 6 (1980): 499–526. A fascinating attempt to establish a distinctive Italian visual culture is M. Baxandall, *Painting and Experience in Fifteenth Century Italy* (Oxford, 1972); for Germany, see his *The Limewood Sculptors of Renaissance Germany*.

28. Panofsky, *Albrecht Dürer*, pp. 266–70.

29. Nuremberg, 1532. Reprinted in H. Rupprich, ed., *Dürer Schriftlicher Nachlass* (Berlin, 1956–69), Vol. I, pp. 307–12. See the excellent discussion by P. Parshall, "Camerarius on Dürer," pp. 11–29, from which these observations are borrowed. Of course, noble subjects and artistic "decorum" are the very backbones of the humanist theory of painting, for which the essential study remains R. Lee, "*Ut Pictura Poesis:* The Humanistic Theory of Painting," *Art Bulletin* 22 (1940): 197–269.

30. The full story of Memling and Italy is yet to be written and is worthy of much further study. McFarlane's *Hans Memling* reminds us of the number of Italian patrons in the Bruges mercantile community who commissioned paintings from Memling and who could have exposed him to the art of their homeland. Panofsky (*ENP*, p. 349) comments on Memling's adoption of Quattrocento architectural features in his Madonna pictures, but he minimizes any Italian figural influence on the Bruges master. The portrait types common to both Memling and Italy that John Pope-Hennessey has argued came from the south may well have flowed the other way instead. Memling had a number of Italian patrons and produced a greater number of portraits using these common formulas, many with earlier dates than the dated comparisons from Italy (see Pope-Hennessey, *Portrait in the Renaissance*, p. 60, n. 85, admitting that Memling also exerted a "reciprocal" influence on later Italian painters and linking the 1462 London *Man* by Bouts to a ca. 1500 Perugino *Self-Portrait* in the Uffizi; also Panofsky, *ENP*, p. 349). The most important Italian comparisons to Memling's works are Perugino's 1494 *Francesco dell'Opere* or Solario's 1505 *Cristoforo Longoni*, which has often been compared to Massys' portraits (see Catalogue, Portraits).

31. Panofsky, *ENP*, p. 272ff.

32. Diffusion of "grotesque" ornament from Italy to the north after its development out of Roman archaeological discoveries has been discussed only in specialized contexts. For the formation of the new ornament style, based in large part on the discovery in Rome of the Golden House of Nero and the study of those wall decorations by Renaissance artists such as Pintoricchio and Raphael, see N. Dacos, *La Découverté de la Domus Aurea et la formation des grotesques à la Renaissance* (London,

1969). On ornamental prints later in the 16th century, see S. Schéle, *Cornelis Bos: A Study of the Origins of the Netherlands Grotesque* (Stockholm, 1965).

33. Some of the iconographic complexity and richness of this scene and the van Eyck *Rolin Madonna* on which it is based is generated precisely by this ambiguous (heavenly or earthly?) palace location. See, on the van Eyck, Philip, *Ghent Altarpiece,* pp. 190–92, 198–99.

34. E. Panofsky, *Renaissance and Renascences in Western Art* (Stockholm, 1960), p. 190, n.1; R. K. J. Reznicek, "De Reconstructie van 't' Altaer van S. Lucas' van Maerten van Heemskerck," *Oud Holland* 71 (1956): 233ff.; R. Grosshans, *Maerten van Heemskerck* (Berlin, 1980), pp. 109ff.

35. The only exception is his placement of donor figures on the wings of his *Crucifixion triptych* (Antwerp, Museum Mayer van den Bergh, cat. 22, F.56), a work with considerable workshop participation. Of course, van Cleve continues to feature donors at the side of holy figures in single panels as well as in altarpieces throughout his career. Gossaert's early works include some archaistic devotional diptychs, particularly the Doria diptych of Antonio Siciliano (ca. 1513–14) and the 1517 Jean Carondelet diptych (Paris). For these archaisms in context, see below.

36. One of the saints is identified as John the Baptist, a saint who also received masses at the altar of the Mechelen painters' guild, by A. Monballieu, "Bij de interpretatie en de datering van J. Gossaerts 'Lucas en de Madonna' uit Mechelen," *Miscellanea Josef Duverger* (Ghent, 1968), pp. 125–38. Monballieu also redates the Mechelen altarpiece to ca. 1513 by means of comparisons to the *Grimani Breviary* (commissioned by Siciliano).

37. Panofsky, *Renaissance and Renascences,* p. 68, fig. 48. The figure may be compared to Gossaert's drawing of a *Standing Hercules* (Lord Wharton coll., London; *Jan Gossaert genaamd Mabuse,* exh. cat., no. 47).

38. A. Katzenellenbogen, *The Sculptural Programs of Chartres Cathedral* (Baltimore, 1959), pp. 15, 66; I. Forsyth, *The Throne of Wisdom* (Princeton, 1972), for the association of the Madonna with Christian wisdom. For Minerva imagery, see R. Wittkower, "Transformations of Minerva in Renaissance Imagery," *JWCI* 2 (1939): 194–205. A more negative view of the owl as a bird of night and evil is summarized in L. Silver, "Of Beggars: Lucas van Leyden and Sebastian Brant," *JWCI* 39 (1976): 256, n.18–20.

39. E. de Jongh, "Speculaties over Jan Gossaerts Lucas-Madonna in Prag," pp. 43–61; P. Hübner, "Der Knabe mit der Gans," *Monatshefte für Kunstwissenschaft* 4(1911), discusses the ancient sculpture. In Bruegel's *Superbia* print, the bird of pride is a peacock rather than an eagle, but de Jongh's ornithology may be off—the "eagle" still resembles a goose—and his allegory correct.

40. M. Meiss, *Painting in Florence and Siena after the Black Death* (Princeton, 1951), pp. 143, 156, and "The Madonna of Humility," p. 434ff.; H. van Os, *Marias Demut und Verherrlichung in der sienisicher Malerei 1300–1450,* p. 77ff.

41. Panofsky, *ENP,* p. 352f.; H. Pauwels, "Jan Gossaert en van Eyck," pp. 4–15. The use of 15th-century models by 16th-century artists is acknowledged but conceived as part of a new vision by G. Brom, "Vernieuwing van onze schilderkunst in de vroege Renaissance," p. 7ff.

42. De Jongh, "Jan Gossaerts Lucas-Madonna."

43. Illustrated in Blum, fig. 54, in the context of a discussion of the popularity of the cult of the eucharist in 15th-century Flanders, p. 63, n. 28–30; see also Philip, *Ghent Altarpiece.* The mystical and fanatical devotion to the miraculous eucharistic host has been pointed out by historians of late medieval piety, such as Toussaert, pp. 116–21; Delaruelle, Labande and Ourliac, pp. 746–52. This phenomenon is also confirmed in the visual arts by the widespread popularity of the great miracle of the host, the Mystic Communion of St. Gregory, as a subject in late 15th-century art; see de Bosque, p. 138, n. 3, discussing the use of this subject in the context of the 1504 Valladolid retable (cat. 8, F. 84); J. Borchgrave d'Altena, "La Messe de Saint grégoire," p. 3–34. The cult of the eucharist and tabernacles as well as local eucharistic miracles are discussed in E. de Moreau, *L'Eglise en Belgique,* pp. 368–72. Most recently, the idolatry of the eucharist has been characterized by F. Oakley, *The Western Church in the Later Middle Ages,* pp. 88–89: "The introduction during the twelfth century of the elevation of the host at mass; the institution during the thirteenth century of the feast of Corpus Christi and processions of the Blessed Sacrament; the growth during the fourteenth and fifteenth centuries of the practice of exposing the previously consecrated eucharistic species for public adoration in an *ostensorium* or monstrance; a comtemporaneous increase, however modest and regional, of the frequency with which the laity actually received communion—all of these practices bear witness to a deepening of devotion to the mystery of the eucharist." Oakley also cites Archbishop Cranmer of England (1489–1556) as inquiring: "What was the cause of all these, and that as well the priest and the people so devoutly did knock and kneel at every sight of the sacrament, but that they worshipped that visible thing they saw with their eyes and took it for very God."

44. The interpretive history of this Late Gothic architectural form has yet to be written, but its visionary character points to a more mystical image of architecture than the "classic" forms of 13th-century "High Gothic" archetypes. Panofsky's *Gothic Architecture and Scholasticism* (Cleveland, 1977) attempts in an elliptical way to associate this later form of Gothic architecture with a "pictorial" experience or "subjectivism" (pp. 11–20). "Late Gothic permitted, even delighted in, flowing transitions and interpenetrations, and loved to defy the rule of correlation by, for instance, over-membrification of the ceiling and under membrification of the supports" (p. 50). For the roots of this attitude to architecture, see J. Bony, *The English Decorated Style Gothic Art Transformed 1250–1350* (Ithaca, N.Y., 1979), p. 62ff. Still fundamental is H. Focillon, *The Art of the West,* ed. J. Bony (London, 1963), vol. 2, pp. 139–57, who characterizes the architecture of the late Middle Ages as having "a quality of magic . . . an art of fantsy" (p. 149). If the notion of "decline" suggested by Panofsky and Focillon could be exorcised from the assumptions about Late Gothic architecture (whose very label points out the inherent assumptions which link it as a "baroque" late phase to "High" Gothic), perhaps it could be viewed as a vital component of a coherent culture. In some ways, a promising beginning has been made, partly through the process of elimination, by J. Bialostocki, "Late Gothic: Disagreements about the Concept," *Journal of the British Archaeological Assn.,* 3rd ser., 29 (1966): 76–105, with excellent bibliography. See also his "Die 'flamboyant Welt': Die zweite Hälfte des 15. Jahrhunderts im Norden," *Spätmittelalter und beginnende Neuzeit,* Propyläen Kunstgeschichte 7 (Berlin, 1972), pp. 98–105. Indeed, Baldass has adapted the term "Late Gothic style" for paintings of the end of the 15th century in Flanders: L. von Baldass, "Die Niederländischen Maler des spätgotischen Stiles," pp. 117–38. For France, see R. Sanfaçon, *L'architecture flamboyante en France* (Quebec, 1971).

45. The quotation is by K.G. Boon, *Jan Gossaert genaamd mabuse*, exh. cat., p. 23. For the Chicago van Cleve, see Hecht, "Infants Christ and John," pp. 222–29.

46. On inspiration of the Evangelists writing the Gospels, cf. I. Lavin, "Divine Inspiration in Caravaggio's Two *Saint Matthews*," *Art Bulletin* 56 (1974): 59–81, 590–91, discussing the Vienna Gossaert.

47. See note 31.

48. Panofsky, *Renaissance and Renascences*, p. 174f. In the case of Joos van Cleve or the conjunction of images between the Master of 1518 (Jan van Doornicke?) and Peter Coeck (G. Marlier, *Pierre Coeck d'Alost* [Brussels, 1966], pp. 109–45), these motifs carry over from works usually considered "Antwerp Mannerist" to succeeding works of the so-called "Flemish Renaissance".

49. As on the left wing of Roger van der Weyden's *Bladelin triptych* (Berlin); see Blum, p. 19.

50. For the *Adorations;* see Friedländer, vol. 9, nos. 7–10, 27, 28. For the icons, nos. 18, 48–64. Joos's development is well sketched by Friedländer in vol. 9, pp. 22–30.

51. *Jan Gossaert genaamd Mabuse*, no. 25.

52. Delaruelle, Labande, and Ourliac, pp. 870–79; S. Ozment, *The Reformation in the Cities*, pp. 1–46, esp. 21–22.

53. Delaruelle, Labande, and Ourliac, p. 875.

54. Ozment, *Reformation in the Cities*, pp. 24–32, 57. See also the full-length study by T.N. Tentler, *Sin and Confession on the Eve of the Reformation*, (Princeton, 1977).

55. The principal Bosch paintings are the Madrid *Tabletop of the Seven Deadly Sins* and the Washington *Death of the Miser*. For the ES print and the theme as a whole, with bibliography, see the exhibition catalogue *Europe in Torment* (Providence, 1974), pp. 79–80. See also Huizinga, pp. 147–51; R. Rudolph, *Ars moriendi* (Cologne, 1959); and for deathbed confessions in 15th-century Flanders, see Toussaert, p. 122.

56. *Jan Gossaert genaamd Mabuse*, pp. 98–104, no. 11.

57. Pope-Hennessey, *Portrait in the Renaissance*.

58. *Jan Gossaert genaamd Mabuse*, pp. 325–26, no. 65.

59. Thompson, *Pretext of Praise*.

60. Friedländer, vol. 12, pp. 49f., 9f.

61. See above, n. 2; also J. Held, "Artis pictoriae amator," p. 53ff.

62. E. Said, *Beginnings Intention and Method* (Baltimore, 1975), pp. 34, 83–84.

63 The *locus classicus* for this truism is Gombrich, *Art and Illusion*.

64. H.-W. von Löhneysen, *Die ältere niederländische Malerei*, p. 320; E. Kris and O. Kurz, *Legend, Myth, and Magic in the Image of the Artist*, Eng. ed. (New Haven, 1979), p. 14ff. Van Mander uses the same legend of an untrained artist for Herri met de Bles and Abraham Bloemart in his 1604 *Schilderboeck*.

65. Fickaert, *Metamorphosis, p. 16:*

> Een wander salck van Quinten Matsijs, dat noch heden deghs/ alsmen iemant van eenigh werck verbaren wilt/ dan seghtmen dese worden: Ey Masus! al aftmen segghen wilde: Ey vrient laet sulcken salck een man ghelyck Matsijs aenvatten/ uwen gheest is al te flecht/ u verstant al te cleyn.

Fickaert also translates Lampsonius's poem (see Chapter 1) from the 1572 engraved portrait by Wiericz of the "much renowned, widely famed, and most artistic" Quinten. I am grateful to Zirka Filipczak for discussing 17th-century Antwerp with me; see her important "The Social Status of Artists in Antwerp during the Seventeenth Century," (Ph.D. dissertation, Harvard University, 1973). A useful study of the concept of "painter" in the 17th-century Netherlands is based on contemporary texts: L. de Pauw–de Veen, *De Begrippen 'Schilder', 'Schilderey', en 'Schilderen' in de Zeventiende Eeuw* (Brussels, 1969).

Catalogue Raisonné
Paintings

I. THE EARLY WORKS Ca. 1491–1507

1. *Madonna and Child Enthroned, with Angels* (London) F. 25
2. Half-length *Madonna and Child with Book* (lost)
3. *Madonna Enthroned* at Half-length (Brussels) F. 20
4. *Salvator Mundi (Christ Blessing)* (Raleigh)
5. Diptych: *Christ Blessing, Virgin in Prayer* (Antwerp) F. 5
6. *St. John the Evangelist* (Padua)
7. *St. Christopher* (Antwerp) F. 32
8. *Adoration of the Magi* (Workshop; St. Louis) F. 59 (cf. F. 84)
9. *Madonna and Child Enthroned* (Brussels) F. 17

II. THE GREAT ALTARPIECES 1507–1513

10. *St. Anne altarpiece* (Brussels) F. 2 *1507–09*
11. *St. John altarpiece* (Antwerp) F. 1 *1508–11*
12. *Seven Sorrows of the Virgin* Polyptych (Lisbon, Worcester) F. 4 *before 1513*
13. *Madonna Standing in a Church with Angels* (Lyons, London / Seilern coll.) F. 27, 165
14. *Madonna with the Sleeping Child* (lost)
15. *Christ Carrying the Cross* (Hague) F. 167

III. PATINIR AND EXPERIMENTATION 1514–1524

16. *Moneychanger and his Wife* (Paris) F. 53 *1514*
17. *Pieta* (Paris) F. 16
18. *Passion altarpiece* (Coimbra) F. 196 *1514–17*
19. *Banker and his Client* (lost)
20. *Crucifixion* (Ottawa) F. 12
21. *Mary Magdalene and Mary of Egypt* (Philadelphia) F. 7
22. *Crucifixion altarpiece* (Antwerp) F. 56
23. *San Bernardino of Siena* (Formerly Lisbon, Salazar coll.)
24. *Lucas Rem altarpiece (Altarpiece of the Trinity with the Virgin)* (Munich) F. 3 *1518–20*
25. *Mystic Marriage of St. Catherine* (London) F. 28
26. *Temptation of St. Anthony* (Madrid) F. 31 *before 1522*
27. *Madonna and Child with Milk Soup* (Rotterdam) F. 168
28. *St. Jerome* (lost) F. 70
29. *Mary Magdalene* (Antwerp) F. 35
30. *Drunkard* (Formerly Dortmund/Becker coll.) F. 191
31. *Ecce Homo* (Madrid) F. 10
32. *Grotesque Pair: Old Woman / Old Man* (London / New York, private coll.) F. 52
33. *Franciscan Saint or Monk* (Barcelona) F. 30
34. *Infants Christ and John the Baptist Embracing* (Chatsworth) F. 29

IV. THE FINAL YEARS 1524–1530

35. *Ill-Matched Pair* (Washington) F. 54
36. *Madonna Nursing* (lost) F. 68
37. *Madonna Enthroned* (Berlin) F. 18
38. *Madonna Enthroned with Angels* (Formerly van Pannwitz coll.) F. 26
39. *Magdalene at a Balustrade* (Paris, private coll.)
40. *Adoration of the Magi* (New York) F. 8 *1526*
41. *Grieving Magdalene* (fragment; Berlin) F. 34
42. *Madonna and Child Outdoors* (Detroit) F. 23
43. *Laughing Man (Democritus)* (lost) F. 55

This is a summary catalogue. It lists major literature and history for each of Massys' authentic paintings. Isolated illustrations or exhibitions without scholarly commentary have been omitted unless they provide some contribution to understanding or dialogue. The condition of a painting should be presumed to be good unless otherwise specified; preservation is mentioned only where it is a subject of controversy or a case of serious damage.

The paintings are in approximate chronological order, clustered into groups anchored by dated or datable works. No attempt is made to date pictures more precisely than these clustered dates. In the author's opinion (which has changed since the writing of the dissertation on which this book is based), style is a highly imprecise way of dating, particularly for an artist like Massys, who establishes his figural types fairly early and maintains them with only minor changes during the course of his entire career. A good case in point is the female figures of the Antwerp *Lamentation* of 1508–11, whose faces reappear for sister saints and Madonna icons in many later incarnations. One must constantly remember that what might at first seem to be "period features"—colors or forms created during a particular moment in an artist's career—could just as easily be "generic features" chosen because of their appropriateness for presenting a particular subject. In no way can Massys' work be seen as a steady progression (Baldass, 1933) from "Gothic" to "Renaissance" features; as his latest Madonna icons make clear, the Virgin's environment can be either a domestic interior in the manner of the 15th-century models of Campin *(Madonna Nursing; Rattier Madonna,* 1529) or a tall, lacy, late Gothic hybrid throne *(Berlin Madonna)* still reminiscent of the artist's earliest icons *(Madonna and Child Enthroned, with Angels;* Half-Length *Madonna and Child with Book),* or else a lavish, novel Renaissance fantasy *(van Pannwitz Madonna; Madonna of the Cherries;* London *Mystic Marriage of St. Catherine).* Moreover, to date pictures with different subjects (hence, different generic forms) is also too tricky a task to permit any more precise dating. Only within the same basic formulas of icon, portrait, or secular picture can relative dates or developments be established. Based upon their different ambitions and their representational premises, portraits cannot be compared with the other pictures by Massys and will be listed as a separate group, again in approximate chronological order.

There is general consensus within accumulated scholarship about the attributions and often about dates of most of Massys' *oeuvre.* Most of these entries, therefore, will not contain major debates; dissent will be noted, particularly concerning dates. For those paintings in which most scholars have seen the hand of Massys but this catalogue demurs, a subsequent section of "Doubtful Attributions" is appended with discussion of authorship and/or date. Omitted paintings have been rejected as authentic Massys originals, and works preserved only in copies have been evaluated as if they were the missing originals and inserted at the place appropriate to their date of origin. Works attributed to Massys in other media (bronze medals, tapestries) will be treated separately in their own appendices.

Dimensions of individual pictures are in centimeters and on panel, except where noted. Each picture is accompanied by an F. number that refers to Friedländer's 1929 catalogue, as updated and amended in the 1971 English language edition. Friedländer's catalogue was arranged according to subject. Information about each painting has been derived from that definitive catalogue and from individual modern collections, whenever available.

I. THE EARLY WORKS (Ca. 1491–1507)

Juvenilia are in many ways the most difficult of all pictures to assign with confidence. They must be inferred, often without any precise information, from the artist's later, mature style. The process is like guessing the identity of a child from comparing its photograph with the facial features of an adult. These pictures must be considered as the embryonic versions of the painter's mature style. Often, they are without documentation, owing to the obscurity of the fledgling artist when he made them. Moreover, the juvenilia often show greater dependence on models and precedents than later works, which are marked by the greater independence of the mature craftsman. In short, the labels for most of these pictures should be taken as tentative in both their attributions and their dates, even though they do not specifically appear in the "Problematic Pictures" section.

The terminal dates of this large period are given by the entry of Massys into the Antwerp St. Luke guild of painters in 1491 *(terminus post quem)* and by his first documented, large-scale product, the St. Anne altarpiece of 1507–09 (cat. 10, F. 2) which begins to define the archetypal Massys forms.

Closest to the *St. Anne altarpiece* in types is the Brussels *Virgin Enthroned* (cat. 9, F. 17), which provides both a female type and a Christ Child for comparison. Mary's right-facing, egg-shaped oval head is very similar to the Mary Cleophas in the lower left of *Pl. 48* the *Holy Kinship*. Her long, brown, flowing hair and spiky halo reappear in the Virgin of the *Anne altarpiece*. Yet the Brussels *Pl. 1* picture offers its own, different qualities, in particular a much more insistent, dark shading. The shadowy modeling follows the curve of the Madonna's jaw and accentuates her features. Mary's hands in the Brussels painting also look stiffer—less delicate in their pose than in the later works of Massys. The Child in the Brussels picture is a type close to the *St. Anne* Infant: high forehead, fuzzy indistinct hair, tiny button nose, and flat, beanlike ears, as well as the same form of nimbus. Younger than the Christ of the *Holy Kinship*, the Brussels Child compares closely to the tiny infant of Mary Cleophas with a prayerbook at the *Pl. 5* lower left corner of the *Holy Kinship*. The colors of the *Virgin Enthroned* are soft in hue, like those of the *St. Anne altarpiece*, but appear thicker and less transparent, along with their more-pronounced interest in light and shadow. The Brussels panel features a basic contrast between the rose of Mary's gown and the various tones of grey in both Christ's mantle and the surrounding architecture. This particular color scheme is one favored by Massys for Madonna pictures, even at the end of his career (e.g., *Detroit Madonna)*. In the Brussels panel, the effect of this simplified color scheme is the powerful isolation of the *Pl. 64* figure of Mary.

The Brussels painting has an architectural framework in its throne structure that is more conventional and Gothic than the fantastic architecture of the *Holy Kinship;* its gabled statuary niches closely resemble contemporary Flemish building ornament. Also traditional is the jewel-bordered gown of the Virgin, which resembles the standard formulas of the School of Bruges, most recently exemplified by Hans Memling but reaching back to the formulations of Jan van Eyck two generations earlier. Massys' dependence on Bruges models for his own earlier pictures is hardly surprising in light of the economic and cultural dominance of Bruges throughout the 15th century, to be eclipsed by Antwerp only during Massys' lifetime. Memling (d. 1494) was the foremost Bruges painter of his generation and would have been the principal artistic figure in the Flanders of Massys' youth.

The close match between the forms of the Brussels *Madonna Enthroned* and the Holy Kinship panel of the *St. Anne altarpiece* suggests that the icon probably dates close in time to the retable, i.e., only a few years before 1507. We can be no more specific, but confirmation of the date's validity comes from a pair of altarpiece shutters in the Church of the Holy Savior, Valladolid, Spain (F. 84). These panels are dated 1504 and are documented as having been donated by Licentiate Gonzalo Gonzales; they *Pl. 74* were originally thought by Justi to be the work of Massys (cf. cat. 8). Friedländer and de Bosque, however, are surely correct to assign the panels to a Massys follower, but these images do offer a barometer of Massys' style as it had developed by 1503-04. Mary's face in the two scenes of the *Nativity* and *Adoration of the Magi* has the same oval shape and features as the Brussels *Madonna Enthroned* and much the same shading for the curve of the jaw and the nose. The Valladolid Child, while hairless, has the same tiny nose, stuck-on ears, and domelike skull as the Brussels Christ, even as this figure appears in its fastidious outlines to be the product of a different artist. The Spanish shutters also present male figures close in type to the Joseph and Joachim of the *St. Anne* scenes. In similar fashion, the angels around the manger of the Valladolid *Nativity* resemble the wavy-haired children of the *Holy Kinship*. What the Spanish altarpiece reveals, in sum, is that most of the mature figure types used by Massys in 1507 had already developed by 1504 in Antwerp, perhaps in Quinten's own studio.

Our ground becomes increasingly less firm on the path toward Massys' first works. The Brussels *Madonna Enthroned* offers a link to another consensus Massys image, the Antwerp *St. Christopher*, whose Christ Child has the same domical head with fuzzy *Pl. 113* hair and delicate features as the Brussels child. But the Antwerp *St. Christopher* has its own distinctive qualities: the pronounced eyelids and staring eyes, shared by both the Child and Christopher. These characteristics contrast with the drowsy-looking, slit eyes of both males and females in Massys' later, mature works and illustrate a habitual formula of the earlier period that would be replaced by another formula later. Another oddity is the prominent nimbus of the Antwerp *St. Christopher*, a striking contrast with the muted halo of the *St. Anne*. Christopher himself is forcefully shaded in the manner of the Brussels Virgin, but his face is blockier in structure (e.g., his nose) than the more-angular, bearded faces of either the *Holy Kinship* or the Valladolid shutters. The form of the saint's face again seems to grow out of another artist's established formulas, in this case the dark male faces of Massys' older Bruges contemporary Gerard David (cf. in particular the faces of David's Bruges Justice panels of 1498).

A stunning novelty of the *St. Christopher* is its deep landscape, receding dramatically to a low horizon with a glowing sunrise. At the left, powerful, rocky cliffs close the composition, as Massys would compose his outdoor scenes for the 1509–11 *Antwerp* *Pl. 20* *Lamentation* or the 1513 Madre de Deus altarpiece scenes (Worcester *Rest on the Flight;* Lisbon *Women at the Tomb;* cat. 12, F. 4). *Pl. 28* The image of St. Christopher in a landscape is the only one of Massys' earliest works that clearly derives from the heritage of his *Pl. 27* own home town; Friedländer has already demonstrated the importance for this picture of the Louvain artist Dieric Bouts (d. 1475) and his sons, who continued to be leading painters of Louvain during the period when Massys grew up there.

Linked to the Antwerp *St. Christopher* but probably predating it by a few years is the Brussels *Madonna at Half-Length* (cat. 3, F. *Pl. 39* 20) with a background brocade supported by putto-like angels. Here the motif is similar to the later Brussels *Madonna Enthroned:* Christ sits on Mary's lap reading a book. The Virgin wears the same mantle, with jeweled borders and a squared v-neck. Her halo, however, is more emphatic—glowing golden rays within a circle of yellow light. The Madonna's hazy soft facial modeling is less pronounced than in the later Brussels work, but the shape of her face is even more distant from the *St. Anne* types than any of the images thus far. This early visage is a broad ellipse, almost without chin or tapering. Like the Antwerp *St. Christopher* type, the Christ Child here has wide-open, staring eyes set off by prominent eyelids. In this image, the overall effect is flatter and more decorative than the solid bodies of later Massys works, but caution reminds us that these forms, reinforced by the fleur-de-lis brocade behind the holy figures, could simply be the result of a different visual goal, one of dematerialization rather than substantiality.

Farthest of all from the mature forms and almost certainly dating from the artist's earliest years is the London *Madonna* *Pl. 38* *Enthroned* (cat. 1, F. 25, formerly Dyson-Perrins collection). This picture achieves much of its effect through a rigid symmetry and an elaborate gilded throne that occupies almost half the picture surface. In contrast to the Brussels *Madonna at Half-Length,* set close to the viewer, the London *Madonna* is set back at greater depth and observed full-length, but again this is a different, more-reserved choice of presentation. This Madonna is the bulkiest, yet most formless of all thus far. Her stiffness is echoed by that of the Child and attendant angels. The faces of all figures are markedly different from previous images by Massys. Mary's face is so rounded and broad as to appear bloated and almost circular. Her radiating golden rays resemble the forms still employed in the later Brussels image, and the soft, flowing brown hair already is established as a Massys trademark. The costume has the same ingredients, but here the jeweled borders of the Bruges School are mere dots of light instead of shapes. The head of Christ deserves comparison to the other types we have seen, especially in the tiny nose and indistinct, fuzzy hair. Here again appear the staring eyes and framing lids, but they are more like dots of color than like the alert features of the later faces. Both figures of this incipient effort seem clumsy, posed, stiff, and lacking in the lustrous glow that infuses Massys' later efforts.

This roster of examples has been chosen for more general discussion because such images offer an unbroken chain of comparisons of Madonna and Child types and because of some of the additional features, such as landscape, costume, haloes. Establishing dates can only be guesswork, although the steady links seem to provide a coherent sequence of successive types representing the very same figures. Only extrapolation from the well-established *St. Anne altarpiece* makes this sequence possible, with any and all other attributed early works in this catalogue filling in the gaps by the same process of comparison.

Cat. 1. *Madonna and Child Enthroned, with Angels* (F. 25). London, National Gallery, no. 6282 (0.62 × 0.43).* *Plate 38*

HIST.: 17 June 1924 Sneyd sale, Keele Hall, lot 69; bought by Buttery; before 1927, coll. C.W. Dyson-Perrins; 1958 bequest to Gallery.

LIT.: Friedländer, "Neues zu Quentin Massys," p. 6f; Friedländer 7, p. 19; Baldass, pp. 139f, 159; Boon, p. 12; Mallé, p. 81; Cuttler, p. 419; Davies, *Early Netherlandish School, National Gallery Catalogues,* p. 90; DB, pp. 106–7.

This conservative panel clearly derives from the hieratic Madonnas made popular by Hans Memling in Bruges. De Bosque has compared the rounded, fleshy face to the model of Robert Campin, such as the London *Madonna Nursing* or *Mérode altarpiece* (N.Y., Cloisters). It is generally accepted as Massys' earliest extant work (excepting, perhaps, the Seilern *Pl. 90* Coll. *Crucifixion,* cat. Suppl. A). Numerous details suggest an early date. The spiky, rigid halo is highly prominent, as is the "unreal" (Boon) golden throne. Spatial construction is awkward, including the arms of the throne and the receding floor tiles. Small, dotted, staring eyes reveal no character or emotion. Faces are tiny in relation to bodies; they are topped by fuzzy mops of hairlike caps. The miniature features sit close together within the simple geometric shapes of the heads. The only real modeling is the shading along the side of the Madonna's broad, round face. Regular symmetry and stiff poses of bodies and hands suggest the cautious hand of a novice.

Cat. 2. *Half-length Madonna and Child with Book* (lost).

A. Vienna, Schottenstift Coll.

LIT.: Baldass, p. 159, n. 34; idem, "Ein Madonnentüchlein aus der Nähe des Quinten Metsys," *Melanges Hulin de Loo* (Brussels/Paris, 1931), p. 31f.

B. Holland, private coll. (38 × 29.5)

LIT.: *Nederlandse Primitieven,* exh. cat. (Laren, 1961), no. 56, plate 20.

C. Liege, coll. Wittert (50 × 35). *Plate 41*

LIT.: L. Dewez, *Les peintures anciennes de la collection Wittert,* (Liege, 1955).

D. New York, Newhouse Gallery (not available) *Plate 40*

From the close correspondence between the various versions of this lost composition, a composite prototype emerges. The Liege panel cannot be the Massys original because it contains additions—an apple in the lower left corner and rosary around the neck of Christ—that are not present in any other copies. The Vienna panel has perhaps the best claim to be original, but its gravely damaged condition is apparent even in photographs, so no definitive judgment is possible.

The composition of the lost Massys original agrees in many ways with the London *Madonna Enthroned* (cat. 1). Behind its half-length figures, another gold throne emphasizes the regal majesty of Mother and Child; however, emphatic dark hatching reduces the spatial awkwardness created by the brilliant glitter. Emphatic halos composed of radial gold "spokes" are used again. Mary's aura forms a circle conforming to the pure, round shape of her head, while Christ's is subdivided like the points of a compass.

As in the London *Madonna Enthroned,* Mary wears a V-neck gown. Her trunk is again a massive pyramidal shape that entirely encloses the body of Christ. A new feature is the three-tiered pearl diadem, which is reproduced exactly in all copies.

The lost half-length represents several improvements on the London panel, such as the greater control over the distracting gold throne. Even its half-length format is symptomatic of an increased desire to suggest greater warmth

*In the following catalogue, all dimensions are in centimeters, unless otherwise indicated.

and intimacy after the stiff distance of London figures. Mary places one hand around Christ, instead of merely holding His prayerbook. Her expression, although still dreamy and thoughtful, has softened and no longer has the effect of a stare. The changes are even more evident in the body of Christ, who no longer seems so rigid. The Child now crosses his feet—a motif borrowed from the followers of Bouts and van der Goes—and twists His body slightly. Although the facial type is the same as the London panel, with fuzzy hair and emphatically outlined eyelids, Massys displays a more developed sense of flesh and roundness, which are apparent even through the copies. Presumably the lost half-length was painted around the time of, or a few years after, the London *Madonna Enthroned.*

Cat. 3. *Madonna Enthroned at Half-Length* (F. 20). Brussels, Musées Royaux, no. 643 (62 × 50). *Plate 39*

HIST.: "anciens depots" (Museum catalogue).

LIT.: Cohen, p. 49; Brising, p. 10; Delen, p. 44f.; Friedländer 7, p. 18f.; Baldass, pp. 139, 159; Mallé, p. 82; *Catalogue de la peinture ancienne* (Brussels, 1957), p. 70; Puyvelde 1970, p. 231; DB, pp. 108–10.

A. Copy by Massys imitator (F. 20a), Brussels, Musées Royaux no. 6647 (47.5 × 35.5 with frame)

HIST.: coll. E. Renders, Bruges; H. Goering, Berchtesgaden; Museum acquisition from Belgian state, 1952.

LIT.: *De Eeuw van Bruegel,* exhibition cat., p. 138, no. 164; DB, pp. 110–12.

Direct comparison of the two panels in the Brussels Museum shows the rounded panel from the Renders collection to be the work of an imitator, however attractive his product. The slender face of the Madonna and the peculiar squat head of Christ fail to conform to the facial characteristics in the previous catalog entries and in Brussels no. 643. Instead, they appear much closer to the copy of the same composition by the Master of the Morrison Triptych (Kreuzlingen, Kisters coll., Friedländer 7, no. 88).

On the other hand, Brussels 643 takes its place in the consistent evolution of Massys' types. The Madonna's face, with its more gracefully tapered chin, is still a fairly broad oval. Christ's head, too, remains round, with characteristic fuzzy hair and "double-lidded" eyes. But the Child exhibits greater activity and expressive movement. He clutches a rosary with one hand and, with the other, absent-mindedly crumples a page He is turning in a prayerbook. This youthful Christ stares self-possessedly at the viewer and is, in turn, carefully watched by a thoughtful Mary. Massys is increasingly interested in the expression of character and emotion in his holy figures.

Although the figures are in half-length, Massys shows them seated in a throne. The throne is awkwardly constructed, with arms that converge too sharply, despite the cloth of honor, held by putto-like angels to disguise the throne's spatial shortcomings. Massys here displays inconsistencies and hesitations that mark him as an inexperienced painter.

The royal nature of the holy figures is expressed by the throne and the cloth of honor, the accompanying angels (who, despite their rounder faces, recall the flying pair of the London *Madonna Enthroned*), and the jeweled borders of Mary's mantle (also more plastic than in the London panel). Christ no longer bears a halo, but the Madonna's is made still more emphatic by a circle of yellow light around the golden rays.

Cat. 4. *Salvator Mundi (Christ Blessing).* North Carolina Museum of Art, Raleigh (no. GL 60.1762) (21″ × 14¼″).

HIST.: Samuel H. Kress Coll; French and Co., New York; ex-coll. Ormanda Ruiz. *Plate 44*

LIT.: Stanley Ferber, "Quentin Matsys' 'Salvator Mundi,'" *Bulletin of North Carolina Museum of Art* 9 (1970): 37–41; Colin Eisler, *European Paintings Excluding Italian from the Samuel H. Kress Collection* (Oxford, 1977), p. 77f.

A. Variant copy: Aachen, Suermondt-Museum (F. 65), no. 295 (66 × 43).

HIST.: Weber Coll.

LIT.: DB, p. 135.

The bareheaded *Christ Blessing* of North Carolina is clearly a close relative of Massys' powerful Antwerp *Salvator Mundi* *Pl. 43* (F. 4, cat. 5). Both figures appear frontally, Raleigh at half-length, Antwerp at bust-length. Both works display an orb of royalty surmounted by a cross of delicate filigree goldwork. The respective figures wear simple monochrome cloaks decorated with golden interlace trim and fastened at the neck with a large brooch clasp. Fine differences still distinguish the two versions. Raleigh's brooch is more elaborate, featuring a seated image of Moses with the decalogue under a lacy Gothic shrine. The Antwerp panel has a simpler configuration of jewels. The crosses offer a complementary degree of elaboration in each case: Raleigh's cross is simpler and jewel-encrusted, whereas Antwerp's highlights a central Christ enthroned in a tabernacle with animal symbols of the four evangelists at the extremities of the cross. Such a marked similarity between the ornamentation of the two panel reveals an essential kinship of sensibility.

Details of presentation separate the two works. The Antwerp Christ appears against a deep blue background with radiating golden rays in the form of his halo. Raleigh's background is bordered by cloud-forms and presents a golden surface articulated by red, measle-like dots; this peculiar vision of heaven reappears in several images associated with a Massys contemporary in Antwerp, the Master of Frankfurt (e.g., in the Washington *Virgin and Child with St. Anne,* where this background appears within a blue daytime sky as a vision of God the Father). The dark circular halo around Christ's head in North Carolina is as unique in Massys' work as that peculiar gold and red sky.

Particular qualities of execution in the Raleigh panel cast further uncertainty about Massys' authorship. Specifically, the sharp linear outlines and darker modeling of face and hands diverge noticeably from the Antwerp technique. If anything, the characteristic long, tapering Massys fingers are even longer and more delicate than usual in the Raleigh image. Assigning comparisons to the North Carolina image also proves difficult. The darker shading and plasticity of the face stand closest to the main figure of Massys' Antwerp

Pl. 113 *St. Christopher* (F. 32, cat. 7), yet the broader and rounder
Pl. 39 shape stands closest to the softly modeled Massys figures like the Brussels *Madonna at Half-Length* (F. 29, cat. 3). In short, the Raleigh picture offers many of the features characteristic of the young Massys and his Antwerp colleagues; yet anomalous elements, particularly the background, prevent any conclusive attribution to Massys or, for that matter, to a follower, copyist, or imitator. Even if it is by the youthful artist, this is a picture with borrowings and experiments, filled with the uncertainties that plague definitive attributions of juvenilia. In the case of the Raleigh panel, the relationship to Massys' Antwerp *Christ Blessing* is even sufficiently undefined to leave open the question of which image lies closer to the maturity of the *St. Anne altarpiece.*

Cat. 5. *Christ Blessing; Virgin in Prayer* (F. 5). Antwerp, Koninklijk Museum, nos. 241–42 (38 × 28.5 each). *Plates 42–43*

HIST.: Visible in the art collection painted by François
Pl. 174 Francken II, *The Party of the Art Lover* (Munich, Alte Pinakothek; ill. 4b)—cf. Speth-Holterhoff 84f., no. 24. The painting was formerly in the collection of N. Rockox (d. 1640)—cf. Denucé, p. 89, no. 23. "Twee contrefeytsels d'eene van onsen Salichmaecker ende dander van onse Lieve Vrouwe, oliewerve op panneel, met twee ledekens aen malcanderen." Acquired in 1828 from the van Ertborn bequest; formerly coll. Countess van der Werve de Vorselaer, Antwerp.

LIT.: Hymans, p. 16ff.; Cohen, pp. 16ff., 81; Bosschere, p. 30ff.; Brising, p. 12f.; Winkler, p. 202; Delen, p. 53; Friedländer 7, p. 32; Baldass, pp. 140, 146, 154, 157, 160, 168; *Beschrijvende Catalogus* (Antwerp, 1959), p. 174; Broadley, p. 209; von der Osten, p. 148; *Deutsche und Niederländische Gemälde bis 1550,* Wallraf-Richartz Museum (Cologne, 1969), p. 69f.; DB, pp. 131–34.

A. Reversed copy (F. 5a), London, National Gallery, no. 295 (58.5 × 33 cm each).
LIT.: Davies, *Early Netherlandish School,* p. 92; Cohen, p. 85 ("maturer than Antwerp"); DB, pp. 134–35.

Numerous other copies, including Lille, Museum; Los Angeles County Museum (no. 62.19; Virgin only, reversed); Cologne, Wallraf-Richartz Museum (F. 5b; no. A 1069; Virgin only, reversed).

Baldass argues that the London copies reveal an even earlier style than the Antwerp diptych, and he postulates the existence of a still-earlier pair of panels by Massys, copied by the London artist and reversed by Massys himself in the Antwerp panels. The only reason for this assertion must be the large number of copies with Mary facing the other direction at the left side of Christ. To have placed her at the right side of Christ makes Him occupy the *sinister* portion of the diptych, thus constituting a reversal of normal heraldic form. Yet the ultimate source of the diptych, Jan van Eyck's Ghent altarpiece, placed Mary to the right of God in her role as intercessor for mankind; in the same altarpiece, John the Baptist appeared at the left side of Christ, so there was no breach of heraldic precedence (cf. the copy by Gossaert, Pl. 47). Since the chief difference between the copies and the Antwerp panels is the "correction" of the figures' relative position and, frequently, the more naturalistic tendency to omit haloes (and, often, Mary's crown), there is no necessary reason to assume an earlier Massys version than the Antwerp diptych. For one thing, the Antwerp panels agree most closely with their Eyckian model, so that all succeeding copies can be seen to be adaptations of the surving diptych. No visible stylistic difference in the London panels or any other copies would establish them as earlier than the Antwerp originals. Indeed, Cohen calls them more mature than the Antwerp panels. And, according to the Francken copy (Pl. 174), the Massys diptych originally had the same orientation as the Antwerp panels.

In terms of verisimilitude, the Antwerp diptych reveals Massys' coming-of-age as a painter. Almost life-size, the faces of Christ and the Virgin are painted with the subtlest of skin tones and a meticulous attention to textural detail, especially as seen in the hare of Christ's beard and Mary's gossamer veil. Jewels and goldwork have a clarity of form not found in the previous Madonna paintings. The pinkish
skin color is related to the earlier Brussels *Madonna* (cat. 3) Pl. 39
but more closely resembles the Antwerp *St. Christopher* Pl. 11
(cat. 7).

Like the Brussels *Madonna,* the Antwerp diptych features rather broad oval faces, along with a firm outline around the eyes. The haloes are bathed in colored light like the Brussels panel, but they have become spikier, with uneven beams of light extending outside the glow. The soft pastel colors—bluish-grey for Mary's gown, pinkish-orange for Christ's—accord well with the Brussels *Madonna.*

The ultimate model of the Antwerp figures are van Eyck's Ghent altarpiece *Virgin in Prayer* and *Holy Trinity.* The Virgin's full, rounded face and long, flowing hair are coupled with details of dress, like the richly ornate crown, in both the Ghent and Antwerp works. Similarly, the beard, blessing gesture, and gilded scepter link the respective Christ figures. In the case of the Antwerp diptych, Massys has not combined two models from the past, as is often his customs (cf.
the Brussels *Madonna Enthroned,* cat. no. 9), but in addition Pl. 48
to the Ghent altarpiece, he has drawn upon the bust-length format made popular by later 15th-century artists, especially Roger van der Weyden and Dieric Bouts. Van Eyck himself had created an early form of the bust-length holy
figure, a *Holy Face* (best version, Swinburne coll., Newcastle), Pl. 4
which might also have been familiar to Massys. Roger van Pl. 4
der Weyden (e.g., *Braque altarpiece*) and Dieric Bouts, with their workshops, greatly increased the number of these portrait-like icons as small-scale votive images (cf. Ringbom, p. 39ff.). Such isolated iconic bust images of Christ and the Virgin were popular personal objects and can often be seen in the background interiors of paintings with pious donors or praying holy figures. The bust-length had a particular association with the gesture of royal blessing from a balcony, so it was additionally appropriate to the depiction of holy figures.

Massys' archaism in this image pair corresponds to another adaptation of the same period by Jan Gossaert, who
also copied the Ghent altarpiece figures for his *Deësis* (Ma- Pl. 4
drid, Prado). There is no information about the donor or circumstances of this painting, but because it was painted on paper, the *Deësis* may have been made for the same kind of

private devotion as the other folios seen tacked on walls within paintings. Gossaert added his own distinctive Late Gothic architectural fantasy to his model, but essentially his *Deësis,* too, replicates a particular famous and venerable devotional image.

Cat. 6. *St. John the Evangelist* (F. 71). Padua, Museo Civico, no. 273 (33.5 × 25.5). *Plate 175*
HIST.: Legacy to Count Leonardo Capodilista.
LIT.: *Zeitschrift für bildende Kunst* N.F. 24 (1913): 268; Friedländer 7, p. 68; Baldass, p. 164; DB, pp. 136–37.

Damaged in both hands and monochrome background, this bust-length picture is probably only a fragment; however, its face is quite well preserved. The attribution to Massys was proposed by Baldass in 1933, who dates it to the early years of the 16th century. The soft modeling and pinkish tonality of the facial features and highlights of the hair mass recall the Antwerp *Christ Blessing* (F. 4, cat. 5). The facial type can
Pl. 1 also be compared to the male saints of the 1507–09 *Holy Kinship,* except for Padua's distinctive, tight-lidded eyes, seen only in earlier Massys works. The only other compara-
Pl. 39 ble Massys original is the half-length *Brussels Madonna* (F. 20, cat. 3), where the eyes of Christ and the relatively flat color surfaces of the drapery suggest conceptions like those of the Padua *Evangelist.* X-rays have revealed, in the rounded upper half of the panel above the Evangelist's head, two gilded acanthus scroll ornaments, thicker but akin to the gold patterns of the Antwerp pendants of *Christ Blessing* and the *Virgin in Prayer.*

Cat. 7. *St. Christopher* (F. 32). Antwerp, Koninklijk Museum no. 29 (1.06 × 0.72 m.). *Plate 113*
HIST.: Van Ertborn legacy, 1841.
LIT.: Bosschere, p. 94; Delen, p. 50; Winkler, p. 196; Friedländer 7, p. 20; Baldass, pp. 140, 146, 154, 157, 160, 168; Friedländer, "Quentin Massys: Reflexions on his Development," p. 53f.; Roosen-Runge, p. 19ff.; Boon, p. 16; Mallé, p. 81; Puyvelde, 1970, p. 231; Robbins, p. 58ff.; DB, pp. 130–31.

Previous scholars have traced the links between Massys' panel and a Dieric Bouts composition of the saint, showing the figure at twilight in midstream between rocky cliffs. Albert Bouts's Modena *Christopher* (Friedländer 3, no. 71) and the right wing of the "Pearl of Brabant" triptych (Dieric the Younger?; Munich, Alte Pinakothek; Friedländer 3, no. 24; fig. 5a) offer the closest comparisons—including the rosy glow of the rising sun in the Munich panel. Common to Massys' work and the Boutsian compositions is the craggy cliff at the left of the composition (showing a guiding monk with a lantern in the Antwerp and Modena versions), contrasted with a more-placid distant landscape. Friedländer has rightfully stressed the more heroic character of Massys' straining saint and the impressive sense of recession created by a lower horizon and point of view.

What has been neglected is the position of the Massys *Christopher* within a long and consistent tradition of images. Bouts himself owes a debt to earlier representations of the saint; like 15th-century manuscript illuminators of the north Netherlands, he goes back to a previous model (cf. Sulzberger, "Dieric Bouts et l'enluminure hollandaise," p. 227ff.). The most striking manuscript example comes from the *Hours of Catherine of Cleves* (New York, Morgan Library; fo. 275); this folio shows numerous parallels with Massys' Antwerp panel. Both pictures feature brilliant lighting effects against low horizons, and they produce a golden nimbus around Christ's head (omitted from the Bouts works). The hermit monk appears with his lantern at the left, inside a cliff grotto; below, in the lower-left corner, a mighty boulder anchors the composition. In the right middle distance is a tiny boat (several in the Massys panel), while opposite, behind the cliff, lies a tiny townscape (more trees in the *Cleves Hours).* The only major discrepancy between the two depictions is the interpretation of Christopher himself: Massys shows the saint burdened and struggling toward the rocky shore, while the miniaturist shows him almost upright, glancing hesitantly away from the cliff to the river bank he has left behind. Both show Christopher holding a long pole across his body with both hands.

Perhaps the best record of the common model is a *Christopher* drawing, attributed by Friedländer (Vol. 1, plate 68a) to Jan van Eyck, but probably by a follower. Since it omits the essential twilight lighting of the Massys and *Cleves Hours* versions, the drawing is not the single source of those two compositions. Yet it provides a missing link that helps clarify what the lost model looked like. The rocky coastlines were more like the manuscript replica; "axe-cut" rocks below the monk (whose pose is identical with the drawing), the tuft of grass at the summit, the towering cliff at the right, and the boulder in front of the saint—all are identical; so Massys altered his model to produce a contrast between the two shores.

But Massys' *Christopher* is probably closer to the original source. Like the Louvre drawing, it shows the giant striding forward but bent over the staff that crosses his body (both the drawing and the Antwerp panel show a staff that is forked at the top). The *Cleves Hours,* however, repeats Christ's orb and fluttering drapery, which Massys eliminated and replaced only with Christopher's flapping headband. The Louvre drawing also preserves the suggestion of background boats and townscape in the same positions as in the *Cleves Hours* and Massys paintings.

Much of the final image is already expressed clearly in the *Beaufort Hours* (London, British Museum Royal 2 AX VIII, fo. llv.; ill. Panofsky, *ENP,* ill. 173): monk, cliffside, nocturne, and foreground rocks. And the composition also found favor among late 15th-century printmakers: Master FVB (P. 146), the Housebook Master (L. 32), and Israhel van Meckenem (G. 269); cf. the illustrations in E.K. Stahl, *Die Legende vom heil. Riesen Christophorus in der Graphik des 15. und 16. Jahrhunderts* (Munich, 1920), nos. 98, 108, 94, respectively. All these examples serve to point out a single famous (or at least often-copied) prototype—most likely a pre-Eyckian panel painting, because it was visible for copies in so many different media. The special cult veneration of Christopher as a protector against sudden death (see Chapter 4) would have created a demand for images of the saint and would have lent a mystical aura to particular panels, which would have been copied for their miraculous powers. Such devotion explains the number of almost identical copies, particularly in prints, which were circulated in multiple replicas, like prints.

Massys' *St. Christopher* can be dated among his earlier works because of details like the prominent halo and staring, double-lidded eyes. Yet vigor and flowing movement are achieved, particularly in the draperies and in the pose of the saint. Brownish shadows are accentuated in comparison to previous works, although pinkish skin tones and pastel coloration resemble the achievement of the Antwerp diptych (F. 4, cat. 5). The darker shadows and the descriptively detailed, masculine facial type of Massys' *Christopher* derive from works of Gerard David, like the bearded Cambyses in the *Judgment of Sisamnes* (Bruges, Stedelijk Museum). A similar Davidian chiaroscuro pervades Massys' Brussels *Ma-*
Pl. 48 *donna Enthroned* (F. 17, cat. 9) and suggests a close relationship between Massys and David and Bruges during the early years of the 16th century.

Cat. 8. *Adoration of the Magi* (Workshop; F. 59a) *Plate 73*
St. Louis Art Museum, no. 93. 26 (F. 59a; 1.288 × 1.003 m.).

HIST.: van den Corput coll., Brussels; Fischer Gallery, Washington; Ehrich Galleries, New York.

LIT.: J. Destrée, *Hugo van der Goes* (Brussels, 1914), pp. 115f., 124; Winkler, *Das Werk des Hugo van der Goes,* p. 198ff.; L. Reis-Santos, *Eduardo, o português* (Lisbon, 1966), p. 13; Friedländer 7, p. 66; L. Silver, *Early Northern European Paintings* (Bulletin; The St. Louis Art Museum, Summer 1982), p. 8f.

Copies and Variants: A. Formerly Berlin, Kaiser Friedrich Museum, no. 569a (F. 59); B. Lübeck, Museum für Kunst und Kulturgeschichte, no. 21 (F. 59e).

Comparative painting: altar shutter, *Adoration of the Magi* (F. 84) Church of San Salvador, Valladolid (2.37 × 1.42 m.) *Plate 74*

LIT.: K. Justi, *Jahrbuch der preussischen Kunstsammlungen* 8 (1887), p. 24ff.; Hymans, p. 206, Cohen, p. 38ff.; Bosschere, p. 36; J. Agapito y Revilla, *La Capilla de San Bautista* (Valladolid, 1912); Friedländer 7, pp. 21, 44, 66, 70; Baldass, p. 174; Malle, p. 82; DB, pp. 137–45.

The stumpy, thick-set figures and their lunging postures in the St. Louis painting are not the work of Massys himself; moreover, their faces reveal a harder outline than the delicate flesh tones and modelling of an authentic Massys. Nonetheless, the painting as a whole agrees in its main figures with a number of other works taken by Friedländer and other scholars to be the surviving variant copies after a lost Massys Adoration composition. In addition, underdrawings, especially visible in the robes of the angel in white in the St. Louis picture, suggest that at the very least this panel was not slavishly copied from some pre-existing image. The bearded magi, with their long faces and chiseled noses, resemble the men from Massys' *Holy Kinship* from the *St.*
Pl. 1 *Anne altarpiece* (F. 2, cat. 10); the Madonna and Child, too, show the softly modeled oval faces and linear features to be found in the Brussels work of 1507–09. The background landscape, which differs considerably from other copies of the composition, nevertheless provides spindly trees, craggy outcrops, and building types akin to the setting behind
Pl. 28 Massys' Worcester *Rest on the Flight* from the *Seven Sorrows Polyptych,* sent to Portugal before 1513 (F. 4, cat. 12). Thus, the St. Louis picture might have been executed by Massys' workshop, but it seems to be the finest surviving version of his design. Given the present information, we cannot be certain whether or not Massys ever completed a better, lost image of this composition himself. Yet it was clearly this Massys composition that served as the basis for a crowded variation (note that the eldest magus kisses the hand of Christ as opposed to his prayer in the Massys version) in Valladolid (F. 84), dated by inscription to the year 1503.

Winkler was the first to point out the heavy debt of this Massys composition to Hugo van der Goes. Two separate Goesian compositions of the *Adoration of the Magi* seem to have played a part in Massys' creation. The first is the *Monforte altarpiece* (Berlin-Dahlem). It features Mary and Pl. 76
Christ along a wall with the magi kneeling or standing in the same relative poses, and it features the same dress and facial types—the presence of a black magus is a distinctive Goesion element. Furthermore, the left background of the *Monforte altarpiece* features buildings and grooms with horses like the background of the Massys version. However, the *Monforte altarpiece* has a right-to-left movement which is reversed in the Massys composition. Additional evidence of Massys' use of the *Monforte altarpiece* comes from the Valladolid wings. The *Nativity* of Valladolid repeats Hugo's formula, originally the left wing of the *Monforte altarpiece,* surviving in a copy by the Master of Frankfurt (Antwerp, Koninklijk Museum, F. 123). Both works show Mary kneeling with angels in adoration of her Child, while Joseph stands beside and removes his cap.

The other Hugo *Adoration of the Magi* is now lost but is preserved in numerous copies of manuscript illuminators and painters like Gerard David (Munich, Alte Pinakothek; Pl. 78
cf. K. Arndt, "Gerard Davids 'Anbetung der Könige' nach Hugo van der Goes. Ein Beitrag zur Kopienkritik," *Münchner Jahrbuch der bildenden Kunst* 12 [1961], 153–75). This *Adoration,* dubbed "the stall in the hill' by Winkler, has the same left-to-right orientation as Massys' work, and it also shows the more closely cropped type of St. Joseph that Massys repeated. Its numerous copies, particularly at Bruges, might have served as the direct source for young Quinten, who need not have seen the original painting firsthand. Manuscript illumination of the late 15th century, particularly of the "Ghent-Bruges School," owed much to the inventions of Hugo and could have served equally well as the means of transmission to a young artist. On the other hand, if the Master of Frankfurt, an Antwerp contemporary of Massys, could make a direct copy after the *Monforte* Pl. 75
altarpiece, then it may also have been accessible to a curious, youthful Quinten (the 16th-century location of the altarpiece is uncertain). The available contacts with Hugo's art seem to have been considerable for Massys, as in the case of the *St. Anne altarpiece* (F. 2, cat. 10). De Bosque has suggested a correspondence between the Valladolid type of black magus and yet another Hugo *Adoration:* the triptych in the Hermitage, Leningrad.

The Valladolid altarpiece, donated by Licentiate Gonzalez in 1503, has frequently been attributed to Massys but is more probably the work of a close follower. Friedländer's tentative attribution to the Master of the Morrison Triptych

is most probable, but the Valladolid shutters do not possess the Geertgen-esque charm of other works by this master
l. 83 (e.g., the *Adoration of the Magi,* Philadelphia, Johnson Coll., F. 87). Instead, they have a monumental gravity and stillness that make them appear as imposing as the contemporary works of Massys (e.g., *St. Christopher,* cat. 5; *Madonna and Child Enthroned,* cat. 7).

Since the Valladolid shutters are dated, they provide a likely 1503 *terminus ante quem* for the Massys *Adoration,* if indeed they depend upon this Massys composition. The shaded oval face of the Virgin and the blocky, bearded face of St. Joseph resemble certain panels from Quinten's output (cats. 7, 9), so that the Valladolid Master's work is helpful in the dating of these panels. The other copies of the *Adoration,* however, show Mary with a softly rounded face that more
l. 42 closely resembles the Antwerp *Virgin in Prayer* (F. 5, cat. 5) and is associated with the David–van der Goes models. Similarly, the closely barbered head of Joseph and the two hovering angels (visible only in the St. Louis image) hark back to the Davidian model. This *Adoration,* like the Antwerp diptych, reveals Massys' close ties in the early 16th century to Bruges painting, particularly the Gerard David workshop.

Cat. 9. *Madonna and Child Enthroned* (F. 17). Brussels, Museés Royaux no. 1497 (1.30 × .86 m.). *Plate 48*

HIST.: Abbey of Büdingen (near Siegburg); coll. of vicar at Willich; coll. J.P. Weyer, Cologne; museum acquisition 1862.

LIT.: Cohen, p. 50ff.; Bosschere, p. 91f.; Brising, p. 9; Winkler, p. 196; Friedländer, 7, p. 29f.; Baldass, pp. 139f., 159f., 178; Roosen-Runge, p. 4ff.; Boon, p. 13ff.; Mallé, p. 82; *De eeuw van Bruegel,* p. 137, no. 163; Puyvelde 1970, 231; DB, pp. 112-14.

This panel demonstrates Massys' creative yet dependent use of the Netherlandish painting tradition, a "synthetic archaism." The Brussels *Madonna Enthroned* (F. 17, cat. 7) incorporates two other famous images of the Christ Child reading a book on the Virgin's lap: Roger van der Weyden's *Madonna*
. 49 *Duran* (Madrid, Prado) and the original version of Jan van
. 50 Eyck's Melbourne *Madonna.* Roger's large panel features Christ dressed in white, Mary in red—a scheme repeated by Massys except for the softer rose hue of Mary's gown in the Brussels panel. From Roger, too, comes the strong background frame of the throne, rounded by Massys into a shape like Roger's niche. And from a detail in the right background of the Brussels painting, Massys reveals his certain knowledge of van der Weyden's image. Over the doorway of the building seen through the window, a tiny sculpted group shows the same figures of the *Madonna Duran* as well as the Gothic tracery of their niche and the projecting ledge below them. Massys' foreground scene, like Roger's painting, is also meant to suggest the effect of a niche sculpture come to life in the presence of a devout beholder.

But the Brussels *Madonna Enthroned* also contains many elements drawn from van Eyck's composition, particularly the pose of the reading Christ Child. The heavy but fluid drapery style and the jeweled borders recall Eyckian models that continued to be popular during Massys' day in the School of Bruges of Memling and David. In the *Seilern Madonna* (F. 27/165, cat. 13) Massys has blended two famous earlier images into his own original creation. He has also managed to provide the same blend of intimate human warmth and divine majesty in the devotional image.

Relative to the Brussels *Anne altarpiece,* the *Madonna Enthroned* appears archaic, e.g., the Gothic throne or the Virgin's prominent nimbus. But, along with the somber colors and the deep shadows, these features recall contemporary Bruges works, particularly those of Gerard David, with whom Massys was probably already in contact at the time. Hulin de Loo claimed to discern the arms of Louvain in the window to the right of the Virgin. Although some scholars have used this observation as evidence that the panel dates from Massys' earliest years, it may be more correct to see the Louvain contact as evidence of Massys' continued ties to his birthplace. Because in 1507, Louvain offered Quinten the commission for the *St. Anne altarpiece,* the Brussels panel need not be dated too early in his career because of the city's arms. Actually, the forms of the Virgin and Child most
closely resemble the figures of the *St. Anne altarpiece* and *Pl. 1*
should probably be dated to only a few years before the period 1507–09.

II. THE GREAT ALTARPIECES (1507–1513)

The great watershed in Massys' career came during the period when he worked on his *magna opera,* his earliest dated authentic works: the *St. Anne altarpiece,* completed between 1507 and 1509, for the Louvain confraternity of St. Anne, and the *St. John altarpiece,* completed between 1508 and 1511 for the chapel of the joiners guild in Antwerp cathedral. These two great projects come at the midpoint of Massys' career, during his early forties. In addition, these were the achievements that were singled out most prominently by the 16th-century biographers, and they remain the cornerstones of any study of Massys' *oeuvre* (see Chap. 2).

With the *St. Anne altarpiece,* Massys can be seen to be exploring new models for his pictorial forms, in all likelihood due to the new subject-matter after all the previous Madonna images. For his interior narratives, Massys turned to the examples of Bouts and van der Goes, and his background landscapes seem to be an outgrowth of the Louvain traditions of Bouts. The complex architecture of the *Holy Kinship* appears to be a fusion of the imagery of Hans Memling of Bruges with some direct contact with
Italian models; the closest parallels can be found in the works of Perugino and Cima da Conegliano. The *Saint Anne altarpiece* *Pl. 1*
offers the largest number of figures, costumes, and settings yet seen in a Massys painting, a complex yet tranquil sequence of dignified, quiet assemblages of saints. In contrast, the more densely packed exterior narratives offer more dramatic interactions

of figures and the first appearance in Massys' work of less-than-saintly onlookers. Most of the later visual vocabulary of Massys' art is revealed *in embryo.*

After the *St. Anne altarpiece,* the *St. John altarpiece* comes as a veritable explosion of energy and action. Even though work on both projects may have overlapped during a brief period, their forms are entirely distinct, owing to the completely different cities and clients for the two works. The nobility of the *Holy Kinship* and St. Anne narratives has given way to an intense, emotional, and human drama of three martyrdoms. Here the models for Massys are modern and foreign: the exotic narratives of Dürer prints, the grotesque visages of Leonardo drawings. The *St. John altarpiece* connects closely with the emerging altarpiece vocabulary that would later crystallize into the formulas of "Antwerp Mannerism" and replaces the more traditional Flemish forms of Bruges, Ghent, and Louvain that had earlier dominated Massys' output (and the *oeuvre* of his contemporary in Antwerp, the Master of Frankfurt). Paradoxically, the *St. John altarpiece* retains one traditional pattern on its exterior, the presentation of the two patron saints John as (gilded) grisaille sculpted figures in niches—a formula derived from the great 15th-century altarpieces of van Eyck, van der Weyden, et al.

Soon after the commission of the joiners' guild for the Antwerp *St. John altarpiece,* Massys embarked upon another major project: the altarpiece of the *Seven Sorrows of Mary* (F. 4, cat. 12) for the church of the Convento da Madre de Deus in Xabregas, near Lisbon (see Chapter 3), in 1509. Assuming that the altarpiece was delivered within a few years of its request, the *Madre de Deus altarpiece* would have been approximately contemporary with the Antwerp *St. John altarpiece;* because the eight large panels were painted during this busy period and were intended for export, the Lisbon pictures are uneven in quality and appear to be largely the work of Massys' assistants, taking second place in the artist's priorities to the local altarpiece. The finest of the Madre *Pl. 28* de Deus panels, the Worcester *Rest on the Flight,* does, however, show many points of contact with the other great altarpieces. Its landscape unfolds along a diagonal into the distance and features elaborate formations and cliffside castles. Corner rocks *Pl. 10* anchor the composition, and the figures occupy the immediate foreground space, like the *Annunciation to Joachim.* As in the *Holy Kinship,* Christ is clad in a full-length garment and bears just the suggestion of a halo with emanating golden rays of light. As in the *Holy Kinship,* Mary is tenderly maternal to her infant; in her sorrow, she lets a tiny tear glide down her cheek.

The facial types of the *Madre de Deus altarpiece* can be seen to develop out of earlier holy figures. Christ most closely resembles *Pl. 48* the reading Child of the Brussels *Madonna Enthroned* with his halo, high forehead, and tiny nose. But there is a new petiteness of features, e.g., the tiny mouths, and the Virgin's face is a narrower, still-perfect oval, with a tiny straight nose running down from *Pl. 1* her forehead. Joseph is a heavier figure than the well-trimmed husbands of the *Holy Kinship;* he resembles Joachim in facial type, but his brooding brows and matted hair have more in common with the richly detailed male figures, such as Joseph of Arimathea, in the Antwerp *Lamentation.* The mobility of the Worcester Joseph shows the same slow decisiveness of Joachim or Joseph of Arimathea in the previous works.

Colors in the Worcester panel have more in common with the Antwerp *St. John altarpiece.* In place of the soft harmonies of the *Holy Kinship,* Mary's bright blue garment and Joseph's red mantle over a violet base recall the contemporary brilliance of the *Pl. 20* Antwerp *Lamentation.* Only Christ's grayish frock harks back to the precedents of the *Holy Kinship* or the Brussels *Madonna Enthroned.*

The autograph portions of the *Madre de Deus altarpiece* permit redating of several works previously considered to be early. In *Pl. 52* particular, the Seilern *Madonna in a Church* can be seen to be quite close to the Worcester *Rest on the Flight* and, to a lesser extent, *Pl. 28* the *St. Anne altarpiece.* It has the narrower, almost chinless head and same straight nose of Mary as the Worcester panel, and it repeats the same bright blue of her mantle. The younger Christ Child of the *Seilern Madonna* does not match the Worcester Infant, although the pug nose and subtle linear halo are comparable; the true matches to the Worcester Christ Child are the sculpted putti on the capitals of the Seilern panel. Moreover, the music-playing angels of the *Seilern Madonna* grow out of types like the older children of the *Holy Kinship,* and their purple and green robes resemble colors in costumes of the *Antwerp Lamentation.* Only the *Banquet of Herod* offers a comparison to the glittering ornament and hybrid, luxury architecture in the *Pl. 13* *Seilern Madonna.* Thus, the icon of the *Madonna in a Church* fits more comfortably into the period of creation of the great altarpieces in its forms.

What has confused previous scholars in dating this image is the conservative nature of iconic images in Massys's day. The *Pl. 54* *Seilern Madonna* is a composite of two traditional images, famous icons of the 15th century: Campin's *Madonna in an Apse* and *Pl. 55* van Eyck's *Madonna in a Church.* As in the case of the Brussels *Madonna Enthroned,* Massys has practiced synthetic archaism to provide his own version of venerated pictures, yielding to what Friedländer called "the compulsion of the iconographic tradition in Flemish art." This process was by no means unique to his youth, as even his late icon of the *Rattier Madonna* (1529, F. *Pl. 68* 24, cat. 48) demonstrates. Thus, habitual scholarly assumption that an artist is more dependent upon his forerunners in his youth must be laid aside in light of the purpose of these iconic images and the importance of heritage in religious art for Massys' Flanders.

Other Madonna icons datable to this period consist largely of workshop products or works surviving only in multiple, weak copies. A number of inferior variants on the *Seilern Madonna* itself survive, and the lost *Madonna with Sleeping Child,* preserved in a variety of lesser copies, displays the very same features of Madonna and Child as the Worcester and Seilern icons. Seeming to date from this same phase of Massys' career are several problematic Mary icons that feature landscape backgrounds like the Worcester *Rest on the Flight;* all ought to be assigned to the large workshop mobilized to produce the *Madre de Deus altarpiece.* Among these icons: Warsaw *Madonna at Half-Length, Aynard Madonna* (F. 21), *Warneck Madonna* (F. 22), bearing a strong likeness to the *Holy Kinship* figures, and the *Hradec Madonna* (F. 197), which combines echoes of the Brussels *Madonna Enthroned* with the Worcester *Rest on the Flight.*

In the wake of the Antwerp and Madre de Deus altarpieces, Massys produced several other Passion scenes with greater or lesser assistance of his enlarged atelier. The Mauritshuis *Christ Carrying the Cross* shows Quinten's own handling of the theme in contrast to the clumsy execution in the Lisbon panel of this action. Ponderous movement, bright colors, and a crowded composition with dark-skinned grotesque tormentors link the Hague *Calvary* to the martyrdom scenes on the wings of the *St. John altarpiece,* but its slender Christ with fine, sharp features also resembles the Passion pictures of the next few years, such as the ca. 1513–17 Coimbra *Passion altarpiece* (F. 196, cat. 18). From this period, too, comes the workshop *Lamentation* (Ottawa, National Gallery of Canada, F. 62), itself a variation on the Antwerp altarpiece and a close relative of a series of altarpieces attributed to Massys' Portugese apprentice in Antwerp, Eduardo Portugalois (Lisbon, *Deposition;* Tomar, *Baptism;* cf. L. Reis-Santos, "Edouard Portugalois," p. 185ff.).

Pl. 89
Pl. 88
Pl. 32
Pl. 33

Cat. 10. *St. Anne altarpiece* (F. 2). Brussels, Musées Royaux no. 299 (2.245 × 2.19 m., central panel). Inscribed on left outer wing: "QUINTE METSYS SCREEF DIT 1509." *Plates 1, 6–10*

HIST.: Commissioned in 1507 by the Louvain confraternity of St. Anne for their chapel in St. Peter's of Louvain; Paris, Louvre 1794; restored to Louvain 1815; museum purchase 1879.

LIT.: Guicciardini, *Descrittione di tutti i Paesi Bassi;* J. Molanus, *Memoria aliquot pictorum Lovaniensium* (1575), IX, fo. 610; van Mander, *Het Schilder-boeck;* Fickaert, p. 16; Fornenbergh, p. 22f.; E. Fetis, "La Descendance apostolique de Sainte Anne, triptyque de Quinten Metsys," *Bulletin des commissions royales d'art et d'archeologie* (1866), 86ff.; van den Branden, p. 67ff.; Hymans, p. 205ff.; Cohen, pp. 18ff., 83f.; Bosschere, p. 54; Brising, p. 20ff.; Winkler, p. 198f.; Delen, p. 49ff.; Friedländer 7, p. 15f.; Prims, "Quinten Massys en de Annadevotie," p. 64ff.; Kleinschmidt, *Die heilige Anna,* p. 346ff.; Baldass, pp. 139ff., 146f., 154, 156f., 174, 178; Roosen-Runge, pp. 35ff., 177ff.; Boon, p. 20f.; Benesch, p. 90f.; Mallé, p. 83ff.; Puyvelde, p. 295ff.; Broadley, p. 27ff.; *De eeuw van Bruegel,* no. 162; Cuttler, p. 419; von der Osten, p. 148; Robbins, p. 11ff.; Puyvelde 1970, p. 225; DB, pp. 92–100.

The *Anne* altar features five scenes from the life of St. Anne, mother of the Virgin. The great central panel displays the *Holy Kinship,* with the *Annunciation of Joachim* and the *Death of St. Anne* on the wings. On the exterior are the *Offering of Joachim and Anne* as a young couple and the later *Rejection of Joachim* at the altar by the high priest. Thus, the narrative sequence begins on the closed exterior and continues chronologically from left to right across the interior. The panels are related as successive events in the lives of the same characters, while the central panel in particular affords a chance for pious contemplation of the saintly figures descended from Joachim and Anne.

The altarpiece of *St. Anne* was commissioned in 1507 by the Confraternity of St. Anne in Louvain, Massys' birthplace, for the brotherhood's chapel in the church of St. Peter. Massys completed work in 1509, signing and dating the painting on the left exterior wing. The overall impression, especially in the central panel of the *Holy Kinship,* is one of dignity and calm. The effect is also maintained within the individual characters throughout the altarpiece.

Pl. 1 The *Holy Kinship* panel features a powerful architectural setting with rounded arches, barrel-vaults, and a central fenestrated cupola. The holy figures are aligned along a foreground balustrade with a mountainous landscape in the distance. Prominently isolated by the central opening of the architecture, Mary and Anne are seated above the other women. Together they enfold the infant Christ at the geometrical center of the composition. Both their glances and their complementary poses center upon the holy Child. Because of the regular architecture and the symmetrically placed figures, a feeling of order and balance dominates the painting. Yet at the same time, subtle rhythms and twists of figures serve to enliven the simple arrangements of the forms. For example, Christ turns to examine a goldfinch perched on His hand, and St. Anne leans slightly forward to offer Him a cluster of grapes. Each person has a measure of directed energy and graceful movement in his pose and his glance. And over all the figures, in harmony with their rounded outlines, is the architectural framework, lending focus to the *Anna Selbdritt* while lending unity to the ensemble.

Space is established in a clear succession of planes. The figures are loosely arrayed across the breadth of the altarpiece. They occupy three clear zones of space, backed first by the balustrade and then by the three vaulted openings, but the regularity of the architecture is replaced by a fantastic realm in the background landscape. Jutting above the head of St. Anne is a towering cleft promontory. The faraway mountains are indistinct in a blue-green haze. This is no longer the almost tactile clarity of the smallest detail, as found in van Eyck's Ghent altarpiece, but a unified, completely visual experience; the viewer observes the altarpiece from a single, fixed position. He cannot expect to see Eyckian fine detail by coming closer. And his own position in real space is accounted for; since the altarpiece is designed to be seen in one specific locale, the figures and the architecture are seen slightly from below. Thus, they appear natural and life-size from a viewer position below the altar for which the painting was intended.

Each of the holy figures possesses a delicate beauty. The women dominate the central panel; theirs is an almost geometrically perfect beauty, expressed in rounded oval-shaped heads with fine features. The men, too, are almost uniform in appearance; each, like the women, has the same angular jaw and narrow face with slit eyes. Massys displays here a taste for exotic courtly or orientalizing costume, including turbans and other unusual headgear.

Perhaps the most remarkable feature in the central panel is the subtle orchestration of color across the entire composition. The Holy Family in the center is the nexus of the entire painting. Mary wears a blue-white gown trimmed in green, with a gold-brown hem. Anne wears a wine-red garment and a deep violet head covering. Between them, Christ mediates coloristically with a blue-gray chemise. Around the central figures is a full panoply of the same colors (green, blue, red, brown) in a variety of combinations and saturations. Even the landscape tones (blue and green) and architectural marbles (green, brown) contribute to the overall harmony. This, again, is a new departure from the juxtaposition of bright primary colors so common in the 15th-century. Massys once again asserts an overall visual harmony over individual details.

Pl. 10 The left wing, the *Annunciation to Joachim*, is a more idyllic outdoor scene, featuring one of the finest examples of Massys' landscape creations. Again, the artist is attentive to surface pattern in his composition: the wings of the angel are made to accord with the shape of the frame, and the background mountains, like Joachim, fall gently downward to the left. The vertical dynamic between the angel and Joachim is counterbalanced by the horizontal spread of the mountainous panorama. The left wing, however, is looser in composition than the delicately balanced central panel. Nonessential details (a dog in the corner, a shepherd in the background, a mountain citadel) fill the right portion of the panel. Colors, too, are more loosely coordinated than in the *Holy Kinship*. The robes of the angel are a daring *couleur-changeant* combination, in which a light green base is shaded with a carmine tone. The landscape is constructed primarily in green with soft suggestion of atmosphere. This tonal working of landscape provides a sense of both continuity and depth, and it marks a departure from the assembled, equally visible particulars of 15th-century backgrounds. In this panel, Massys has invested landscape with a new prominence and independence—an important trend throughout his career.

In contrast to the uncrowded, outdoor scene of the left
Pl. 6 wing, the right-wing *Death of St. Anne* presents a tightly unified, crowded interior. As in the central panel, all the figures are gathered around the holy mother, but here the death bed is arranged at a sharp diagonal, with the viewer almost at its foot. Again, the point of view is clearly defined; the observer finds himself beneath (and behind) even the kneeling young woman (Mary Cleophas) beside the bed. The visible space of the room is completely closed off by walls and curtains. With almost a *horror vacui* Massys has filled the central horizontal space of the panel with a succession of heads, belonging to figures at varying heights and depths in space. The predominant color is rose, defined by the large areas of bedcovers and hangings. Thus, the side panels move centrifugally outward from the balanced central panel, each one asserting a dominant color (green, red) and a dominant space that are synthesized into a unity within the *Holy Kinship*. And just as all the elements of the holy family revolve around its center, so do all the elements of the altarpiece interior derive from that center.

After the interior panels' three separate casts of characters and emotional situations, the exterior panels, with two scenes for a simple narrative of youth and old age for the same characters, appear very unified, indeed. The locations are analogous (temples), the actions are analogous (presentation of offerings), and the compositions, too, are analog-
Pl. 8 ous. In the *Offering of Joachim and Anne*, the kneeling couple present their gifts to the priest, who forms the tallest point of the group at the right edge of the panel (the center of the exterior). In the *Rejection of Joachim*, an older, white-bearded
Pl. 9 priest is the tallest point (now along the left side) at the center of the exterior, and Joachim bows away toward the right. Thus, a gentle ascent to the center at the left is complemented by an equally gentle descent on the right. In both compositions other figures are included, with much the same succession of heads as in the *Death of St. Anne*. The two architectural settings also tend to reinforce the principal directions of movement. There are differences, of course; the left panel has an open window with a mighty background church tower (like the one that Antwerp was then building for its cathedral) and temple portal. The right panel is closed, framed by a large column at the right and the baldachin over the priest at the left. The colors are more saturated and warm than in the interior panels; in particular, the *Rejection of Joachim* panel is composed in lively blue and gold tones not used elsewhere on the altarpiece.

The exterior wings, which bear Massys' signature (on the left wing: "QUINTE METSYS SCREEF DIT 1509"), thus appear stylistically to be a different development among the portions of the altarpiece. They were probably the last sections to have been completed.

The *St. Anne altarpiece*'s condition has been a major bone of contention among scholars. The principal strife has concerned the soft colors of the *Holy Kinship* panel. Friedländer asserts that this softness was the result of overcleaning; van Puyvelde (whose museum affiliations may have made him a more partisan observer), Marlier (in the 1963 catalogue), and others have contended, based upon the 19th-century work of Fetis, that the panel is painted in distemper (rather than oil-based pigment) with a light, transparent oil glaze, and that the warmer tones of the exterior are the result of darker varnish (and, presumably, more exposure over the centuries). Roosen-Runge gives the fullest discussion of the problem, and he, too, calls attention to the differences in varnish between the interior and the yellowed exterior. The soft colors of faces and garments are consistent throughout the interior and are so harmonious in appearance that their modelling cannot have been affected substantially by any restorations. Even the most delicate layers of paint, such as the veil of the women of the *Holy Kinship*, remain intact. Of course, some differences between interior and exterior are also the result of changes in Massys' use of color; this development is elucidated by Roosen-Runge.

The contention of Cohen and Broadley that a dove of the Holy Spirit was painted above the heads of St. Anne and the Virgin is erroneous; the spot of repair they cite in the upper panel is off-center, and the anonymous 1577 Liege woodcut showing the Holy Spirit within the *Kinship* composition (*DB*, ill. 80) is an unreliable document with respect to other details (including the arms of Liege, see Roosen-Runge, p. 179). The early history of the panel is given by E. Fetis, "La Descendance apostolique de Sainte Anne," p. 86ff. The altarpiece was last cleaned in 1881.

The architecture of the *Holy Kinship* has frequently been compared to the forms of Italian painting; for example, Broadley, p. 105, suggests comparison with Perugino's Dublin *Pieta* (ca. 1495). De Bosque cites a visually convincing source in Cima da Conegliano's *John the Baptist with Saints* (Venice, Santa Maria dell' Orto, 1493–94), for the unusual fenestrated rotunda construction of Massys. Another good analogy is the 1491 altar of Giuliano della Rovere (Rome, Villa Albani) by Perugino, or the same artist's 1493 *Madonna*

and Saints (Florence, Uffizi; see W. Bombe, *Perugino* [Stuttgart / Berlin, 1914], nos. 23, 24, 28). Perugino's architecture has the same square pilaster crowns as Massys, and his constructions, like Quinten's, are all viewed from a single point of view that reveals the ceiling vaults. The triple-arched opening of the *Holy Kinship* is unique in Northern painting of the time, while it was much more of a commonplace for Italian painters. The spaces of Perugino, however, normally involve a series of arches rather than a single vault. Furthermore, the extended breadth of the figure composition, the use of a balustrade to divide the space, and the developed background are all distinctive Northern features found in Memling (e.g., the Vienna *Madonna)*, but not in Perugino. Massys' own hybrid fantasy creations, like the cupola and the complex half-column / half-pilaster structure, are combinations drawn from several models. Massys might have seen a Perugino or a Cima picture—perhaps among the possessions of the Italian trading communities of Bruges or Antwerp. But it cannot be used as conclusive evidence to support a hypothetical journey by the artist across the Alps. As in the classical putti-and-swags motif of
Pl. 52 the *Seilern Madonna* (F. 165, cat. 13), the *sacra conversazione* convention and the architecture of the *Holy Kinship* owe as much to Hans Memling of Bruges as to any Massys experience of Cisalpine art (Memling's Italianisms are an important neglected topic for research). Memling, moreover, was an important model for Massys' early Madonna icons (see Chap. 4) and for many of his later portraits (see Chap. 8).

The variety of sources for the *St. Anne altarpiece* is impressively extensive and may owe much to the novelty of subjects for Massys, who until then had specialized, for the most part, in Madonna icons. Dieric Bouts provided the kneeling posture, astonished gesture, and basic composition (rocks at the left, sheep at the right) of the left interior wing, the
Pl. 11 *Annunciation of Joachim*, with his *Moses at the Burning Bush* (Philadelphia, Johnson coll.). Also from Bouts came the orientalizing costumes of the male figures, as in the two altarpieces of *St. Erasmus* (Friedländer 3, no. 8) and the *Holy Sacrament* (Friedländer 3, no. 18), both found in the same church as the *St. Anne altarpiece*—St. Peter's, Louvain. Massys has adopted Bouts's facial types for his younger men: half-closed eyes, prominent noses, and thrusting, bearded chins. The hazy, atmospheric background of the *Holy Kinship* parallels Bouts's *Elijah* panel of the *Holy Sacrament altarpiece;* even closer in its rock forms is the landscape with trees and crags of *Christ with the Baptist and Donor* (Friedländer 3, no. 22; Munich) or the background of the *Baptist* wing of the *Pearl of Brabant triptych* (Friedländer 3, 24; Munich). The Louvain commission for the St. Anne altarpiece seems to have encouraged Massys to make use of the local Bouts tradition in addition to the other models (Memling, van der Goes) from Netherlandish tradition.

Pl. 12 Van der Goes's *Death of the Virgin* (Bruges) inspired Massys' right wing, the *Death of St. Anne*, as well as the hovering angel in the *Annunciation to Joachim*. The oblique placement of the bed, with the viewer at its foot, the dying women shrouded in a white head-covering, and the monochrome tonality of the *Death of St. Anne* (pink in the Massys, blue in the Hugo van der Goes) are common to both pictures. Hugo's hovering Christ with His distinctive curve along His lower robe evoked the form of Massys' angel, who is also a brother to the boyish angels of Hugo. From Gerard David's
Baptism triptych exterior (Bruges) comes Massys' Madonna Pl. 4
and Child in the *Holy Kinship;* here, in contrast to his previous youthful types, borrowed from 15th-century painted models, Massys' Christ Child is older, clad in a smock, and turning in space. Mary's posture, turning right, and her flowing brown hair are also repeated after David. In addition, David's turbaned Magdalene from the exterior gave rise to Massys' Mary Cleophas in the *Holy Kinship*.

Gerard David may also have contributed to Massys' compositional structure. The 1498 *Arrest of Sisamnes* (Bruges), already mentioned as a source for Massys' forceful head of *St. Christopher* (Antwerp, F. 32, cat. 7) is arranged like the scene of the *Offering of Joachim and Anna*. David shows an oblique view with a portico room opening onto two rounded-arch doorways, and Massys' temple space is laid out the same way, although he had to compress it into the narrower dimensions of the wing panel. Both artists show an adjacent porch through the right doorway—a motif that makes much more sense in David's spatially coherent painting than in Massys' jumble of background buildings. And both painters display municipal towers through the left doorway, giving Massys the chance to exhibit civic pride by showing the nearly finished tower of the Antwerp cathedral. (David's work featured the famous Bruges Chapel of the Holy Blood). Massys' reliance on David for this composition reveals further that the *St. Anne altarpiece* was an unprecedented step for him into large-scale narrative, of which David was a leading master at the time.

The document in Joachim's hands in the *Offering* contains Massys' name and may be a contract or other public document connected with the altarpiece, but it is difficult to decipher in the gallery. Marlier in the 1963 exhibition catalog asserts that it is the 15 March 1508 donation by Massys of his payments for the altarpiece to the sons of his first marriage (de Bosque, p. 424, / document 4, illustrated on p. 40), but it is in a more formal script and differs from that document as preserved in the Antwerp City Archive.

St. Anne was an increasingly popular object of veneration in the early 16th century, particularly with respect to the doctrine of Immaculate Conception (see Chap. 2). Her history fills out the scenes of the wings, and the more devotional *Holy Kinship* in the center glorifies her offspring. In this image, the symbolic still-life elements (see Chap. 4) further amplify the theological content behind the attractive figural forms. In the lower-left corner, devotional prints (including the Holy Name monogram of Jesus popularized by St. Bernardino of Siena) and a prayerbook elicit a pious response from the viewer.

The portraitlike face staring out at the observer from the right exterior wing, the *Rejection of Joachim*, has been rightly considered by most scholars as Quinten's probable self-portrait. The only comparison is the 1572 Wierix engraving (Friedländer 7, plate 134c), a formal profile view, but the features of the two works tally well. The Wierix print was possibly based on a self-portrait Massys presented to the St. Luke guild (lost in transit to France in 1794; see Lost Works, no. 7).

Both Hymans and Prims stress the fact that the original commission (before 1503) was given to a pair of sculptors, van Kessel and Peterceels, whose price was considered too high by the Louvain St. Anne confraternity. In 1503, an Antwerp sculptor replaced the two previous carvers, only to yield to Massys in September of 1508. This historical note serves to point out the relative importance of sculpture in early 16th-century Antwerp, especially for altarpieces (see Bosschere, *La Sculpture anversoise*).

Cat.11. *St. John altarpiece* (F.1). 1508–11, Antwerp, Koninklijk Museum nos. 245–49 (260 × 270 center). *Plates 13, 15, 17–20*

HIST.: Commissioned 1508 for the chapter of the joiner's guild in Antwerp Cathedral. Completed before 26 August 1511, when payment was converted into a trust fund for the children of Massys' first marriage; to Antwerp town hall 1582; returned to Cathedral on the altar of the city 1589.

LIT.: Guicciardini, *Descrittione di tutti i Paesi Bassi;* Molanus, *Memoria aliquot pictorum Lovaniensium* (1575) IX, fo. 610; van Mander, *Het Schilder-Boeck;* Fickaert, p. 13ff.; Fornenbergh, p. 16ff.; van den Branden, pp. 54ff., 148n., 234; Hymans, pp. 204, 215ff.; Cohen, pp. 24ff., 81ff.; Bosschere, p. 69ff., Brising, pp. 26ff., 50; Conway, p. 324f.; Winkler, p. 202; Delen, p. 61ff.; Friedländer 7, p. 16f.; Baldass, pp. 141, 143, 147f., 155f., 162, 165, 178ff,; Prims, "De Schilderijen van het Kuipersaltaar," p. 296ff.; Roosen-Runge, pp. 125ff., 182ff,; Boon, p. 22ff.; Benesch, p. 89ff.; Mallé, p. 98ff.; Bialostocki, "Opus Quinque Dierum," p. 23; Broadley, pp. 49ff., 132, 185ff.; Puyvelde, p. 295ff.; Cuttler, p. 420f.; von den Osten, p. 148n.; Puyvelde, 1970, p. 227; Robbins, p. 5ff.; DB, pp. 101-6.

The *John altarpiece* is Massys' most fully documented painting, and it stands as the very cornerstone of his *oeuvre*. The earliest sources, Guicciardini and Molanus, mention it in the late 16th century. Van Mander also gives it a lengthy description, but in 1604 he mentions difficulties about seeing the details of the painting. Modern viewing shows no major problems of preservation; what van Mander objected to was probably a darkened varnish that obscured the clarity of a few heads.

Massys' second great altarpiece, the *St. John altar,* must have been begun at the very time when the *St. Anne* exterior panels were being painted. The altarpiece consists of a central panel, the *Lamentation* over the body of Christ, and two wings. The left depicts the martyrdom of John the Baptist; its principal scene is *Salome before Herod* with the head of the Baptist. On the right wing is the *Martyrdom of John the Evangelist.* The exterior wings bear painted sculpture of the two St. Johns, patrons of the guild.

The *John altar* compositions reveal a marked intensification of some of the later developments on the exterior of the *St. Anne altarpiece.* Again, Massys displays a *horror vacui* by crowding a variety of figures into his compositions. The movement of the exterior Joachim panels has been stepped up, and the new, dramatic twisting poses of hateful, grotesque figures provide conflict and tension.

Painted only a few years after the *Anne altarpiece,* the *John altarpiece* almost appears to come from a different artist. Its energetic figures, fanciful costumes, and grisly emotional scenes are a different world from the calm balance of the *Holy Kinship.* Even the colors of the later work are richer and fuller than the soft pastels of a few years previous. The change in patrons from a conservative religious confraternity in Louvain to a professional trade guild in prosperous Antwerp accounts for the change in artistic vocabulary under the influence of fashionable Flamboyant trends. Furthermore, the rivalry of the joiner's guild with their former professional allies, the coopers, evoked the joiner's desire for a decidedly "modern" altarpiece by the same artist—Massys—who had painted a joint altarpiece for the coopers and joiners only a decade earlier (now lost; see Prims). For Antwerp in 1508, that style was "Antwerp Mannerism" or "Flamboyance," and Massys delivered an altarpiece filled with the poses, the costumes, the decorative details, and the active energy so characteristic of this artistic fashion. The central panel, a traditional theme determined by the guild's history, depends more strongly on earlier models.

Flamboyant style is most evident on the two wings. On the left wing Salome and a young page swerve and turn with no comprehensible purpose. All the figures are resplendent in magnificent gowns: the wing is a dazzling essay in gold, green, and red, filled with rich brocades but also featuring a broken-color blue-with-orange mantle for Herod and a silver-and-gold gown for Salome. To create a sharp spatial contrast, Massys places the distant scene of the beheading of John the Baptist near the center of the composition—exactly between the large figures of Salome and Herodias. *Pl. 13*

The densely packed right wing is even more unsettling. Here only John the Evangelist is not in some energetic twisting activity or lively discussion. The grotesquely evil faces of his executioners stand out in contrast to the delicate features of St. John (who looks like a close relative of the men in the *Holy Kinship*). Although the figures are in separate layers of space, their diminution of scale seems altogether too rapid; moreover, many of them are almost entirely cut off by the frame. The colors are kaleidoscopic, in no apparent order, with strong contrasts between light and dark tones. Here, particularly, the millinery is endlessly varied in color and shape. Only the trees at the sides of the panel and the background architecture at the top give any sense of stability to this crowded, chaotic composition. *Pl. 15*

It is the central panel, the *Lamentation,* which is at once most subtle and most simple, continuing much of the harmony of the *St. Anne altarpiece.* As in the latter, the figures are spread horizontally across the panel, and they are isolated in the foreground by a massive landscape background. Once again the most-important figures, John and Mary, are in the center; they cast their full attention on the other compositional focus, the body of Christ (just as the youthful Christ was a focus of the *Holy Kinship*). Compositionally, the figures are inextricably entwined like links in a chain, and the eye moves continuously back and forth over them, always with the main emphasis on Christ or on the two central holy figures. At the left, Joseph of Arimathea forms a ponderous parenthetical close to the picture; he is complemented by the stooping female form at the right. This weight distribution is counterbalanced by the landscape, open into the distance behind the man but thrusting craggily *Pl. 20* upward behind the women. The composition is basically a series of interlocking triangles with John the apex of the central triangle. The triangular landscape promontory echoes this scheme, jutting upward from the heads of John and Nicodemus. But the crag also picks up the rising movement from the women at the right, beginning with the parenthetical corner figure and moving up through the next two mourners.

Landscape has achieved a heightened importance in the *Lamentation* panel. It continues its background supportive
Pl. 10 function, as in the *Annunciation to Joachim* or the *Holy Kinship*, but it is now assertive enough to eliminate the need for an architectural matrix. At the same time, the landscape enhances the evocative emotional qualities of the theme, creating a natural counterpart to the sharp, empathetic pains of the mourners. No longer is there a strict separation of green
Pl. 1 and blue bands according to distance, as in the *Holy Kinship*. Instead, Massys has achieved a new fusion of color around a green tone that grades into gold in nearer areas and blue in the far distance. Jerusalem and the distant mountains are even more hazily indistinct than the atmospheric backgrounds of the *St. Anne altar*, but the sense of texture and material substance is even more convincing. Once again, Massys assumes a certain viewer distance to create an overall visual reality.

Color in the *Lamentation* panel is as carefully unified as is the composition. The two central figures are painted in bright, pure tones—John in tomato red. Mary in sky-blue. Christ, too, is prominent; His skin tones are the panel's lightest portion. The remainder of the colors are carefully coordinated with the two central figures. All the men beside John echo his red mantle in warm, less-saturated reds, oranges, and umbers. Beside Mary's blue the women wear cool tones of green and violet (although the right corner figure wears bright red sleeves and that to close the composition coloristically, as her posture closes it formally). The two principal colors are picked up by the dress of two tiny figures on the crag above, while the landscape forms a harmonious neutral background of brown and green tones.

The scene of the *Feast of Herod* appears frequently in late 15th-century representations of the Martyrdom of John the Baptist, as in the illustrated Dutch *Vita Christi*, printed by Gerard Leeuw in 1487 (illustrated in Bosschere, p. 50) or a panel by Juan de Flandes (*De eeuw van Bruegel*, exh. cat. [Brussels, 1963], cat. no. 92, ill. 16). Rubens freely copies the Massys *Feast of Herod* for his own depiction of the event (Edinburgh, National Gallery of Scotland, no. 2195).

The central scene of the *Lamentation* was derived from a pair of famous van der Weyden models (today in Madrid, Prado, and The Hague, Mauritshuis). Roger's Prado paint-
Pl. 21 ing was easily accessible to Massys, since it was exhibited in the Crossbowmen's Chapel in the Louvain Church of Our Lady Outside the Walls. Young Quinten could have seen the work while growing up or, later, during his 1509 delivery of the *St. Anne altarpiece* to Louvain. Although its mournful character contrasts with the more active character of the scenes on the wings, the *Lamentation* scene was dictated by historical circumstances, inasmuch as it was the central panel of the previous altarpiece of the coopers. In a sense, the *Lamentation*, too, is a scene of martyrdom like the events on the wings of the *John altarpiece*, but its devotional character is removed from the frenzied narrative of the saints' lives. From the *Prado Deposition* Massys borrowed Roger's sense of tightly closed composition, and he intensified the visual flow by crowding the figures even closer together. He also retained individual characters, like the fleshy, brocaded Joseph of Arimathea, who supports the body of Christ as in Roger's painting. John and Mary continue to wear the same pure red and blue garments in the Massys adaptation, where the older woman's pitiful expression of grief is drawn from the Magdalene of the *Deposition*.

From the Rogerian *Lamentation* (The Hague, Maurit- *Pl. 22*
shuis), perhaps executed by a talented workshop assistant, Massys used Mary's kneeling posture of prayer and the protective embrace of John behind her. The Hague *Lamentation* also provided the peculiar, half-upright, half-lengthwise extension of Christ's body along the central foreground of the picture, with Joseph of Arimathea at the left to support it. Roger's bilateral composition was divided into separate groups of men and women by Massys, and even the grief-stricken gesture of wringing hands appears in The Hague panel with the shrouded woman behind Joseph.

The *St. John altarpiece* is thus an amalgam of foreign models, fashionable forms, and traditional themes and models. Viewed as a whole, the triptych is fairly conservative in format, particularly in featuring grisailles on the exterior. The two saints John, although depicted in more flamboyant twisting poses, still retain the same attributes, niche, and socle as their famous precedents on the exterior of the Ghent altarpiece. Again, Massys adapts famous models from Netherlandish tradition, in his personal fashion, to take advantage of the special veneration held for certain popular images. We have already seen his contact with the Ghent altarpiece in the Antwerp diptych (cat. 5), suggesting Mas- *Pl. 42*
sys' possible visit to Ghent as well as Bruges early in his *Pl. 43*
career.

Cat. 12. *Seven Sorrows of the Virgin altarpiece* (F. 4, Add. 193). Ca. 1509–12. *Plates 24–28, 30, 31*

1. *Mater Dolorosa*. Lisbon Museum Nacional, no. 1275 (171.5 × 151).
2. *Three Maries at the Tomb*. Lisbon, no. 1830 (82.5 × 79.5).
3. *Christ among the Doctors*. Lisbon, no. 1692 (62.5 × 80.5).
4. *Christ Carrying the Cross*. Lisbon, no. 1821 (82.5 × 82.5).
5. *Calvary*. Lisbon, no. 1702 (92 × 90.5).
6. *Rest on the Flight*. Worcester Art Museum, no. 1937.4 (82.6 × 79).
7. *Presentation in the Temple*. Lisbon, no. 1830 (82.5 × 79.5).
8. *Pieta*. Rio de Janeiro, Escola Nacional de Belas-Artes (83 × 79.5).

HIST.: Painted for the Church of the Convento da Madre de Deus founded by Queen Leonor in 1509 in Xabregas (near Lisbon).

1. Church of Madre de Deus; 1912, Lisbon Museum.
2. Church of Madre de Deus; L. Harris, London; Lisbon Museum 1938.
3. Church of Madre de Deus; before 1885, Countess of Edla Coll.; 1929 Lisbon Museum.

4. Church of Madre de Deus; 1937 Lisbon Museum.
5. Church of Madre de Deus; 1933 Lisbon Museum.
6. Church of Madre de Deus; by 1874 coll. J. M. Fidie; after 1882 King Ferdinand of Portugal; ca. 1922 L. Harris, London; 1928 Worcester Museum.
8. Church of Madre de Deus; coll. Fidie; coll. King Ferdinand; J. M. d'Almeida Garcia Fidie; J. Ferreira das Neves; 1945 Rio de Janeiro Escola.

LIT.: C. Justi, "Die Portugiesische Malerei des XVIe Jahrhunderts," *Jahrbuch der kön. Preuss. Kunstsammlungen* 9 (1888): 147f; Friedländer 7, p. 29; Winkler, "Quinten Massys' Ruhe auf der Flucht," p. 345f; de Figueiredo, "Metsys et el Portugal," p. 175ff; Baldass, pp. 142, 155, 165f; dos Santos, *O Poliptico da Madre de Deus de Quintino Metsys;* Richardson, p. 170f; Boon, p. 22; Reis-Santos, p. 83f; Mallé, pp. 87, 92; J. R. Texeira Leita, "Un quadro de Metsys no Brasil," *Coloquio* 8 (1960), p. 25; Cuttler, p. 423; von der Osten, p. 149; Puyvelde 1970, p. 229f; Robbins, p. 95ff; E. Haverkamp-Begemann, *European Paintings in the Collection of the Worcester Art Museum* (Worcester, 1974), pp. 190–97; DB, pp. 149–55.

The origin of this altarpiece is documented for a Portuguese, royally sponsored cloister and evidences Antwerp's strong commercial and political ties with Portugal during the early years of the spice trade (Chap. 3). Massys' choice of theme was the recent, immensely popular cult which had been exported previously to Spain in the Palencia altarpiece of Jan Joest of Calkar (1505; Friedländer 9a, no. 2). A central *Mater Dolorosa* was flanked by the seven narrative panels that recount her sorrows. As reconstructed by E. Haverkamp-Begemann and de Bosque, the sequence read as follows: left (top to bottom) *Christ among the Doctors,* the Worcester *Rest on the Flight,* and the *Presentation in the Temple;* center *Calvary,* right *Crucifixion, Pieta,* and *Three Maries at the Tomb.*

The dating of the panel is uncertain but definable. Queen Leonora founded the monastery in 1509 *(terminus post quem),* and on 20 July 1513 King Manuel ordered cloth for a curtain for the altarpiece of the main altar (*terminus ante quem;* quoted by R. dos Santos, p. 5f.), which probably indicates that the paintings were available for viewing by that time. As Haverkamp-Begemann points out, the *retablo* format of multipaneled altarpieces is a Spanish feature divergent from typical Flemish triptychs or polyptychs or Italian panel sequences then favored in Portugal.

For a *Rest on the Flight* theme, Massys was directly depen-
Pl. 29 dent on a model by Gerard David painted only a few years earlier (e.g., New York and Prado panels). More frequently in Flemish versions of the *Seven Sorrows* theme, the *Flight into Egypt* itself is depicted. Massys replaced the more usual Entombment scene as well, substituting the *Three Maries* theme. For comparison, see the *Seven Sorrows* panels of Bernard van Orley, Friedländer 8, nos. 94–95.

Pl. 28 The Worcester *Rest on the Flight into Egypt* depends upon David's representation of this same subject, beginning late in the first decade of the 16th century; most typically for David, the Virgin is suckling the Child with the Flight into Egypt or Joseph procuring fruit in the background. Massys adopts this overall theme, and he also includes a typical Davidian detail, the Holy Family's humble wicker basket (Massys shows it open, filled with a supply of bread and apples.) Details of posture, essential in David's version, are repeated without significance in Massys' Worcester panel. Where David's Mary held her fingers parted in order to offer her breast, Massys' Virgin holds only her head covering; her arm, which enfolded Christ naturally when the Child was on her lap, appears disjointed and anatomically impossible because it appears in the same position—even though Christ has been moved over onto a rock. Massys also repeats the Child's feet crossed one over the other, proving even more clearly that he did not invent the image but borrowed it from Gerard David.

The bright colors of the Worcester scene recall the gar-
ments of John and Mary in the Antwerp *Lamentation* (cat. *Pl. 20*
11). Similar connections link the elaborate rock arches and hillside castles of both works, and the craggy head of St. Joseph compares closely with Joseph of Arimathea in the Antwerp centerpiece.

Uneven quality of execution is a problem in the altarpiece, suggesting that, while Massys may have designed all the panels, their actual painting was largely done by workshop assistants. The large number of smaller-scale separate panels would have facilitated this process, which is unusual for this date in Massys' career. In all probability, the demands of the great Antwerp altarpiece necessitated heavy workshop participation in this second major project; at the same time, the artist probably would have found it difficult to turn down a royal commission from Portugal. But the distant destination of the altarpiece and its non-Flemish (hence less style-conscious) audience also permitted Massys to cut corners in preparing the altarpiece.

Of the eight panels, only the Worcester *Rest on the Flight*
and Lisbon *Christ among the Doctors* (excepting Mary and *Pl. 31*
Joseph) display the subtle modeling, rich coloration, and natural sense of movement that marks the contemporary *St.*
John altarpiece. Other works, most notably the *Crucifixion* and *Pl. 30*
Pieta, contain stumpy, stiffly awkward figures with wooden *Pl. 26*
expressions. Even the *Mater Dolorosa,* a beautifully designed *Pl. 24*
panel, certainly a Massys conception akin to the Virgin of the Antwerp *Lamentation,* has a general flatness of execution in the blue robes, a lack of precision in landscape detail (which also mars the handsome *Three Maries*), and a certain emptiness of facial expression. De Bosque's scenario assigns only the central *Mater Dolorosa* to Massys himself; she sees the Worcester *Rest* as the finest of the narrative scenes and assigns it to a known Massys apprentice, Eduardo Portugalois.

Diane T. Robbins has carefully divided the workshop painters into two hands. "Hand A" painted the *Crucifixion, Pieta,* and *Three Maries* panels. His work is characterized by a certain lack of detail, repetition, and dryness of execution; his figures are stunted and stock shapes without grace of movement. "Hand B" is associable with other works ascribed to Massys' Portugese apprentice, Eduardo Portugalois, by Reis-Santos ("Edouard Portugalois—discipline et collaborateur de Quentin Metsys," p. 185ff.). Robbins assigns the grisailles of the Antwerp *John altarpiece* to Hand B (although not convincingly to this author) and compares the *Mater Dolorosa* to another Massys-related altarpiece in Lisbon, the *Descent from the Cross* (Reis-Santos, ibid., ill. 5). De Bosque also has connected this Lisbon *Deposition* to a Massys workshop variant on the Antwerp *Lamentation:* the Ottawa *Lamentation.* Like the other works of the presumed Eduardo, the *Mater Dolorosa* shows a lanky, gently swaying figure mass without the emotional compassion of Massys' greatest works. That Hand B differs in all essential points from Hand A is clear from a comparison of *Christ Carrying the Cross* between the *Seven Sorrows altarpiece* and the *Descent from the Cross altarpiece* (Reis-Santos, ibid., ill. 6a). Both works go back to a Massys design (see the same theme in The Hague, cat. 15) but clearly reveal personal characteristics that distinguish them from the master. To the *Mater Dolorosa* should be added the *Presentation in the Temple* as the work of Hand B.

Cat. 13. *Madonna Standing in a Church with Angels* (F. 165). Ca. 1510–11, Coll. Count A. Seilern, London (47.5 × 33). *Plate 52*

HIST.: Duchess of Holstein-Sonderburg (?); Count P. Sinzendorf, 1728; Count Thurn-Valsassina, Carinthia (previously the central panel of a small silver gilt altar).

LIT.: Brising, p. 48; Delen, p. 47f; Winkler, p. 196; Friedländer 7, p. 31; Baldass, p. 138f; M. J. Friedländer, "Über den Zwang der iconographischen Tradition in der vlämischen Kunst," p. 211ff; Boon, p. 32ff; Benesch, p. 82; Panofsky *ENP*, p. 353f., p. 175, n. 2; Seilern, *Flemish Paintings at 56 Princes Gate,* p. 5f, no. 3; Mallé, p. 88; Cuttler, p. 49; DB, pp. 119–20. *Plate 53*

A. Replica: Lyons Museum no. 170 (54.5 × 37.5) (F. 27)
   HIST.: coll. Jourdeuil, Dijon; coll. L'Homme, Besançon; 1859 museum purchase.
   LIT.: M. Vincent, "La vierge a l'Enfant entourée d'Anges de Quentin Metsys au Musee des Beaux-Arts de Lyons," p. 21ff; DB, pp. 115–19.

B. Variant: *Virgin Standing Outdoors.* Private coll., Switzerland (F. 166) (48 × 33).
   HIST.: Friedländer 1938; DB, p. 121.

In 1929, Friedländer called the Lyons painting the original and the Seilern panel a "precise replica." By 1938, he cited the Swiss variant as the first of the three, presumably because of its similarity to van Eyck's Antwerp *Madonna by a Fountain.* Baldass, who first published the *Seilern Madonna,* argued convincingly for its priority, and he found support from Panofsky, who called the Lyons *Madonna* a "competent replica." The Lyons painting features an uncharacteristically ornate decoration (a product of later taste, according to Baldass) and a more complete vision of the architectural setting around Mary. This has the effect of diminishing the prominence of both Madonna and angels and is inconsistent with such truncated architectural spaces as the *Holy Kinship* (Pl. 1) or the Brussels *Madonna Enthroned* (cat. 91) (Pl. 48). Baldass argues, however, that the *Seilern Madonna* dates before the *Anne altarpiece* (cat. 10) on account of its "Gothic" forms rather than the "Renaissance" elements of the *Holy Kinship.* But this dating on the basis of progressive "Italianizing" does not hold for Massys' development. The dating of the painting can more easily be established by comparison with dated or datable works.

Most scholars have assigned the *Seilern* /Lyons *Madonna* to the earliest period of Massys' career (e.g., Delen, who feels that the weaknesses in the painting make it an uncertain work, if not an early one). But the bright blue gown of the *Seilern* Virgin recalls the colorful garments of the Madonnas in the Antwerp *Lamentation* (cat. 11) (Pl. 20) and the Worcester *Rest on the Flight* (cat. 12) (Pl. 28) from the *Seven Sorrows altarpiece.* Similarly, the facial types of Worcester and Antwerp (e.g., the woman washing Christ's feet) feature the same high forehead, tiny chin, and firm, straight nose as the *Seilern* Virgin. The Lyons replica, however, with its even finer features, more closely resembles such small-scale figures of a few years later as the Ottawa *Crucifixion* (cat. 25) (Pl. 91). These connections date the *Seilern Madonna,* not to Massys' earliest years, but to his years of early maturity during the time of the great altarpieces. The Lyons panel, in turn, appears to be a later Massys original.

The *Seilern Madonna* creatively combines models by both van Eyck and Campin. The Eyckian model was the *Madonna in a Church* (Berlin-Dahlem) (Pl. 55), an influential picture that was copied during the 15th and early 16th centuries by a number of artists (Friedländer 1, plates 39, 107; 4, no. 37; 8, no. 3). In 1513, perhaps around the time Massys was completing the *Seilern Madonna,* Jan Gossaert was making a much more literal replica of the van Eyck work for Antonio Siciliano, an emissary from Milan (*Jan Gossaert genaamd Mabuse,* exh. cat., p. 76ff., no. 7; Panofsky, *ENP,* p. 353). In contrast, Massys adapts the figure of the Madonna to entirely new surroundings, but he maintains the visual identification of the Virgin with the Church which lay at the heart of van Eyck's image, even though the *Seilern Madonna* offers a more natural relationship of scale between the figures and their surroundings. In place of the Gothic nave of van Eyck, Massys has substituted a complex building more properly described as a heavenly palace, although sculpted portal figures of prophets recall the exteriors of churches.

Quinten has retained the dominant figure of the Virgin; her face is the Eyckian chinless type with long, flowing brown hair. She stands in three-quarter view, holding the tiny, naked Child with a white cloth pressed close against her body. In the background are angels with tapers; in van Eyck's panel, they sing from a book, but Massys shows them preparing a royal throne, above which a canopy is marked with their names: "———us" and "Maria." For both paintings, the total effect is a subtle combination of maternal intimacy and regal majesty. Massys has absorbed his Eyckian model with understanding and empathy. He has even "added" to his source, by bringing the holy figures into more central prominence. This creative assimilation of tradition is what Panofsky terms Massys' "peripheral yet comprehending archaism."

Robert Campin's famous panel, the *Virgin in an Apse,* now lost but preserved in copies (Pl. 54), also served as a source for the *Seilern Madonna.* Campin's Virgin, who stands full-length in white robes, was flanked by two music-playing angels, who held lute and harp. The *Seilern Madonna* also shows a lute-playing angel, and it has the same characteristic Campinesque spill of drapery on the floor around the feet of the Virgin. Ironically, the *Sailern Madonna* repeats the blue robes of van Eyck, while the Lyons replica adopts Campin's dress of white.

Cat. 14. *Madonna with the Sleeping Child* (lost).
Versions:

1. Basel, Kunstmuseum, no. 1141 (65 × 52) (F.69).
   LIT.: Friedländer 7, p. 68; DB, pp. 145–46.

2. Oslo, National Gallery, no. 1348 (55 × 43).
   LIT.: Friedländer 7, 68; DB, pp. 147–48.
3. Troyes, Musée des Beaux-Arts (52 × 38.5).
   LIT.: F. Voigtländer, "Ein Madonnenbild des Quentin Massys," *Cicerone* 4 (1912): 295f.; Friedländer 7, p. 68; DB, pp. 146–47.
4. Ghent, Museum voor Schone Kunsten, no. 1907 (43 × 31.5).
   LIT.: DB, p. 148
5. Lisbon, National Museum, no. 1524 (42.5 × 31).
   LIT.: L. Reis-Santos, *Eduardo o Português* (Lisbon, 1966); DB, p. 148.

Voigtländer and Friedländer were the first to recognize that a Massys composition underlay the cluster of mediocre, surviving copies of this composition. The Madonna and Child are repeated exactly in all surviving versions except for the Ghent panel, which slightly alters the Madonna's hand and cuts off the figures at bust-length rather than half-length. For the rest of the examples, the Virgin can be seen wearing a transparent veil that reveals her hairline and ear; her mantle is drawn back, exposing her left breast for nursing. The Child nestles close against her body, His head and tiny hands perched above the breast on Mary's shoulder. The Madonna's hands and her long, slender fingers support Jesus from below and behind, enfolding Him within a white cloth.

Aside from the main figures, all the copies show variations in the settings and accessories. The Basel panel is the only one to show the scene outside, although de Bosque reports that x-rays taken in the museum reveal traces of a Renaissance-style architectural background beneath the present surface. A similar framework of columnar construction is preserved in the Troyes image (and to a lesser extent in Oslo); the Renaissance vocabulary here recalls the forms of the throne in the London canvas of the *Marriage of St.*
Pl. 176 *Catherine* (F.28, cat. 25), a work whose Christ Child de Bosque compares to the *Madonna with Sleeping Child.* These correspondences, however, fail to add up to a convincing dating, as de Bosque places the London canvas around 1518–20 but situates the *Sleeping Child* around 1503–05.

Another element is a foreground ledge with symbolic fruits, a feature of many Joos van Cleve Madonna images
Pl. 64 and of later Massys icons, such as the Detroit *Madonna*
Pl. 63 *Outdoors,* Berlin *Madonna Enthroned,* and Paris *Rattier Ma-*
Pl. 68 *donna.* Basel, Troyes, and Oslo present exactly the same configuration of fruit, so we can conclude with some confidence that the original composition also offered it: a bunch of grapes at the left, followed by two apples, the first seen from below, the second with its upper stem facing left. As Eddy de Jongh has pointed out ("Grape Symbolism in Paintings of the 16th and 17th Centuries," pp. 166–91), the metaphor of Mary as the grape vine is a reference to her support of Christ as the true source of life. If we consider the traditional association of the apple with sin and Christ with the redemption of sin as the New Adam, then the placement of these two fruits before the Madonna and Child, respectively, is entirely appropriate.

As de Bosque's comments suggest, the dating of this composition is a difficult task, the more so with the original forms of Madonna and Child is the *Seilern Madonna in the* *Pl. 52*
Church (F.165, cat. 13), particularly as shown in the replica in *Pl. 53*
Lyons (F. 27). The sharp features and chinless oval head of the Lyons *Madonna* are quite close to the face of the *Virgin with the Sleeping Child.* The pudgy, pug-nosed, curly-haired Sleeping Child is older than the Christ of the Lyons *Madonna,* but His age and features compare closely to the sculpted putti above the main figures. The difficulty of dating purely on the basis of figure types can be seen by comparing the Sleeping Child to such later (?) Christ figures as the Rotterdam *Madonna with Milk Soup* (F.168, cat. 27) or *Pl. 65*
the Detroit *Madonna Outdoors* (F.23, cat. 42). Moreover, the *Pl. 64*
date of the *Madonna of the Church* is often placed by scholars quite early in Massys' career. There are also correspondences between the *Madonna with the Sleeping Child* and the female types of the *Madre de Deus altarpiece,* 1510–13, and the presence of a substantial Massys workshop in the completion of that retable project provides the opportunity for diffusing this composition in numerous copies. The origins of the lost *Madonna with Sleeping Child* seem to lie in the later years of the period of the great altarpieces.

Cat. 15. *Christ Carrying the Cross* (F. 167). The Hague, Mauritshuis, on loan from Amsterdam, Rijksmuseum (83.8 × 57.1). *Plate 89*

HIST.: Colnaghi, London 1934: coll. de Bruyn van der Leeuw, Spiez; gift to museum 1961.

LIT.: Friedländer 7, p. 80; Boon, p. 28; Mallé, pp. 92, 94f; *Bulletin van het Rijksmuseum* 9 (1961), p. 65; DB, p. 158.

The isolated panel in The Hague is Massys' first extant Passion scene other than an altarpiece. Its closest relatives are the scenes in Lisbon from Massys' *Seven Sorrows* altarpiece (cat. 12) and from the *Deposition* altarpiece by a Massys follower (Lisbon), presumably Eduardo Portugalois (see cat. 12). What distinguishes the Mauritshuis panel as an original Massys, rather than the work of a collaborator, is the subtle working of both colors and modeling. The bluish-grey robes of Christ, set off against a bright yellow turban and banner, and the rose of the man at the right recall color experiments of the *Anne* altarpiece and the *John* altar (cats. 10, 11). The grotesque faces, carefully modeled in tones of brown, have a vitality absent from the comparable Lisbon scenes. And the religious feeling of The Hague panel is heightened by having Christ gazing out at the viewer, imploring assistance with His burden. To this end, Massys eliminates the man behind Christ who helps with the load in both Lisbon panels and emphasizes compositionally the size and weight above Christ.

The closest comparisons to the types of both Christ and His tormentors are the figures in the Coimbra *Passion retable* *Pl. 3*
(ca. 1513–17, F. 196, cat. 18) or the lanky Christ of the *Pl. 3*
Louvre *Pieta* (F. 17, cat. 16). *Pl. 9*

An ineffective portion of the panel is the topmost section, featuring a round, stepped building (the Temple of Jerusalem) and clouds, which are uncharacteristic of Massys' delicate, atmospheric heavens (e.g., the *Seven Sorrows* or *Lamentation* scenes). Since there is no damage evident from the picture's surface, the highly contrasted clouds and the dark blue sky seem to be the products of a workshop assistant rather than of a modern restorer.

III. PATINIR AND EXPERIMENTATION (1514–1524)

To a certain extent, this most creative period of Massys' career can be defined by his contact in Antwerp with the landscape
specialist Joachim Patinir (R. Koch, *Joachim Patinir*), who is recorded as a master in the guild of St. Luke in 1515. We can be
certain that Massys knew and liked Patinir, for in a document of 5 October 1524 (de Bosque, no. 20, p. 425) he was declared
custodian, along with Karel Alaerts, Jan Buyst and the artist's widow, for the two daughters of Patinir. Moreover, the two
painters collaborated on a single painting, the Prado *Temptation of St. Anthony* (F. 31, cat. 26). A later, 16th-century Escorial *Pl. 114*
inventory lists the picture as being the work of "Maestre Coyntin y M. Joachim," and the visual division of labor suggests that the
foregound figures were the work of Massys, while the background figures and landscape were the creation of Patinir.

Patinir is already named as "the good landscape painter" by Dürer in his Diary of the 1520 trip to the Netherlands, and much
scholarly attention has been given to Patinir's impact on Massys in terms of landscape. Of course, Massys' talents for picturing
scenery were already manifest in the sensitive riverside sunrise of the early *St. Christopher* (Antwerp, F. 32, cat. 7). In the great *Pl. 113*
altarpieces, Massys placed significant background landscapes, shrouded in hazy, atmospheric distance, behind the large *Pl. 20*
foreground figures. In the Antwerp *Lamentation*, the religious drama is localized against the backdrop city of Jerusalem in the
distance at the left and the hill of Golgotha with its three corpses above the figures in the center. In addition, the landscape
details of the *Lamentation*, like the crosses or the rock-cut tomb at the right, serve to position the principal event within the flow
of biblical narrative. The same is true of the Worcester *Rest on the Flight into Egypt* (F. 4, cat. 12), which shows the Massacre of the *Pl. 28*
Innocents behind the foreground scene, or in the *Annunciation to Joachim*, where a tiny Meeting at the Golden Gate is visible in *Pl. 7*
the distance along the walls of Jerusalem.

Patinir's landscapes also might contain background scenes of this type, just as the *Temptation of St. Anthony* features other trials
of the holy man in various spatial pockets of the distance. But the principal characterization of a Patinir landscape is quite
distinct from the Massys constructions we have seen before now. Patinir's settings are termed "world landscapes": vast
panoramas seen from a high viewpoint, receding unbroken to a distant high horizon. Patinir landscapes seem to have a
sampling from almost every conceivable earthly location. Towering craggy rocks on one side are balanced by flatlands on the
other; tiny rural hamlets alternate with distant urban seaports. Even the sky seems to mix dark, stormy clouds with bright, open
heavens in Patinir's constructs. Contrasted with these epic vistas, Massys' landscapes are seen along with larger figures from a
lower viewpoint. Visual details lack the sharpness of Patinir's careful paintings, where even the most distant items are as clear as
the features of the foreground; Massys' distance is suffused by a hazy atmosphere that affords only a generalized view of objects
but situates the viewer in a fixed relationship toward near and far. One feature of Massys landscapes that is absent from Patinir
is a coordinated totality, where the contours of the foreground principals are echoed in the background. The *Holy Kinship* *Pl. 1*
mountains conform to the arrangement of the *Anne Selbdritt*, just as the shape of Golgotha echoes the massing of the foreground
mourners of the Antwerp *Lamentation*. The same harmonies are coordinated into the compositions of the Worcester *Rest on the
Flight* and *Women at the Tomb* from the Madre de Deus altarpiece. This contrast of images of landscape between Massys and *Pl. 27*
Patinir is carefully articulated by L. von Baldass, "Die niederländische Landschaftsmalerei von Patinir bis Bruegel," p. 111ff.).

Yet as distinct as Massys' early forms of landscape are from Patinir's world landscapes, it is also true that after Patinir's arrival
in Antwerp, Quinten's settings, particularly behind his Passion scenes, show signs of an accord with the specialist's formulations.
In works such as the Louvre *Pieta* (F. 16, cat. 17), the Ottawa *Crucifixion* (F. 12, cat. 20), and the Antwerp *Crucifixion triptych* *Pl. 94*
(Museum Mayer van den Bergh, F. 56, cat. 22), smaller-scale figures act against a broader landscape with ever more visible *Pl. 95*
details. It should be noted that, even in these instances, Massys' settings seem to be correlatives of the inward emotions of the
religious figures. In scenes like the Worcester *Rest on the Flight* or Antwerp *Lamentation*, the soaring crags and rugged terrain
vividly suggest the agony of mournful stress of the holy actors. The Louvre *Pieta* continues this parallel, and the Ottawa
Crucifixion complements the quiet despair of the *Stabat Mater* and St. John with falling curves in its background mountains.

Despite the influence of Patinir,works like the Louvre *Pieta* show smooth continuity with earlier Massys creations. Not only do
the mountains of this work continue to echo the outlines of Mary's dark blue silhouetted mantle, but the figure types also
suggest earlier Massys characters. The head of Mary is sharp-featured and narrow like the Worcester and Seilern *Madonnas*, *Pl. 52*
while the face of St. John bears the features of the same saint from the Lisbon *Women at the Tomb*, of the *Madre de Deus altarpiece*,
or the young,unbearded Joachim from the *Offering in the Temple* of the *St. Anne altarpiece* exterior. A tendency toward thin, *Pl. 8*
angular outlines can also be seen in both the face and the anatomy of the dead Christ, a softly modeled, unified slender body
that departs from the detailled modeling and anatomy of the Antwerp *Lamentation*.

Increasingly, the landscapes of this Patinir phase of Massys' career are filled with tall, lanky figures. The Ottawa *Crucifixion*
continues this trend, as does the Antwerp *Crucifixion triptych*, a work that displays workshop participation. Even a work with no
interest in landscape, the *Passion altarpiece* of Coimbra (F. 196, cat. 18) situates similar slender figures within a spacious, *Pl. 32*
predominant architecture. The Coimbra altarpiece is datable between 1513 and early 1517, so it provides external corrobora- *Pl. 33*
tion for the timing of this reorientation in Massys *oeuvre* around the time of Patinir's arrival in Antwerp. Moreover, the central
panel at Coimbra, today preserved only in an oval fragment, preserves a *Mater Dolorosa* which is virtually the twin of the *Stabat* *Pl. 36*
Mater of the Ottawa *Crucifixion* or the grieving mother of the Louvre *Pieta*. The Madonna pose of tilted head with her hands
crossed over her breast, the Madonna costume of indigo mantle with gold trim, and the Madonna facial type of narrow oval face
with sharp, straight nose are common to all of these works. In similar fashion, the tall, bony, small-faced Christ of the Coimbra
wings, a *Flagellation* and an *Ecce Homo*, is a cousin to the crucified savior of the Ottawa and Louvre panels. And the Hague *Way to
Calvary* (F. 167, cat. 15), mentioned earlier as an outgrowth of the *Madre de Deus altarpiece*, belong in this company. *Pl. 89*

The Coimbra panels have a new prominence of bright colors. Blues, purples, and golds dominate the *Ecce Homo* wing; in *Pl. 9* colors and in the use of brown-toned grotesque faces, this Coimbra wing most closely resembles the *Rejection of Joachim* shutter from the exterior of the *St. Anne altarpiece*. But the similarities of the two wings only serve to point out the changes in Massys' style over the time separating them. Increasingly, the sufferings and vulnerability of holy figures have been emphasized through contrast with the horrific, inhuman tortures who mock them. The relatively motionless figures of the first great altarpiece have given way to ever more theatrical actors in the religious drama, whose powerful poses and gestures are underscored by their colorful silhouettes. The taller, thinner figures of the later decade are crowded tightly together to enhance their lively interaction.

The Coimbra *Passion retable* is a rare example during this time of a major altarpiece commission undertaken entirely by Massys himself, although the Antwerp *Crucifixion altarpiece* seems to be largely his work. But during this period, Master Quinten seems to have continued his Madre de Deus pattern by generating a number of lesser workshop products, such as the *Crucifixion altarpieces* now in Brussels and the collection of Count Harrach (F. 58, 57). An isolated panel from the same period by the workshop is the *Seven Sorrows of Mary* (Brussels, F. 63), which allegedly served for the worship of that cult by the Antwerp painters' guild of which Massys was a member. And the large *Lamentation* panel, formerly in the Wetzlar collection, Amsterdam (F. 14), should probably also be seen as the work of Massys' atelier; its slender figures clustered against the Golgotha hillside are much closer as types to the Coimbra *Ecce Homo* or even the Prado *Temptation of St. Anthony* than they are to the actors in the Antwerp *Lamentation*.

Shortly after the Coimbra and Ottawa panels, Massys painted a small, devotional altarpiece (Munich, Alte Pinakothek, F. 3, *Pl. 37* cat. 24) for a private patron, the German trade representative from Augsburg, Lucas Rem. The *Rem altarpiece* bears the arms of both the donor and his wife, so it can be dated to after his 1518 marriage; most likely it was commissioned during Rem's visit to Antwerp in late 1518 or, alternatively, during a 1520 visit. The conservative subject matter of the *Rem altarpiece* includes two visionary main figures, the Holy Trinity and Maria in Sole, on the central panel, and protector saints, Sebastian and Roch, on the wings. Undoubtedly, these themes, like the grisaille exterior of the couple's patron saints, Luke and the *Anna Selbdritt*, were specified by the patron, Rem. Massys seems to have left most of the execution of the wings to his assistants, and the quality of painting is uneven. For the perfect visages of the sacred visions, Massys has adapted forms that appeared earlier in the Antwerp *Lamentation*—the patriarchal bearded figure above the head of Christ and the smooth, oval faces of the female mourners—but the more uniform coloration and symmetrical, fine features offer a regularity appropriate to the celestial visions. The figure of Christ on the crucifix is derived from the types of the Coimbra *Ecce Homo* or Ottawa *Crucifixion*—thin arms, triangular head, straight nose—and while the Madonna is youthful and unlike the Coimbra *Mater Dolorosa*, her regular, broad, oval head repeats *Pl. 35* the form of the *Virgin Annunciate* grisaille on the exterior of the *Coimbra altarpiece*. This fuller oval facial type, a standard Massys *Pl. 176* formula for the young Mary, will continue to dominate his output. In contrast, other fair-featured females, such as the two *Pl. 112* saints in the *Mystic Marriage of St. Catherine* (F. 28, cat. 25), or the two hermit saints in Philadelphia (F. 7, cat. 21), or even the *Pl. 114* siren temptresses of the Prado *Temptation of St. Anthony*, made in collaboration with Patinir, have narrow, almost angular faces *Pl. 13* with fine, etched features, a form prefigured by the Salome of the Antwerp *St. John altarpiece*.

Personal piety was served during this period by another pair of images from the Massys workshop. The *San Bernardino of Siena*, which survives in a trio of exemplars (best version Lisbon, coll. Salazar), is a characteristically Mediterranean saint and was probably one of Massys' exports through the Antwerp trading community. Another devotional image with devotional purposes, made by the Massys workshop, is the *Descent from the Cross* (Madrid, Lazaro coll. F. 61). This close-up narrative is derived from a Roger van der Weyden model (Ringbom, *Icon to Narrative*, p. 25f.) and is related to the Man of Sorrows icon type, which was associated with a special prayer of indulgence. The wings of Lazaro triptych bear one of the "Seven Prayers of St. Gregory," stipulated for the Man of Sorrows image and frequently included in prayerbooks. The exterior of the *Descent from the Cross* wings shows grisaille miniatures in elaborate Late Gothic decorative shrines of two saints, John the Baptist and Elizabeth of Hungary, who in all probability were the patron saints of the married donors, like the Rems.

For the most part, these preoccupations of Massys are not major shifts of direction, despite the influence of Patinir's *Pl. 118* landscapes and the new figure types. But with the creation of the 1514 Louvre *Moneychanger and his Wife* (F. 53, cat. 16), Massys shows a new concern with ethical decisions and the temptations of both saints and sinners. For the most part, these ethical themes are presented like the example of the first of the series, the Louvre *Moneychanger*—as half-length close-ups. Before this time, only portraits or iconic devotional images had been pictured in this manner, and they conspicuously lack both the action and the interaction of the principal characters. These two figures show the same soft modeling and delicate features that will dominate the religious pictures of the Patinir period; the Louvre *Moneychanger*, painted the year before Patinir's arrival in Antwerp, provides a reference point or benchmark with its secure date.

Probably not long after the Louvre *Moneychanger*, Massys' lost composition of the *Banker and his Client* continued the secular *Pl. 120* theme of money and its temptations with another pair of figures within a boothlike room. In this case, however, the handsome *Pl. 121* faces and poised, unresolved ambiguity of the Louvre picture are replaced by moral repulsion in the ugly, grimacing faces and even more outlandish costumes of the two financiers. Massys was also to use the brown-skinned, gruesome face of aging, overdressed decadence in his admonitory withered hag in the *Temptation of St. Anthony*. But it was with the direct use of *Pl. 122* Leonardo drawings, in particular for the London *Grotesque Old Woman*, that Massys' most acerbic secular pictures were *Pl. 124* developed (see Chap. 7). For these characters, the skin is a muddy brown color with lustrous white highlights and the ugliness *Pl. 33* even more assertive than in Passion scenes like the Coimbra *Ecce Homo*. The ultimate contrast between this visual image of moral *Pl. 86* turpitude and holiness comes from this same period in the Prado *Ecce Homo*, where the bright, smooth skin of Christ acts as a foil to the dark, leering rabble.

In both theme and conception, the Prado *Ecce Homo* is the a change from the Coimbra panel, as the Madrid work offers a distinctive new focus on the characters rather than on the environment. Just as the Grotesque *Old Man and Woman* had adjured the wooden room that was the setting for the earlier secular works, the Madrid *Ecce Homo* replaced theatrical gestures and three-quarter length figures with a new concentration on facial expression viewed close up in half-length. The net result is greater concentration on the figures and heightened emotional impact. Christ's suffering becomes more important than the dramatic spectacle and stage space of His presentation to the crowd. This new emphasis on religious and secular characters and their inner emotions will be the major feature of Massys' final period of creativity during the 1520s. With this human component dominating over incidentals of setting, Massys returns to the half-length format of the devotional images that had comprised his earliest work.

The combination of ethical concerns already revealed by the first secular works and the increased focus on inner emotions can be found in Massys' other great experiment of this phase of his career: the half-length saints in distress. The *St. Jerome* in his cell (F. 70, cat. 28), for example, uses almost exactly the same setting as the Louvre *Moneychanger* and presents the saint in the same half-length format. *Pl. 106* But whereas the wife of the moneychanger turned aside from her prayers to glance at her husband, the holy man glances deeply at the prayerbook illumination of the Last Judgment and thoughtfully fingers a skull, which keeps the presence of death constantly before him. *St. Jerome* is not an icon for cultic devotion, like the *St. Bernardino,* but an image intended as much for moral instruction as the secular images. Here the "role model" is positive rather than ambiguous or negative. Again, in the case of the *Magdalene* (Antwerp, F. 35, cat. 29), who already wears a cross and opens her unguent jar to *Pl. 110* adorn the feet of Christ, the process of conversion and internal spiritualization takes place before the viewer's eyes in the averted and meditative glance of the wealthy young woman. These works can be related to previous products. The face of the Magdalene recalls the *Moneychanger*'s wife or the *Madonna with St. Catherine;* her rich golden sleeves are the same as those of Pilate in the Prado *Ecce Homo.* The *Jerome* has the coloration of the first secular pictures and both the brown tones and careful delineation of detail of the God the Father from the *Rem altarpiece.* Circumstantially, it is datable through its resemblance to the study environment and intellectual circumstances of the 1517 Erasmus portrait (F. 36, cat. 58) and by the fact that it almost *Pl. 99* certainly served as the model for another famous image of the saint: Dürer's 1521 Lisbon *St. Jerome,* yet another export from Antwerp to Portugal.

Cat. 16. *Moneychanger and his Wife* (F. 53). 1514, Paris, Louvre no. 2029. Inscribed: "Quinten Matsys Schilder 1514." (71 × 68). *Plate 118*

Copy: Brussels, Musées Royaux no. 1069. Inscribed: "Quinten Matsys schilder inventor 1519" (70 × 66.5).

HIST.: Possibly identical with painting no. 186 in inventory of P. P. Rubens, 1640 (Denucé, p. 64): "Een portret van een koopman in juweelen, door Meester Quintinus." Collection Peter Stevens, Antwerp, as "Wisselaer en vrouwe, 1514," according to Fickaert, 1648, and Fornenbergh, 1658. 1676 inventory of Diego Duarte, Amsterdam, no. 130: "Een seer curieus stuck van twee figuren man en vrouw, met veel bywercken genaemt het juweelierken" (G. Dogan, "De inventaris der schilderijen van Diego Duarte," *Jaarboek van het Koninklijk Museum Antwerp,* 1971, p. 215). Acquired by Louvre 1806.

LIT.: Fickaert, p. 15; Fornenbergh, p. 26f.; van den Branden, p. 70f.; Hymans, p. 202f.; Cohen, p. 86; F. de Mely, *Gazette des Beaux Arts* 50 (1908): 216f.; Conway, pp. 317, 325; Winkler, p. 206; Delen, p. 83f.; Friedländer 7, p. 24f.; Baldass, pp. 146ff., 165, 170; Boon, p. 44; E. Michel, *L'ecole flamande du XVe siecle au musee du Louvre* (Brussels, 1944), p. 63f.; G. Hartlaub, *Zauber des Spiegels,* p. 98; H. Schwarz, "The Mirror in Art," p. 103; E. Michel, *Catalogue raisonné,* p. 207ff., no 2029; Panofsky *ENP,* p. 354; Marlier, pp. 186, 238ff.; I. Bergström, "Disguised Symbolism in 'Madonna Pictures' and Still Life," p. 346; Puyvelde, p. 301; *De eeuw van Bruegel,* no. 167; S. Sulzberger, "Considerations sur le chef d'oeuvre de Quentin Massys," p. 27ff.; Benesch, p. 88; Völker, 175ff.; Cuttler, p. 423; von der Osten, p. 151; J. Bialostocki, "The Eye and the Window," p. 159ff.; P. Schabacker, "Petrus Christus' *St. Eloy*: Problems of Provenance, Sources, and Meaning," p. 108ff.; DB, pp. 202–6.

The *Moneychanger and his Wife* (Paris, Louvre, signed and dated 1514), is a half-length close-up of the two main figures, a new departure in format for Massys as well as his earliest known secular subject. Up to this point, his only half-compositions had been portraits or devotional images. Despite its anomalies, the painting carries the personal stamp of Massys' touch. Most striking are the hands of the couple—long, elegant fingers, gently bent, with the little finger poised apart. The delicate features of the woman recall the female faces around the body of Christ in the Antwerp *Lamentation*; Massys repeats the sharp, straight *Pl. 20* nose, the lightly shaded brows, and the blonde tonality of the earlier 1508–11 panel. The moneychanger's wife, however, is also one of the earliest developed examples of the female head type that marks Massys' later creations. She has a characteristic spade-shaped head, which is broader at the top and tapers downward to a prominent chin. Increasingly, Massys favors the three-quarter pose, since it emphasizes the contours of the head for the side turned away from the viewer. In the Louvre picture, the modeling of the wife's head is extremely subtle and is carefully graded.

Her husband, on the other hand, is placed so that half his face and half his hand are in shade. Again, parallels from the *John altar* show this heavier modeling, which Massys seems to reserve for male figures as early as the Antwerp *St.* *Pl. 113* *Christopher.* The type for an unbearded male head is almost unprecedented in Massys' earlier works, but again the *John altar* offers the closest comparison: the boy in the tree above the *Martrydom of St. John.* Not only are the noses, eyes, hands, and relative poses nearly identical for the two figures, but they also share much the same color tonality.

In overall color, too, the *Moneychanger and his Wife* grows out of the achievements of the *John altar.* Both characters are dressed in large color blocks, which emphasize the regularized contours of their bodies (especially the lines of their shoulders). The wife is dressed in bright red, but the bluish tint of her fur trim harmonizes with the color of her husband's garb; he, in turn, is dressed in a grey-blue gown but has reddish fur trim and red cuffs that match his wife. His dark olive cap is balanced by her brown hat, just as the brown color of the picture's top half is countered below by a green table cover.

Beginning with the 1514 Louvre *Moneychanger*, Massys inaugurated a new category of secular subjects within his *oeuvre*. And for this everyday theme he turned to traditional models. The closest extant source for the *Moneychanger* is yet another Bruges painting, Petrus Christus's 1449 *St. Eloy* (New York, Lehmann Coll.), although this, in turn, may depend on an older Eyckian model. The *St. Eloy* contains many of the features incorporated into Massys' *Moneychanger*: a stall with foreground ledge, measuring scales, a rich background still-life, and a bull's-eye convex mirror in the corner that reflects offstage action for the viewer. Doubtless, the professional activity of Christus's principal character appealed to Massys in his choice of model; St. Eloy, as a goldsmith, had many of the accessories, including a sales booth, of a moneychanger. And the novelty of Massys' social criticism could also have determined his reference to the older painting. The costumes of the Louvre *Moneychanger* are distinctly archaic; in fact, the turban headdress on the red pleated cassock more closely resemble fashions found in Eyckian portraits a decade earlier than the *St. Eloy* panel. The outmoded costumes have the effect of removing Massys' *Moneychanger* from its contemporary setting. This historical distance serves to soften the sting of the social criticism in the panel (see Chap. 7), and it also links the *Moneychanger* to a tradition of painting in the Netherlands. Christus's *St. Eloy*, along with Roger van der Weyden's *St.*
Pl. 168 *Luke and the Virgin* (Boston), was a generalized professional portrait, where the patron saint of a guild or trade embodied the occupational activity. Massys himself painted a *St. Luke*, now lost, for the Antwerp guild (see Catalogue: Lost Works). When, in 1514, he painted a secular subject, Quinten returned to the professional models of Petrus Christus to evoke a similar generalized activity in his *Moneychanger.* Using older Netherlandish models enabled Massys both to legitimize his unusual subject matter and to make more universal social criticism.

Part of the seriousness of the painting is expressed via traditional religious symbols transferred into the new context. Candle and scales recall man's brief existence and the Judgment to come. Apple and plate suggest original sin and Christian redemption. The foreground mirror is a complex symbol associated with both Prudence and Vanity; it cautions mankind to think of the way of religion, as it features a man at devotion seen before a church spire.

In the 17th-century, van Fornenbergh reported an inscription on the frame of the painting, which tallies with its moralizing content: "Let the balance be just and the weights equal (Lev. 19,35)."

A number of derivatives from the Louvre *Moneychanger* were painted by Marinus van Reymerswaele (see Friedländer 12, no. 70), but these exaggerate the unusual costumes and emphasize the greed of the central figures without allowing for the ambiguity and uncertainty of human choice, as Massys had done. For example, the prayerbook of the woman is later seen as an account book, so that the religious component of the picture has disappeared entirely.

A copy of the *Moneychanger* appears in the lower right-
hand corner of Willem van Haecht's *Atelier of Apelles* (Speth- *Pl. 181*
Holterhoff, 104ff., ill. 38; The Hague, Mauritshuis). But there one detail disagrees with the Louvre picture: the wife's prayerbook shows a scene of Adam and Eve, rather than the Madonna and the Child of the preserved original. Since the careful Brussels copy repeats the Louvre picture and not the image of van Haecht, the 17th-century artist must have worked after a copy or freely adapted the original to make a theological point about worldly temptation.

Cat. 17. *Pieta* (F. 16). Paris, Louvre, no. 2203 (36 × 50). *Plate 94*

HIST.: Gallery Sedelmeyer sale to Louvre 1983; previously reported to have been in a 19th-century English collection.

LIT.: Cohen, pp. 29, 87; Bosschere, p. 48; Brising, p, 14f.; Conway, p. 316; Winkler, p. 203; Friedländer 7, p. 29; Baldass, pp. 143, 146, 155, 167; Boon, p. 40; Michel, *Catalogue raisonné*, p. 210; Panofsky, *ENP*, p. 261 n. 4; Mallé, p. 81; Robbins, p. 41ff.; DB, pp. 158–62.

Copy: Coll. E. Traumann, Madrid (39 × 50.5).

The Louvre *Pieta* is one of Massys' most direct borrowings from Dieric Bouts, whose *Pieta* is also in the Louvre. The principal correspondence is the main figure composition, where the dead Christ is stretched out stiffly, His shoulders resting on Mary's lap of dark blue. His head is supported by a genuflecting St. John, who bears a white towel and is dressed in red. Mary is depicted as a subdued mourner with her head covered; John is bareheaded, and his angular jaw and movemented posture suggest a more externalized grief.

Yet Massys' panel does show changes from its model. Bouts's theatrial Magdalene is omitted, and the cross itself is consigned a more minor role in the distance to focus attention on the main figures. Massys' figures are spread across the foreground, rather than aligned at an angle into the painting. As a result, they acquire isolated, heroic stature, reemphasized by the background hills that echo their outlines. Within the group, Massys subtly reverses Bouts's arrangement to give Mary greater prominence through her raised height and centrality.

The landscape background contains elements of self-quotation, almost a pastiche of Quinten's great altarpieces.
The natural arch in the left distance repeats the *Holy Kinship* *Pl. 1*
background, while Golgotha's three crosses and the candle-
lit tomb at the right recall the Antwerp *Lamentation.* Reced- *Pl. 20*
ing Jerusalem and its wall suggest the *Annunciation to Joachim* *Pl. 7*
and compare closely with the near-contemporary Ottawa
Crucifixion (F. 12; cat. 20), especially in its soldiers on horse- *Pl. 91*
back—an Eyckian "highlands" motif.

The Louvre *Pieta*, then, is an evocative combination of landscape and figures. Its sources are varied and include previous Massys works as well as Bouts and van Eyck. It
should be dated close to the 1514 Louvre *Moneychanger* (cat. *Pl. 11*
16) because of its stress on contours, tight figure grouping,

and a facial type like St. John. On the other hand, its broad landscape vista, diminished figure scale, and Madonna type recall the datable 1513–17 Coimbra *Passion* altarpiece (cat. 18) and the Ottawa *Crucifixion*, a work that probably post-dates the 1515 arrival of Patinir in Antwerp. *Pl. 32–36*

Cat. 18. *Passion altarpiece* (F. Add. 196). 1514–17, Coimbra, Museu Machado de Castro, nos. 2518–19 (191 × 92 cm. wings). Central panel missing except for an oval fragment of the *Mater Dolorosa* (47 × 31.5). *Plates 32–36*

HIST.: Commissioned in Flanders by Silvester Nunes, Antwerp factor of King Manuel I of Portugal (16 November 1513—1 March 1517); given to Monastery of Santa Clara, Coimbra, by Manuel I.

LIT.: J. de Figueiredo, "Metsys e Portugal," *Melanges Hulin de Loo* (Brussels / Paris, 1931): 167; Baldass, pp. 143, 148, 165; Boon, p. 29; L. Reis-Santos, "Quentin Metsys, seus discipulos e continuadores em Portugal," p. 10; F. J. Sanchez-Canton, "Notas sobre Quinten Massys en la Peninsula," p. 313; Reis-Santos, p. 85f.; idem, Museu Machado de Castro, *Catalogo de Arte Flamenga do Seculo XVI* (Coimbra, 1954), p. 19f.; Mallé, p. 95; Broadley, p. 215; Cuttler, p. 423; Völker, p. 108; DB, pp. 156–57.

This three-paneled altarpiece, closely datable from receipts of Silvester Nunes, whose Antwerp sojourn was brief (late 1513–early 1517), has remained in Coimbra since its initial delivery to Portugal. Its destination and commission reveal the close ties between Antwerp and Portugal during the early years of the 16th-century spice trade (see Chap. 3), and this royal patron evidences Massys' local prominence in Antwerp.

Reis-Santos, p. 85f., hypothesizes that river flooding may have damaged the central panel of the triptych during the 17th century, judging from the frame of the preserved oval fragment. The *Mater Dolorosa* figure was probably part of some Calvary scene, such as the *Lamentation* or *Christ Being Nailed to the Cross*.

The slender, elongate figures and their disposition in space recall works of Memling, such as the *Passion* panel (Turin, Galerie Sabauda; Friedländer 7, no. 34), and works of the late 15th-century Ghent-Bruges school of manuscript illumination. Comparable small figures and gruesome tormentors can be found in Simon Bening's *Grimani Breviary* Crucifixion page margins or the miniature *Ecce Homo* by Juan de Flandes (Prague; ill. in J. Bialostocki, *Spätmittelalter und Beginnende Neuzeit Propyläen Kunstgeschichte* 7 [Berlin, 1972], no. 35). Since one of Memling's panels was painted in 1478 for the Bruges illuminator Willem Vrelant, it is not surprising that such miniature scenes found easy transfer into local manuscripts. For a discussion of the Turin panel, see C. Aru and E. de Giradon, *La Galerie Sabauda de Turin Les Primitifs Flamands* 1, no 5 (Antwerp, 1952), p. 16. A close connection can also be made between Memling's gray-blue *Christ Carrying the Cross* and Massys' Hague composition (cat. 15), where Christ also looks outward at the viewer. *Pl. 89* The fanciful architecture, bright colors, and lively movement all recall Memling, although there is no evidence of any direct borrowing.

Massys' theme is traditional, reflecting late medieval preoccupation with the Passion of Christ (Chaps. 3, 5). In the *Ecce Homo* wing, however, the artist involves his audience directly in the event by means of a defined viewpoint and a glance from the man in the right foreground of the crowd of tormentors.

Because the painting is datable, it serves as a useful reference point in assigning undated works to Massys' chronology. In particular, the angular but fine features of the shrouded Virgin, the lanky figures and their movement, and the increased importance of architecture and space characterize the non-portrait products of the middle of Quinten's third decade (ca. 1515–20).

Cat. 19. *Banker and his Client.* (lost; see Friedländer 12, no. 167), ca. 1514–15.

Copies and variants:

1. Windsor Castle, no. 234 (115.5 × 82.5); replica: Detroit Institute of Arts, no. 89.62 (46″ × 38″). *Plate 120*
2. Formerly coll. O. Strauss, Berlin (88.5 × 60); ex-coll. Oppenheim, Berlin. Includes inscription: "Le roy doict a Maistre Corneille de la Chapelle son painctre sur la Gabelle du Sel la somme de Deux mille Liv(res)."
3. Coll. Cailleux, Paris (87 × 70). *Plate 121*
4. Munich, Alte Pinakothek, no. 136 (88 × 72).
5. Sale, Christie's (23 Dec. 1954; no. 106); dated 1549 in book.
6. Swiss coll. (96 × 89); ex-coll. G. Agnew.
7. Geneva, Musee d'Art, no. 1910–31 (leg. van Roberti; 122 × 98).
8. Nancy, Museum no. 96.

Marinus van Reyemerswaele variant: Antwerp, Koninklijk Museum, no. 244 (65 × 52); numerous copies.

LIT.: Hymans, p. 216; Friedländer 12, no. 167; Hoogewerff, *De noord-nederlandsche schilderkunst* 4 (The Hague, 1941–42), pp. 463, 467; 5, p. 162; R. deRoover, *Money, Banking, and Credit in Medieval Bruges*, pp. 201, 262; H. van Werveke, "Aantekeningen bij de zoogenaamde *Belastingspachters* en Wisselaers van Reymerswaele," p. 43ff.; Marlier, p. 266ff.; Mallé, p. 106; L. van Puyvelde, "Un portrait de marchand par Quentin Metsys et les percepteurs d'impots par Marin van Reymerswale," p. 3ff.; Puyvelde, p. 301; Völker, p. 186f.

Some documentation associates Quinten Massys with this subject, and several 17th-century inventories mention such a painting. In 1616 (Sept. 22), the collection of Jacques Dassa (formerly coll. N. Rococx): "A painting on panel of a taxcollector or money-changer made by Master Quinten" (Denucé, p. 28). Later, in 1652, the painting appeared in the inventory of Jan van Meurs of Antwerp (ibid., p. 133): "A painting, painted by master Quinten Metsys, showing the Tax-Collectors."

Only Puyvelde believes any of the extant versions (no. 3; Paris, coll. Cailleux) to be an original by Massys. Marlier, in turn, believes the Windsor panel to be an accurate replica of a lost Massys prototype. From the various copies, the original Massys seems to have been a more close-up composition than the Windsor painting, which should be considered a variant, since it also includes additions of a parrot and moneybags not found in most of the copies.

The subject matter is that of a lost van Eyck panel (1440),

seen around 1530 by Marcantonio Michiel in Milan. The Eyckian date supports the authenticity of the statement, although neither the original painting nor copies have survived to convey its appearance. Presumably, it was a commissioned portrait, perhaps by the Bruges community of Italian financiers (e.g., Giovanni Arnolfini, who ordered other panels from van Eyck).

Its many copies indicate the picture's continued popularity. Doubtless, its criticism of avarice (see Chap. 7) continued to be timely during the 16th century. The exact interpretation of the scene is not clear and, in light of inscriptions on later versions and adaptations by van Reymerswaele, it has been seen as a municipal tax collector rather than as a banker (van Werveke). It is possible, however, that later copyists misunderstood or intentionally altered the painting's meaning. Moreover, the Cailleux Collection ledger has a biblical paraphrase critical of avarice instead of the tax accounts found on other copies. As for the Windsor version, van Werveke argues (p. 54) that the two men cannot be banker and client unless funds are being deposited, because no second entry appears. He cites the anachronistic use of a profession which had almost entirely disappeared by the 16th century. Yet the Windsor entries are also currency exchanges rather than tax revenues, and the ledger contents could have been altered, since the listed exchange rates date from a period between 1548 and 1551 (van Werveke, Appendix, p. 57).

Pl. 118 The archaistic costumes are carefully studied, as in the 1514 *Moneychanger.* They betray none of the caricatural excess of Reymerswaele's creations (see also his *Tax Collectors* [London, National Gallery, no. 944]). A comparison of faces also shows a less grotesque distortion in the *Banker and Client* copies than in the Antwerp Marinus version. Particularly with the suggestion of an Eyckian model, Massys would have been the likeliest creator of the *Banker* original. We have already seen Marinus adapting the Louvre *Moneychanger* to his own purposes, and the Antwerp version also reveals the same dependence on an earlier work: the lost Massys original.

The colors of the copies (e.g., Munich, Windsor) show the same sense of inversion and balance as the Louvre *Moneychanger.* The banker wears a red turban and blue-green jacket, which are complemented by the client's red coat and olive turban. Together with the archaic costumes, the boothlike space, and the green table-cover, the coins and other still-life elements, the original *Banker and his Client* seems to belong to the earliest, archaizing phase of Massys' secular paintings, dating close in time to the 1514 *Moneychanger.*

Either the original or (more likely) one of the numerous variations on Massys' *Banker and his Client* is itemized in the 17th-century Spanish inventory (1642) of the Marquis of Leganés, Diego Messía: no. 31, "a banker counting coins on a table," and no. 328, "a painting with two bankers with papers, one writing in a book." Both paintings are specifically credited to "Mro. Quintin." Another reference of the inventory (no. 248) surely refers to Massys' *Praying Monks* (F. 80, cat. 45). This reference was called to my attention by Prof. John Elliot; the full citation appears in the publication of the inventory by J. Lopez Navió, "La gran collección de pinturas del Marqués de Leganés," *Analecta Calasanctiana* 7–8 (1962), pp. 262–330. Recently, an art historian has analyzed this very inventory: Mary C. Volk, "New Light on a Seventeenth-Century Collectora The Marquis of Leganés," *Art Bulletin* 62 (1980): 256–68, especially 260–67, Appendix Two.

Cat. 20. *Crucifixion* (F. 12). Ottawa, National Gallery of Canada, no. 6190 (51 × 36.5). *Plate 91*

Copy: Munich, Alte Pinakothek (as Patinir School), no. 149 (95 × 70).

HIST.: Coll. Weyer, Cologne; Prince of Liechtenstein, Vaduz; 1954 museum purchase.

LIT.: Hymans, p. 198; Hulin de Loo, *Catalogue critique* (Bruges, 1902), p. 53f.; Cohen, pp. 28, 85; Bosschere, p. 43; Brising, p. 15; Winkler, p. 203; Friedländer 7, p. 28; Baldass, pp. 143ff., 155f., 169; Boon, p. 37ff.; Strohmer, *Gemäldegalerie des Fürsten Liechtenstein* (Vaduz, 1943), p. 95; Mallé, p. 82f.; *National Gallery of Canada Catalogue of Paintings and Sculpture* 1 (Ottawa/Toronto, 1957), p. 63; Broadley, p. 90f.; Puyvelde, 1970, p. 230; Robbins, p. 31ff; DB, pp. 192–93.

Variant: London, National Gallery, no. 715 (F. 13).

HIST.: Ex-coll. Ottinger-Wallerstein.

LIT.: M. Davies, *Early Netherlandish School National Gallery Catalogues,* no. 715; DB, pp. 194–95.

This panel and its mate in London have long been associated with Massys, but a number of authors have expressed belief that the landscape is by Patinir. Certainly, its high viewpoint and panoramic vista reflect the influence of Massys' friend Joachim, who enrolled in the Antwerp guild in 1515. But the careful integration of background elements with the foreground figures is a feature of Massys' landscapes, not of Patinir's, and the lyrical coordinated setting lacks Patinir's sense of epic breadth. Nothing in the picture offers any reason to attribute any part of the Ottawa panel to a collaborator, although the Patinir influence suggests a date shortly after 1515.

There is general agreement that the Ottawa figures are by Massys. The balanced shapes of the figural composition and their layered effect across the foreground plane recall other works, like the Louvre *Pieta* (cat. 17). Once the Ottawa Pl. 94
Crucifixion is admitted into Massys' *corpus,* however, the differences of its London variant become clearer. Even in a detail like the clouds, London's overly studious, crowded forms depart from Massy's usual effects. Similarly, additional figures (including a ludicrous grinning mourner at the right edge of the panel) disturb the normal figural balance, and their drapery, particularly the Magdalene's scarf, flutters distractingly. Moreover, the London panel introduces a new strong movement into depth on the right side of the cross; this uncharacteristic movement is reinforced by the overlap of figures and the spaces between them. The London panel also smooths away physical details and the sense of firm structure, especially in the face and thorns of Christ.

For this traditional subject, Massys turned to famous Netherlandish models. An Eyckian composition, preserved in the *Turin-Milan Hours* and a panel in the Ca d'Oro, Pl. 92
Venice, is one model. These pictures show the same balanced poses of the Virgin and St. John, the same posture of Christ on the cross, and an elevated viewpoint with Jerusa-

lem in the background. Other features—Christ's fluttering loincloth and the Magdalene clutching the base of the cross—ultimately derive from Roger van der Weyden's Vienna *Crucifixion.*

The Ottawa *Crucifixion* can be approximately dated because of its points of contact with the Coimbra *Passion altarpiece* (cat. 18). The slender, lanky figures and the face of the Virgin have their counterparts in the 1514–17 panels, and the Patinir features provide a narrower 1515 *terminus post quem.* *Pl. 32* *Pl. 33*

Cat. 21. *Mary Magdalene and Mary of Egypt* (F. 7). Philadelphia, Johnson Coll., nos. 366–67 (29.5 × 20 cm each). *Plate 112*

HIST.: Coll. P. & D. Colnaghi, London, 1902; Sale Müller, Amsterdam, 27 April 1909 (no. 92).

LIT.: Winkler, p. 204; Friedländer 7, p. 60; Baldass, pp. 153, 160, 168; B. Knipping, *De iconografie van de contra-reformatie in de Nederland,* pp. 98f., 140ff.; Puyvelde 1970, p. 230; *John G. Johnson Collection Catalogue of Flemish and Dutch Paintings* (Philadelphia, 1972), p. 54; DB, pp. 172–74.

These two panels emphasize penitential grief of beautiful female saints, who become pious hermits at the end of their days. Mary Magdalene is identifiable from her ointment jar attribute; according to legend, she retreated into a mountain grotto, where she was nourished by angels for 30 years. Paired with her on the pendant wing is the less familiar Mary of Egypt, another sinner who fled to the desert in repentance and survived there for 47 years on three morsels of bread (illustrated by Massys in the Philadelphia panel). Her long hair is a frequent identifying attribute, as it covered her nakedness after her clothes had been worn away during the long years in the desert.

Female saints repenting in the wilderness, like Jerome, the favorite male saint in the wilderness, were not unknown in the early 16th century. Adrian Isenbrant's *Magdalene in the Desert* (Friedländer 12, no. 210) and Lucas van Leyden's early engraving (ca. 1508, B. 123) both carry out the same theme. But Lucas's print may be Mary of Egypt rather than the Magdalene, for Mary of Egypt was discovered in the desert and visited twice by St. Zosimas, while Mary Magdalene, according to the *Golden Legend,* was protected by a divine force field from any intrusion. Later, the penitent Magdalene (also painted by Massys in his later Antwerp panel, cat. 29) became a favorite theme of the Counter-Reformation. She was frequently shown by 17th-century artists in a cell with a skull, like Massys' *St. Jerome* (F. 70, cat. 28). For bibliography on the cult of the Magdalene, see J. Bialostocki, "The Descent from the Cross in Works by Peter Paul Rubens and His Studio," *Art Bulletin* 46 (1964): 521f., n. 39ff., esp. n. 43. *Pl. 106*

The Philadelphia panels are so beautifully matched with regard to their presentation of figures and landscapes that it is difficult to imagine any central panel in between to form a triptych. Perhaps they appeared as a diptych; after all, the two panels together complete a tree and the green bank where each saint resides. Nevertheless, the programmatic pairing of the two female penitents may have included a central hermit saint in the wilderness, like St. Jerome (e.g., Patinir's New York altarpiece, Metropolitan Museum) or other popular hermit saints, like Giles or Anthony (e.g., Bosch's *Hermits altarpiece,* Venice, Palazzo Ducale; Friedländer 5, no. 98).

Dating the saints is possible by their elongate proportions and fine, angular features, like the Virgins of Patinir-influenced compositions just after 1515 (e.g., Ottawa *Crucifixion,* F. 12, cat. 20, or the *Mater Dolorosa* of the Coimbra *Passion altarpiece,* F. 196, cat. 18). The figures also resemble the Magdalene from a workshop altarpiece of the *Crucifixion* (F. 56, cat. 22) now in the Antwerp Museum Meyer van den Bergh. *Pl. 91* *Pl. 36*

Cat. 22. *Crucifixion altarpiece* (F. 56). Antwerp, Mayer van den Bergh Museum no. 27 (156 × 92.7).

LIT.: Cohen, p. 82; Bosschere, p. 42ff; Brising, p. 16; Delen, p. 60f; Friedländer 7, p. 29; Baldass, pp. 143f, 155f, 168; Boon, p. 39; Broadley, p. 89; J. de Coo, *Mayer van den Bergh Catalogue* (Antwerp, 1966), p. 96f. (with full bibliography); DB, pp. 188–91.

Friedländer assigns the Antwerp altarpiece to the Massys workshop, but some passages in its panels are of higher quality than the rest. In particular, the Magdalene and donor on the right wing are painted with a subtle precision and sense of body movement that suggest the work of Quinten himself. In contrast, the donor with St. Jerome on the left wing is flat in appearance and empty in expression. The central landscape is clearly not by Massys; the town in the distance, the rocks, and the skull are loosely painted and insubstantial. The figures of the central panel are also uneven in quality, although they are all competent executions of typical Massys designs. Like the male donor, Mary Magdalene appears as a flat surface pattern at the foot of the cross. In contrast, the older woman mourner behind the Virgin is painted in subtle brown harmonies that suggest comparison with portraits and half-lengths of the late teens. The Virgin's robe is an unusual luminous blue that might be the result of restoration.

In brief, the design and some of the figures seem to be Massys originals. Weaker figures, such as the male donor and the central Magdalene, appear out of place and may, like the landscape, be the work of studio assistants. The slender figure types, broad landscape setting, and use of browns associate the altarpiece with panels like the Philadelphia *Maries* (cat. 21) and with later works of the 1515–20 period. Its types resemble but seem slightly to postdate the Ottawa *Crucifixion* panel (F. 12, cat. 20), and they recall works from the end of the decade, e.g., the 1518–19 *Rem altarpiece* (F. 3, cat. 24) or the pre-1522 Prado *Anthony* (F. 31, cat. 26). For de Bosque, however the very closeness of resemblance between the Ottawa *Crucifixion* and this Antwerp *Crucifixion triptych* is proof enough that the retable is the prime object with the single panel as the derivative, possibly even by Patinir. *Pl. 91* *Pl. 37* *Pl. 114*

Cat. 23. *San Bernardino of Siena.* Lisbon, Salazar collection (31.7 × 24.7).

HIST.: From the collection of the Almadas, "Provedores da Casa da India," to Quinta da Malpartilha at Azeitão, with the legacy of the first Count of Carvalhais, D. José Joaquim Lobo da Silveira e Almada, coll. Dr. Alberto James Gomes de Oliveira. Probably purchased, according to Reis-Santos, by Rodrigo Fernandes de Almada, factor of Portugal, from Massys in Antwerp. Donation by Dr. Ricardo de Espirito Santo Silva to President Salazar of Portugal.

LIT.: Reis-Santos, *Le portrait de Saint Bernardin de Sienne par Quentin Metsys;* idem, *Masterpiece of Flemish Painting of the Fifteenth and Sixteenth Centuries in Portugal,* p. 87ff.; DB, pp.170–71.

A. Replica: Cloister of Descalzas Reales, Madrid (3.0 × 1.5).
B. Copy: Feltre, Museo Civico (29.5 × 21.5).

As noted in Chapter 3, the Lisbon *St. Bernardino* is the likely outcome of the Massys' contact in Antwerp with the Portugese trading community, specifically with the aristocratic factor Rodrigo Fernandes de Almada. It was Fernandes who helped to welcome Dürer to Antwerp in 1521, who received numerous prints and drawings from the German artist, and who commissioned from Dürer the magnificent *St. Jerome* (1521) now in the Lisbon Museum. In all likelihood, it was Fernandes who exposed Dürer to Massys' own
Pl. 106 earlier *St. Jerome* (cat. 28) as a model for that commission. San Bernardino (d. 1444) was a distinctly Mediterranean saint, famous in the 15th century as a major Observantine reformer of the Franciscans and as a popular preacher. His legacy to popular piety of the late Middle Ages was the cult of the monogram of Christ, the IHS that appears within his hand in the Massys image as a glowing disk with golden rays
Pl. 43 akin to the halo of the Antwerp *Christ Blessing* (F. 5, cat. 5). This formulation conforms to the standard image of Bernardino created by the saint's contemporary painters in Siena, such as Sano di Pietro (ill. de Bosque, fig. 182). Massys' saint, like the Siena versions, also appears in his brown Franciscan habit. One of the rare other appearances of San Bernardino in Flemish painting is Gerard David's inclusion of the saint within a group of holy figures and a donor (London, National Gallery); in that case, too, the reason was tied to the ca. 1501 commission, for Bernardino was the name saint of the donor, Bernardinus de Salviatis, canon of St. Donatian's, Bruges. In David's image, Bernardino's monogram appears in a more-naturalistic guise as the tooled gold cover of a leather-bound prayerbook.

The brownish background (illustrated in color in Reis-Santos, 1962) is unusual for Massys' monochrome bust-length images, but it harmonizes with the brown skin tones and robes of the aged ascetic. The use of a portrait convention adds to both the verisimilitude of this recent saint (canonized in 1474) and to his iconic presence before the viewer. The wrinkled brown skin, in fact, links this painting to other Massys' images of aged saints, in particular to the *St. Jerome,* preserved today in a replica in Vienna; the *St. Jerome* also features distinctive long fingers and a characteristic flexed little finger found in this *San Bernardino.* The leathery dark skin of this saint can also be found among the grotesque tormentors of Christ and the saints in Massys' religious works. Bernardino and Jerome are both exceptional cases in the artist's assignments, since they are not beautiful nor youthful images of sainthood.

Undisputable attribution to Massys is problematic for all these works, although the Feltre picture is clearly a careful copy. The Madrid replica offers sharper linear outlines and seems to be the derivative version, but considerable workshop involvement is possible even for the Lisbon image.

Cat. 24. *Altarpiece of the Trinity with the Virgin—Rem altarpiece* (F. 3). 1518–20, Munich, Alte Pinakothek, nos. 141–43 (90 × 78 center). *Plate 37*

HIST.: Hofgarten Gallery 1781; to Paris 1800; restored to Schleissheim 1815; Alte Pinakothek 1836; Sebastian wing added 1911.

LIT.: Braune, *Münchner Jahrbuch* 9 (1914–15), p. 151f.; Friedländer 7, p. 26; *Catalogue of Alte Pinakothek,* 17th ed. (1930), p. 91f.; Baldass, pp. 141, 147, 154, 160ff., 168, 170; Boon, p. 35ff.; Mallé, p. 100; H. von Welser, "Der Globus des Lukas Rem," *Mitteilungen des Vereins für Geschichte der Stadt Nürnberg* 48 (1958); 96ff.; von der Osten, p. 147; R. Koch, *Joachim Patinir,* p. 9ff.; Puyvelde 1970, p. 229; Robbins, p. 20ff; DB, pp. 198–202.

The triptych is datable because of what is known about the biography of the patron, Lucas Rem. He was a member of a patrician Augsburg family, who worked in Antwerp as the representative of the prosperous Welser trading firm (see Chap. 3). His first visit to the city was in 1508, and he resided there periodically between 1511 and 1518 (see B. Greiff, *Tagebuch des Lucas Rem* [Augsburg, 1861]). Rem's diary records that in 1516 and 1517, his profits were converted into "paintings, gems, and fabrics" in Antwerp. The Massys altarpiece is specifically identified because it bears not only the arms of the merchant (along with his patron saint, Luke), but also those of his wife, Anna Ochainen (and her patron saint, Anne). The couple were married in Augsburg on 17 May 1518, the *terminus post quem* for the altarpiece. According to the diary, Rem was back in Antwerp between September 1518 and January 1519, and also between April and July 1520. Only during these periods could he have commissioned the panels from Massys.

Baldass has argued that the arms were added, after the marriage, to a panel painted considerably earlier, i.e., during the first stay in Antwerp in 1508. His arguments are stylistic, based on figure types and the execution of folds, landscapes, and heads. The figure of St. Anne, however, could not have been added before the donor's 1518 marriage. Although the saints—Sebastian and Roch—on the wings were invoked against plague while Rem was in Portugal in 1505, there was also a plague scare in Antwerp in 1519, according to Boon. The archaic forms of the central figures—Trinity and Apocalyptic Woman—need not be the product of an earlier phase of Massys' development; their traditional appearance is the result of conservative subject matter requested by Rem. The image of the Trinity appears substantially unaltered from 15th-century versions, e.g., the sculpture above the fireplace in Robert Campin's *Werl altarpiece* (1438; Madrid, Prado; Friedländer 2, no. 67). Similarly, the *Virgin on a Crescent* was a popular image for the Immaculate Conception, and its frequent appearance was promoted by allying this votive picture with a 15th-century prayer of indulgence. Numerous prints—e.g., Israhel van Meckenem—portrayed the Apocalyptic Virgin along with the associated prayer. As Koch has demonstrated, Rem's diary invokes the Trinity, the Virgin, and all the saints in the diary passage dealing with his marriage.

For the pose of Sebastian, which was new to Massys' work, the figure by Hans Memling (Friedländer 6a, no. 45), now in Brussels, may have served as a source. It, too, features the saint tied to a tree with one arm raised. Massys has lowered the position of the bowmen to conform with space restrictions of the wing.

As for the forms of the *Rem altarpiece,* the types of the
Pl. 33 Crucifix and the Virgin developed out of the *Ecce Homo* and
Pl. 35 the *Virgin Annunciate* grisaille, respectively, of the Coimbra *Passion altarpiece* (1514–17, F. 196, cat. 18). Christ's thin arms, triangular head, and straight nose can also be found
Pl. 91 in the Ottawa *Crucifixion* (F. 12, cat. 20). The regularized, broad oval head of the Madonna will be the standard for the full-face Virgins in Massys' later icons.

The present state of the altarpiece betrays alteration. An original bell-shaped frame has been squared off, in the center, with gray wedges, and in the wings with additional patches of sky. The surface of the panels is well preserved.

Friedländer and Robbins have argued that portions of the altarpiece (grisailles and Roch, or both wings, respectively) were painted by Massys' workshop. Robbins compares the landscapes to the Ottawa *Crucifixion* (F. 12, cat. 25), a work whose landscape she also considers to be the product of an assistant ("Hand C"); however, the carefully integrated, lyrical *Crucifixion* background differs in execution from the more prosaic buildings and crags of the *Rem* wings. The figures of God, the Virgin, and Sebastian reveal Massys' own careful execution. The Virgin may be compared to the Coimbra *Virgin Annunciate* grisaille exterior, the crucified Christ to the crucifix in Ottawa (although, after the *Coimbra altarpiece,* the figure appears even more attenuated in the Rem panel). The pinkish skin tones and soft modeling of *St. Sebastian* recall a dated portrait: the 1517 Karlsruhe *Man* (F.
Pl. 152 194, cat. 57), particularly in the coarsely textured depiction of hair. St. Roch, however, is painted much more flatly with a discordant gray skin color, and the angel beside him is awkwardly foreshortened and painted mechanically (hair, folds).

Von Welser discusses the globe at the feet of the Trinity, dating it ca. 1502–3. He claims that its view of Asia and Africa relates to a journey organized by Rem to India for the Welser merchants during his stay in Lisbon. However, the reference to Rem's earlier career need not serve as a date for the altarpiece but only as a *terminus post quem;* it could still be dated later in the donor's life, as both Massys' style and the patron's saints suggest. Rem continued to serve the Welsers as trade representative during his later years in Antwerp.

Cat. 25. *Mystic Marriage of St. Catherine* (F. 28). London, National Gallery no. 3664; canvas (93 × 110).
Plate 176

HIST.: Ex-coll. J. Linnell (d. 1882); to museum 1922 from C.B.O. Clarke.

LIT.: T. Borenius, "An Unknown Quentin Massys," *Burlington Magazine* 33 (1918): 3; Conway, p. 323; Delen. p. 77; Friedläuder 7, p. 31; Baldass, p. 166; Davies, p. 89f; von der Osten, p. 148 n. 15; Völker, p. 117f: DB, pp. 176–78.

This painting is noteworthy as the only surviving example of Massys' work on canvas, a support that already posed problems of preservation in the damp Netherlands by van Mander's time (1604; *Het Schilderboeck,* p. 147, in discussing canvases by Lucas van Leyden). Its subject, too, is unique for Massys. According to medieval legends, the saint prayed at her martyrdom and was answered by Christ, "Come my dear fiancee, the doors of Heaven are open before you." Saints Barbara and Catherine, who appear together on the London canvas, were paired frequently as holy representatives of the active and comtemplative lives. Both were considered members of the Fourteen Auxiliary Saints, who were invoked in all perilous situations.

Most scholarly comment about the London canvas attempts to date it within Massys' *oeuvre.* Von der Osten dates it early, based on the compositional symmetry. Yet both the general conception and the individual types grow out of later works. The puffy-cheeked Christ Child with domed skull is quite similar to the Infant of the 1526 New York
Adoration (F.8, cat. 40), but both reflect a distinctive Joos van *Pl. 79*
Cleve type (see Friedländer 9, nos. 52–54). Mary's face, unlike the tapered-chin, almond-shaped type of the New York *Adoration,* is completely round; in this respect, she
more closely resembles the *Maria in Sole* of the *Rem altarpiece* *Pl. 37*
(F.3, cat. 24), or the Antwerp *Mary Magdalene* (F. 35, cat. 29). *Pl. 110*
The sharp-featured female saints suggest the pointed-
chinned temptresses of the Prado *Temptation of St. Anthony* (F. *Pl. 114*
31, cat. 26) but have a stronger sense of volume. Their
jutting noses recall the *Magdalene wings* (Philadelphia; F.7, *Pl. 112*
cat. 21) or the Virgin in the Louvre *Pieta* (F. 16, cat. 17). *Pl. 94*

The layered space of the *Mystic Marriage* is not deep but has a convincing volume. Its hybrid Italianate architecture of the throne with its bottle-shaped marble columns and slender capitals recalls the playfulness of earlier images,
such as the *Seilern Madonna* (F. 165, cat. 13) or the late *Pl. 52*
Madonna of the Cherries, yet its solidity is comparable to the *Pl. 58*
massive marble throne of the *van Pannwitz Madonna* (F. 26,
cat. 38). The Troyes copy of the lost *Madonna with Sleeping* *Pl. 57*
Child (cat. 14) is the design closest to the throne of this London canvas.

Another characteristic Massys feature is the tall, slender tree visible through the door. This type of tree in the artist's
work first appears in the backgrounds of the Antwerp *Pl. 20*
Lamentation, of the Madre de Deus *Mater Dolorosa,* and of the *Pl. 24*
workshop icons like the Warsaw *Madonna and Child* or *Aynard Madonna* (F. 21). Closest comparisons to this lanky tree appear in later works: the trees behind the Berlin *Madonna*
Enthroned (F. 18, cat. 37) or the Rotterdam *Madonna with* *Pl. 63*
Milk Soup (F. 168, cat. 27), as well as Massys' backgrounds for *Pl. 65*
his late portraits, including the Vaduz *Canon* (F. 39, cat. 65) *Pl. 143*
or the Frankfurt *Scholar* (ca. 1521, F. 46, cat. 61). Joos van *Pl. 146*
Cleve's more delicate tree forms, seen on the wings of his earlier altarpieces of the teens, may have intervened to affect Massys.

Cat. 26 (with Joachim Patinir) *Temptation of St. Anthony* (F. 31). Before 1522, Madrid, Prado, no. 1615. Signed at bottom: "OPUS JOACHIM *AT*NIER" (155 x 173).
Plate 114

HIST.: In Escorial inventory by 1574, coll. Philip II; to Prado 1837.

LIT.: C. Justi, "Altflandrische Bilder in Spanien und Portugal, Joachim Patinir und Quentin Metsys," p. 93ff; Cohen, p. 85f; Bosschere, p. 127; Brising, pp. 16, 31; Baldass, "Die niederländische Landschaftsmalerei von Patinir bis Bruegel," p. 120; Winkler, p. 204; Friedländer 7, p. 25; Baldass, p. 169; Boon, p. 55f; Benesch, p. 90; Mallé, p.

104; Puyvelde, p. 222; *Museo del Prado Catalogo* (Madrid, 1952), p. 469; Koch, *Joachim Patinir*, pp. 21, 39f, 44, 49f, 78; Puyvelde 1970, p. 229; Robbins, p. 56ff; DB, pp. 178–80.

This picture has long been attributed to the collaboration of Massys and Patinir. The 1574 Escorial inventory reference, published by Justi in 1886, credits the figures "de mano de maestre Coyntin," the landscape "de maestre Joaquin." Boon (p. 56 n. 1) refers to a 1542 Spanish inventory reference to this picture; I have been unable to trace his reference.

The background displays Patinir's typical "world landscape" rather than Massys' more tightly unified forms; it may be compared with Patinir's Madrid *St. Jerome* (Koch, ill. 28), a signed work. But the elegant temptresses of the foreground tie in closely with Massys' work. There is an aged hag in an archaic wimple like the London *Old Woman*
Pl. 122 (F. 52, cat. 32). St. Anthony's unified features grow out of
Pl. 33 forms like the Christ of the Coimbra *Ecce Homo* (F. 196, cat. 18). His brown skin and wrinkles, like those of the hag, can be compared to the icons of *St. Bernardino* (cat. 23); the smooth, white, delicate faces of the sirens are constructed
Pl. 65 like the Rotterdam *Madonna* (F. 168, cat. 27) or the saints of
Pl. 176 the London *Mystic Marriage of St. Catherine* (F. 28, cat. 25).

The painting also can be dated to a *terminus ante quem* because it was adapted for a dated woodcut, attributed to Jan de Cock, of *St. Anthony* (1522; Koch, ill. 48). In particular, the wimpled old woman appears in the same position in the print, and the four background scenes are placed in the same relative positions as in the Prado panel.

Massys' earthly temptation is a derivation from the *Judgment of Paris,* reversed so that the women, like modern Eves, tempt the reluctant saint with an apple. Such a Christianized interpretation of the Paris scene found expression in a popular 15th-century text, the *Ovide moraliseé.* More frequently (e.g., Bosch, Grünewald), St. Anthony was depicted as attacked by demons or as a wilderness hermit—scenes consigned to the background of the Prado panel. See C. Cuttler, "Some Grünewald Sources," *Art Quarterly* 19 (1956), 101–24; idem, "The Lisbon *Temptation of St. Anthony* by Jerome Bosch," *Art Bulletin* 39 (1957): 109–26.

Cat. 27: *Madonna and Child with Milk Soup* (F. 168). Rotterdam, Museum Boymans-van Beuningen, no. 2460 (41 x 28). *Plate 65*

HIST.: Private coll., Paris; coll. D. G. van Beuningen.

LIT.: Friedländer 7, p. 81. Boon, *Catalogus Museum Boymans van Beuningen,* 1962; DB, p. 218.

Stylistically, the handling of pink skin tones, highlighted by white, and the brilliant red mantle of the Virgin recall the
Pl. 37 *Apocalyptic Woman* of the 1518–20 *Rem altarpiece* (F. 3, cat. 24) and serve to date the Rotterdam panel to approximately the same period. The fine features of the Madonna are even more delicately rendered than in the Antwerp *Magdalene* (F.
Pl. 110 35, cat. 29); they announce the fuller versions of the narrow
Pl. 114 facial types in Massys' Prado *Temptation of St. Anthony* (F. 31, cat. 26, before 1522). The plump, blonde, curly haired Child also appear in the *Rem altarpiece;* this type derives ultimately from Leonardo da Vinci and was probably transmitted through Joos van Cleve. Van Cleve's half-length Madonnas were popular in Antwerp during the teens and were frequently replicated in his workshop. Several of them show the Virgin outdoors (Friedländer 9, nos. 51a, 53, 57, 59); almost all feature a symbolic foreground still-life, adopted by Massys for the Rotterdam panel but uncommon in his work before then, except for the *Virgin with Sleeping Child* (cat. 14).

The milk soup motif was established by Gerard David in his large-scale *Virgin with Milk Soup* (Brussels); it may be a *Pl. 66*
reference to the relic of the milk of the Virgin. Paired with sacramental bread, referring to grace through Christ, the milk would be equivalent to grace via the Virgin. David's panel also combines the intimate maternal care for her Child, the foreground still-life on the table, and the right-hand corner view of a landscape that together inform Massys' Rotterdam picture. Massys adopted these features in the 1529 *Rattier Madonna* (Paris, Louvre; F. 24, cat. 48), where *Pl. 68*
he also includes the fuller face and transparent veil of his David model.

Massys' soft atmospheric blue-green background is more finely painted than other landscapes by him from around this time (e.g., the Antwerp *Magdalene,* Louvre *Pieta*) and *Pl. 94*
suggests the forms of his later style. The spindly trees are an important feature that also continues into the 1520s. Again, van Cleve seems to have been a source for this motif in the wings of his early altarpieces (Friedländer 9, nos. 7–14, 16–17).

Cat. 28. *St. Jerome* (lost; F. 70). Before 1521.

Copies: Vienna, Kunsthistorisches Museum, no. 691 (57 x 77). Munich, Alte Pinakothek, no. 5320/2888. *Plate 106*

LIT.: Hymans, pp. 19, 194; Cohen, p. 90; Bosschere, p. 123; G. Ring, *Beiträge zur Geschichte niederländische Bildnismalerei im 15. und 16. Jahrhunderte,* p. 66f.; Friedländer 7, p. 68; Baldass, p. 166f.; Friedländer, "Der heilige Hieronymus von Marinus van Reymerswael," *Pantheon* 13 (1934): 33ff.; Winkler, "Dürers Lissaboner Hieronymus," pp. 12, 14; Reis-Santos, *Le portrait de Saint Bernardin de Sienne par Quinten Metsys,* p. 21f.; Marlier, p. 179ff.; Reis-Santos, "Jan Quinten Massys Discipulo e Colaborador de seu Pai Mestre Quinten Metsys," p. 4f.; DB, pp. 100–103.

The difficulties of determining the originality of the Vienna painting are graphically ilustrated in Friedländer's writings. In 1929, he called the Vienna painting "close to the master, possibly a work by Jan Massys." In 1934, he implied that Massys' composition lay behind Reymerswaele's 1521 Berlin *Jerome* and Dürer's 1521 Lisbon saint. But his 1936 volume 13 of *Die altniederländische Malerei* (pp. 185, 227) places the Vienna panel squarely under the listing of Jan Massys. In 1949 correspondence with Reis-Santos (1964, p. 9, n. 12), Friedländer reversed himself and reconsidered the Vienna painting to be an authentic work of Quinten.

According to Reis-Santos, the painting has suffered extensive cleaning, although its condition appears to be generally good. Hymans cites a 1574 Escorial inventory: "Maestre Coynthin Tabla S. Geronimo con el dedo sobre una calavera." Nevertheless, this reference almost certainly describes a panel, now in the Prado and ascribed to Jan Massys, that derives, in its turn, from the original Massys *Jerome.* Modern scholars are also divided about the authorship of the Prado painting; a summary of opinions is given by V. Scaff, "Johannes Quintini Massiis Pingebat," p. 276.

The Vienna panel seems to be the product of the same anonymous master who painted the Prado picture. In particular, the gray tones of the aged saint's skin are unparalleled in the authentic Massys works. And while certain features such as fingers and hair are finely painted in the manner of the Massys idiom, notable and uncharacteristic weaknesses in spatial construction mar the composition. Jerome's right shoulder and arm are weakly coordinated with the other side of the body. Similarly, the depth of the table and the construction of the cell are ambiguous. These lapses are difficult to reconcile with the artist's earlier accomplishments, achievements such as the 1514 Louvre *Moneychanger* (F. 53, cat. 18) and the 1517 *Friendship Diptych* of *Erasmus* and *Gillis* (F. 36–37, cat. 58). Yet the close-up, half-length figures and paneled interiors associate Massys' original composition with these two works. *Pl. 118* *Pl. 99* *Pl. 100*

Jerome was a favorite model for Erasmus (see Chap. 6), and the painting may have been painted for a friend or associate of the Rotterdam humanist. If so, it would probably have been produced after Erasmus's 1516 publication of Jerome's letters and his new edition of the New Testament—the first since Jerome. Also, the visual association with Massys' 1517 *Erasmus* portrait was probably a request of his patron.

This interpretation of *St. Jerome* is an unusual combination of the patriarch's penitence (normally a scene in the wilderness) and his contemplative work in a scholar's cell. For the latter tradition see Strümpell, "Hieronymus im Gëhäus," pp. 173–244. A Dresden painting of uncertain date from the circle of Hugo van der Goes (Winkler, *Das Werk des Hugo van der Goes,* p. 236f.) is the only precedent for such a vision of Jerome. As Friedländer, Winkler, and Marlier have pointed out, the close-up of the saint with skull was enormously influential, particularly on Dürer and Marinus, but also for more conventional artists such as Joos van Cleve.

Cat. 29. *Mary Magdalene* (F. 35). Antwerp, Koninklijk Museum, no. 243 (45 × 29). *Plate 110*

Copies: Paris, coll. Baron E. de Rothschild; Lucca, Palazzo Mansi.

HIST.: Ex-coll. Jan van Hal; 1836 coll. van Ertborn; museum bequest 1841; mentioned in 17th-century inventory: 1621 Nicolas Cornelis Cheeus: "A painting of Saint Mary Magdalene, made by Quinten Massys, estimated at 60 guilders" (Denucé, p. 33f.); possibly to be equated with a "Saint Mary Magdalene by Quinten Massys," coll. Arnold Lunden, Antwerp (1639–49).

LIT.: van den Branden, p. 72; E. Jacobsen, "Die 'Magdalena' Quinten Matsys," *Gazette des Beaux-Arts* 60 (1898); Cohen, pp. 73f., 82; Bosschere, p. 96; Brising, p. 29; Conway, p. 319; Winkler, p. 204; Delen, p. 73f.; Friedländer 7, p. 32; Baldass, pp. 146, 165f.; Boon, p. 46f.; Benesch, p. 88; Marlier, p. 156; Mallé, p. 98; Broadley, p. 131; Cuttler, p. 421; Robbins, p. 62ff; DB, pp. 184–86.

Cohen and Delen have expressed their conviction in a generalized influence from Leonardo da Vinci on the Antwerp *Magdalene.* As Broadley points out, however, the modeling and lighting of Massys' work differ greatly from such Leonardesque creations as the *Mona Lisa.* And the facial type of the *Magdalene* is entirely consistent with earlier Massys types from the great altarpieces, so that it requires no new outside influence as a source.

The tonalities of the Antwerp *Magdalene* panel mark a shift for Massys. After the firm shadows of the great altarpieces, he has produced a new evenness of modeling, painting so thin that underdrawings are visible in the brows. There are delicate highlights in hair and skin surfaces, and colors are harmonized just as carefully into an ensemble. Like the 1517 *Friendship Diptych* (F. 36–37, cat. 58), the *Pl. 99* Antwerp panel is a coordinated study in brown. And the *Pl. 100* landscape background, a strip of blue and blue-green, tallies with backgrounds such as the Louvre *Pieta* (F. 16, cat. 17) *Pl. 94* and the Ottawa *Crucifixion* (F. 12, cat. 20). *Pl. 91*

This representation of the Magdalene is an innovative combination of two traditions—those of the penitent, already painted by Massys in the Philadelphia wings (F. 7, cat. *Pl. 112* 21) and the wealthy woman of leisure (see Chap. 6). Increasingly in the 16th century, the Magdalene was depicted as an elegant, courtly personality, engaged in reading, music, or writing, and identifiable only by her ointment jar attribute. The Master of the Female Half-Lengths derives his name from such pictures, and they also enjoyed a vogue in Bruges (see Marlier, *Ambrosius Benson,* p. 188ff.). No cult of the Magdalene existed in the Netherlands, but the widespread popularity of other penitent saints (Anthony, Jerome) points to an interest in the saints' sinful, fallible natures. The indulgent use of wealth would also have served as a particular warning to prosperous Netherlandish burghers in a time of expanding trade.

Massys' *Magdalene,* in contrast to other representatives of the fashionable lady, repents of her pleasures. She seems to be at a turning-point—the moment of conversion, expressed when she thoughtfully fingers her ointment jar. Like the figure of *Jerome* (F. 70, cat. 28) with his skull, Mary Magda- *Pl. 106* lene represents a saint turning away from worldly affairs to the issue of personal salvation.

Massys painted the worldly Magdalene with her jar once again in his later years (cat. 39). Interest in the saint may well be tied to her representation as a convert in popular religious drama in the Netherlands as well as the confirmation of her identity and history after a philological dispute among the northern humanist community.

The history of the picture in the 17th century has recently been considered by Hans Vlieghe, "Une grande collection anversoise du Dix-Septième Siècle: Le cabinet d'Arnold Lunden, beau-frère de Rubens," *Jahrbuch der Berliner Museen* 19 (1977), p. 189, no. 77. Vlieghe identifies the picture in this important inventory, probably compiled in the mid-1640s, as the Massys image in Antwerp today; moreover, he argues (n. 70) against the assertion (*Antwerp Jaarboek* 1971, 251, no. 132) that the Antwerp painting is to be identified as "a praying Magdalene with some accessories" by Massys in the Amsterdam inventory of Diego Duarte, 1682.

Cat. 30. *Drunkard* (F. Add. 191). Formerly Dortmund, coll. Dr. H. Becker (Oil on parchment; 31.6 × 21.5).

HIST.: sale P. de Boer, Amsterdam.

LIT.: Friedländer, "Quentin Massys as a Painter of Genre

Pictures," p. 119; R. Fritz, *Sammlung Becker* (Dortmund, 1967), no. 36.

The closest comparison for this delicately ugly little picture is the softly modeled, brown-skinned Grotesque *Old Man*
Pl. 123 (New York, cat. 32). The brown harmonies and delicate highlights of the jug and cloths relate this picture to Massys'
Pl. 110 *Magdalene* (F. 35, cat. 29). The excessively pudgy fingers are unusual for Massys, and this is perhaps his clumsiest grotesque face, but the quality of execution shores up the lapses in conception. The soft support of parchment points to an informal or less expensive commission, which is in keeping with the satirical subject.

For the contemporary satires and attacks on drunkenness, see Chapter 7. Both Erasmus and the *rederijkers* (especially the latter) inveighed against this vice. According to Fritz, the bagpipe could be tied in this context to the pleasures of the flesh; he mentions a French proverb, "Quand le cornemuse est pleine, on en chante mieux."

Cat. 31. *Ecce Homo* (F. 10). Madrid, Prado, no. 2801 (160 × 120). *Plate 86*

HIST.: Ex-coll. D. M. Lanuza; Madrid 1936; coll. Marques de Remisa in 19th century.

LIT.: Friedländer 7, p. 28; Baldass, pp. 143, 148; Boon, p. 29; Mallé, p. 95; Broadley, p. 214f; Cuttler, p. 423; von der Osten, p. 149; Völker, p. 105ff.; *Museo del Prado Catalogo de las Pinturas* (Madrid, 1972), p. 399f; Friedländer, "Quentin Massys as a Painter of Genre Pictures," p. 115ff.; DB, p. 210.

Broadley rejects this painting as too "coarse" to be attributed to Massys, and he criticizes what he terms excessive "linearity and a disconcerting preoccupation with insignificant details." But both the forms and the execution of the powerful figure of Pilate dominate from above like God the Father
Pl. 37 from the *Rem* altarpiece (F. 3, cat. 24). The curly-haired children of the Caritas sculpture group repeat the form of the *Rem* Christ Child. The female Caritas figure has the same fine features and angular chin of Virgins from the
Pl. 91 teens (e.g., Ottawa *Crucifixion,* F. 12, cat. 20; Rotterdam
Pl. 65 *Madonna* F. 168, cat. 27). The rounded regular-featured heads around Christ in the Prado *Ecce Homo* find analogies in the faces of *St. Sebastian* and *St. Roch*, the *Rem altarpiece* wings.

The treatment of forms also recalls the *Rem altarpiece* and other Massys works of the same period. An overall brown
Pl. 140 tonality suggests comparison with the New York *Woman* (F.
Pl. 110 48, cat. 60), the Antwerp *Magdalene* (F. 35, cat. 29), and the Becker *Drunkard* (F. 191, cat. 30). Golden robes and red and blue garments have much the same glitter and shading in the *Magdalene* (sleeves), *Drunkard* (bagpipe), and the Berlin
Pl. 180 *Man* (F. 76, cat. 59).

There are new features in the Prado *Ecce Homo*—features that stand out in comparison with the Coimbra *Ecce Homo* of
Pl. 33 1513–17 (F. 196, cat. 18). Massys has introduced a new grandeur, a monumentality that will characterize the close-up visions of his final period. There is also a new virtuosity in the artist's treatment of surfaces. Meticulous foreground detail in brocades, gleaming brown faces, and architectural ornament heighten the vividness of the religious event. While its concept of viewer involvement is the same as that of the Coimbra panel (see Chap. 5), the Prado panel intensifies a close-up, finely observed, spiritual confrontation.

The dense system of sculpture in the Prado *Ecce Homo* serves several purposes. Barely visible in photographs is a relief along the front of the balustrade that shows an extremely painful version of the Crowning with Thorns, the scene preceding the main scene of Christ's Presentation. Above the figures two sculptures offer images associated with the Roman Empire. Alongside the balustrade relief is an imperial soldier with a shield and a sinister owl on his helmet; atop a column at the right sits a pagan deity, possibly Apollo, with a star. Two of the sculpted groups have ironic overtones for the figure scene below: a Caritas, to contrast with the jeering crowd, and a seated king, whose feet are being washed as he is guarded by an attendant. Christ's own foot-washing of the Apostles had occurred earlier, and He had had His feet salved by the Magdalene. After these gestures of humility during Christ's mission, in this *Ecce Homo* the King of Heaven is brought low at the mercy of imperial forces and an abusive rabble. Instead of being anointed here, He is tormented. Instead of being protected by guards, He is a prisoner. These references to pagan divinities and to deference or charity around Christ serve to deepen the irony of His pitiful situation. Of course, the entire complex, like Herod's banquet hall in the *St. John altarpiece,* is also intended to suggest the wealth and power of the historic Roman Empire.

Cat. 32. *Grotesque Pair.*

A. *Old Woman* (F. 52). London, National Gallery no. 5796 (64 × 45.5). *Plate 122*

B. *Old Man;* New York, private coll. *Plate 123*

HIST.: A. Coll. H. D. Seymour by 1854; 1920 H. Blaker; museum bequest 1957.

B. Gallery Heinemann, 1955; Rosenberg & Stiebel, New York, 1976; NY private coll.

LIT.: Van Fornenbergh, p. 31; G. F. Waagen, *Treasures of Art in Great Britain* vol 2 (London, 1854), p. 243; Brising, p. 37; Friedländer 7, p. 33f.; Baldass, pp. 148f., 166; Boon, p. 43; Friedländer, "Quentin Massys as a Painter of Genre Pictures," p. 115ff; Panofsky, *ENP,* p. 355f; Marlier, p. 223f; E. Tietze-Conrat, *Dwarfs and Jesters in Art* (London, 1957), pp. 19, 91; Puyvelde, p. 301; Broadley, p. 133ff; Davies, *Early Netherlandish School National Gallery Catalogues,* p. 92ff; von der Osten, p. 151; Panofsky, "Erasmus and the Visual Arts," p. 214; DB, pp. 246–47; Viridis, "Moralismo e satira nella tarda produzioni di Quentin Metsys," pp. 19–24; Silver, "Power and Pelf," pp. 63–92.

This pair is perhaps to be equated with the 17th-century reference by van Fornenbergh: "several monstrous and comical mugs." They were engraved by Wenzel Hollar Pl. 127
(1607–77; Parthey no. 1603), who attributed the figures to Leonardo da Vinci. In fact, a da Vinci drawing was the immediate source for Massys' London *Woman;* it closely copies a drawing after Leonardo in Windsor Castle (fig. 37d, Pl. 124
no. 12492; see Clark and Pedretti, *The Drawings of Leonardo da Vinci at Windsor Castle,* p. 83). No original drawing for the

Old Man has been found, but virtually the same profile head appeared earlier in Massys' work in the Madre de Deus
Pl. 31 *Seven Sorrows altarpiece* (F. 4, cat. 12) and the isolated
Pl. 157 Jacquemart-Andre *Man* (F. 51, cat. 54). Such pairings of grotesques of both sexes have other parallels in Leonardo's work. That the Hollar engraving is derived from the two Massys panels instead of their Leonardo originals is evident from the print's exact replication of the figures' hands—hands which cannot be found in the surviving drawing. Moreover, the Hollar engraving adds confirmation to the presumption that the Massys works and their linked balustrades were indeed pendants.

According to Davies, the Germanic headdress of the woman could be "as early as ca. 1450, but it continued to be worn at the beginning of the sixteenth century." The low-necked dress, an Italian fashion, seems to have arisen in the late 1480s. Leonardo's drawing is dated ca. 1495 by Clark and Pedretti. But according to Davies, the additions to the drawing betray later Netherlandish fashion. These include the goffered edge of the veil and the frill inside the dress (ca. 1510). The man's cap recalls the hat worn by Cosimo de'
Pl. 158 Medici on mid-15th-century portrait medals (see Silver, fig. 12) but it also resembles earlier Netherlandish millinery; e.g., the copies of a lost portrait of Philip the Bold.

Panofsky argues that the *Old Woman* is tied to Erasmus's *The Praise of Folly,* in which foolish oldsters "play the goat." Not knowing the *Old Man* pendant, Panofsky did not assign it to a corresponding theme, but the texts of Erasmus also describe the vanities of old men. The pompous gesture of Massys' painting indicates a measure of pride connected to the *Man*'s wealth and status as indicated by both his clothes and his prominent aldermanic thumb-ring. If the reference to Cosimo de' Medici in the *Man*'s features is indeed correct and intended, the avarice connected with that master banker of Europe could be associated with the New York picture.

The New York *Old Man* can be regarded as the source for Hollar's engraving because it features the same hand gesture. Its imitation marble balustrade also links it with the London *Old Woman.* Massys used such a balustrade in his
Pl. 152 1517 Karlsruhe *Man* (F. 194, cat. 57), and he had recently used parallel architectural forms to unite the portraits with
Pl. 140 columns in Schloss Au and New York (F. 48, 69; cat. 60). The high quality of both works speaks for Massys' authorship, despite Davies' reservations about the London *Old Woman* and certain weaknesses in the hand of the *Old Man.*

The meticulous detail—and especially the brown skin with shiny white highlights—links these works most closely with
Pl. 86 the Prado *Ecce Homo* (F. 10, cat. 31).

Cat. 33. *Franciscan Saint or Monk* (F. 30) Barcelona, Palacio de la Virreina, no. 64.998 (37.2 × 31.2). *Plate 177*

HIST.: Ex-coll. Cambo, Barcelona; in Vienna before 1926; sale by Fischer, Lucerne.

LIT.: Friedländer 7, p. 32f.; Baldass, p. 166; F. J. Sanchez-Canton, *La colleccion Cambo* (Barcelona, 1955), p. 91f., no. 35; DB, p. 256.

Pl. 99 This painting of an old man in monastic robes dates from a
Pl. 100 period not long after the 1517 *Erasmus* and *Gillis* pendants. Full of character, the blocky head looks like a one-quarter profile of the Jacquemart-André *Man* of 1513 (F. 51, cat. 54) Pl. 157
or the New York *Old Man* (cat. 32), but the linear refinements of eyelids, hair, and other facial features are closer to the 1517 *Gillis* or the New York *Woman* (F. 48, cat. 62) as well Pl. 140
as the Antwerp *Magdalene* (F. 35, cat. 29). These delicately Pl. 110
modeled skin tones, now in partially damaged condition (especially the right half of the saint's face) contrast with more heavily modeled, earlier heads, such as the 1509 Winterthur *Pilgrim* (F. 38, cat. 53) and correspond most Pl. 136
closely with works like the brownish, lustrous grotesque, the London *Old Woman* (F. 52, cat. 32) or the Prado *Ecce Homo* Pl. 122
(F. 10, cat. 31). Presumably, the original *St. Jerome,* now lost Pl. 86
(F. 70, cat. 28), was the closest analogue to this Barcelona saint. The dark tones and finely painted hair of the Barcelona figure can, however, also be compared to the heads of the 1526 New York *Adoration of the Magi* (F. 8, cat. 40). Pl. 79

Without any of the usual attributes of tau cross, bell, and pig, this elderly saint cannot be specifically identified as St. Anthony, as previously asserted by scholars, nor is his costume definite enough to fix his ecclesiastical station as an abbot. Most likely the picture has been cut down, thus eliminating recognizable attributes; it does seem to be an image of a saint rather than a portrait of a monk, although de Bosque sees it as a portrait. But the distinctive brown habit invites identification with some elderly Franciscan saint.

Cat. 34. *Infants Christ and John the Baptist Embracing* (F. 29). Chatsworth, Devonshire Coll. (34 × 45.5). *Plate 69*

LIT.: Glück, "Schicksale einer Komposition Leonardos," p. 502ff.; Friedländer 7, p. 33; Baldass, pp. 147, 171, 173; Boon, p. 44f.; Broadley, p. 150ff.; DB, pp. 234–36; Hecht, "The Infants Christ and John Embracing," *Apollo* (1981): 222ff.

Boon identifies this panel with an inventory item of Margaret of Austria (17 July 1516): "ung tableau de deux petitz josnex effans qui se baisent l'ung l'autre" (Le Glay, ed., *Correspondence de l'Empereur Maximilien ler et de Marguerite d'Autriche, sa fille, gouvernante de Pays-Bas de 1507 a 1519,* vol. 2 [Paris, 1839], p. 482; cited by Broadley, p. 152 n. 1). Nothing identifies the inventory listing with Massys, however. In fact, the motif of embracing holy infants goes back to a design by Leonardo da Vinci, preserved in a drawing at Windsor Castle (no. 12564; see Clark and Pedretti, *Leonardo* Pl. 70
da Vinci Drawings at Windsor Castle, vol. 1, p. 107f); Clark postulates a completed Leonardo painting, now lost, which would have been visible in Flanders. By far the largest number of versions of the image were adapted by Joos van Cleve and his workshop (Friedländer 9, no. 37). Massys probably drew upon van Cleve, as he did for the still-life foreground elements and domestic Madonna pictures of his final decade.

The style of the Chatsworth panel dates from Massys' period of the early 1520s. The curly-haired blond infant type, found earlier in Joos van Cleve, makes its appearance most frequently after the *Rem altarpiece* (F. 3, cat. 32; 1518– Pl. 37
20) in Massys' work. The glossy skin and fine features point to later works like the Rotterdam *Madonna with Milk Soup* (F. Pl. 65
168; cat. 48) or the *Van Pannwitz Madonna* (F. 26, cat. 47). Pl. 57

Yet the singularly flat appearance of the panel, the literalness of the copying, and the uncoordinated composition argue against Massys' authorship. Seen against interior Pl. 67 works like the *Madonna Nursing* (lost, F. 68, cat. 42) or the Pl. 68 *Rattier Madonna* (F. 24, cat. 56), the arrangement of elements like the bed, spread, and pillow is flimsily laid out and incompletely finished. The matron in the background corner also appears flat and wooden; her gesture of surprise is mechanical and unconvincing, although in type her features are close to the Massys design of the mourner in the van den Bergh *Crucifixion* alterpiece (F. 56, cat. 22).

Broadley challenges the work's authenticity on the basis of its monochromatic coloration. This effect, while more characteristic of paintings from the late teens, would indeed be out of place within the later features mentioned above, although it would be consonant with works from the late teens. The hard contours of the children are also uncharacteristic of Massys.

IV. THE FINAL YEARS (1524–1530)

From the documents that survive of his life, Massys is at his most silent during the final years. Most of these records are merely rental agreements, testimony to the fact that Quinten had achieved a measure of prosperity and had become a man of property (1522–30, de Bosque, Appendix, documents 8–15, pp. 44, 424–25). Massys had long ago ceased to register apprentices with the St. Luke guild; his last official pupil had been Eduardo Portugalois in 1504. Yet almost certainly Quinten's own sons, who would go on to become important Antwerp painters in their own right, were unofficially learning their father's trade in his workshop during this time. Both Cornelis and Jan Massys became masters in the Antwerp guild during the first year after their father's death in 1531. Several scholars have naturally sought to identify the collaborations of these two talented offspring within the late works of Quinten—Cornelis as a landscape painter and Jan as a figure painter (de Callatay, "Cornelis Massys paysagiste, collaborateur de son père et de son frère et auteur de l'album Errera," p. 49ff; Dunbar, "The Landscape Art of Cornelis Massys," pp. 148–52; Reis-Santos, "Jan Quinten Massys discipulo e colaborador de son pai Mestre Quinten Metsys": V. Scaff, "Johannes Quintini Massiis Pingebat," *Mélanges d'archeologie et d'histoire de l'art au Prof. Lavallege* [Louvain, 1970], pp. 259ff).

A typical dilemma of these later works and their afterlife is the *Madonna and Child with the Lamb* (Poznan, F. 19), here rejected as an original Quinten Massys and associated with the name of Cornelis Metsys (cf. cat. Supp. D). The painting is clearly derived from Leonardo da Vinci's Louvre *Anna-Selbdritt* or one of its numerous variants and copies, such as the version of Cesare da Sesto in the Poldi-Pezzoli Museum, Milan, which, like the Poznan picture, eliminates St. Anne but retains the Leonardo Virgin, Child, and lamb (de Bosque, ill. 257). Quinten's authorship for the Poznan painting has been championed by Gustav Glück and Baldass, while Friedländer, Boon, Bosschere, and de Bosque saw in it a collaboration with Patinir, like the Prado *Temptation of St. Anthony*. Advocates of Cornelis as painter have also not been lacking: Cornelis van de Wetering and Jan Bialostocki, who also has pointed to the Patinir-like artist, the Master of the Female Half-Lengths. Dunbar also sees the hand of a Patinir follower in the landscape, but demurs from naming Cornelis Metsys. The figure types are clearly related to Massys' authentic works, such as Pl. 65 the Madonna of the Rotterdam *Virgin with Milk Soup* (F. 168, cat. 27) or the two figures of the Berlin *Virgin Enthroned* (F. 18, cat. Pls. 63, 57 37) or *Van Pannwitz Madonna* (F. 26, cat. 38, although the delineation of the features of the Poznan figures lacks the firm drawing and delicacy of Massys' mature paintings. In short, the Poznan picture strongly suggests the authorship of a talented workshop artist, possibly the young Cornelis Metsys, who was to go on to derive much of his future landscape art from the example of Patinir and the next generation of landscape artists in Flanders. Moreover, it testifies to the increased interest in Leonardo's compositions and figures in Antwerp during the 1520s and 1530s.

Joos van Cleve, Massys' younger contemporary who was so active in the St. Luke guild during the 1520s, was a major leader in the move toward Leonardo da Vinci and other Italianate forms in Flemish art during Massys' final decade. Joos had registered apprentices in 1516, 1523, 1535 (two), and 1536, and he was dean of the painters' guild in 1519, 1520, and 1525, so he was a painter with considerable influence locally. Early in his career, Joos had adapted Massys compositions for himself, as in his use Pl. 91 of the Ottawa *Crucifixion* for an altarpiece in Naples and a panel in Boston. But in this final decade, Joos van Cleve in turn exercised his own influence on the older Quinten. For example, Joos set the pace as far as Madonna images were concerned: Pl. 58 many of Massys' late icons, such as the enthroned Madonnas (Berlin, Van Pannwitz, and the lost *Madonna of the Cherries)* or the Pl. 64 Detroit *Madonna Outdoors* and its copies, bear the stamp of Joos's formulations, or at the very least a common vocabulary, which Pl. 79 is unusual for Massys. Massys' New York *Adoration of the Magi* (F. 8, cat. 40) owes as much to van Cleve as to van der Goes. The setting—a ruined pagan temple with ornate Italianate pilasters—is based upon Joos's numerous Adorations during the previous ten years, and the figures with their gifts owe much to previous van Cleve formulations. These correspondences are especially close for the two younger magi, a swarthy man with dark beard and a black magus, who can be found on van Cleve's Detroit Pl. 84 *Epiphany* (or its Naples replica). Even the type of the infant Christ is common to both van Cleve and Massys.

It was in the Italianate architectural forms and the more elegant poses of the infant Christ that Joos showed the way for Pl. 166 Massys and other Antwerp painters during the 1520s. Joos's workshop turned out numerous versions of the *Infants Jesus and* Pl. 70 *John the Baptist Kissing*, a composition based upon Leonardo da Vinci. Massys' variant on this theme (Chatsworth, Devonshire Pl. 69 coll., F. 29, cat. 34) places the event in a domestic bedchamber, rather than the more regal surroundings of the several van Cleve examples. Art historians inevitably tend to assume that the "greater" artist spreads images by diffusion to "lesser" artists, and thus they assign Massys priority for the innovation in Flanders, even though the original Leonardo composition was not place-specific and even though van Cleve was to use that composition on many more occasions. Of course, numbers of replicas are no Pl. 107 index to priority, for van Cleve freely repeated numbers of versions of *St. Jerome in his Study* after the example of Massys and

Dürer. In similar fashion, the van Cleve studio turned out many replicas of another Leonardo-based compostion of the *Madonna of the Cherries* (Friedländer 9, no. 63). This work was not borrowed exactly by Massys, but was echoed instead in his own enthroned Madonnas, including the lost *Madonna of the Cherries* and the *Van Pannwitz Madonna,* whose standing, twisting Child also echoes van Cleve's *Infant Jesus on a Globe* (formerly Becker coll, Dortmund; Friedländer 9, no. 35).

During his final years, Massys principally painted his pictures at half-length in what appears to be an attempt to promote closer proximity between the viewer and the holy figures. Even narratives, such as the *Pieta, Ecce Homo,* or *Adoration of the Magi,* employ this format, which seems to grow out of the portraitlike icon tradition (see Ringbom, *Icon to Narrative).* In his late works, too, Massys adopts a facial type for his female figures. Lustrous, almost oily in their skin tones, these female faces have broad, oval outlines that taper along ridgelike noses to narrow chins; usually the exposed jawline is softly modeled with transparent shadows. Such facial types can be seen as early as the Washington *Ill-Matched Pair* (F. 54, cat. 35) and in firmly dated works such *Pl. 129* as the 1526 New York *Adoration* (F. 8, cat. 40) or the 1529 *Rattier Madonna* (Louvre, F. 24, cat. 48). Other secure works that *Pl. 63* display this late form of the Virgin include the Berlin *Madonna Enthroned,* the Detroit *Madonna Outdoors,* the *Van Pannwitz* *Pl. 64* *Madonna,* and lost works like the half-length *Pieta* (F. 15, cat. 36). Massys' male types during this period appear less frequently *Pl. 95* but are often marked by the brown or ruddy skin tones first seen in the Antwerp *Lamentation.* In these last years, moreover, new *Pl. 20* features appear, such as glistening, almost watery eyes, leathery, wrinkled skin, and frequent use of the peculiar scalloped eyelids that also appear on the faces of late Massys Madonnas. These grizzled male faces can be seen in the Washington *Ill-* *Pl. 87* *Matched Pair,* the 1526 New York *Adoration,* the Venice *Ecce Homo* (F. 11, cat. 46), and the *Praying Monks* (F. 80, cat. 45), as well as *Pl. 108* in the more admirable faces of the Gaeta *Deposition* (Jan Massys?; F. 195, Supp. F) and the 1529 Madrid *Christ Blessing* (cat. 49). *Pl. 72* In most of his late pictures, including the numerous Madonna icons, Massys stresses the emotional states of his principal figures and concentrates on their relationships through his half-length heads and hands. Interlocked poses, such as the embrace of the lecher and the girl of the *Ill-Matched Pair* or the kisses of the Berlin or Rattier *Madonnas,* the lost *Pieta,* and the Chatsworth *Kissing Infants,* offer one demonstrative example. To these gestures could be added the theatrical, expressive hand poses seen in the 1526 New York *Adoration,* the Venice *Ecce Homo,* and the 1529 Prado pendants of *Christ Saying Farewell to His Mother (Virgin in Prayer* with *Christ Blessing).* Even more than in his previous pictures, Massys' latest images at half-length sharpen the distinction between the beautiful and the grotesque, between the sacred and the profane, with these heads and gestures. In light of this contrast, Massys' attempt to stress the otherworldly and extraordinary beauty of the holy figures is reinforced by his adoption of Italianate forms and compositions (see Chap. 9) for his Madonna images, alongside the grotesque heads he had previously borrowed from Leonardo da Vinci (and Bosch) for lesser humanity.

Cat. 35. *Ill-Matched Pair* (F. 54). Washington, National Gallery (42 × 62).

Copies: A. coll. Wittert, Liege University Library (76.2 × 64). *Plate 129*
B. Switzerland, private coll. (48 × 65).

HIST.: Ex-coll. E. de Pourtalés, Paris; museum purchase 1972. Seventeenth-century inventory references: coll. Steven Wils the Younger (d. 1628), "A panel of Master Quinten, in which a young woman frees the old man of his purse" (no. 62, Denucé, p. 49); coll. Herman de Neyt (d. 1642), "A panel of Quinten showing an old man with a young woman and a fool, in an ebony frame" (Denucé, p. 94).

LIT.: van den Branden, p. 68f; Hymans, p. 205; Cohen, pp. 76, 88; Bosschere, p. 117; Brising, p. 34; Delen, p. 84; Winkler, p. 206; Friedländer 7, p. 33; Baldass, pp. 150, 173; Boon, p. 53; Marlier, p. 228ff; Mallé, p. 106; Puyvelde, p. 301; Broadley, p. 146; *De eeuw van Bruegel,* exh. cat., no. 168 (Liege copy); Cuttler, p. 423; von der Osten, p. 151; Völker, 189ff. Puyvelde 1970, p. 230; Silver, "The *Ill-Matched Pair* by Quinten Massys," p. 104ff.; DB, pp. 206–7.

The *Ill-Matched Pair,* acquired by the National Gallery in 1972, is in excellent condition except for a restoration of its dark background. Unfortunately, this dark paint was carelessly allowed to cover the contours of both the old man's right hand and the young girl's facial profile.

The colors of this painting are the same as in the *Temptation* *Pl. 114* *of St. Anthony* (F. 31, cat. 26): tomato red, olive green, and a dark charcoal gray. Furthermore, the painting contrasts the lustrous ivory skin of the young girl with the brown, wrinkled face of the aged lecher. For the later painting in Washington, however, Massys is even more meticulous in describing the ravisher's skin than he had been for the smaller-scaled old woman of the Prado *St. Anthony.* As in the Prado picture, human emotions are the basic subject-matter here, and in the Washington painting they are highly visible in close-up half-lengths rather than being lost against a vast background panorama. In both its forms and its half-length presentation, the *Ill-Matched Pair* anticipates the 1526 New York *Adoration of the Magi* (F. 8, cat. 40), *Pl. 79* with its greater sense of volume and textured detail.

For visual sources, Massys turned to two works. The first was Leonardo's Five *Grotesque Heads* (Windsor Castle no. *Pl. 16* 12495), already a model for several of the executioners in the *Evangelist* wing of the John altarpiece (F. 1, cat. 11). In *Pl. 17* the *Ill-Matched Pair* Leonardo's leftmost head has been transformed, reversed, into Massys' grinning old man. Lucas van Leyden's *Prodigal Son* woodcut (Paris; Bibliotheque *Pl. 130* Nationale) also contributed to Quinten's work. Both the tilted, oval face and clothing of the young girl, her chin chuck, and the grasping pose of her suitor were transposed from the tavern scene of the Lucas print to the Washington panel.

His combination of two sources suggests that Massys' theme inspired him to search for visual models, rather than the reverse. Literary sources provided him with the subject of the *Ill-Matched Pair.* Both Erasmus *(Praise of Folly)* and contemporary *rederijker* verses contributed to this subject. Presumably, Massys' image would have fitted into this context; it could have been commissioned by either the humanist circle around Erasmus or the broader bourgeois world of the *rederijkers*.

Cat. 36. *Madonna Nursing* (lost; F. 68).
Copies: A. Munich, Alte Pinakothek no. 132 (F. 68a) (89 × 70). *Plate 67*
B. Werner Coll; Luton Hoo, England (F. 68b) (60 × 45).
HIST.: A. Perhaps to be identified with a panel in the collection of Maximilian I, 1630 (see text below).
B: Wildenstein Gallery, London, 1946.
LIT.: Cohen, p. 86; Brising, p. 32; Winkler, p. 204; Friedländer 7, p. 68; Baldass, p. 157; DB, p. 24.

The Munich version is so heavily damaged that its authorship cannot be settled definitively. Nevertheless, Brising calls it "zweifellos echt." Winkler accepts it without comment, while Friedländer calls it "possibly an original." Hardness of execution, particularly in the Madonna's face and hair, and anatomical weaknesses (e.g., shoulders) argue against the originality of the Munich panel.

The subject is an old one, first finding expression in Flemish art in the circle of Robert Campin (see Friedländer 2, nos. 58, 60, 64). As in Campin's works, the Massys composition features a bourgeois environment, warmed by a fire in the hearth. A detail that recalls van Eyck's *Arnolfini Wedding* (London, Friedländer 1, plate 20) and Roger van der Weyden's Paris *Annunciation* (Friedländer 2, no. 9) is the background bed. Massys repeats the bed in the Virgin's
Pl. 68 chamber in his 1529 *Rattier Madonna* (F. 24, cat. 48).

The narrow, tapered oval head of the Virgin is closest to
Pl. 114 the forms of the Prado *Anthony* sirens although fuller in its suggestion of volume (F. 31, cat. 26) while the curly-haired
Pl. 37 Child appears as early as the *Rem altarpiece* (F. 3, cat. 24) and
Pl. 65 Rotterdam *Madonna* (F. 168, cat. 27). The stronger sense of figure volume and the complex figure poses recall both the
Pl. 129 *Ill-Matched Pair* (F. 54, cat. 35) and the Berlin *Madonna*
Pl. 63 *Enthroned* (F. 18, cat. 37), which also seem to date from the same period of figure types.

Brising and Cohen identify the original panel with an inventory listing of Maximilian I (ca. 1630): "Ein unser liebe fraw, wie sie das Khindelein seugt, is gar von ainem alten Niederlendischen Maister Quintin Metsys, sonst Schmidt genannt."

Cat. 37. *Madonna Enthroned* (F. 18). Ca. 1523–24, Berlin-Dahlem, no. 5052 (84.5 × 74.5).
Variant: Brussels, Musées Royaux, no. 5052, (84.5 × 74.5) *Plate 63*
Copy: Antwerp, Church of St. Jacques (65 × 53).
HIST.: Identified with a painting in the Coudenberg collection of Archduke Albert and Isabella: "A painting in oil on wood panel, which served as altar retable of the rectory of Her Highness [the Archduchess]. It shows Our Lady dressed in blue with red mantle, seated on a throne kissing the nude Child, and below a table with a glass of wine, a plate of butter, bread, and various fruits. The painting has a round frame, painted and gilded." [*Una pintura sobre table al olio, que solia servir de retablo al altar del oratorio de Su Alteza—el Archiduquesa—de Nuestra Senora vestida de azul con manto roxo, sentado en un alto besando al Nino desnudo; y abaho una mesa con un vidrio con vino, manteca, pan, y algunas frutas, tiene su marco a modo de portada, pintado, y dorado*] (no. 72; 10 July 1639). Sold between 1643–52. Possibly identical with Amsterdam inventory item of Diego Duarte (1682): "A Mary picture with the Child, sitting in an oratory. Sold to Princess Nassau [Mary Stuart? 1662–95]." 1816 Nurenburg coll. Frauenholz; 1823 museum bequest.
LIT.: van den Branden, p. 202; Cohen, pp. 32, 82; Bosschere, p. 102; Brising, p. 31; Delen, p. 74f; Winkler, p. 204; Friedländer 7, p. 30f; *Beschreibendes Verzeichnis der Gemälde in Kaiser-Friedrich Museum und deutschen Museum* (Berlin, 1931), p. 284; Baldass, pp. 143, 172f; Boon, p. 47f; Benesch, p. 89; Mallé, p. 102; Bergström, 1956; Broadley, p. 160f; M. Smeyers, "Schilderijen van Kwinten Metsys in het Bezit der Aartshertogen Albrecht en Isabella," *Miscellanea Josef Duverger* vol. 1 (Ghent, 1968), p. 139ff; Cuttler, p. 421; von der Osten, p. 149; Robbins, p. 45ff; DB, 214–16.

Largest of the Massys Madonna panels, the Berlin *Madonna Enthroned* is approximately lifesize. Its 17th-century whereabouts have been established by M. Smeyers: the panel served as altarpiece in the oratory of Archduchess Isabella in the Coudenberg palace in Brussels. This location, the other Massys paintings known to be important in collections, and the contemporary biographies of Massys all attest to the artist's lofty reputation in 17th-century Flanders.

In this full-length *Madonna Enthroned* Massys has transposed the intertwined arms and complementary rhythms of the *Ill-Matched Pair* to the embracing holy figures of Virgin *Pl. 12*
and Child. Color is used to focus attention on the figures, particularly the brilliant red of Mary's mantle, which dominates the center of the panel. The dark-green leaves of the trees behind the characters silhouette the two heads and echo their contours. The emphatic vertical of the throne also isolates the holy figures, and Massys uses a diagonal foreground table like the balustrade of the Prado *Ecce Homo* *Pl. 86*
to situate the figures in space. The facial type of Christ has been adapted from the curly-haired youths like the sculpted children in the Prado Caritas group; however, the Berlin Christ is an older child—no longer an infant—with a lithe body in a complicated posture. Mary's face, with an assertive contour and prominent chin, repeats the type of the girl in the *Ill-Matched Pair.* Both characters have the typical shiny skin tone of Massys' later period.

A variety of religious symbols fill the panel. In the background landscape are two traditional emblems: the enclosed garden and the fountain of living waters. In addition, the foreground still-life features sacramental bread and cherries of salvation along with an unusual large mound of butter on a plate, whose possible symbolic meaning remains unclear.

The painting is undated, but its brilliant red and electric-blue garments recall the 1519–20 *Rem altarpiece* (F. 3, cat. 24) *Pl. 37*
and the Rotterdam *Madonna* (F. 168, cat. 27). It also shares *Pl. 65*
the leafy stone ornament of the *Rem* central panel and of the New York *Woman in Prayer* (F. 48, cat. 60). The Berlin *Pl. 14*
panel, however, has a greater sense of volume and modeling for its faces and shapes than these works and, compared with the Rotterdam *Madonna*, its landscape distance is both more carefully detailed and more atmospherically convincing. The Berlin panel also incorporates the same interlaced movement between Madonna and Child as the amorous

couple displays in the *Ill-Matched Pair* (F. 54, cat. 35). For these reasons, a later date, during the 1520s, seems correct. De Bosque dates the work between 1515–20 on the basis of its mixture of Gothic and Renaissance elements in the throne.

A kiss between Madonna and Child has been linked to Leonardesque influence, particularly the works of Leonardo followers like Giampetrino or Pseudo-Boltraffio (see W. Suida, *Leonardo und sein Kreis* [Munich, 1929]. But similar tenderness occurs in paintings by Flemish masters who also
Pl. 62 had considerable influence on Massys: Gerard David and
Pl. 60 Dieric Bouts. The kiss, therefore, was also a native tradition, which might have received reinforcement (perhaps influencing the longer proportions of Massys' Christ) from the circle of Leonardo.

The still-life and oratory reflect the popular current forms of Joos van Cleve.

Cat. 38. *Madonna Enthroned with Angels* (F. 26). Present location unknown (83.8 × 53.3). *Plate 57*

Copy: Lisbon, Museu Nacional (without angel at right), no. 222 (89 × 59.5).

Hist.: Formerly van Pannwitz coll., Hartekamp; sold by Rosenberg and Stiebel, New York, 1958.

Lit.. DB, pp. 154–55.

The van Pannwitz panel is Massys' most thoroughly "Renaissance" composition, reflecting the popularity of Italianate creations by Jan Gossaert or Bernard van Orley of Brussels in the 1520s (see Friedländer 8). The standing Christ Child, twisting to receive an apple from the angel at His right, is closely related to a Joos van Cleve composition of the *Christ Child on a Globe* (formerly Dortmund, Coll. Becker). Massys' solution makes sense in its context, but he seems to have borrowed the posture from the blessing motion of van Cleve's panel. The puffy-cheeked Child with curly blond hair is also a characteristic van Cleve form.

The van Pannwitz panel shows numerous affinities with
Pl. 63 the great Berlin *Madonna Enthroned* (cat. 37). The older Christ, the complicated pose, and the delicately colored sleeves are repeated. Moreover, the van Pannwitz panel conveys the same precise execution of ornament as the 1526
Pl. 79 New York *Adoration* (F. 8, cat. 40). Folds and features (e.g., brows, eyelids) also have a greater hardness than the Berlin *Madonna.*

De Bosque assumes that the Lisbon copy is by Eduardo Portugalois, Massys' Portugese apprentice, who became an Antwerp master in 1506. She argues that Eduardo would have seen the Massys composition during the period of the *Seven Sorrows Polyptych* (F. 4, cat. 12), i.e., before 1513. She also compares this *Madonna Enthroned with Angels* to the
Pl. 24 Lisbon *Mater Dolorosa* and the Virgin in the Worcester *Rest on*
Pl. 28 *the Flight,* both from the Madre de Deus retable—a distant analogy to the eye of this author.

Cat. 39. *Magdalene at a Balustrade.* Paris, Private coll. (85 × 73).

Lit.: De Bosque, p. 186.

This unknown painting was first published in the de Bosque monograph; but its existence might have been postulated from the several imitations it spawned among Massys' followers. For example, the name painting of the Master of the Mansi Magdalene (Berlin, F. 89) shows the saint at three-quarter length before a landscape, dressed in her worldly finery yet displaying her open ointment jar to the viewer. The more frontalized Mansi Magdalene picture omits the handsome balustrade and marble columns that relate this Massys painting to his portrait half-lengths before a land-
scape, such as the Frankfurt *Scholar* (F. 46, cat. 61) or the *Pl. 146*
Edinburgh *Notary* (F. 45, cat. 64). Another Mansi Magdalene *Pl. 145*
picture (Dessau, F. 101) is even a more-literal replica of the Paris Massys *Magdalene.*

Like the earlier Antwerp *Magdalene,* this conception of the *Pl. 110*
saint is initially a pseudo-portrait. The framing columns and balustrade and the background landscape form the basis of Massys' portraits during the 1520s. In addition, the expensive finery (jewel-encrusted bodice, embroidered sleeve, fur-trimmed velvet dress) points to the wealth and status of the saint in all her worldly prosperity. But this image also depicts the future conversion of the worldly saint within the background landscape. In the cave above the ornate filigree jar can be discerned the full-length figure of the saint after her conversion. Mary Magdalene retreated into the wilderness and became a saint, her nude body covered only by long flowing hair, as she had been depicted earlier by Massys in
the Philadelphia shutter (F. 7, cat. 21). *Pl. 112*

Once more, as in the Antwerp *Magdalene,* Massys has stressed the drama of the saint's shift from a worldly and courtly background to her total renunciation of prosperity and privilege. And the Paris Magdalene makes the contrast explicit within a single picture, as the kneeling nude penitent in the background raises both her hands above her head in an anguished and abject act of prayer. The juxtaposition
recalls Lucas van Leyden's 1519 engraving of the *Worldly Life* *Pl. 111*
of the Magdalene (B122), which shows the saint promenading in the foreground, hunting in the middle ground, but nourished by angels in her wilderness retreat in the most distant background.

The colors of the Paris painting are precisely those of the
Berlin *Madonna Enthroned* (F. 18, cat. 37), a brilliant assem- *Pl. 63*
blage of bright red over blue and white alongside purplish-gray in the garments of the Virgin. Moreover, the Paris landscape is quite close in its execution to the background of the Berlin painting. In discrete, successive layers the atmospheric sequence of spaces is conveyed through delicate colors: first browns, then greens, and finally soft blues. This
formula had already appeared in the interior of the *St. Anne* *Pl. 1*
altarpiece of 1507–09, but in the late works the landscape *Pl. 10*
colors have a more delicate transparency and a more separate layering effect. A similar technique can be seen through
the window of the 1529 Paris *Rattier Madonna* (F. 24, cat. 48). *Pl. 68*

A number of late Massys works offer close comparisons to the smooth, perfect, tapering oval face of the Paris *Magda-*
lene. For example, the 1526 New York *Adoration* (F. 8, cat. *Pl. 79*
40) features the same face, if humbler raiment, for the Madonna. The tapering, softly modeled face of the Berlin *Madonna Enthroned* (F. 18, cat. 37) also compares closely, as do the colors and landscape forms. Also close in facial features, although more fully modeled, is the Berlin frag-
ment of the *Grieving Magdalene* (F. 34, cat. 41). *Pl. 178*

Cat. 40. *Adoration of the Magi* (F. 8). 1526, New York, Metropolitan Museum no. 11.143 (101 × 79). Inscribed "26" on pilaster ornament. *Plate 79*

HIST.: Coll. H.R. Hughes, Kenmel (North Wales); R. Kann, Paris 1907; museum purchase 1911.

LIT.: Cohen, pp. 73, 88; Bosschere, p. 39; Brising, p. 52, no. 68; Burroughs, *Metropolitan Museum Bulletin* 6 (1911): 228; Conway, p. 319; Winkler, p. 203; Friedländer 7, p. 26f; Baldass, pp. 139, 166; Boon, p. 48; Wehle and Salinger, *Catalogue of Early Flemish, Dutch, and German Paintings*, p. 108ff; Reis-Santos, *Le portrait de Saint Bernardin de Sienne par Quentin Metsys*, p. 21f; Mallé, p. 104; Cuttler, p. 423; von der Osten, 149; Völker, pp. 102f., 113ff.; Puyvelde 1970, 231; DB, pp. 241–42.

Parts of the New York painting have suffered damage. The Virgin's blue robe was restored in 1934, and the color overlaps her white collar. The upper-right corner is largely restoration; neither the sky nor the masonry of this area can be ascribed to Massys. In addition, a few of the background faces, particularly the grimacing man, have been repaired slightly, although they are largely intact.

In this picture the Virgin appears with a more rounded chin and more ivory-colored skin tone, but her facial type is *Pl. 63* still much the same as the Madonna in Berlin, or, for that *Pl. 37* matter, the *Mary in Sole* of the *Rem* altar. The infant Christ is a distinctive new type—bald and pudgy with large eyes and puffy, almost swollen cheeks. The figures of Mary and Christ are silhouetted against a dark curtain and highlighted by the white cloths wrapped around them. Further isolation for the holy pair is provided by the ornately decorated reddish pilaster behind them.

The other half of the painting is crowded with the gaily dressed magi and onlookers from their retinue. A broad spectrum of colors—gold, purple, green, red—for the costumes fills the panel, and Massys uses an unusual amount of gold filigree ornament for the magi's clothing and their gifts. Especially for the oldest, white-haired magus, there is a careful execution of facial detail, and the facial shadows, glistening eyes, and skin tones of all the figures receive special attention. Massys continues to employ the muddy brown skin tones for the human participants in religious drama, and he again contrasts the ideal perfection of the holy figures with the evil and unattractive humans around them. And he retains the close-up to focus attention on the individual characters rather than on the landscape or architectural setting.

The New York *Adoration* basically derives from the *Monforte Altarpiece* of Hugo van der Goes, a popular composition *Pl. 76* replicated by the Master of Frankfurt and other Antwerp *Pl. 75* artists. Hugo's old magus in prayer and black magus at the right are repeated in the New York *Adoration of the Magi*. However, Massys concentrates his composition and intensifies its devotional content by presenting the figures in half-length (cf. Chapter 4) rather than in Hugo's full-length.

From Joos van Cleve, who also adapted Hugo's basic composition, come some of the Flamboyant or Antwerp mannerist details that fill the New York panel. Gilded sceptre and sword of the eldest magus and filigree gifts of all *Pl. 84* three men derive from van Cleve's altarpieces in Detroit and Naples. Also from van Cleve comes the puffy-cheeked Christ Child typical of later Massys works.

Leonardo da Vinci's drawings also influenced the New York *Adoration*. Massys' impressive oldest magus has the hook nose, open mouth, and flowing beard of a Leonardo profile drawing in Windsor Castle (no. 12500). The angry, *Pl. 80* grimacing background face (also repeated in Massys *Ecce Homo*, F. 11, cat. 46) likewise derives from a da Vinci model *Pl. 87* like the "nutcracker" face, now in Rome. *Pl. 85*

Alternatively, Massys could have returned to Hugo's *Monforte* altarpiece, for the wing of the *Circumcision*, where the old priest also has a long white beard, hook nose and balding head. Viewed in profile, Hugo's old man is dressed in rich robes like the Massys magus and could also have served as an available model.

Most striking about the New York *Adoration* is its splendor. Not only the ornate Flamboyand gilding and filigree but also the rich rainbow of unusual colors—gold, purple, green, red—in the costumes combine to dazzle the eye. To this extent, the panel is more closely related to the popular pictures of Joos van Cleve than to the older model of Hugo.

Because of Massys' basic continuity of figure types, here closely akin to the Leonardesque faces of the *St. John Altarpiece*, Völker dates the New York panel (as well as the Madrid *Ecce Homo*) to the same early period, i.e., before ca. 1510. While these similarities of types certainly exist, the relationship to Joos van Cleve and other Antwerp painters, plus the altered handling of modeling and coloration clearly indicate a later phase of Massys' career.

Cat. 41. *Grieving Magdalene* (fragment; F.34). Berlin-Dahlem, no. 547c (33 × 24). *Plate 178*

HIST.: Ex-coll. Rev. Heath, Enfield 1896.

LIT.: Cohen, pp. 33, 83; Bosschere, p. 103; Conway, p. 319; Delen, p. 77; Friedländer 7, p. 30; Baldass, p. 173; Reis-Santos, *Le Portrait de Saint Bernardin de Sienne, par Quentin Metsys*, p. 26 n. 18; Mallé, p. 104; Broadley, p. 88 n. 2; DB, p. 184.

Iconoclastic riots in Antwerp in 1566 eliminated numerous famous local art works, including a Holy Cross panel ("Heyligh Cruys tafereel, gemaecht van meester Quinten") in the Cathedral (cf. Lost Works, no. 1), which might have contained such a mourning saint. We find the identical pose of the *Grieving Magdalene*, reversed, however, in another Massys-related composition (here considered a workshop creation), not a Crucifixion, but a *Lamentation* (F. 62, Ottawa, National Gallery of Canada). This *Lamentation*, although called an early work by Friedländer ("Quentin Massys: Reflections on His Development," p. 53f), actually seems to postdate as a pastiche, rather than to predate the Antwerp *Lamentation* (F. 1, cat. 11). Furthermore, the Ottawa panel's *Pl. 20* elongate, heavily shaded figures seem not to be the product of Massys himself, but rather of the workshop assistant (Eduardo Portugalois?) who painted the Lisbon *Deposition* altarpiece mentioned above (see cat. 12). For photographic comparisons of other works by this assistant, see L. Reis-Santos, "Paneis de Metsys em Portugal anteriores ao Retablo de Lovaina," p. 13ff, ills. 4–19. Another late Massys work is copied in much this same fashion in the Lisbon replica of the

Pl. 57 *Van Pannwitz Madonna* (F.26, cat. 38), attributed by Reis-Santos and de Bosque to the same hand (ibid., ills. 25–26).

Possibly, then, the Ottawa *Lamentation* also replicates a large, lost Massys composition, of which only the *Magdalene* survives. Its relationship to the Antwerp *Lamentation* would be no different from the self-quotation already seen in the
Pl. 26 *Seven Sorrows Lamentation* (F. 4, cat. 12) or the Louvre *Pieta*
Pl. 94 (F. 16, cat. 17).

The Berlin panel can be dated close in time to the 1526
Pl. 79 New York *Adoration* (F. 8, cat. 40). In particular, the *Magdalene*'s oval face and glossy skin repeat the head of the New York Virgin, even in terms of position. A lovely burgundy mantle shows the same indulgent taste for color and introduces a tone that becomes commonplace in Massys' latest works.

Cat. 42. *Madonna and Child Outdoors* (F. 23). Detroit, Institute of Arts, no. 89.60 (55.2 × 39.7). *Plate 64*

Copies:

1. (F.23a). Formerly H. Kisters Coll., Kreuzlingen (51 × 37.5).
2. (F. 23b). Formerly Arnot Gallery, London (1935) (58 × 43).
3. (F. 23c). Budapest Museum, Palffy Coll., no. 74 (56.5 × 35.8).
4. Sale Fievez, Brussels (1928; 57 × 37).
5. Coll. Ehrich, New York 1933.

HIST.: Ex-coll. Murata, Florence; Scripps bequest 1889.

LIT.: Friedländer 7, p. 62; Baldass, p. 170 n. 55; Richardson, p. 171f; idem, *Catalogue of Paintings Detroit Institute of Arts* (1944), p. 84; *Holbein and his Contemporaries*, exh. cat. (Indianapolis, 1950), no. 51; Robbins, p. 100ff; DB, pp. 237–38.

The Detroit *Madonna* is close in time to both the 1526 New
Pl. 79 York *Adoration of the Magi* (F. 8, cat. 40) and the Berlin
Pl. 178 *Magdalene* fragment (F. 34, cat. 41), sharing the same egg-shaped head and glossy skin. In addition, it displays the pudgy-cheeked Christ Child (with additional blond curls) of New York and the burgundy mantle of the Berlin *Magdalene*. The background rock appeared first in the Ottawa
Pl. 91 *Crucifixion* (F. 12, cat. 20) of a decade earlier. Most recently, it had served as a landscape element in the Edinburgh
Pl. 145 *Notary* portrait (F. 45, cat. 64). But this rolling and loosely painted landscape may well be the work of a collaborator in the Detroit panel—possibly even the young Cornelis Massys. Robbins identifies the collaborator as "Hand C" and associ-
Pl. 37 ates the Detroit picture with the *Rem altarpiece* wings (cat. 24) and with the Ottawa, Berlin, and Edinburgh panels. These other works appear to be of higher quality, however; they form the source for Detroit's forms rather than being products by the same hand.

Massys continues to use symbolic still-life in the foreground: the apple of Original Sin and the grapes of redemption through Christ. The uncharacteristically detailed execution of the head of the Child may indicate some workshop participation, although the work is of high quality. The Madonna clearly is by Massys alone.

De Bosque places the work earlier, ca. 1515–20, and assigns it to the studio.

Cat. 43. *Laughing Man* (Democritus?) (F. 55). Present location unknown (46.5 × 35). *Plate 115*

HIST.: London market, Agnew 1928; P. de Boer, Amsterdam, 1930.

LIT.: Friedländer 7, p. 66; *Drei Jahrhunderte vlämischer Kunst,* exh. cat. (Vienna, 1930), no. 67; Baldass, pp. 151, 170; Silver, "Prayer and Laughter," pp. 20–23.

In format, the *Laughing Man* resembles the portraits of the
period 1510–20, like the Altrincham *Man* (F. 170, cat. 55) or Pl. 153
the Oldenburg *Man* (F. 49, cat. 56): a bust-length, heavily Pl. 102
modeled sitter against a neutral backdrop, which itself shows the shadow of the picture frame. But the costume of the *Laughing Man* features a rounded cap like the Edinburgh
Notary (F. 45, cat. 64), suggesting a date of at least a decade Pl. 145
later. Furthermore, there is a new handling of textures and surfaces. A glimmer of light brightens the eyes of the *Laughing Man*, as in the adoring eyes of the 1526 New York
Magi (F. 8, cat. 40). Deep shadow defines the brow, as in the Pl. 79
reddish face of the middle magus. And the tightness of detail in the drawn, thin eyelids or the raised shirt buttons suggest comparison with the crisp handling of very late
works like the *Pieta* (F. 15, cat. 47) or the Venice *Ecce Homo* Pl. 95
(F. 11, cat. 46). Pl. 87

The meaning of this enigmatic character is suggested by Pl. 116
an engraving of Cornelis Cort, labeled "Democritus" (see Chap. 6 for a fuller discussion of the Democritus identification). Cort's work copies Massys' panel, adding a beard and hat to suggest that the subject was an ancient Greek philosopher. Democritus was the man who, according to classical tradition, laughed at the follies of the world. Paired with the weeping philosopher, Heraclitus, he served as a pictorial *topos* in Netherlandish art through the 17th century (A. Blankert, "Heraclitus en Democritus," p. 31ff.). Cort also engraved a *Heraclitus* that displays long fingers on a balustrade in the manner of Massys, but whether this reflects a lost work must remain speculative.

Both the classical subject and the lack of identification or attributes suggest that Massys' *Democritus* was created for a friend from the circle of Erasmus who would have understood the subject without any accessory details. The *Praise of Folly* text makes frequent references to the laughing philosopher, so Erasmus and his readers were well acquainted with the figure of *Democritus* (see Chap. 6).

Cat. 44. *Fool* or *Allegory of Folly*. Coll. J. Held, New York (60 × 47.5); inscribed: "Mondeken toe" (the word "Mot" is a later addition). *Plate 135*

HIST.: Ex-coll. N. Smith, Montreal 1938.

LIT.: *Flemish Painting*, exh. cat. (Worcester-Philadelphia, 1939), p. 35, no. 45; *Holbein and His Contemporaries*, exh. cat. (Indianapolis, 1950), no. 50; E. Tietze-Conrat, *Dwarfs and Jesters in Art* (London, 1957), p. 19, 94; W. Willeford, *The Fool and His Sceptre* (London, 1969), p. 6; DB, p. 209.

The Held *Fool* is one of Massys' latest essays into grotesque secular art. This persona is identified by the familiar costume of cowl with ass's ears, bells, and obscene marot (see Chap. 7). Moreover, the *Fool* is characterized by the "stone of folly" on his forehead. Despite the finger over his lips and the inscription "Mondeken toe" (Hold your tongue), the cock's head of the fool's head covering is betraying his secrets. According to Erasmus, this simple blurting out of truth makes fools instructive despite their unwise words. In similar fashion, Massys' secular grotesques are humorous, but they also carry along an important form of instruction.

The carefully modeled features, such as the regular, scal-
Pl. 108 loped brows, most closely resemble Massys' two *Praying*
Pl. 109 *Monks* (F. 80, cat. 45), or the elders of the dated 1526 New
Pl. 79 York *Adoration of the Magi* (F. 8, cat. 40). The *Fool* also exhibits the same monochrome (dark green) background and half-length format as later secular pictures or portraits. Similar grotesque faces and brownish skin tones, as well as the elongate proportions and stooped postures, can already be found among Christ's tormentors on the wings of the
Pl. 32 Coimbra *Passion altarpiece* (F. 196, cat. 18) and in later
Pl. 33 versions of the Passion, such as the Venice *Ecce Homo* (F. 11,
Pl. 87 cat. 46), where the figure at the right bears a close resemblance to the Held *Fool.*

The picture is in good condition. I am most grateful to Professor Held for his cooperation regarding the painting, for an informative, lengthy letter concerning it (8 December 1973), and for the opportunity to view it in his home.

William Robinson has graciously shared his own researches on the topic of fools unable to control their tongues. A phrase from Juvenal's satires, "Digito compesce labellum," was translated among the Christian proverbs of J. David (*Christelijcke waersegghen* [1603], pp. 94, 148, 225) as "finger on lip" or "mondeken toe," the same cautionary words already found on the Held panel. Juvenal, in turn, was cited by Alciati in his 1531 emblem book—a work that postdates Massys but which, like Erasmus's adages, grows out of a blend of biblical, proverbial, and classical phrases. The Alciati Latin text reads as follows: "Cum tacet, haud quicquam differt sapientibus amens: / Stultitiae est index linguaque voxque suae. / Ergo premat labia, digitoque silentia signet / Et sese Pharium vertat in Harpocratem." (One prizes a fool as witty / Who's silent, but he's soon betrayed / As he chatters with a sage / Like a crowd who harbored ill / And therefore keeps his mouth well shut / With finger and who speaks not much / As God painted Harpocras / Who wants to learn such virtue.)

The images of Harpocrates, Greek god of Silence, are described by Plutarch according to K. Langedijk, "Silentium," *NKJ* (1964): 3ff. The Held image also calls to mind passages from Proverbs: "Even a fool when he is silent is thought to be wise, and he who keeps his lips closed is considered intelligent" (17: 28), or "A fool's mouth is his ruin, and his lips are a snare to his soul" (18: 7). Massys, of course, has transformed the fool of the Old Testament into the professional fool of the late Middle Ages. Jacob Jordaens produced a mid-17th century engraving, *The Fool and the Cat* (ca. 1645), where rooster-crowns adorn the fool's caps on the base of the frame (inscribed "Fatuo ridemur in uno").

Cat. 45. *Praying Monks* (lost; F. 80).
Copies:

1. (F. 80). Palazzo Doria, Rome (30 × 43; fig. 51a). *Plate 108*
2. (F. 80a). Munich, Alte Pinakothek, no. 23 (34 × 48; fig. 51b). *Plate 109*
3. Formerly London trade F.A. Drey, 1945 (29 × 37).
4. Drawing by Jacob de Gheyn II, East Berlin, with added foreground elements (13 × 16).

HIST.: Mentioned by van Fornenbergh (1658) in a Brussels collection: "Worshippers from life, appearing to read piously with paternosters in hand."

LIT.: Van Fornenbergh, p. 31; Cohen, p. 89; Bosschere, p. 124n.; Winkler, p. 206; Friedländer 7, p. 69; Baldass, pp. 151, 167; van Puyvelde, *La peinture flamande à Rome*, p. 112; Marlier, p. 247 n. 16, xiv (L. Reis-Santos); Puyvelde, p. 301; Puyvelde 1970, p. 231; DB, p. 208; Silver, "Prayer and Laughter," pp. 20–23.

Van Fornenbergh's reference indicates the satirical meaning of the picture, a contrast between the earnest prayer of the man at the left and the uncomprehending curiosity of his companion. The same attack on pious hypocrites can be found in the words of Erasmus (see Chap. 6).

None of the surviving versions appears to be by Massys' own hand, although Reis-Santos claims to have found the original in a Lisbon private collection (he never published the picture). This subject was mentioned by the Portugese humanist Damião de Gois in his heresy trials and would have been acquired by him from Massys in Antwerp around the same time as a now-lost *Crucifixion altarpiece* (see Documented Lost Works, no. 2).

The Doria version, according to Puyvelde, is a Massys original finished later because of the different thicknesses of pigment. Nevertheless, weaknesses of execution, as in the anatomy of the hands or in the head and shoulders of the praying monk, disqualify the Doria design as well as its producer.

Massys' original should be placed close in date to the 1526 New York *Adoration* (F. 8, cat. 40). The scallop-shaped eyelids, heavy modeling, and textured detail of hair or wrinkles recall the elderly magus and the swarthy central king from that panel.

A variant or copy of this picture is mentioned in the 1642 inventory of the Spanish Marquis of Leganés: "no. 248, a painting at half length in a frame of two old men by Master Quintin, one holding a rosay in his left hand and the other with hands clasped [in prayer]" *(una pintura de media basa en quadro de dos biejos de maestro Quintin, uno tiene un rrosario en la mano yzquierda, y otra enclabğadas las manos).* Reprinted by Jose Lúpez Navío, "La gran colección de printuras del Marqués de Leganés," *Analecta Calasanctiana* 8 (1962): 262–330, a reference provided by Prof. John Elliott. Also discussed by Mary C. Volk, "New Light on a Seventeenth-Century Collector: The Marquis of Leganés," *Art Bulletin* 62 (1980): 256–68, esp. 267, Appendix 2.

Cat. 46. *Ecce Homo* (F. 11). Ca. 1528–29, Venice, Palazzo Ducale (95 × 74). *Plate 87*

LIT.: Brising, p. 30; Friedländer 7, p. 28; Baldass, pp. 148, 173; Boon, p. 30, Mallé, p. 95; Völker, p. 11f.; DB, p. 212.

The Venice *Ecce Homo* is Massys' latest known depiction of a
theme found earlier at Coimbra (F. 196, cat. 18) and Madrid Pl. 33
(F. 10, cat. 31). No longer does a balustrade separate the Pl. 86
viewer from Christ and Pilate; the expressive heads must be confronted directly—a departure from the historical narrative sense of the *Ecce Homo* in late 15th-century scenes. As in

Pl. 79 the 1526 New York *Adoration*, the viewer is made an intimate participant in the religious drama. And like the pilaster of the New York *Adoration*, the Venice archway serves to isolate and emphasize the principals.

Leonardesque heads again appear among Christ's tor-
Pl. 85 mentors. The glowering face over Pilate's shoulder had already appeared behind Pilate in the Prado *Ecce Homo* and above the magi in the New York *Adoration*. Along with the other angry man with the rope, this Venice head can be compared to a Leonardo grotesque in Rome.

The *Ecce Homo* colors have the soft harmonies of other late panels with burgundy, royal blue, and cream tones. Hard-edged patterns of folds recall sleeves of the New York *Adoration*. And there is a crispness of texture found only in the late pictures. Facial wrinkles and crinkly fabrics, especially Christ's loincloth, have a new physical immediacy. The
Pl. 68 *Rattier Madonna* (F. 24, cat. 48) still-life or the lost *Pieta* (F.
Pl. 95 15, cat. 47) headcovering present the same carefully studied surfaces. Christ's facial type presents a fuller, more rounded, broad head with heavy eyelids akin to Massys' later Madonna types.

Cat. 47. *Pieta* (lost; F. 15).
Versions:
A. 1. Brussels, Musées Royaux no. 4705 (112 × 103).
2. Madrid, Coll. Lazaro-Galdiano no. 976. *Plate 95*
3. Munich, Alte Pinakothek no. 134 (123 × 103) (forms altered considerably by W. Key).
B. 1. Antwerp, Koninklijk Museum no. 565 (62 × 49) (F. 64; other copies in Seville, Cathedral, Coll. Cremer, Dortmund, etc.) *Plate 96*
LIT.: Brising, p. 30; Conway, p. 316; Friedländer 7, p. 61; Baldass, pp. 155, 173; DB, p. 168.

A host of copies and variants of varying qualities testify to the existence of a late Massys original, now lost. The best version is the Brussels panel, showing a slightly elevated Christ with Calvary visible over His head. Only Mary's right arm is visible. A varient composition (B), best represented at Antwerp, shows Calvary over the Virgin's head, and her left arm is also evident behind the head of Christ. Essentially, the two versions agree in other respects, except that the Brussels panel shows a foreground ledge, which features both the nails and the crown of thorns. Mary is shrouded in a white head covering with crinkly edges; her burgundy mantle is trimmed at its cuffs with a grey ring of fur. Christ's sharp nose and bulging, closed eyelids intensify the effect of suffering in the slender, angular body.

Key's Munich copy, which has been called a later completion of an unfinished Massys panel, seems to be a completely independent work. Neither the loosely painted landscape nor the head of the Virgin shows Massys' touch, and there is no inconsistency within the parts of the panel. Furthermore, the number of copies of Massys' panel indicates that at least one (and possibly a second, slightly different variant) original panel was fully completed by the artist.

The soft, cool coloration of the *Pieta* panel associates it with late works, most notably the 1529 *Rattier Madonna* (F.
Pl. 68 24, cat. 48). In addition, the fuller, more rounded face of the Virgin links it to the dated Paris work. The ruffled white
Pl. 87 linen resembles Christ's loincloth in the Venice *Ecce Homo* (F. 11, cat. 46). Christ's and the Virgin's sharp features resemble the Massys workshop's half-length *Deposition* (Madrid, Museo Lazaro-Galdiano, F. 61) more than the Venice *Ecce Homo* (F. 11, cat. 46). The *Pieta*'s greater sense of volume and texture is evident in comparison with the Louvre *Pieta* (F. 16, cat. 17) of the middle teens. *Pl. 94*

Two similar, complementary sources lie behind the *Pieta* composition. Mary's crinkled white headpiece and embrace, along with the type for Christ, comes from Roger van der Weyden's Pieta composition (London), but in the latter the *Pl. 97* Madonna does not reach across the chest of her Son, as in Massys' composition.

This motif is more closely approximated by a Gerard David Pieta composition (Friedländer 7, no. 194a, 203), extracted from his own large composition of the *Lamentation* (London; Friedländer 6, no. 194), itself possibly influenced by Massys' Antwerp altarpiece. But David's *Pieta* is further from the Massys version, for it eliminates the mount of Calvary, it has a fuller, more athletic Christ, and it eliminates the cloth under his head. And Massys' composition moves from left to right, the reverse of David's first close-up but consistent with the second image. Once again, as in his early Madonna images, Massys has produced his own version of traditional images through the creative combination of two separate models.

Cat. 48. *Rattier Madonna* (F. 24). 1529, Paris, Louvre no. 20 (68 × 51); inscribed: "Qu. M. *529" *Plate 68*
HIST.: Identified as a painting in the collection of Archduke Albert and Isabella, Coudenberg, 1639 (no. 77, see below); transported to Brussels, St. Gudule, 1652; acquired 1902 from Rattier collection.
LIT.: H. de Chennevières, "Les recentes acquisitions du department de la peinture au Louvre," *Gazette des Beaux-Arts* 30 (1903): 501f.; Cohen, pp. 33. 87; Brising, p. 32; J. Guiffrey, *La Musee du Louvre, les peintures, les dessins, la chalcographie* (Paris, 1909), p. 138; L. Demonts, *Musee national du Louvre Catalogue des peintures*, vol. 3 (Paris, 1922), p. 59; Winkler, p. 204; Friedländer 7, p. 27; Baldass, pp. 146, 172f.; Boon, p. 46; E. Michel, *Catalogue raisonné . . . Peintures flamandes du XVe et du XVIe siècles*, p. 211; Mallé, p. 106; Broadley, p. 154f.; von der Osten, p. 149; Cuttler, p. 421; M. Smeyers, "Schilderijen van Kwinten Metsys in het Bezit der Aartshertogen Albrecht en Isabella," *Miscellanea Josef Duverger*, vol. 1 (Ghent, 1968), p. 139ff.; Puyvelde 1970, p. 229; DB, 123–34; de Jongh, "Grape Symbolism in Paintings of the 16th and 17th Centuries," pp. 183–86.
Copy: Location unknown (F. 24a); formerly Paris coll. (83 × 64.5).

The *Rattier Madonna* is a dated work, with the year (1)529. It again shows the Virgin and Child embracing, though Christ is now an older long-limbed youth (still with curly hair and glossy skin) adapted from the type of the Berlin *Madonna*. *Pl. 63*
The Virgin's face has a new rounded fullness and almost no suggestion of the sharply thrusting chins in earlier Massys visages. The artist has fully mellowed the bright colors of his previous pictures into a harmonious play of mild purple, blue, and burgundy for Mary's clothes. The landscape, visible through the window, is thinly painted in soft green

tints with the gentle suggestion of distant blue mountains. But the painter's attention to minutiae of texture is at a height; the foreground still-life even reveals the smallest veins in a leaf or the reflected glimmer of a plate, while a similar care is bestowed upon the gentle pressure of Mary's hand on her child. Massys, in this final effort, exerts all his powers to suggest the domestic intimacy between holy mother and child.

The domestic interior and close-up view contribute to an intimate version of the Virgin—particularly in contrast to the earliest Madonna images. A similar close-up view occurs
Pl. 71 in the 1529 *Virgin in Prayer* (Prado; cat. 49) and the undated
Pl. 64 Detroit *Virgin Outdoors* (F. 23, cat. 42) or Venice *Ecce Homo* (F.
Pl. 87 11, cat. 46).

The visual source for Massys' panel has been ascribed to the followers of Leonardo—Giampetrino or Marco d'Oggiono. But both in its domestic emphasis and its facial type, the *Rattier Madonna* is derived from the late works of David,
Pl. 62 particularly the *Holy Family* (formerly, Paris coll. Leroy), which even features a view out a window on the right. The Virgin wears the same diaphanous veil in both the David and Massys pictures. A similar facial type (and window view)
Pl. 66 occurs in the David *Virgin with Milk Soup* (Brussels). Like the
Pl. 95 late *Pieta* (cat. 47) or the Prado diptych of *Christ and the*
Pl. 71 *Virgin* (cat. 49), the *Rattier Madonna* reveals Massys' continu-
Pl. 72 ing interest in mature compositions by David.

A 17th-century inventory listing of the Archduke Albrecht has been identified by Smeyers with the *Rattier Madonna:* "A painting on panel in oil of two *anas* in height and a little more in width which contains in the center in half circle frame and in the center an image of Our Lady with the undressed Child, embracing Him in her arms and on a table a bunch of grapes and a pared peach on a plate and a small knife and a glass; the frame is worked and gilded, with reliefs of several seraphim, angels, and other figures; its doors hold scriptures, a few verses written on them in Latin and in the heights the Eternal Father painted on the panel in oil following the contours of the retable" (no. 77). This description confirms the 17th-century location of the picture, and it sketches a vision of its original (?) frame, now lost.

De Jongh's discussion of the symbolism of the bunch of grapes alludes to the usual association of Christ as the true vine (John 15:1) and the late medieval eucharistic representation of Christ spilling his blood in the winepress. He adds citations from verses of 16th-century *rederijkers,* such as Anna Bijns (see Chap. 1) that go further and call Mary the tendril in wine for Christ as grape. Bijns's verse reads as follows: "Pure body, free of sinful stink, / You have borne / The grape, whose wine, the sweetest drink, / Reconciled the Pharaoh—oh fertile tendril . . . "

Cat. 49. *Christ Blessing and Virgin in Prayer.* 1529, Madrid, Prado nos. 1561/2; inscribed on reverse of Christ Panel: "OPUS QUINTINI METSYS AN MDXXIX" *Plates 71, 72*

Copies: (Virgin) Dortmund, coll. Becker; (Christ) Winterthur, Kunstverein (46 × 36).

HIST.: Escorial inventory of 1597; to Prado 1837.

LIT.: Van den Branden, p. 71; Friedländer 12, p. 185, no. 172; L. van Puyvelde, "Der segnende Christus," *Hauptwerke des Kunstmuseums* (Winterthur, 1949), p. 15ff.; Reis-Santos, "Jan Quinten Massys Discipulo e Colaborador de seu Pai Mestre Quinten Metsys," p. 3ff.; Puyvelde 1970, p. 229; *Museo del Prado Catalogo* (Madrid, 1972), p. 339.

The counterpart to the *Rattier Madonna,* also dating from Pl. 68
1529, is a pair of panels, *Christ Blessing* and *Mary in Prayer* (Madrid, Prado, signed and dated in Latin on the verso of the Christ panel). Here appears the same facial type for the Virgin as the *Rattier Madonna,* with a sharper light upon the individual facial details. Christ, too, is seen in bust length under bright light; His skin has a ruddy cast like that of the
central magus of the New York *Adoration* (F. 8, cat. 40). The Pl. 79
deep blue and maroon of the garments correspond to the colors in the *Rattier Madonna* and reinforce the quiet dignity of Massys' final works.

The *Christ Blessing* is a change from Massys' early Antwerp
Salvator Mundi (F. 5, cat. 5), eliminating the trappings of Pl. 43
royalty and facing the Redeemer toward the Virgin. Mary, too, is now dressed humbly, with a headdress similar in type to that of the *Rattier Madonna.* No longer is the visual source the same. From van Eyck's Ghent altarpiece for the earlier work, Massys has turned, late in his career, to Gerard
David's *Christ Saying Farewell to the Virgin* (Friedländer 6, nos. Pl. 98
168, 169) which features both Mary's prayerful pose and Christ's gesture of benediction. In harmony with his Antwerp precedent, Massys places Mary on Christ's right, thus reversing the direction of David's panel.

A curious detail is the legible Hebrew lettering embroidered on Mary's neckline, the opening words of Genesis. Christ's letters are not actual words and seem to be purely decorative.

Cat. 50. *Madonna of the Cherries; Enthroned Virgin and Child Embracing* (lost; F. 67). Ca. 1529.

Versions:

A. Amsterdam, Rijksmuseum, no. 1529 (75 × 63); on loan to The Hague, Mauritshuis.
B. Coll. E. W. Edwards, Cincinnati.
C. Northbrook Coll., London, no. 23 (72.5 × 50).
D. Ringling Museum, Sarasota, no. 200 (29½″ × 24¾″). *Plate 58*
E. G. Gerlachuis Foundation, Mantta, Finland (27 × 32).
F. Coll. Baron T. de Budai (82.5 × 65).

HIST.: 1628 Antwerp coll. Cornelis van der Geest; featured in foreground of gallery picture by Willem van Haecht (Antwerp, Rubenshuis); to Peter Stevens 1638; sold 1668. Pl. 59

LIT.: Fickaert, p. 15; Fornenbergh, p. 24f.; van den Branden, 73; Hymans, p. 201f.; Cohen, p. 33; Brising, p. 32; Conway, pp. 316, 318; Winkler, p. 204; Friedländer 7, p. 68; Baldass, p. 172f.; Boon, p. 47; Mallé, p. 104; Held, "Artis Pictoriae Amator. An Antwerp Art Patron and His Collection," p. 63 n. 21; Broadley, pp. 152, 162ff.; Puyvelde 1970, p. 229; DB, pp. 221–32; L. Silver, *Flemish and Dutch Paintings 1400–1900,* Ringling Museum (Sarasota, 1980), no. 30.

Hymans attempted to identify this picture with a 1676 inventory item of the Amsterdam dealer Diego Duarte: "A Mary panel with the Child and a prospect, very good" (no. 131). Smeyers, however, has identified this entry with the

Pl. 63 Berlin *Madonna Enthroned* (F. 18, cat. 37); in addition, the Pl. 68 1529 *Rattier Madonna* (F. 24, cat. 48) features a similar "prospect" behind the holy figures. In 1615, Albrecht and Isabella attempted to purchase the lost Massys picture from van der Geest for the royal collection; van Fornenbergh mentions this visit, and van Haecht's gallery picture also commemorates the visit.

The van Haecht panel presumably features the missing Massys original in its foreground. From this record, the veracity of copies can be determined. The Hague panel, although of high quality, reverses the arrangement of a foreground still-life of apple and grapes in van Haecht's picture. Other copies are consistent with the gallery painting and with each other, but not with the version in The Hague, which also lacks the greyish plum-colored dress of the original. The Hague picture, featuring a blue dress, also has a much more ornate throne with a brocade, rather than the simpler marbleized throne of the other copies. None of the other copies displays comparable quality (except, perhaps, the Edwards Coll. panel, which Puyvelde calls an original), so the authentic Massys may still be presumed missing.

For this particular image of the Madonna embracing her Child, the obvious source is Bouts, who made two versions of Pl. 60 the theme, one with a brocade background (San Francisco, Pl. 61 De Young Museum) and one without (New York, Metropolitan Pl. 68 Museum; Florence, Bargello). The Gerard David works that influenced the 1529 *Rattier Madonna* (cat. 48) play less of a role, although the corner window view recalls works like the Pl. 62 Leroy *Holy Family* or the Brussels *Madonna with Milk Soup.* Pl. 66

The original van der Geest *Madonna* may be considered one of Massys' very last works, because it has many features in common with the *Rattier Madonna.* The atmospheric landscape (with a spindly tree recalling the Vaduz *Canon,* F. 39, cat. 65) in the corner, and the round face and prominent, straight nose of the Virgin repeat forms of the Paris panel. The red of Mary's mantle, the curly-haired smaller Child, and the foreground still-life recall Madonna panels of the previous decade.

V. PORTRAITS

Because portraits in the post-medieval period allegedly resemble their sitters and must, therefore, conform to the features of their referent, they do not offer the relatively continuous and imagined features of the Madonna, Christ, and saints. Those more generalized types offer a more recognizable "signature" of Massys' visual "handwriting" because of their independence of external constraints of reference. For this reason, Massys' portraits will be considered separately here, and they will be more broadly assigned to periods of the artist's activity. Comparisons to figure types from religious or secular pictures by Massys are often based more on coloration, brush strokes, or some other technical element of manufacture than on facial features, or else they depend on such secondary, but equally imaginary, ingredients as background landscapes or architectural ornament within the portraits.

As in the case of the great altarpieces, Massys began his career as a portraitist rather late, and only the portraits after 1509 can be dated with any precision. The earliest inscribed likeness, the Winterthur *Pilgrim* (F. 38, cat. 53), has a date of 1509, precisely Pl. 138 the period of the completion of the *St. Anne altarpiece* and the beginning of the *St. John altarpiece.* In this case, the date presents uncertainty about whether it refers to the year of the commemorated pilgrimage or to the actual date of the portrait. Therefore, it is a *terminus post quem,* an important personal event marked by the portrait panel.

Other dated or datable portraits offer a sequence from the remainder of Massys' career. The Paris *Old Man* (F. 51, cat. 54) Pl. 157 bears an inscription with the date 1513. If the Oldenburg *Man and Wife* are truly Peter Gillis and his first wife, Cornelia Sandrin, Pl. 102 then their marriage date of 1514 would be the *terminus post quem* of these pendants. (On the other hand, some scholars have Pl. 103 assumed that Gillis is portrayed with his second bride from the year 1526, because the man in the picture appears to be older than the sitter for Massys' *Gillis* of the 1517 *Friendship Diptych.)* Pl. 100

The Friendship Diptych is datable precisely to mid-1517 through the letters of Erasmus and Thomas More, the recipient of the Pl. 99 pendants *Erasmus* and *Gillis* (see Chap. 6). Another dated portrait, bearing the year 1517 on a cartellino attached to a foreground balustrade, is the Karlsruhe *Man* (F. 194, cat. 57). With the depiction of a study interior filled with scholarly books, Pl. 152 Massys began to amplify the monochrome backgrounds he had borrowed from 15th-century portrait models and to include additional environments, possibly offering further information or suggestive connotations about his sitters. This development was to be particularly striking in the portraits of the 1520s, those containing landscapes and/or architectural backgrounds.

One of these later portraits is datable ca. 1520–22 if the identification of the sitter as Cornelius Grapheus (see Chap. 6,8) is Pl. 146 correct, for Grapheus was exiled from Antwerp (temporarily, but during the remainder of Massys' career) in 1522. Also dated positively in this period is Massys' portrait of King Christian II of Denmark, who first visited Antwerp in 1521 but returned to Pl. 155 the Netherlands in 1523, when he was exiled by the Danish nobility for attempting to introduce the Reformation into Denmark. The king's gold chain of the Order of the Golden Fleece provides a *terminus post quem* of 1519, the year of Christian II's induction into the Order.

Only one other Massys portrait is dated: the Windsor Castle *Man* (F. 171, cat. 63) of 1527, and this painting is as vexing as it is Pl. 182 informative, for it marks a return to the earliest portrait formulas of the artist. Monochrome background, oblique glance, and linear modeling once again tie this image to 15th-century portrait conventions, e.g., Roger van der Weyden and Hans Memling. By coming full circle to a bare minimum of information and the simplest presentation of an effigy, Massys' Windsor portrait reveals fully and once more the degree to which the artist could alter his pictorial formulations to suit either a particular client or a particular effect. Such variability (or versatility) should remind us to be extremely cautious about dating any Massys picture, including his portraits, solely on the basis of technique or formal features.

Massys' early and repeated use of monochrome backgrounds depends upon the previous portraits of van Eyck, van der

Weyden, and Memling. By the time of the Winterthur *Pilgrim*, however, Massys had introduced a strong, angled light into his portraits and had showed a dark shadow cast against the neutral ground. His 1517 adaptation of the formula of a scholar at work in his study, long a cliché in the frontispieces of illuminated manuscripts, was a breakthrough use of environment for a portrait of a living individual, Erasmus. For later images of learned men, Massys borrowed Memling's portrait formula of an individual at a table and in front of a sunny, summery landscape vista, often mediated by an open arcade. These portraits have often been associated with Italian models, such as Perugino's portraits or the school of Leonardo da Vinci (especially Solario). But after Memling's frequent portrait commissions from the Italian merchant community of Bruges, the distinction of a Northern or Southern source for Massys is moot. Just as Massys' later religious icons seem to owe a considerable debt to Leonardo in the 1520s (see Chap. 4) as well as to Memling's own Italianate Madonnas, so this set of portraits may well be tied to both Renaissance forms and Memling's earlier experimentation with transalpine ideality.

From Memling in particular, Massys attempted to emulate a portrait model which could be, in Panofsky's words (*ENP*, 348): "a genuine synthesis of stylization and verisimilitude, a happy medium between Rogerian character and Eyckian individuality." To this end, he employed interior settings or background landscapes as well as the costumes and distinctive attributes placed in sitters' hands. But he never settled on a routine or repeated formula, and he never seems to have become a "professional" portraitist in the manner of Holbein, Antonis Mor, or Hals—yet another reason for treating his portraits with special caution and in isolation from his other works.

Cat. 51. *Wealthy Man* (F. 41). New York, Metropolitan Museum no. 32. 100 (45, 8 × 34.6, rounded top). *Plate 151*

HIST.: Coll. Earls of Harrington, Elvaston Castle (Derbyshire) by 1857; London sale 1924; Michael Friedsam Coll.; museum bequest, 1931.

LIT.: Friedländer, "Neues zu Quentin Massys," p. 7; idem, unpublished catalogue of Friedsam Coll., p. 125; Friedländer 7, pp. 34, 65f.; B. Burroughs and H. B. Wehle, *Metropolitan Museum Bulletin* 27 (1932): 28; Baldass, p. 163; Richardson, p. 169; Wehle and Salinger, *The Metropolitan Museum of Art Catalogue of Early Flemish, Dutch and German Paintings*, p. 106; Mallé, p. 98; DB, p. 243.

The date of this portrait panel is controversial. Mallé places it ca. 1514, and he is joined by Friedländer (7), who, however, had previously dated it earlier in preceding publications (1927, 1505; unpublished, 1510). Other authors consider it to be one of Massys' earliest portraits, dating before 1509.

The light green background of the piece, which bears the marks of damage and restoration, is a simple variant of the shaded ground of later portraits, such as the Winterthur
Pl. 138 *Pilgrim* (cat. 53), which can be dated after 1509. The picture's surface has suffered greatly and is heavily crazed. Much of the detail is lost, e.g., in the fur, but what remains exhibits meticulous attention to embroidery and goldwork. The Wealthy Man's face bears pronounced shadows along the bridge of the nose and the line of the jaw; these modeling effects would have been even more striking in the picture's original condition. The combination of crystalline detail and shaded contours relates this portrait to the Brus-
Pl. 48 sels *Madonna Enthroned* (F. 17, cat. 9), giving an approximate date of ca. 1505.

Pl. 139 Jan van Eyck's *Jan de Leeuw* (1436) appears to have been a model for Massys. Both sitters look directly out at the viewer and raise their right hands to chest level to display a small object. In addition, both subjects turn away from the light source and leave their left sides in shadow.

The blue flower in the Wealthy Man's right hand has been identified (Wehle and Salinger) as a sprig of borage, a sign of bethrothal; his sword pommel resembles North Italian varieties of the early 16th century. His collar bears the embroidered inscription "LEVER," and his cuff has the letters "C [lover's knot according to Richardson] M F O."

Several notes of caution deserve expression. The very pomp and display so prominent in this image are also anomalous among Massys' portraits, including his one image of royalty, *King Christian II* (F. 172, cat. 62). Moreover, *Pl. 15*
the condition of this painting makes dating it, even in relation to other portraits, quite difficult. The unshaded monochrome background is a Massys hallmark, but the shaded features and positioning of the head of the New York portrait are closest to the Winterthur *Pilgrim* (F. 38, cat. 53); moreover, the features of the sitter are delineated in a manner closely approximating that of the Altrincham pen- *Pl. 15*
dants (F. 170, cat. 55) or of the Oldenburg *Man* (Peter Gillis, *Pl. 15*
F. 49, cat. 56), here dated ca. 1514—15 (but often consid- *Pl. 10*
ered a decade later by scholars for extrinsic reasons). In this *Pl. 10*
respect, de Bosque's recent analysis is provocative: She considers the attribution to Massys "improbable" and dates the costume to around 1515–20.

Cat. 52. *Man with a Flower* (F. 47). Chicago, Art Institute, no. 94. 1025 (43.9 × 29.2). *Plate 149*

HIST.: Paris, des Beurnonville coll.; Paris, May coll.; Pratolino, Prince Demidoff coll. 1890; Chicago, Glessner coll.; gift to museum 1894.

LIT.: Conway, pp. 319, 327; Winkler, p. 199; Friedländer 7, p. 34; Baldass, 163; H. Tietze, *Meisterwerke Europäische Malerei in America* (1935), pl. 141; Richardson, p. 169; Boon, p. 51; Benesch, p. 88; Mallé, p. 100, n. 31; *Paintings in the Art Institute of Chicago* (Chicago, 1961), p. 296f.; I Bergström, *Den symboliska nejlikan*, p. 101; Cuttler, p. 421; Puyvelde 1970, p. 231; DB, pp. 243–44.

The *Man with a Flower* is Massys' most impressively archaistic portrait. Its light blue background and supple contours recall van der Weyden's portraits from devotional diptychs. At the same time, the clasped flower and hand on the lower edge of the frame recall Eyckian portraits, e.g., *Jan de Leeuw* *Pl. 13*
(1436; Vienna) and "Timotheos" (1432; National Gallery, *Pl. 13*
London). The most immediate source seems to have been Gerard David's *Goldsmith* (Vienna) where the figure, against *Pl. 15*
a soft green background, clasps the attribute of his occupation.

The flower of the Chicago portrait has not been firmly

identified. Cuttler calls it a member of the compositae family; in shape, it resembles a carnation, but its blue coloring is *Pl. 52* unusual. Massys also shows carnations in the *Seilern Madonna* (cat. 13) *Pl. 1* and the *Holy Kinship* panel (cat. 11), where they refer to the Incarnation and Passion of Christ. In 16th-century portraiture, however, the flower seems to have had more of a *vanitas* association (e.g., the Dirk Jacobsz. portrait of Occo, Amsterdam) and to express hope for the resurrection and redemption of the sitter. A Bruyn portrait (1537; Cologne, Wallraf-Richartz Museum) of *Petrus van Clapis* bears the inscription "Spes mea deus," and a second portrait reads "Dum spiro, spero" (Bergström, p. 106, n. 1, 105f.).

The Chicago painting is usually considered one of Massys' first efforts at portraiture, and it is frequently dated before the *St. Anne altarpiece*. Nonetheless, its nut-brown skin tones, color scheme, and sense of outline link this portrait to the *Pl. 8* heads on the exterior shutters of the *St. Anne altarpiece*. Note, *Pl. 9* for example, the "self-portrait" of Massys on the right wing, or the man reading, adjacent to the high priest on the left wing. The darker skin tones can be seen on the grotesque head, seen in three-quarter view over Joachim's shoulder on the right wing. The surface of the picture is abraded (note the skin tones), and its unusual hat is a modern restorer's invention.

Cat. 53. *Pilgrim* (F. 38). Ca. 1509–12. Reinhart collection, Winterthur (46 × 33). Inscribed on a paper in the subject's hand: "ETAS MEA 51 DUM SCRIBERETUR 1.5.0.9. FUI IN TERRA SANCTA." *Plate 138*

LIT.: G. Hulin de Loo, "An Unknown Portrait by Quinten Metsys," p. 212; Friedländer 7, p. 22f; Baldass, p. 163f; Boon, p. 51; Mallé, p. 89; Broadley, p. 95ff; Cuttler, p. 421; von der Osten p. 150; Puyvelde 1970, p. 229 (reads inscription as 1508); DB, pp. 242–43.

The Winterthur *Pilgrim* has a solid, blocky head with a slightly pinkish cast. The jowls and cheeks are modeled in fairly dark shadow, but elsewhere, including the hands, the accents are more subtle. The Pilgrim's hair appears coarse and stringy; it accentuates the contour and shape of his head. The fur and dark brown velvet of his costly garments are convincingly portrayed but quietly understated.

Closest to the *Pilgrim* in both facial types and execution are the older men painted by Massys himself, rather than by assistants, in the *Seven Sorrows* altarpiece (ca. 1509–12, F. 4, *Pl. 28* cat. 12). The face of St. Joseph in the Worcester *Rest on the Flight* displays the same blocky solidity and features the same stringy hair, although painted a bit more loosely. Another *l. 113* close analogue is the Antwerp *St. Christopher* (F. 32, cat. 7). In Worcester, as in Winterthur, the shading is careful and delicate around the brows (the heavy shadows are lacking because the *Rest on the Flight* is an outdoor scene without a spotlight effect). Another good comparison from the Madre *Pl. 31* de Deus altar is the group of old men from *Christ among the Doctors* (Lisbon). There, the treatment of fur, facial tonalities, and regularized features all relate closely to the Winterthur *Pilgrim*, suggesting a date for the portrait to around 1510–12.

Also close to the Winterthur *Pilgrim* is one of the rare *. 150* portraits ascribed to Gerard David, the *Goldsmith* (Vienna, Kunsthistorisches Museum). Both works have distinct shading, hands visible above the lower frame, and a solid background against which the sitter casts a shadow (avocado green in Massys' case, a turquoise for David). The two paintings also share a common relation of sitter to field. Apparently Massys drew inspiration from a portrait model of David at the same time as he turned to the Davidian composition of the *Rest on the Flight*.

But the Massys portrait with its averted glance has a liveliness and interior mental quality that cannot have come from David. Not surprisingly, the closest analogies come from much earlier models—the works of Jan van Eyck. Eyck's Goldsmith *Jan de Leeuw* (Vienna) and his *Man in a Red* *Pl. 139* *Turban* (London, National Gallery) peer intensely out of the frame at the viewer, and they both feature a simple dark background with a spotlight effect on the face. In addition, de Leeuw's hand is visible at the bottom of the picture. Other Eyckian portrait figures hold letters in their hands; this feature may have inspired the inscription held by the *Pilgrim*. Like David, van Eyck and his followers were active in Bruges, so it is quite possible that Massys saw these or other examples of Eyckian portraiture during youthful visits to that city. As in his religious pictures, Massys creatively combines a variety of pictorial sources to produce his own distinctive portrait forms.

The portrait is identified as a Jerusalem *Pilgrim* by the inscription and by the heraldic Jerusalem cross on the paper; however, the date of 1509 can as easily be taken as the date of the commemorated pilgrimage as it can the date of the panel (for which it is a *terminus post quem*). A few years later, Jan van Scorel painted five paintings of *Jerusalem Pilgrims* in Haarlem (1527–30; Friedländer 12, nos. 345–49), all of them lined up in a row in a narrow horizontal panel and each of them carrying a palm branch.

Cat. 54. *Old Man* (F. 51). Museum Jacquemart-Andre, Paris, no. 829, 1513 (48 × 37 cm.) Paper mounted on canvas; inscribed in upper left: "QUINTINUS METSYS / PINGEBAT ANNO 1513." *Plate 157*

HIST.: Ex-coll. d'Oultremont, Paris; coll. Jacquemart-Andre, Paris.

LIT.: Hymans, *Gazette des Beaux-Arts* XXVIII (1902): 82; M. J. Friedländer, *Repertorium für Kunstwissenschaft* 26 (1903), p. 155; Cohen, pp. 75f, 87; Bosschere, p. 107; Brising, p. 37; Conway, p. 320; Winkler, p. 203; Delen, p. 79; Friedländer, pp. 24, 65; Baldass, pp. 146, 149f, 166; Boon p. 43f; Friedländer, "Quentin Massys as a Painter of Genre Pictures," p. 116; Panofsky, *ENP*, p. 354f; Marlier, p. 223ff (introduction by L. Reis-Santos, xii); Mallé, p. 95; Broadley, p. 140ff; *De eeuw van Bruegel*, exh. cat., p. 131, no. 65; Puyvelde, p. 301; von der Osten, p. 151; Cuttler, p. 422; G. Kauffmann, *Die Kunst des 16. Jahrhunderts* (Berlin, 1970), p. 197f; Puyvelde 1970, p. 230; DB, pp. 244–46; Silver, "Power and Pelf," pp. 70-72.

This profile head can perhaps be identified as one of the "several monstrous and comical mugs" seen by Fornenbergh (p. 30) in the 17th century. Most of the scholarly discussion has involved the sources of the painting, which Baldass compares to the presumed *Robert des Masmines*, attributed to the Master of Flemalle. Boon cites its resemblance to remaining copies of a lost portrait of Philip the Bold, Duke of

Burgundy. Another possible model for the Old Man was a hypothetical Leonardo drawing, now lost, but intended as a Pl. 122 satirical grotesque like the *Old Woman*, which served as a model for Massys' London panel. Massys' later panel of the Pl. 123 *Old Man* drawing, made as pendant to the London *Old Woman* (F. 52, cat. 32), was engraved in the 17th century by Pl. 127 Wenzel Hollar, Parthey 1603, who thought that the two paintings were by Leonardo.

The da Vinci drawing, if it existed, was based, like the Jaquemart *Old Man*, on a 15th-century portrait medallion of Pl. 158 Cosimo de' Medici. A similar prototype inspired Pontormo's Pl. 159 posthumous portrait of *Cosimo* (Florence, Uffizi), which bears a striking resemblance to Massys' images. Massys, himself a designer of portrait medals (cf. Appendix A), would in all likelihood have been exposed to the *Cosimo* bronze.

Massys had used the same Cosimo prototype before 1513 Pl. 31 for one of the hideous Pharisees in *Christ among the Doctors* from the Seven Sorrows altarpiece (cat. 12). This repetition of the head suggests that the Jacquemart head lay very near to the artist's satirical grotesques of evil and ugliness, and it was only a few years afterward that Massys reused it, with added balustrade and hands, as a pendant to the London Pl. 122 *Grotesque Old Woman* (F. 52, cat. 32).

The Latin inscription of the *Old Man* is unique in Massys' *oeuvre*, other than a disputed work of 1529, *Christ Blessing* Pl. 72 (Madrid, Parado; cat. 49); because of its oddness, Delen rejects the signature entirely. Possibly this image was intended for an Italian or humanist patron who would have elicited the prominent, prideful letters laid down by Massys. The inscription appears to be genuine, inasmuch as the distinctive letters (S, T, E) tally with the inscriptions on bronze medals attributed to Massys (Appendix A). The medal of Cosimo could have inspired Massys' patron, in which case the figure would have to be regarded as a posthumous portrait, like the image of Pontormo. Reis-Santos hypothesizes further that Erasmus himself may have commissioned the work from Massys as a gift to the new Medici Pope Leo X. It seems unlikely from Erasmus's silence in his frequent correspondence that the humanist had contact with Quinten much before 1517; nevertheless, the concordance of the year 1513 and the Latin signature could point to an Italian audience for the work, which is also possible based on the unusual support of paper. It is even conceivable that Pontormo somehow borrowed the softer hat form from Massys' own image in Italy in addition to utilizing the 15th-century medal of Cosimo.

Stylistically, the painting accords with some of the carefully modeled, brownish-skinned old men of Massys' early maturity. Examples like the man directly above Christ in the Antwerp *Lamentation* or the Pharisee closest to the Child in *Christ among the Doctors* show the same meticulous detailing of features as the *Old Man*. Yet the shadows of the Jacquemart-Andre head have a delicate, almost transparent lightness that differs from the earlier works and bears comparison with a masterwork like the 1514 Louvre *Moneychanger* (F. 53, cat. 16; especially the hands) from the same period.

Cat. 55. *Man and Woman*. Badminton, coll. Lady Altrincham (31 x 25). Signed on paper in Man's hand: "Q. Matsys" (in script). *Plates 153–154*

HIST.: Christie's auction, 1863; ex-coll. Poyndor.

LIT.: DB, pp. 248–49.

Copy: *Man and Woman* (F. 170). Polesden Lacey, Surrey (33.1 x 26.4). Signed on paper in Man's hand: "Q. Matsys."

HIST.: Ascribed to Lord Braye coll.; Artemus Tooth; to Mrs. R. Greville, Polesden Lacey, 1934.

LIT.: Friedländer 7, p. 81; *Polesden Lacey Catalogue* (The National Trust, 1971), p. 21, no. 12.

These pendant portraits, originally united within a single frame, have a common green background, partly darkened with shadows like the Massys Oldenburg pendants (F. 49; Pl. 10 cat. 56) or the 1509 Winterthur *Pilgrim* (F. 38, cat. 53). Like Pl. 10 the Winterthur panel, the Altrincham figures cast shadows Pl. 13 onto the background, although this effect is exaggerated in the lighter green coloration of the Polesden Lacey copies. The form and shading of the *Man*, such as the cleft chin and its sharp shadow, resemble the Winterthur *Pilgrim* and the Oldenburg *Gillis*. From the religious works of Massys, the two sitters most closely resemble Joseph of Arimathea or Mary Magdalene from the Antwerp *Lamentation*. The Al- Pl. 20 trincham pendants also offer a delicacy of outline and execution quite like that of the Antwerp retable. They could, however, also be compared to the 1517 portraits of the Pl. 99 *Friendship Diptych* or the Karlsruhe *Man*. De Bosque, in Pl. 10 particular, sees the Altrincham portraits as close in time to the Radnor *Gillis*.

The signature of the artist is unique among Massys' portraits, along with the Latin block letters of the Paris *Old Man* Pl. 15 (F. 51, cat. 54), but it conforms closely with the signature in script on the 1514 Louvre *Moneychanger and his Wife* (F. 53, Pl. 11 cat. 16). Perhaps this dual portrait was an important one for Massys, a cause for pride that led him to sign the panel. The Altrincham panels are the first surviving portrait pair by the artist. The social position of these unknown sitters may also have occasioned artistic pride, for they both wear golden chains, emblems of honor (see J. Held, *Rembrandt's Aristotle and Other Rembrandt Studies* [Princeton, 1969], pp. 32–37; Z. Filipczak, "The Golden Chain in the Portraits of Rubens and Van Dyck," lecture, College Art Assn., 1978; S. Sullivan, "Rembrandt's Self-Portrait with a Dead Bittern," *Art Bulletin* 62 [1980]:238, n. 16–17). Within Massys' portraits, such prominent subjects are unusual (except for the New York *Wealthy Man*, F. 41, cat. 51), and this in itself could have Pl. 15 evoked a signature from the painter.

The Polesden Lacey portraits are extremely careful copies except for the lighter green of the background, and the meticulous rendition is extended even to the accurate replication of the signature.

Cat. 56. *Man and Woman* (F. 49, 50). Ca. 1514–15 (presumably portraits of Peter Gillis and Cornelia Sandrin), Oldenburg, Museum (33 x 28 each). *Plates 102, 103*

HIST.: Coll. W. Tischbein; 1804 coll. Duke P.F. Ludwig von Oldenburg.

LIT.: W. Bode, *Die Grossherzögliche Gemälde-Galerie zu Oldenburg* (Vienna, 1888), p. 81; F. Schmidt-Degener and A. Bredius, *Die Grossherzögliche Gemäldegalerie im Augusteum zu Oldenburg* (1906), p. 28; K. Schaefer, *Führer durch die Grossherzögliche Gemäldegalerie im Aug. zu Oldenburg* (1912), p. 6; Winkler, p. 206; Friedländer 7, p. 34; Baldass, p. 164; Mallé, p. 100; W. Müller-Wulckow, *Vier Bildnisse des Petrus Ägidius;* Oldenburg Museum catalogue (Oldenburg, 1966), p. 42; DB, p. 258.

Only in recent times have these pictures been attributed to Massys. In the early 19th century, Holbein was believed to be the artist; later, Bartel Bruyn. Most recently, Müller-Wulckow reascribed the works to Holbein. Her argument is as follows: the male portrait is Peter Gillis, *stadsgreffier* of Antwerp who was portrayed in a dual portrait with his
Pl. 100 friend Erasmus by Massys in 1517. Since he appears older than the 1517 version, the pair of portraits would date later in time, according to Müller-Wulckow. Since Gillis remarried in 1526 (his first marriage of 1514 predates the Friendship Diptych), the pendants would most likely have commemorated that event. Inasmuch as Hans Holbein visited Gillis (on Erasmus's introduction) in 1526, he would be the likeliest painter of the two sitters in that year.

The pendants, however, do not accord with any of Holbein's earlier portraits (i.e., before his first trip to England; see, for example, his early portrait of Erasmus in Gerlo). Yet their green background and strong lighting are characteris-
Pl. 138 tic of Massys' early efforts, such as the Winterthur *Pilgrim* (F.
Pl. 153 38, cat. 53) or the Badminton pendants (cat. 55). The
Pl. 154 arrangement of the two figures with the woman on the sinister side is consistent for both Oldenburg and Polesden Lacey pairs and, in each case, the stronger lighting falls on the head of the male, while the woman's face is lit evenly.

The Oldenburg panels are less schematic and dependent on models than Massys' earlier portraits. Quinten eliminates the half-length arrangement in order to concentrate on the figures' heads. By so doing, he achieves a closer contact with the observer, and his sitters' character is more directly communicated than in the more formal and distant Polesden Lacey couple.

The man's panel retains the contrast between light and dark areas, with strong light on one side of the face and his shadow cast upon the background. The woman's panel is uniformly lighted, and her face is delicately modeled and appears almost without shadows. These complementary lighting effects may also be observed in the painting technique for the two figures. The man's hair and fur collar are loosely painted, while everything about his wife appears smooth, in broad, almost flat surfaces. Such a contrast can also be observed in the 1514 Louvre *Moneychanger and his*
Pl. 118 *Wife* (F. 53, cat. 16) where the dark shading of the husband is counterbalanced by the smooth delicacy of his wife. And the refined, almost brittle features of the Louvre panel invite comparison with the Oldenburg *Pair*, which may then be dated around the middle of the decade.

Müller-Wulckow's identification of the Oldenburg *Man* as Peter Gillis is not without merit. His hair color, strong, slightly uptilted nose, and dimpled chin all agree with Massys' 1517 portrait. The more mature appearance of the sitter for the Oldenburg panel might be explained as a result of its close-up format and strong lighting and also as part of its formal commemorative character as a marriage portrait. According to the letters of Erasmus, Gillis was ill during the sitting for the *Friendship Diptych*, and this might have affected his appearance in the 1517 panel.

If the Massys portrait does represent Gillis, then the woman depicted is his first wife, Cornelia Sandrin, whom he married in August 1514. This marriage was commemorated by Erasmus in the colloquy *Epithalamium of Peter Gillis* (Chap. 6). Perhaps that marriage also led to Massys' double portrait in Oldenburg.

Cat. 57. *Man in Half-Length* (F. Add. 194). 1517, Karlsruhe, Staatliche Kunsthalle, no. 2458 (54.3 x 39.3). Inscribed: "Cosuelmo [Quintino?] de[?] Laro qui / Veretur[?] . . . egit[?] amn . . .[?] / Ano 1517 13 die Martij" *Plate 152*

HIST.: Formerly coll. Barons de Rothschild; purchase 1959.

LIT.: P. Wescher, "Des Erasmus Bildnisse von Jean Clouet and Quinten Massys," *Pantheon* 18 (1960): 242ff.; J. Lauts, *Staatliche Kunsthalle Karlsruhe Katalog Alte Meister bis 1800* (Karlsruhe, 1966), p. 180f; DB, pp. 247–48.

Like earlier Massys portraits (e.g., the Winterthur *Pilgrim* or Pl. 138
Oldenburg *Pair*), the Karlsruhe *Man* appears against a Pl. 102
green background, where he casts a shadow. The painting is Pl. 103
dated on a cartellino at the center. A novelty is the imitation marble balustrade to which the inscription is affixed; this has the effect of anchoring the sitter in space, between the parapet and the backdrop. Such a device first appears in the
inscribed stone balustrade of Jan van Eyck's "Timotheos" Pl. 136
(1432; London, National Gallery). Imitation marble frames are commonly found in Hans Memling's portraits (e.g., Florence, Uffizi *Young Man*).

In contrast to the Oldenburg *Man*, the Karlsruhe portrait has more subtle facial modeling, with mottled lighting and no harsh shadows. The paint texture has become thicker, although pinkish skin tones still resemble those of the Oldenburg *Woman*. Massys again paints the hair and the fur collar with a sense for texture, but the energetic brushstrokes and strong contrasts of the Oldenburg panel are missing, replaced by a new visual softness.

According to X-ray studies mentioned by de Bosque, the imitation marble balustrade was a later addition to the panel. But the 1517 date is consistent with both the panel's technique and costume.

Cat. 58. "Friendship Diptych" (F. 36–37). 1517.

A. *Desiderius Erasmus* (lost?). Hampton Court, no. 331 (50.3 × 45).

HIST.: Ex.-coll. Charles I of England.

Copies:

1. Replica: Palazzo Barberini, Rome (58.4 × 46).
   HIST.: Ex-coll. Stroganoff; Palazzo Corsini, Rome. *Plate 99*
2. Amsterdam. Rijksmuseum no. 1530 (39 × 27).
3. Coll. A.A. Azzoni (43 × 31.5).

B. *Peter Gillis* (Petrus Aegidius), Coll. Lord Radnor, Longford Castle (74.6 × 52.2).

HIST.: Purchase 1754; ex-coll. Dr. Mead; recorded 1648 in coll. King Charles I of England (Fickaert, p. 18: "Peter, with his friend Erasmus, 2 learned men / painted from life in two half ovals / joined together by Quinten Matsijs, to be seen with great admiration in the Cabinet of the King of England [Charles I]" *(Petrus, met sijnen vrint Erasmus, twee gheleerde mannen / naer het leven gheschildert zijn in twee half ovalen / by een ghevoeght van Quinten Matsijs, te sien met groote verwonderingh' in het Cabinet van den Coninck van Enghelant);* Charles II, 1667.

Replica: Antwerp, Koninklijk Museum, no 198 (59 × 46). *Plate 100*

Copy: Formerly Paris, Sedelmeyer auction 1907, no. 219 (57 × 41).

LIT.: H. Hymans, "Quinten Metsys et son portrait d'Erasme," *Bulletin des commissions royaux d'art et d'archeologie* 12 (1878): 616ff.; van den Branden, p. 75; Hymans, p. 208; Cohen, p. 85; Bosschere, p. 111; Brising, p. 37f.; G. Ring, *Beiträge zur Geschichte niederländische Bildnismalerei im 15. und 16. Jahrhunderte,* p. 17f.; Conway, pp. 319, 327; Winkler, p. 206; Friedländer 7, p. 23f.; Baldass, p. 170; A. Gerlo, "Erasme en Quinten Metsijs," *Revue belge d'archeologie et d'histoire de l'art* 14 (1944): 33ff.; Boon, p. 48f.; Benesch, p. 87f.; Marlier, p. 72ff.; Mallé, p. 99f.; E. Treu, *Die Bildnisse des Erasmus von Rotterdam,* (Basel, 1959), p. 22ff.; Broadley, pp. 68ff, 121ff., 190f.; J. Pope-Henessey, *The Portrait in the Renaissance,* p. 92ff.; Cuttler, pp. 418, 422; von der Osten, p. 150f.; Gerlo, p. 1ff.; E. Panofsky, "Erasmus and the Visual Arts," p. 214; *Erasmus en zijn tijd,* exh. cat., nos. 237–38; Puyvelde 1970, p. 229; DF, pp. 250–53; M. Mann Phillips, "The Mystery of the Massys Portrait," pp. 18–21; Trapp and Schulte-Herbrüggen, *Sir Thomas More,* pp. 41–42; Campbell, Phillips, Schulte-Herbrüggen, and Trapp, "Quentin Matsys, Desiderius Erasmus, Pieter Gillis, and Thomas More," pp. 716–24, with bibliography.

This double portrait, painted for Thomas More in 1517, probably remained in his collection until his arrest and execution in 1535. Whether they were kept by More's family or confiscated with his property by the Crown, they are reported to have been in the collection of King Charles I (see van den Branden; Broadley) by Isaac Bullart (1682) and later writers. Their trace disappeared until Lord Radnor's 18th-century purchase of the *Gillis.* The original *Erasmus* has not definitely been recovered (see below), although the Hampton Court image has a strong claim.

As a portrait pair, these pendants differ significantly from Massys' previous solid-color portrait backgrounds. The two panels depict a visually unified interior space that connects the pair, and each man is surrounded by work materials. The friends pause in their activity to discuss a letter from Thomas More. A very specific point in time is suggested by Erasmus's work-in-progress, his *Paraphrasis* on the Epistle to the Romans (1516–17).

In construction, the Erasmus-Gillis portraits recall the
Pl. 118 1514 Louvre *Moneychanger* (F. 53, cat. 16). The sitters appear at half-length behind a table whose front edge, with the same greenish cover and gold tacks, is visible in the foreground. At the rear of the interior is a bookshelf, filled with the items of daily activity for the persons portrayed: Erasmus's and other scholarly texts labeled with the names of classical authors. One further attribute—scissors—may refer to Erasmus's editing of texts; frequently, scissors are associated with depictions of the scholarly work of St. Jerome.

In format, the portraits recall a medieval tradition of "author portraits" frequently found as manuscript frontispieces. A 15th-century version of this idea is Petrus Christus'
Jerome in his Studio (Detroit), a working portrait of the *Pl. 101*
scholar-saint. Massys might have known a copy or adaptation of this work. In any case, the resonances with Jerome would have appealed especially to Erasmus, who had a special empathy with the holy editor (see Chap. 6). The
working cell of Erasmus and Gillis also recalls the Massys *St.* *Pl. 106*
Jerome (cat. 28) and the earlier Louvre *Moneychanger* (cat. *Pl. 118*
16).

The correspondence of Erasmus (see Gerlo) dates the panels to the period between 30 May and 8 September 1517. The pendant portraits were a gift of the Antwerp pair to their mutual friend, Thomas More, whose letter is reproduced in the *Gillis* panel. Erasmus's letters do not suggest any continuing intimacy between him and Massys, although the artist produced a portrait medal of the humanist in 1519
(Appendix A; Chap. 6). If the Oldenburg *Man* (cat. 56) can *Pl. 102*
actually be identified with Peter Gillis at the time of his first marriage (1515), Massys enjoyed a longer acquaintance with the Antwerp *stadsgreffier* and would have met Erasmus through his introduction. Certainly, the *Gillis* panel's greater sense of vitality and careful observation (compared with the *Erasmus*) may reflect Massys' greater familiarity with his hometown sitter. Furthermore, the existence of a high-
quality replica of the *Gillis* portrait (Antwerp, seemingly by *Pl. 100*
Massys himself) points to the importance for Quinten of Erasmus's lesser-known Antwerp friend.

The Radnor *Gillis* can be identified as the original Massys by More's description, for it is the only panel of high quality displaying More's handwriting on the letter in Gillis' hand: "Dear Peter, since our Quinten has expressed all so marvelously, what admirable imitation is he not capable of? For he has imitated the heading of my letter to you so well, that I could not do it again myself so faithfully . . . "

The Barberini *Erasmus* has also been called an original *Pl. 99*
Massys by most scholars, excepting Winkler, Brising, and Broadley. While of high quality, it differs from the Longford Castle *Gillis* in one important respect: it has no labels on the books depicted. Furthermore, More's description mentions that Erasmus writes his own name: "the identity of the first will be revealed to you by the letter which has been written to him; the other, to keep you from ignorance, writes his own name; yet, even if it were not revealed, the titles of the books . . . will be able to inform you who it is." Like the Antwerp *Gillis,* the Barberini *Erasmus* seems to be a replica by Massys himself.

The Hampton Court version, although seemingly inferior in quality, features titles of works by Erasmus on the volumes within the panel. And the inscription in the open book before Erasmus features his name—the only version of the *Erasmus* portrait that corresponds to More's description.

Therefore, the Massys original, either surviving or copied in the Hampton Court panel, once served as the pendant to Lord Radnor's *Gillis.* Quite possibly the Rome *Erasmus* and Antwerp *Gillis,* sharing similar dimensions and replica quality, are also pendants made for another of Erasmus's many friends throughout Europe. Detailed discussion of dimensions, historical provenance, and condition for these pictures is given in the 1978 *Burlington Magazine* article. The principal problem with the authenticity of the Hampton Court *Erasmus* remains the "rubbed" and undefined quality of the sitter's face, probably the result of damage or overcleaning (described by the 1978 authors as "worn, but relatively free of overpaint").

Cat. 59. *Young Man,* aged 20 (F. 76). Berlin-Dahlem, no. 574 (51 × 37). Inscribed on a letter in the sitter's hand: "Annum Agens 20." *Plate 180*

HIST.: Ex-coll. Soley, 1821.

LIT.: Friedländer 7, p. 69; *Beschreibendes Verzeichnis der Gemälde im Kaiser-Friedrich Museum und Deutschen Museum,* 9th ed. (Berlin, 1931), p. 284, no. 574.

Described by Friedländer as "done about 1520, close to the master in shape and expression of the head," this neglected portrait is a worthy original by Massys. Its subtle shading and overall unity tally with Friedländer's proposed date. Its pinkish skin tones and green background most closely resemble the 1517 Karlsruhe *Man* (F. 194, cat. 57), but there is l. 152 an even more meticulous rendering of the prosperous sitter's rich fur trim, velvet sleeves, and hair (foreshadowing the great Frankfurt portrait, F. 46, cat. 61). l. 146 There are visible *pentimenti* in the hat.

Cat. 60. Portrait Diptych, ca. 1519–20.

A. *Woman in Prayer* (F. 48). New York, Metropolitan Museum, no. 32.100.47 (48.3 × 43.2). *Plate 140*

HIST.: Ex-coll. J. Goudstikker, Amsterdam; F. Kleinberger, New York; M. Friedsam, New York.

B. *Man* (F. 169). Schloss Au (Switzerland, coll. Mrs. H. von Schulthess-Bodmer.

HIST.: Ex-coll. Lenbach, Munich; Bodmer Coll., Zurich.

LIT.: M.J. Friedländer, *Repertorium fur Kunstwissenschaft* 24 (1901), p. 323; idem, "Bildnisse von Quentin Massys," p. 171; Friedländer 7, pp. 35, 65, 81; *Metropolitan Museum of Art Bulletin* 27 (1932): 28, no. 39; Baldass, p. 163; Boon, p. 51; Wehle and Salinger, *Catalogue of Early Flemish, Dutch, and German Paintings,* p. 107; Mallé, p. 101; Cuttler, p. 422; von der Osten, p. 151; DB, p. 254.

General consensus dates these portraits around (or shortly after) 1520; an exception is Cuttler, who dates the New York *Woman* ca. 1510–15 and compares it to the 1509 Winterthur l. 138 *Pilgrim* (F. 38, cat. 53).

The *Woman* continues the brown tonalities and the active movement of the 1517 portraits; the pendant *Man* shares the same arch framework. Both pictures are flanked by two marble columns with capitals, surmounted by imitation carvings of acanthus ornament. The same leafy decoration Pl. 37 occurs on the central panel of the *Rem altarpiece* (Munich, F. 3, cat. 24); more meticulously painted, it appears a few years Pl. 63 later on the arms of the throne of the Berlin *Madonna Enthroned* (F. 18, cat. 37). The whitish skin tonalities of the New York *Woman* also link the portrait to the Virgin of the *Rem* altar.

Comparison of the *Man* and *Woman in Prayer* with the Pl. 102 Oldenburg pendants reveals just how much Massy's portrai- Pl. 103 ture has become enlivened. He still uses the same device of casting stronger light on the male partner and setting off the woman's head by means of her cap. But by introducing their hands, Massys animates the pictures and gives the suggestion of movement to his subjects. The quality is heightened by the momentary gesture and glance of the *Woman in Prayer.* Like the Winterthur *Pilgrim,* she glances to the side, out of the picture space; but, holding her place in an attractive prayerbook, she appears to be distracted only temporarily from concentration. The cap of the New York *Woman* suggests a date between 1515 and 1520, without the archaic chin covering of the Oldenburg *Woman* yet not as abbreviated as the modish headgear of the 1520 Joos van Cleve *Woman with Rosary* (Florence, Uffizi).

Also indicative of the period of origin is the two portraits' new architectural framework. The Schloss Au *Man* incorporates a marble balustrade across the bottom of the panel along with marble columns within the frame. Another dual portrait/marble frame format appears around the same time in the grotesque portrait *Pair* (F. 52, cat. 32; London Pl. 122 *Old Woman; Old Man*). Pl. 123

Although he interpreted the invention in quite an original fashion, Massys developed the idea of dual portraits with columns from the works of Memling. The *Moreel Portraits* Pl. 141 (Brussels, Museés Royaux) show the sitters between Pl. 142 columns, facing each other in prayer; a landscape is visible over a balustrade in the background. Memling also shows a *Praying Youth* (London, National Gallery) situated with his prayerbook between two columns.

In general, the appearance and execution of the Bodmer *Man* can be compared to the 1517 Karlsruhe *Man* (F. 194, Pl. 152 cat. 57), but his face is even more delicately and evenly modeled, with no dark shadows. Drawing of facial features has been especially meticulous for this portrait pair.

Like the Badminton and Oldenburg portrait pendants, the Bodmer/New York duet are placed with the wife on the *sinister* side and the husband facing her. With a bold new informality, Massys shows the woman glancing out of the frame, turned even more emphatically away from the viewer than the Winterthur *Pilgrim* (F. 38, cat. 53). Furthermore, the architectural framing devices of both marble columns at the side and acanthus stone scrollwork above the figures is an experimental step further than the recent marble balustrade of the Karlsruhe *Man.*

Cat. 61. *Scholar (Man Reading;* perhaps a Portrait of Cornelius Grapheus) (F. 46). Ca. 1520–22, Frankfurt, Staedel Kunstinstitut, no. 113 (69 × 53). *Plate 146*

HIST.: Acquired in 1829; formerly in 17th-century Antwerp collection of Cornelis van der Geest (see gallery panel by Willem van Haecht; Antwerp, Rubenshuis; 1628). Pl. 181

LIT.: Hymans, p. 212; Cohen, p. 84; Bosschere, p. 111; Brising, p. 37; G. Ring, *Beiträge zur Geschichte niederländische Bildnismalerei im 15. und 16. Jahrhunderte,* p. 13ff; Conway, p. 319; Winkler, p. 206; Friedländer 7, p. 35;

Baldass, pp. 156, 173; Boon, p. 52; Mallé, p. 102; Broadley, pp. 99ff, 188f; von der Osten, p. 150; DB, pp. 262–65.

This energetic portrait represents a number of innovations by Massys. Both the momentary gesture and strong glance out of the frame suggest a frozen action and a lively character. In the background, visible through an arcade, is a panoramic landscape with a tall tree and distant vista at the left and a cliffside fortress at the right. The broad view of the landscape, together with the carefully painted foliage, derives from Patinir, with whom Massys collaborated on a *Temptation of St. Anthony* (Madrid, Prado, F. 31, cat. 26). The combination of architecture and landscape with a portrait was the invention of Hans Memling, who had influenced the recent Massys dual portraits (F. 48/169, cat. 60). *Pl. 114* *Pl. 141* *Pl. 140*

There is no precedent anywhere in portraiture for this suddenness and force from a sitter. The Frankfurt panel reveals just how much Massys was striving to reveal individuality through action and setting. Just what is the landscape of Massys' Frankfurt portrait meant to express? The two halves of the pictures are contrasted; one is dominated by a mighty cliffside fortress, while the second contains a gentle, expansive river valley. Perhaps the two sections are meant to convey a dual nature of the sitter. His active gesture contrasts his contemplative nature, which is revealed by his open book and reading glasses.

The distinctive head of the Frankfurt *Man Reading* identifies him as Peter Gillis's close friend and associate Cornelius Grapheus (d. 1558), an Antwerp city secretary, Latin scholar, and member of local humanist circles (Graephus and Gillis together composed the tributes for the city's 1520 reception of the young Charles V). Dürer sketched him and befriended Grapheus during his visit to Antwerp in 1521. Unfortunately, the drawing cannot be identified, though a lost charcoal portrait (formerly Weimar, Schlossmuseum, W811) of an unknown sitter looks impressively like Massys' *Pl. 147* Frankfurt *Scholar* and could well be Grapheus himself. The principal portrait of Grapheus shows him as an older man, bearded according to a fashion introduced by Charles V in the 1530s; it was published as an engraving by P. Galle for *Pl. 148* the 1572 volume *Virorum doctorum Effigies*. But in spite of the beard and the passage of more than a decade, the engraving shows the same prominent nose, fleshy lower lip, and powerful massive head as the Frankfurt *Man Reading*.

Massys' portrait must have been painted before a major misfortune in Grapheus's career. Strongly attracted by Erasmus's suggestions for Church reform, Grapheus published his own zealous ideas as the preface to a book, *De Libertate Christiana* by Johann van Goch. On 22 April 1522, Grapheus was forced to recant his ideas publicly in the Antwerp cathedral in the wake of a strong reaction against "Lutheran" sympathizers. Eventually, he returned to Antwerp and again became city secretary and the designer of future civic pageants. But his portrait by Massys could not have been possible after the 1522 stigma of heresy. From the clothing and the features of Massys' style, the portrait was painted at the height of Grapheus's fame, ca. 1520-22. The distinctive cap with tied side flaps was a brief but very popular style of those years, recorded by Dürer during his trip to the Lowlands and by other portraits, such as the drawing of Lucas van Leyden (W. 816 Lille, Musée Wicar) from 1521. (For Netherlandish fashions, see J. H. der Kinderen-Besier, *Mode-Metamorphosen* [Amsterdam, 1933], 71ff; and de Jonge, "Bijdrage tot de Kennis van de Kleedracht in de Nederlanden in de XVIe Eeuw.")

The Frankfurt portrait is a skillful combination of previous portrait elements. The glance out of the frame appeared as early as 1509 in the Winterthur *Pilgrim* (F. 38, cat. 53) and the New York *Woman in Prayer* (F. 48, cat. 60). Both the *Erasmus* (1517; F. 36, cat. 58) and the *Woman in Prayer* contain characters with open books. The portrait of Peter Gillis also involves an active personality who interrupts his reading and looks away; however, unlike the *Gillis*, no pendant is known for the Frankfurt *Man Reading*.

This portrait agrees with stylistic features of Massys during the early 1520s. The pink skin tonalities with white highlights accord with foreground tormentors in the Prado *Pl. 86* *Ecce Homo* (F. 10, cat. 31) with the *Rem altarpiece* figures (F. 3, *Pl. 37* cat. 24), and with the portrait in Berlin (F. 76, cat. 59). *Pl. 18* Furthermore, the Patiniresque landscape suggests a date in the early 1520s—around the time of the Prado *Anthony* collaboration. Therefore, in its dating, the Frankfurt portrait complies with the historical requirements of its sitter's biography.

Cat. 62. *Christian II of Denmark* (F. 172). Kroměrice (Moravia), Episcopal Museum. (57 × 40 cm original measurements, enlarged to 73 × 51.5 cm)*Plate 155*

HIST.: Cited in Kremsier inventory by 1680 (by 1670 according to Broadley, p. 94, n. 2).

LIT.: A. Breitenbacher, *Dějiny arcibiskupské obrazárny a Koměriži* (Kremsier, 1925), App. xxi; Friedländer 7, p. 81; idem, "Bildnisse des Dänenkönigs Christian II," p. 96f; G. Glück, "Portraetter af Christian II og Hans Hustru Isabella," p. 15f; Boon, p. 50; Broadley, p. 93ff; DB, pp. 254–56.

During King Christian's 1521 visit to Antwerp, he ordered his portrait painted by Massys. A document records the payment from the king's chancellor to the Amsterdam banker Occo: "Meer betalt Mester Quinten de maeler t'Antwerpen van myns g.h.k. Ansicht the conterfeyten, als ick anders niet weet, 20 gulden" (Glück; also cited by Broadley, p. 93, n. 1). The figure, except for the Golden Fleece emblem on his neck which dates the picture after 1519, does not appear to be a monarch. Compared with the recent Frankfurt *Grapheus* portrait (F. 46, cat. 61), the king's hands *Pl. 14* are strikingly still; they repose on a tabletop, arranged as in the *Gillis* portrait of 1517 (F. 37, cat. 58). Nor is there a *Pl. 10* suggestive environment to identify the sitter or present his character—only an undifferentiated dark background. Except for the table, this portrait has an isolated concentration on the sitter like the earliest portraits (e.g., Chicago *Man*, F. *Pl. 14* 47, cat. 52) and the recent Berlin *Man* (F. 76, cat. 59). *Pl. 18* Christian II was a monarch who sought out artists, including Gossaert, Dürer, Cranach, Sittow, van Orley, and Jacob Cornelisz. (see Friedländer, 1938). Therefore, Massys' only royal portrait commission does not necessarily imply court connections, and it is significant that the portrait has a definite nonceremonial quality.

Cat. 63. *Man* (F. 171). 1527, Windsor Castle (18½ × 13¾ inches). Inscribed on paper in hand: "ANNO 1527" (also read as "1537" or "1521"). *Plate 182*

HIST.: In Royal collection by 1697; inventory of James II, Kensington; possibly the "Head to the Wast [sic] donne by ould Quinten," in the ca. 1624 inventory of Charles I.

LIT.: Friedländer 7, p. 81; C. H. C. Baker, *Catalogue of the Principal Pictures in the Royal Collection at Windsor Castle* (London, 1937), p. 235; Boon, p. 50; L. Cambell (correspondence, 1979); based on forthcoming catalogue of English royal collection.

This portrait, whose date has been read incorrectly as 1537 by Baker, marks a reversal from Massys' more-daring portraits with landscape or architecture of the 1520s (New York, *Pl. 140* Frankfurt, Edinburgh; cat. nos. 60, 61, 64). Instead, it *Pl. 145* follows the neutral dark background, the oblique stare, and *Pl. 146* the hand with attributes of Roger van der Weyden's por- *Pl. 150* traits or Gerard David's Vienna *Goldsmith.* Massys had al- *Pl. 149* ready used this portrait format in his Chicago *Man with a* *Pl. 153* *Flower* (F. 47, cat. 52) and the Badminton *Pair* (cat. 55); more *Pl. 154* recently, the 1521 portrait of *Christian II* (F. 172, cat. 62) *Pl. 155* resumed this presentation, introducing a tabletop foreground. Such a conservative portrait was perhaps the result of a request by Massys' sober-looking patron, because he painted another portrait with landscape at about the same *Pl. 143* time (Vaduz *Canon,* F. 39, cat. 65). The smaller scale may also have limited the artist's inventiveness. In the late 18th century (George III inventory of 1778; see Baker), the sitter was identified as being Dr. Thomas Linacre, but there is no evidence to support this claim (see F. Maddison, M. Pelling, C. Webster, eds., *Essays on the Life and Work of Thomas Linacre* [Oxford, 1977]).

The picture surface appears to be "rubbed" or overcleaned, particularly the areas of hands and hair. Nevertheless, carefully modeled brows, jaw, and hands recall details *Pl. 79* (e.g., the black magus) of the 1526 New York *Adoration* (F. 8, *Pl. 87* cat. 40) or the Christ of the Venice *Ecce Homo* (F. 11, cat. 46). There is no comparable late portrait in Massys' *corpus.* Possibly the more traditional portraits by Joos van Cleve (Friedländer 9, nos. 74–107) also helped shape this late Massys work.

The costume is close to that of the Edinburgh *Notary* and helps to confirm the date inscribed on the panel.

Cat. 64. *Notary* (F. 45). Edinburgh, National Gallery of Scotland, no. 2273 (80 × 64.5). *Plate 145*

HIST.: Ex-coll. Spencer-Churchill, Northwick Park; museum acquisition 1965.

LIT.: Conway, p. 327; Friedländer 7, p. 35; Baldass, p. 173; Boon, p. 52; Mallé, p. 101; Broadley, p. 97ff; Robbins, p. 67; DB, p. 262.

The portrait shows a man with writing implements, seal, and wax—the paraphernalia of a notary. In his hand he holds quill pen, rose, and cross, indicating perhaps that he served within one of Antwerp's religious confraternities. The Brotherhood of the Holy Cross, for example, traditionally included as its treasurer one of the city's secretaries (Prims, p. 123f.), and its dozen members were generally members of Antwerp's "spiritual or worldly aristocracy." Massys could have known one of the city's secretaries through Peter Gillis, if not on his own.

Broadly has identified the accessories of the *Notary* as those of St. Fiacre, but the only saint by this name was a patron of gardeners, rather than scribes. In all probability, the halo around the sitter's head is a later addition.

Tiny details of the background reveal peasant activities—milking, chopping, and dancing. Their meaning is unclear; perhaps they are analogous to the urban vigor of the sitter or a reference to his country origins. Perhaps they were intended only as staffage to fill the landscape. Whatever their meaning, these scenes are precedents for the work of Peter Bruegel two generations later.

The idyllic broad landscape creates a harmony between sitter and setting that Panofsky (*ENP,* p. 316f) calls a "Stimmungsporträt." The soft green colors recall the background of the Berlin *Madonna Enthroned* (F. 18, cat. 37), although *Pl. 63* there is a firmer sense of structure in the Edinburgh panel. This quality is reinforced by the tightly integrated architecture, whose three rounded arches echo the cap and brows of the sitter as well as the tripartite background valley.

In addition to the landscape elements, the rounded, reddish, deeply modeled face of the *Notary* relates him to the middle magus of the 1526 New York *Adoration* (F. 8, cat. 40) *Pl. 79* and helps to date the picture.

Cat. 65. *Canon* (F. 39). Vaduz, Liechtenstein Coll. (74 × 60 cm.). *Plate 143*

HIST.: Purchased in Paris 1889; ex-coll. J. W. Wilson, Paris.

LIT.: Cohen, pp. 74f., 90; Bosschere, p. 106; Brising, p. 36 n. 2; G. Ring, *Beiträge zur Geschichte niederländischer Bildnismalerei im 15. und 16. Jahrhundert,* p. 50; Conway, p. 319; Winkler, p. 206; Delen, p. 78; A. Kronfeld, *Führer durch die Fürstlich Liechtensteinsche Gemäldegalerie in Wien,* (Vienna, 1927), p. 189f., no. 927; Friedländer 7, pp. 34, 64; Baldass, pp. 156, 173; Boon, p. 52; Benesch, p. 89; Mallé, p. 101; Broadley, pp. 103ff., 124; Cuttler, p. 422; Puyvelde 1970, p. 231; Robbins, p. 65; DB, p. 260.

The Vaduz *Canon* was previously attributed to Hans Holbein, as were so many other Northern portraits during the 19th century (see also the Oldenburg pendants, F. 49, 50, *Pl. 102* cat. 56). It also was erroneously identified as a portrait of the *Pl. 103* Grand Chancellor of England and Bishop of Winchester, Stephen Gardiner. When it was correctly reattributed to Massys, this label also fell away.

Like the Frankfurt *Grapheus* portrait (F. 46, cat. 61), the *Pl. 146* Vaduz *Canon* displays scholarly attributes with the spectacles and book in his hands; in addition, his headdress is an academic *biretta.* Although the name of Massys' sitter is unknown, one candidate is the brother of Peter Gillis: Nicolai Claesz. (Egidius). Nicolai was the only Antwerp canon during Massys' later years who was also a doctor of theology and entitled to wear a *biretta* (see Chap. 8).

The rolling landscape background has been compared by many authors with Italian paintings, such as Perugino's 1494 *Francesco delle Opere* (Uffizi) or Andrea Solario's 1505 *Senator* (London). While similar Italian creations may have reinforced Massys' own ideas, he need not have turned only to foreign sources for inspiration. A local tradition, founded by Memling, favored placing sitters before unbroken landscape backdrops. These paintings, which were popular among the Italian community of Bruges (many are now in Italian museums—e.g., Uffizi *Young Man* or *Man with a Cap*, Palazzo Vecchio) probably influenced the Italian portrait forms of Perugino and Solario (see J. Pope-Hennessy, *The Portrait in the Renaissance*, p. 60, n. 85), just as it influenced the Massys *Canon* two decades later. *Pl. 144*

Massys' Vaduz *Canon* should be placed among his latest works. Its firmly shaded, regular brows grow out of forms like the central magus of the New York *Adoration* of 1526 (F. 8, cat. 40), yet it has a harmony of cool colors characteristic of later works (e.g., *Rattier Madonna*, 1529, F. 24, cat. 48). The soft blue sky, punctuated by thinly painted clouds amid atmospheric haze, may be compared with the Venice *Ecce Homo* (F. 11, cat. 46). Such spindly trees in the background appeared almost a decade earlier in works like the Rotterdam *Madonna* (F. 168, cat. 27), but the gentle rolling landscape resembles more recent works like the Edinburgh *Notary* (F. 45, cat. 64) or the Detroit *Madonna Outdoors* (F. 23, cat. 42). Unlike these precedents, the Vaduz landscape has no hilly terrain to disturb its calm. Its tranquility suggests an analogue to the stable pyramidal composition of the sitter's body and provides a connotation of spiritual peacefulness akin to prayerfulness (see Chap. 8) for the donor. *Pl. 79* *Pl. 68* *Pl. 87* *Pl. 65* *Pl. 145* *Pl. 64*

DOCUMENTED LOST WORKS

1. *Crucifixion*, Antwerp Cathedral, destroyed in 1566 iconoclastic riots. "They also destroyed many artistic and precious paintings by various outstanding masters such as the *Crucifixion* by Quinten, the *Ascension of our Lady* above the high altar by Frans Floris, that of the Holy Name of Jesus, and many others." F.G.V., *Antwerpsch Chronijkje sedert den jare 1500 tot het jaar 1574* (Leyden, 1743), p. 88; quoted by D. Freedberg, "Iconoclasm and Painting in the Netherlands 1566–1609" (Ph.D. dissertation, Oxford University, 1972), p. 118; also Bosschere, p. 103 n. 1; Delen, p. 71; Broadley, p. 52 n. 2.
2. *Crucifixion altarpiece*, Nossa Senhora de Vareza (Alenquer)—see Chapter 4. Commissioned by Damião de Gois, Portuguese factor in Antwerp (1523–45); documented during a heresy trial (1571). "A retable with wings on which is painted a Crucifixion made by Master Quinten and valued at more than one hundred *cruzados* because of its great perfection." J. de Figueiredo, "Metsys et le Portugal," *Revue belge d'archeologie et d'histoire de l'art* 3 (1933):9.
3. *Self-Portrait* for Antwerp St. Luke guild; removed to France in 1794 (according to the list of Odevaere) and lost afterward.

   LIT.: Hymans, p. 18; van den Branden, p. 76; J. van Nieuwenhuizen, "Antwerpsche schilderijen te Paris," *Antwerpen* 8 (1962): 81.
4. Grisaille frescoes in Massys' house, "St. Quinten," Schuttershofstraat. Described by van Fornenbergh, 1658, p. 29f. The decorative program featured foliate ornament, including motifs of putti and swags. Beside the door to the courtyard were imperial columns and the "Plus Oultre" slogan of Charles V on two pennants. Van Fornenbergh also mentions a gallery with four flute players, but this had already been "spoiled" with extensive damage by the 17th century.
5. Four figures around a table playing cards (Fornenbergh, p. 27f): "The third is a piece of four figures, two men and two women, who are around a table playing a foreign game, known mostly in Poland and Germany and called Krimpen. It is played with two cards." Possibly one of several works by Lucas van Leyden, although van Fornenbergh had extensive contact with authentic Massys works.
6. *Altarpiece of the Lamentation*, Oratory of Albrecht and Isabella (van Fornenbergh, p. 28f). The centerpiece featured a Lamentation. One wing showed St. Agnes as shepherdess with straw hat and crook staff before a background landscape; on the other wing, St. Barbara stood beside her tower. According to van Fornenbergh, the altarpiece was in damaged condition, and it was sold in 1651-52 to Thomas Lopes, Baron de Lemale (see M. Smeyers, "Schilderijen van Kwinten Metsys in het Bezit der Aartshertogen Albrecht en Isabella," *Miscellanea Josef Duverger* vol. 1 [Ghent, 1968], p. 139ff).
7. *St. Luke Painting the Virgin*. Painted for the Antwerp St. Luke guild; replaced in 1602 by Marten de Vos. If the replacement indicates the loss of Massys' panel, then it cannot be identified with a November 1653 inventory listing of the Antwerp merchant, Pompeo Petrobelli: "van Meester Quinten . . . een schilderye van Sinte Lucas conterfeytende Onse Lieve Vrouwe" (cited by van den Branden). An engraving of *St. Luke and the Virgin* by A. Wierix (1559-1624) bears the inscription "N. Quintin Mazzys, inventor." L. Reis-Santos discovered a painting, now in the Lisbon Museum (no. 1459; 104 × 62.5) and a drawing (Rotterdam, Museum Boymans-van Beuningen; 20 × 12.5) that replicate the figure of St. Luke preserved in Wierix's engraving. The precise hatching of the drawing indicates its affinities with van der Goes, as both Winkler (1964) and Reis-Santos have contended. The painting, however, is by an unknown copyist, although Reis-Santos believes it, too, to be a van der Goes original. The group of Virgin and Child, preserved only in the engraving, is characteristically Goesian, with no trace of Massys. The round-faced Madonna and the informal, energetic Child closely resemble Hugo originals like the Frankfurt *Virgin and Child* or the central figures of the Berlin *Nativity* (Friedländer 4, nos. 5, 15). The Wierix inscription, therefore, is erroneous, and the painting he copied cannot be equated with the Massys original cited in documents.

LIT.: Alvin, *Catalogue raisonné de l'oeuvre des freres Jean et Antoine Wierix* (Brussels 1966), no. 484; van den Branden, p. 80; Hymans, p. 20; Cohen, p. 10ff; Bosschere, p. 34f; Brising, p. 16f; Winkler, p. 196; Delen, p. 48ff; Friedländer 7, p. 88 (editor's note); Baldass, p. 160; L. Reis-Santos, "A Lost Work of Massys and a Hitherto Unknown van der Goes," p. 162ff; Boon, p. 16; Mallé, p. 81; Reis-Santos, p. 61f; F. Winkler, *Das Werk des Hugo van der Goes* (Berlin, 1964), p. 221ff.; H. Pauwels, "Naar aanleiding van een gravure naar Quinten Metsys," pp. 248-62.

SUPPLEMENT: DOUBTFUL ATTRIBUTIONS

Supp. A. *Christ on the Cross with Virgin, St. John, and Donors.* London, Seilern Coll. no. 295 (50 × 34.5).
Plate 90

HIST.: Coll. Lippmann, Berlin; 1912 coll. Liechtenstein, Vienna.

LIT.: A. Kronfeld, *Führer durch die Fürstlich Liechtensteinssche Gemäldegalerie* (Vienna, 1931), p. 189, no. 133; O. Benesch, "Ein Frühwerk von Gerard David," p. 154f; A. Seilern, *Flemish Paintings and Drawings Addenda* (London, 1969), p. 3f; DB, pp. 135–36.

This painting, if by Massys, would be one of the earliest of his pictures. The carefully modeled donors have the fine features, dot eyes, and hazy hair caps of the music-playing *Pl. 38* angels from the London *Madonna* (cat. 1). Furthermore, the frontal Madonna of the Seilern panel exactly repeats the features of Massys' medal of *Cristina Metsys* (1491; Antwerp, Museum Mayer van den Bergh; see Appendix A). Although unlike the ponderous form of the London Virgin, the slender Seilern Madonna has the same stiffness of pose and an analogous rigidity in her hands and fingers.

The difficulty in accepting this picture lies in its uniqueness. Because Massys' remaining *Crucifixion* panels are much *Pl. 91* later in date (e.g., Ottawa, F. 12, cat. 20), there are no early adult Christ figures for comparison. Similarly, the earliest landscapes appear only as corner traces within larger com- *l. 40* positions, e.g., the gabled buildings visible through the *l. 41* window of the *Madonna and Child with Book* (lost; cat. 2) or *l. 39* the fleecy clouds at the top of the Brussels *Madonna in Half-length* (F. 20, cat. 3). The *Seilern Crucifixion* also appears to be slightly abraded in the areas of the background landscape, and the fanciful clouds and rooftops differ from the comparisons cited above. These, however, can be explained away as youthful experiments not repeated later; thus, the panel could be regarded as a possible Massys.

Supp. B. *Portrait of a Man* (F. 40). Present location unknown.

HIST.: Formerly coll. Hahn, Berlin; formerly Austrian coll.

LIT.: Friedländer, "Bildnisse von Quentin Massys," p. 171; Friedländer 7, p. 34; Baldass, p. 163 n. 38; Mallé, p. 89.

The present location of this picture is not known. Its solid blue background relies on Rogerian portrait models (see Chap. 8).

The closest comparison is Massys' Chicago *Man with a* *149* *Flower* (F. 47, cat. 52), which, however, is painted solely in harmonious brown tones, whereas the Hahn picture features a red hat. The crisp handling of details (eyes, mouth) *l. 20* associate this panel with the 1508–11 *John altarpiece* and with *153* other ca. 1510 portraits like the Badminton *Man* (cat. 55) *138* and the Winterthur *Pilgrim* (F. 38, cat. 53). This painting is listed here as "doubtful" only because I have seen neither the original nor a modern color reproduction.

Supp. C. *Portrait of a Mature Man* (F. 43). Sale, Parke-Bernet, New York (14 March 1951; 49 × 36).

HIST.: Ex-coll. Semmel, Berlin 1929; Simon Coll., Berlin.

LIT.: Friedländer 7, p. 34; Baldass, p. 173 n. 63; Richardson, p. 170; J. Held, "Alterations and Mutilations of Works of Art," *South Atlantic Quarterly* 63 (1963): ills. 39–41.

The older photographs of this portrait suggest that it shares the warm brown tonalities and mild chiaroscuro of the *Erasmus* and *Gillis* portraits (1517; F. 36/37, cat. 58). Rich- *Pl. 99* ardson, however, dates it to the late 1520s because of its *Pl. 100* sobriety and close awareness of the sitter—subjective criteria at best but also inconsistent with the calm distance of the 1527 Windsor *Man* (F. 171, cat. 63). The Semmel portrait is *Pl. 180* closest in type to the Barcelona *Saint* (F. 30, cat. 33) of *Pl. 177* around the same time as the *Erasmus* portrait. According to Held, the picture has been greatly altered since it was last discussed in print. I regard it as probably authentic but must reserve conclusive judgment because I know the picture only through old photographs.

Supp. D. *Madonna and Child Outdoors* (F. 19). Poznan, Nationalmuseum, no. Mo 114 (111 × 87).

HIST.: Ex-coll. Raczynski; 18th-century coll. Pfinzinger, Nuremburg; coll. H. von Hallerstein, Nuremburg; 1820 A. Raczynski.

LIT.: A Raczynski, *Katalog der Raczynskischen Bildersammlung* (Berlin, 1841), no. 13; Cohen, p. 61, 80; Bosschere, p. 128f; G. Cagnola, "Note intorno a quadri italiani in una galleria tedesca," *Rassegna d'Arte* 12 (1913): 1ff; Conway, p. 318; W. Suida, *Leonardo und sein Kreis,* p. 258; Friedländer 7, p. 25; G. Glück, "Zwei unveröffentlichte Gemälde von Quinten Metsys," p. 84ff; Baldass, pp. 157, 158, 171; C. van Wetering, *Die Entwicklung der niederländischen Landschaftsmalerei vom Anfang des XVI. Jahrhunderts bis zur Jahrhundertmitte* (Berlin, 1938), p. 56; Boon, p. 44; J. Bialostocki, "Leonardo i Nederlandczycy," *Biuletyn Historii Sztuki* 17 (1955): 369ff; idem, "Poznanskie Leonardianum Vwagi o Manonnie Quentina Massysa w Muzeum Naradowym w Poznaniu," *Studia Muzealne* 2 (1957): 127ff; idem and M. Walicki, *Europäische Malerei in Polnischen Sammlungen,* p. 497f, no. 128; Broadley, p. 148ff; Puyvelde, p. 195; R. Koch, *Joachim Patinir,* p. 55, n. 24; Callatay, pp. 56–58; Cuttler, p. 421; von der Osten, p. 149; Puyvelde 1970, p. 226; Robbins, p. 48ff.; B.L. Dunbar, "The Landscape Art of Cornelis Massys," pp. 1972, 148ff.; DB, p. 218ff.; Dunbar, "The Question of Cornelis Massy's Landscape Collaboration with Quinten and Jan Massys, "*Antwerp Jaarboek* (1979), p. 129f.

The Poznan picture has generally been accepted as a Massys, although many see in the landscape the work of a collaborator, specifically Patinir. As the *corpus* of Patinir has become better known, certain atmospheric elements and the blended color harmonies argue against his authorship. Koch says that the picture is in Patinir's most mature landscape formula (i.e., 1520–24) but the product of a follower. Such a follower, who also drew upon the atmosphere and colors of Quinten, was Cornelis Massys (see the 1538 *Return of the Prodigal Son,* Amsterdam); van de Wetering and von der Osten assign the landscape to Cornelis. Dunbar, a specialist on Cornelis, demurs, comparing the forms to other Massys followers, such as the Master of the Mansi Magdalene.

Many authors have pointed out the picture's relationship to the figures of Leonardo's *Virgin, Child, and St. Anne* (Paris, Louvre), although Bialostocki indicates properly that the direct source was probably a work by a Leonardo follower. Such a copy, omitting St. Anne, appears in the Poldi-Pezzoli Museum, Milan. Its isolated Virgin has much the same weightlessness as the Poznan picture.

If Massys drew directly on Leonardo's Madonna, it would be one more example of his use of the Italian master (see Chap. 2), but the principal borrowings are from grotesque drawings, not Madonna images (an exception might be the
Pl. 69 Chatsworth *Embracing Infants,* cat. 34). Leonardo's Madonna and Child imagery was more popular in the circle of Joos van Cleve.

Close inspection makes more doubtful the attribution of the Poznan picture to Massys. The small grins on the faces of both Madonna and Child are wholly uncharacteristic of Quinten's characters (excepting only the Detroit *Madonna*
Pl. 64 *Outdoors,* F. 23, cat. 42, which has a more-intense gaze by both characters than in the Poznan work). Furthermore, the pinkish skin tones and tangerine skirt of the Virgin are unique to the Poznan picture. Again, the closest analogy is Cornelis Massys' *Prodigal Son,* where the standing frontal figure has the same facial smirk. Cornelis Massys is the leading candidate for authorship of the Poznan picture, although his early *oeuvre* is uncertain.

Supp. E. *"Paracelsus"—Portrait of a Man before a Landscape* (lost, F. 78).

Copies: Paris, Louvre, no. 2567a) (72 × 55). Inscribed: "FAMOSO DOCTOR PARACELSUS."
Brussels, Musées Royaux no. 388 (77 × 54)—Rubens. *Plate 183*

HIST.: In 17th-century coll. Cornelis van der Geest, Antwerp, according to the gallery painting by Willem van Haecht (1628; Antwerp, Rubenshuis), although the painting depicted is possibly the Rubens copy.

LIT.: P. Bautier, "Le portrait de Paracelse par Rubens," *Bulletin Museés Royaux de Cinquantenaire* 11 (1912): 86f; G. Ring, *Beiträge zur Geschichte niederländische Bildnismalerei im 15. und 16. Jahrhunderte,* pp. 14ff., 50; Friedländer 7, p. 69; E. Michel, *Catalogue raisonée des peintures . . . flamandes du XVe et XVIe siecle,* p. 212f; A. Tschinkel, "Paracelsus—bildnisse in neuer Sicht I." *Salzburger Museum Carolino Augusteum* 10 (1964): 41ff; G. von der Osten, "'Paracelsus'—Ein verlorenes Bildnis von Wolf Huber," *Wallraf-Richartz Jahrbuch* 30 (1968): 201ff; Robbins, p. 71ff; DB, pp. 265–67.

Von der Osten was the first modern scholar to remove the "Paracelsus" portrait original from Massys' *oeuvre.* He argues that the background motifs are more typically upper-German than Netherlandish, and that Massys never shows as much sky above the heads of his sitters among the 1520s Pl. 14
portraits with landscapes (cats. 38, 44, 52). Massys' charac- Pl. 14
teristic integration of sitter and background lacks the plastic Pl. 14
contrast of cliff and portrait that von der Osten sees in the "Paracelsus." A Patinir collaboration is ruled out because of the depiction of water, according to von der Osten, and he asserts that the double chin, plump hand, and lowered viewpoint are also uncharacteristic of Massys' portraits.

These arguments are overly dogmatic about Massys' portraits and certainly not persuasive in favor of von der Osten's new ascription: Wolf Huber. The few Huber portraits with landscapes have nothing in common with the so-called "Paracelsus." The attribution seems partly to derive from identifying the picture as Paracelsus himself, based on the Paris inscription and the common Germanic regions of both the doctor's and Huber's activity (von der Osten, p. 210). Nevertheless, the forceful face of the Louvre-Brussels copies does not resemble the "authentic" portraits discussed by Tschinkel, nor can the divergences be explained away by von der Osten as posthumous painting (p. 208). As a matter of fact, the same head was painted in a tondo frame by the Master of Frankfurt, Massys' Antwerp contemporary (Friedländer 7, no. 162; formerly H. Jonas, Coll., New York). Except for the (spurious) inscription in the Louvre copy, there is no reason to associate the picture with Paracelsus or even with a Germanic artist or sitter.

But there are reasons for reassigning the attribution to an artist other than Massys. The principal objection to Quinten's authorship is the panoramatic, unintegrated landscape and its unusual turbulent sky. A few details of the background link the original to Joos van Cleve. In particular, the motif of a bridge over arches with fortification at one end can be found as a commonplace in works by van Cleve and his workshop (see Friedländer 9, nos. 11, 12, 29, 30, 33, 45, 49a, 50). In nos. 11, 45, and 50, dated by Friedländer to the middle teens, the bridge is associated with a steep Patiniresque cliff, a combination found in the "Paracelsus" landscape. It is possible that Joos van Cleve followed Massys' lead in combining portraits with landscape; however, his preserved portraits are generally more conservative and uniform than Massys' experiments. More probably, the "Paracelsus" was the work of a follower, borrowing van Cleve's landscape formulas in combination with Massys' format from works like the Vaduz *Canon* (F. 39, cat. 65). A large work by a Massys follower (New York, Metropolitan Museum, no. 32.200.52; 95.3 × 76.9; F. 66), derived ultimately
from the Detroit *Madonna Outdoors* (F. 32, cat. 42), features Pl. 6
both bridge and cliff in its background and a cloudy sky above. Its competent author might have been responsible for the "Paracelsus" original. But the *Paracelsus* also evokes suggestions of the landscapes of Cornelis Massys, e.g., the Patiniresque 1538 Amsterdam *Prodigal Son,* which features both bridge and cliff in its right background. No portraits by Cornelis have survived, however.

Supp. F. *Pieta* (F. 195). Gaeta, Cathedral, Diocesan Museum (90 × 131)

HIST.: On altar of family of Jacopo de Vio; possibly purchased by Cardinal Tommaso de Vio (1469–1534), bishop in the years 1519–34, papal legate to counter Luther in Germany in 1518.

LIT.: E. K. Waterhouse, "An Unnoticed Quentin Massys," *Burlington Magazine* 89 (1947): 280; Friedländer 7, p. 84; DB, p. 165ff.

According to de Bosque, a 1690 inventory of P. Rossello (*Breve descrittione delle cose più notabili di Gaeta,* Naples, 1690) already mentions this panel as located in Gaeta, although at that time the work was ascribed to the Venetian master Paolo Veronese. Waterhouse rediscovered the painting and quite properly associated it with Massys. Although it is accepted as the authentic work of Quinten by de Bosque, she nonetheless points out several anomalies within the panel: "The landscape loses its importance to the end that the gaze is directed toward the figures and principally to the body of Christ, of which the forms show a very clear evolution since the Louvre *Pieta* [F. 16, cat. 17]." This muscular, Italianate body of Christ is indeed a striking novelty within Massys' work, especially in comparison to the gaunt, bony type for Christ in the late half-length *Pieta* (F. 15, cat. 47), where the Madonna type compares closely. Only the Venice half-length *Ecce Homo* (F. 11, cat. 46), also a late work, presents similar figures, where a rounder, fuller Christ and a venerable Pilate come close to the actors (and colors) of the Gaeta *Pieta.* If this work is by Massys, then surely it is a late work. Yet the landscape, whose rocks, according to de Bosque, are unusually well painted for a Quinten setting, and the fully modeled skin tones go well beyond the faces of other late Madonnas. The workmanship seems rather to lie closer to Massys' workshop and followers, quite possibly the work of his son, Jan Massys. DeBosque indicates kinship to the "brutal realism" of Jan's later Brussels *Susannah and the Elders* and suggests a collaboration of father and son, ca. 1520–25. While such a collaboration is certainly possible, it should rather be dated closer to 1530 and with stress on Jan's role over Quinten's.

Pl. 94 *Pl. 95* *Pl. 87*

Supp. G. Drawing: *Portrait of a Man.* Munich, Graphische Sammlung, silverpoint on parchment, reoutlined in lead pencil (13.6 × 10.8).

LIT.: A. E. Popham, *Drawings of the Early Flemish School* (London, 1926), p. 31, pl. 51; DB, p. 279.

Popham relates this drawing to the Chicago portrait of a *Man with Flower* (F. 47, cat. 52), but the stylized features of the head in the drawing seem more closely related to Massys' later portrait style. Angular, heavy lids and an emphatic bridge of the nose are closest in type to the Barcelona *Saint* (F. 30, cat. 33) or the later portraits of the teens and 1520s (cat. nos. 56–63). The cap is not distinctive enough to be firmly datable, although de Bosque sees it as late 15th century, citing the Massys self-portrait engraved later by Wierix (cf. "Lost Works").

Pl. 149 *Pl. 177*

If authentic, this drawing would be Massys' only surviving original in the medium. Certainly its forms derive from the Massys idiom. Yet, being unique, it should probably not be considered authentic. Possibly comparisons to Massys underdrawings, revealed by infrared inspection of his painted panels, will eventually settle this issue.

In some thinly painted panels, like the Antwerp *Magdalene* (F. 35, cat. 29), underdrawing is visible under the brows and mouth, indicating that Massys worked out his composition directly on the panel. And repetition of individual forms, such as Leonardesque heads, also demonstrates that Massys must have had a sketchbook repository of such motifs. His craftsmanlike contours betray Quinten's draftsmanlike spirit in many a composition. *Pl. 110*

The drawing has a finished quality instead of the appearance of a preparatory sketch (note the hair and shading), yet its quality of refinement seems rough in comparison with Massys' normal standard of painted panels. If it is a completed portrait, the work would be even more exceptional within Massys' *oeuvre,* because his painted portraits during the teens and 1520s usually involve bust-length poses and often include additional elements of landscape and/or architecture.

APPENDIX A. PORTRAIT MEDALS

LIT.: E. van Even, "Quelques observations sur trois medallions attribués a Quentin Metsys," *Revue belge de numismatique* (1900): 441ff.; L. Forrer, *Biographical Dictionary of Medallists,* vol. 3 (London, 1904–30), p. 607; J. Simonis, *L'art du medailleur en Belgique,* vol. 1 (Brussels, 1900–04), p. 29ff., 83ff.; V. Tourneur, "Quentin Metsys medailleur," *Revue belge de numismatique* (1920): 139ff.; Friedländer 7, p. 23; F. Ballion, "Quentin Metsys," *Bulletin de l'alliance numismatique Européenne* (1958): 25f., 33ff., 41ff., 49f.; E. Treu, *Die Bildnisse des Erasmus von Rotterdam* (Basel, 1959), p. 26ff.; *Medailleurs et numismates de la Renaissance aux Pays Bas,* exh. cat. (Brussels, 1959), p. 32ff.; Pope-Hennessey, *The Portrait in the Renaissance,* p. 92ff.; A. Gerlo, *Erasme et ses portraitistes,* p. 18ff.; L. Smolderen, "Quentin Metsys Medailleur d'Erasme," *Scrinium Erasmianium,* Vol. 2 (Leyden, 1969), p. 513ff.: *Erasmus en zijn tijd,* exh. cat., nos. 239, 269–72; E. Panofsky, "Erasmus and the Visual Arts," pp. 204, 208 n. 34, 214ff; DB, pp. 59–62.

Four medals have been attributed by numismatic scholars to Quinten Massys. The artist's familiarity with bronze metal casting must have begun early, when the young Quinten grew up in the Louvain forge of his father. As early as Molanus (*Rerum Lovaniensium Libri XIV* [1575], cited by Brising, p. 22, n. 2), Massys was credited with the bronze baptismal font of Louvain's St. Peter's church. Traditionally, Quinten is also cited as the creator of a fount with leaf grillwork, and he is mentioned as a smith-turned-painter in early biographies, even though there is no documentation for either assertion. Of course, a variety of 15th-century artists worked in several media, and Quinten Massys may have been no exception. However, in addition to his father, Quinten's brother Joos was also a smith, so there is no necessity to believe that Quinten himself cast the medals. He might simply have been the designer and his brother the medal caster.

Support for this view comes from Massys' first bronze

portrait medal: *Cristina Metsys* (1491), wife of his smith brother, Joos. The medal survives in a unique impression (Antwerp, Museum Mayer van den Bergh); its high relief, large letters, and raised edges reveal an exaggerated grandeur of expression that suggests the artist's immaturity. The frontal face and gesture of Cristina reappear in the Virgin of the small *Seilern Crucifixion* panel (supp. A). Smolderen thinks that the frontal pose and high relief point to Joos's direct authorship instead of to Quinten's softer style as revealed in later works. *Pl. 90*

Massys' second medal, also dated 1491, is *Willem Schewez,* a Scottish archbishop of St. Andrew's who resided in Louvain in 1491 (d. 1497). This portrait is seen in profile, in the manner of Italian precedent and, in comparison with *Cristina Metsys,* it shows more-refined edges and more-restrained lettering.

In 1495 another dated medal, a self-portrait inscribed *Quintinus Metsys,* appeared (Friedländer, pl. 133a). The character of the letters is identical with preceding works; however, in addition to an unusual oval shape, the medal is more softly modeled in low relief. If the portrait is compared with both the 1491 *Schewez* or the 1519 *Erasmus* medal, its authorship seems inconsistent with the other two, and it is the least convincing of the medals attributed to Massys. Yet its letters are formed identically with the block signature of the Jacquemart-Andre *Old Man* (1513; F. 52, cat. 54). Possibly its stylistic discrepancies derive from the personal nature of the product. Like the *Cristina Metsys,* the *Quintinus Metsys* features large letters not isolated from the portrait head; like other Massys portrait medals, the sitter is seen in profile, cut off at bust length. This portrait either served I. H. Wierix as a source for his 1572 *Quintinus Mesius* portrait engraving (in D. Lampsonius, *Pictoriae;* see Chap. 1, Introduction) or it likewise derived from the lost Massys self-portrait for the St. Luke guild (see Lost Works, no. 3; Smolderen, p. 521 n. 31, thinks the self-portrait medal is a copy of the self-portrait from the first third of the 16th century). *Pl. 157*

The most famous of all Massys' portrait medals is his *Erasmus,* which survives in several states. Thomas More's praise of Massys in 1517 for the *Erasmus* and *Gillis* portrait panels had already expressed the desire for portraits in "a more durable matter in order to conserve them for ever" (see Chap. 6.) Dated 1519, the *Erasmus* medal is inscribed on its obverse with a Greek phrase that translates: "The better image will my writings show." Dürer used the same motto on his 1526 engraved portrait of Erasmus. Massys' portrait bust is seen in profile to the left, and it also contains the Latin inscription "Portrait after life" *(Imago ad viva effigie expressa).*

Massys is identified as the creator of the 1519 medal by Erasmus himself in a letter (29 March 1528) to Henricus Botteus in Brou: "Where did your sculptor procure my portrait unless by chance he possessed that which Quinten cast in bronze at Antwerp. Dürer painted me but in a bad likeness" (see Gerlo, p. 18). A later medal, dated 1531, may be the work of this second "sculptor" (see *Medailleurs . . . aux Pays Bas,* no. 22).

Erasmus sent the portraits to his friends, and copies met the additional demand. A correspondence during 1524 between Erasmus and Willibald Pirckheimer in Nuremburg discusses the problems of casting new replicas (Gerlo, p. 21ff.). In one passage (8 February 1524), he mentions the obverse of the medal, the god Terminus, without which the casting of a copy would be simpler. In a letter of 3 June, Erasmus speaks of making the obverse relief lower by turning the bust of Terminus in profile; this detail has led Smolderen to hypothesize that there was an original medal, now lost, where Terminus was seen *en face.* Therefore, all surviving versions showing Terminus in profile would be later emendations. Yet this passage could also be understood to mean shifting the relief away from the center of the medal to get a better impression on both sides when recasting.

The obverse with Terminus features the Roman god of boundaries, a bust on a base in profile to the left. Beside the head is the motto "Concedo nulli" (I yield to none). Around the circumference of the medal is an adage from Horace (*Epistolae* I, 16, 79): "Mors ultima linea rerum" (Death is the ultimate boundary of things), and a Greek inscription: "Contemplate the end of a long life." Panofsky (p. 215 ff.) elegantly sketches the significance of Terminus and his motto for Erasmus.

For stylistic types, the young, fine-featured Terminus head may be compared with Massys' paintings and such figures as St. John from the Ottawa *Crucifixion* (F. 12, cat. 20), St. Luke of the *Rem altarpiece* grisaille exterior (F. 3, cat. 24), and St. Anthony of the Prado *Temptation* (F. 31, cat. 26). *Pl. 91* *Pl. 114*

APPENDIX B. TAPESTRIES

LIT.: Brising, p. 40ff.; Winkler, p. 198; Delen, p. 53; Baldass, 173ff.; W. Schöne, "Bildteppiche von Quinten Massys," Art History Congress, London, July 1939, Section IVa, abstract; DB, pp. 274-77.

To account for the lack of early painted works by Massys, these several authors (excepting Brising) have attempted to connect him with the large designs for tapestries—then a major industry in the Netherlands, especially at nearby Brussels. There are evident similarities between the tapestries and earlier Massys paintings (see the *Anne* altarpiece, cat. 10, at the close of the first period). Both employ small-featured, slender facial types seen in three-quarter profile, a favorite pose of Massys. Like Quinten's works, tapestries also use large-scale figures within a narrow foreground space parallel to the picture plane. *Pl. 1*

Tapestries are difficult to date precisely, and most were executed over a long period of time. No Massys cartoons for tapestries have survived, and original designs can only be inferred from the surviving weavings. Another possible explanation of the connection is that Massys' painting style might have drawn upon tapestry designs as guidelines for his first monumental panel paintings.

Brising is the only author who believes that Massys' tapestry designs would have dated from his final years, i.e., the decade of the 1520s. He incorrectly assigns the Paris series of *David and Bathsheba* (Cluny Museum) to Massys. They are now known to be the design of Jan van Roome (see below).

Schöne adds the following attributions:

1. *Story of Mary* (Madrid). Illustrated in H. Göbel, *Wandteppiche Niederlande* (Leipzig, 1923), vol. 2, no. 115f. The tapestries are dated ca. 1500 and attributed "mit Sicherheit" to Massys by Schöne.
2. *Mass of St. Gregory* (1495, Nuremburg, Germanisches Museum)—Göbel, no. 120. A full discussion is in R. A. d'Hulst, *Tapisseries flamandes* (Brussels, 1960), p. 115ff. "Concept by Massys but not cartoon," says Schöne.
3. *Veneration of Mary, Presentation of Jesus* (Madrid), *Transfiguration* (formerly Morgan Coll., New York), all dated 1495–1505 and given to Massys "in concept" by Schöne.
4. *Life of Christ and Mary* (Aix-en-Provence cathedral, ca. 1510; Baldass, ill. 145; DB, ills 318–20).
5. *Nativity* (Budapest, Kunstgewerbemuseum; Baldass, ill. 144).
6. *Prodigal Son* (ca. 1525; Morgan Coll.; Göbel, no. 90).
7. *Last Judgment* (ca. 1525; Paris, Louvre; Göbel, no. 130).
8. *Moralidades* and *Honores* (Madrid; see Conde de Valencia, *Tapices de la Corona de España* (Madrid, 1903), nos. 20–23, 32–40).
9. *Mary* tapestries (ca. 1525; Vatican, Salle Borgia; Göbel, no. 136).
10. *Pieta* (ca. 1510; Vienna, Kunsthistorisches Museum; Baldass, pl. 13; DB, pl. 321).
11. *Assumption of the Virgin* (Berlin, Schlossmuseum; see Baldass, p. 178 n. 76).

Winkler cites two other individual tapestries: *Ecce Homo* (Paris, coll. Le Roy) and *Prodigal Son* (coll. Nardus).

The Cluny Museum *David* series has received careful recent discussion: G. Souchal, *Masterpieces of Tapestry from the Fourteenth to the Sixteenth Century*, exh. cat. (New York, 1973), p. 214ff., nos. 94–7; *Tapisseries bruxelloises de la pré-Renaissance*, exh. cat. (Brussels, 1976), pp. 25–51, nos. 1–10 (with bibliography). The artist of these designs has been revealed by Elisabeth Dhanens, "The David and Bathsheba Drawing, *Gazette des Beaux-Arts* 53 (1959): 215ff. (see also idem, "Jan van Roome alias van Brussel, schilder," *Gentsche Bijdragen tot de Kunstgeschiedenis* 11 [1945–48], pp. 41–46; idem, "L'Importance du peintre Jean van Roome, dit de Bruxelles," *Tapisseries bruxelloises de la pré-Renaissance*, p. 231ff.). The documented tapestry of the *Legend of Herkinbald* was ordered from him in 1513 by the Brotherhood of the Holy Sacrament (compare Massys' 1507–09 altarpiece for another Louvain confraternity, St. Anne). The tapestry is now in Brussels (Museum of Art and History, no. 865; *Tapisseries bruxelloises de la pré-Renaissance*, p. 78ff., no. 19, with bibliography). Indeed, much of the style of Brussels tapestries in the crucial years 1511–20 of Massys' career can be termed the "style of Jan van Roome," according to scholars; he was much more likely the entrepreneurial head of studio than actual cartoon designer and was also noted for his designs for sculptures and stained glass.

Except for Jan van Roome, the names of most tapestry designers are known only from documents but unattached to specific works (see the overviews by M. Crick-Kuntziger, "La Tapisserie Bruxelloise au XVme siècle," *Bruxelles au XVme siècle*, exh. cat., p. 87ff.; J.-K. Steppe, "Inscriptions décoratives contenant des signatures et des mentions du lieu d'origine sur des tapisseries bruxelloises de la fin du XVe et du debut du XVIe siècle," *Tapisseries bruxelloises de la pré-Renaissance*, 193ff.).

The most universally cited series in connection with Massys is the nine scenes of the *Life of the Virgin and of Christ* from the Cathedral of the Holy Savior, Aix-en-Provence (G. Souchal, *Masterpieces of Tapestry*, pp. 187–91, nos. 83–84, with bibliography); indeed, it has also been compared to Jan van Roome. M. R. James ("The Tapestries at Aix-en-Provence," *Proceedings of the Cambridge Antiquarian Society* 11, n.s. 5 [1903–07], pp. 506ff.) discovered that the series was made for the primates of the Church in England (the arms of Dean, Morton, and Warham, archbishops of Canterbury, are on the set) and purchased in Paris for Aix in 1656. An inscription on the border refers to a donor named Richard Dering, cellarer in the time of Henry VIII, and gives the date 1511. There is no firm evidence tying the series to Massys or to anyone else.

Most tapestries include features that would be exceptional in the works of Massys: densely packed figures, prominent architectural stage settings, and emphasis on drapery and ornamental surface design. The features shared by Massys and cartoon designers do not appear in the painter's work before the monumental altarpieces of 1507–11, yet they occur within a consistent tapestry tradition datable to at least a decade earlier (e.g., the 1495 *Gregory Mass*, no. 2 above). The most reasonable conclusion, therefore, is that the prestigious and costly medium of tapestry influenced or paralleled the large-scale compositions of Massys, but only up to a point. His name cannot be associated with tapestries in the documents of either Brussels or Antwerp, and his presence, if any, within the history of tapestry design had no significant effect. The premier scholar of Antwerp's tapestry industry during Massys' era has justly concluded: "Formal indication of Quinten's direct collaboration is lacking in tapestry works" (J. Denucé, *Antwerpsche Tapijtkunst en handel* [Antwerp, 1936], p. xvi).

Plates

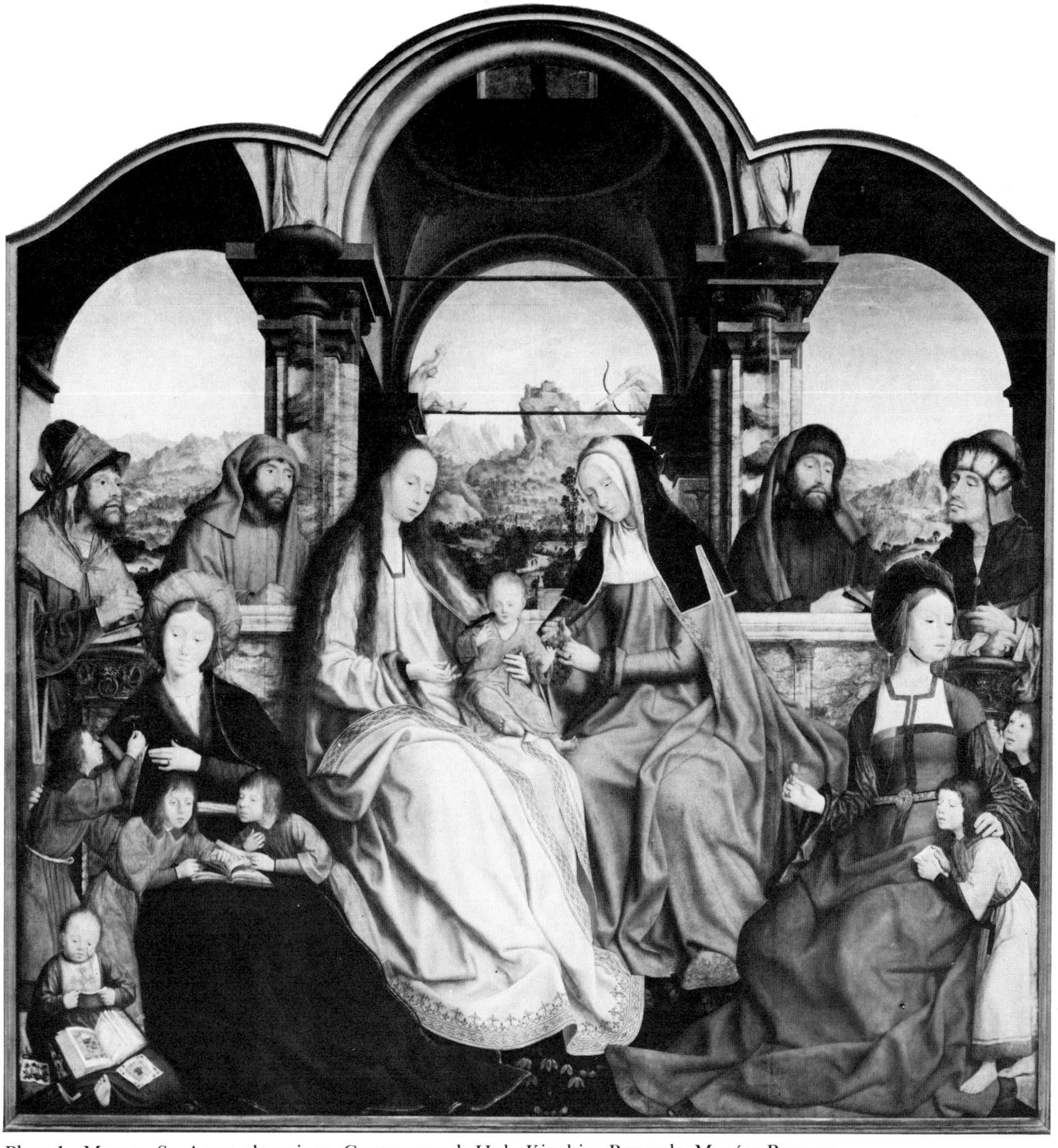

Plate 1. Massys. St. Anne altarpiece. Center panel: Holy Kinship. Brussels, Musées Royaux.

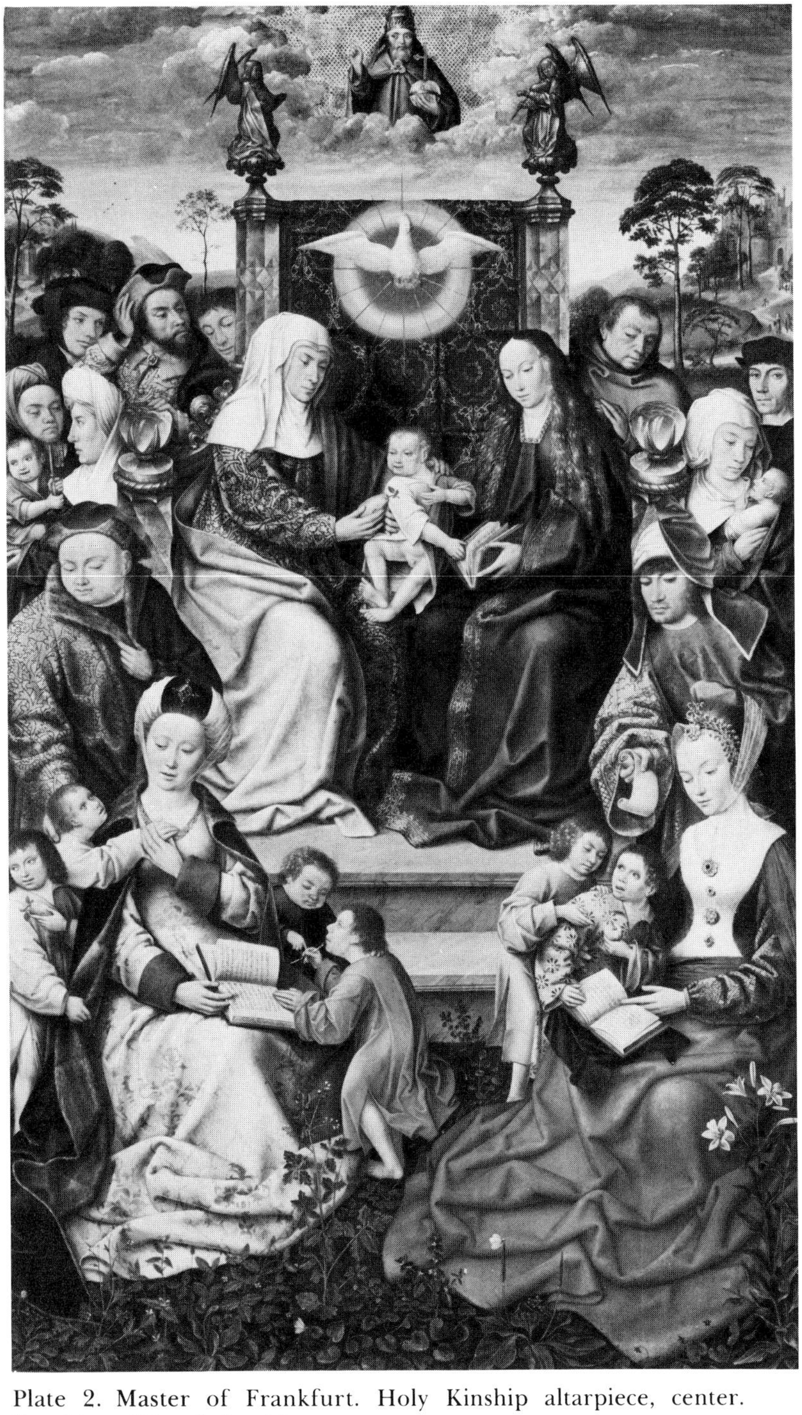

Plate 2. Master of Frankfurt. Holy Kinship altarpiece, center. Frankfurt, Historisches Museum.

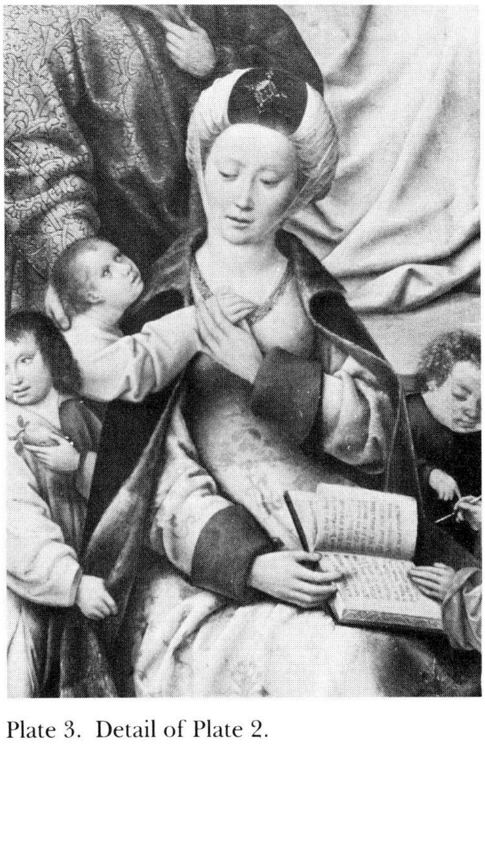

Plate 3. Detail of Plate 2.

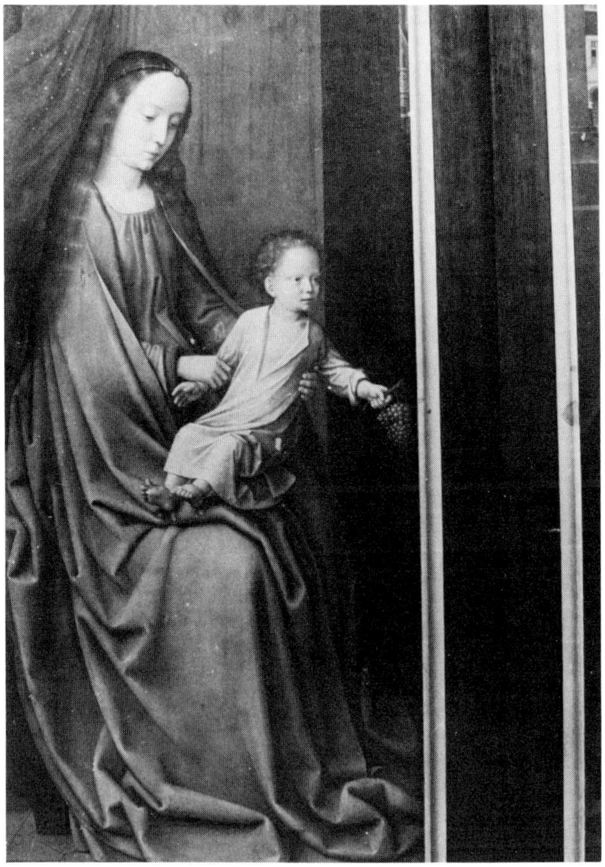

Plate 4. Gerard David. Baptism triptych. Exterior (detail): Madonna and Child. Bruges, Groeninge Museum.

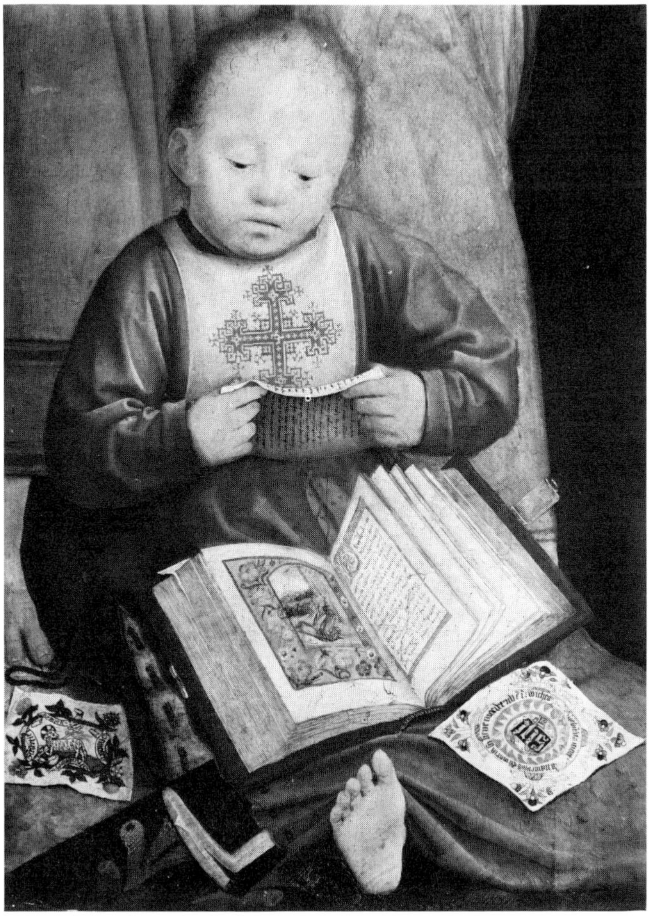

Plate 5. Detail of Plate 1.

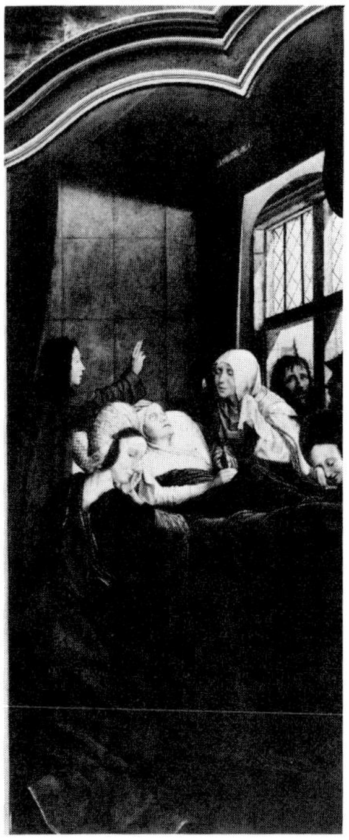

Plate 6. Massys. St. Anne altarpiece. Right panel: Death of St. Anne.

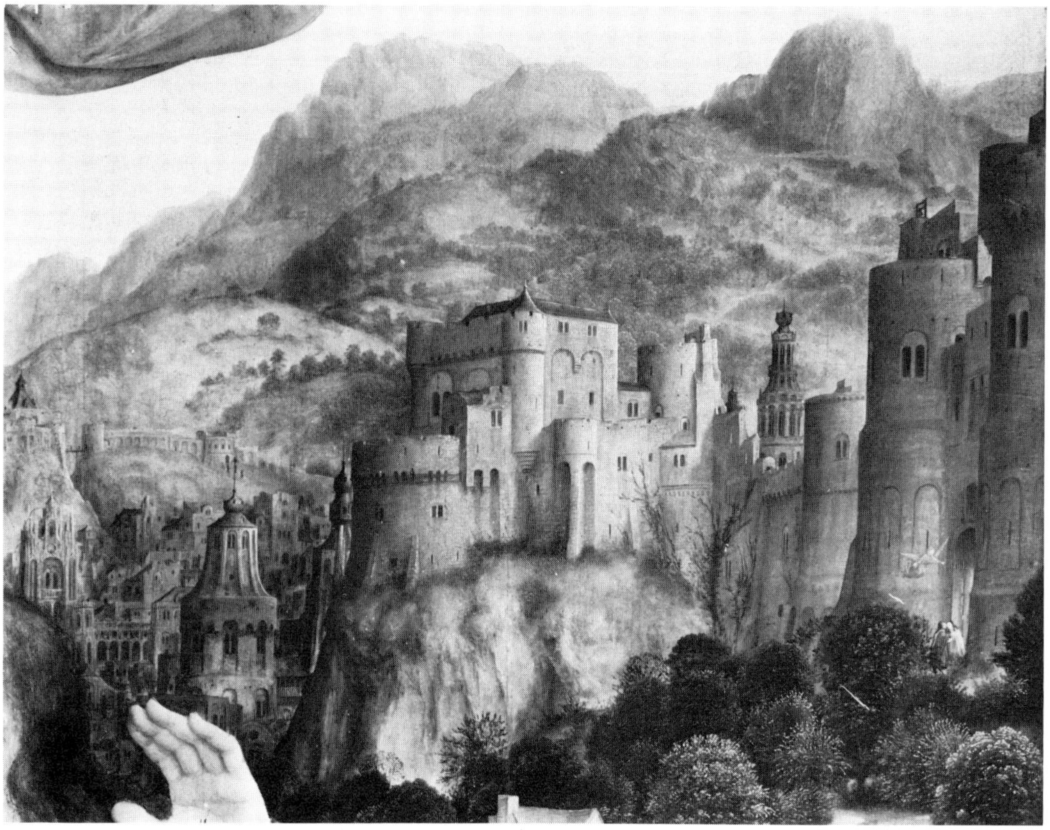

Plate 7. Massys. St. Anne altarpiece. Left panel (detail): Annunciation to Joachim.

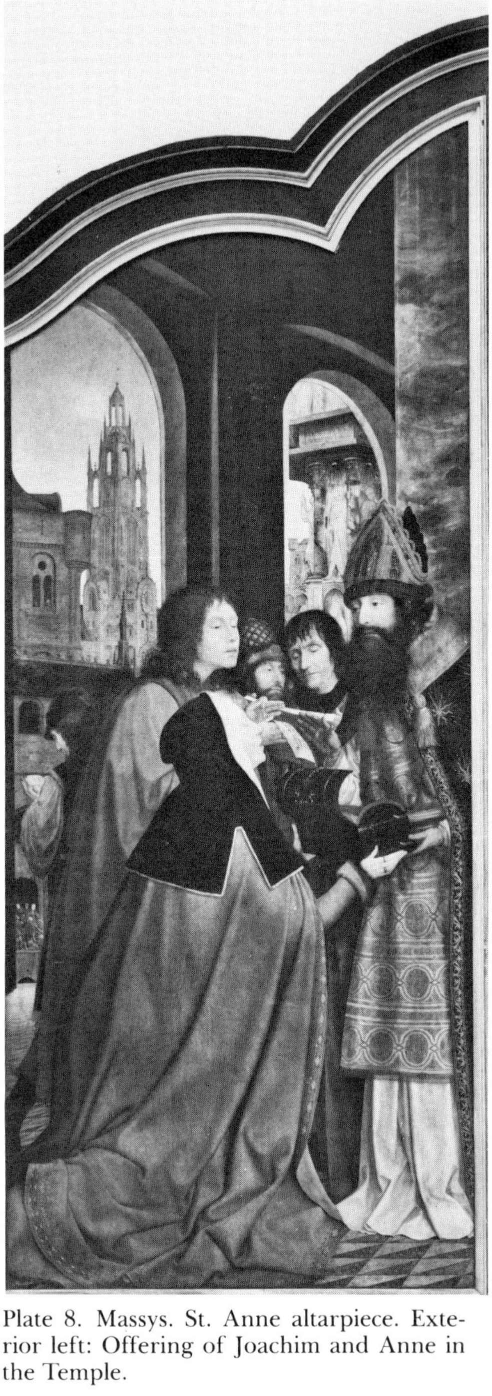

Plate 8. Massys. St. Anne altarpiece. Exterior left: Offering of Joachim and Anne in the Temple.

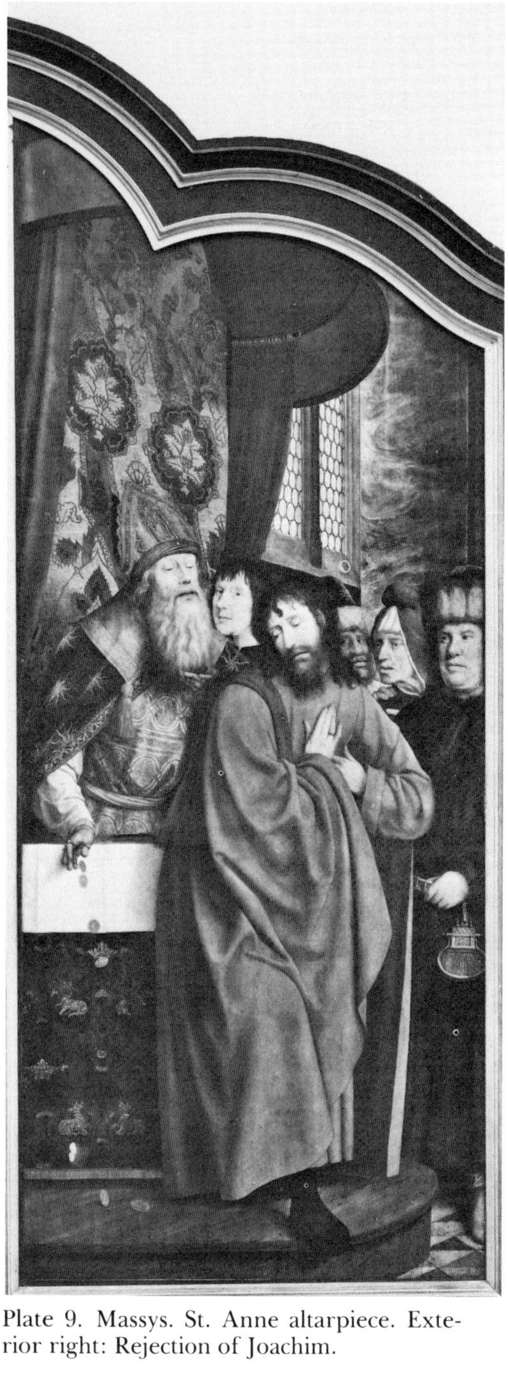

Plate 9. Massys. St. Anne altarpiece. Exterior right: Rejection of Joachim.

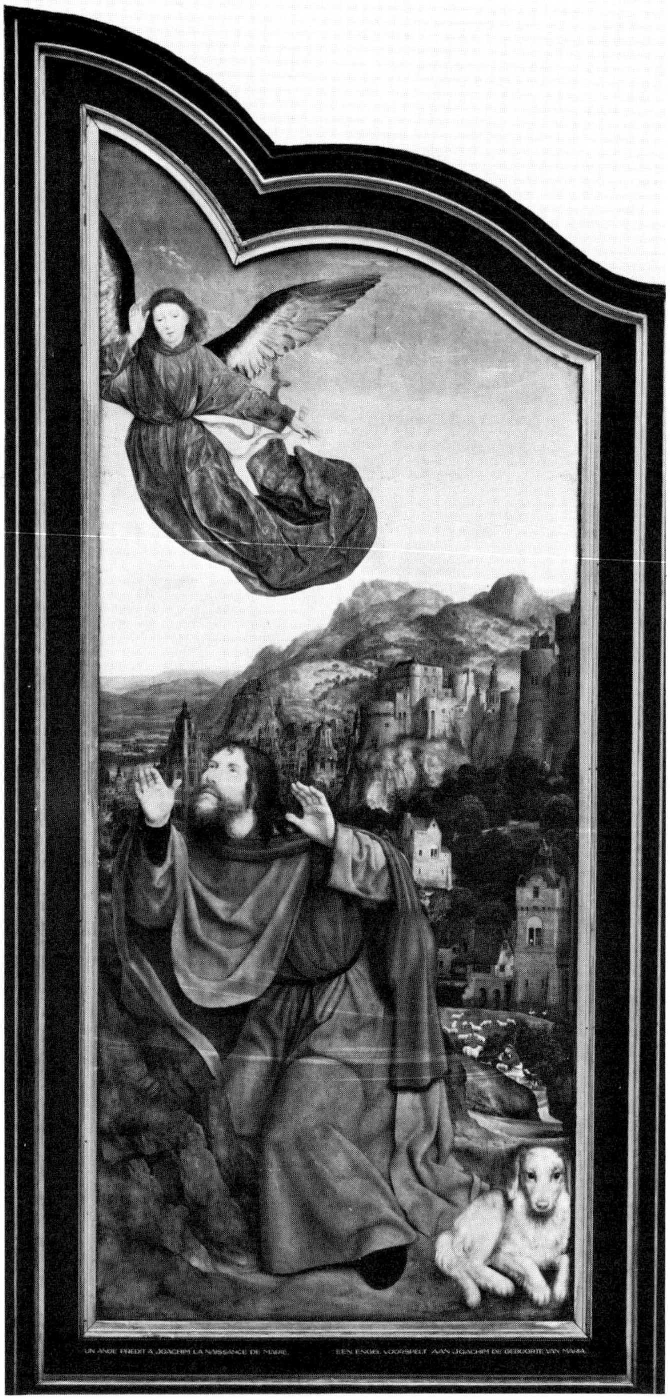

Plate 10. Massys. St. Anne altarpiece. Left panel: Annunciation to Joachim.

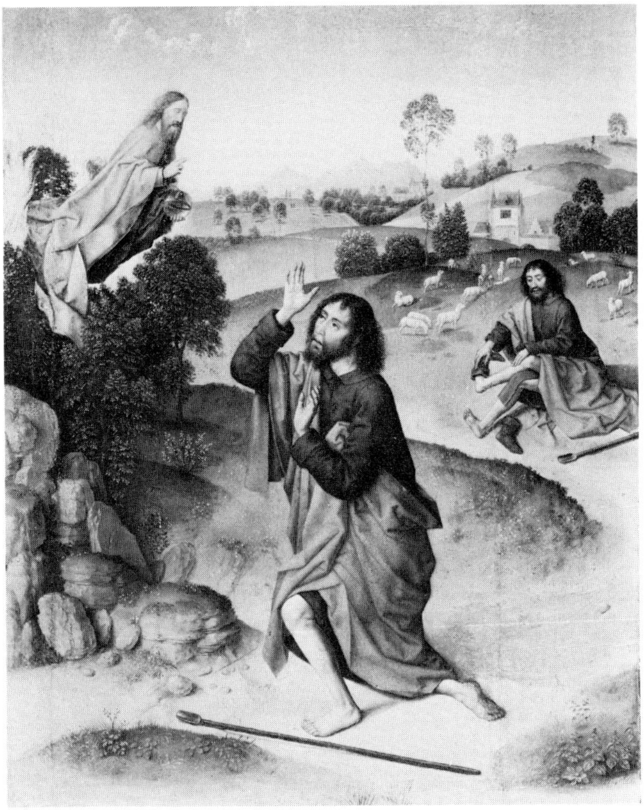

Plate 11. Dieric Bouts: Moses before the Burning Bush. Philadelphia, Johnson collection.

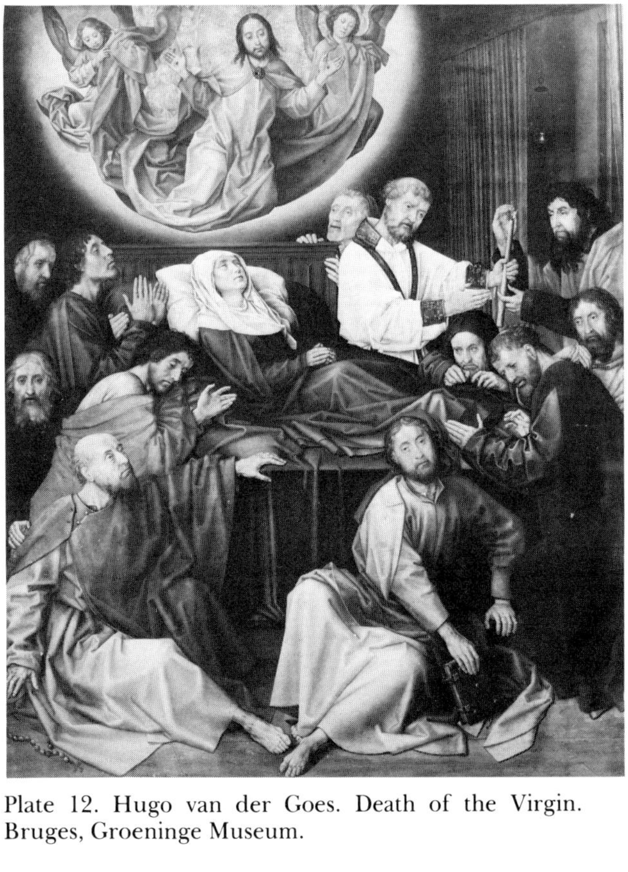

Plate 12. Hugo van der Goes. Death of the Virgin. Bruges, Groeninge Museum.

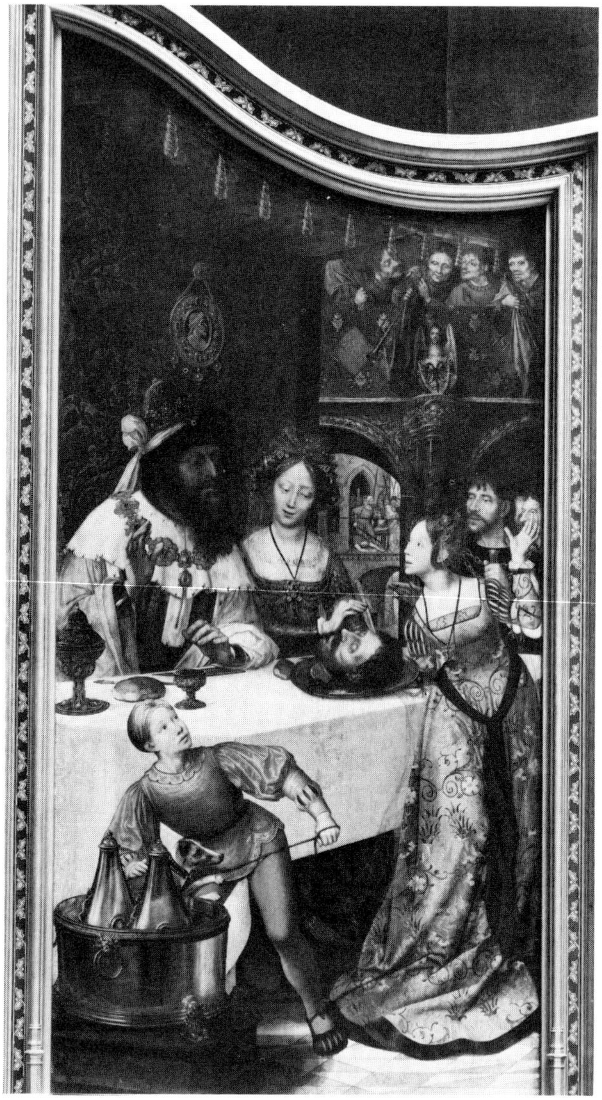

Plate 13. Massys. St. John altarpiece. Left wing: Dance of Salome. Antwerp, Koninklijk Museum.

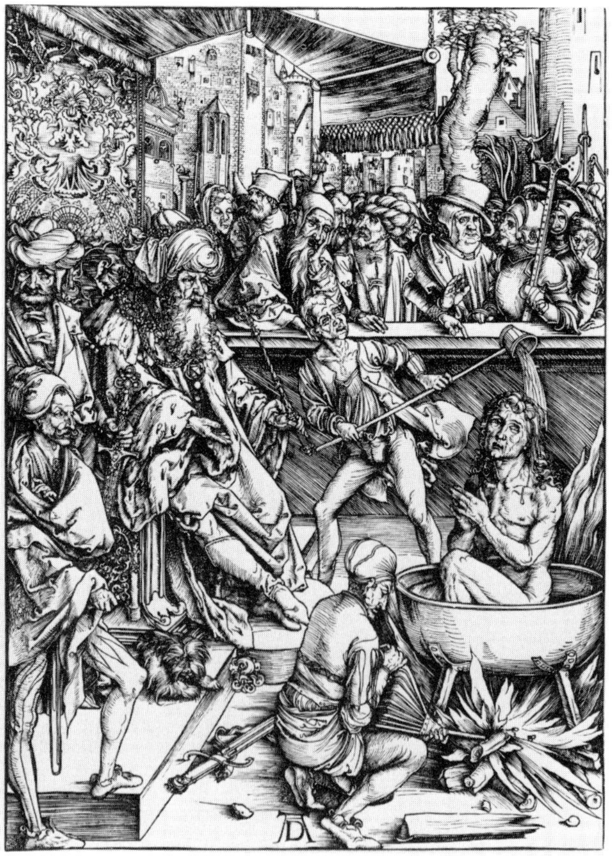

Plate 14. Albrecht Dürer. woodcut. Martyrdom of St. John Evangelist from *Apocalypse*.

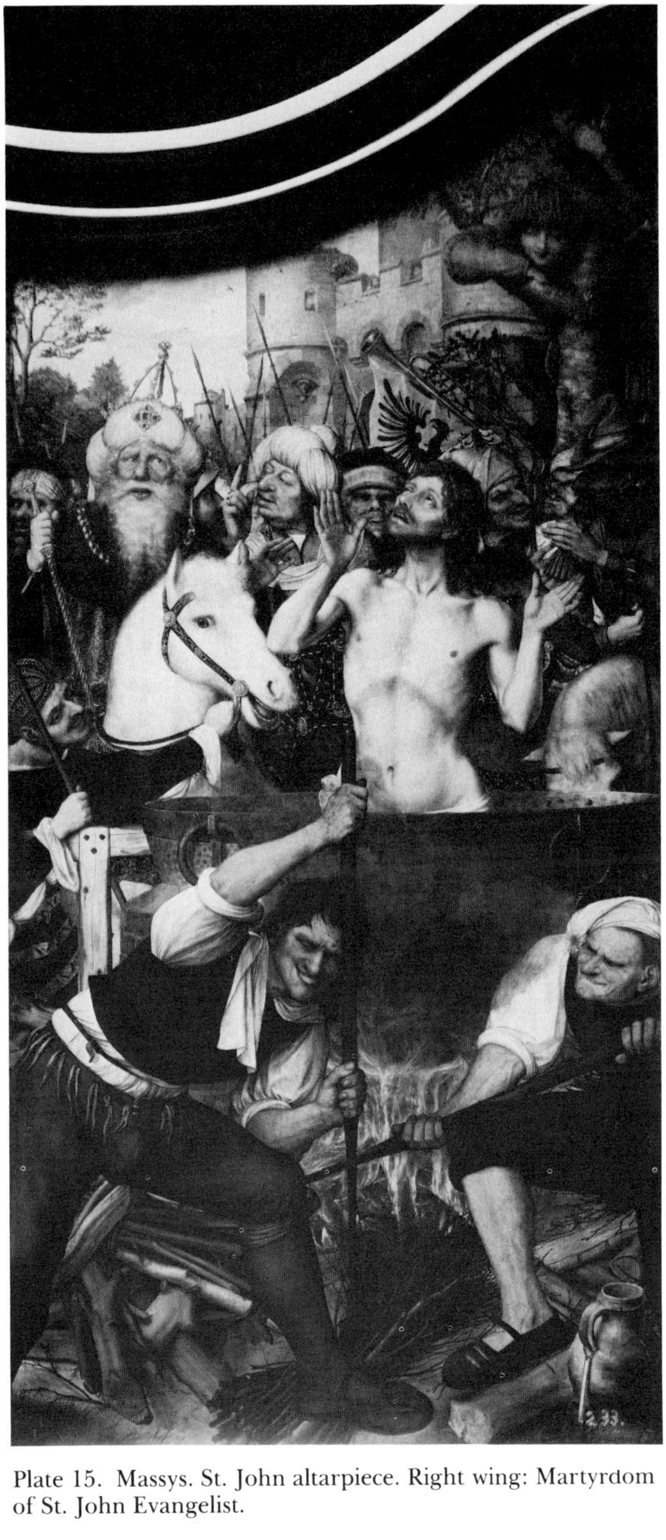

Plate 15. Massys. St. John altarpiece. Right wing: Martyrdom of St. John Evangelist.

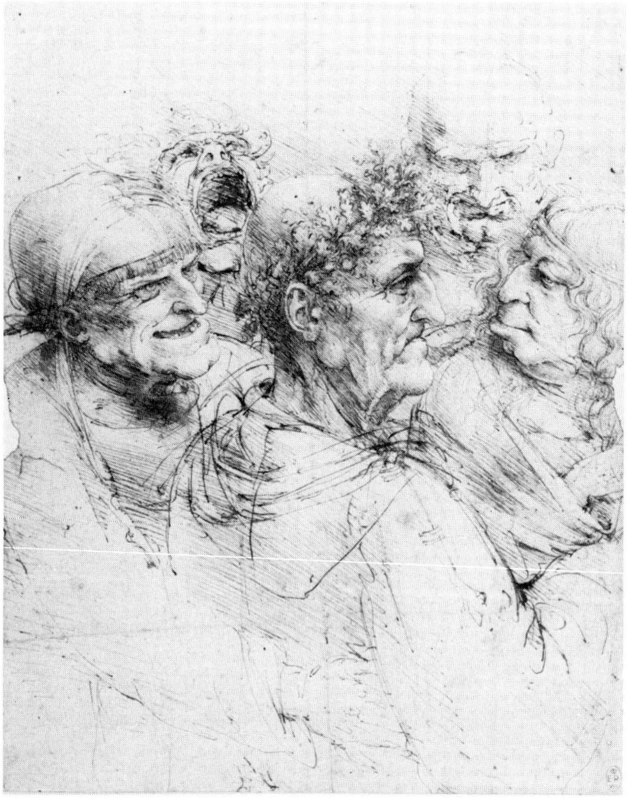

Plate 16. Leonardo da Vinci. Five Grotesque Heads. Windsor Castle.

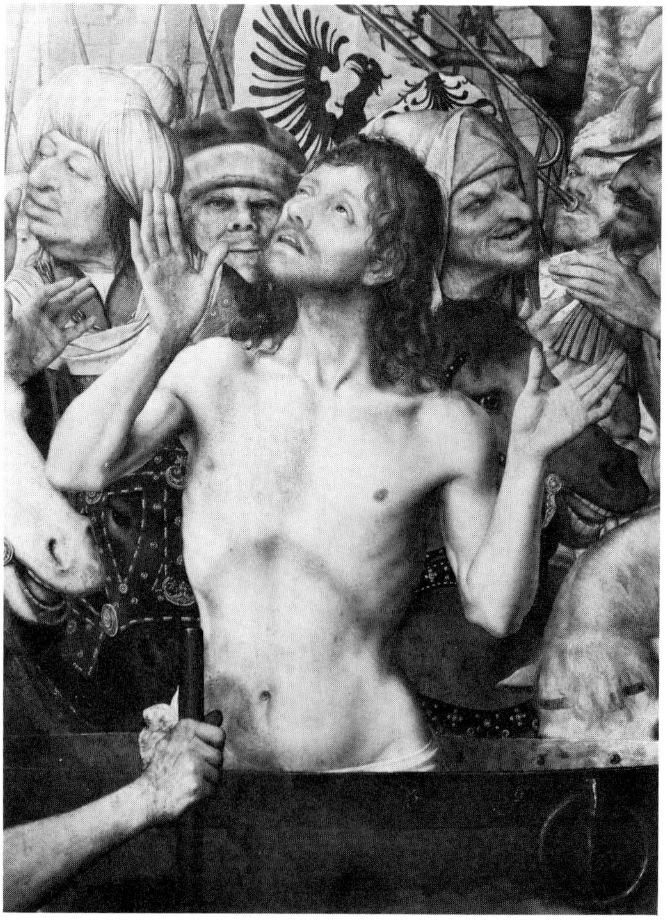

Plate 17. Detail of Plate 15.

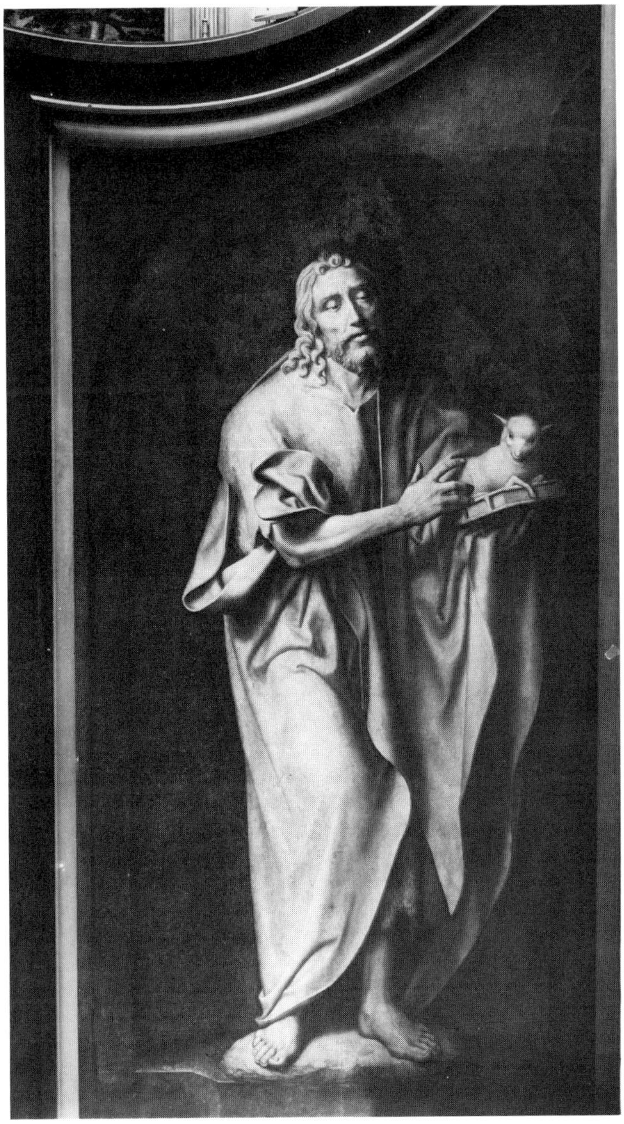

Plate 18. Massys. St. John altarpiece. Exterior left: St. John Baptist.

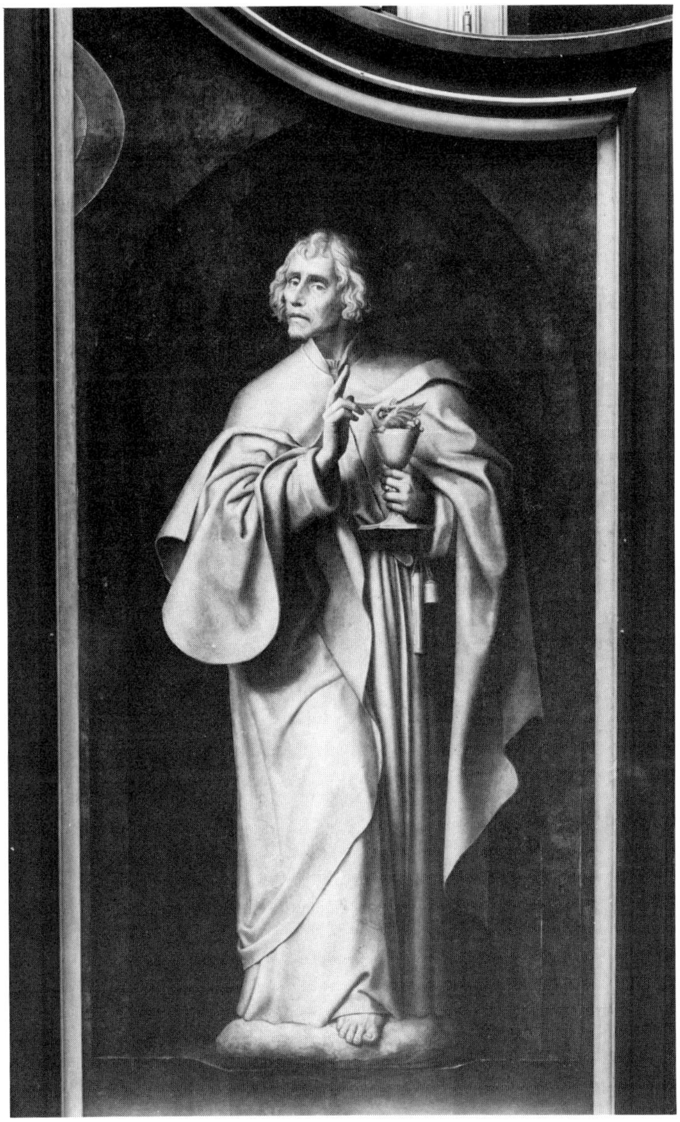

Plate 19. Massys. St. John altarpiece. Exterior right: St. John Evangelist.

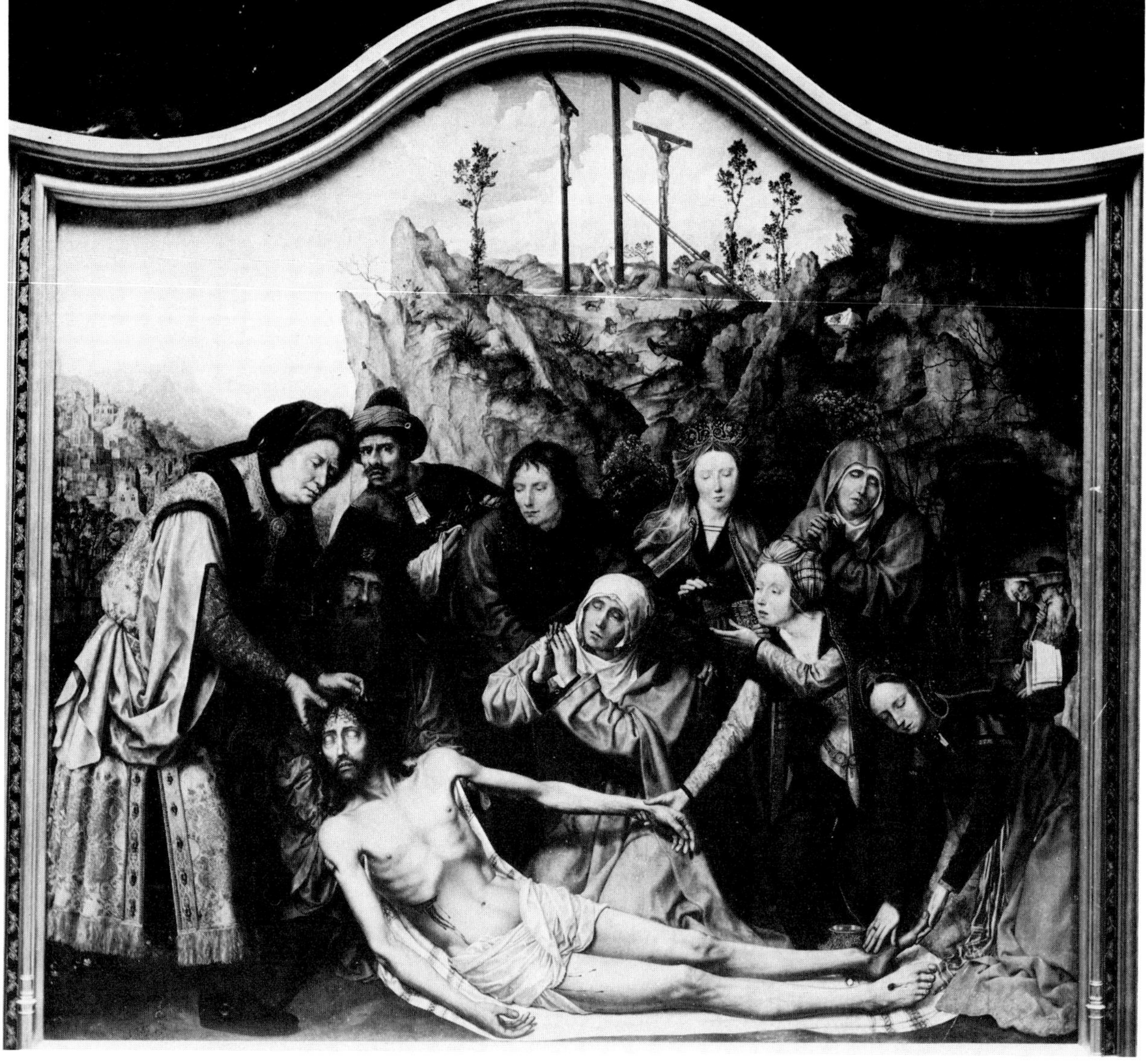

Plate 20. Massys. St. John altarpiece. Center: Lamentation.

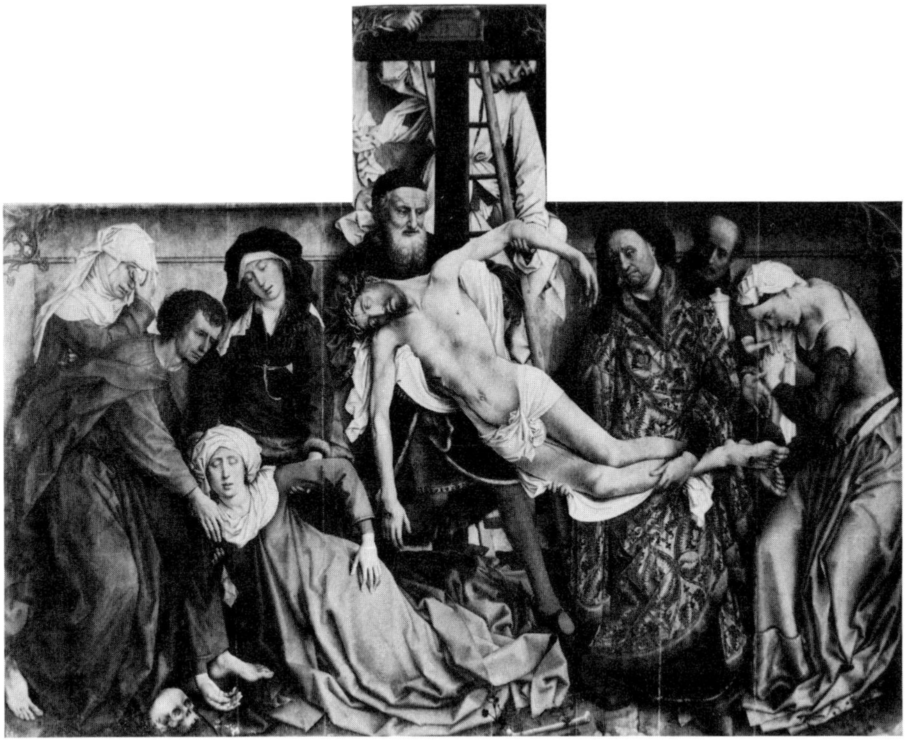

Plate 21. Roger van der Weyden. Deposition retable. Madrid, Prado.

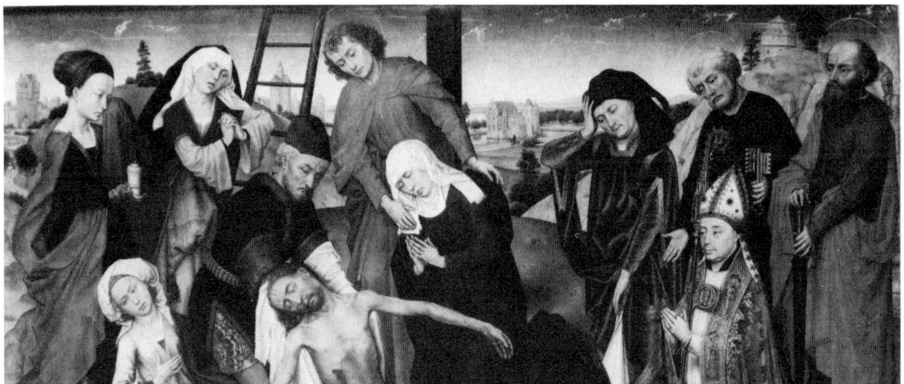

Plate 22. Roger van der Weyden. Lamentation. The Hague, Mauritshuis.

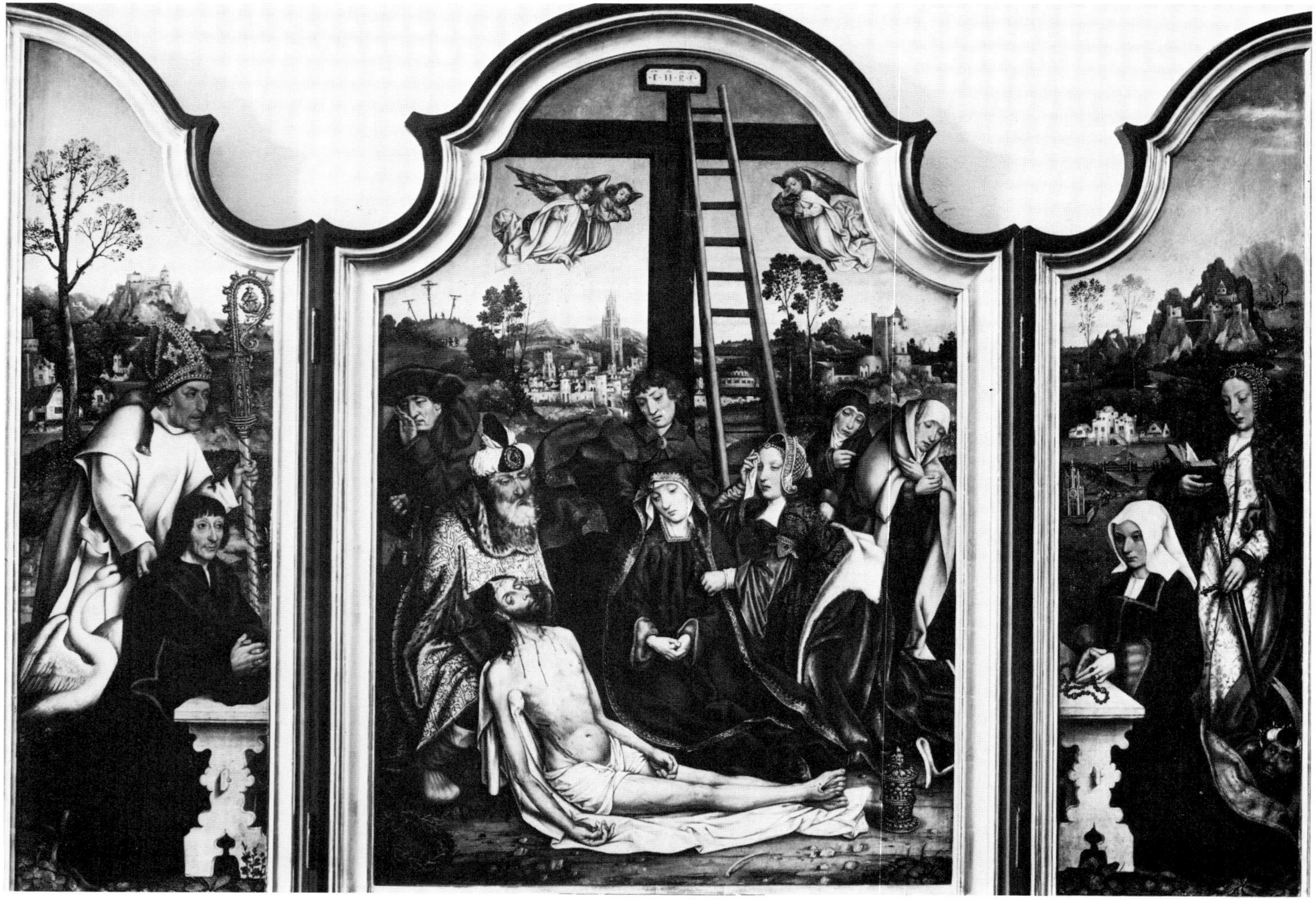

Plate 23. Master of Frankfurt. Lamentation altarpiece. Munich, Alte Pinakothek.

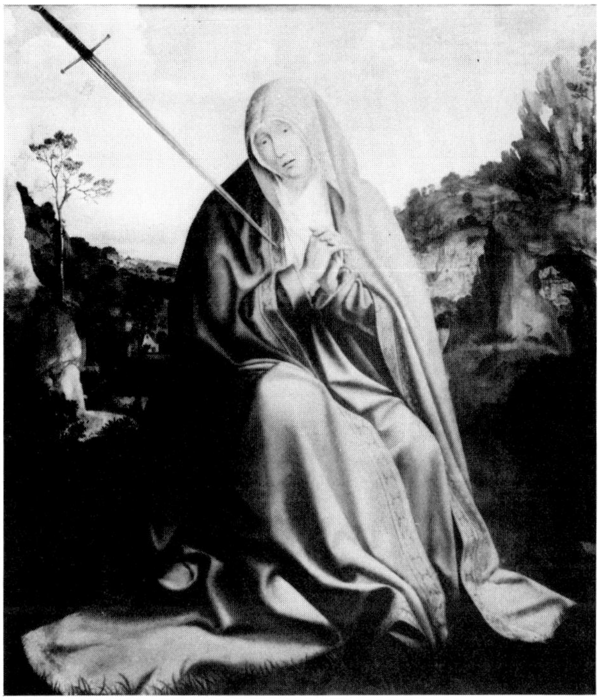

Plate 24. Massys. Madre de Deus altarpiece. Center: Mater Dolorosa. Lisbon, Museu Nacional.

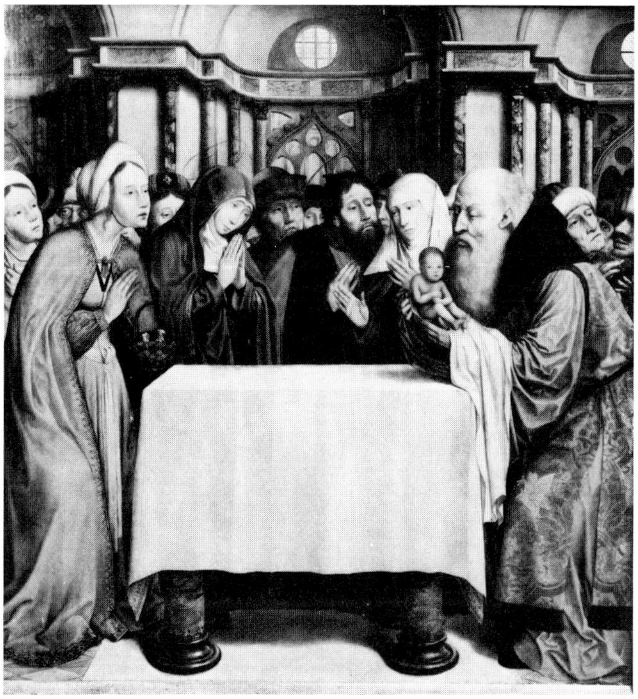

Plate 25. Massys. Madre de Deus altarpiece. Presentation in the Temple. Lisbon, Museu Nacional.

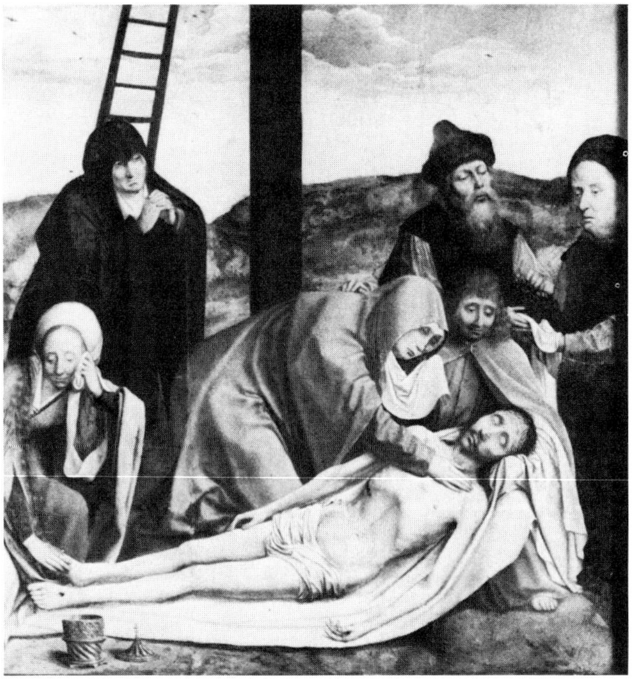

Plate 26. Massys. Madre de Deus altarpiece. Pieta. Rio de Janeiro, Escola Nacional de Belas-Artes.

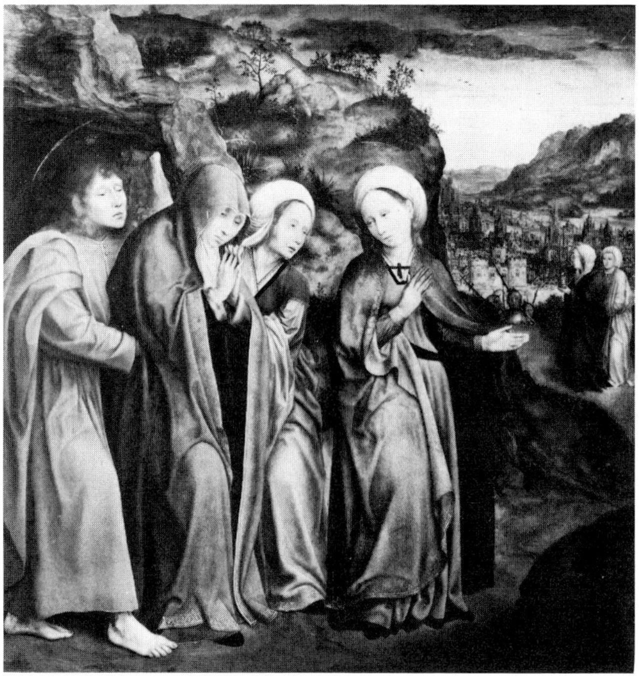

Plate 27. Massys. Madre de Deus altarpiece. St. John and Three Maries at the Tomb of Christ. Lisbon, Museu Nacional.

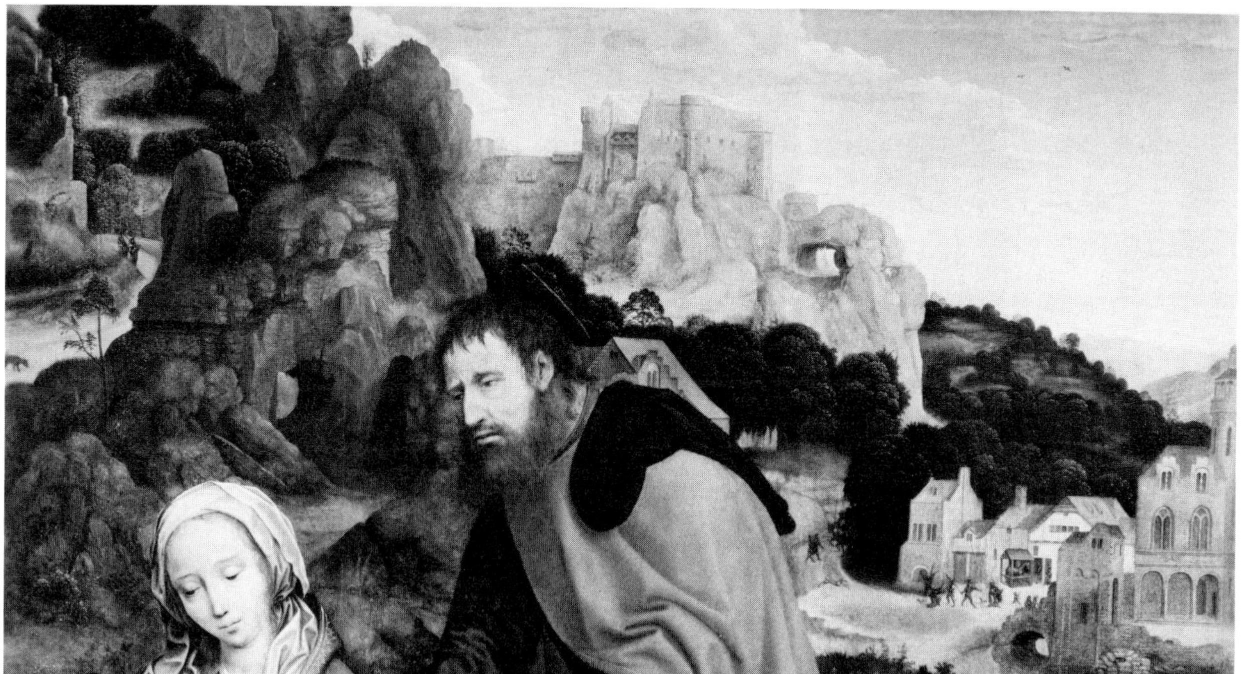

Plate 28. Massys. Madre de Deus altarpiece. Rest on the Flight into Egypt. Worcester Art Museum.

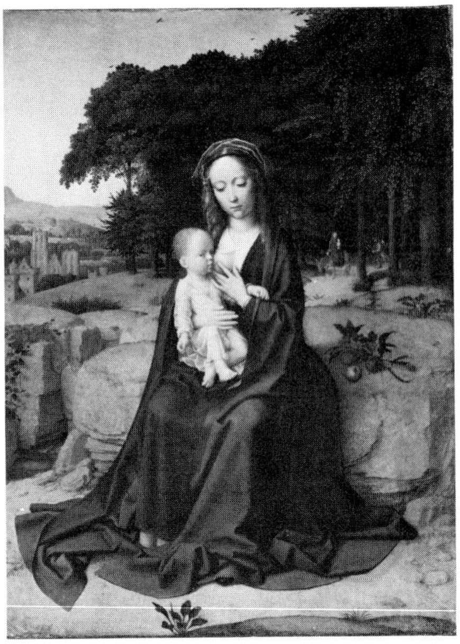

Plate 29. Gerard David. Rest on the Flight into Egypt. New York, Metropolitan Museum of Art.

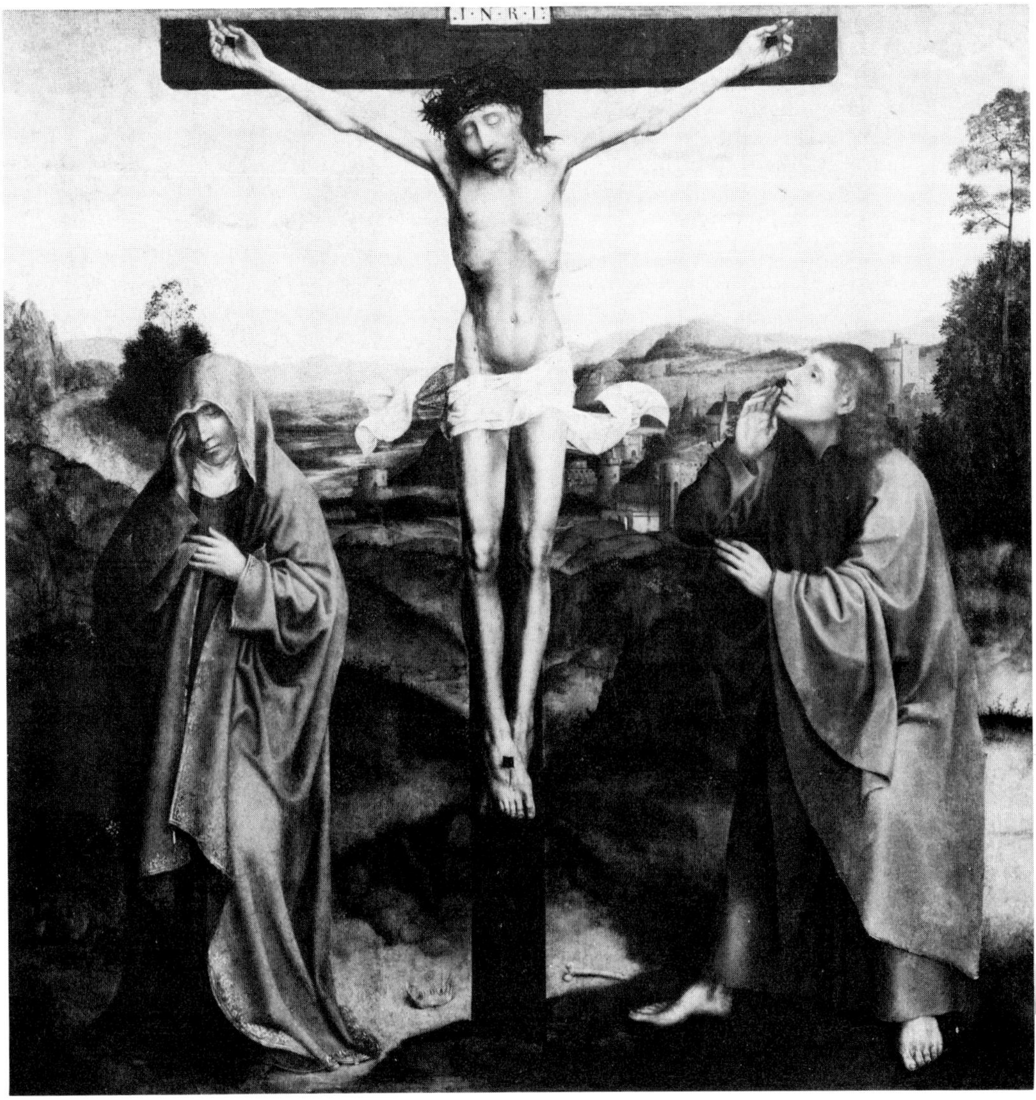

Plate 30. Massys. Madre de Deus altarpiece. Crucifixion. Lisbon, Museu Nacional.

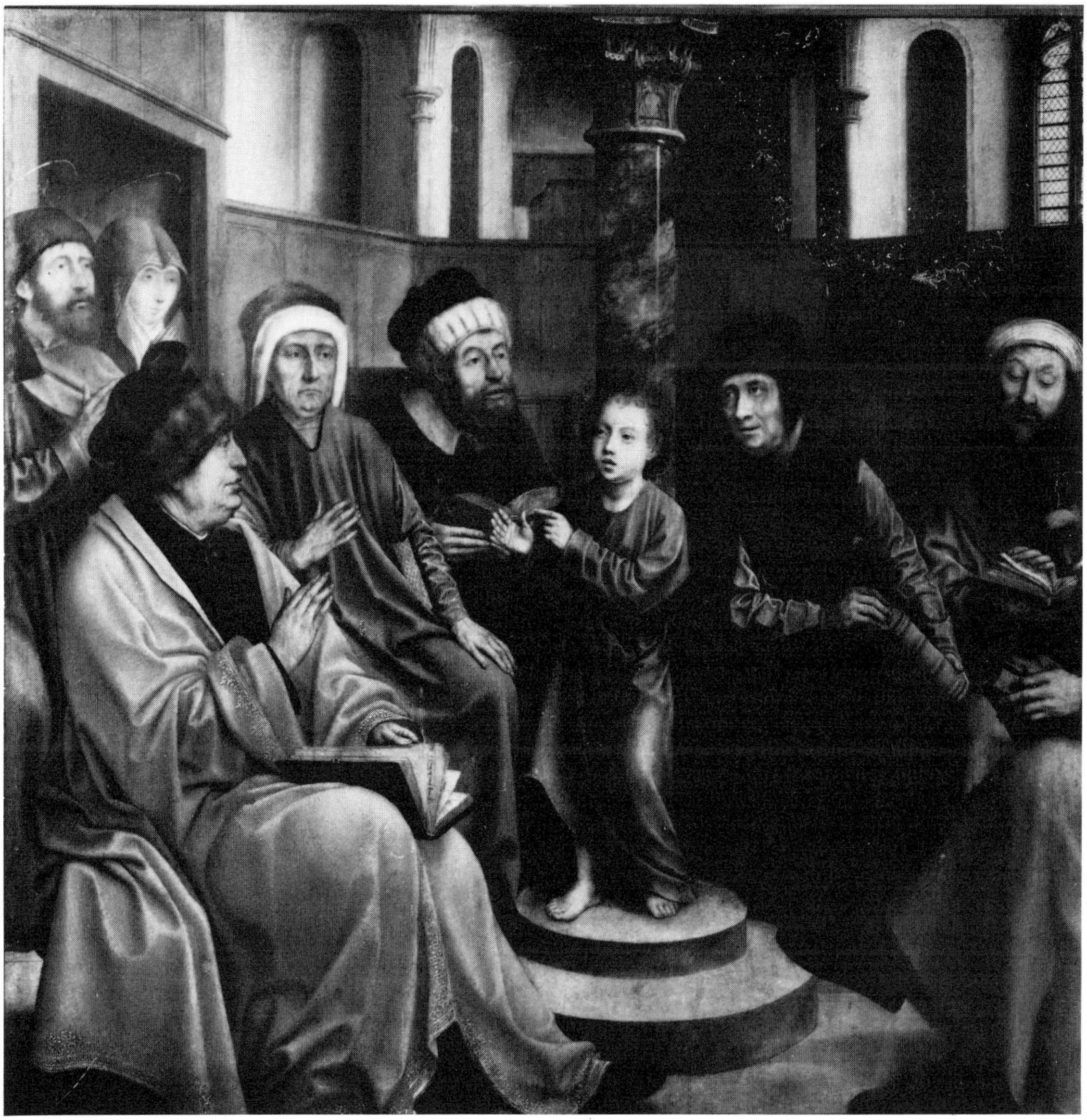

Plate 31. Massys. Madre de Deus altarpiece. Christ among the Doctors. Lisbon, Museu Nacional.

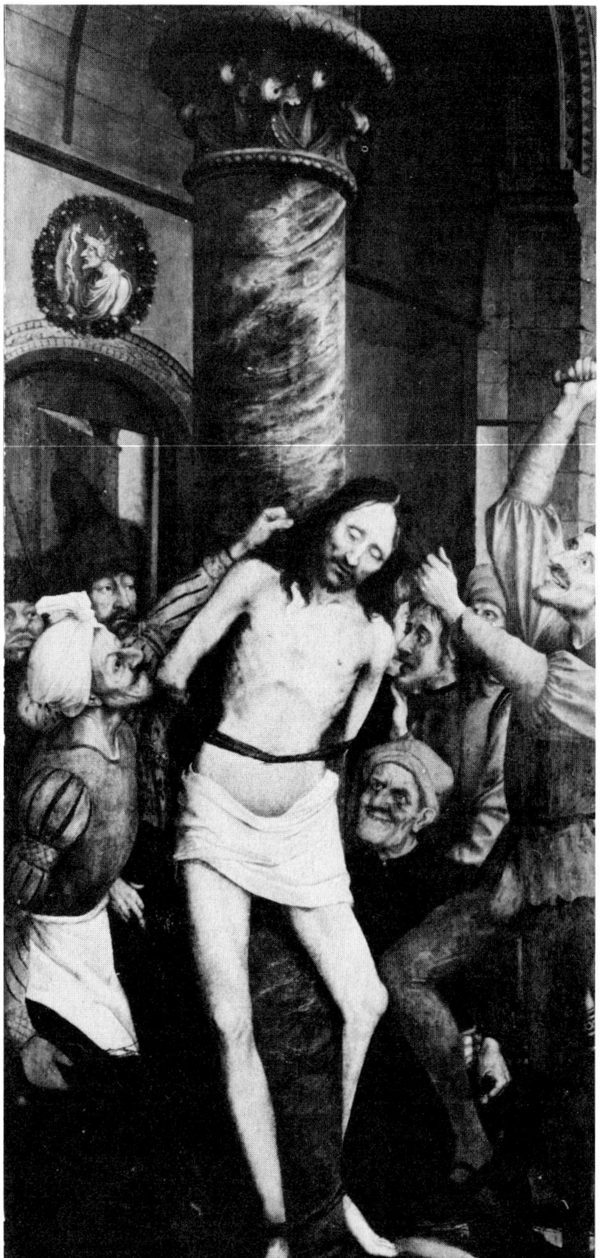

Plate 32. Massys. Passion altarpiece. Left panel: Flagellation. Coimbra, Museu Machado de Castro.

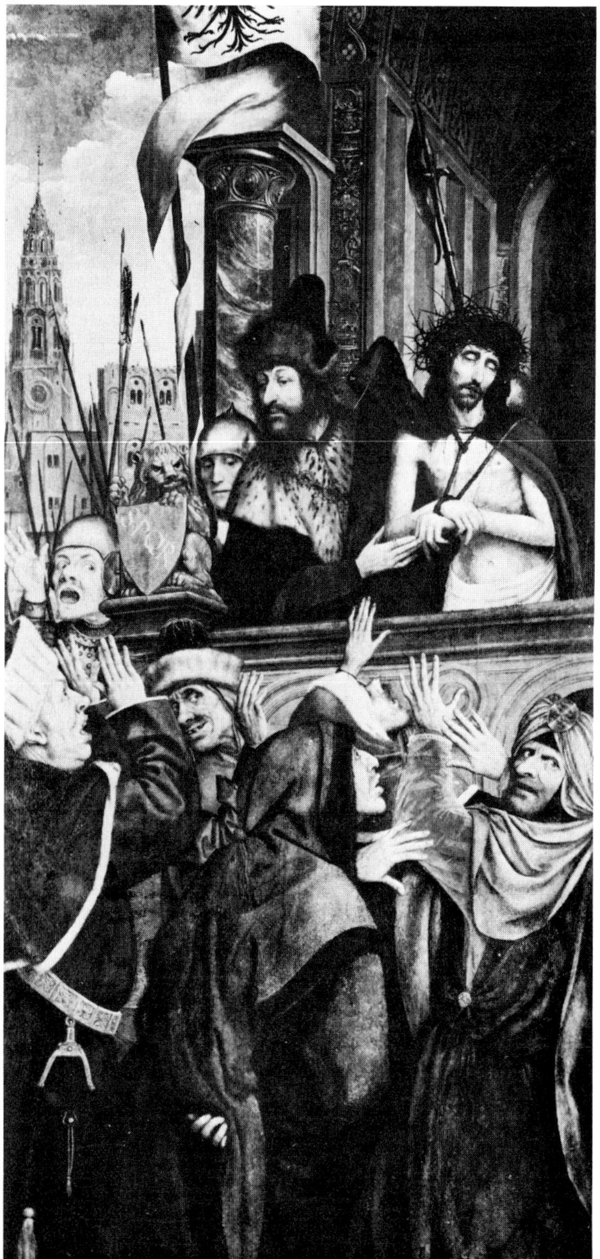

Plate 33. Massys. Passion altarpiece. Right panel: Ecce Homo. Coimbra, Museu Machado de Castro.

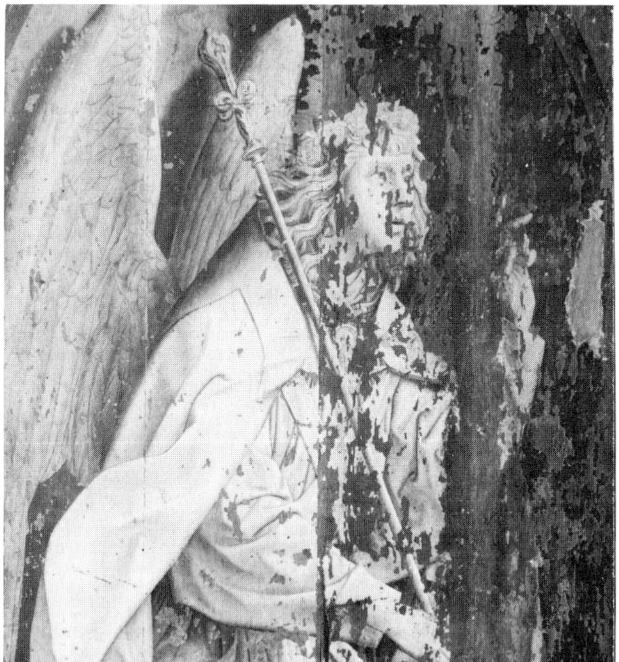

Plate 34. Massys. Passion altarpiece. Left exterior: Gabriel of Annunciation. Coimbra, Museu Machado de Castro.

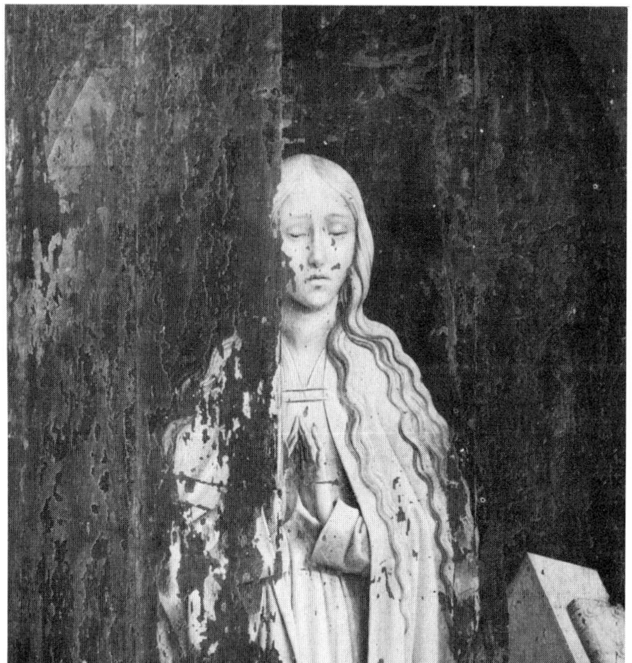

Plate 35. Massys. Passion altarpiece. Right exterior: Virgin Annunciate. Coimbra, Museu Machado de Castro.

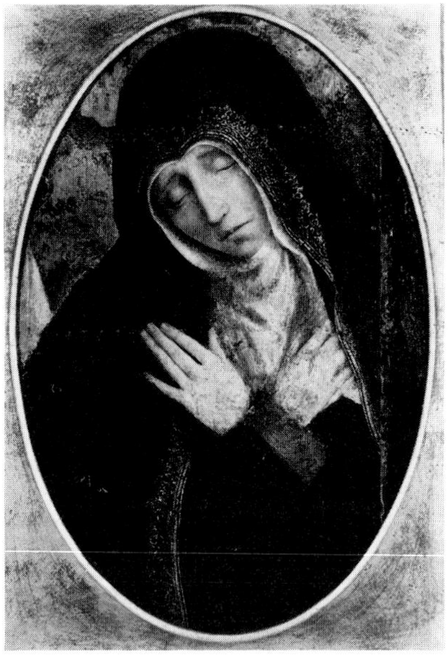

Plate 36. Massys. Passion altarpiece. Center (fragment): Grieving Madonna. Coimbra, Museu Machado de Castro.

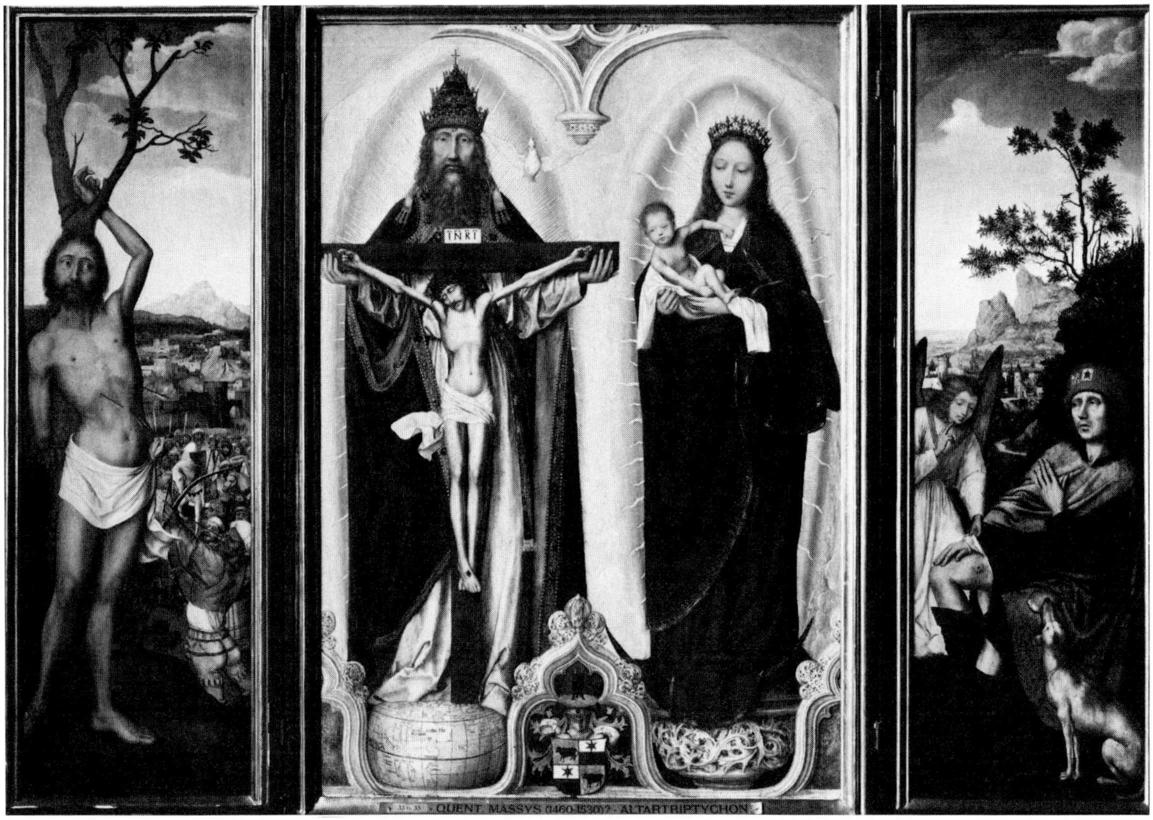

Plate 37. Massys. Rem altarpiece. Munich, Alte Pinakothek.

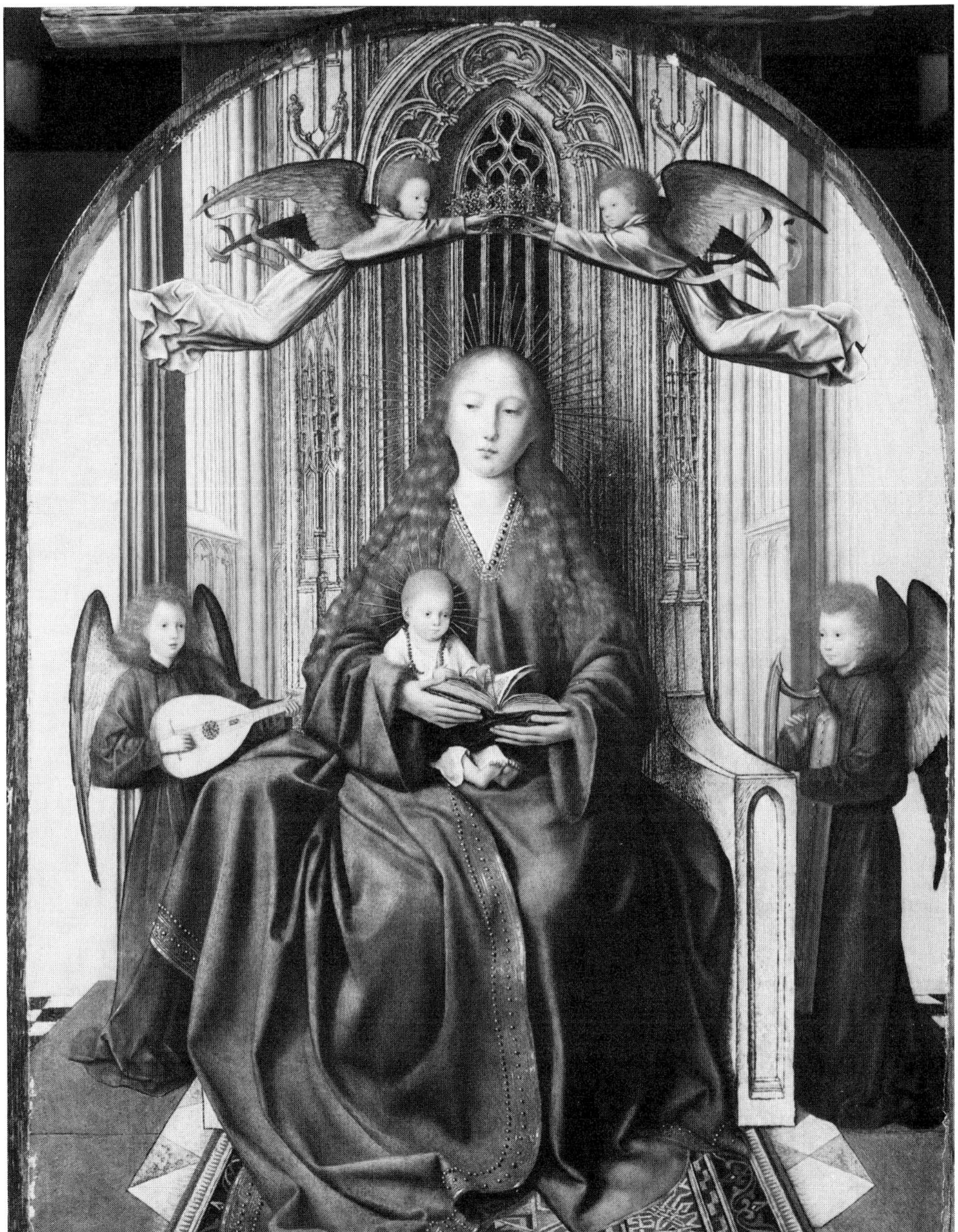

Plate 38. Massys. Madonna Enthroned (Dyson-Perrins). London, National Gallery.

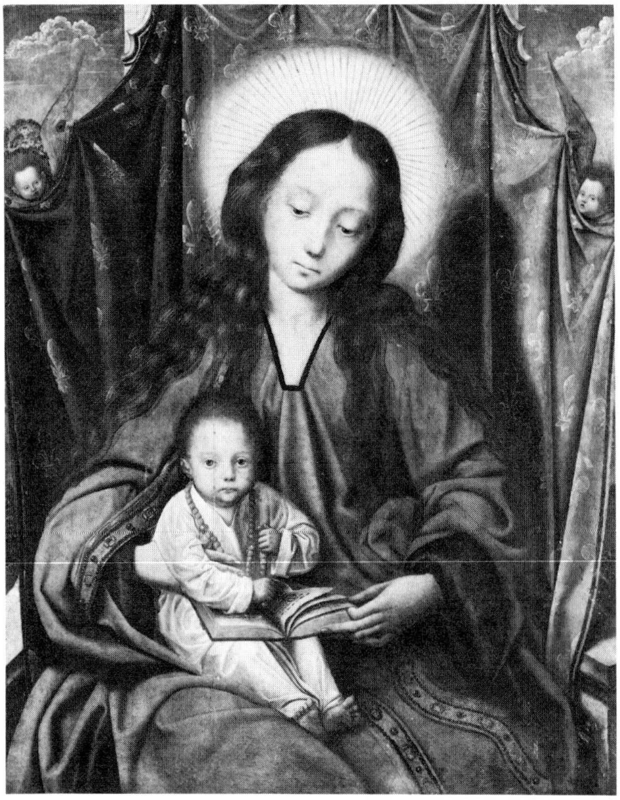

Plate 39. Massys. Madonna at half-length with Angels. Brussels, Musées Royaux.

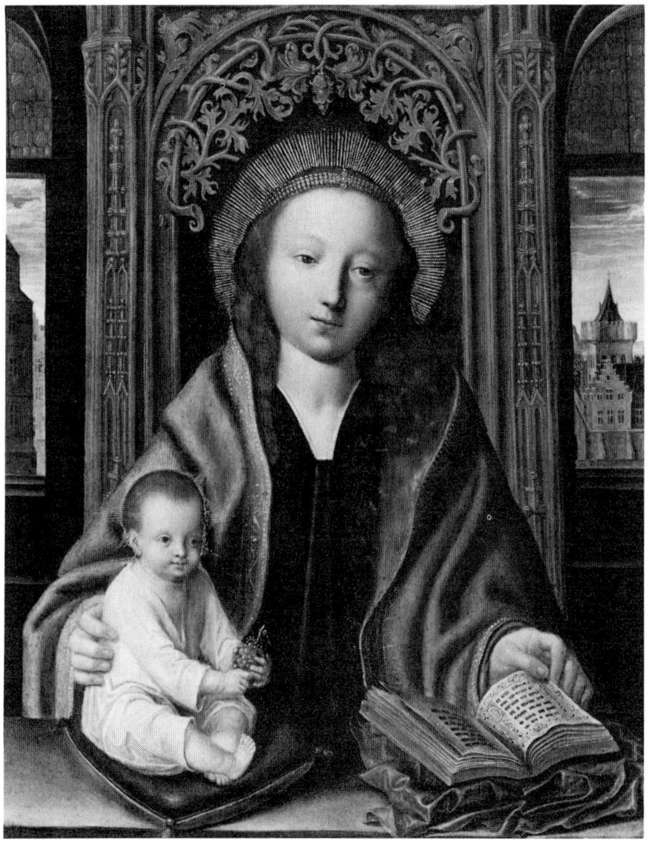

Plate 40. Massys, copy. Madonna and Child at half-length with Grapes. New York, Newhouse Gallery.

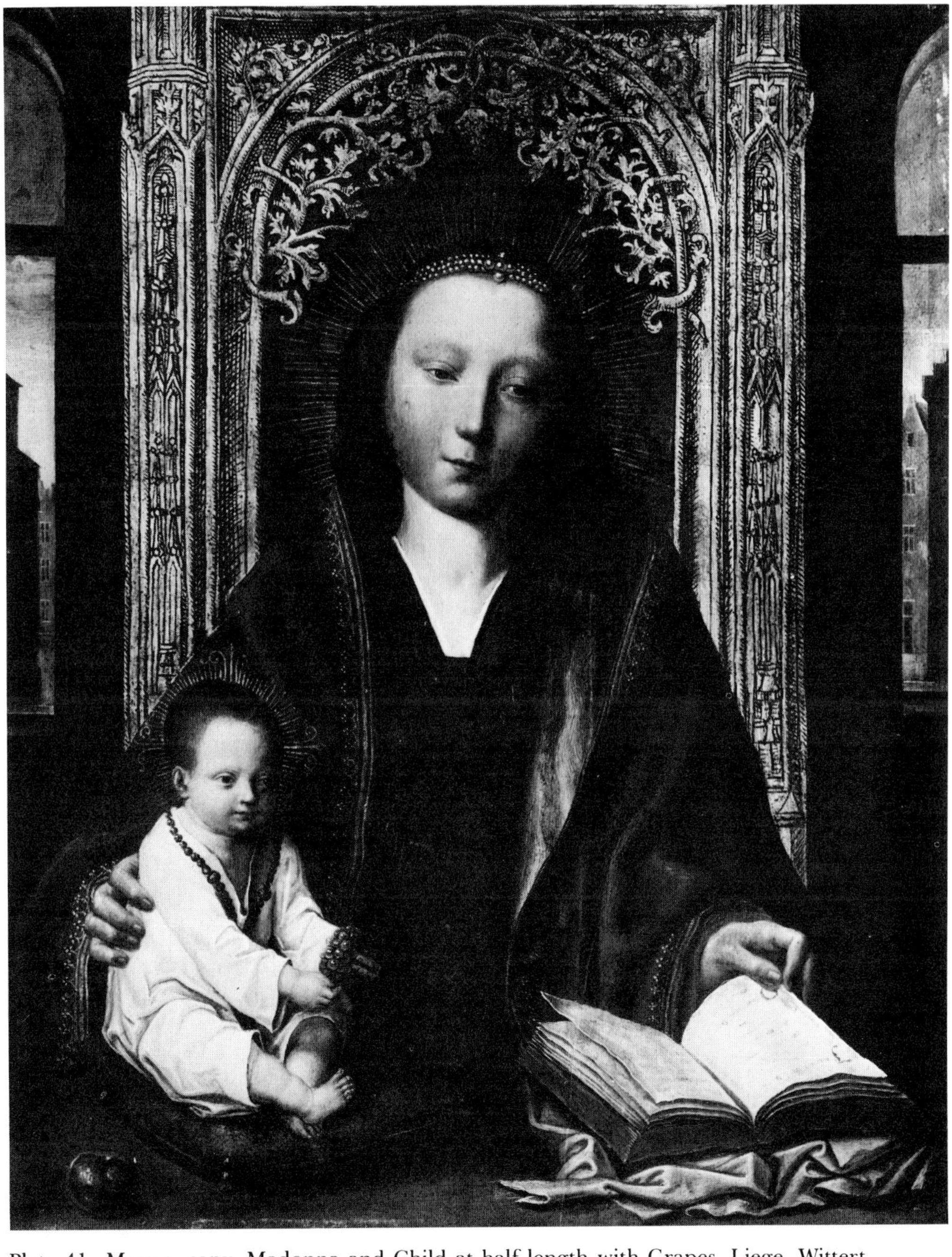

Plate 41. Massys, copy. Madonna and Child at half-length with Grapes. Liege, Wittert coll.

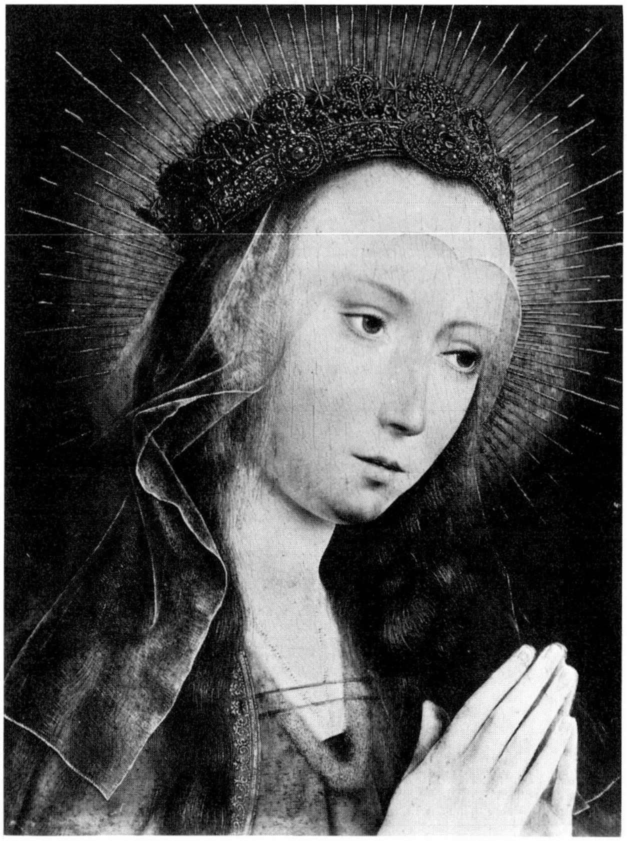

Plate 42. Massys. Madonna in Prayer. Antwerp, Koninklijk Museum.

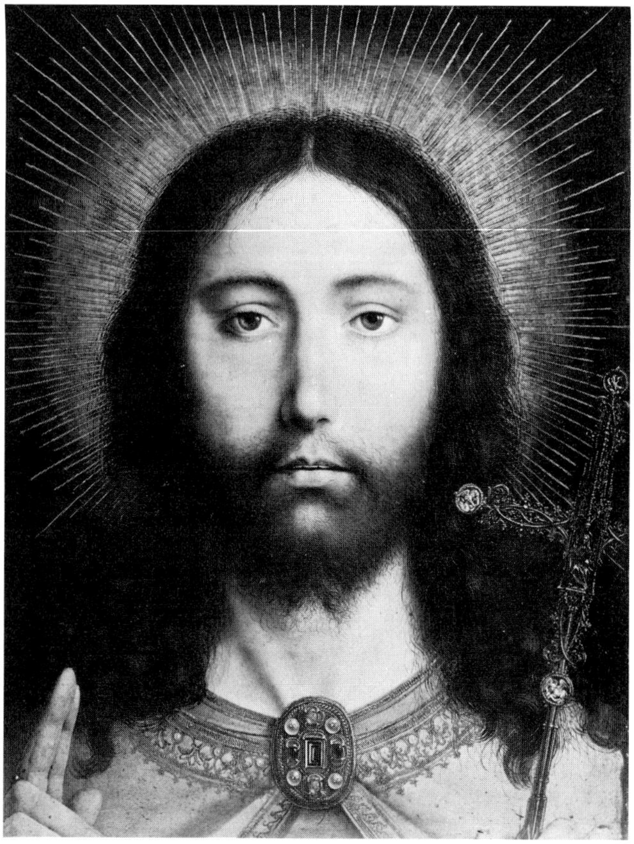

Plate 43. Massys. Salvator Mundi. Antwerp, Koninklijk Museum.

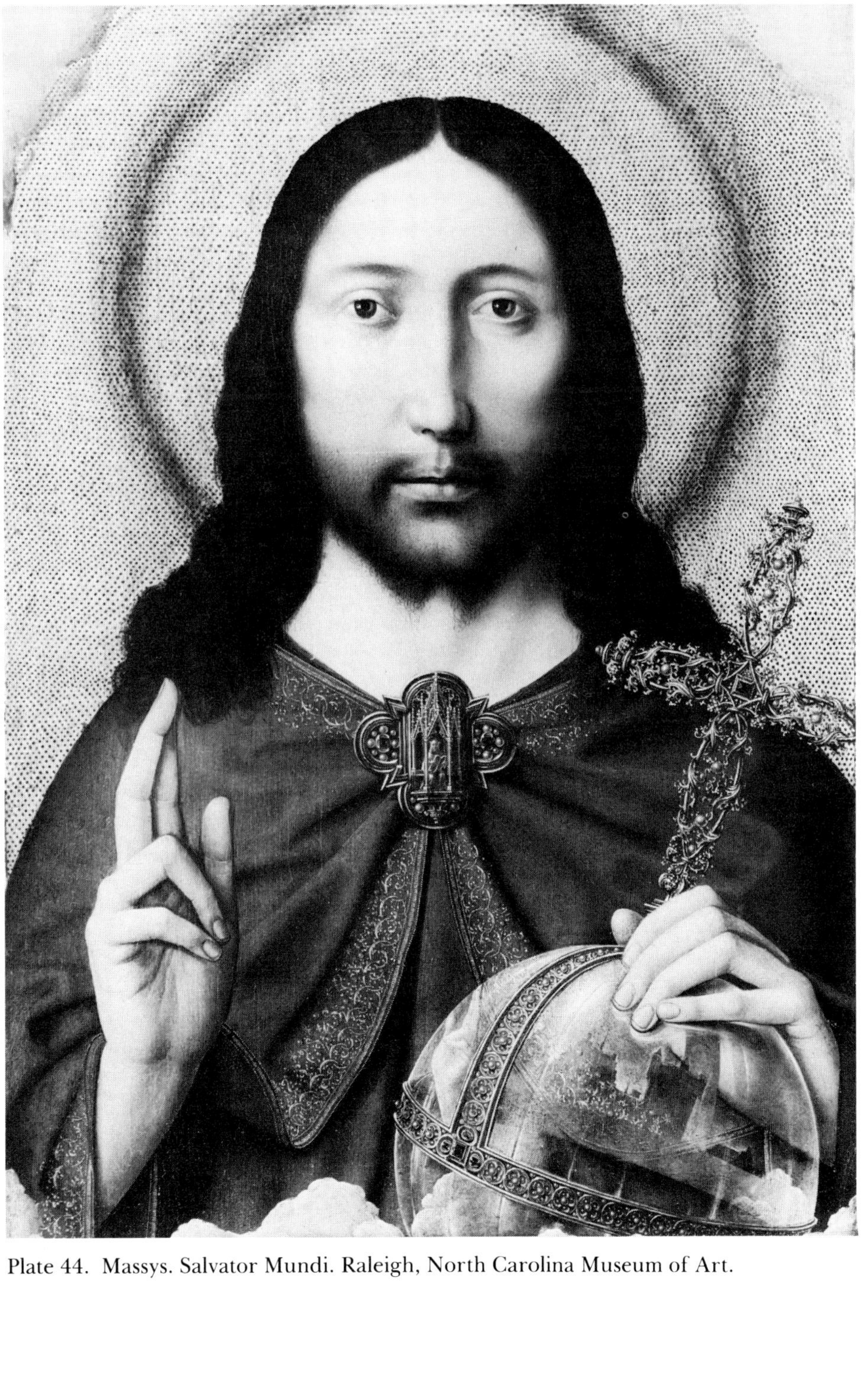

Plate 44. Massys. Salvator Mundi. Raleigh, North Carolina Museum of Art.

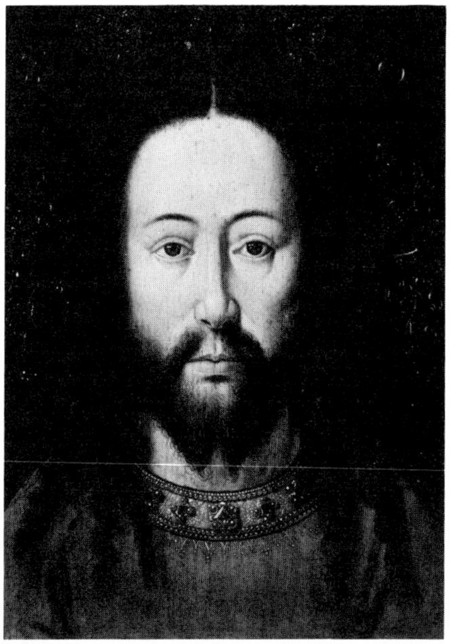

Plate 45. Jan van Eyck, copy. Holy Face. Bruges, Groeninge Museum.

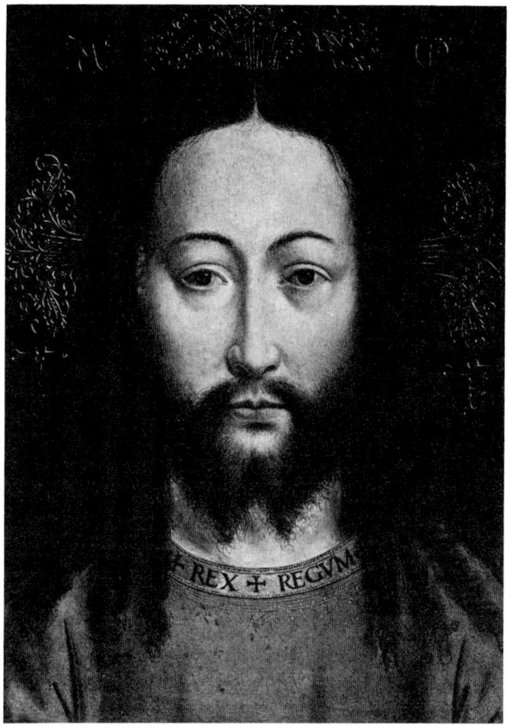

Plate 46. Jan van Eyck, copy. Holy Face. Berlin-Dahlem.

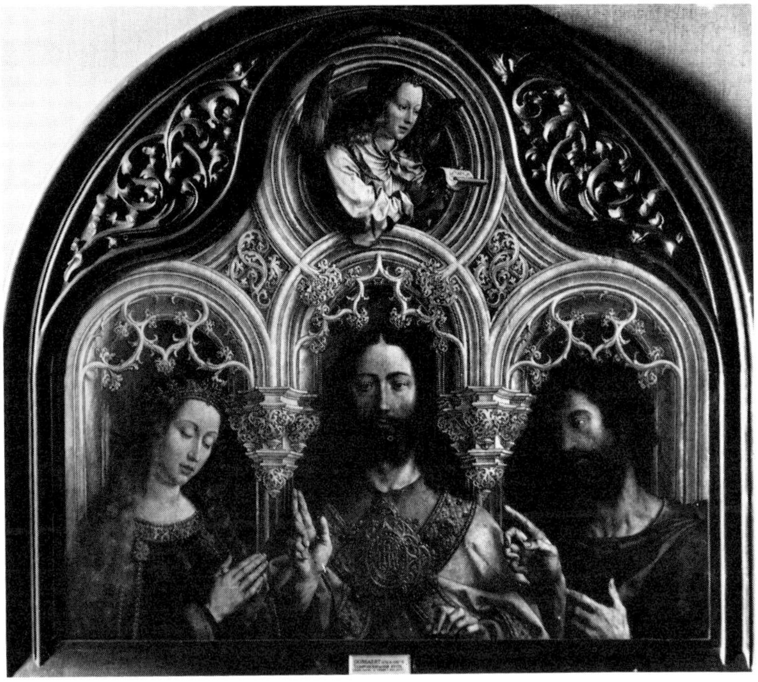

Plate 47. Jan Gossaert. Deësis. Madrid, Prado.

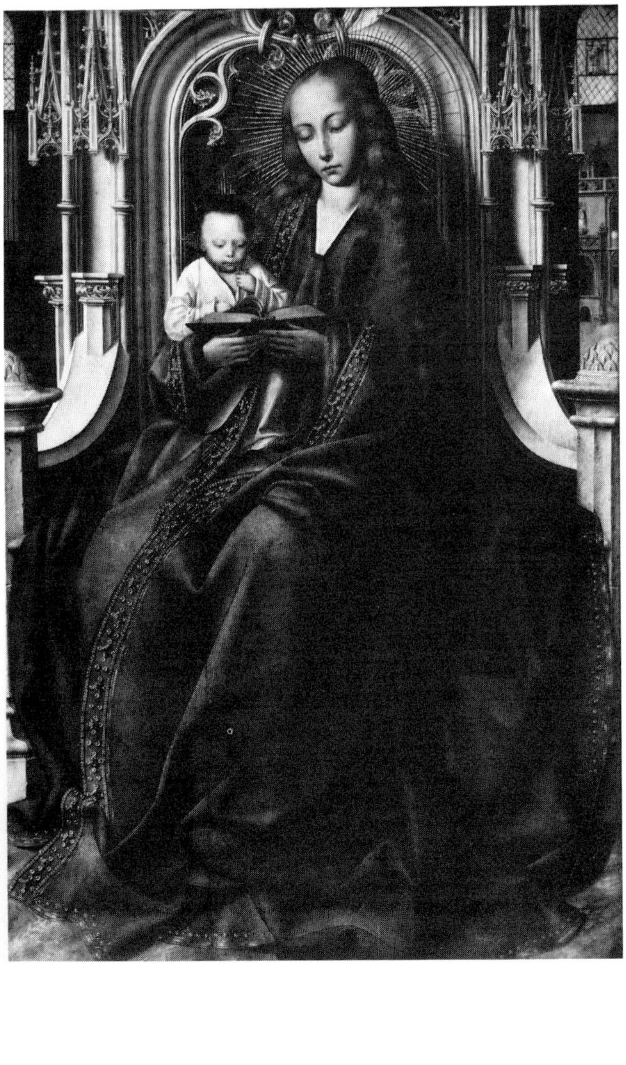

Plate 48. Massys. Madonna Enthroned. Brussels, Musées Royaux.

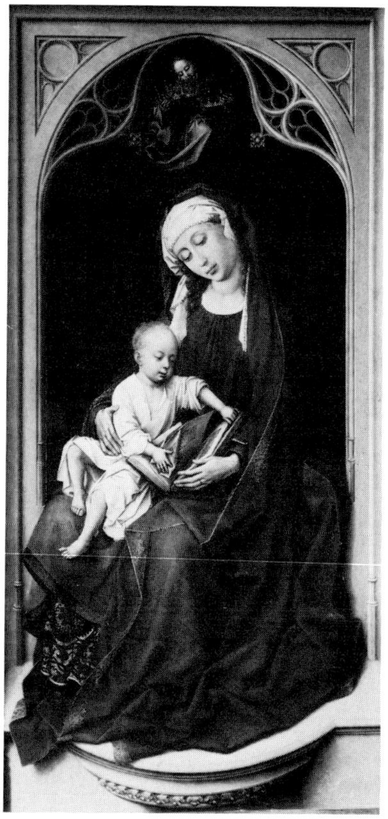

Plate 49. Roger van der Weyden. Madonna in a Niche (Madonna Duran). Madrid, Prado.

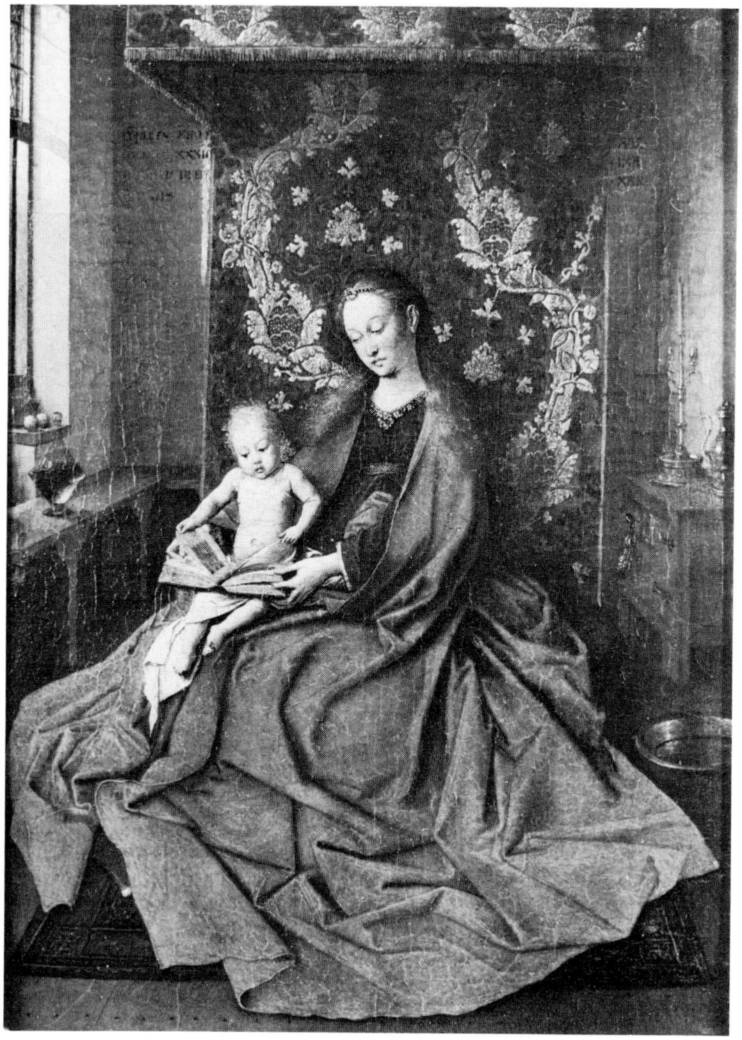

Plate 50. Jan van Eyck, copy. "Ince Hall Madonna." Melbourne, National Gallery.

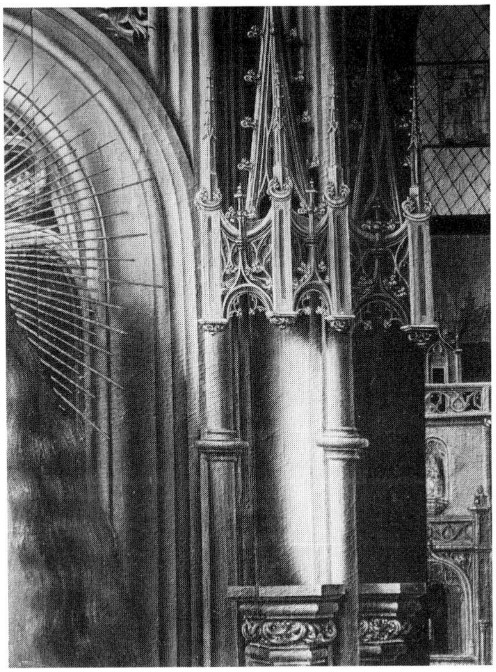

Plate 51. Detail of Plate 48.

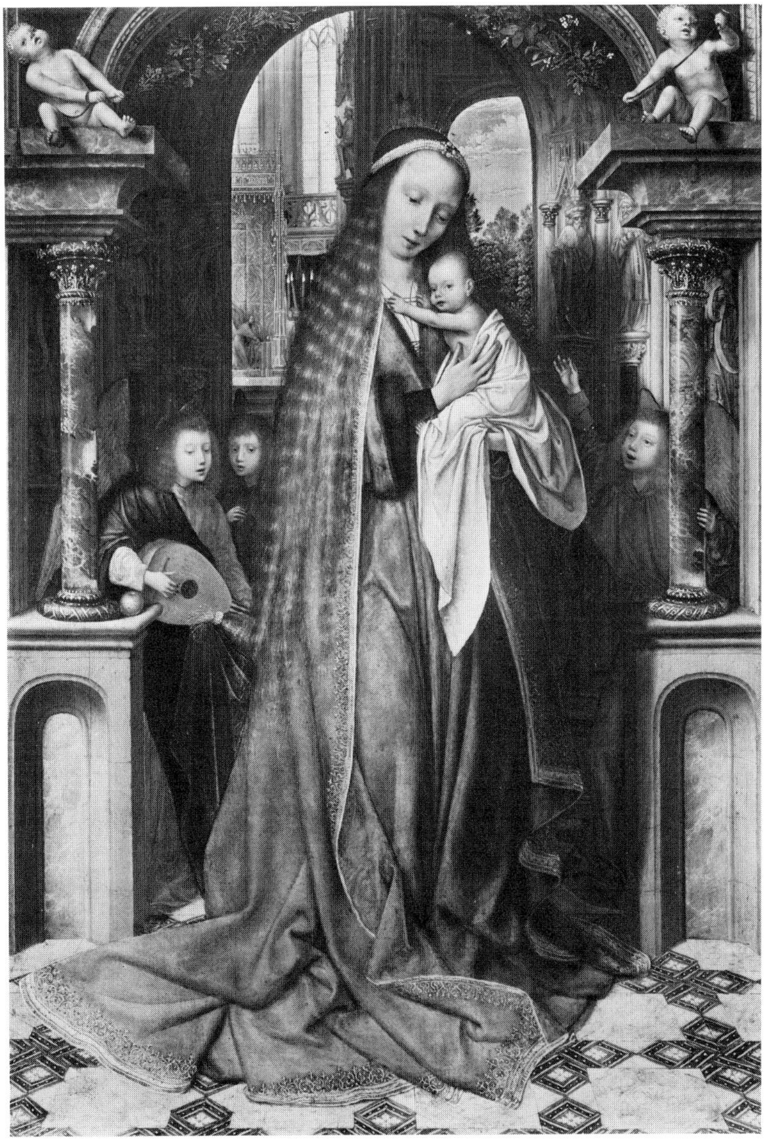

Plate 52. Massys. Madonna Standing with Angels. London, Seilern collection.

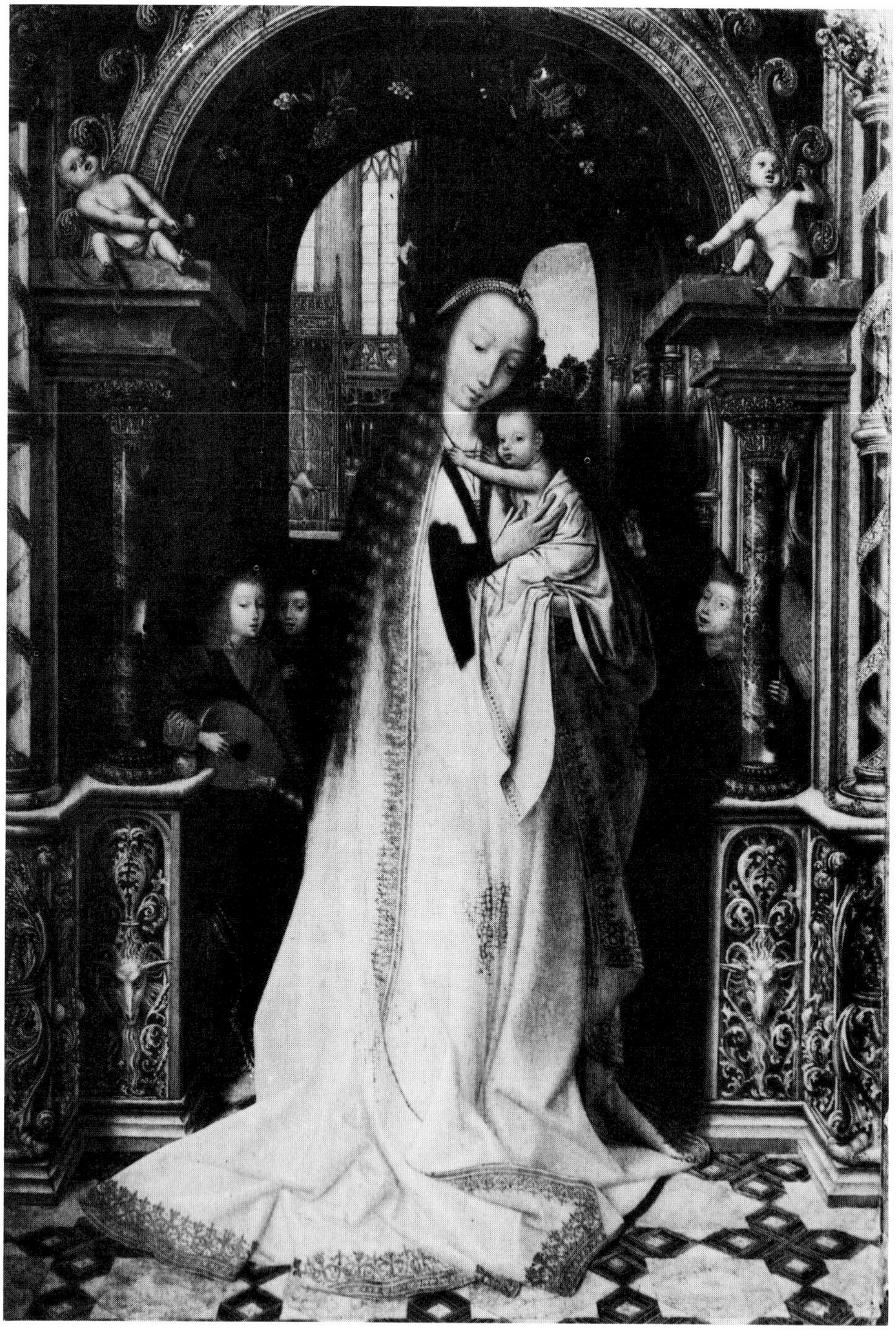

Plate 53. Massys, replica. Madonna Standing with Angels. Lyons, Musée des Beaux-Arts.

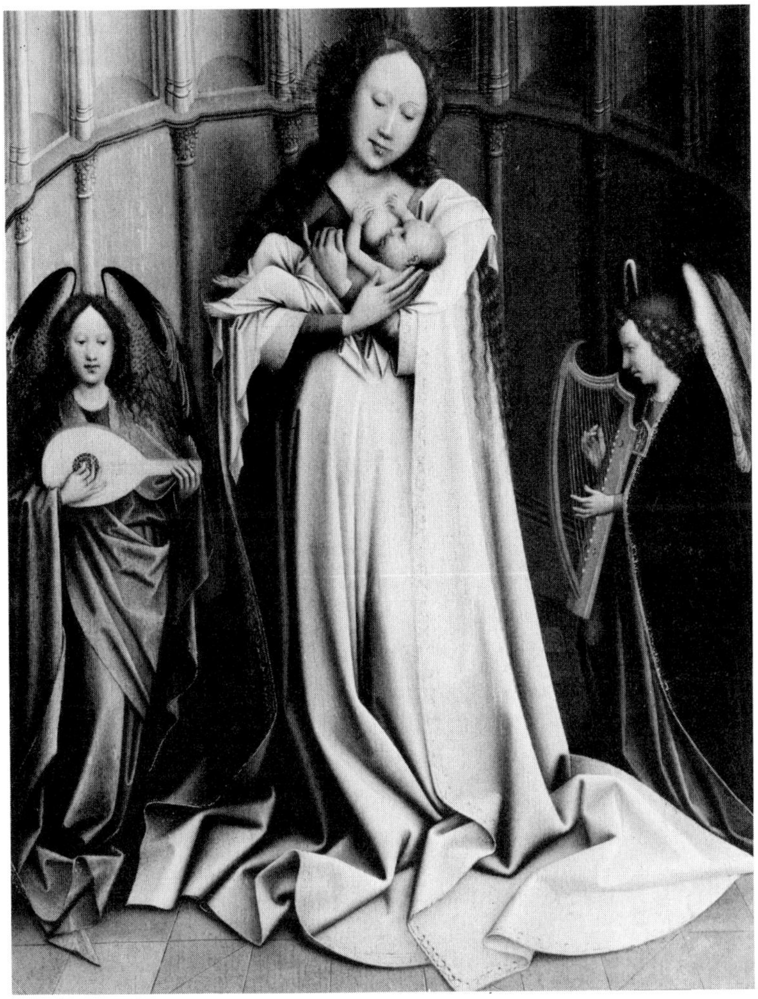

Plate 54. Robert Campin, copy. Madonna in an Apse. Sarasota, Ringling Museum.

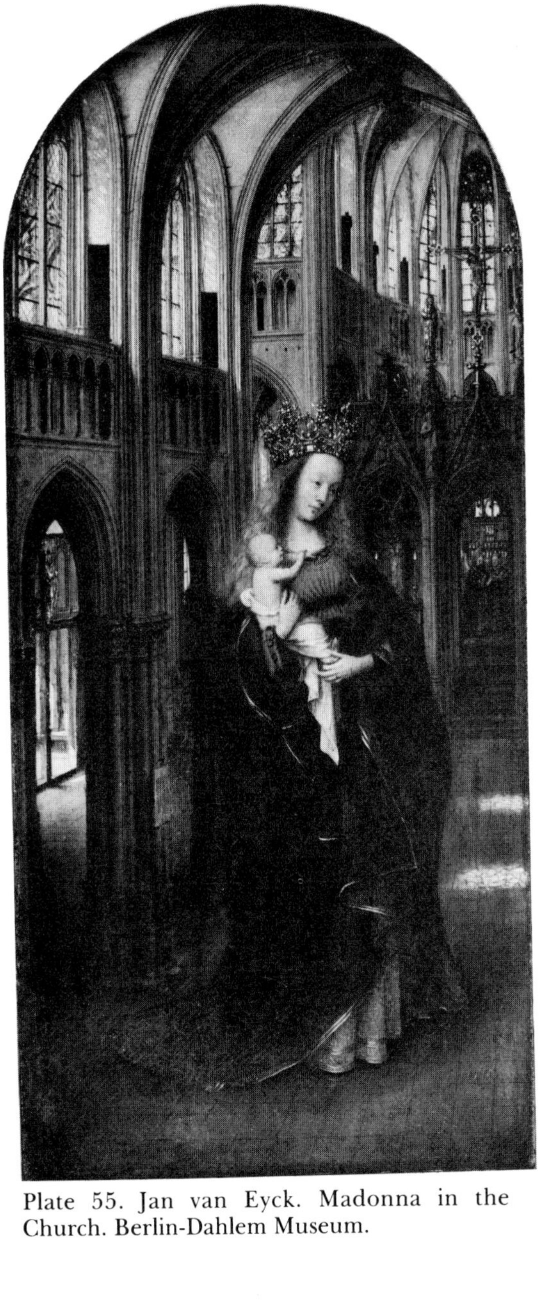

Plate 55. Jan van Eyck. Madonna in the Church. Berlin-Dahlem Museum.

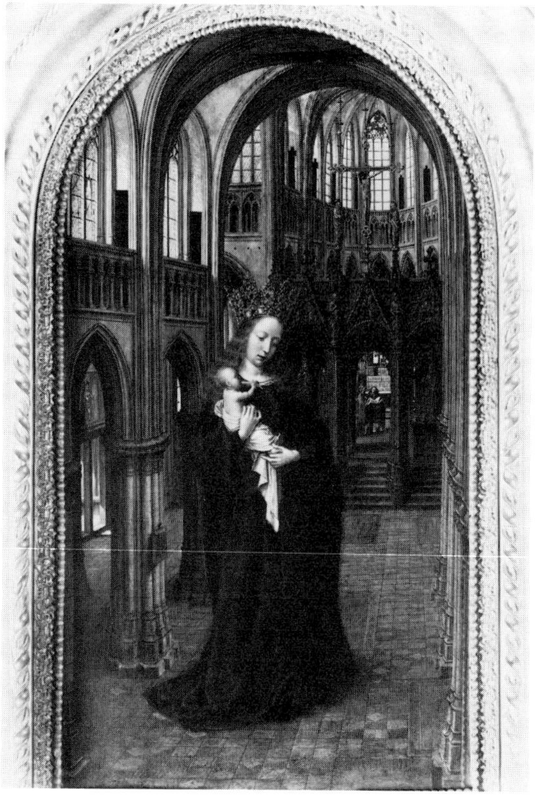

Plate 56. Jan Gossaert. Madonna in the Church. Rome, Palazzo Doria.

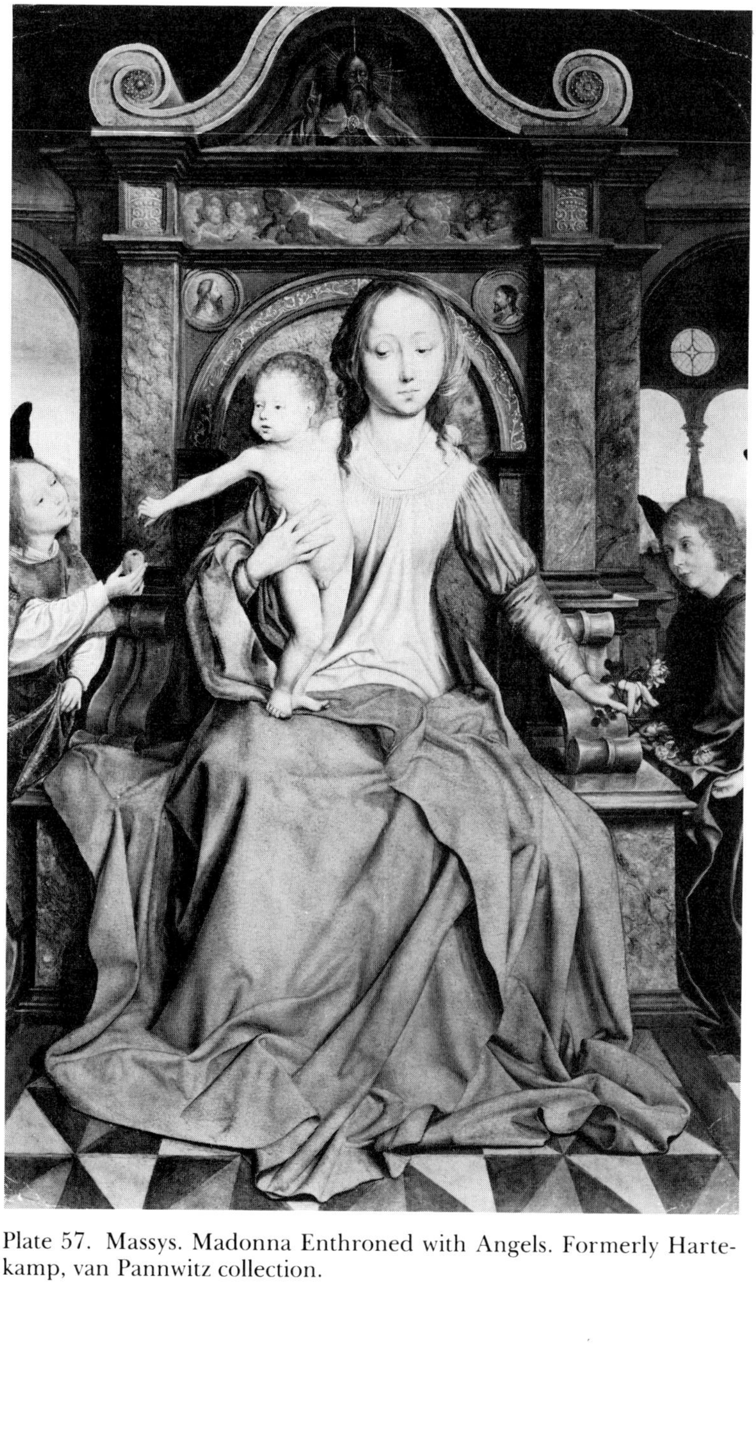

Plate 57. Massys. Madonna Enthroned with Angels. Formerly Hartekamp, van Pannwitz collection.

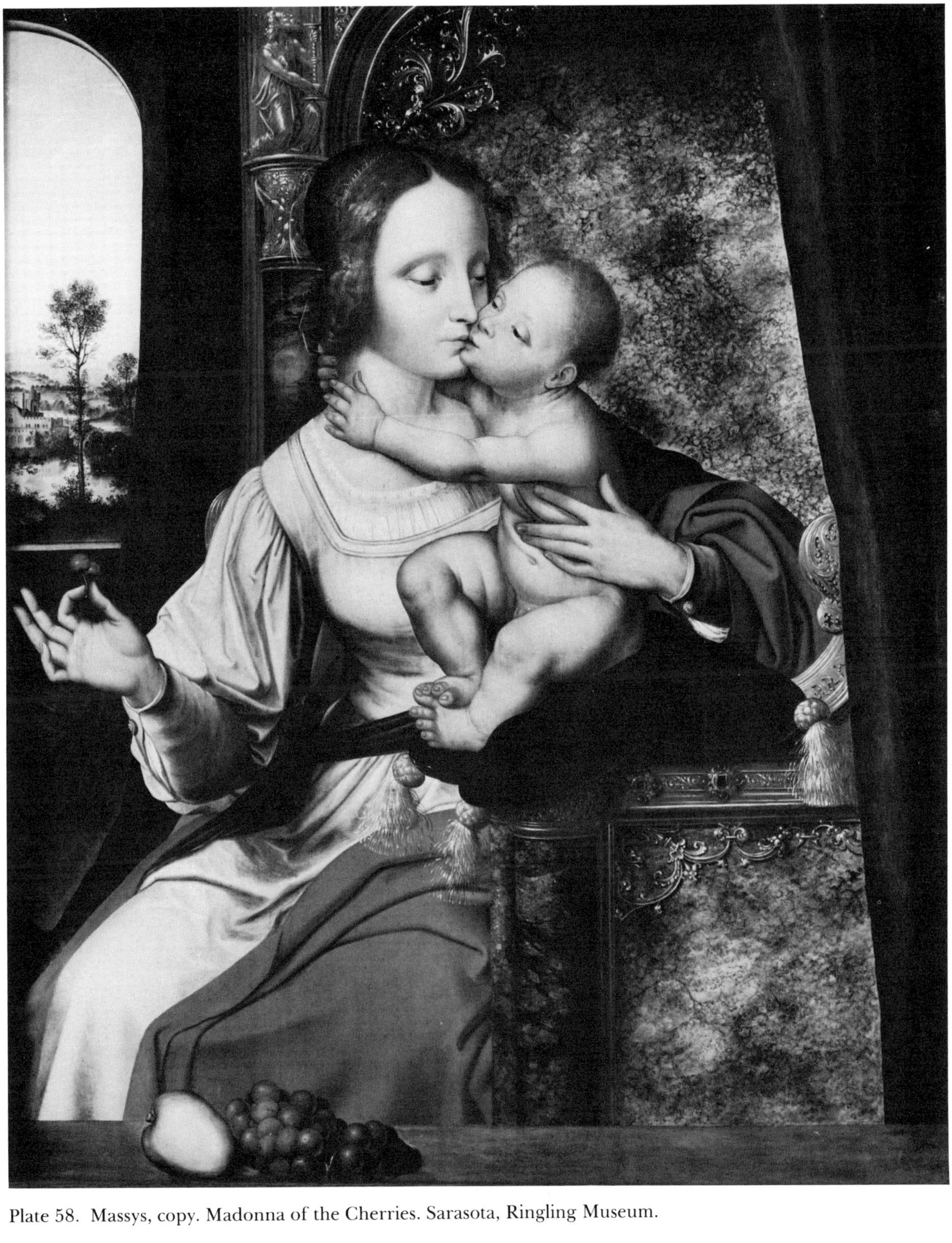

Plate 58. Massys, copy. Madonna of the Cherries. Sarasota, Ringling Museum.

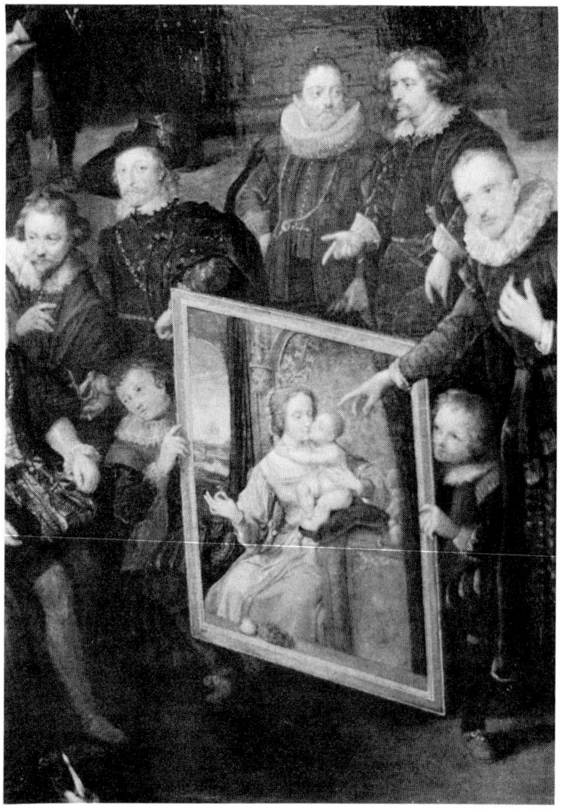

Plate 59. Willem van Haecht. Gallery of Cornelis van der Geest (detail, showing original of Plate 58). Antwerp, Rubenshuis.

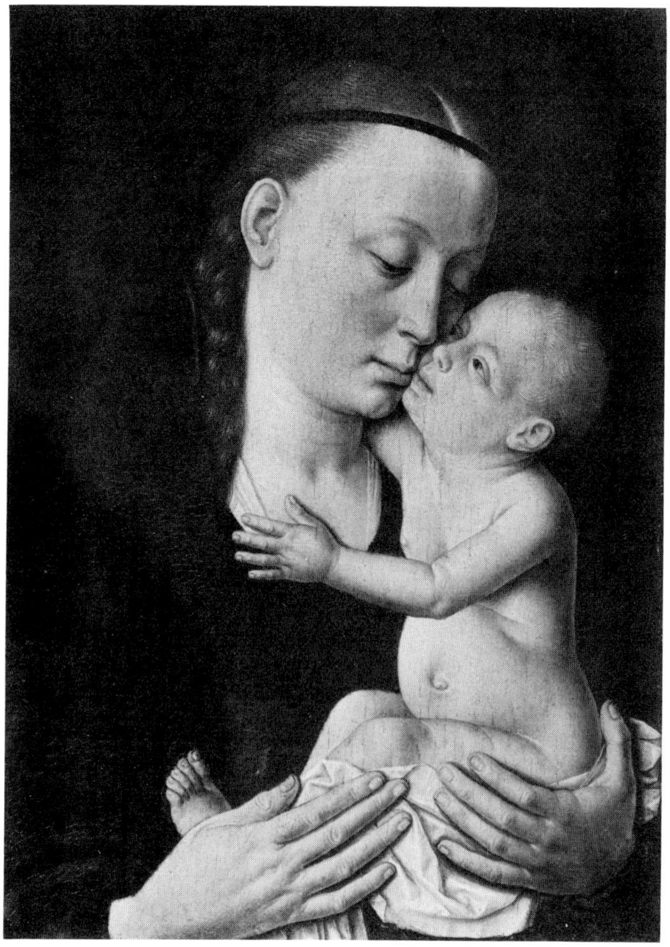

Plate 60. Dieric Bouts. Madonna and Child Embracing. New York, Metropolitan Museum.

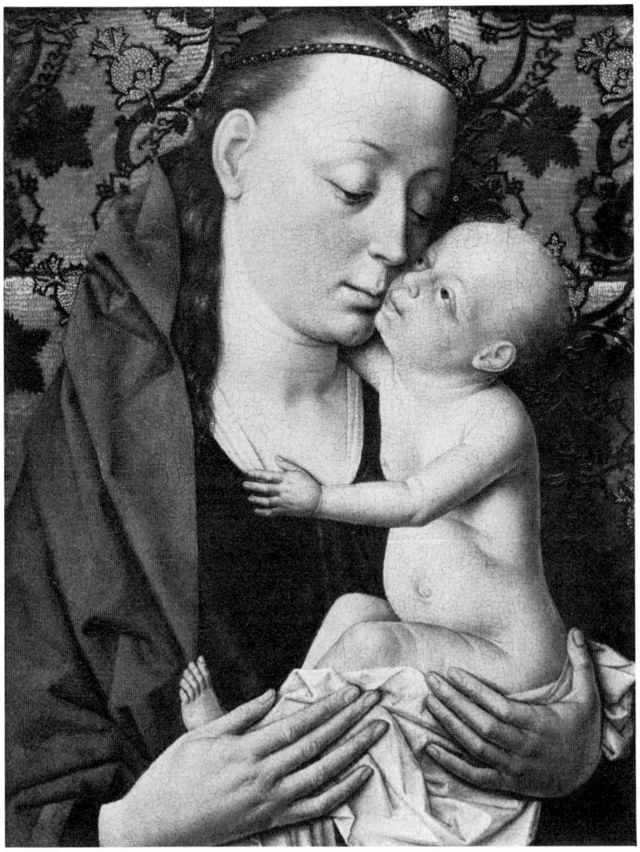

Plate 61. Dieric Bouts. Madonna and Child Embracing. San Francisco, de Young Museum.

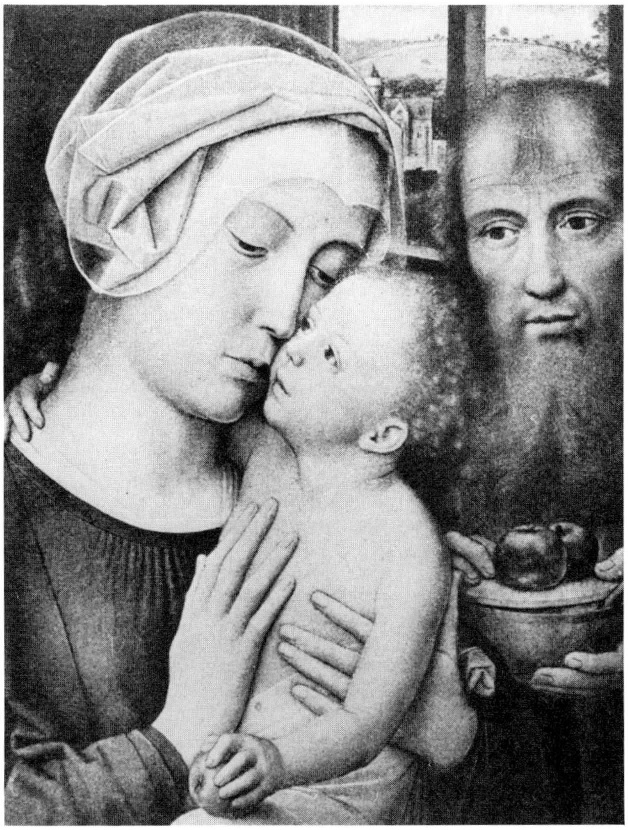

Plate 62. Gerard David. Holy Family. Formerly Paris, Leroy collection.

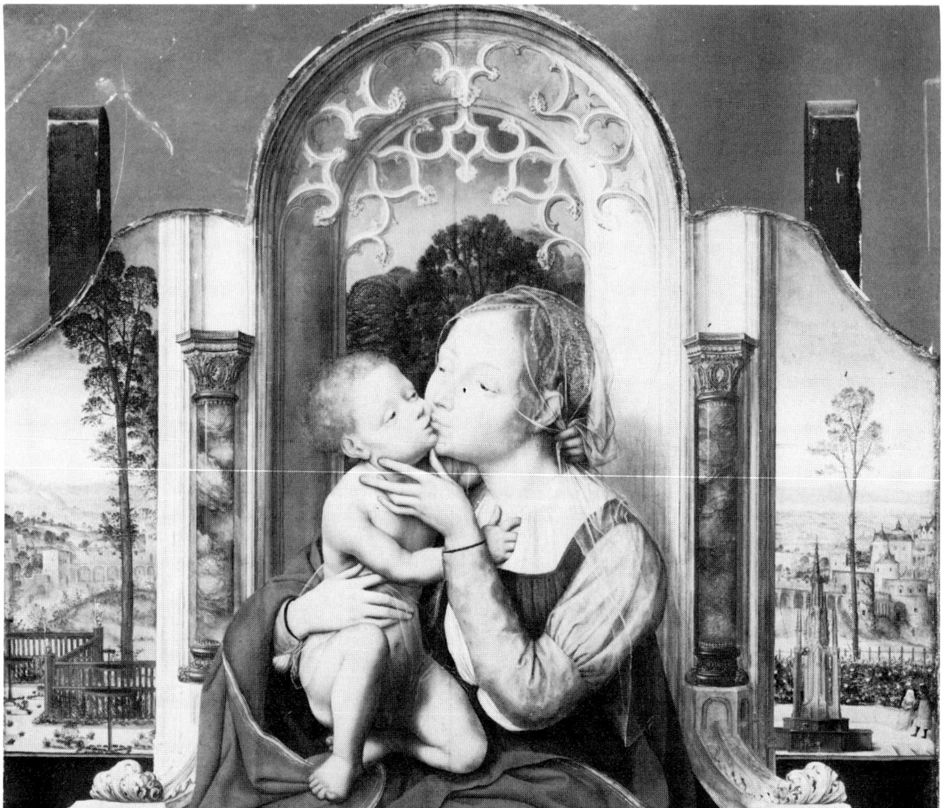

Plate 63. Massys. Madonna and Child Enthroned. Berlin-Dahlem Museum.

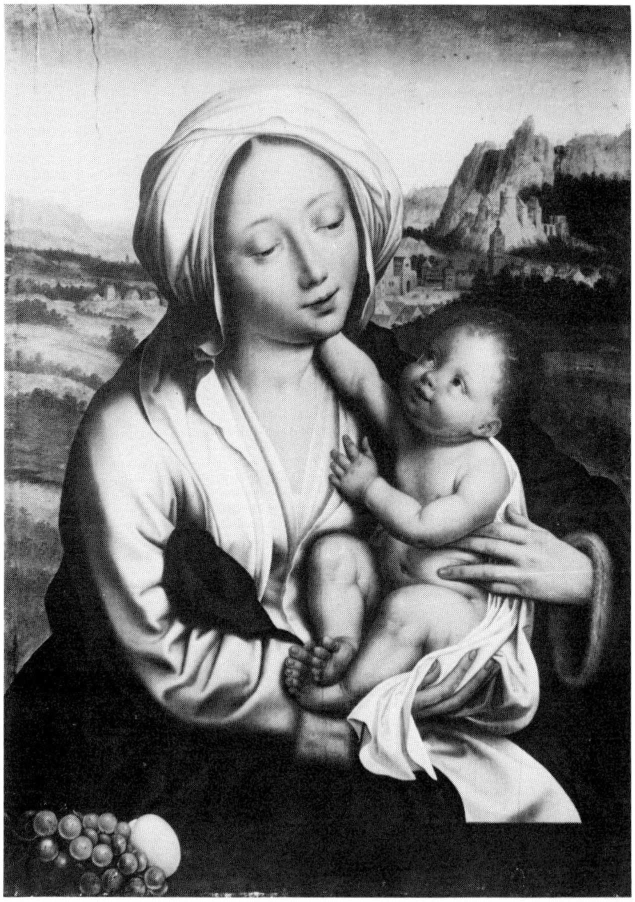

Plate 64. Massys. Madonna and Child Outdoors. Detroit Institute of Arts.

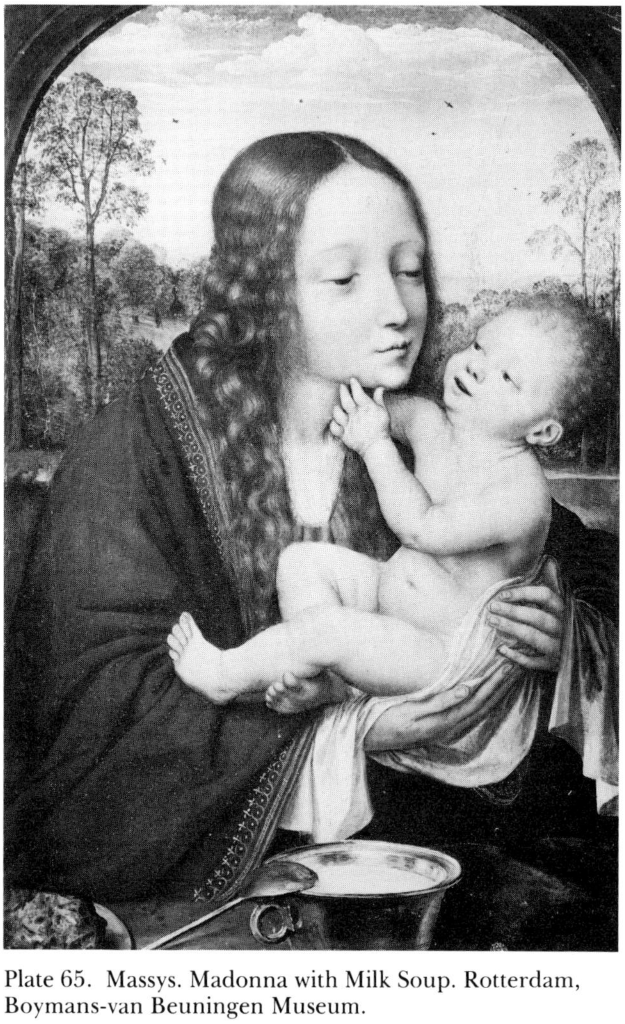

Plate 65. Massys. Madonna with Milk Soup. Rotterdam, Boymans-van Beuningen Museum.

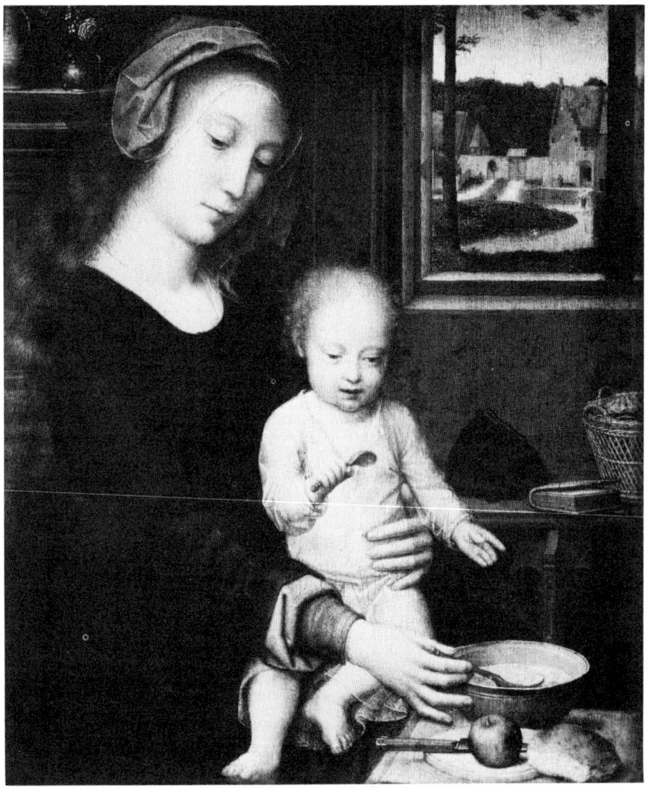

Plate 66. Gerard David. Madonna with Milk Soup. Brussels, Musées Royaux.

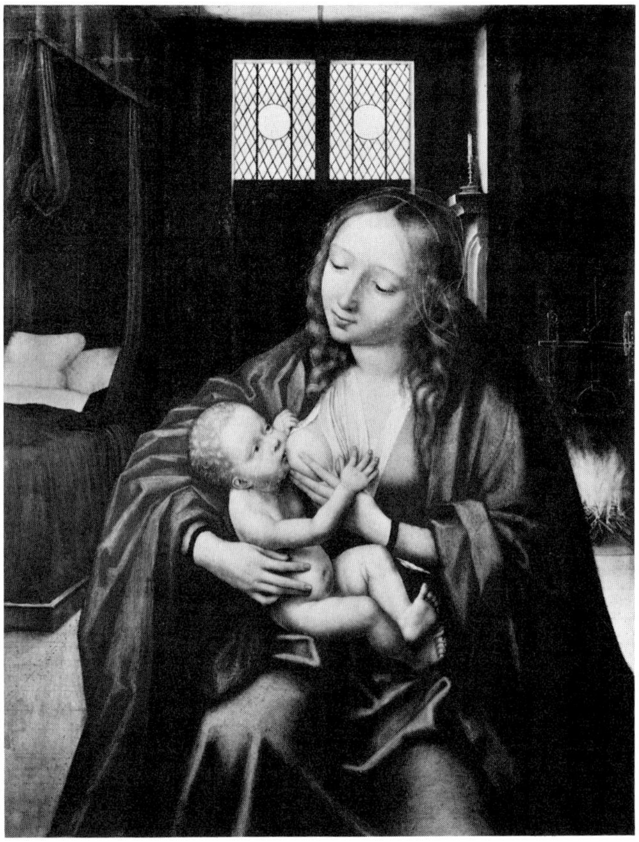

Plate 67. Massys, copy. Madonna Nursing in an Interior. Munich, Alte Pinakothek.

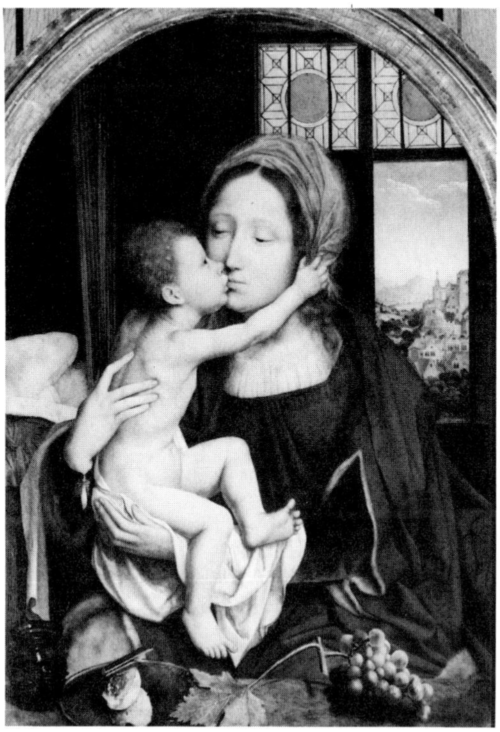

Plate 68. Massys. Madonna and Child Embracing ("Rattier Madonna"). Paris.

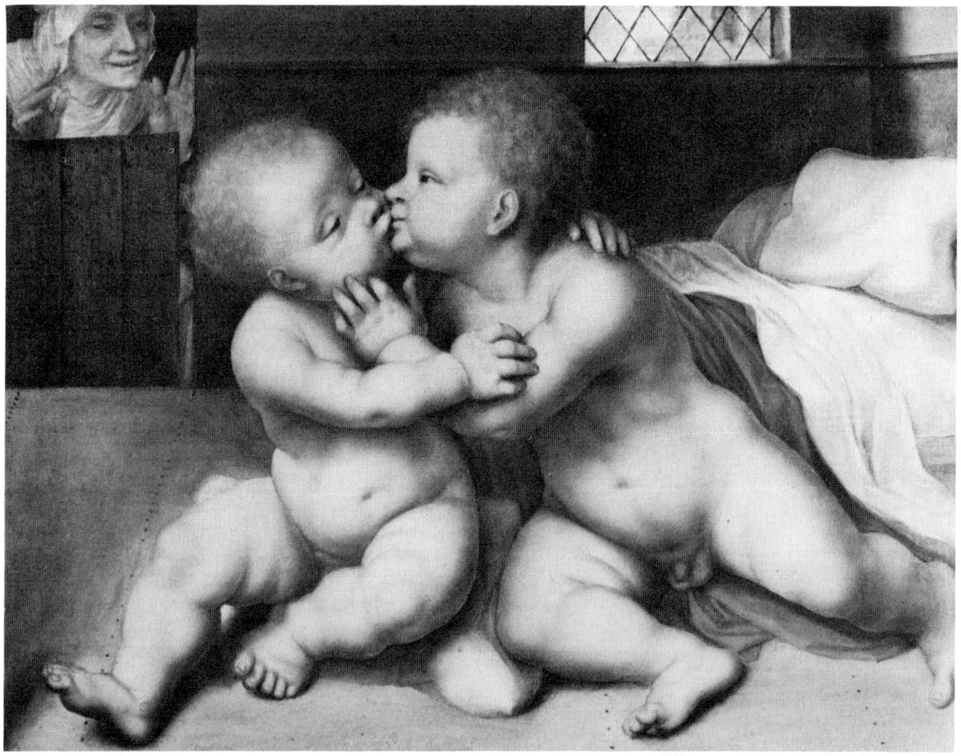

Plate 69. Massys. Infants Jesus and John the Baptist Embracing. Chatsworth, Devonshire Collection.

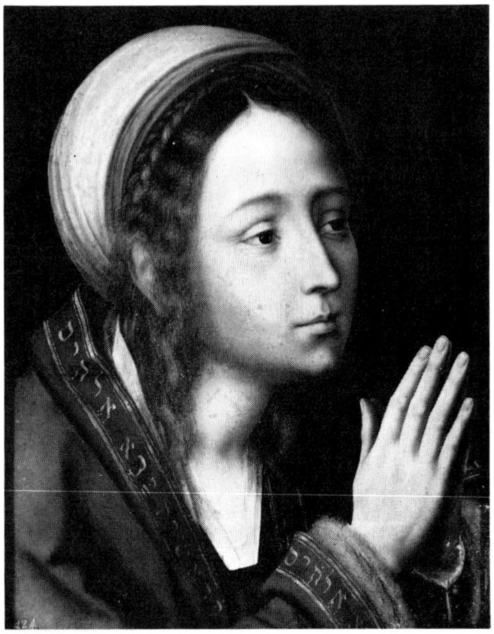

Plate 71. Massys. Virgin in Prayer. Madrid, Prado.

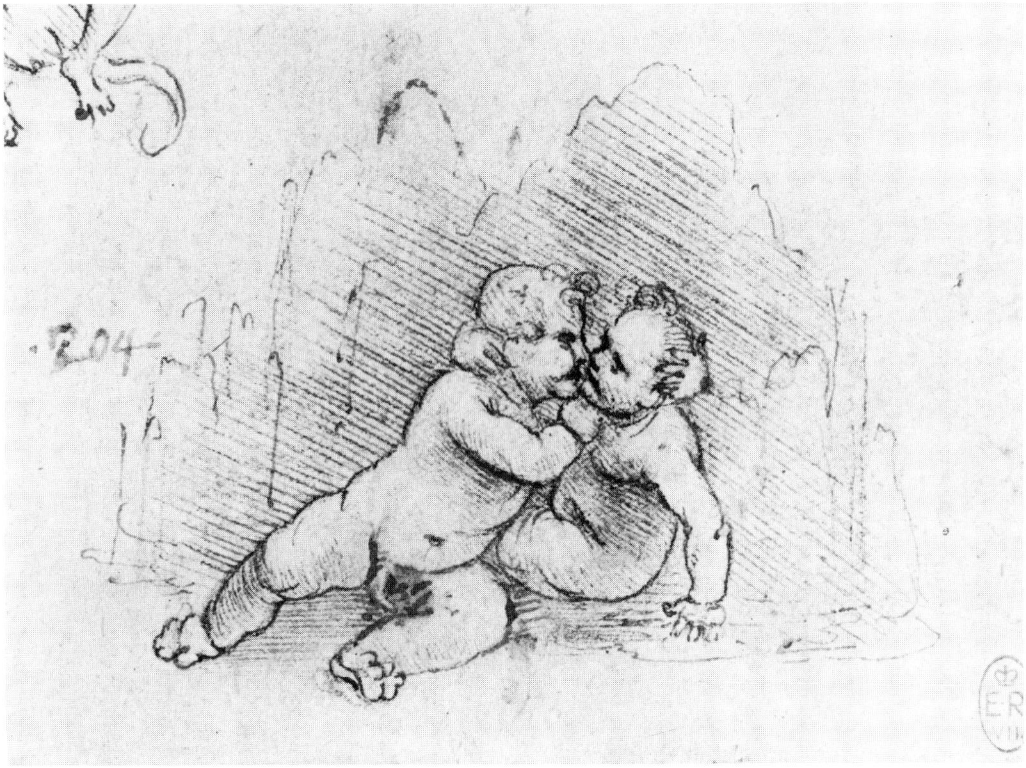

Plate 70. Leonardo da Vinci, copy. Drawing (detail): Infants Jesus and John the Baptist. Windsor Castle (no. 12564).

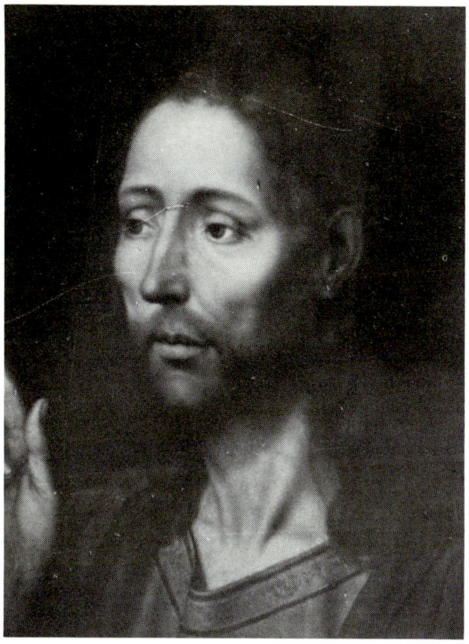

Plate 72. Massys. Christ Blessing. Madrid, Prado.

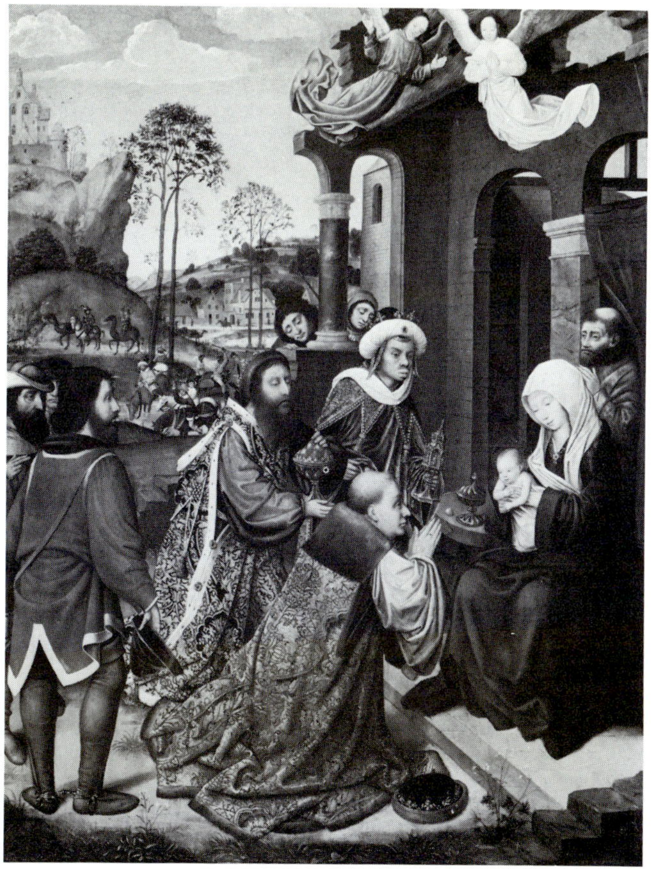

Plate 73. Massys, workshop. Adoration of the Magi. St. Louis Museum.

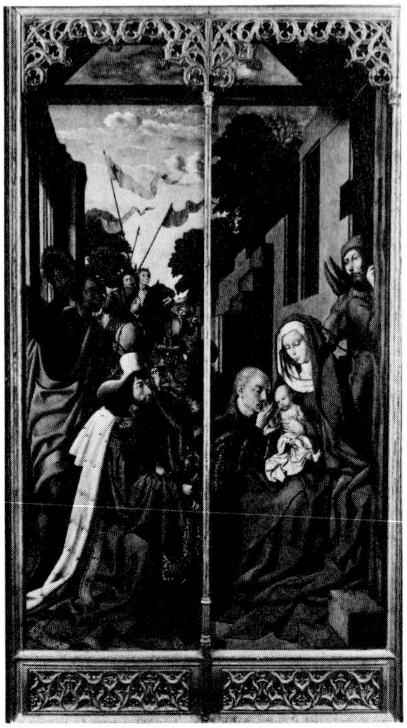

Plate 74. Antwerp Master. Adoration of the Magi (Gonzalez retable). Valladolid, San Salvador.

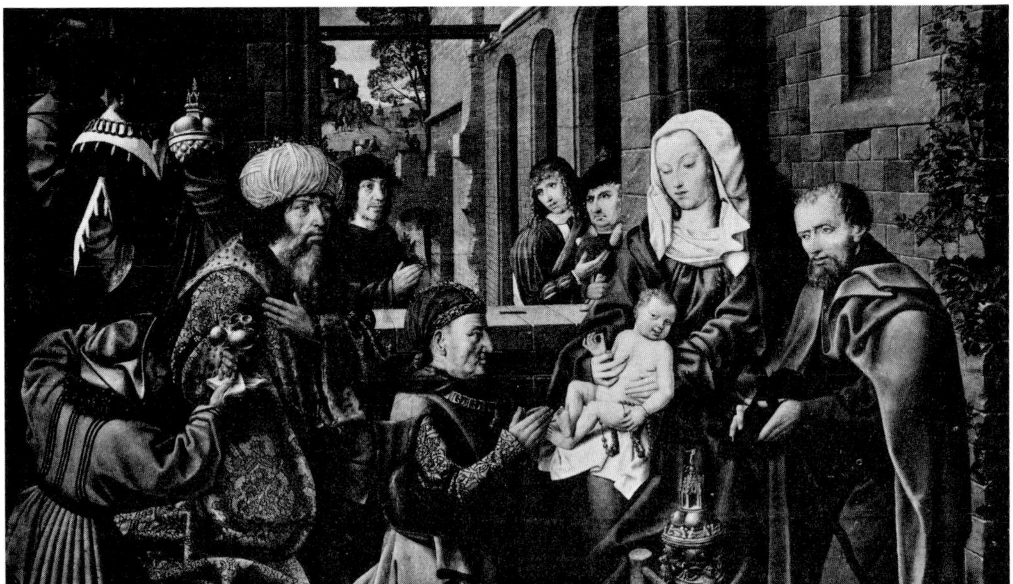

Plate 75. Master of Frankfurt. Copy of Hugo van der Goes, Adoration of the Magi (Monforte altarpiece). Antwerp, Koninklijk Museum.

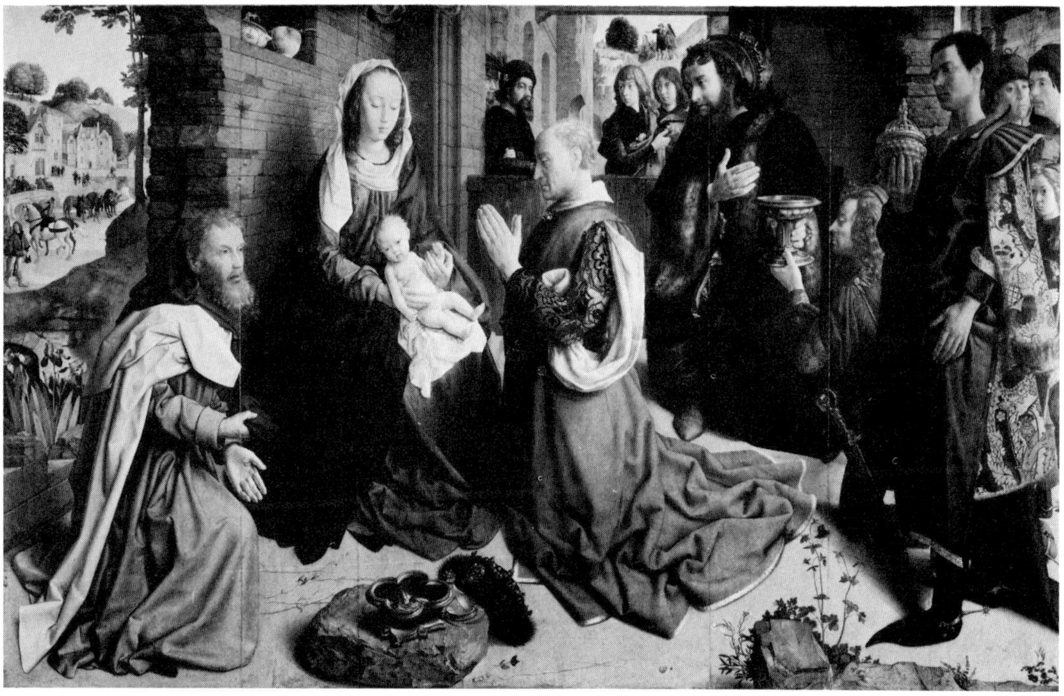

Plate 76. Hugo van der Goes. Adoration of the Magi (Monforte altarpiece). Berlin-Dahlem.

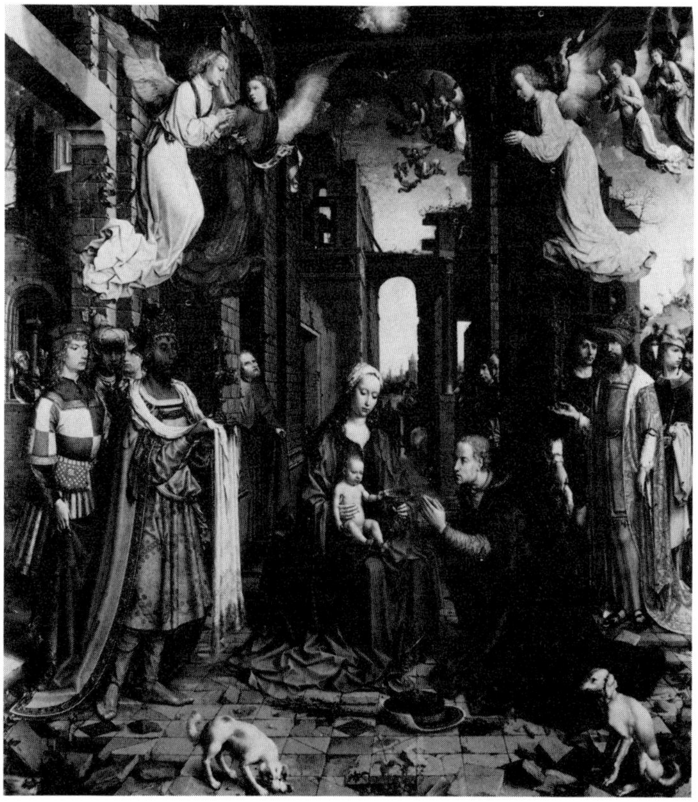

Plate 77. Jan Gossaert. Adoration of the Magi. London, National Gallery.

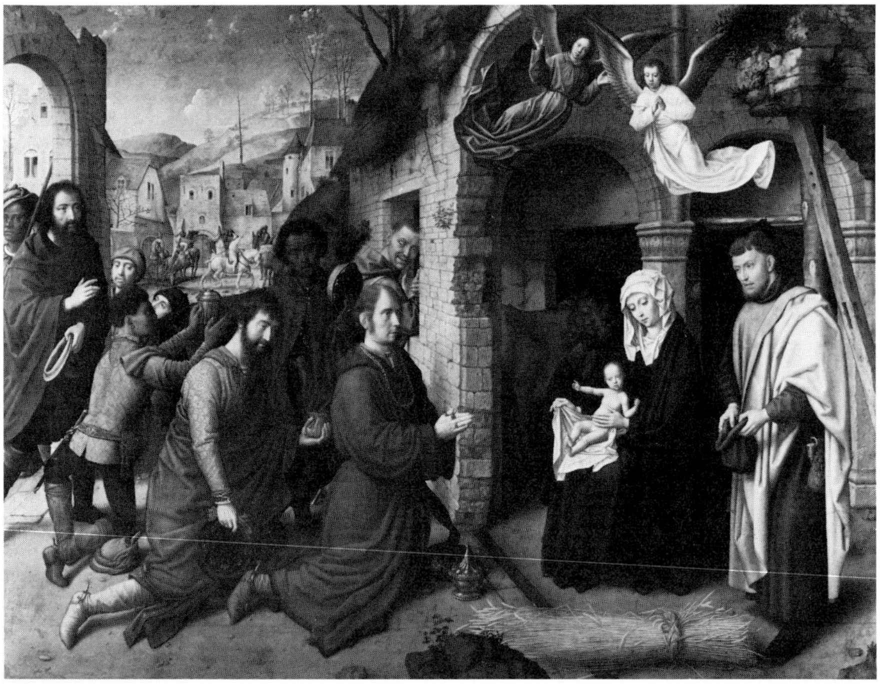

Plate 78. Gerard David. Copy of Hugo van der Goes, Adoration of the Magi. Munich, Alte Pinakothek.

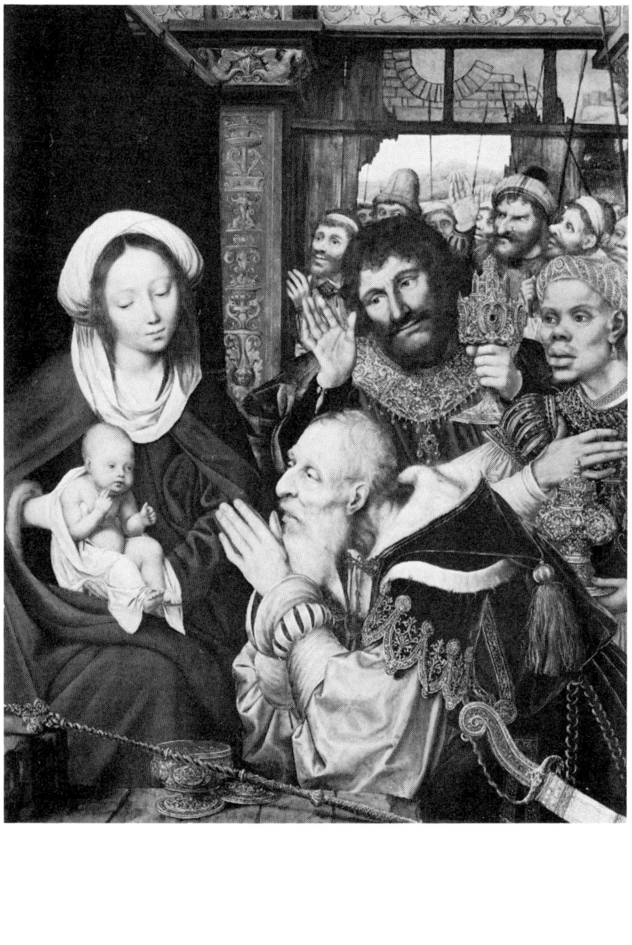

Plate 79. Massys. Adoration of the Magi. New York, Metropolitan Museum.

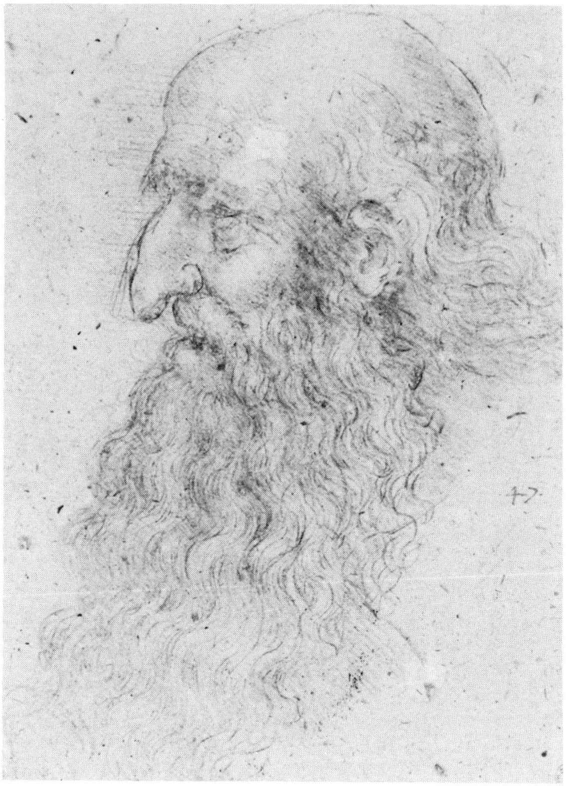

Plate 80. Leonardo da Vinci. Head of Old Man. Windsor Castle.

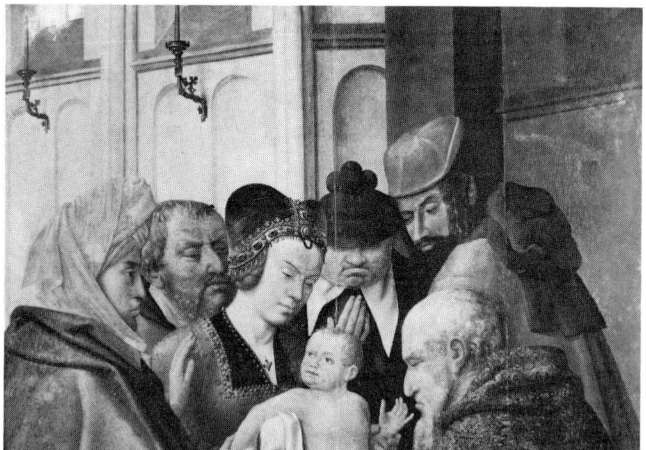

Plate 81. Master of Frankfurt. Copy of Hugo van der Goes, Circumcision (Monforte altarpiece). Antwerp, Koninklijk Museum.

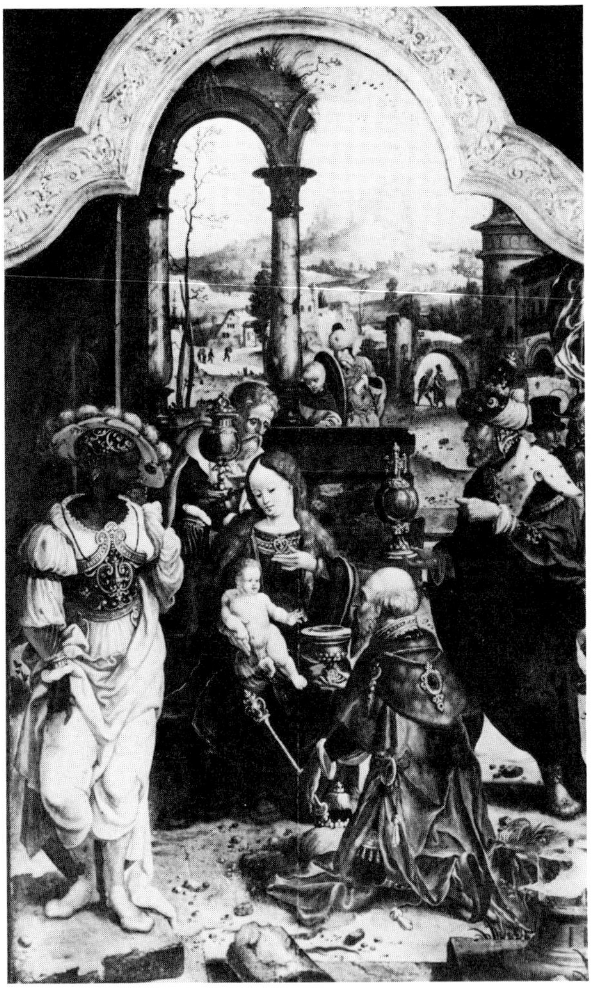

Plate 82. Antwerp Artist of 1520s (Circle of Pieter Coecke van Aelst). Adoration of the Magi. Sarasota, Ringling Museum.

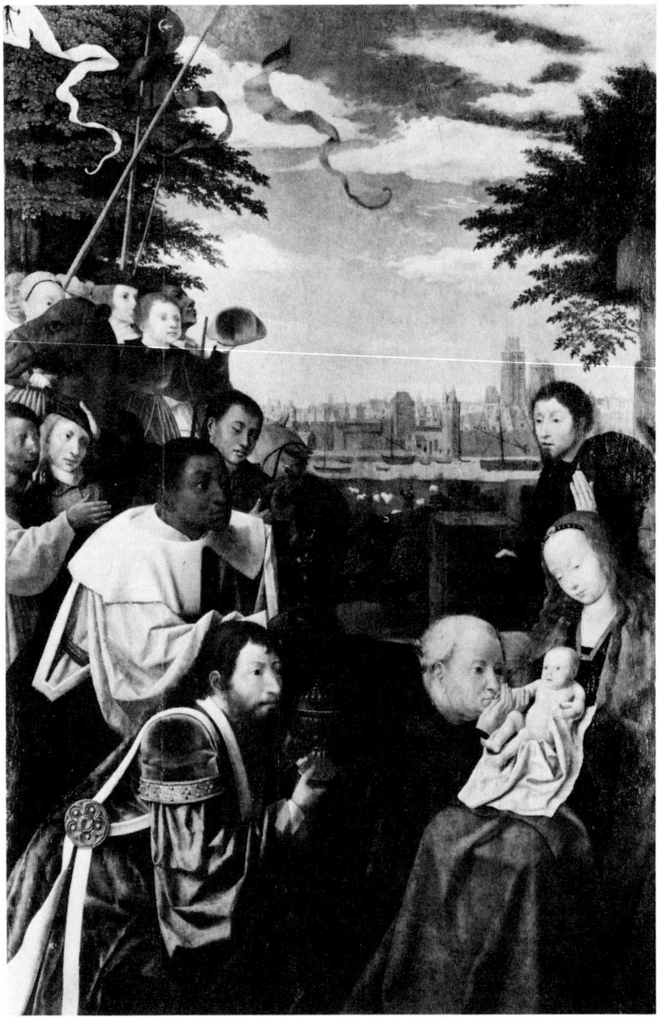

Plate 83. Master of the Morrison Triptych. Adoration of the Magi. Philadelphia, Johnson collection.

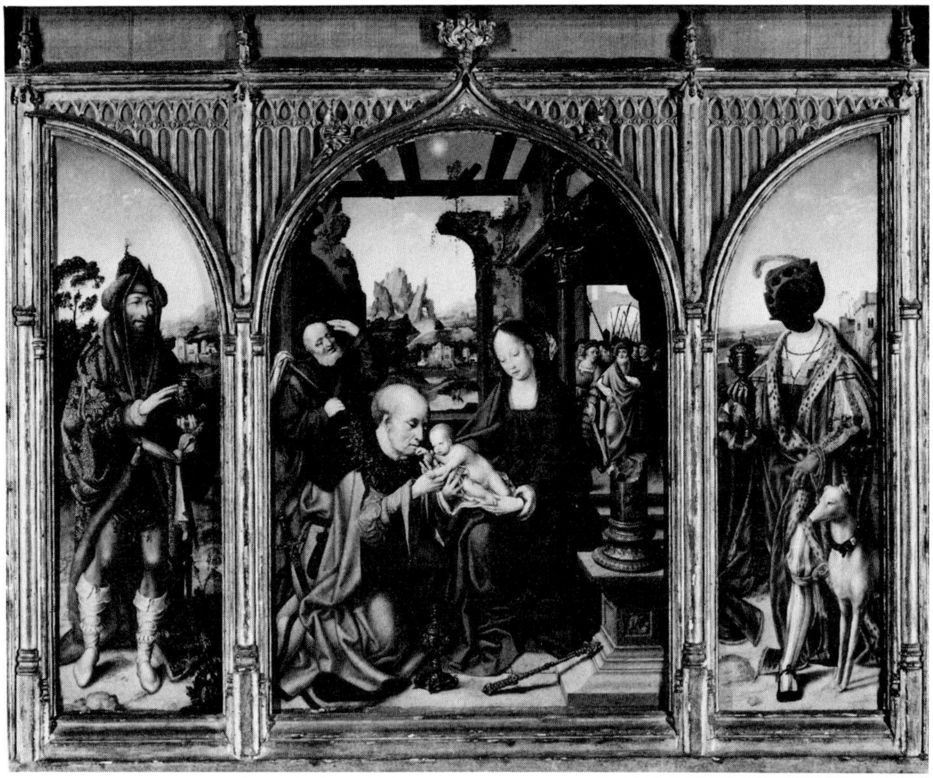

Plate 84. Joos van Cleve. Altarpiece of the Adoration of the Magi. Detroit Institute of Art.

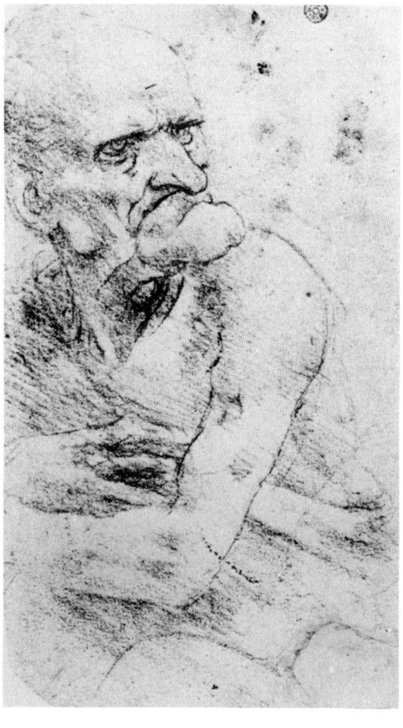

Plate 85. Leonardo da Vinci. Angry Old Man. Rome, Galleria Nazionale di Stampi.

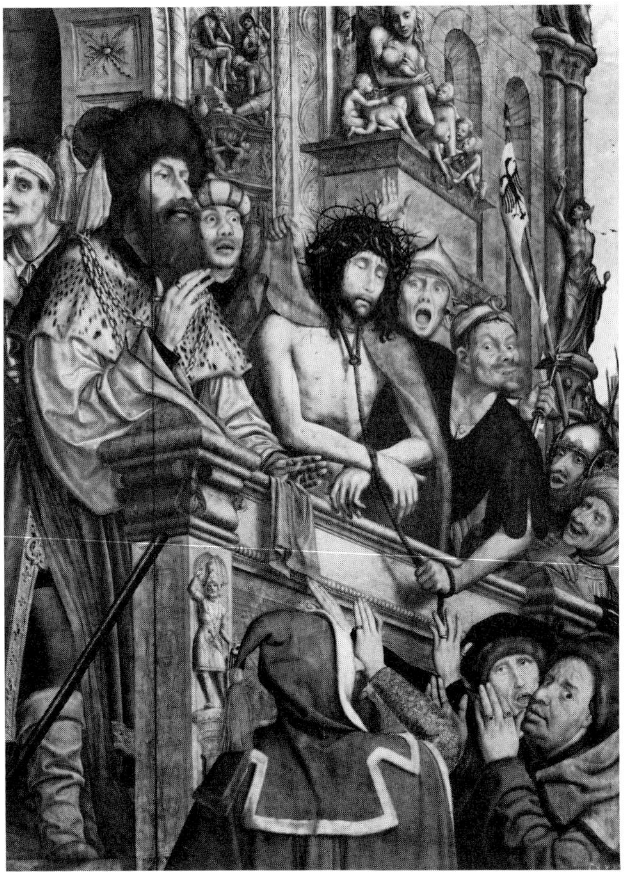

Plate 86. Massys. Ecce Homo. Madrid, Prado.

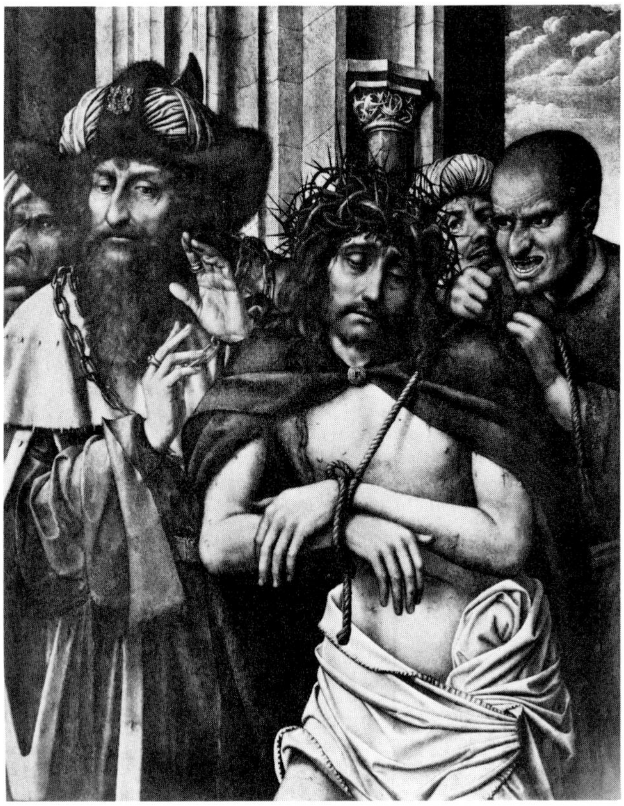

Plate 87. Massys. Ecce Homo. Venice, Palazzo Ducale.

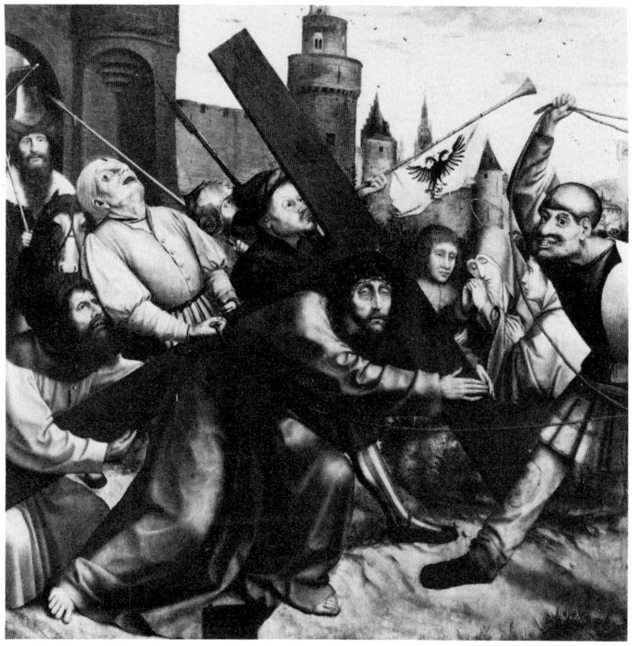

Plate 88. Massys. Madre de Deus altarpiece. Lisbon, Museu Nacional. Christ Carrying the Cross.

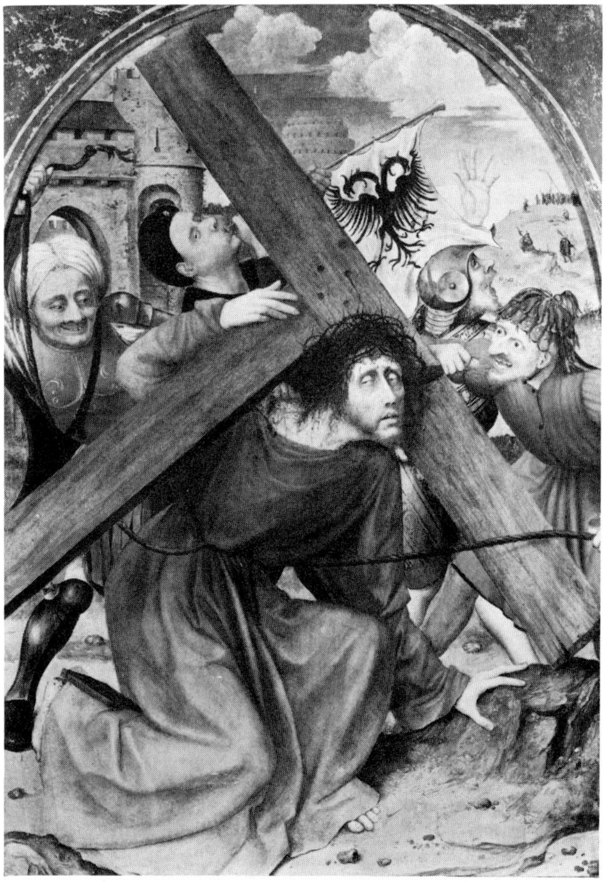

Plate 89. Massys. Christ Carrying the Cross. The Hague, Mauritshuis.

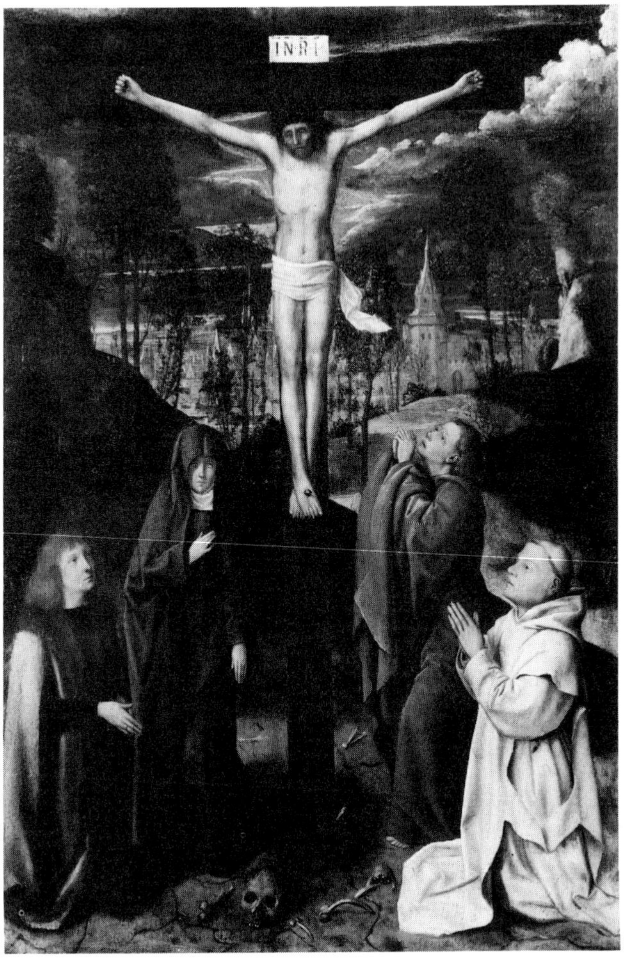

Plate 90. Massys (?). Crucifixion with donors. London, Seilern collection.

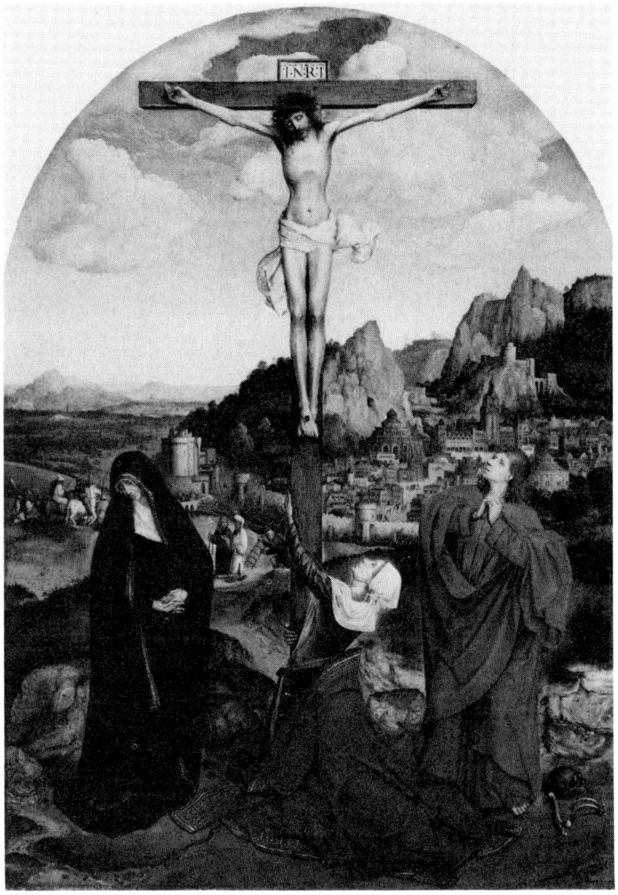

Plate 91. Massys. Crucifixion. Ottawa, National Gallery.

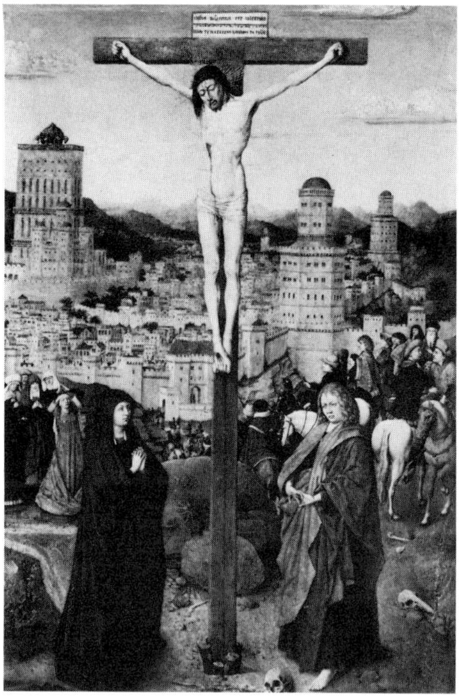

Plate 92. Jan van Eyck, copy. Crucifixion. Venice, Ca d'Oro.

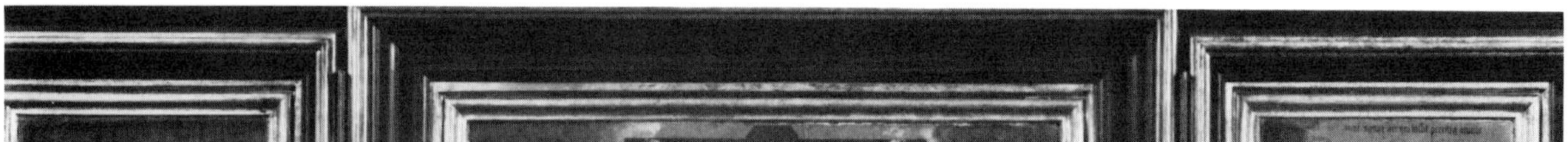

Plate 93. Roger van der Weyden, workshop. Sforza Crucifixion altarpiece. Brussels, Musées Royaux.

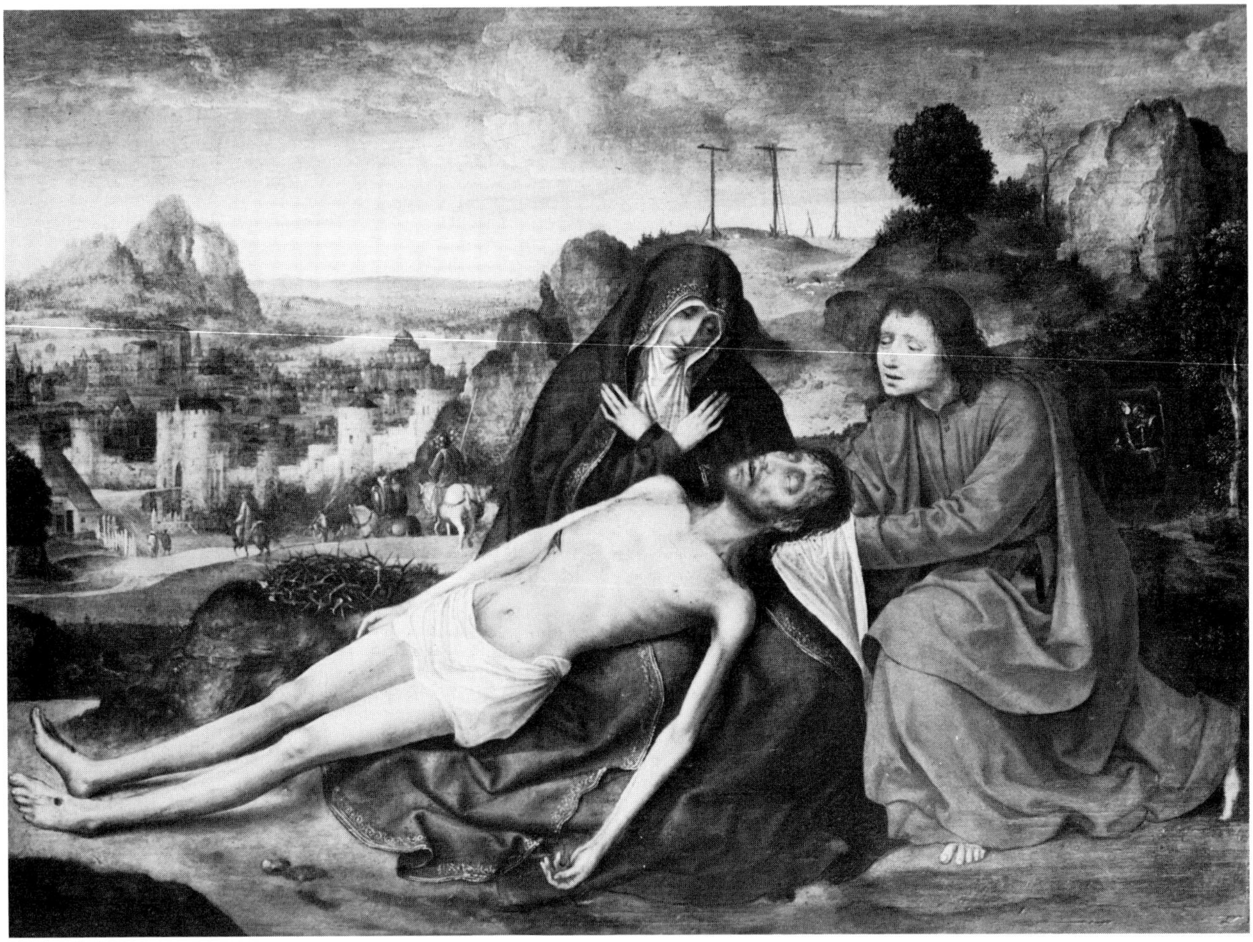

Plate 94. Massys. Pieta. Paris, Louvre.

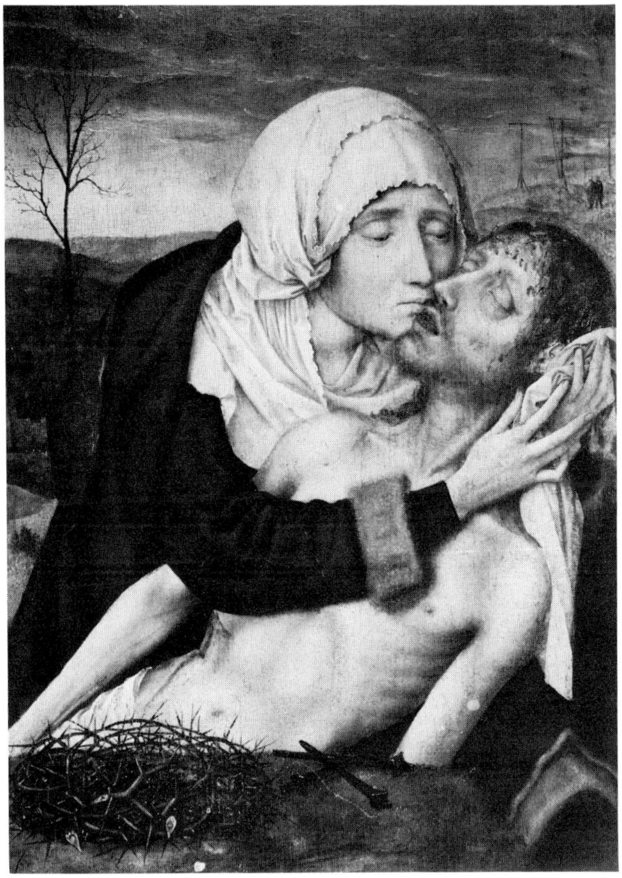

Plate 95. Massys, copy by workshop. Pieta at half-length. Brussels, Musées Royaux.

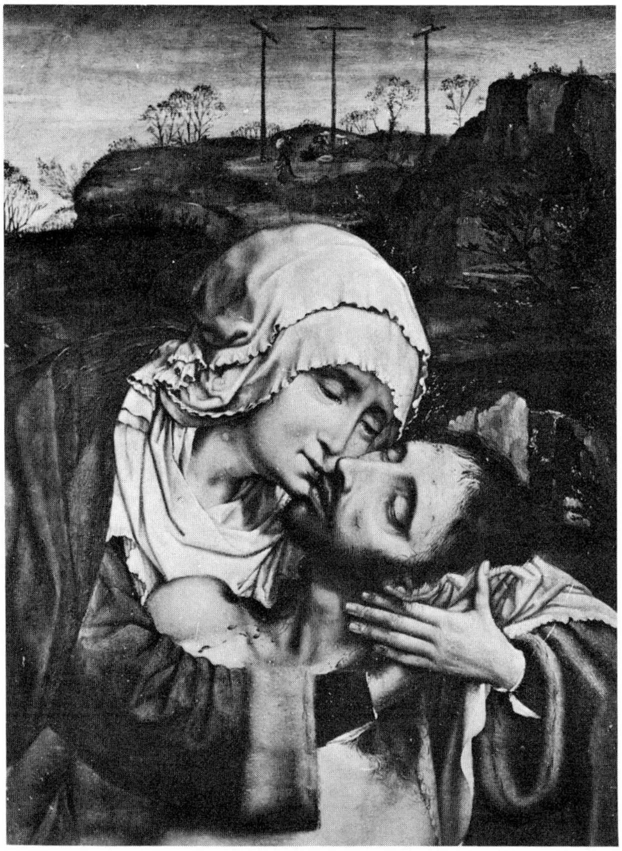

Plate 96. Massys, copy. Pieta at half-length. Antwerp, Koninklijk Museum.

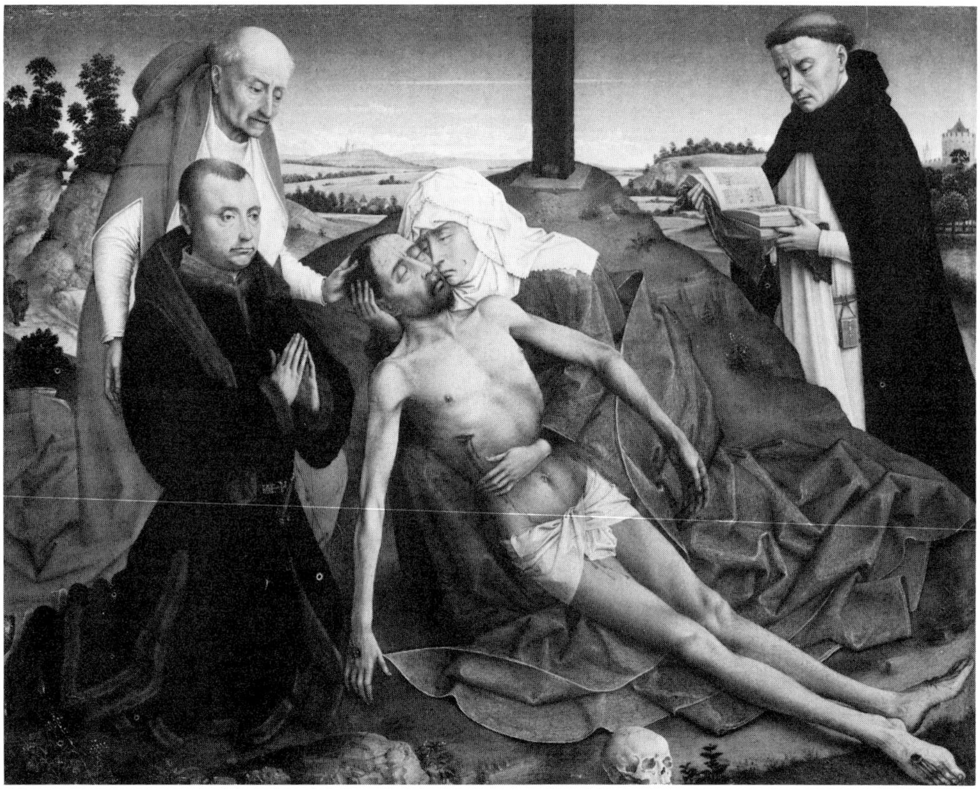

Plate 97. Roger van der Weyden. Pieta with Donor and Saints. London, National Gallery.

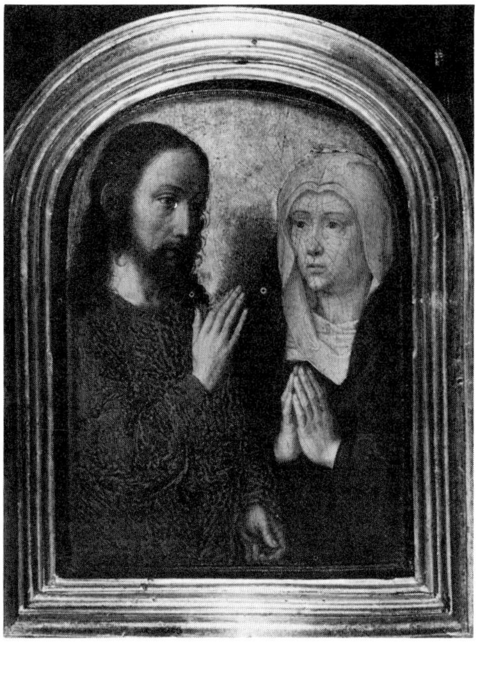

Plate 98. Gerard David. Christ Saying Farewell to the Virgin. Munich, Alte Pinakothek.

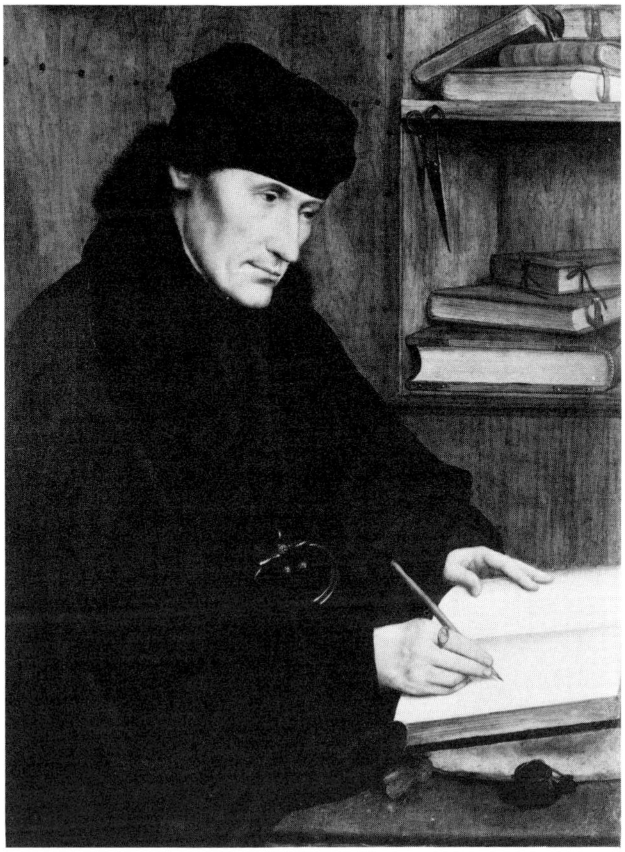

Plate 99. Massys, replica. Erasmus of Rotterdam. Rome, Palazzo Barberini.

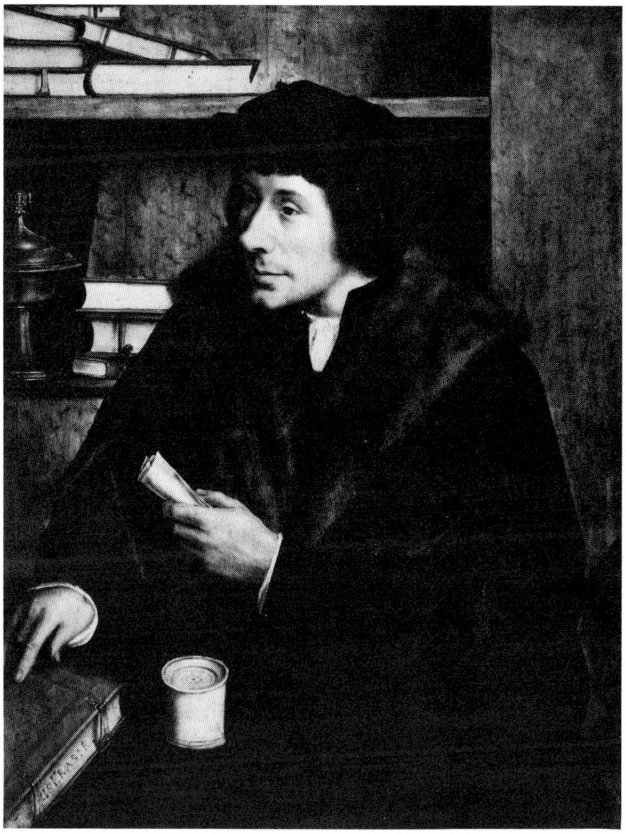

Plate 100. Massys, replica. Pieter Gillis (Petrus Aegidius). Antwerp, Koninklijk Museum.

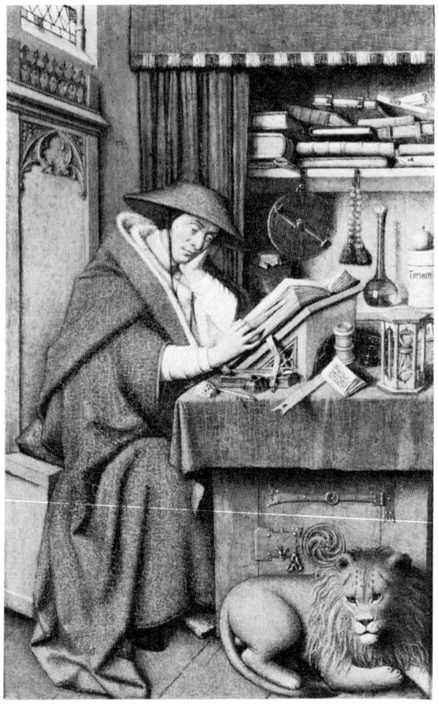

Plate 101. Petrus Christus. St. Jerome in his Study. Detroit Institute of Art.

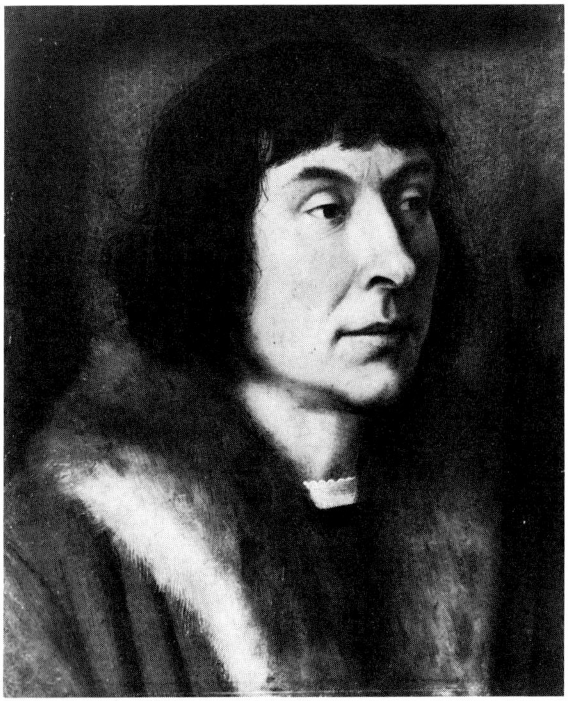

Plate 102. Massys. Portrait of a Man (Pieter Gillis). Oldenburg, Museum.

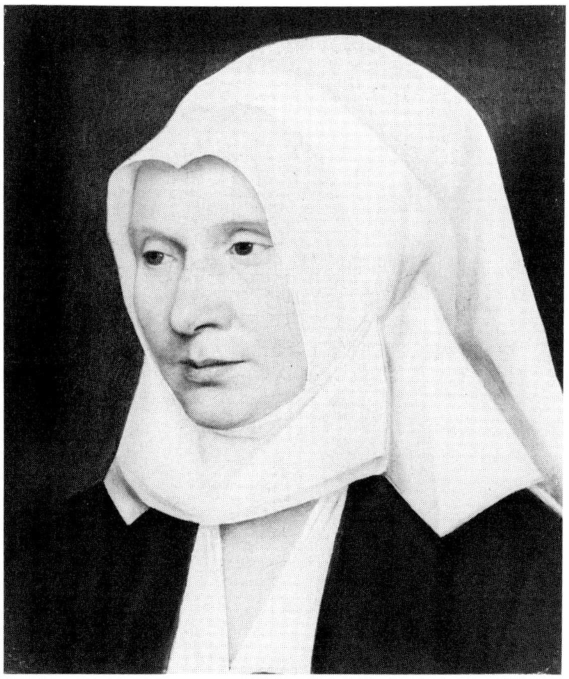

Plate 103. Massys. Portrait of a Woman (here identified as Cornelia Sandrin). Oldenburg, Museum.

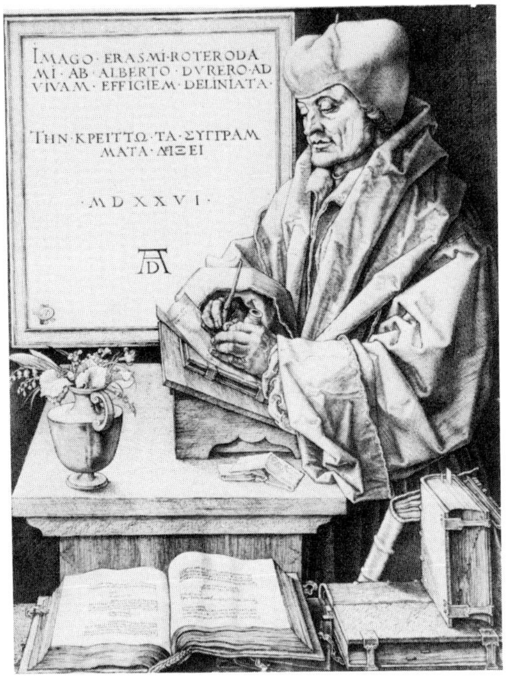

Plate 104. Albrecht Dürer. engraving. Erasmus of Rotterdam.

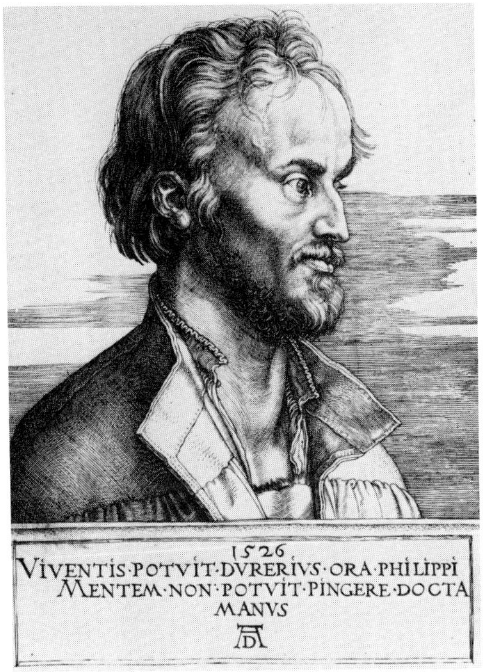

Plate 105. Albrecht Dürer. engraving. Philip Melanchthon.

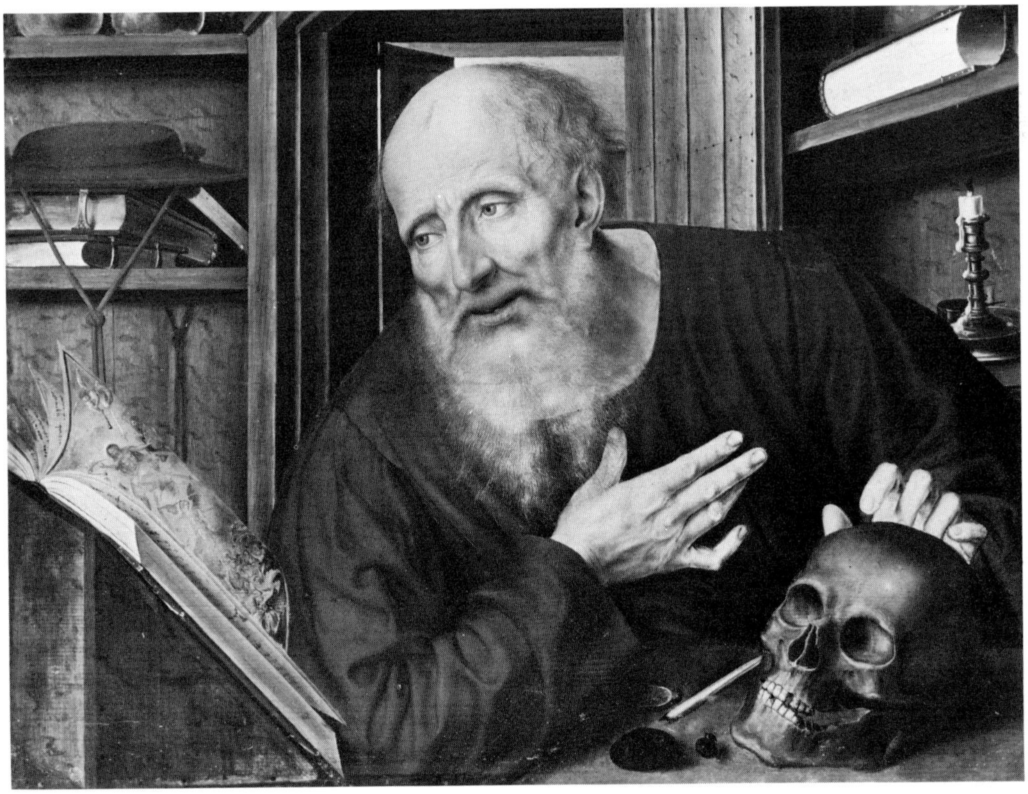

Plate 106. Massys, copy. St. Jerome in his Study. Vienna, Kunsthistorisches Museum.

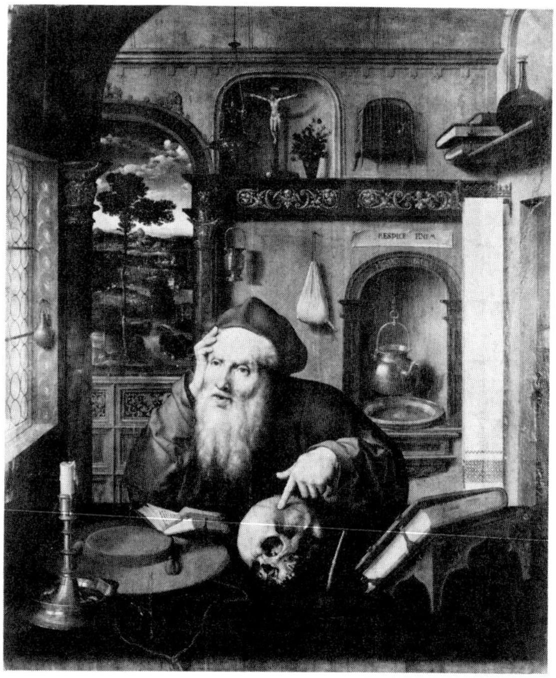

Plate 107. Joos van Cleve. St. Jerome in his Study. Cambridge (Mass.), Busch-Reisinger Museum.

Plate 108. Massys, workshop copy. Two Praying Monks. Rome, Palazzo Doria.

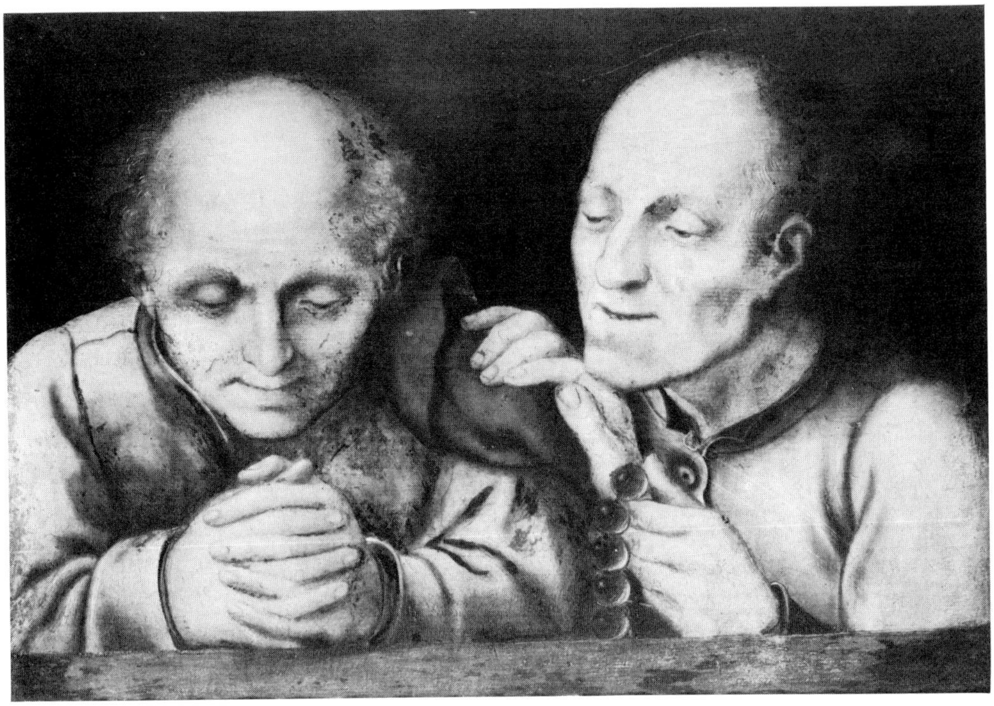

Plate 109. Massys, copy. Two Praying Monks. Munich, Alte Pinakothek.

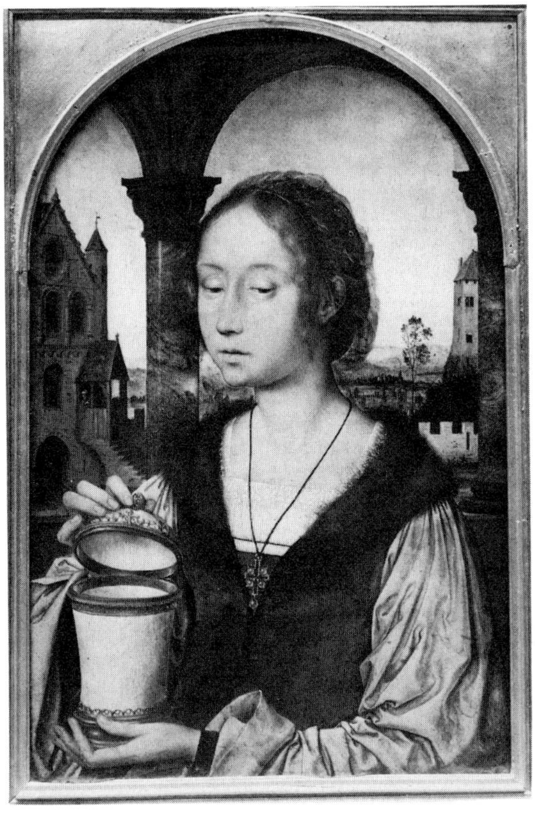

Plate 110. Massys. Mary Magdalene. Antwerp, Koninklijk Museum.

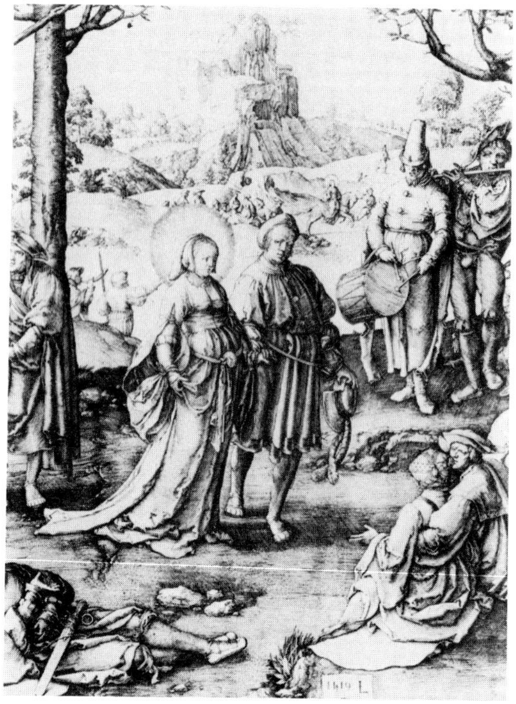

Plate 111. Lucas van Leyden. engraving. Worldly Life of the Magdalene (detail).

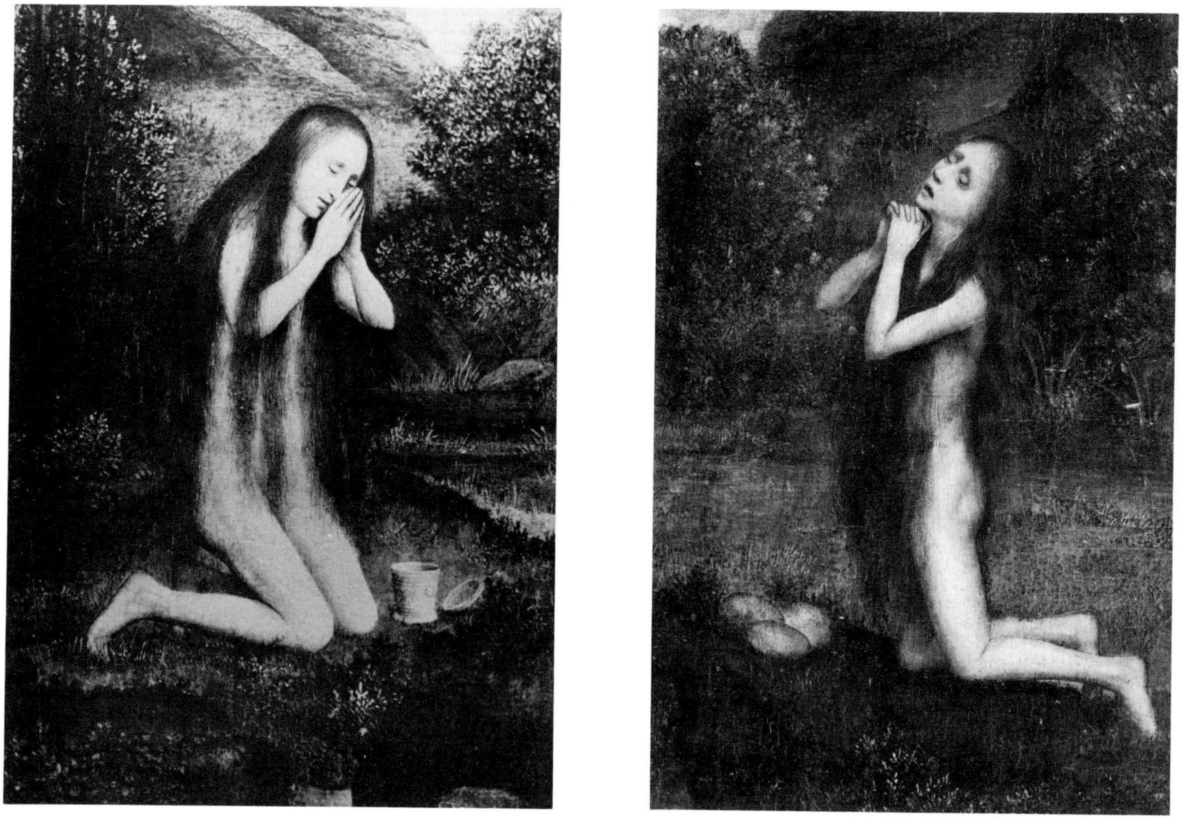

Plate 112. Massys. Mary Magdalene *(left)* and Mary of Egypt in the Wilderness. Philadelphia, Johnson collection.

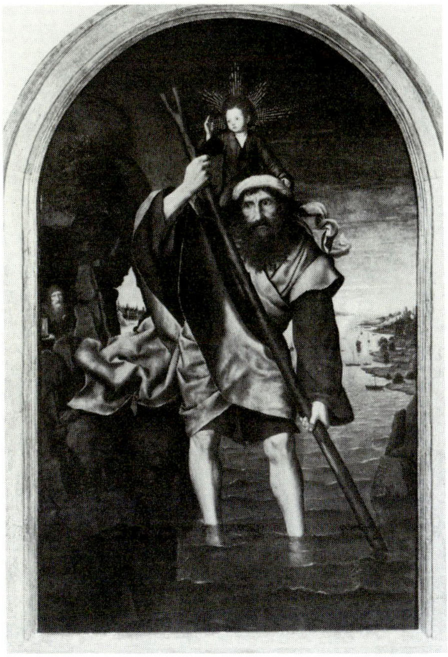

Plate 113. Massys. St. Christopher. Antwerp, Koninklijk Museum.

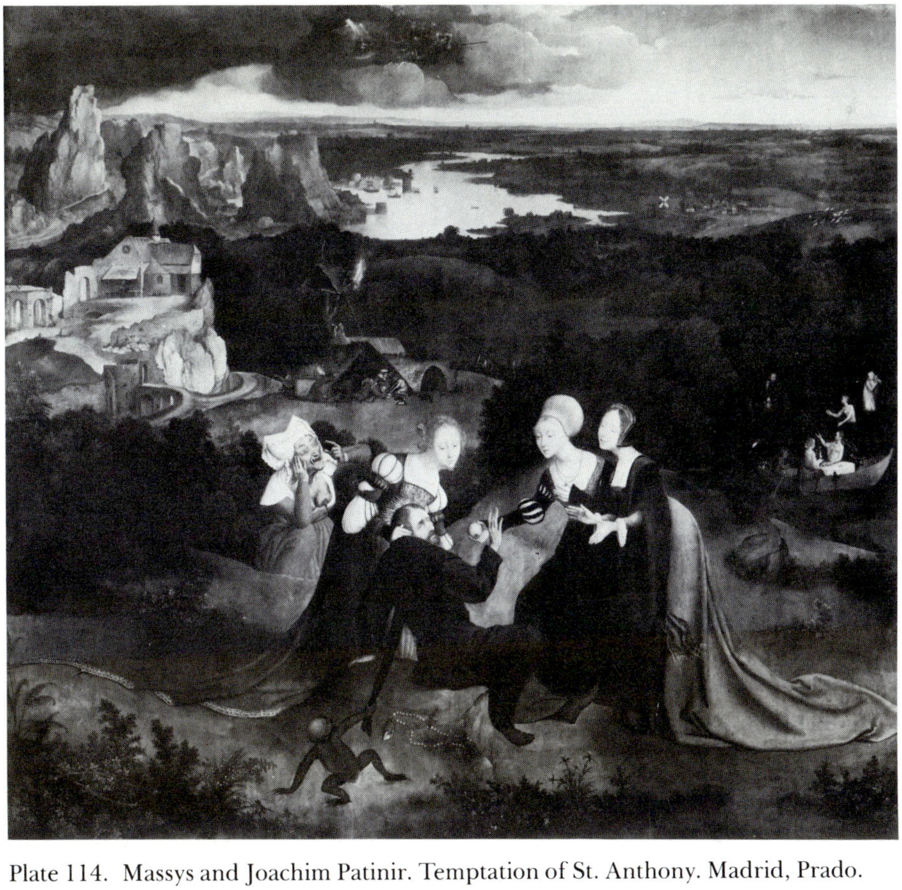

Plate 114. Massys and Joachim Patinir. Temptation of St. Anthony. Madrid, Prado.

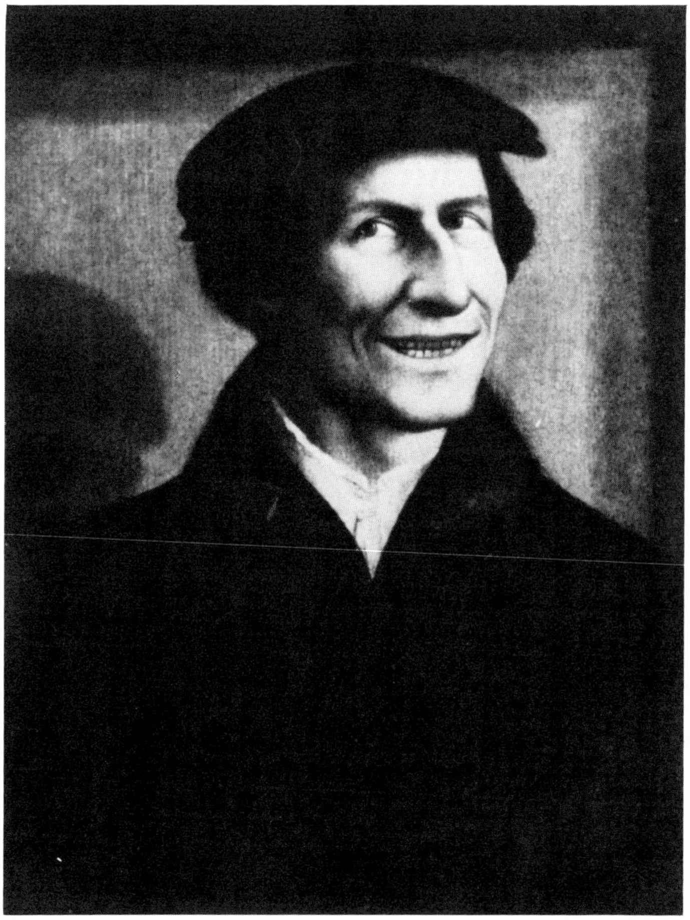

Plate 115. Massys. Democritus. Location unknown.

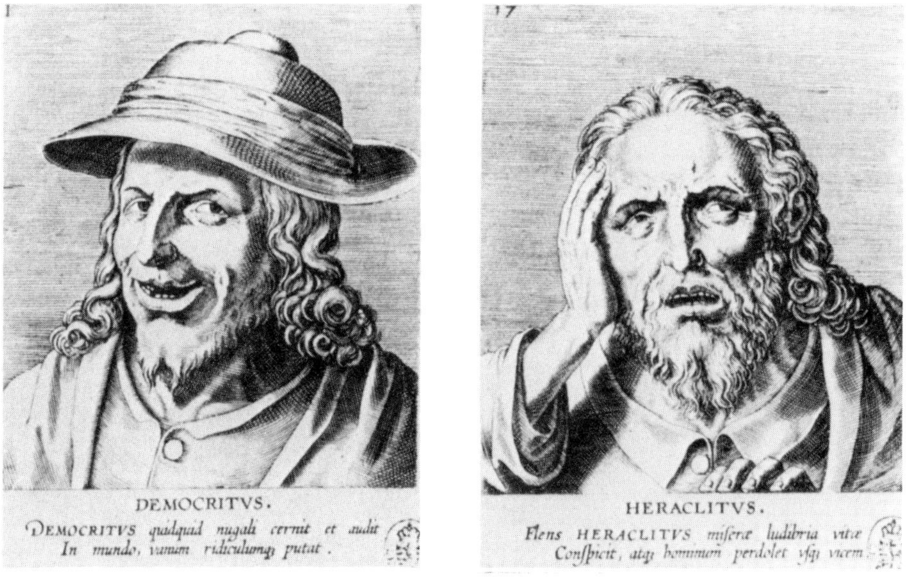

Plate 116. Cornelis Cort. Engravings. Democritus and Heraclitus.

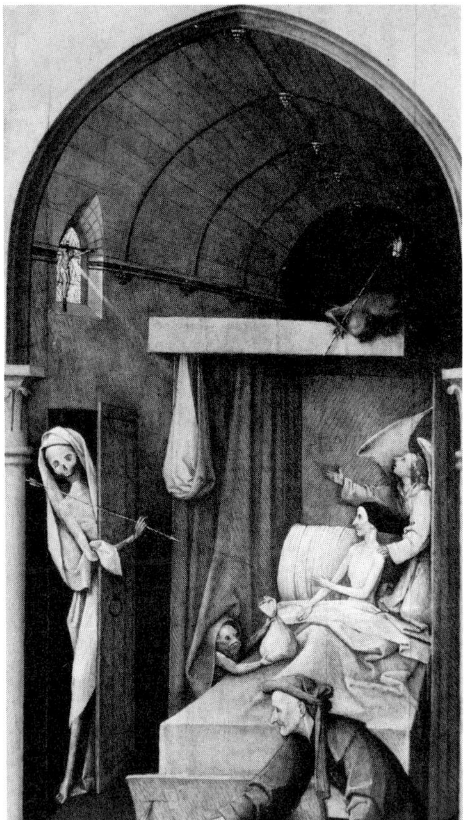

Plate 117. Hieronymus Bosch. Death and the Miser. Washington, National Gallery.

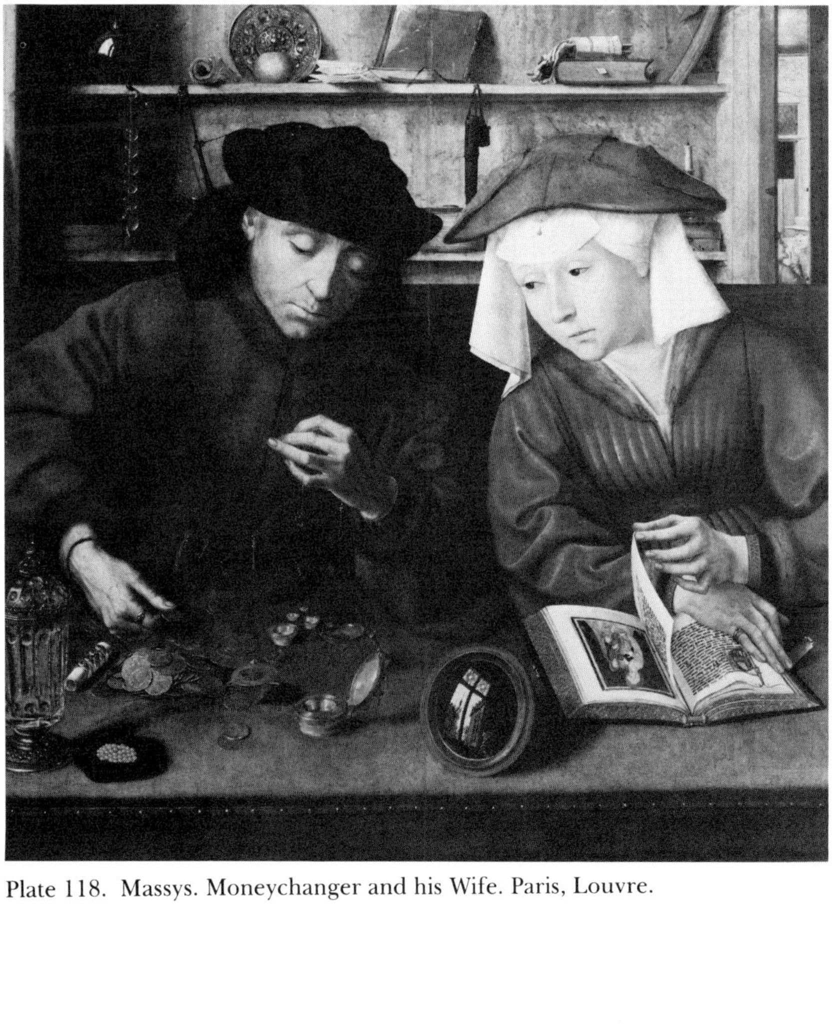

Plate 118. Massys. Moneychanger and his Wife. Paris, Louvre.

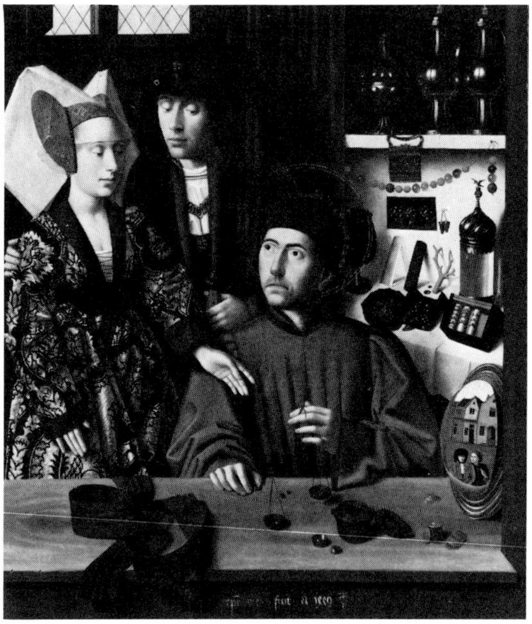

Plate 119. Petrus Christus. St. Eloy (Eligius). New York, Lehmann collection.

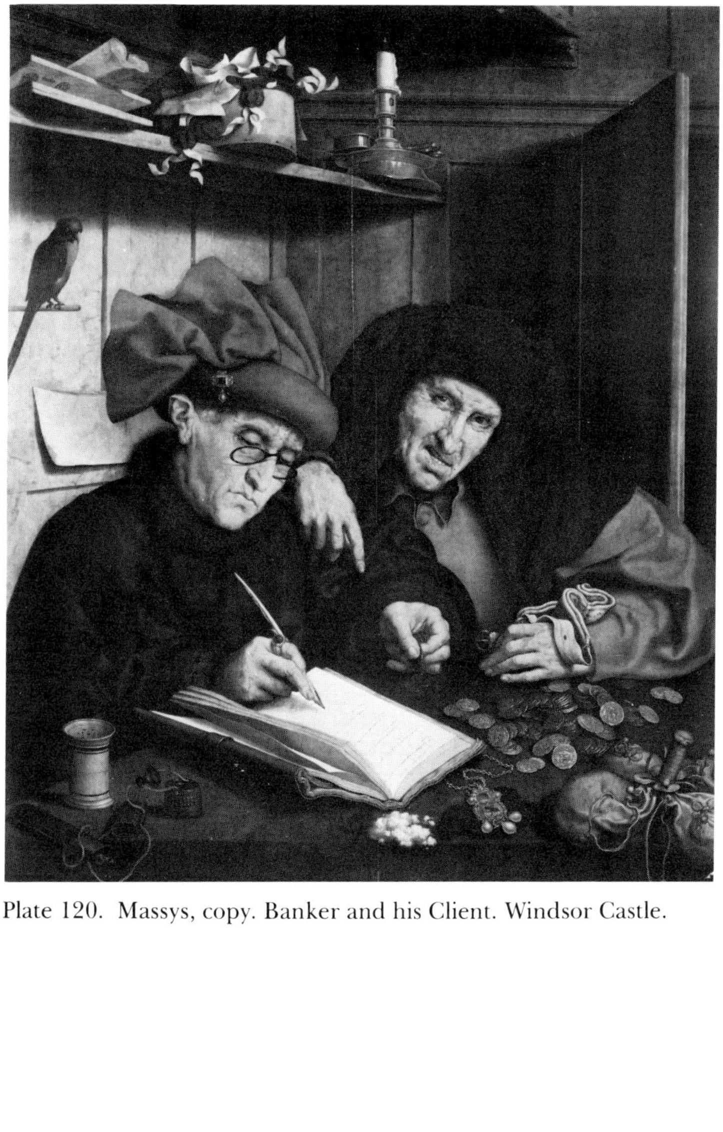

Plate 120. Massys, copy. Banker and his Client. Windsor Castle.

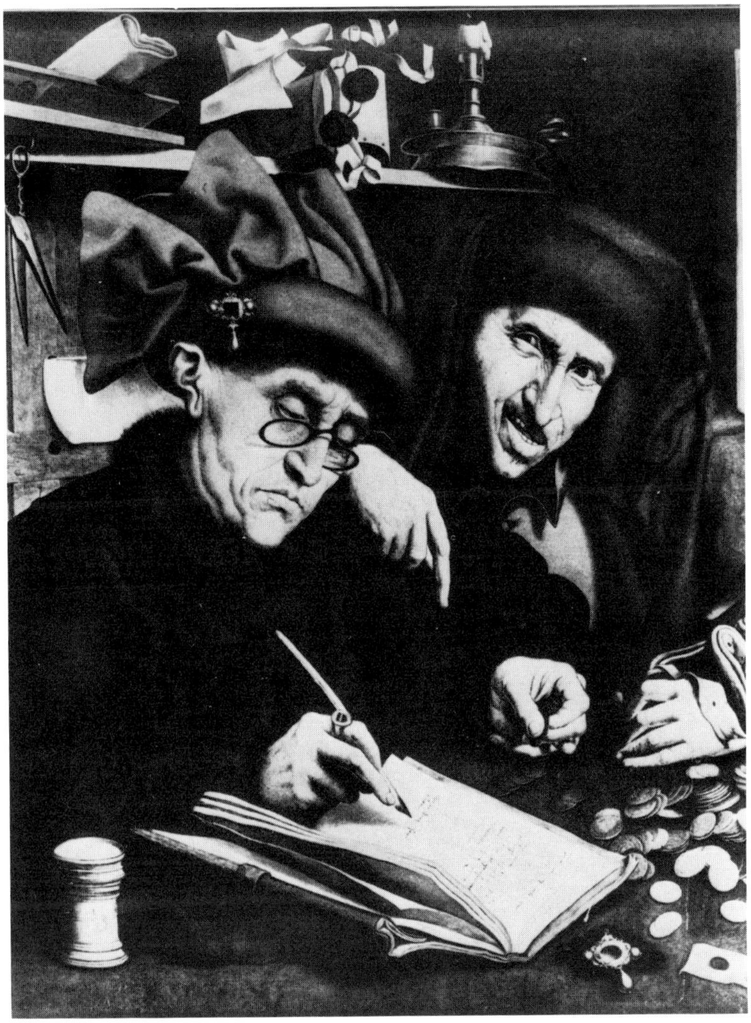

Plate 121. Massys, copy. Banker and his Client. Paris, Cailleux collection.

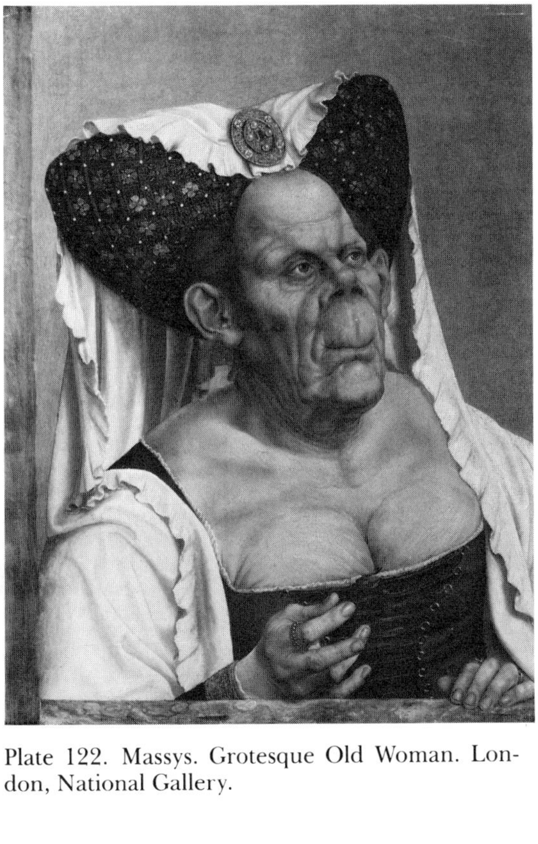

Plate 122. Massys. Grotesque Old Woman. London, National Gallery.

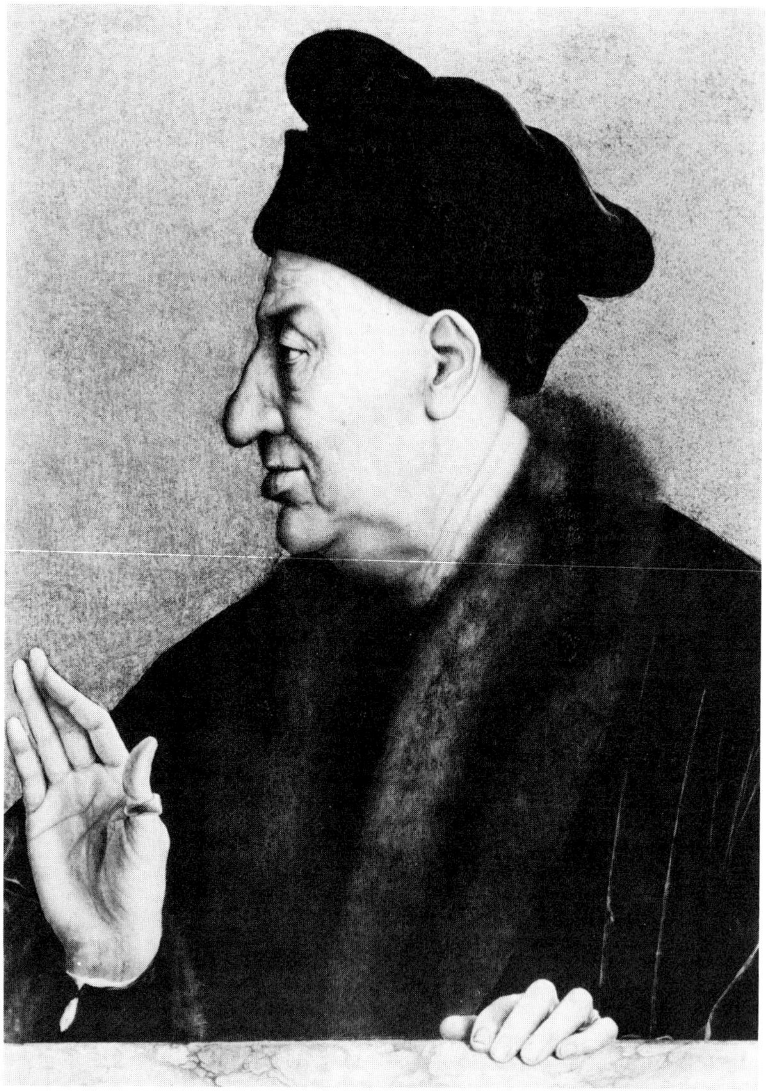

Plate 123. Massys. Old Man. New York, private collection.

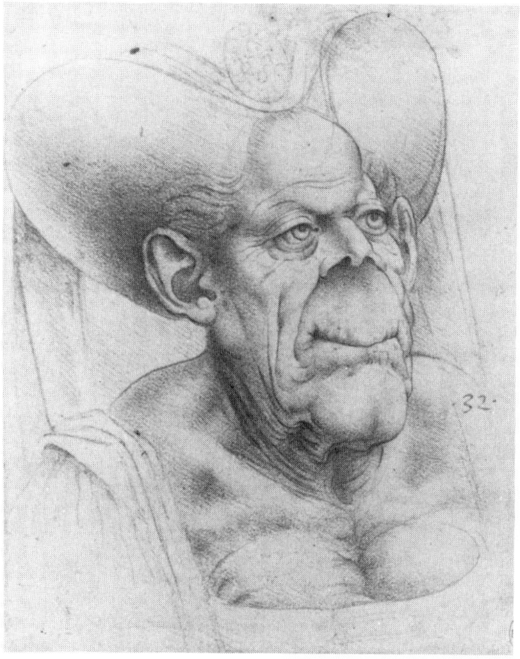

Plate 124. Leonardo da Vinci, copy. Grotesque Old Woman. Windsor Castle.

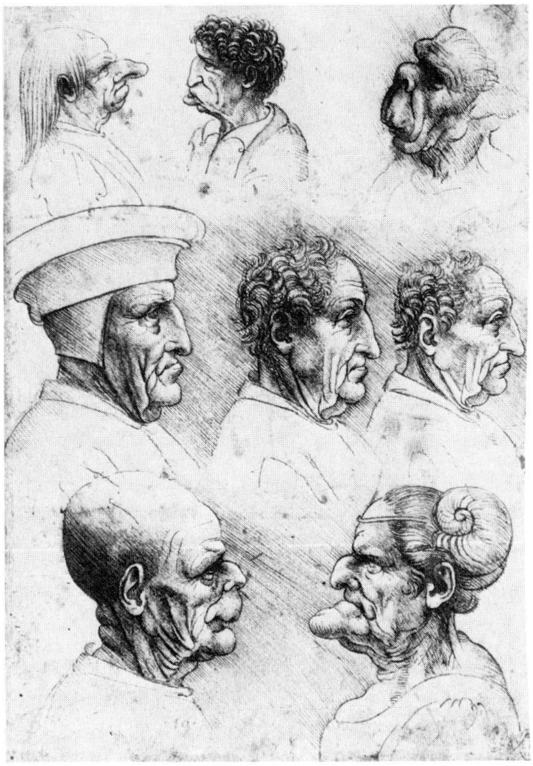

Plate 125. Leonardo da Vinci, copy. Grotesque Heads. Windsor Castle.

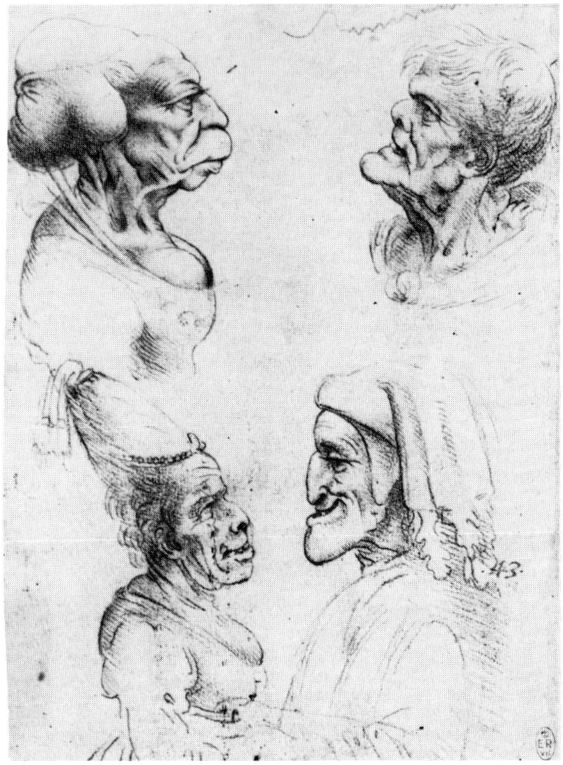

Plate 126. Leonardo da Vinci, copy. Grotesque Heads. Windsor Castle.

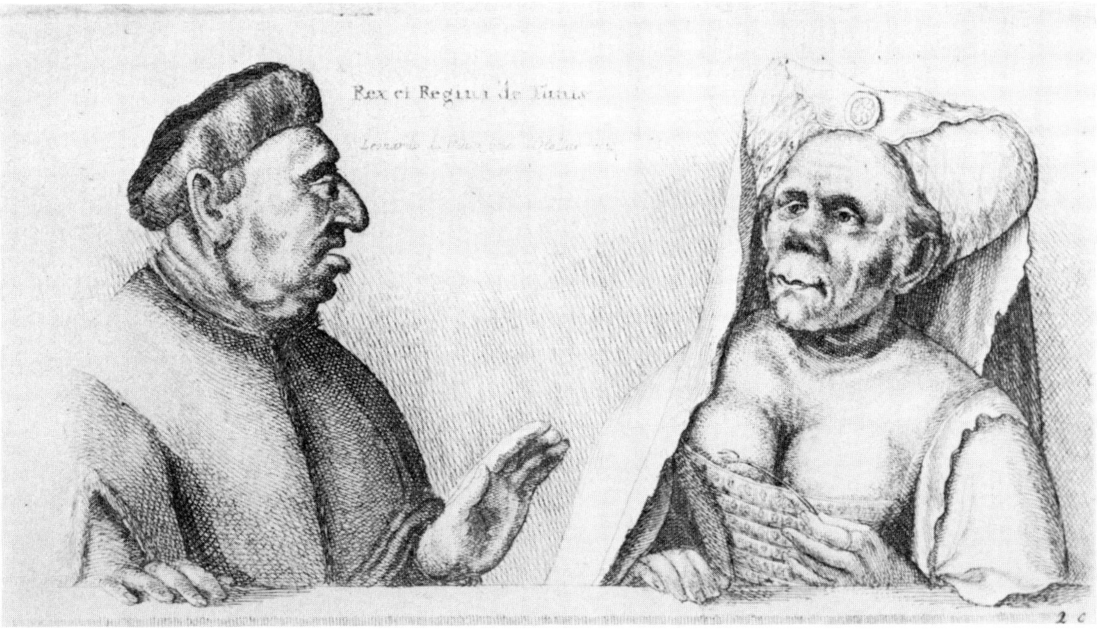

Plate 127. Wenzel Hollar. engraving. Copy after Plates 122–123.

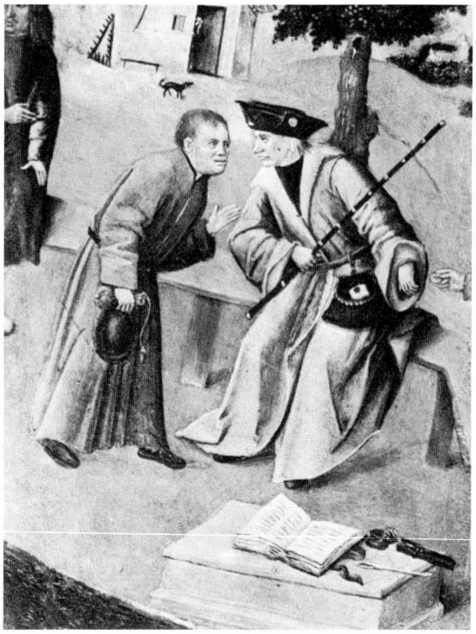

Plate 128. Hieronymus Bosch. Seven Deadly Sins. (detail): Avarice. Madrid, Prado.

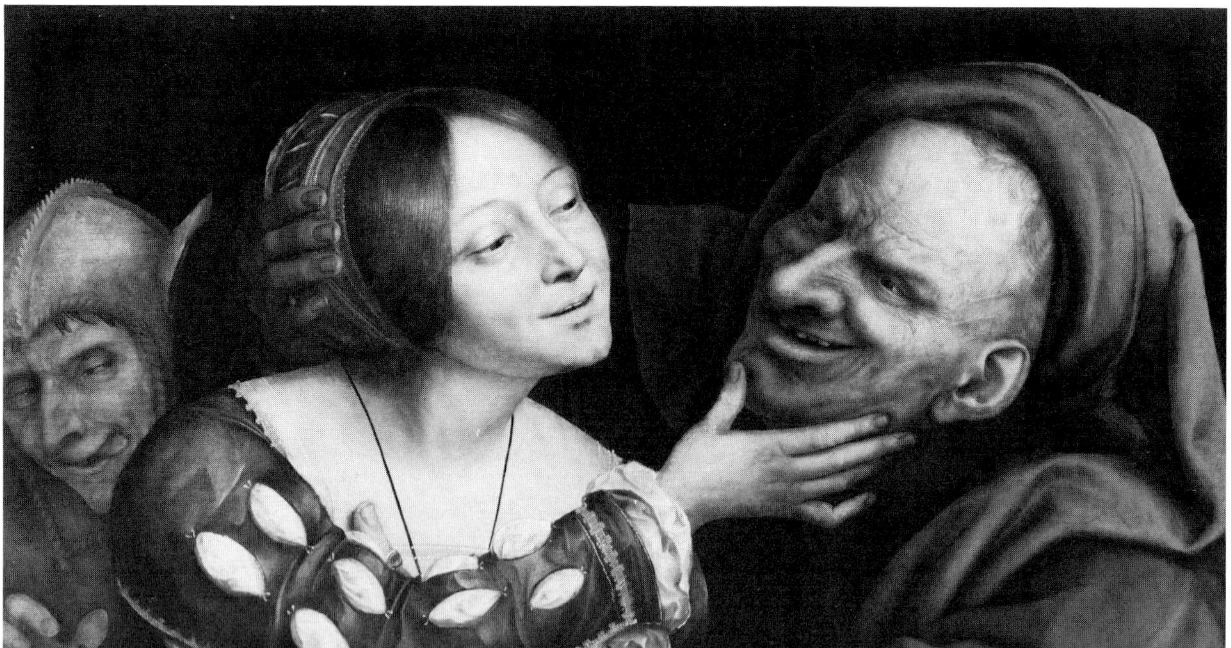

Plate 129. Massys. Ill-Matched Pair. Washington, National Gallery.

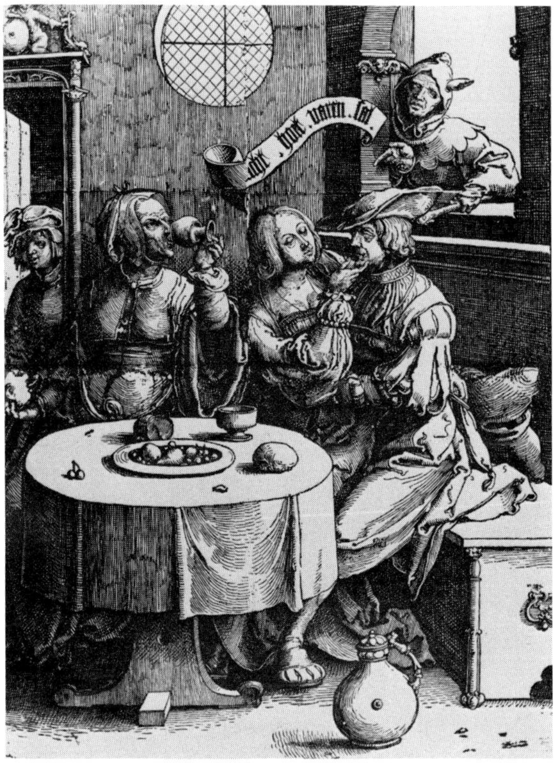

Plate 130. Lucas van Leyden. woodcut. Tavern Scene (Prodigal Son?).

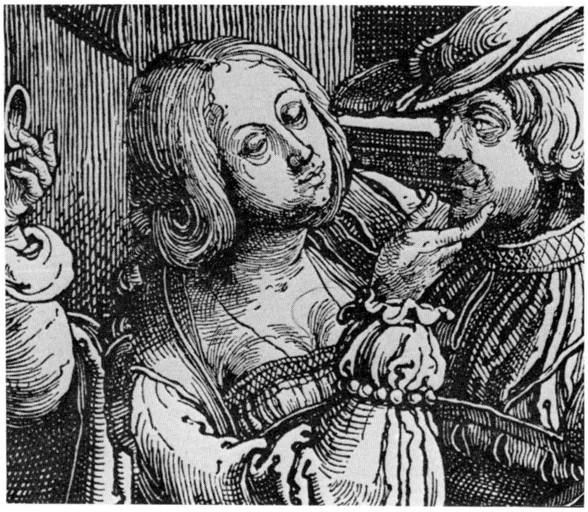

Plate 131. Detail of Plate 130.

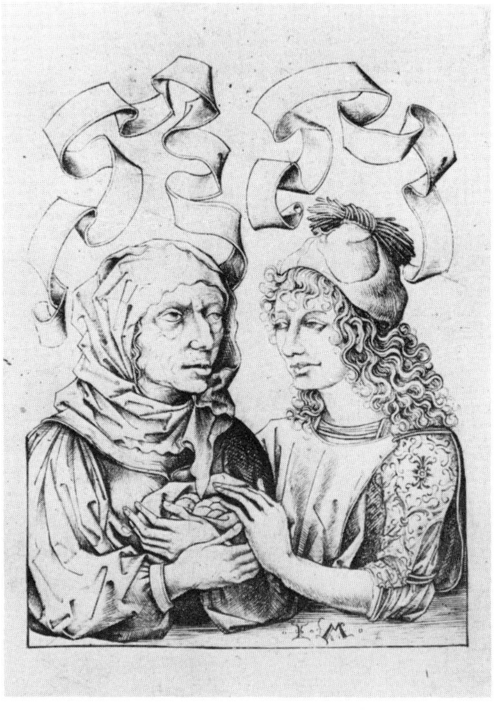

Plate 132. Israhel van Meckenem, copy after the Master of the Housebook. engraving. Ill-Matched Pair (Old Woman/Young Man).

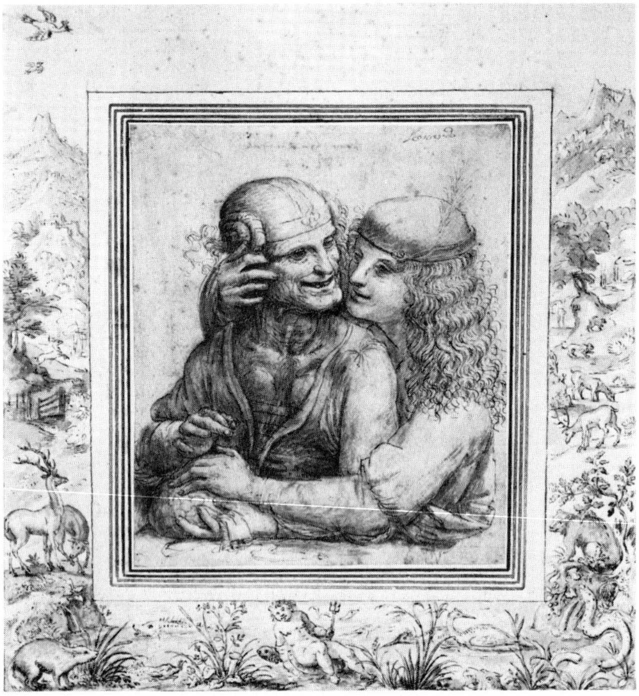

Plate 133. Leonardo da Vinci, copy (ascribed to Jacob Hoefnagel). Ill-Matched Pair (Old Woman/Young Man). Vienna, Albertina.

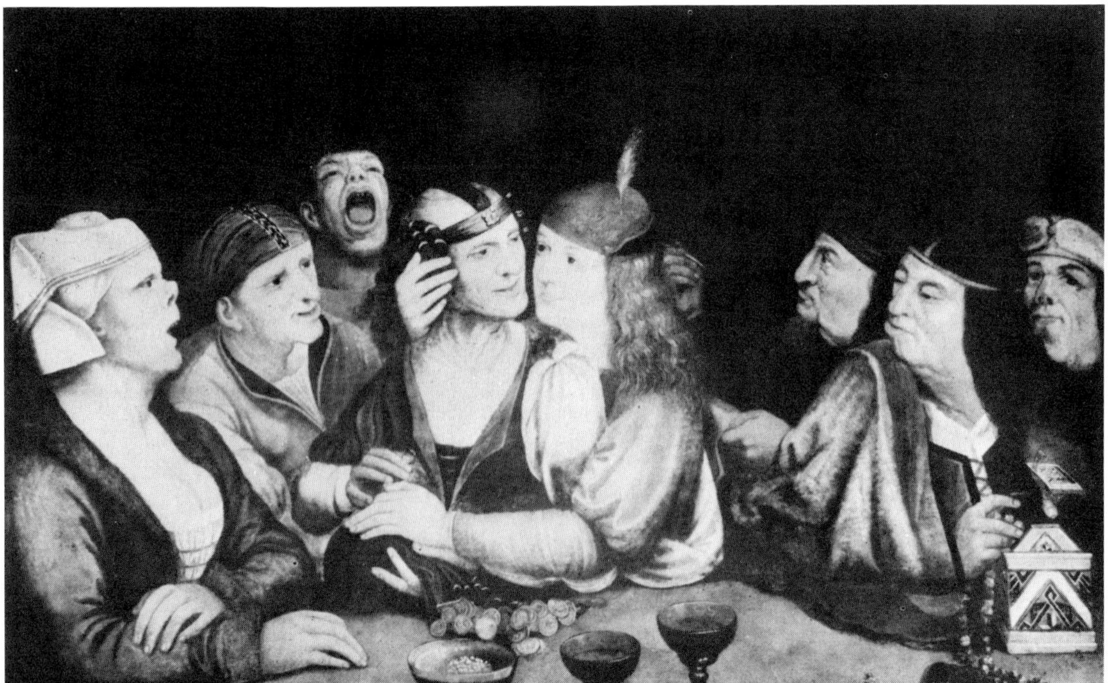

Plate 134. Imitator of Massys. Ill-Matched Pair and Merry Company. Location unknown.

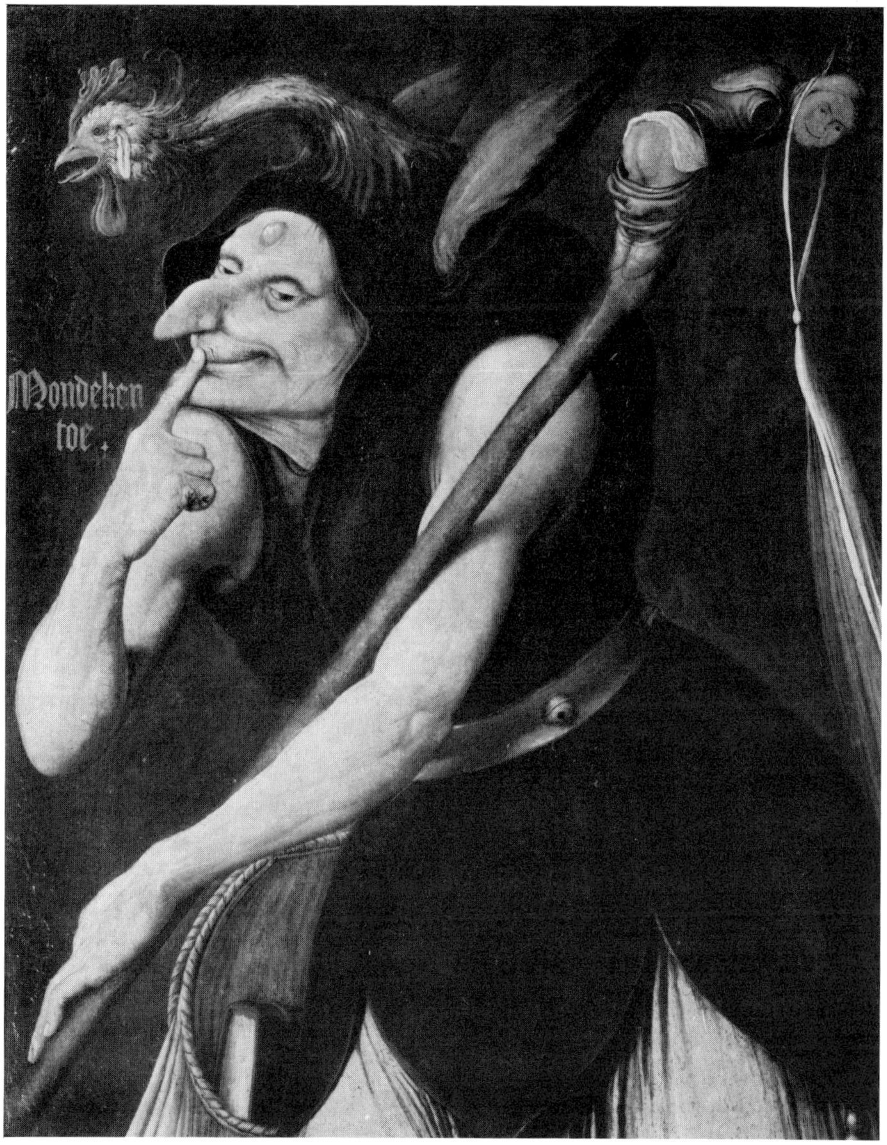

Plate 135. Massys. Fool. Old Bennington, Held collection.

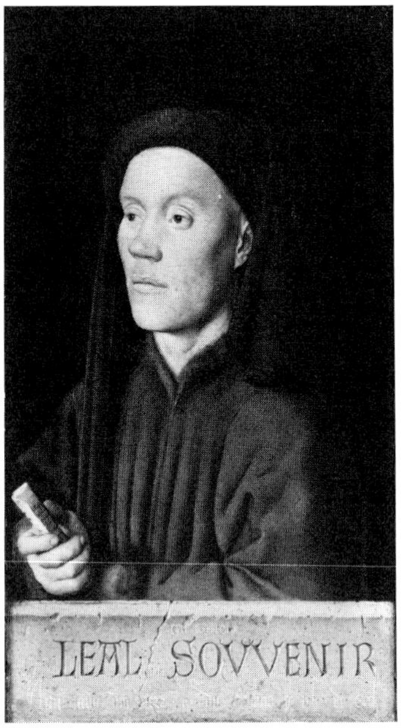

Plate 136. Jan van Eyck. "Timotheos" Portrait. London, National Gallery.

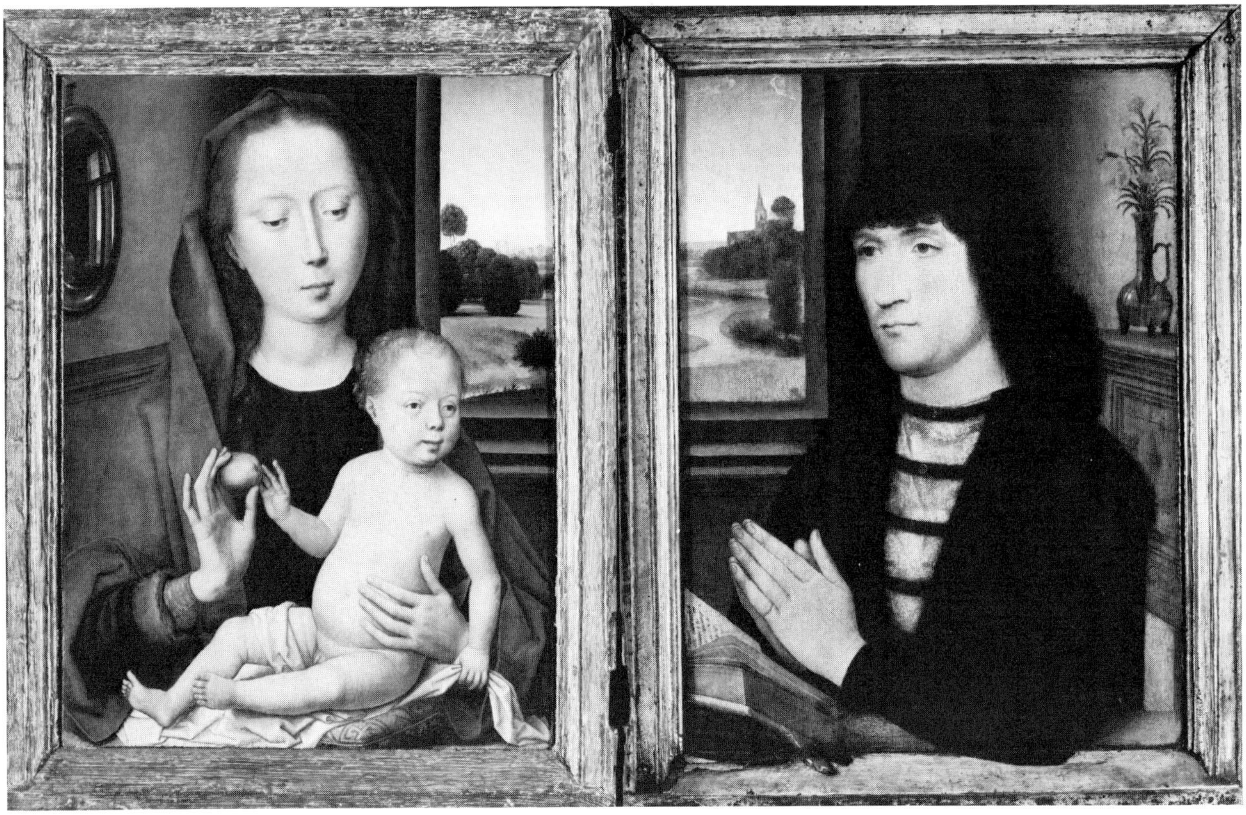

Plate 137. Hans Memling. Diptych: Madonna and Child with Donor. Chicago, Art Institute.

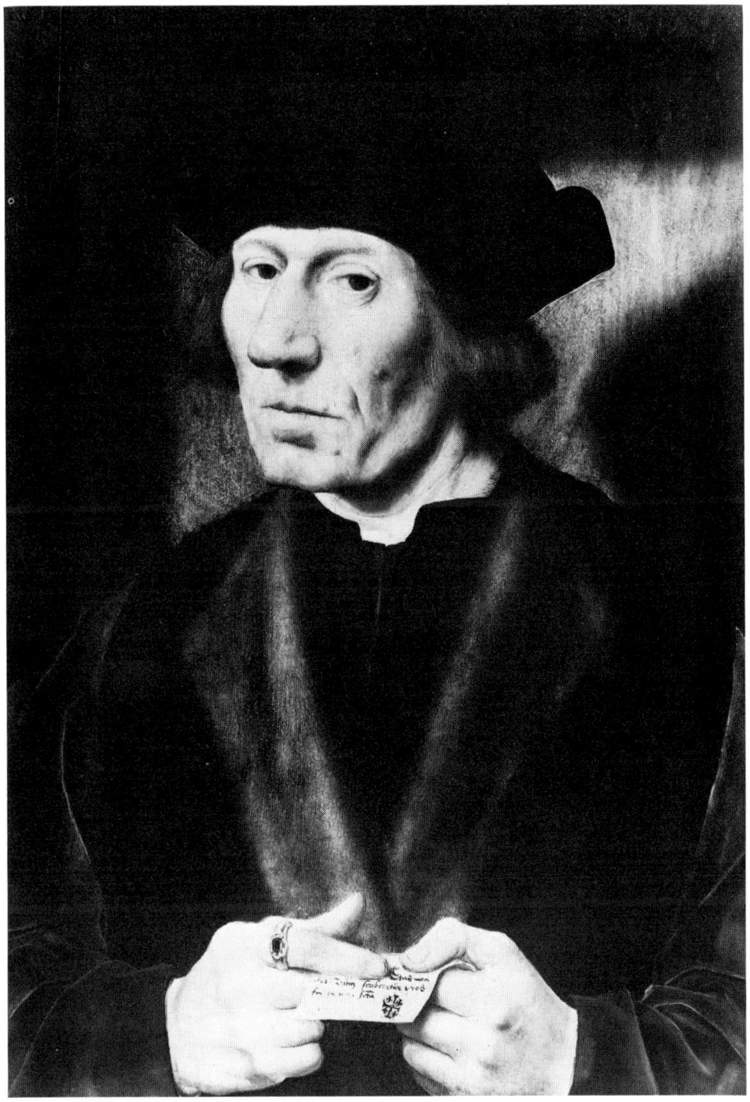

Plate 138. Massys. Portrait of a Pilgrim. Winterthur, Reinhart coll.

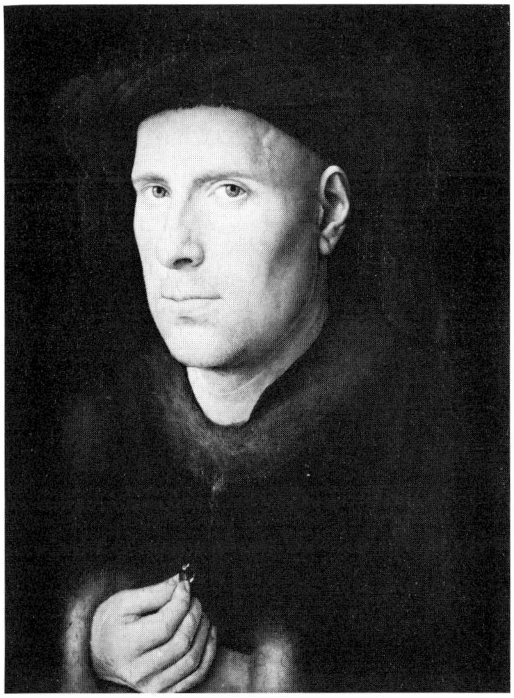

Plate 139. Jan van Eyck. Portrait of Jan de Leeuw. Vienna, Künsthistorisches Museum.

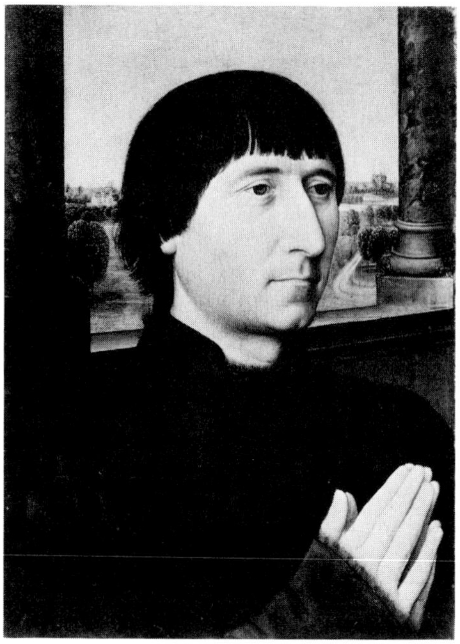

Plate 141. Hans Memling. Portrait of Willem Moreel. Brussels, Musées Royaux.

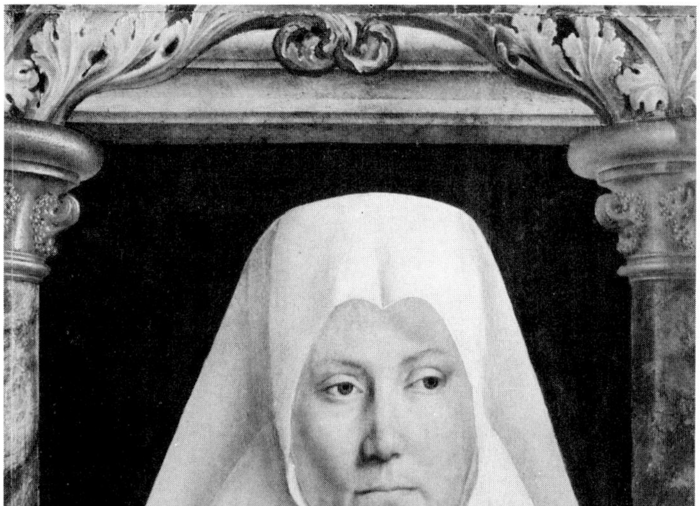

Plate 140. Massys. Portrait of Woman with Prayerbook. New York, Metropolitan Museum.

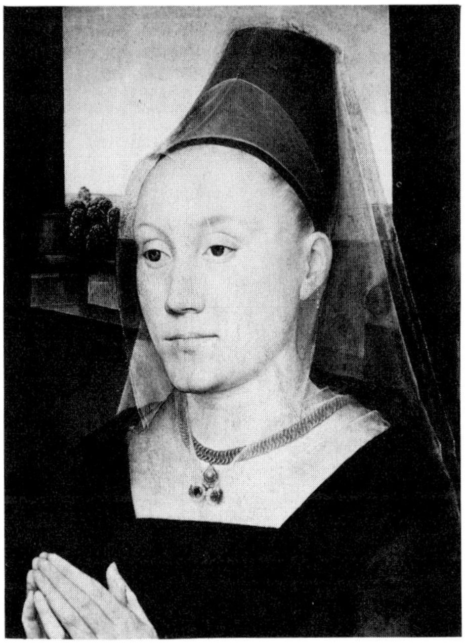

Plate 142. Hans Memling. Portrait of Barbara Moreel. Brussels, Musées Royaux.

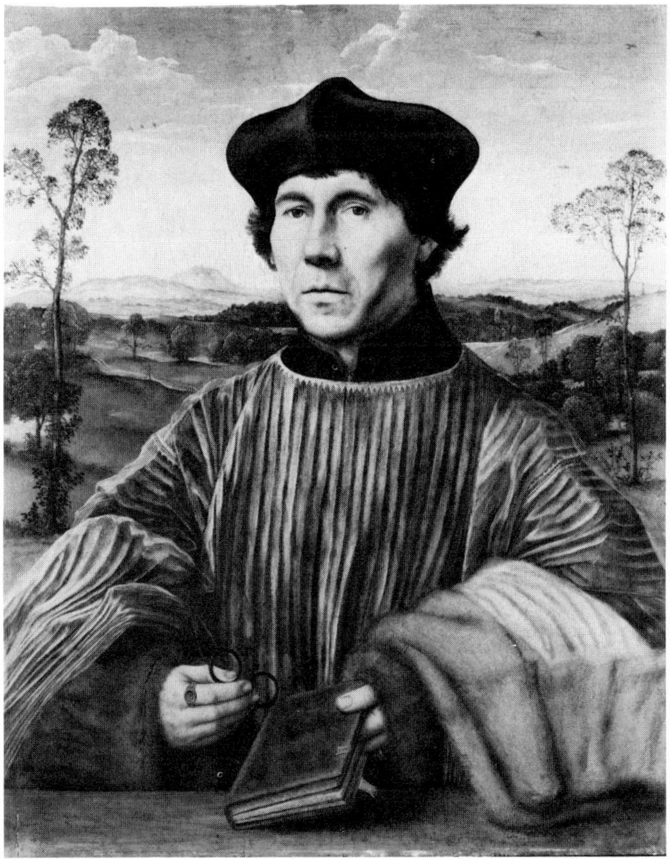

Plate 143. Massys. Portrait of a Canon (here identified as Nicolai Aegidius). Vaduz, Liechtenstein collection.

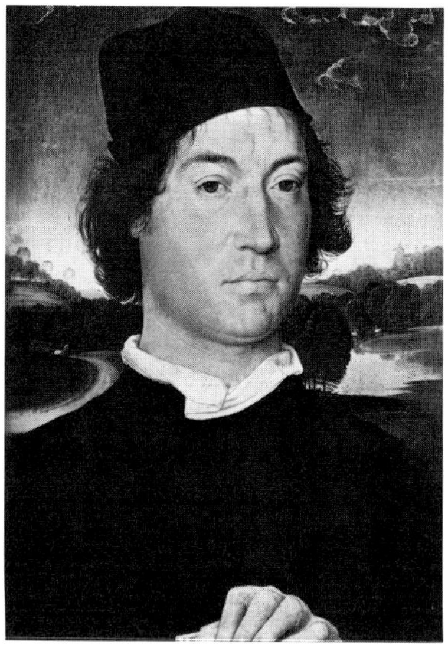

Plate 144. Hans Memling. Portrait of a Man in Open Air. Florence, Corsini Gallery.

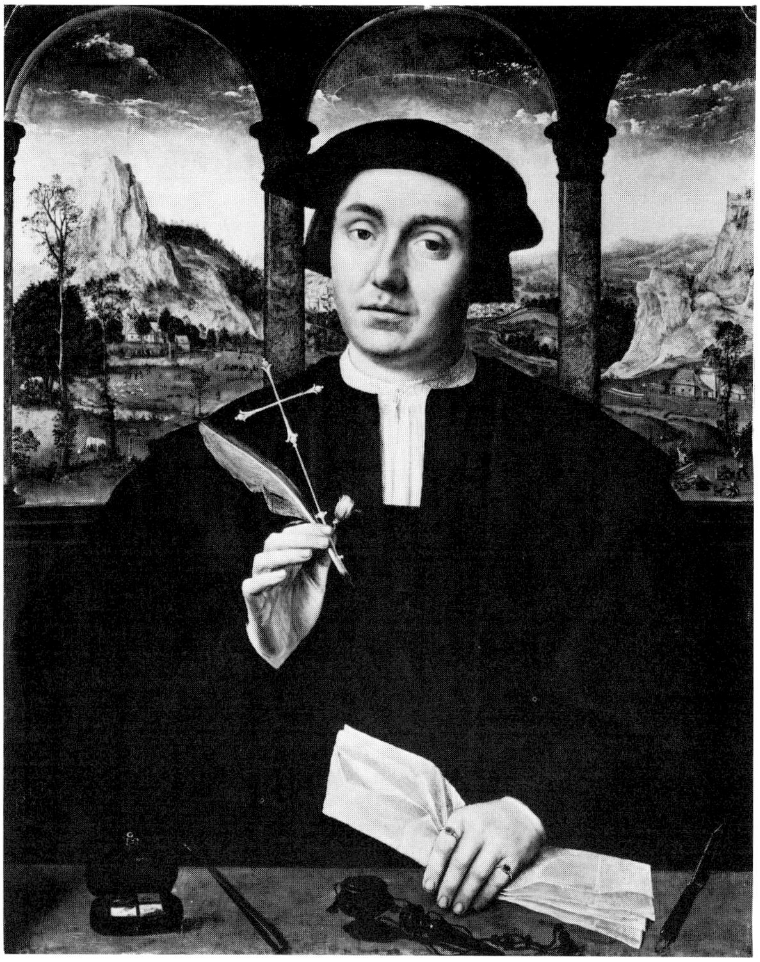

Plate 145. Massys. Portrait of a Notary. Edinburgh, National Gallery.

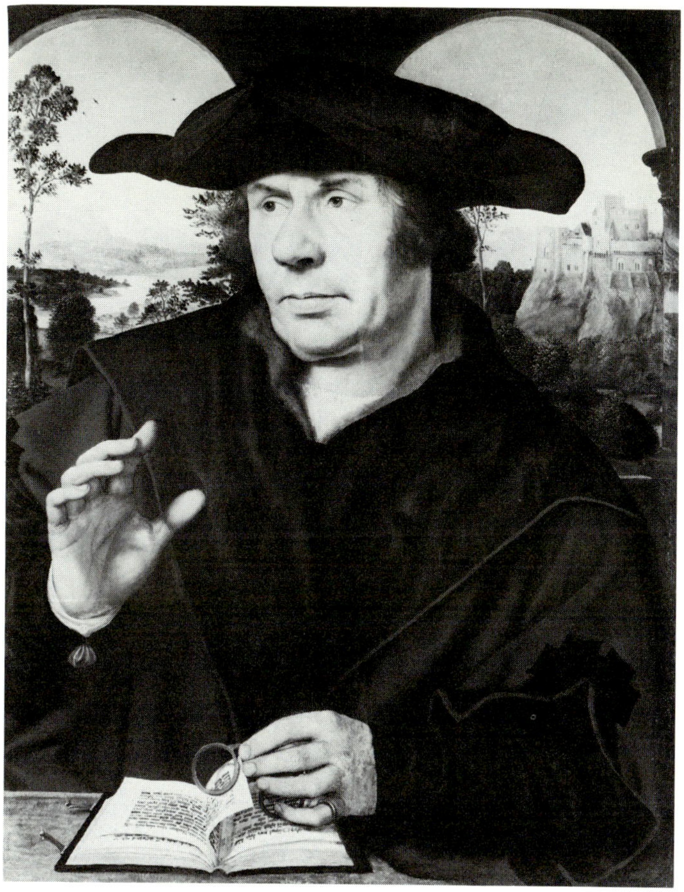

Plate 146. Massys. Portrait of a Scholar (here identified as Cornelius Grapheus). Frankfurt, Staedel Institute.

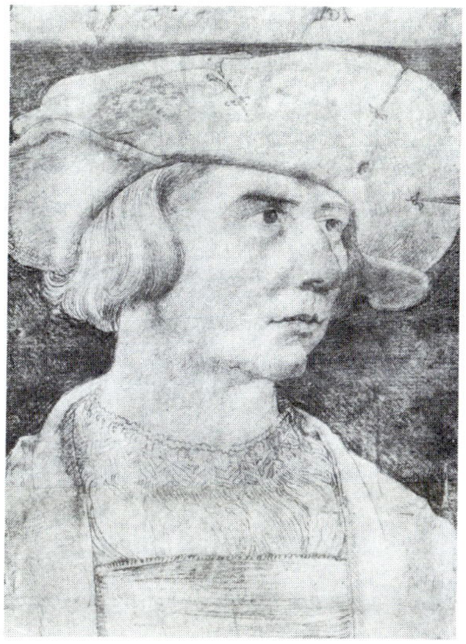

Plate 147. Dürer, Portrait of a Man (here identified as Cornelius Grapheus). Formerly Weimar, Schlossmuseum.

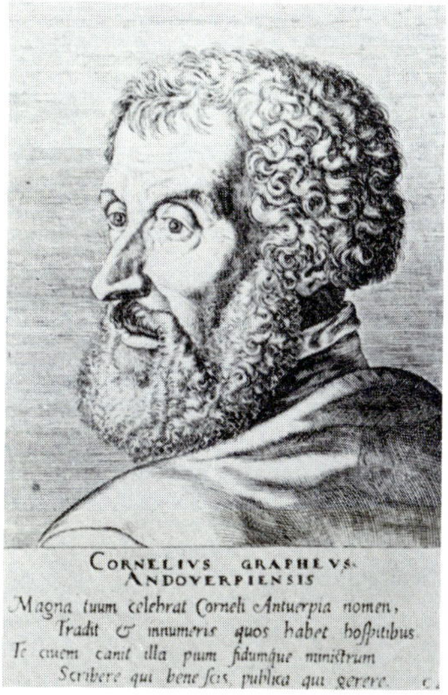

Plate 148. Philips Galle. engraving. Portrait of Cornelius Grapheus.

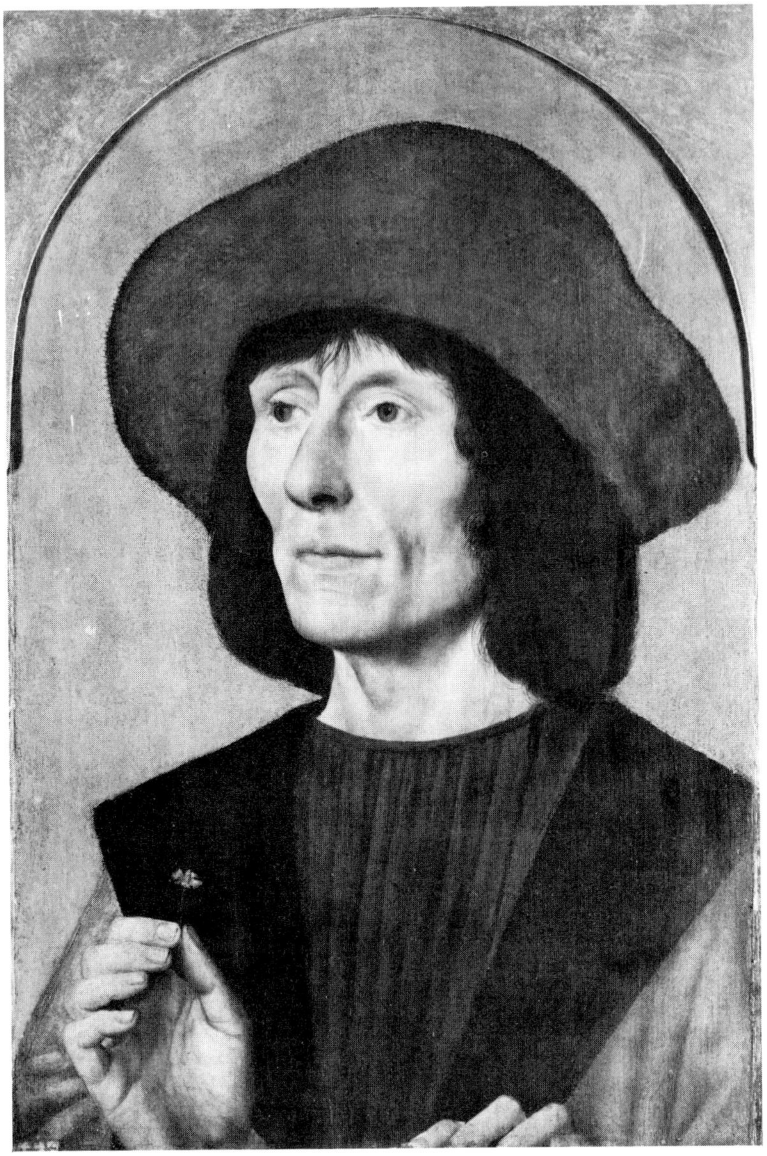

Plate 149. Massys. Portrait of a Man with a Flower. Chicago, Art Institute.

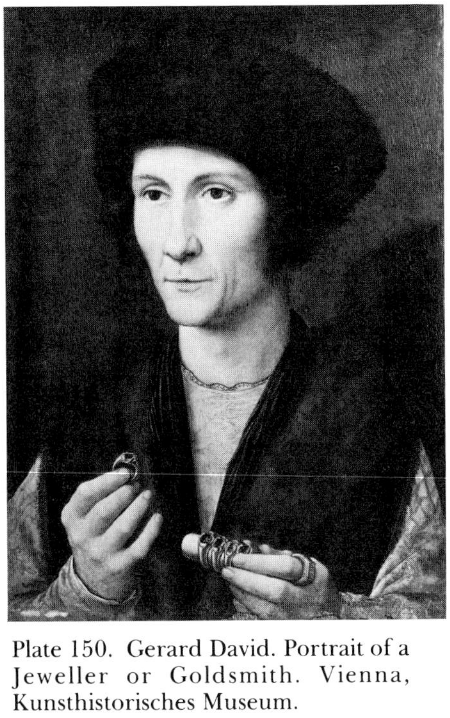

Plate 150. Gerard David. Portrait of a Jeweller or Goldsmith. Vienna, Kunsthistorisches Museum.

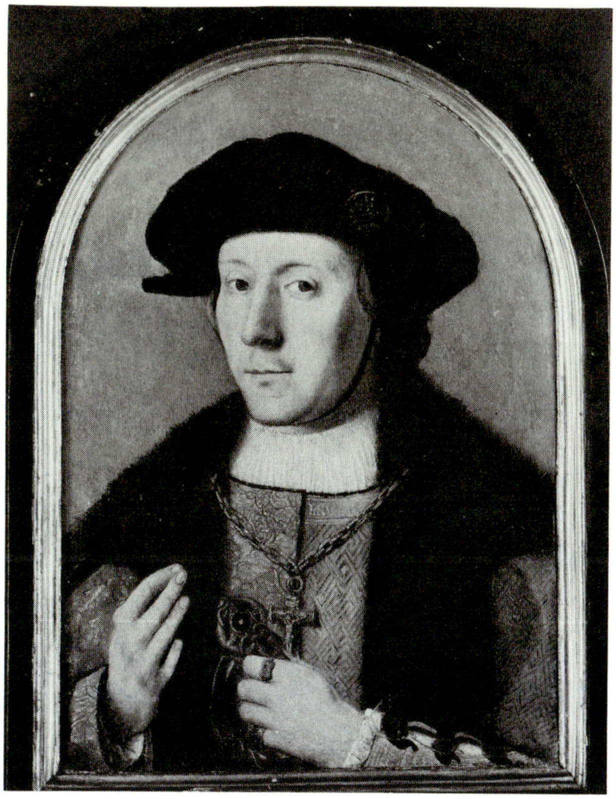

Plate 151. Massys. Portrait of a Wealthy Man. New York, Metropolitan Museum.

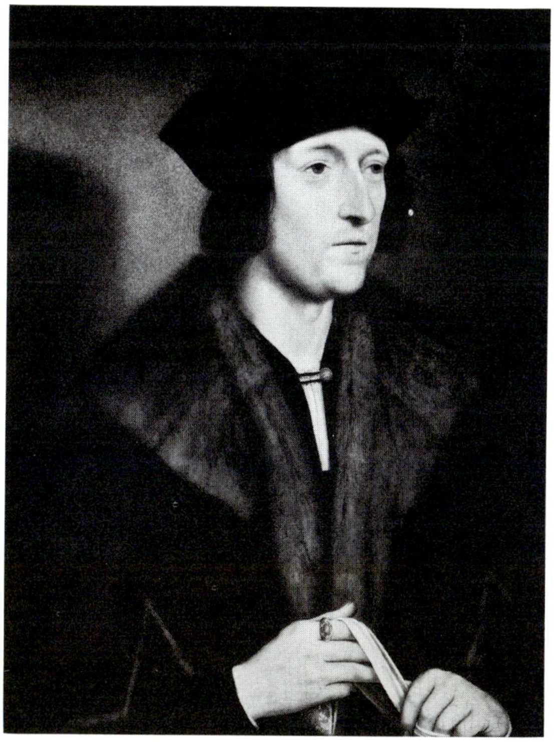

Plate 152. Massys. Portrait of a Man. Karlsruhe, Kunsthalle.

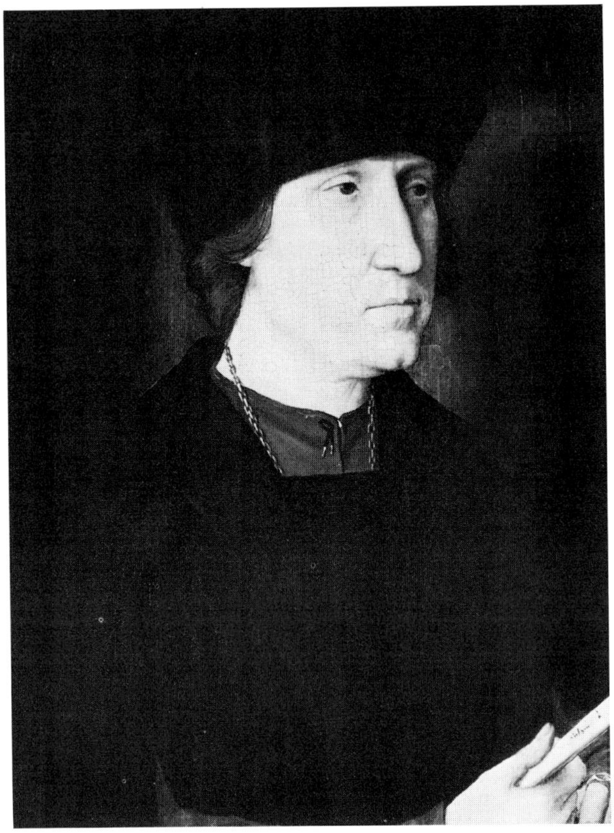

Plate 153. Massys. Portrait of a Prominent Man. Badminton, collection Lady Altrincham.

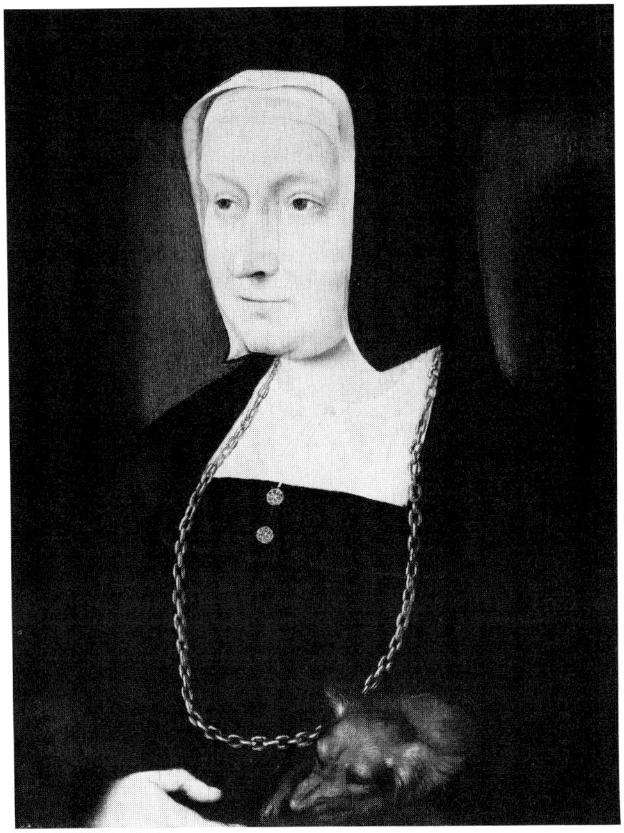

Plate 154. Massys. Portrait of a Prominent Woman. Badminton, collection Lady Altrincham.

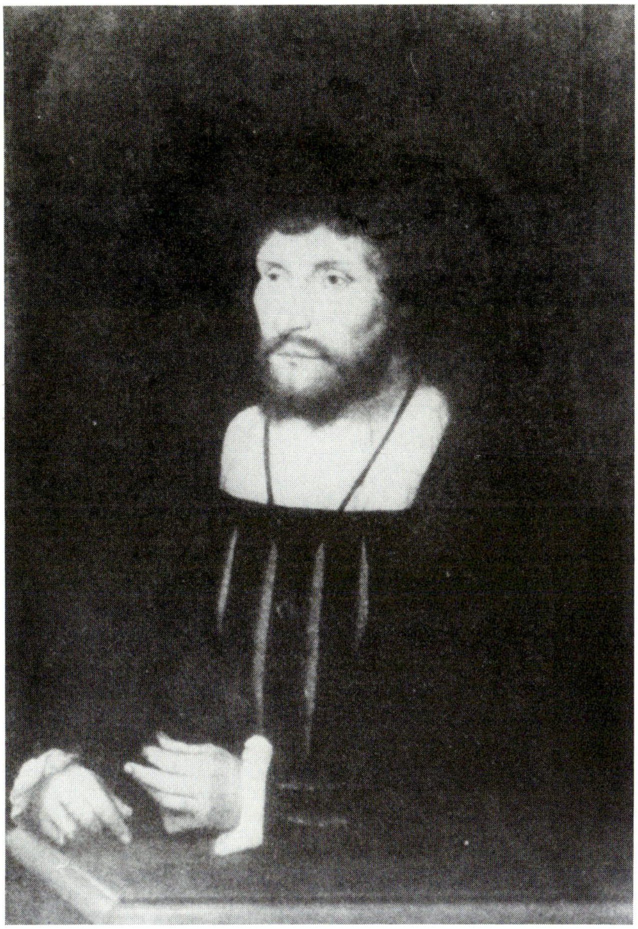

Plate 155. Massys. Portrait of Christian II of Denmark. Kroměřice, Episcopal Museum.

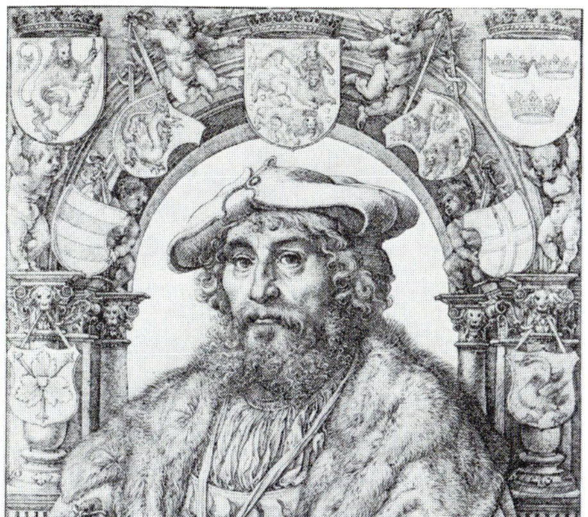

Plate 156. Jan Gossaert. Drawing: Portrait of Christian II of Denmark. Paris, Institut Néerlandais.

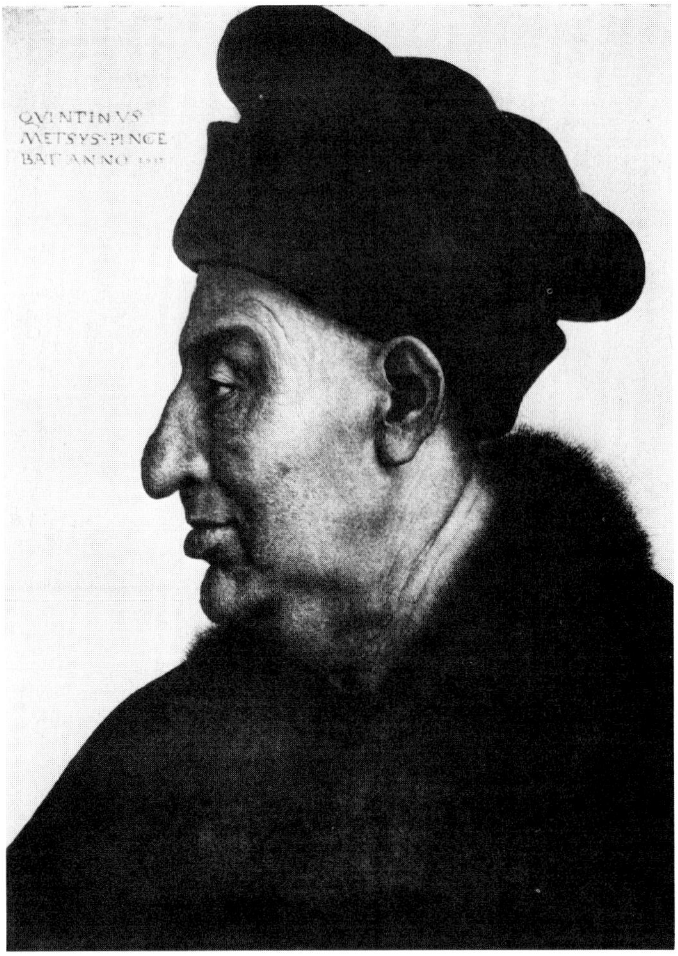

Plate 157. Massys. Portrait of Cosimo de' Medici. Paris, Musée Jacquemart-Andre.

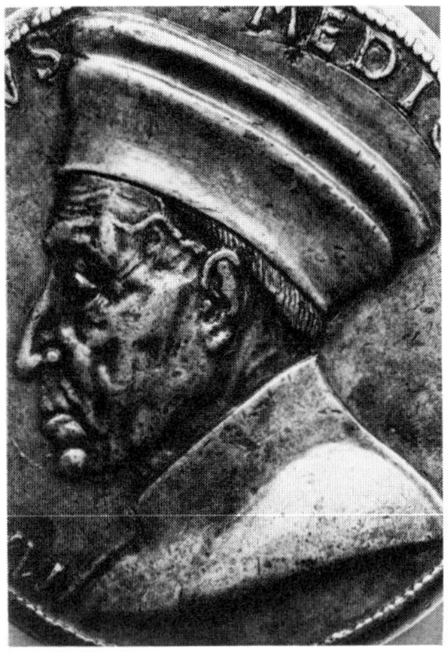

Plate 158. Bronze portrait medal. Florentine. Cosimo de' Medici.

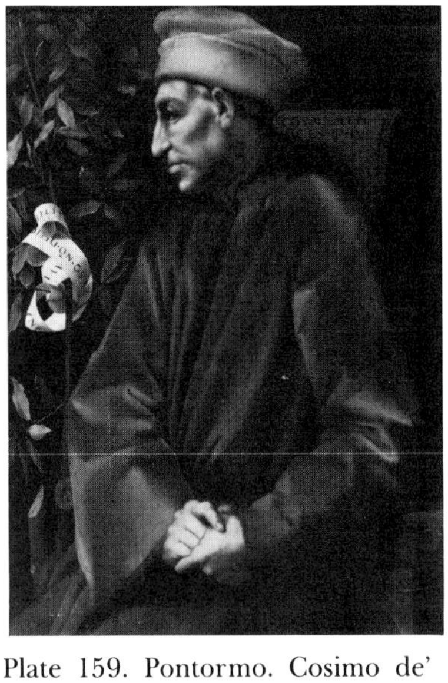

Plate 159. Pontormo. Cosimo de' Medici. Florence, Uffizi.

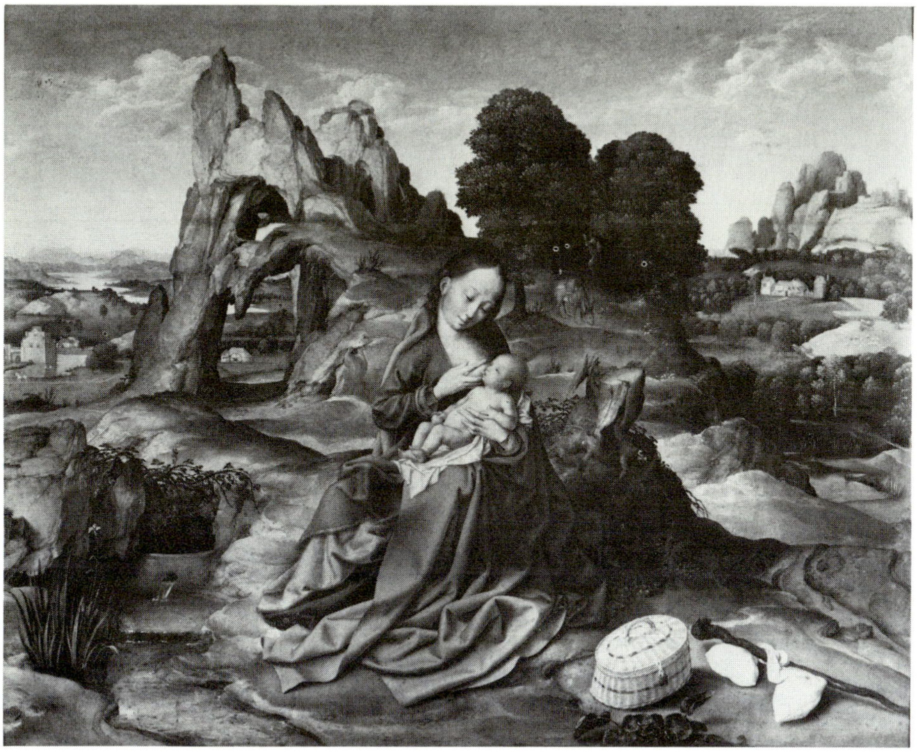

Plate 160. Joos van Cleve. Rest on the Flight into Egypt. Brussels, Musées Royaux.

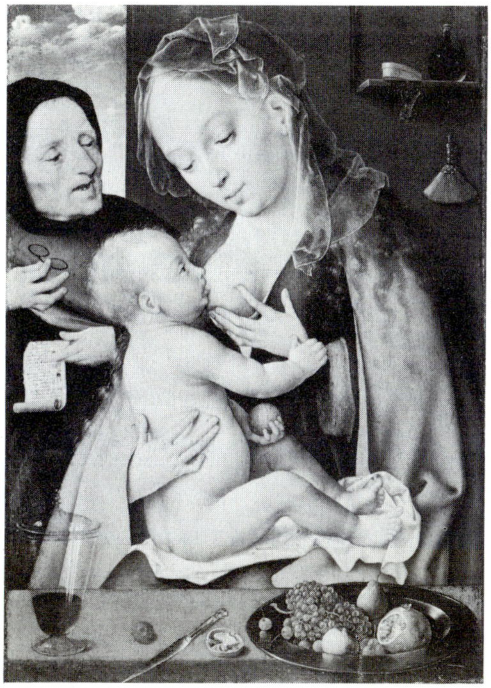

Plate 161. Joos van Cleve. Holy Family. New York, Metropolitan Museum.

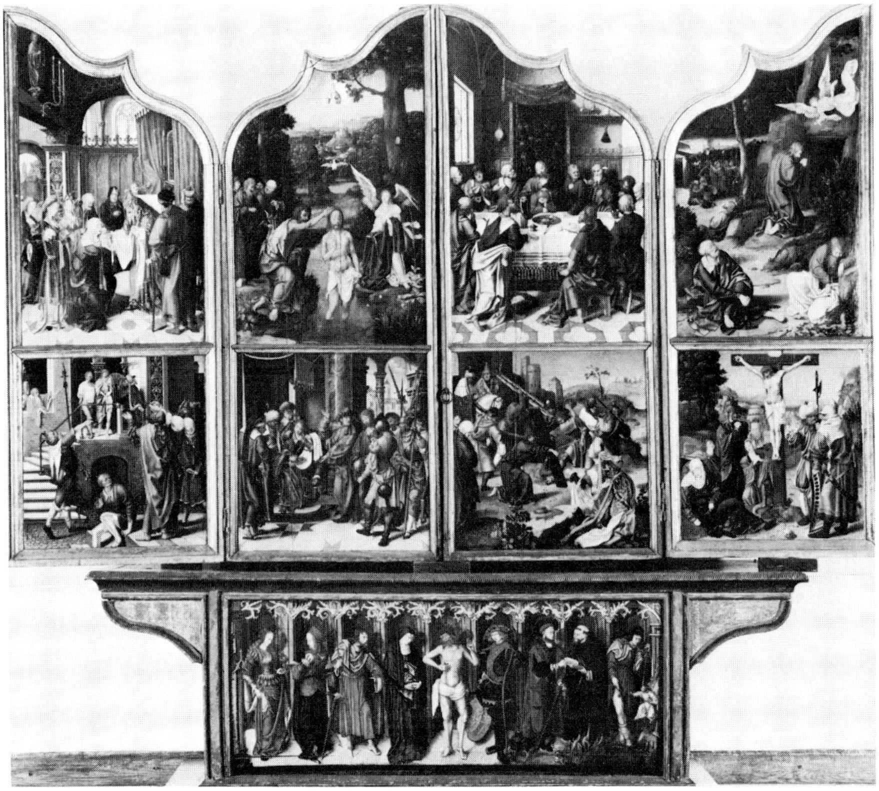

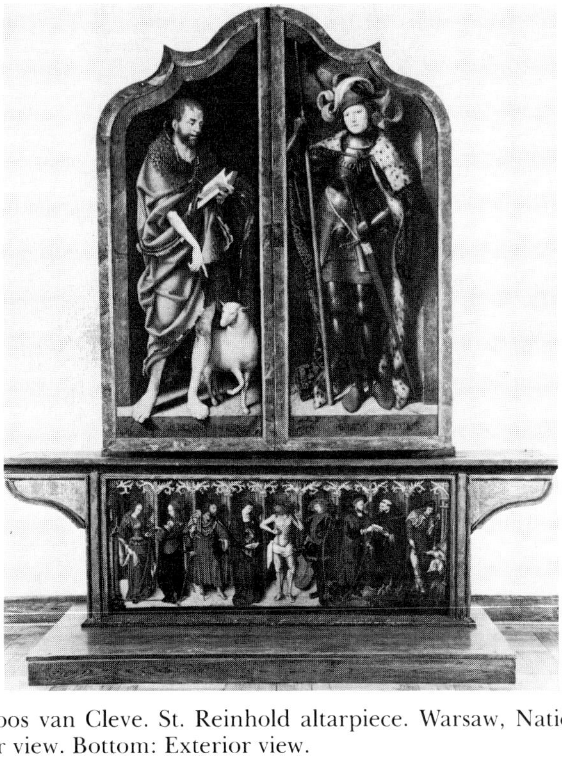

Plate 162. Joos van Cleve. St. Reinhold altarpiece. Warsaw, National Gallery.
Top: Interior view. Bottom: Exterior view.

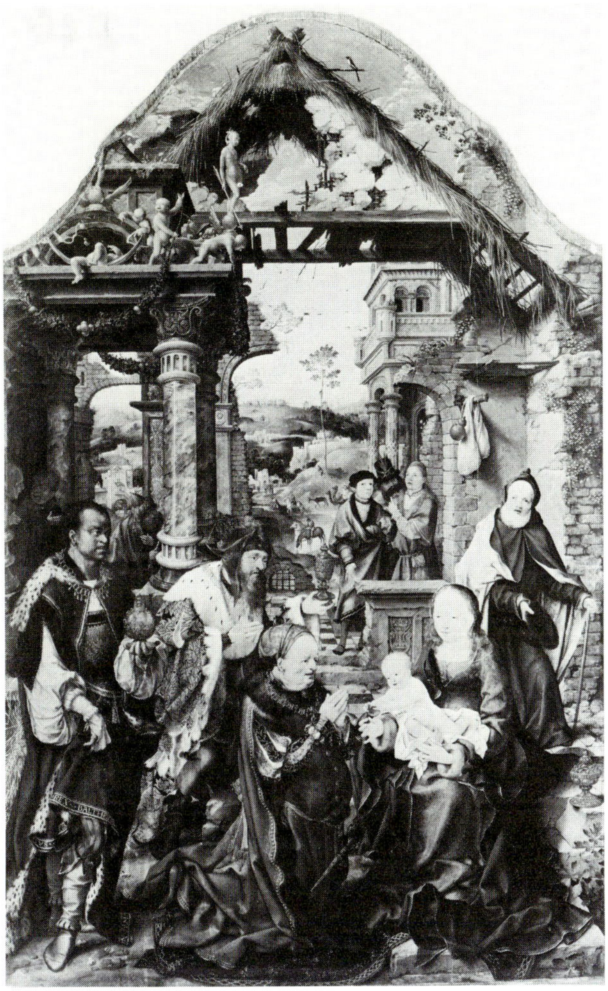

Plate 163. Joos van Cleve. Adoration of the Magi. Dresden, Gemäldegalerie.

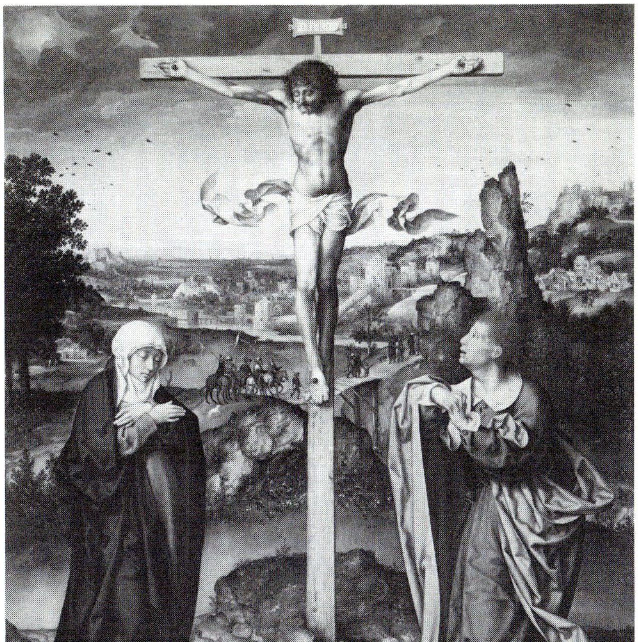

Plate 164. Joos van Cleve. Crucifixion. Boston, Museum of Fine Arts.

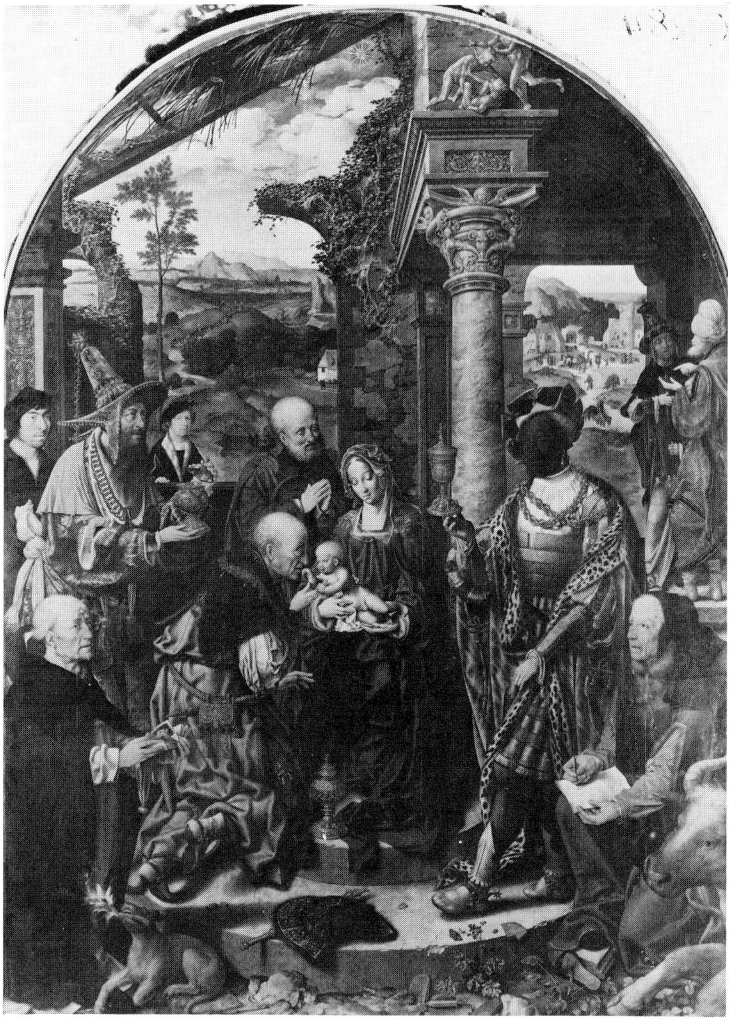

Plate 165. Joos van Cleve. Adoration of the Magi. Dresden, Gemäldegalerie.

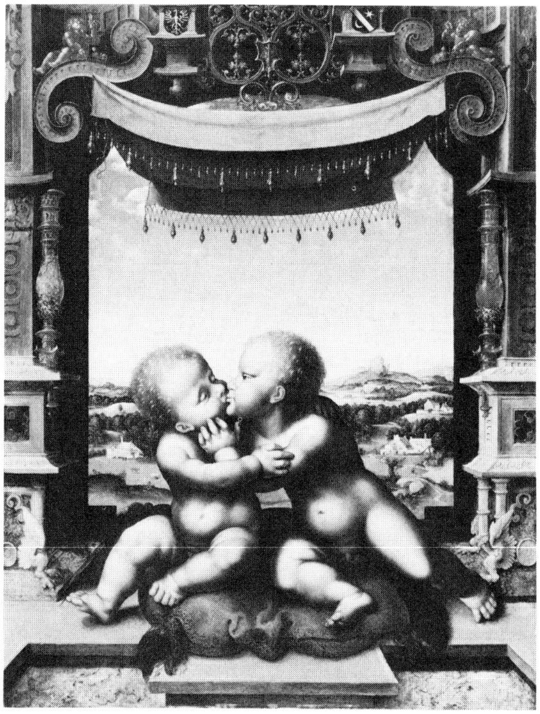

Plate 166. Joos van Cleve, workshop. Infants John and Jesus Kissing. Chicago, Art Institute.

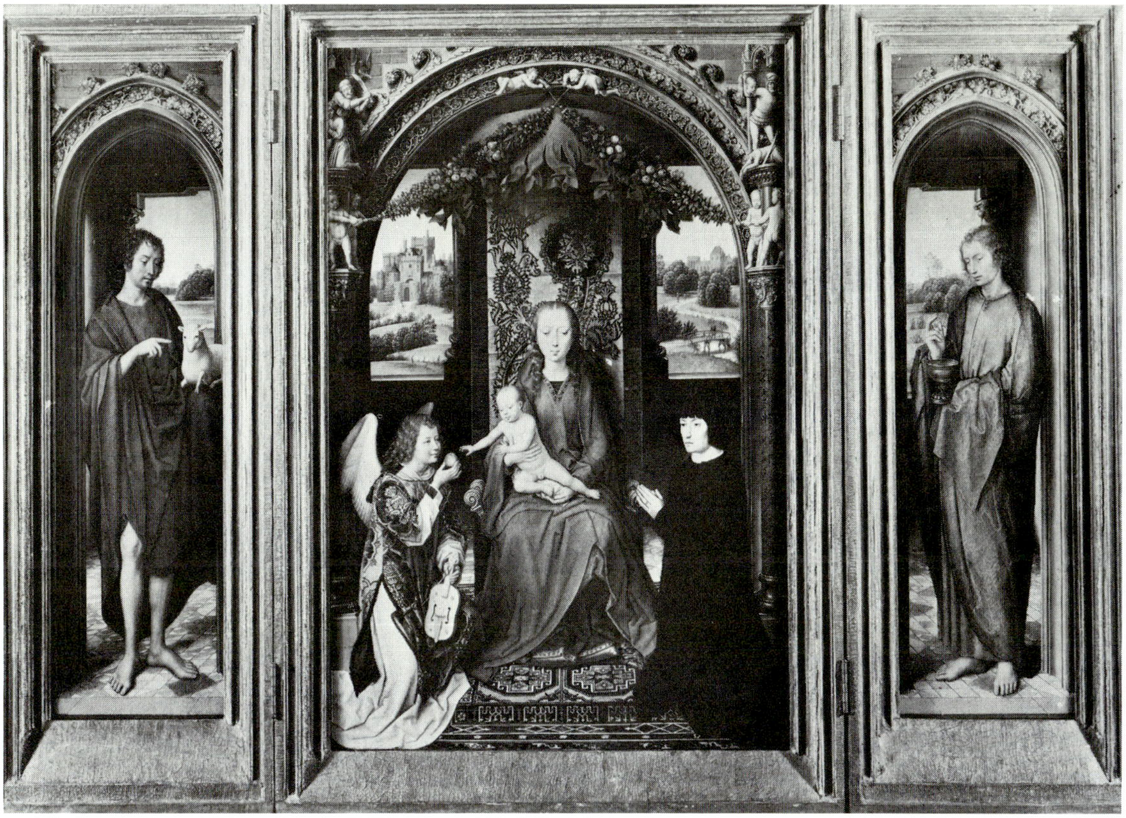

Plate 167. Hans Memling. Triptych with Madonna and Ss. John. Vienna, Kunsthistorisches Museum.

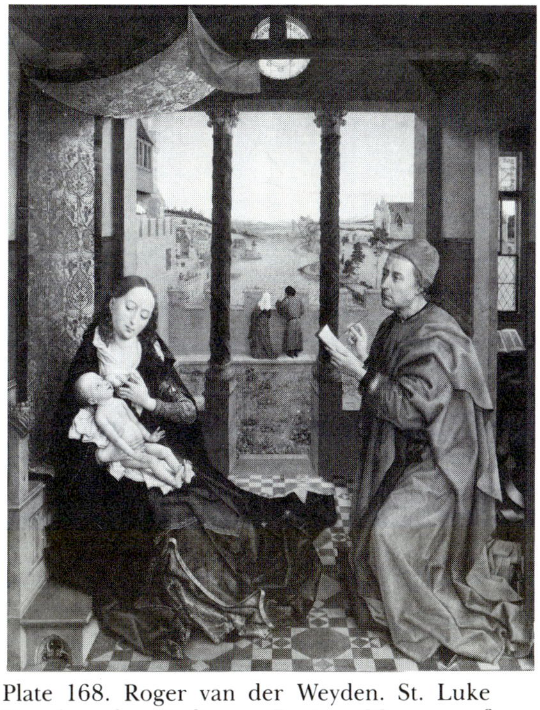

Plate 168. Roger van der Weyden. St. Luke Drawing the Madonna. Boston, Museum of Fine Arts.

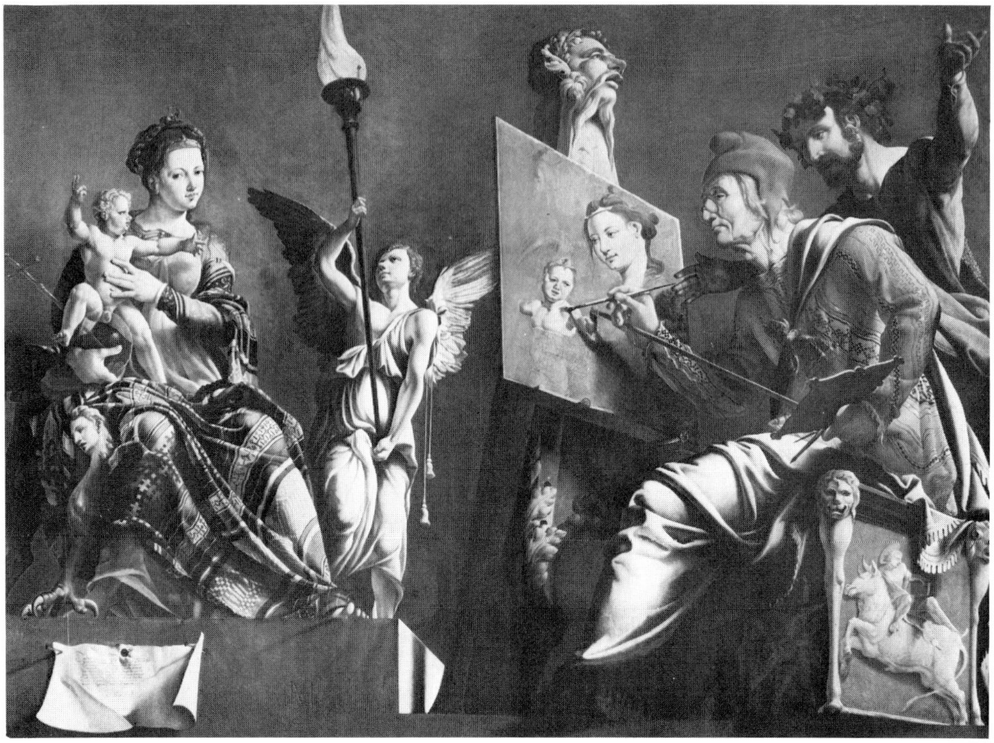

Plate 169. Maarten van Heemskerck. St. Luke Painting the Madonna. Haarlem, Frans Hals Museum.

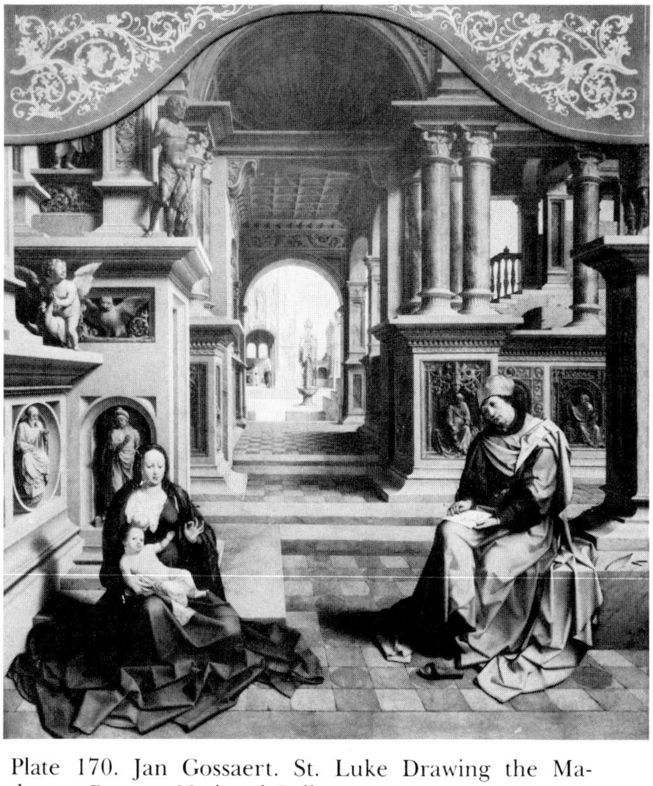

Plate 170. Jan Gossaert. St. Luke Drawing the Madonna. Prague, National Gallery.

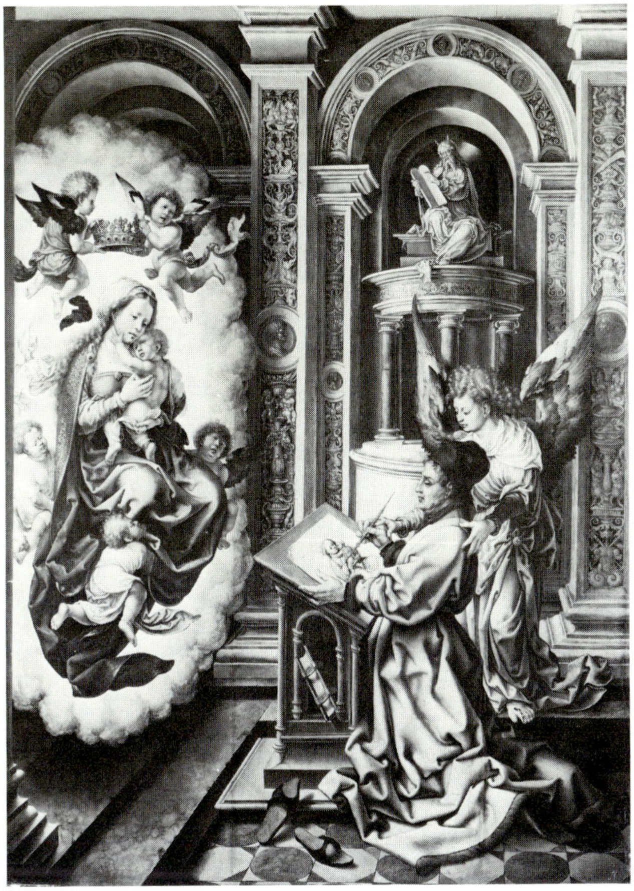

Plate 171. Jan Gossaert. St. Luke Drawing the Madonna. Vienna, Künsthistorisches Museum.

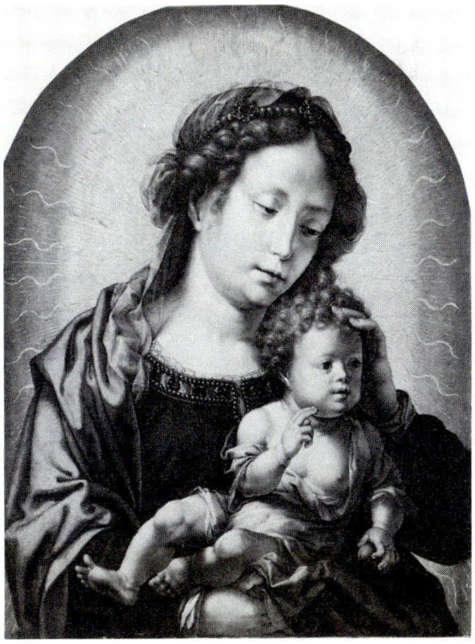

Plate 172. Jan Gossaert. Madonna and Child in a Glory, half-length. Chicago, Art Institute.

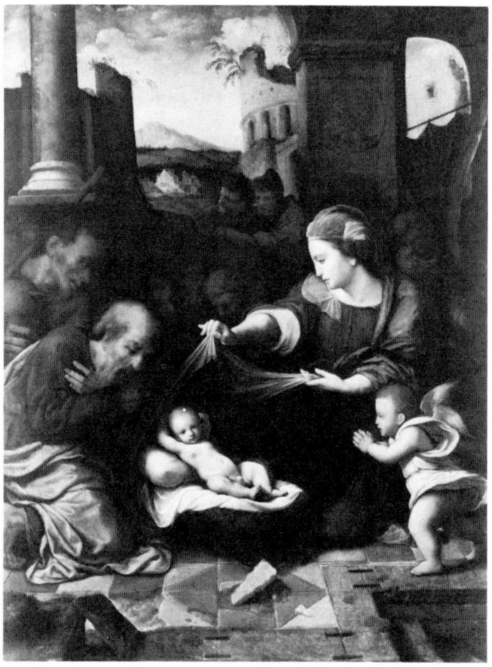

Plate 173. Joos van Cleve (or Cornelis van Cleve). Adoration of the Shepherds. Sarasota, Ringling Museum.

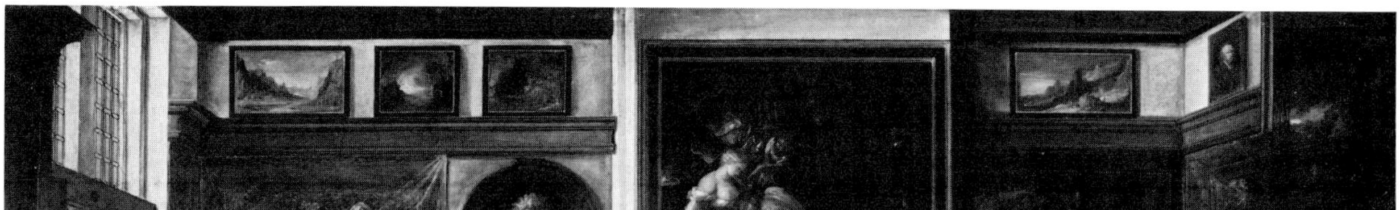

Plate 174. François Francken II. The Party of the Art Lover. Munich, Alte Pinakothek.

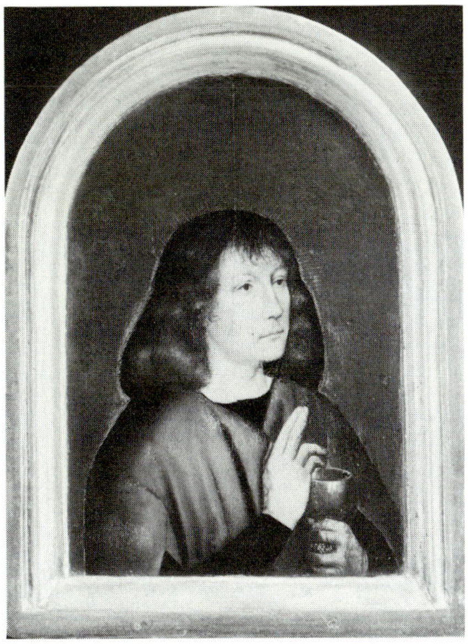

Plate 175. Massys. St. John the Evangelist.
Padua, Museo Civico.

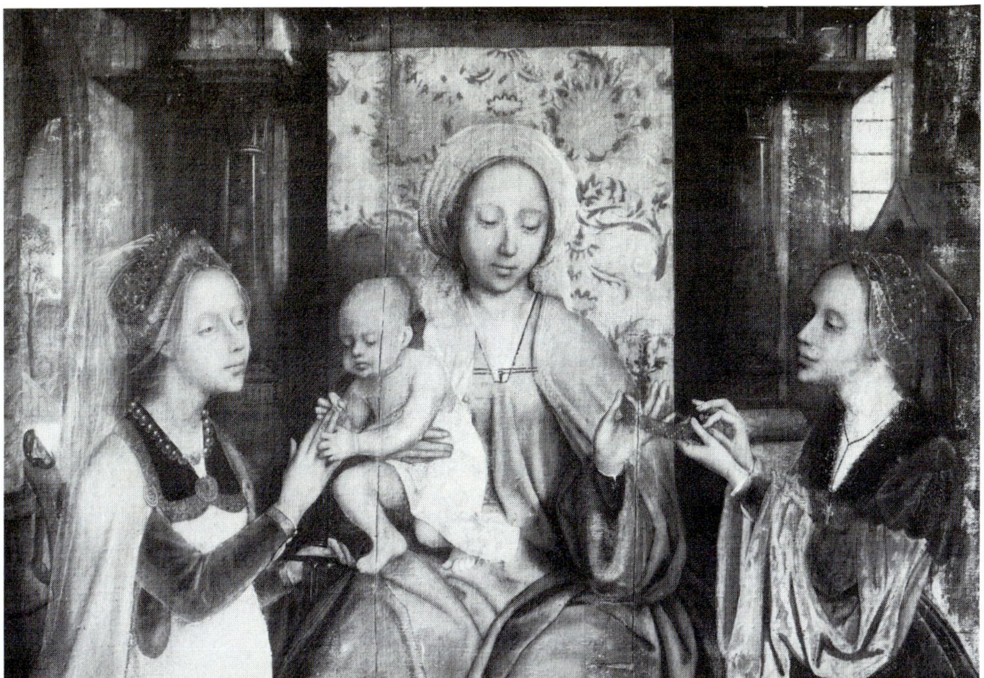

Plate 176. Massys. Marriage of St. Catherine. London, National Gallery.

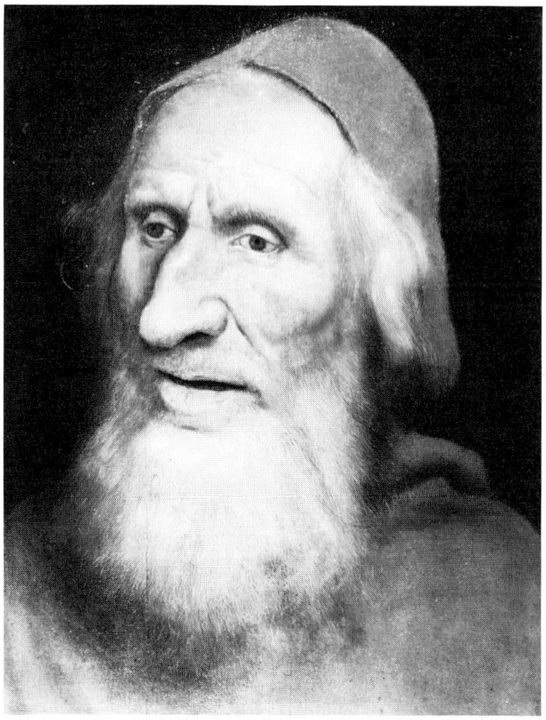

Plate 177. Massys. Head of Saint. Barcelona, Museo Catalan.

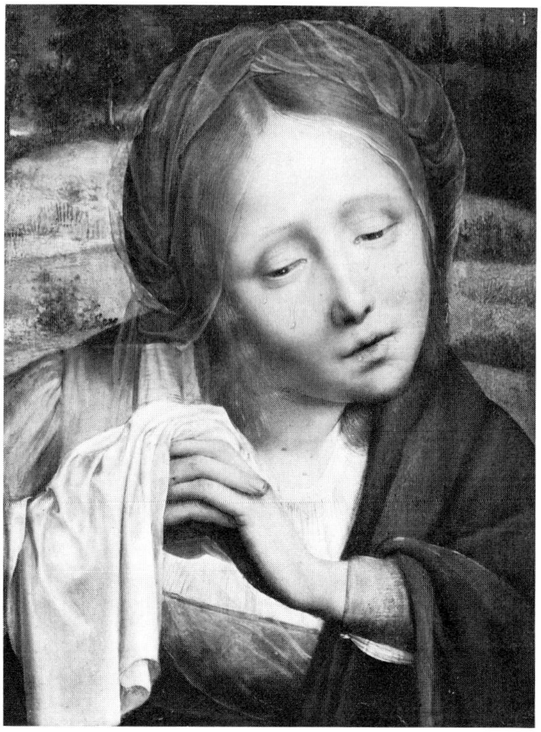

Plate 178. Massys. (fragment) Grieving Magdalene. Berlin-Dahlem.

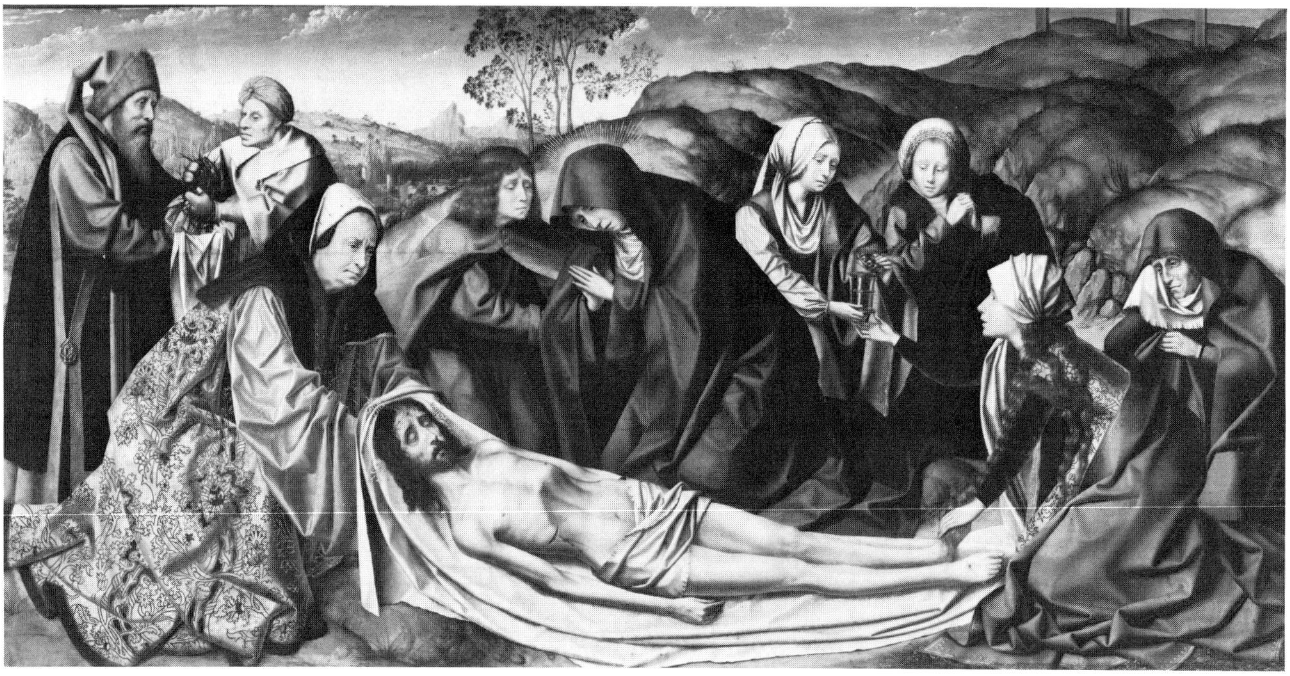

Plate 179. Massys, follower. Lamentation. Ottawa, National Gallery of Canada.

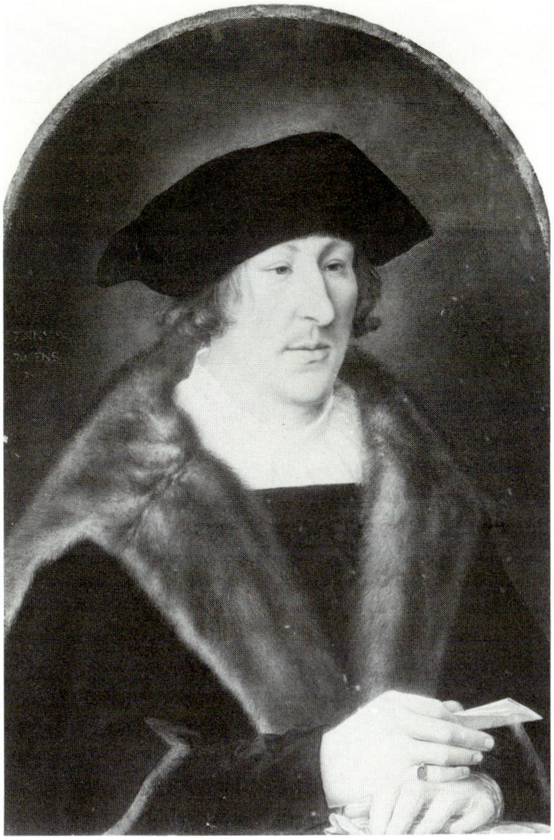

Plate 180. Massys. Young Man. Berlin-Dahlem.

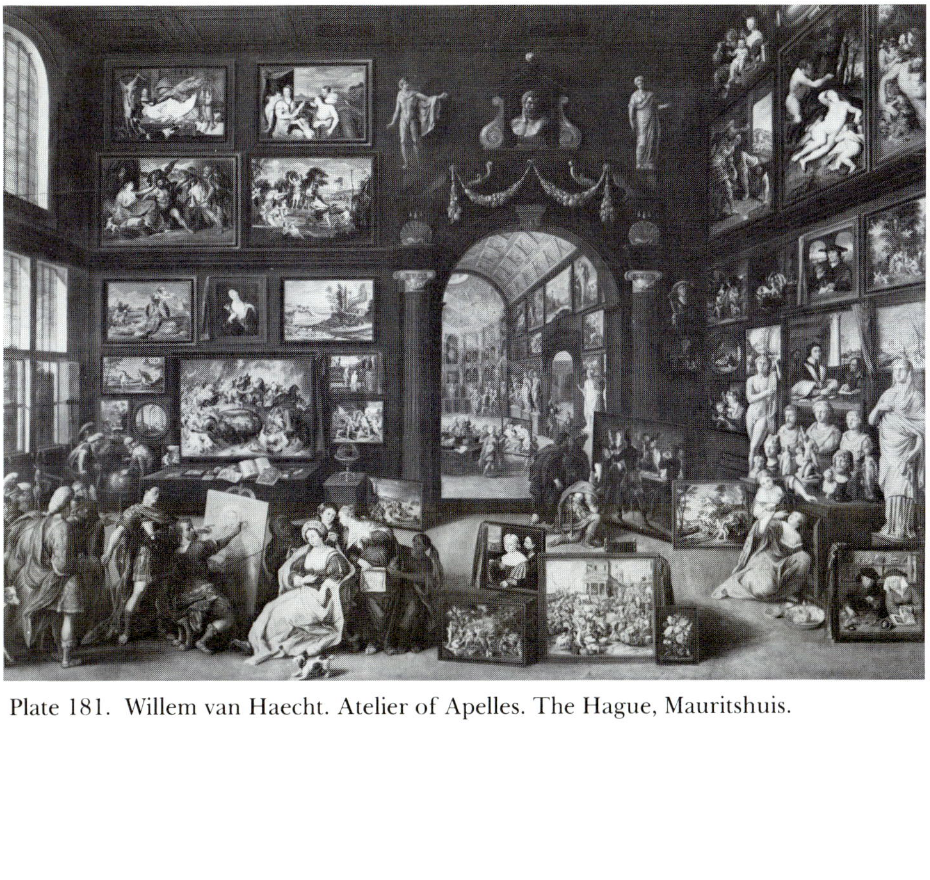

Plate 181. Willem van Haecht. Atelier of Apelles. The Hague, Mauritshuis.

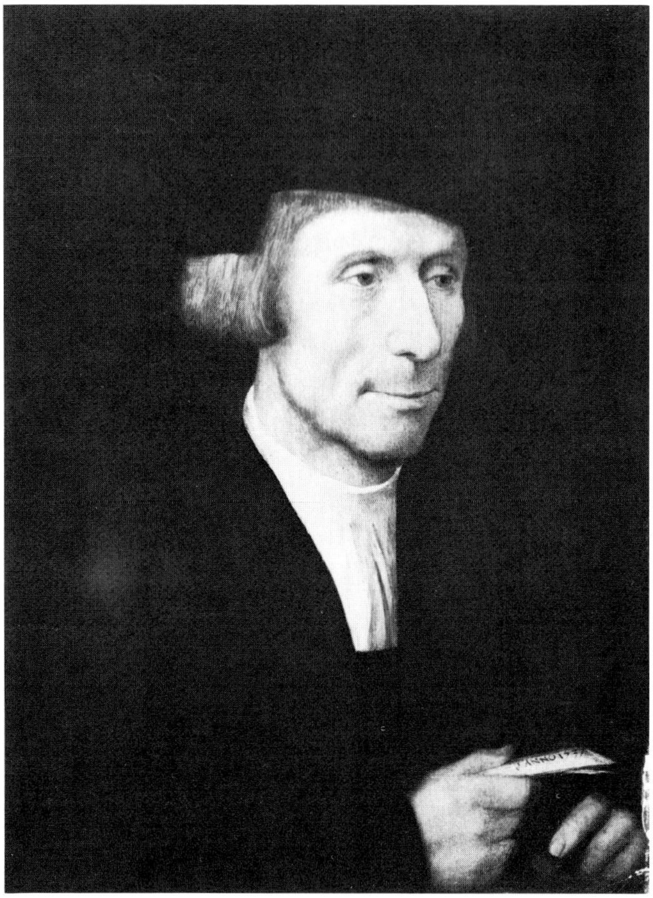

Plate 182. Massys. Portrait of a Man. Windsor Castle.

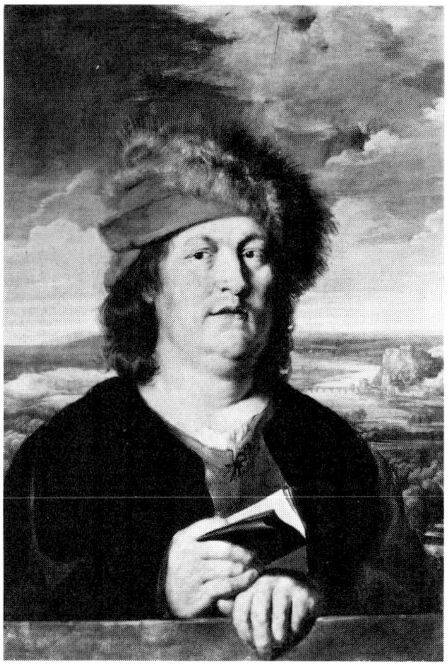

Plate 183. Peter Paul Rubens. Portrait of "Paracelsus." Brussels, Musées Royaux.

Photographic Credits

ANTWERP: Koninklijk Museum voor Schone Kunsten (A.C.L., Brussels), Pls. 13, 15, 17, 18, 19, 20, 42, 43, 75, 81, 96, 100, 110, 113; Rubenshuis, Pl. 59. BADMINTON: Coll. Lady Altrincham (Derek Balmer), Pls. 153, 154. BARCELONA: Museo Catalan (A & R Mas), Pl. 177. BENNINGTON: Coll. Julius S. Held, Pl. 135. BERLIN-DAHLEM: Staatliche Museen Preussischer Kulturbesitz, Pls. 63, 178; (Jorg P. Anders) Pls. 55, 76; (Gust. Schwarz) Pls. 46, 180. BOSTON: Museum of Fine Arts, Pls. 164, 168 (Gift of Mr. and Mrs. Henry Lee Higginson). BRUGES: Groeninge Museum (A.C.L., Brussels), Pls. 4, 12, 45. BRUSSELS: Musées Royaux (A.C.L., Brussels), Pls. 1, 5, 6, 7, 8, 9, 10, 39, 48, 51, 66, 93, 95, 141, 142, 160, 183. CAMBRIDGE: Busch-Reisinger Museum, Pl. 107. CHICAGO: Art Institute, Pls. 137, 149 (Gift of John J. Glassner), 166 and 172 (Charles H. and Mary F.S. Worcester Fund). (All courtesy of the Art Institute of Chicago.) COIMBRA: Museu Machado de Castro (FOCUS), Pls. 32, 33, 34, 35, 36. DETROIT: Institute of Arts, Pls. 64 (Gift of James E. Scripps), 84 (Gift of Mr. and Mrs. Edgar B. Whitcomb), 101. DRESDEN: Staatliche Kunstsammlungen, Pls. 163, 165. EDINBURGH: National Gallery of Scotland (Annan, Glasgow), Pl. 145. FLORENCE: Galleria Corsini (Ed. Alinari), Pl. 144; Galleria Uffizi (Gabinetto Fotografico), Pl. 159. FRANKFURT: Historisches Museum, Pls. 2, 3; Staedelschen Kunstinstituts (Ursula Edelmann), Pl. 146. HAARLEM: Frans Hals Museum (A. Dingjan), Pl. 169. THE HAGUE: Foundation Johan Maurits van Nassau (Mauritshuis), Pls. 22, 89, 181 (A. Dingjan). KARLSRUHE: Staatliche Kunsthalle, Pl. 152. KROMĚŘICE: Episcopal Museum, Pl. 155. LIEGE: Coll. Wittert (A.C.L., Brussels), Pl. 41. LISBON: Museu Nacional, Pls. 24, 25, 27, 30, 31, 88. LONDON: The National Gallery, Pls. 38, 77, 97, 122, 136, 176; Seilern Coll., Pls. 52, 90; The Warburg and Courtauld Institute, Pls. 14, 69, 104, 105. LYONS: Musée des Beaux-Arts, Pl. 53. MADRID: Prado, Pls. 21 and 49 (A & R Mas), 47, 71, 72, 86, 114, 128. MELBOURNE: National Gallery of Victoria, Pl. 50 (Felton Bequest). MUNICH: Alte Pinakothek, Staatsgemäldesammlungen, Pls. 23, 37, 67, 78, 98, 109, 174. NEW YORK: Metropolitan Museum of Art, Pls. 29, 60, 79, 119 (Robert Lehman Coll.), 140, 151 (Michael Friedsam Coll.), 161; Newhouse Gallery, Pl. 40. OLDENBURG: Landesmuseum für Kunst- u. Kulturgeschichte, Pls. 102, 103. OTTAWA: National Gallery of Canada, Pls. 91, 179. PADUA: Museo Civico (Gabinetto Fotografico), Pl. 175. PARIS: Cailleux Coll., Pl. 121; Musée Jacquemart-André, Pl. 157; Institut Néerlandais (Fondation Custodia, Coll. F. Lugt), Pl. 156; The Louvre (Service de documentation photographique), Pls. 68, 94, 118. PHILADELPHIA: Museum of Art (John F. Johnson Coll.), Pls. 11, 83, 112. PRAGUE: National Gallery, Pl. 170.

PROVIDENCE: Rhode Island School of Design, Pl. 127 (Gift of Mrs. Gustav Radeke). RALEIGH: North Carolina Museum of Art, Pl. 44. RIO DE JANEIOR: Escola Nacional de Belas-Artes, Pl. 26. ROME: Galleria Nazionale di Stampi, Pl. 85; Palazzo Barberini (Galleria Corsini) (Alinari), Pl. 99; Palazzo Doria (Ed. Alinari), Pl. 56, 108. ROTTERDAM: Boymans-van Beuningen Museum (A. Frequin), Pl. 65. ST. LOUIS: Museum of Art, Pl. 73. SAN FRANCISCO: de Young Memorial Museum (Fine Arts Museums of San Francisco), Pl. 61. SARASOTA: John and Mabel Ringling Museum of Art, Pls. 54, 58 (Burnell the Photographer), 82, 173. VADUZ: Liechtenstein Coll., Pl. 143. VALLADOLID: San Salvador (A.C.L., Brussels), Pl. 75. VENICE: Ca' d'Oro (Alinari), Pl. 92; Palazzo Ducale (Ed. Alinari), Pl. 87. VIENNA: Albertina, Pl. 133; Kunsthistorischen Museum (Sindhöringer), Pls. 106, 139, 150, 167, 171. WARSAW: National Gallery (Waldemar Jerke), Pl. 162. WASHINGTON: National Gallery of Art, Pls. 117, 129. WINDSOR CASTLE: (Reproduced with Gracious Permission of H.M. the Queen), Pls. 16, 70, 80, 120, 124, 125, 126, 182. WINTERTHUR: Oskar Reinhart Coll., Pl. 138. WORCESTER (Mass.): Art Museum, Pl. 28. PRIVATE COLLECTION: New York, Pl. 123. LOCATION UNKNOWN: Pl. 134 (Brussels, Galerie Trussart).

Frequently Cited Sources

Baldass: L. von Baldass, "Gotik und Renaissance im Werke des Quinten Massys," *Jahrbuch der Kunsthistorischen Sammlungen im Wien* N.F. 7 (1933): 137ff.

Benesch: O. Benesch, *The Art of the Renaissance in Northern Europe,* 2nd ed. (London, 1965).

Blum: S. N. Blum, *Early Netherlandish Triptychs* (Berkeley, 1969).

BMRBA: *Bulletin Musées Royaux des Beaux-Arts de Belgique.*

Boon: K. G. Boon, *Quinten Massys* (Amsterdam [1942]).

Bosschere: J. de Bosschere, *Quinten Metsys* (Brussels, 1907).

Brising: H. Brising, *Quinten Matsys und der Ursprung des Italianismus in der Kunst der Niederlände* (Leipzig, 1908).

Broadley: H. T. Broadley, "The Mature Style of Quinten Massys" (Ph.D. dissertation, New York University, 1961).

Cohen: W. Cohen, *Studien zu Quinten Metsys* (Bonn, 1904).

Conway: M. Conway, *The Van Eycks and Their Followers* (New York, 1921).

Cuttler: C. Cuttler, *Northern Painting from Pucelle to Bruegel* (New York, 1968).

DB: A. de Bosque, *Quentin Metsys* (Brussels, 1975).

Delaruelle: E. Delaruelle, E.-R. Labande, and P. Ourliac, *L'Eglise au temps du Grand Schisme et de la crise conciliaire (1378–1449). L'Histoire de l'Eglise 14* (Paris, 1964).

Denucé: J. Denucé, *De Konstkamers van Antwerpen in de 16e en 17e eeuwen Inventarissen van kunstverzamelingen* (The Hague, 1932).

Dolan: J. P. Dolan, *The Essential Erasmus* (New York, 1964).

ENP: See Panofsky.

Fickaert: F. Fickaert, *Metamorphosen ofte wonderbare veranderingh ende Leven van den vermaarden Mr. Quinten Matsys* (Antwerp, 1648).

Fornenbergh: A. van Fornenbergh, *Den Antwerpschen Protheus ofte Cyclopschen Apelles, dat is het Leven ende Konstrijcke Daden des uytnemenden ende hoogh-beroemden Mr. Quinten Massys* (Antwerp, 1658).

Friedländer: M. J. Friedländer, *Early Netherlandish Painting,* Eng. ed. *VII. Quinten Massys* (Leyden, 1971). All F. numbers refer to this volume; all other volumes from the 14-volume series are designated by volume number.

Hymans: H. Hymans, "Quentin Matsys," *Gazette des Beaux-Arts* 37 (1888); 5–20, 104–23; 38 (1888); 193–216.

JKSW: *Jahrbuch der Kunsthistorischen Sammlungen in Wien.*

JWCI: *Journal of the Warburg and Courtauld Institutes.*

KG: see Post, KG.

KV: see Post, KV.
Mallé: L. Mallé, "Quinten Metsys," *Commentari* 6 (1955); 79ff.
Marlier: G. Marlier, *Erasme et la peinture flamande de son temps* (Damme, 1954).
Panofsky, *ENP:* E. Panofsky, *Early Netherlandish Painting* (Cambridge, Mass., 1953).
Post, KG: R. R. Post, *Kerkgeschiedenis van Nederland in de Middeleeuwen*, 2 vols. (Utrecht, 1957).
Post, KV: R. R. Post, *Kerkelijke verhoudingen in Nederland vóór de Reformatie* (Utrecht, 1954).
Prims: F. Prims, *Geschiedenis van Antwerpen VII*. 3 (Antwerp, 1939–40).
Puyvelde: L. van Puyvelde, *La Peinture flamande au siècle de Bosch et Bruegel* (Paris, 1962).
Puyvelde 1970: L. van Puyvelde, *Flemish Painting from the van Eycks to Metsys*, Eng. ed. (New York, 1970).
RDK: *Reallexikon zur deutschen Kunstgesschichte*, edited by D. Schmitt (Stuttgart, 1937).
Reis-Santos: L. Reis-Santos, *Masterpieces of Flemish Painting of the XV and XVI Centuries in Portugal*, Eng. ed. (Lisbon, 1962).
Richardson: E. P. Richardson, "Quentin Massys," *Art Quarterly* 4 (1941): 163ff.
Ringbom: S. Ringbom, *Icon to Narrative* (Abo̊, 1965).
D. T. Robbins: D. T. Robbins, *Landscape in the Art of Quentin Massys* (Master's thesis, University of Washington, 1972).
Roosen-Runge: H. Roosen-Runge, *Die Gestaltung der Farbe bei Quentin Metsys* (Munich, 1940).
Speth-Holterhoff: S. Speth-Holterhoff, *Les Peintres flamands de cabinets d'amateurs au XVIIe siécle* (Brussels, 1957).
Toussaert: J. Toussaert, *Le Sentiment religieux en Flandre à la fin du Moyen-Age* (Paris, 1963).
von der Osten: G. von der Osten and H. Vey, *Painting and Sculpture in Germany and the Netherlands 1500–1600* (Harmondsworth, 1969).
Winkler: F. Winkler, *Die altniederländische Malerei* (Berlin, 1924).

Bibliography

Antwerpen in de XVIe eeuw. Antwerp, 1975.

Antwerp's Golden Age. Exhibition Cat. Washington, 1973–75.

Aurenhammer, H. "Marienikone und Marienandachtsbild. Zur Entstehung des halfigurigen Marienbildes nördlich des Alpen." *Jahrbuch der Österreichischen Byzantinischen Gesellschaft* 4 (1955): 135ff.

Axters, S. *Geschiedenis van de vroomheid in de Nederlanden III. De Moderne Devotie, 1380–1550.* Antwerp, 1956.

Bainton, R. *Erasmus of Christendom.* London, 1969.

Baldass, L. von. "Die niederländische Landschaftsmalerei von Patinir bis Bruegel." *JKSW* 24 (1918): 111–58.

———. "Sittenbild und Stilleben in Rahmen des niederländischen Romanismus." *JKSW* 36 (1923): 15ff.

———. *Joos van Cleve Der Meister des Todes Maria.* Vienna, 1925.

———. "Gotik und Renaissance im Werke des Quinten Metsys." *JKSW* N.F. 7 (1933): 137–82.

———. "Die niederländischen Maler des spätgotischen Stiles." *JKSW* N.F. 11 (1937): 117–38.

Baxandall, M. *The Limewood Sculptors of Renaissance Germany.* New Haven, 1980.

Benesch, O. "Ein Frühwerk von Gerard David." *Pantheon* 17 (1936): 154–55.

———. *Art of the Renaissance in Northern Europe.* 2nd ed. London, 1965.

Bergström, I. "Disguised Symbolism in 'Madonna' Pictures and Still Life." *Burlington Magazine* 97 (1955): 303–8, 342–49.

———. *Dutch Still-Life Painting in the Seventeenth Century.* London, 1956.

———. *Den symboliska nejlikan* [Malmö] [1958].

———. "Nejliksymbolen än en gång." *Kunsthistorisk Tidskrift* 30 (1961): 30–41.

Bialostocki, J. "Opus quinque dierum: Durer's 'Christ among the Doctors' and its Sources." *Journal of the Warburg and Courtauld Institutes* 22 (1959): 17–34.

———. *La Peinture néerlandaise dans les collections polonaises 1450–1550.* Exh. Cat. Warsaw, 1960.

———. *Stil und Ikonographie.* Dresden, 1966.

———. "The Eye and the Window." *Festschrift für Gert von der Osten.* Cologne, 1970. Pages 159–76.

Bialostocki, J., and M. Walicki. *Europäische Malerei in Pölnischen Sammlungen 1300–1800.* Warsaw, 1957.

Blankert, A. "Heraclitus en Democritus," *Nederlands Kunsthistorich Jaarboek* 18 (1967): 31–124.

Blockx, K. "Das religiöse Leben zur Zeit des Hieronymus Bosch." *Hieronymus Bosch.* Edited by R.H. Marijnissen Ghent, 1972. Pages 121–38.

Blum, S. N. *Early Netherlandish Triptychs.* Berkeley/Los Angeles, 1969.

Bodenhausen, E. von. *Gerard David und seine Schule.* Munich, 1905.

Bologna, F. "Nuove attribuzione à Jan Provost." *Bulletin Musées Royaux des Beaux-Arts Belgique* 5 (1956): 13–31.

Boon, K. G. *Quinten Massys.* Amsterdam [1942].

———. *Gerard David,* Amsterdam [1946].

Borchgrave d'Altena, J. de. "Des Characteres de la sculpture brabançonne vers 1500." *Annales de la Societé Royale d'Archéologie de Bruxelles* 38 (1934): 188ff.

———. *Les Retables Brabançons 1450–1550.* Brussels, 1943.

———. *Les Retables Brabançons conservés en Suéde.* Brussels, 1948.

———. "La Messe de Saint Gregoire. Etude iconographique." *Bulletin Musées Royaux des Beaux-Arts de Belgique* 8 (1959): 3–34.

———. *La Passion du Christ dans la sculpture en Belgique du XIe au XVIe siecles.* Brussels/Paris, n.d.

Bosque, A. de. *Quentin Metsys.* Brussels, 1975.

Bosschere, J. de. *Quinten Metsys.* Brussels, 1907.

———. *La Sculpture anversoise aux XVe et XVIe siècles.* Brussels, 1909.

Branden, F. J. van den. *Geschiedenis der Antwerpsche Schilderschool.* Antwerp, 1883.

Brant, S. *The Ship of Fools.* Edited and translated by E.H. Zeydel. New York, 1944.

Briels, J. "Amator Pictoriae Artis. De Antwerpse Kunsthandelaar Peeter Stevens (1590–1668) en zijn Constkamer." *Jaarboek Koninklijk Museum Antwerpen* (1980). Pages 139–226.

Brising, H. *Quinten Matsys und der Ursprung des Italianismus in der Kunst der Niederlände.* Leipzig, 1908.

Broadley, H. T. "The Mature Style of Quinten Massys." Ph.D. dissertation, New York University, 1961.

Brom, G. "Vernieuwing van onze schilderkunst in de vroege Renaissance." *Gentsche Bijdragen tot de Kunstgeschiedenis* 7 (1941): 7–36.

Bruxelles au XVe siècle. Exhibition Cat. Brussels, 1953.

Burke, P. *Popular Culture in Early Modern Europe.* New York, 1978.

Cahill, J. "Style as Idea in Ming-Ching Painting." *The Mozartean Historian: Essays on the Works of Joseph R. Levenson.* Edited by M. Meisner and R. Murphy. Berkeley, 1975. Pages 137–56.

Callatay, E. de. "Cornelis Massys paysagiste, collaborateur de son père et de son frère et auteur de l'album Errera." *Bulletin Musées Royaux des Beaux-Arts de Belgique* 14 (1965): 49–70.

Campbell, L. "The Art Market in the Southern Netherlands in the Fifteenth Century." *Burlington Magazine* 118 (1976): 188–98.

Campbell, L., M.M. Phillips. H. Schulte-Herbrüggen, and J.B. Trapp. "Quentin Metsys, Desiderius Erasmus, Pieter Gillis, and Thomas More." *Burlington Magazine* 120 (1978): 716–24.

Clark, K., and C. Pedretti. *The Drawings of Leonardo da Vinci in the Collection of Her Majesty the Queen at Windsor Castle.* 2nd ed. London, 1968.

Cohen, W. *Studien zu Quinten Metsys.* Bonn, 1904.

Conway, M. *The van Eycks and Their Followers.* New York, 1921.

Coupe, W. A. "Ungleiche Liebe—a Sixteenth Century Topos." *Modern Language Review* 62 (1967): 661–71.

Cuttler, C. *Northern Painting from Pucelle to Bruegel.* New York, 1968.

Davies, M. *Early Netherlandish School National Gallery Catalogues.* 3rd ed. London, 1968.

———. *Rogier van der Weyden.* London, 1972.

Davis, N. Z. *Society and Culture in Early Modern France.* Stanford, 1975.

Debaene, L. *De nederlandse volksboeken.* Antwerp, 1951.

Degroote, G. "De poezië der Rederijkers." *Dietsche Warande en Belfort* 48 (1948). Pages 292ff, 362ff.

———. "Erasmus en de Rederijkers van de XVIe eeuw." *Revue belge de philologie et d'histoire* 29 (1951): 389–420,1029–62.

———. "Erasmofilie te Antwerpen in de eerst helft van de zestiende eeuw." *Commemoration Nationale d'Erasme Actes.* Brussels, 1970. Pages 225–35.

Delaruelle, E., E.-R.Labande, and P. Ourliac. *L'Eglise au temps du Grand Schisme et de la crise conciliaire (1378–1449). Histoire de l'Eglise 14.* Paris, 1964.

Delen, A. J. J. *Metsys.* Brussels, 1926.

———. "Wie was de Meester van Frankfort." *Miscellanea Leo van Puyvelde.* Brussels, 1949. Pages 74–83.

Denucé, J. *De Konstkamers van Antwerpen in de 16e en 17e eeuwen Inventarissen van kunstverzamelingen.* The Hague, 1932.

Doesborch, J. van. *De Refreinbundel van Jan van Doesborch.* Edited by C. Kruyskamp. Leyden, 1940.

Dogan, G. "De Inventaris der schilderijen van Diego Duarte." *Jaarboek van het Koninklijk Museum Antwerp* (1971): 195–221.

Dolan, J. P. See Erasmus.

Dunbar, B. L. "The Landscape Art of Cornelis Metsys." Ph.D. dissertation, University of Iowa. 1972.

———. "The Question of Cornelis Massys' Landscape Collaboration with Quinten and Jan Massys." *Jaarboek van het Koninklijk Museum Antwerpen* (1979): 125–41.

Dvořak, M. "Ein Stilleben des Beuckelaer oder Betrachtingen über die Entstehung der neuzeitigen Kabinettmalerei." *JKSW* 36 (1923): 1–14.

De eeuw van Bruegel. Exhibition Catalog. Brussels, 1963.

Elslander, A. van. "De Mariavereering bij de rederijkers." *Jaarboek van 'De Fonteine'.* 1945. Page 57ff.

———. *Het Refrein in der Nederlanden tot 1600.* Ghent, 1953.

———. "Letterkundig leven in de Bourgondische tijd. De Rederijkers." *Rederijkerstudiën* 5 (1969): 3ff.

Erasmus. *The Essential Erasmus.* Edited by J.P. Dolan. New York, 1964.

———. *The Colloquies of Erasmus.* Edited by C.R. Thompson. Chicago, 1965.

———. *Desiderius Erasmus: Christian Humanism and the Reformation. Selected Writings.* Edited by J. Olin. New York, 1965.

———. *Erasmus on His Times. A Shortened Version of the Adages of Erasmus.* Edited by M. Mann Phillips. Cambridge, 1967.

———. *Erasmus and His Age. Selected Letters of Desiderius Erasmus.* Edited by H.J. Hillerbrand. New York, 1970.

Erasmus en zijn tijd. Exhibition catalog. Rotterdam, 1969.

Even, E. van. *Notice biographique sur le peinture Quentin Metsys.* Louvain, 1846.

———. *L'Ancienne école de peinture de Louvain.* Brussels, 1870.

Fetis, E. "La Descendance apostolique de Sainte Anne, triptyque de Quentin Metsys." *Bulletin des commissions royales d'art et d'archeologie* 5 (1866): 86ff.

Fickaert, F. *Metamorphosis, ofte wonderbaere veranderingh' ende leven van den vermaerden Mr. Quinten Matsys, constigh grof-smit, ende schilder binnen Antwerpen.* Antwerp, 1648.

Figueiredo, J. de. "Metsys et le Portugal." *Revue belge d'archeologie et d'histoire de l'art* 3 (1933): 1–16.

Flanders in the Fifteenth Century: Art and Civilization. Exhibition catalog. Detroit, 1960.

Floerke, H. *Studien zur niederländischen Kunst- und Kulturgeschichte. Die Formen des Kunsthandels, das Atelier, und die Sammler in den Niederlanden vom 15.–18. Jahrhundert.* Munich/Leipzig, 1905.

Fornenbergh, A. van. *Den Antwerpschen Protheus, ofte Cyclopschen Apelles; dat is: Het leven, ende konstrijcke daden des uyt-nemenden, ende hoogh-beroemden Mr. Quinten Matsys: van grof-smidt in fyn-schilder verandert . . .* Antwerp, 1658.

Friedländer, M. J. "Neues zu Quentin Massys." *Der Cicerone* 19 (1927): 1ff.

———. "Bildnisse von Quentin Massys." *Pantheon* 1 (1928): 171ff.

———. *Die altniederländische Malerei.* 14 vols. Berlin/Leyden, 1924–37. English ed., Leyden, 1967–74.

———. "Quentin Massys: Reflexions on his Development." *Burlington Magazine* 72 (1938): 52–54.

———. "Über den Zwang der ikonographischen Tradition in der vlämischen Kunst." *Art Quarterly* 1 (1938): 19–22.

———. "Bildnisse des Dänenkönigs Christiaan II." *Annuaire des Musées Royaux des Beaux-Arts* 1 (1938): 89–97.

———. "Quentin Massys as a Painter of Genre Pictures." *Burlington Magazine* 89 (1947): 114–19.

———. *Early Netherlandish Painting from van Eyck to Bruegel.* English ed. London, 1956.

Gallo, G. Nieto. "El retablo de San Juan Bautista . . . de Valladolid: ¿Quentin Metsys o Adriaen Skilleman?" *Boletin del Seminario de Estudios de Arte y Arquelogia de la Facultad de Historia de Valladolid* 13–21 (1936–39): 47–70.

Geertz, C. *The Interpretation of Cultures.* New York, 1973.

———. "Art as a Cultural System." *MLN* 91 (1976): 1473–99.

———. "Centers, Kings, and Charisma: Reflections on the Symbolics of Power." *Culture and Its Creators.* Edited by J. Ben-David and T. N. Clark. Chicago, 1977. Pages 150ff.

Gelder, H. A. Enno van. *Erasmus Schilders en Rederijkers.* Groningen, 1959.

Génard, P. *Nasporingen over de geboorteplaats en de familie van Quinten Massijs.* Antwerp, 1870.

Gerlo, A. *Erasme et ses portraitistes.* 2nd ed. Nieuwkoop, 1968.

Gibson, W. *Hieronymus Bosch.* New York, 1973.

———. "Hieronymus Bosch and the Mirror of Man." *Oud Holland* 87 (1973): 205–26.

———. *Bruegel.* Oxford, 1977.

Glück, G. "Schicksale einer Komposition Lionardos: Der einander küssenden Kinder Jesus und Johannes." *Pantheon* 2 (1928): 502–7.

———. "Zwei unveröffentlichte Gemälde von Quinten Metsys." *Pantheon* 11 (1933): 84–86.

———. "Portraetter af Christian II og Hans Hustru Isabella." *Kunstmuseets Aarsskrift* 27 (1940): 1–33.

Goffin, A. "Vlaanderen en Italië: Quinten Metsijs, Joost van Cleef, Hieronymus Bosch, Joachim Patinir, Bles." *Onze Kunst* 40 (1922).
Goris, J. A. *Etude sur les colonies marchandes méridionales (Portugais, Espagnols, Italiens) à Anvers de 1488 à 1567.* Louvain, 1925.
Goris, J. A., and G. Marlier. *Albrecht Dürer Diary of His Journey to the Netherlands 1520–1521.* Greenwich, 1971.
Jan Gossaert genaamd Mabuse. Exhibition catalog. Rotterdam/Bruges, 1965.
Guicciardini, L. *Descrittione di tutti i Paesi Bassi altrimenti detti Germania inferiore.* Antwerp, 1567. French ed., 1625.
Hand, J. "Joos van Cleve: The Early and Mature Paintings." Ph.D. dissertation, Princeton University, 1978.
Hartlaub, G. F. *Zauber des Spiegels.* Munich, 1951.
Hecht, I. "The Infants Christ and John Embracing." *Apollo* (1981): 222–29.
Held, J. *Dürers Wirkung auf die niederländische Kunst seiner Zeit.* The Hague, 1931.
———. "Artis Pictoriae Amator. An Antwerp Patron and his Collection." *Gazette des Beaux-Arts* 50 (1957): 53–84.
Hill, G. F., and G. Pollard. *Renaissance Medals at the National Gallery of Art.* London, 1967.
Hillerbrand, J. J. See Erasmus.
Houtte, J. A. van. "Anvers aux XVe et XVIe siècles, expansion et apogée." *Annales* 16 (1961).
Huizinga, J. *The Waning of the Middle Ages.* New York, 1924.
———. *Erasmus and the Age of Reformation.* New York, 1957.
Hulin de Loo, G. "An Unknown Portrait by Quentin Massys." *Burlington Magazine* 44 (1924): 212–16.
———. "Diptychs by Rogier van der Weyden." *Burlington Magazine* 43 (1923): 53–58; 44 (1924): 179–89.
d'Hulst, R. *Flemish Tapestries.* Brussels, 1966.
Hummelen, W. M. H. *De sinnekens in het rederijkersdrama.* Groningen, 1958.
———. *Repertorium van het Rederijkersdrama 1500–ca. 1620.* Assen, 1968.
Hymans, H. "Quentin Matsys." *Gazette des Beaux-Arts* 37 (1888): 5–20; 204ff; 38 (1888): 193–216.
Jacquot, J., ed. *Les Fêtes de la Renaissance II. Fêtes et ceremonies au temps de Charles Quint.* Paris, 1960.
Jacquot, J., and E. Konigson, eds. *Les Fêtes de la Renaissance III.* Paris, 1975.
Jonge, C. H. de. "Bijdrage tot de Kennis van de kleederdracht in de Nederlanden in de XVIe eeuw." *Oud Holland* 36 (1918): 133–69.
Jongh, E. de. "Speculaties over Jan Gossaerts Lucas-Madonna in Prag." *Bulletin Museum Boymans-van Beuningen* 19 (1968): 43–61.
———. "Grape Symbolism in Paintings of the 16th and 17th Centuries." *Simiolus* 7 (1974): 166–91.
Justi, K. "Altflandrische Bilder in Spanien und Portugal, Joachim Patinir und Quentin Metsys." *Zeitschrift für bildenden Kunst* 21 (1886): 93–95.
———. "Der Altarschrein des Licenciaten Gonzalez in San Salvador zu Valladolid." *Jahrbuch der königlich preussischen Kunstsammlungen* 7 (1887): 24–29.
Kinderen-Besier, J. H. *Mode Metamorphosen.* Amsterdam, 1933.
Kitzinger, E. *The Art of Byzantium and the Medieval West,* Edited by E. Kleinbauer. Bloomington, 1978.
Kleinschmidt, B. *Die heilige Anna, Ihre Verehrung in Geschichte, kunst, und Volkstum.* Düsseldorf, 1930.
Knipping, J. B. *De iconografie van de contra-reformatie in de Nederlanden.* Hilversum, 1939–40.
Knuvelder, G. *Handboek tot de Geschiedenis der nederlandse Letterkunde.* 5th ed. 's-Hertogenbosch, 1970.
Koch, G. F. *Die Kunstausstellung.* Berlin, 1967.
Koch, R. "Flower Symbolism in the Portinari Altarpiece." *Art Bulletin* 46 (1964): 70–77.
———. *Joachim Patinir.* Princeton, 1968.
Kronenburg, J.A.F. *Maria's Heerlijkheden in Nederland,* 8 vols. Amsterdam, 1904–14.
Krönig, W. *Der italienische Einfluss in der flämischen Malerei im ersten Drittel des 16. Jahrhunderts.* Wurzburg, 1936.
Laet, A. de. "Quinten Massys, voorgeslacht, leven, en kunst." *De Schakel* 9 (1954).
Lanc, E. *Die religiösen Bilder des Joos van Cleve.* Vienna, 1972.
Larsen, E. "Un Quentin Metsys inconnu à New York." *Revue belge d'archeologie et d'histoire de l'art* 19 (1950): 171–74.
Lassaigne, J., and R. Delevoye. *Flemish Painting from Bosch to Rubens.* Geneva, 1958.
Lefebvre, J. *Les Fols et la folie.* Paris, 1968.
Levi d'Ancona, M. *The Iconography of the Immaculate Conception in the Middle Ages and the Early Renaissance.* New York, 1957.
Lindeboom, J. *Het bijbelsche humanisme in Nederland.* Leyden, 1913.
Löhneysen, H.-W. von. *Die ältere niederländische Malerei.* Eisenach / Kassel, 1956.

McConica, J. *English Humanists and Reformation Politics under Henry VIII and Edward VI.* Oxford, 1965.
McFarlane, K. *Hans Memling.* Oxford, 1971.
Mak, J. J. *De Rederijkers.* Amsterdam, 1944.
Mâle, E. *L'Art religieux à la fin du Moyen Age en France.* Paris, 1925.
Mallé, L. "Quinten Metsys." *Commentari* 6 (1955) 79–107.
Mander, C. van. *Het Schilder-Boeck.* Edited by A. F. Mirande and G. S. Overdiep. Amsterdam, 1936.
Mann Phillips, M. See Erasmus.
———. *Erasmus and the Northern Renaissance.* London, 1949.
———. "The Mystery of the Matsys Portrait." *Erasmus in English* 7 (1975): 18–20.
Marle, R. van. *Iconographie de l'art profane au Moyen Age et à la Renaissance.* The Hague, 1931–32.
Marlier, G. *Erasme et la peinture flamande de son temps.* Damme, 1954.
———. *Ambrosius Benson.* Damme, 1957.
———. *La Renaissance flamande Pierre Coeck d'Alost.* Brussels, 1966.
Meiss, M. "The Madonna of Humility." *Art Bulletin* 18 (1936): 434–64.
———. *The Painter's Choice.* New York, 1976.
Meller, P. "Drawings by Francesco Cossa in the Uffizi." *Master Drawings* 3 (1965): 3–20.
Mertens, F. H., and K. L. Torfs. *Geschiedenis van Antwerpen.* Vol. 4. Antwerp, 1848.
Michel, E. *Catalogue raisonné des peintures du Moyen-Âge, de la Renaissance, et des temps modernes—peintres flamandes du XVe et du XVIe siècle.* Paris, 1953.
Mierlo, J. van, ed. *De middelnederlandsche Letterkunde Geschiedenis van de Letterkunde der Nederlanden II.* 's-Hertogenbosch, 1949.
———. "Nieuwe studiën over Anna Bijns en andere opstellen." *Verslagen en Mededelingen van de koninklijk Vlaamse Akademie.* Ghent, 1951.
Mirimonde, A. P. "Jan Massys dans les musées de provinces français." *Gazette des Beaux-Arts* 60 (1962): 543–64.
———. "Les Anges musiciens chez Memlinc." *Jaarboek Koninklijk Museum Schoone Kunsten Antwerp* (1962–63): 5–55.
Miskimin, H. *The Economy of Later Renaissance Europe 1460–1600.* Cambridge, 1977.
Moeller, B. "Religious Life in Germany on the Eve of the Reformation." In *Pre-Reformation Germany,* Edited by G. Strauss. London, 1972. Pages 13ff.
Moreau, E. de. *L' Eglise en Belgique,* Vol. 4. Brussels, 1949.
Moxey, K. *Pieter Aertsen, Joachim Beuckelaer and the Rise of Secular Painting in the Context of the Reformation.* New York, 1976.
———. "The *Ship of Fools* and the Idea of Folly in Sixteenth-Century Netherlandish Literature." In *The Early Illustrated Book Essays in Honor of Lessing J. Rosenwald.* Edited by S. Hindman. Washington, 1982. Pages 86–102.
Müller-Wulckow, W. *Vier Bildnisse des Petrus Aegidius.* Oldenburg, 1961.
Muls, J. "Erasmus en Quentin Metsys." *Katholieke vlaamse Hogeschool uitbreiding* 47 (1953): 1ff.
Nauwelaerts, M. A. "Un Ami Anversois de More et d'Erasme." *Moreana* 15–16 (1967): 83ff.
Nijhoff, W., and M. Kronenberg. *Nederlandse bibliografie van 1500 tot 1540.* The Hague, 1923.
Norris, C. "Rubens' *Adoration of the Kings* of 1609." *Nederlands Kunsthistorisch Jaarboek* 14 (1963): 129–36.
Oakley, F. *The Western Church in the Late Middle Ages.* Ithaca, 1979.
Os, H. van. *Marias Demut und Verherrlichung in der sienesischer Malerei 1300–1450.* The Hague, 1969.
Ozment, S. *The Reformation in the Cities.* New Haven, 1975.
Pächt, O. "The Ancestry of the Avignon Diptych." *De Artibus Opuscula XL. Essays in Honor of Erwin Panofsky.* New York, 1961. Pages 402–21.
Panofsky, E. "Imago Pietatis." *Festschrift Max J. Friedländer zum 60. Geburtstage.* Leipzig, 1927. Pages 261–308.
———. *Early Netherlandish Painting.* Cambridge, Mass., 1953.
———. *Life and Art of Albrecht Dürer.* Princeton, 1955.
———. "Jean Hey's 'Ecce Homo'." *Bulletin Musées Royaux des Beaux-Arts de Belgique* (1956): 95–138.
———. "Erasmus and the Visual Arts." *Journal of the Warburg and Courtauld Institutes* 32 (1969): 200–228.
Parshall, P. "Camerarius on Dürer—Humanist Biography as Art Criticism." In *Joachim Camerarius (1500–1574).* Edited by F. Baron. Munich, 1978. Pages 11ff.
———. "Lucas van Leyden's Narrative Style." *Nederlands Kunsthistorisch Jaarboek* 29 (1978). Pages 185–237.
Pauwels, H. *Catalogue Musée Groeninge.* Bruges, 1963.
———. "Jan Gossaert en van Eyck." *Bulletin Museum Boymans-van Beuningen* 19 (1968): 4–15.

———. "Naar aanleiding van een gravure naar Quinten Metsys." *Bijdragen tot de geschiedenis van de grafische Kunst opgedragen aan Prof. Dr. L. Lebeer.* Antwerp, 1975. Pages 248–62.
Pešina, J. "An Unknown Painting by Quentin Massys." *Art Bulletin* 48 (1966): 406–8.
Philippot, P. "La fin du XVe siècle et les origines d'une nouvelle conception de l'image dans la peinture des Pays-bas." *Bulletin Musées Royaux des Beaux Arts de Belgique* 11 (1962): 3–38.
———. "Les grisailles et les 'degrés de realité' de l'image dans la peinture flamande des XVe et XVIe siecles." *Bulletin Musées Royaux des Beaux Arts de Belgique* 15 (1966): 225–42.
———. *Pittura fiamminga e Rinascimento Italiano.* Turin, 1970.
Pirenne, H. *Early Democracies in the Low Countries.* English ed. New York, 1971.
Pochat, G. *Der Exotismus während der Mittelalters und der Renaissance.* Stockholm, 1970.
Pope-Hennessey, J. *The Portrait in the Renaissance.* New York, 1966.
Post, R. R. *Kerkelijke verhoudingen in Nederland vóor de reformatie.* Utrecht, 1954.
———. *Kerkgeschiedenis van Nederland in de Middeleeuwen.* Utrecht/Antwerp, 1957.
———. *The Modern Devotion,* Leyden, 1968.
Primitifs flamandes anonymes, Les. Exhibition catalog. Bruges, 1969.
F. Prims. "De Familie van Quinten Massys." *Antwerpiensia* 4 (1930): 45ff.
———. "Quinten Massys in de Kempen." *Antwerpiensia* 4 (1930): 56ff.
———. "Quinten Massys en de Annadevotie." *Antwerpiensia* 4 (1930): 64ff.
———. "Vrienden ende magen van Quentine Massijs." *Bijdragen tot de Geschiedenis* 9 (1931): 203 ff.
———. "De 13 Hypothesen van Pieter Gillis 1520." *Antwerpiensia* 12 (1938): 159ff.
———. "De Schilderijen van het Kuipersaltaar." *Antwerpiensia* 12 (1938): 296ff.
———. "Het ontluiken van het Humanisme te Antwerpen." *Verslagen en mededelingen van de Koninklijk Vlaamse Akademie.* Brussels, 1938. Pages 523 ff.
———. "Cultuurwaarden en cultuurtekorten te Antwerpen in de eerste helft der XVIe eeuw." *Verslagen en mededelingen van de Koninklijk Vlaamse Academie.* Brussels, 1939. Pages 15ff.
———. *Geschiedenis van Antwerpen VII,* parts 1–3. Antwerp, 1939–40.
Puyvelde, L. van. *La Peinture flamande á Rome.* Brussels, 1950.
———. "Eduardo Portugalois." *Pantheon* 18 (1960): 288–95.
———. "Un portrait de marchand par Quentin Metsys et les percepteurs d'impôts par Marin van Reymerswale." *Revue belge d'archéologie et d'histoire de l'art* 26 (1957): 3–23.
———. *La Peinture flamande au siécle de Bosch et Bruegel.* Paris, 1962.
———. *Flemish Painting from the van Eycks to Metsys.* New York, 1970.
Rapp, F. *L'Eglise et la vie religieuse en Occident á la fin du Moyen Age.* Paris, 1971.
Reallexikon zur deutschen Kunstgeschichte. Edited by O. Schmitt. Stuttgart, 1937ff.
Reis-Santos, L. "A Lost Work of Massys and a Hitherto Unknown van der Goes." *Burlington Magazine* 75 (1939): 162–67.
———. "Quentin Metsys, seus discipulos e continuadores em Portugal." *Panorama* 11 (1942): 7ff.
———. *Le Portrait de Saint Bernardin de Sienne par Quentin Metsys.* Lisbon, 1949.
———. "Paneis de Metsys em Portugal anteriores ao retablo de Lovaina." *Belas Artes* 12 (1958): 13–19.
———. *Masterpieces of Flemish Painting of the XV and XVI Centuries in Portugal.* Lisbon, 1962.
———. "Jan Quinten Massys Discipulo e colaborador de seu Pai Mestre Quinten Metsys." *Belas Artes* 20 (1964): 1–12.
———. "Edouard Portugalois—disciple et collaborateur de Quentin Metsys." *Pantheon* 26 (1968): 185–96.
Richardson, E. P. "Quentin Massys." *Art Quarterly* 4 (1941): 162–76.
Ring, G. *Beiträge zur Geschichte niederländische Bildnismalerei im 15. und 16. Jahrhunderte.* Leipzig, 1913.
———. "Additions to the Works of Jan Provost and Quentin Massys." *Burlington Magazine* 80 (1942): 71–73.
Ringbom, S. "*Maria in Sole* and the Virgin of the Rosary." *Journal of the Warburg and Courtauld Institutes* 25 (1962): 326–30.
———. *Icon to Narrative.* Abo, 1965.
———. "Nuptial Symbolism in Some Fifteenth Century Reflections of Roman Sepulchral Portraiture." *Temenos* 11 (1966): 68ff.
Robbins, D. T. "Landscape in the Art of Quentin Massys." Master's thesis, University of Washington, 1972.
Rogier van der Weyden. Exhibition catalog. Brussels, 1979
Rombouts, P., and T. van Lerius, eds. *De Liggeren der Antwerpsche Sint-Lucasgilde.* 2 vol. The Hague, 1864–76.

Roose, L. *Anna Bijns*, Ghent, 1963.

Roosen-Runge, H. *Die Gestaltung der Farbe bei Quentin Metsys*. Munich, 1940.

Rooses, M. *Geschiedenis der Antwerpsche Schildershool.* Ghent / Antwerp / The Hague, 1879.

Roosval, J. "Retables d'origine néerlandaise dans les pays nordiques," *Revue belge d'archeologie et d'histoire de l'art* 3 (1933): 136–38.

———. "Les peintres des retables néerlandais en Suède." *Revue belge d'archeologie et d'histoire de l'art* 4 (1934): 311–20.

Roover, R. de. *Money, Banking and Credit in Medieval Bruges.* Cambridge, Mass., 1948.

———. *The Rise and Decline of the Medici Bank 1397–1494.* Cambridge, Mass., 1963.

Sabbe, M. "Erasmus en zijn Antwerpsche vrienden." *Vondel en Zuid-Nederland.* Antwerp, 1939. Pages 61ff.

Sanchez-Canton, F. J. "Notas sobre Quentin Massys en la Peninsula." *Archivo Español de Arte* 65-66 (1944): 308–15.

Santos, R. dos. *O Poliptico da Madre de Deus de Quintino Metsys.* Lisbon, 1939.

Saxl, F. "Holbein's Illustrations to the *Praise of Folly* by Erasmus." *Burlington Magazine* 83 (1943): 275–76.

Scaff, V. "Johannes Quintini Massiis Pingebat." *Mélanges d'archeologie et d'histoire de l'art offerts au Prof. Lavalleye.* Louvain, 1970, Pages 259–79.

Schabacker, P. " 'Petrus Christus' *St.Eloy:* Problems of Provenance, Sources, and Meaning." *Art Quarterly* 35 (1972): 103–22.

———. *Petrus Christus.* Utrecht, 1974.

Schmid, H. A., ed. *Erasmi Roterodami Encomium Moriae, i.e. Stultitia Laus.* (facsimile) Basel, 1931.

Schwarz, H. "The Mirror in Art." *Art Quarterly* 15 (1952): 96–118.

———. "The Mirror of the Artist and the Mirror of the Devout." *Studies in the History of Art Dedicated to William Suida.* London, 1959. Pages 90–105.

Segurado, J. "Damião de Goes." *Belas Artes* 28–29 (1975): 133–84.

Seilern, A. *Flemish Paintings at 56 Princes Gate.* London, 1955.

Silver, L. "The *Ill-Matched Pair* by Quinten Massys." *Studies in the History of Art* 6 (1974): 104–24.

———. "Power and Pelf: A New-Found *Old Man* by Massys." *Simiolus* 9 (1977): 63–92.

———. "Prayer and Laughter: Erasmian Elements in Two Late Massys Panels." *Erasmus in English* 9 (1978). 17–21.

———. "Fountain and Source: A Rediscovered Eyckian Icon." *Pantheon* 41 (1983): 95–104.

Simson, O. von. "*Compassio* and *Co-redemptio* in Roger van der Weyden's *Descent from the Cross.*" *Art Bulletin* 35 (1953): 9–16.

Snyder, J. "The Early Haarlem School of Painting II. Geertgen tot sint Jans." *Art Bulletin* 42 (1960): 113–32.

Southern, R. W. *Western Society and the Church in the Middle Ages.* Harmondsworth, 1970.

Speth-Holterhoff, S. *Les Peintres flamands de cabinets d'amateurs au XVIIe siecle.* Brussels, 1957.

Steenbergen, G. J. *Het Landjuweel van de Rederijkers.* Louvain, 1950.

Stewart, A. *Unequal Lovers.* New York, 1979.

Stridbeck, G. *Bruegelstudien.* Stockholm, 1956.

———. "Den gatfulla nejlikan." *Konsthistorisk Tidskrift* 29 (1960): 81–97.

Strümpel, A. "Hieronymus im Gehäus." *Marburger Jahrbuch* 2 (1925-26): 173–244.

Styevoort, J. van. *Jan van Styevoorts refreinenbundel Anno 1524.* Edited by F. Lyna and W. van Eeghem. Antwerp, 1929–30.

Suida, W. *Leonardo und sein Kreis.* Munich, 1929.

Sulzberger, S. "L'Influence de Léonard de Vinci et ses repercussions à Anvers." *Arte Lombarda* 1 (1955): 105–11.

———. "Considérations sur le chef d'oeuvre de Quentin Massys." *Bulletin Musées Royaux des Beaux-Arts de Belgique* 14 (1965): 27–34.

———. "Dieric Bouts et l'enluminure hollandaise." *Scriptorium* 23 (1969): 227–29.

Swain, B. *Fools and Folly during the Middle Ages and the Renaissance.* New York, 1932.

Terner, R. "Bemerkungen zur 'Madonna des Kanonikus van der Paele.' " *Zeitschrift für Kunstgeschichte* 42 (1979): 83–91.

Thompson, C. R. See Erasmus.

Thompson, G. *Under Pretext of Praise: Satiric Mode in Erasmus' Fiction.* Toronto, 1973.

Tolnay, C. de. *Hieronymus Bosch.* 2nd ed. London, 1965.

Toussaert, J. *Le Sentiment religieux en Flandre à la fin du Moyen-Age.* Paris, 1963.

Tracy, J. D. *The Politics of Erasmus.* Toronto, 1978.

Trapp, J. B., and H. Schulte-Herbrüggen. *Sir Thomas More 1477/8–1535: 'The King's Good Servant'.* Exhibition catalog. London, 1977–78.

Valentiner, W. R. "Simon van Herlam, the Master of the Morrison Triptych." *Gazette des Beaux-Arts* 45 (1955): 5–16.

Vanbeselaere, W. "Quentin Metsijs." *Gentsche Bijdragen tot de Kunstgeschiedenis* 9 (1943): 255–67.

Van Buren, A. H. "The Canonical Office in Renaissance Painting, Part II: More about the Rolin *Madonna.*" *Art Bulletin* 60 (1978): 617–33.

Vervaet, J. "Catalogus van de altaarstukken uit de Onze-Lieve-Vrouwenkerk te Antwerpen en bewaard in het Koninklijk Museum." *Jaarbaek van het Koninklijk Museum Antwerpen* (1976): 197–244.

Vincent, M. "La Vierge à l'Enfant entourée d'anges de Quentin Metsys au Musée des Beaux-Arts de Lyons." *Bulletin des Musées Lyonnais* 2 (1957–61): 21–29.

Viridis, C. L. "Moralismo e satira nella tarda produzioni di Quentin Metsys." *Storia dell'Arte* 20 (1974): 19–24.

Voet, L. *Antwerp The Golden Age.* Brussels, 1973.

Völker, B. "Die Entwicklung des erzählenden Halbfigurenbildes in der niederländischen Malerei des 15. und 16. Jahrhunderts." Ph.D. dissertation, Göttingen, 1968.

von der Osten, G., "Studien zu Jan Gossaert." *De artibus Opuscula XL. Essays in Honor of Erwin Panofsky.* New York, 1961. Pages 454–75.

von der Osten, G., and H. Vey. *Painting and Sculpture in Germany and the Netherlands 1500–1600.* Harmondsworth, 1969.

Voragine, J. da. *The Golden Legend.* New York, 1969.

Wallerstein, I., *The Modern World-System. Vol. 1: Capitalist Agriculture and the Origins of the European World-Economy in the Sixteenth Century.* New York, 1976.

Waterhouse, E. K. "An Unnoticed Quentin Massys." *Burlington Magazine* 89 (1947): 280.

Watson, D. G. "Erasmus' *Praise of Folly* and the Spirit of Carnival." *Renaissance Quarterly* 32 (1979): 333–53.

Wee, H. van der. *The Growth of the Antwerp Market and the European Economy.* The Hague, 1963.

Wegg, J. *Antwerp 1477–1559.* London, 1916.

Wehle, H., and M. Salinger. *Catalogue of the Early Flemish, Dutch, and German Paintings Metropolitan Museum.* New York, 1947.

Welsford, E. *The Fool.* London, 1935.

Werveke, H. van. "Aantekening bij de zogenaamde *Belastingpachters* en Wisselaars van Marinus van Reymerswael." *Gentsche Bijdragen tot de Kunstgeschiedenis* 12 (1949–50): 43-58.

Wescher, P. "Beiträge zu Simon von Haarlem, dem Meister des Morrison Triptychons." *Jahrbuch der Berliner Museen* N. F. 7 (1965): 175–88.

Wind, E. "Aenigma Termini." *Journal of the Warburg and Courtauld Institutes* 1 (1937–38): 66–69.

———. "The Christian Democritus." *Journal of the Warburg and Courtauld Institutes* 1 (1937–38): 180–82.

Winkler, F. *Die altniederländische Malerei.* Berlin, 1924.

———. "Quinten Massys Ruhe auf der Flucht." *Pantheon* 6 (1930): 345–46.

———. "Dürers Lissaboner Hieronymus." *Pantheon* 17 (1944): 12–16.

———. *Das Werk des Hugo van der Goes.* Berlin, 1964.

Wolffhardt, E. "Beiträge zur Pflanzensymbolik." *Zeitschrift für Kunstwissenschaft* 8 (1954): 178–96.

Zucker, W. "Reflections on Reflections." *Journal of Aesthetics and Art Criticism* 20 (1962): 239–50.

Zwollo, A. "De Landschaptekeningen van Cornelis Massys." *Nederlands Kunsthistorisch Jaarboek* 16 (1965): 43–65.

Index

LOCATIONS OF ART WORKS